Ultimate Guide to Becoming a Teacher

Ultimate Guide to Becoming a Teacher

Ben Wildavsky and the Staff of U.S.News & World Report

Anne McGrath, Editor

Robert Morse, Director of Data Research

Ulrich Boser, Associate Editor

Sara Sklaroff, Series Editor

SOURCEBOOKS, INC.®
NAPERVILLE, ILLINOIS

Table of Contents

Chapter One: The Trouble with Teaching—and How to Fix It 1

Chapter Two: Alternative Routes to the Classroom 17

Chapter Three: Which Is the Right School for You? 27

Chapter Four: Inside Five Grad Schools 41

Chapter Five: Finding the Money 57

Chapter Six: Getting Licensed in Your State 67

The *U.S. News* Insider's Index: How Do the Grad Schools Stack Up? 77

    Which are the hardest and easiest education schools to get into? 78

    Which are the largest and smallest education schools? 88

    In which states will first-year teachers make the most money?

    Where will they make the least? 101

    In which cities do teachers with master's degrees make the most and the least? 103

    Whose graduates are most likely to pass the state certification test? The least? 106

Schools of Education Offering Graduate Degrees 123

    How to Use the Directory 124

    Directory 126

Index of Schools 505

About the Authors and Editors 518

Chapter One

The Trouble with Teaching—and How to Fix It

For anyone who wants to become a teacher, from young and idealistic college grads to disgruntled midcareer professionals seeking a nobler calling, this is both the best of times and the worst of times.

Why the best? In part, because of sheer demand. A wave of retirements, plus growing enrollment and persistent teacher turnover (especially in troubled high-poverty districts), mean that an estimated two million additional teachers will be needed over the next decade. There's an increasingly urgent call for more teachers with specialized training in high-growth subfields like bilingual and special education and in shortage-plagued subjects like math and science. Add in the federal No Child Left Behind Act's mandate that a "highly qualified" teacher be in every classroom by the 2005–2006 school year, and the first part of the twenty-first century would seem to be a most opportune moment for a would-be shaper of young minds.

So why is this also the worst of times? Because the state of teaching in general—and of teacher training in particular—has come under unprecedented scrutiny from policymakers and the public. Poorly qualified or unmotivated teachers, one-size-fits-all pay scales, ed school classes that are long on trendiness and short on substance—all are regularly denounced by reformers who believe today's system needs some serious shaking up if American students are going to start learning more. "Mamas, Don't Let Your Babies Grow Up to Be Teachers," cautioned the headline of one recent plea for an overhaul of teaching—published in, of all places, the newsletter of the Harvard Graduate School of Education.

It would be a shame if the raging debate over teacher quality discouraged talented individuals from entering the field, because their efforts and dedication are needed more than ever. But anyone contemplating a career in the classroom these days should go in with eyes wide open, aware of the problems he or she is likely to face—and the changes that may be on the horizon.

Many of the difficulties plaguing the profession today are the same ones cited two decades ago by the National Commission on Excellence in Education in its clarion call for education reform, *A Nation at Risk*. Among that report's findings:

"that not enough of the academically able students are being attracted to teaching; that teacher preparation programs need substantial improvement; that the professional working life of teachers is on the whole unacceptable; and that a serious shortage of teachers exists in key fields."

After little progress in the 20 years since, however, there are now ever-more-urgent efforts underway to make the necessary changes to attract better candidates into teaching—and to help make them stay. Will those efforts succeed? That will depend on whether policymakers and teachers alike are at last ready to make far-reaching reforms in how teachers are prepared for the classroom, and how they're treated once they get there.

What went wrong?

Many of us have fond memories of an inspirational, sharp-as-a-whip second grade teacher, or perhaps an uncommonly talented and dedicated high school English teacher who managed to take a daunting reading list, mix in impossibly exacting writing assignments, and keep a roomful of teenagers enthralled. Those types are still out there. But for a complex combination of reasons— low prestige, modest pay that bears no relationship to performance, stressful working conditions, and unpromising career paths—the best and brightest college graduates too often don't even consider a teaching career. In part, this is an unintended consequence of the wide career opportunities now open to talented women and minorities. Their numbers have soared in the past few decades in fields like law, medicine, and business (although women still make up the majority of the teaching ranks). Today, new teachers are "drawn disproportionately from the bottom third of American college students," writes Harvard economist and education researcher Caroline Hoxby, pointing to the relatively low scores of college education majors on English, math, science, and history tests.

Similarly, the U.S. Department of Education reports that college graduates whose SAT or ACT scores were in the bottom quarter of all test-takers were more than twice as likely to have majored in education as those in the top quartile. And among those sitting for the Graduate Record Examination, or GRE, test-takers planning to study elementary education in graduate school score beneath future English grad students in math and beneath future math grad students in English, observes Frederick Hess, director of education policy studies at the American Enterprise Institute, a Washington, D.C., think tank, and author of *Common Sense School Reform*.

To be sure, good test scores don't measure things like an ability to motivate and inspire children. "You can't predict that just because you have a high score on the Praxis series [of teacher-certification exams] you're going to be a highly effective teacher," says David Imig, president of the American Association of Colleges for Teacher Education (AACTE). But there's significant evidence that teachers with strong verbal and cognitive skills—the kind measured by standardized tests such as the SAT—are most likely to boost student achievement. According to a presentation by Grover Whitehurst, who heads the Department of Education's research division, "Every study that has included a valid measure of teacher verbal or cognitive ability has found that it accounts for more variance in student achievement than any other measured characteristic of teachers."

Meanwhile, many schools of education have earned reputations as academically undemanding institutions that serve as cash cows for the universities that house them. "An American master's degree in education is probably the least challenging graduate program on the planet," write veteran educators Vivian Troen and Katherine Boles in their recent reform manifesto, *Who's Teaching Your*

Today, new teachers are "drawn disproportionately from the bottom third of American college students."

Children? Undergraduate programs, which educate the majority of new teachers, are the target of similar criticisms. Ed schools, the argument goes, have paid too much attention to faddish educational theory and methods, too little to subject-area classes and practical topics like classroom management—and less still to whether their graduates are actually able to improve student learning.

Many ed school deans call such criticisms dated and vigorously defend their efforts to address these shortcomings. Imig, whose organization represents 760 colleges of teacher education, notes that the AACTE endorses the requirement—now common in most states—of an academic major for new teachers. He adds that many ed schools are beefing up their curricula (making classes on teaching methods more practical, for instance) and requiring more student teaching to give their graduates real-world classroom exposure. Still, even the American Federation of Teachers (AFT), the nation's second largest teachers' union, bemoans the fact that schools of education suffer from the lack of any core consensus—common in fields such as economics or physics—on precisely what they should teach. "There is, in short, no body of knowledge that the profession has determined that all teacher candidates need to know," AFT delegates declared in a 2002 resolution. "It is vital that we identify what science tells us about how people learn in order to improve the teacher education curriculum."

"It is vital that we identify what science tells us about how people learn in order to improve the teacher education curriculum."

The trouble with teacher preparation goes well beyond ed school, however. State certification standards are another oft-cited culprit: They're frequently too low to keep poorly prepared teachers out of the classroom, and involve way too much red tape to suit many of the really talented. Certification typically requires completion of a certain number of education courses and passage of a licensure exam. (As of 2004, 38 states and the District of Columbia required a basic skills exam for new teachers, while 35 states and the nation's capital required teaching candidates to pass a subject-knowledge test.) But the rigor of such tests varies widely. Some measure little more than rudimentary math or English skills. Even the more challenging content-area tests are often subject to different cutoffs in different states, which means that in some places it's possible to pass with a relatively low score.

Moreover, even these minimal requirements are sometimes bypassed by districts facing teacher shortages—typically in large, troubled urban systems. That happened in the 1990s in California,

which implemented a statewide initiative to reduce average class size and faced an unplanned outcome: A shortage of certified teachers for the resulting increased number of classes left many students taught by unqualified instructors, particularly in schools with heavy concentrations of low-income or minority students.

Ironically, the sorry result of poorly designed certification requirements is that the state's stamp of approval doesn't necessarily ensure good teaching. Just 5 percent of superintendents and 11 percent of principals surveyed in a November 2003 poll by Public Agenda, a nonprofit public opinion group, said that full certification meant teachers had what it takes to succeed. A debate on the topic continues to rage among researchers. Stanford education professor Linda Darling-Hammond, a prominent fan of certification, argues that the process is an important quality-assurance benchmark, and that differences in teacher credentials explain a substantial share of state-by-state variation in students' test scores. But other analysts have cast a far more skeptical eye on the value of traditional certification. Economist Dan Goldhaber of the University of Washington's Center on Reinventing Public Education found in a 2000 study of several thousand students that certified instructors fared no better at raising student achievement than their uncertified peers. In other words, as education scholar Chester Finn, Jr., president of the Thomas B. Fordham Foundation, once said in a debate with Darling-Hammond at a gathering of the Education Commission of the States, "There are plenty of teachers who are certified, yet have

---

A pilot program that pays for results

Three years after graduation, many of Jason Culbertson's high-achieving college classmates are well on their way to lucrative careers in fields like law and consulting. It frustrates him that so few have joined him in public school classrooms. "The best and the brightest don't go there," says the honors graduate of the University of South Carolina, who now teaches social studies at Bell Street Middle School in Clinton, South Carolina. "And it drives me nuts."

One big reason, as Culbertson sees it, is that public schools traditionally offer no incentives to the best performers. "The person who leaves at 3 p.m. is treated the same as the person who stays til 5 p.m," he says. Not so at Bell Street: When Culbertson took on extra duties as a mentor to other teachers and earned the highest possible performance appraisal (based on observations of his teaching, his students' academic results, and schoolwide test-score gains), he boosted his $33,476 base pay by 20 percent. A second promotion netted him an additional $4,000. The extra income has helped keep him in this economically depressed former mill town. "It's not all about the money," he says, "but it certainly makes a difference."

Bell Street Middle School is one of more than 70 schools participating in the Teacher Advancement Program (TAP), a project started in 2000 by the Milken Family Foundation to attract and retain high-caliber teachers and improve the performance and career satisfaction of those already in the classroom. TAP partnerships, which have sprung up at schools in Arizona, Arkansas, Colorado, Florida, Indiana, Louisiana, Minnesota, and South Carolina, have four goals: to create multiple career paths for teachers, to provide market-driven compensation, to use a performance-based appraisal system, and to offer ongoing professional development.

"We're working to help turn teaching into more of a profession," says Lewis Solmon, former dean of the University of California–Los Angeles Graduate School of Education and director of the TAP initiative. "People look for jobs where they can grow.... We felt that people needed to be rewarded for accomplishment."

In the TAP model, for example, ambitious teachers don't need to become administrators to advance: They, like Culbertson, can become "mentor teachers." Besides handling their regular courseload, mentors lead once- or twice-weekly "cluster" meetings with a group of colleagues, touching on lesson plans, teaching techniques, and ways to be more effective in the classroom. In one recent session led by mentor Karen Childress, for example, seventh grade teachers shared ideas about how to get across the concept of meiosis (cell division). Mentor teachers also give occasional demonstration lessons and help observe and evaluate their colleagues. Each of Bell Street's six mentors earns an extra $3,600 a year.

At the highest rung on the TAP career ladder, veteran "master teachers" spend only one period instructing a class and the rest of their time observing colleagues and serving as coaches and quality-control monitors. The payoff at Bell Street? An additional $7,700 a year.

Teachers there say TAP has forced them to reevaluate techniques they have sometimes used for years. Seventh grade science teacher Cathy Dailey didn't want to take part in the program at first—"I don't like change"—but says it has helped her become much more methodical about planning and structuring her lessons. Most important, TAP has motivated her to keep improving. "I don't want to be the teacher that everybody talks about [being] bad," she says. "I want to be the teacher that everybody says, 'I want my child to have Cathy Dailey!'"

The frequent classroom observations (typically from four to six per year) take some getting used to. In the past, administrators sat in only "if you weren't doing a good job," says one teacher. "TAP is sort of the reverse of that." And while the same teacher called the oversight "intimidating" at first, making the adjustment can be well worth it: All teachers are eligible for bonuses (of up to $3,100 at Bell Street) that are

based on how well they rate in a series of observations (50 percent of the rating) as well as their students' academic gains (30 percent) and schoolwide improvements (20 percent).

Teachers have largely bought into the new system, says Bell Street principal David O'Shields, because they're given detailed information about criteria for good performance and have numerous chances to get feedback on how they're doing, rather than being judged on a single snapshot. Because Bell Street's once-dismal test scores have risen continuously since the program was introduced, every teacher at the school received a $750 bonus last year on top of what they merited for their own performance.

The elaborate "rubric" on which TAP teachers are judged breaks good teaching down into a series of concrete and measurable components. First, teachers are coached in each aspect of the rubric, from recognizing exemplary student assignments (those that ask students to "organize, interpret, analyze, synthesize, and evaluate information rather than

reproduce it") to keeping up a brisk pace in the classroom. The rubric is used as a checklist during observations: teachers are evaluated on a scale that ranges from "Emerging" (a euphemism for unsatisfactory for anybody but a novice) to "Proficient" to "Exemplary." Next, they're given a written review, or discuss their performance at a "post-conference" with the observer, or both. At English teacher Josie Kate Haupfear's recent post-conference, for example, assistant principal Dennis Dotterer gave her high marks for lesson structure and pacing and for motivating her students, and encouraged her to work harder on their problem-solving skills. She proposed that when she teaches an upcoming lesson on haiku poetry, which is usually about something in nature, she'll give her students a sample poem about a person instead. When they sit down to write their own poems, she reasons, she'll ask for a more conventional nature haiku, which will force the students to come up with something original and not simply imitate what she has done.

If Bell Street's experience is any indication, one goal of TAP—recruitment of excellent teachers to struggling schools and retention of those already in the classroom—seems to be within reach. The school, where 70 percent of students come from families with incomes low enough to qualify them for free or reduced-price school lunches, once suffered from very high turnover and problems recruiting new teachers. "We used to scramble to find teachers as the [new] school year approached," O'Shields says. "Now we already have six or seven people interested in teaching for next year.... There's not a soul looking to leave." Meanwhile, TAP officials can point to the many teachers in Arizona and South Carolina who have already moved from affluent schools to TAP schools in disadvantaged communities, drawn by the financial awards and career development potential.

It's no accident that TAP schools have spread most quickly in states with weak or nonexistent teachers unions—which have traditionally resisted moving to merit pay because of fears that it will be doled out unfairly. So it's significant that TAP earned the cautious approval of Sandra Feldman, former president of the nation's second-largest teachers union, the American Federation of Teachers. TAP "is well worth a look," Feldman wrote in the March 2004 issue of *American Teacher*, the union's quarterly magazine. "It exemplifies the principle of putting teacher compensation in the context of improving student achievement, and it offers everyone who is concerned with teacher quality and teacher retention plenty of food for thought."

At Bell Street, mentor-teacher Karen Childress says observing the strengths and weaknesses of other instructors has improved her own teaching style, even after 12 years in the classroom. And TAP's focus on finding ways to reach all pupils, no matter where they start out, has changed how she views her students. "You try not to label, but in the back of your mind you may say 'Jimmy isn't going to be a doctor but he could maybe be a factory worker,'" she says. "TAP made me see that wasn't my decision.... I wasn't giving them an equal opportunity to learn. I was pushing Samantha harder than Jimmy. But now I can push Jimmy just as hard." By making the profession more rewarding, TAP aims to help teachers in participating schools feel equally empowered.

abysmal track records when it comes to boosting student learning. These teachers are not qualified even if they are certified."

By contrast, there's a growing consensus among education policymakers backing the commonsense notion that strong subject-content knowledge—the area where teacher-preparation most often falls short—is a prerequisite for effective instruction. Nevertheless, many teachers in middle school and high school lack specialized training in the field they're assigned to teach. According to research by University of

Pennsylvania education and sociology professor Richard Ingersoll for *Quality Counts,* an annual study of the state of American K–12 education published by *Education Week,* 22 percent of secondary school students take at least one class with a teacher who lacks even a college minor in the subject he or she teaches.

The problem is worse in high-poverty schools, where students are nearly twice as likely as their counterparts in low-poverty schools to have a teacher who isn't certified in the subject he or she teaches—the figures are 26 percent and 13 percent, respectively. "No matter which way you measure teacher quality—in-field or out-of-field, certified or uncertified, or data on effectiveness—poor kids and kids of color get more than their fair share of low-end teachers," says Kati Haycock, head of the Education Trust, a Washington-based group devoted to improving the academic achievement of low-income and minority students.

Underlying the difficulty of attracting more talented men and women to teaching is the well-known problem of modest salaries and, in some cases, difficult working conditions. Beginning public school teachers, according to an annual survey conducted by the American Federation of Teachers, make an average of $30,719 (together with long summer vacations during which some teachers earn additional income), while the national average for all teachers was $44,367 in the 2001–2002 school year, compared to about $54,000 for mid-level accountants and $75,000 for engineers. At private and parochial schools, salaries are even lower.

Some veteran teachers can do quite well financially. In Montgomery County, Maryland, for instance—an affluent district with a strong academic reputation, where newly minted teachers start at $38,683 annually—more than two thousand 25-year veterans among the district's 11,189 teachers earn more than $80,000 annually. The highest-paid classroom teacher in Georgia—a P.E. teacher—made $90,895 in the 2001–2002 school year, a figure that reflects the doctorate he holds as well as his extra duties as a high school football coach. Still, most teaching salaries are hardly inspiring, even to the most public-spirited college grads.

An even more serious problem, according to many analysts, is how undifferentiated the salaries tend to be. In other words, terrific performers aren't rewarded. The typical public school teacher's salary is determined entirely by a combination of years of experience and graduate school credits earned (the "step and scale" system). The more years in the classroom and the more degrees you have, the more you earn. Critics point out that this approach (they call it the "factory model") doesn't take into account differences between teachers' qualifications and abilities, the subjects they teach, and the enormous variations in their working conditions. School districts and principals generally can't give star teachers raises or bonuses. They can't pay higher salaries to science or math grads who face lucrative career opportunities in other fields. Nor can they offer more money to teachers willing to take jobs in the most challenging schools—usually in urban areas where most students are disadvantaged and simply keeping control of a classroom can be a struggle.

A workplace in which good teachers make no more than bad teachers (who are often protected from sanctions or dismissal by union-negotiated tenure and seniority rules) contributes to what Andrew Rotherham, director of the 21st Century Schools Project at the Progressive Policy Institute, a Washington think tank, calls "adverse selection."

In other words, good people often don't want to stay and bad people won't leave. The situation is exacerbated by limited career growth ("You can very easily be doing the same thing on your last day after 30 years as you were on your first day," Rotherham says), which leads frustrated teachers either into higher-paid administrative jobs or out of education altogether.

Indeed, despite the unusually good job security most teachers enjoy, the shortcomings of their professional lives, from inflexible salary structures to insufficient mentoring and support, lead many talented teachers to quit the field. High turnover is such a big problem—one third of new teachers leave within three years and retention is even worse in urban schools—that there's considerable controversy over whether the much-bemoaned teacher shortage should be considered a shortage at all. An influential 2003 report from the National Commission on Teaching and America's Future used the metaphor of a leaky bucket to describe the problem of high attrition: Even as more candidates come through the pipeline, the system loses so many teachers that its demands are not met. "When we read the laments over how many teachers need to be hired each fall, and the cries of alarm over where they will come from," the report says, "we should be asking a more useful question: 'How many teachers left last spring—and why?'"

The sense of urgency—some would say crisis—surrounding calls for sweeping change stems in large part from mounting evidence that high-quality teachers are a uniquely important factor in raising student achievement. That's a key departure from the view, still held by many educators, that characteristics such as race, poverty, and parental education dwarf all other influences on how well children do in school. Some of those fac-

tors certainly play a role in school achievement, but researchers such as economists Steven Rivkin of Amherst College and Eric Hanushek of Stanford University's Hoover Institution have shown that having a good teacher makes a critical difference in how much students learn. Their analysis of Texas data found that if low-income students were given a really good math teacher for four or five years in a row, they could nearly close the gap in test scores that usually separates low-income and high-income students. The implications are striking: For all the attention that has been paid to promising reforms like increasing parental involvement and creating smaller schools, great teaching has a distinct and crucial transformative power.

Change is in the wind

Fortunately for those considering careers in the classroom, multiple efforts are underway to make teaching more attractive and rewarding for new recruits—and more effective for their students. Most reform initiatives embrace one of two contrasting philosophical approaches: Making it easier for candidates without traditional ed school credentials to teach—the so-called alternative certification movement, discussed at greater length in Chapter 2; and boosting training and certification requirements in an effort to ensure that all teachers are meeting rigorous standards. Not every reform effort, of course, falls neatly into one or the other camp, and some try to combine both approaches.

At the federal level, for instance, the No Child Left Behind Act includes a major teacher-quality component that requires every public school classroom to have a "highly qualified" teacher by the 2005–2006 school year. That means every teacher

Claudia Aceves-Rocha had planned to be an engineer ever since she spent the summer after eleventh grade taking science classes at the University of California–Los Angeles as part of the Upward Bound program. But as a junior at the University of California–Irvine, she took a work-study job tutoring elementary school kids. It was thrilling. So much so that after graduation she decided to teach kindergarten at Longfellow Elementary in the city of Compton (while simultaneously working toward her teaching certificate), just a couple miles from where she'd attended high school. "I felt I owed something to the community where I came from," Aceves-Rocha says.

Eight years later, Aceves-Rocha is still at Longfellow, now teaching first grade, but it hasn't been an easy ride. Many of her students are from struggling families; almost all participate in the government-assisted lunch program. "Half my class has parents who don't work, and some are staying in homeless shelters or living in a single room with six siblings," she says. "They're not worried about doing homework because they have more immediate problems." In other words, before she can get around to teaching reading and math, Aceves-Rocha finds herself dealing with everything from sleep deprivation to hunger to a student's anger at being shuffled to yet another foster home.

The biggest obstacle to helping her kids learn is getting them to school in the first place. Low attendance has been a constant problem for Aceves-Rocha; a third of her twenty students were absent just before and after Christmas. "Some of their parents are passive," she says. "If their kids say they're sick, they just stay home." Inevitably, they miss out on class content. "We'll review, but it's not in-depth and they're still way behind."

While the combination of California's state curriculum and the No Child Left Behind Act leave scant room for teacher creativity, Aceves-Rocha works hard to make learning fun. "I sell what I do," she says. "The approach I take is, 'What would make them want to learn?'"

When teaching a lesson about shapes, for example, she hands out soft foam cubes, cones, and spheres for students to touch and describe, rather than reading about them in the textbook. She occasionally strikes up a game of "time bingo," where students have to match digital with analog time on their game cards, and she keeps a box of glue sticks, rubber stamps, colorful erasers, and other "treasures" to reward good behavior.

But Aceves-Rocha's doesn't rely on carrots alone. Mounted on a wall in her classroom is a behavioral chart, where a green dot gives way to a yellow one if a student misbehaves, and a red dot triggers a call home. Aceves-Rocha sends a biweekly progress report home with every student. The secret to keeping students' attention, she believes, is maintaining absolute control of the classroom. She avoids even the briefest moments of downtime, distributing worksheets to students' desks before they arrive so they always have something to do.

Aceves-Rocha—who's married and has two young children of

her own—also leans heavily on fellow teachers for advice and pep talks. A group of them meets for dinner every couple of weeks to swap tales of failure and success in the classroom and to talk about life outside Longfellow. Aceves-Rocha has also spent some of that outside time working toward her master's in education, which she recently received. What keeps her going, despite the challenges of Longfellow, is the same thrill she experienced as a college tutor: the satisfaction of helping kids succeed. "My students come in sometimes not knowing how to read or write, with a blank stare on their faces," she says. "At the end of the year, they can open books and share [them] with their class. It's worth it just to see that smile."

must hold a bachelor's degree, possess full certification (as defined by each state), and also show competency in the subjects he or she teaches. The rules for veteran teachers allow considerable flexibility in demonstrating subject-matter competency. But newly hired elementary teachers must pass a test demonstrating their knowledge of core subjects such as reading, writing, and math, while new middle or high school teachers have to either pass a test or hold a degree in the subject they teach.

The requirements have already taken effect for schools receiving federal Title I money for disadvantaged children, and will soon be in place for all public schools. Across the country, states are scrambling to comply with this new mandate in a variety of ways. Some are defining certification so as to make it easier for teachers with nontraditional credentials to join the profession. In Texas, for instance, the State Board of Education recently approved a controversial proposal that would allow individuals with bachelor's degrees to teach in middle school and high school without having completed any education coursework, so long as they pass a subject-area exam and a state certifica-

tion test, and have a major related to the subject they would teach. The plan would grant candidates two-year temporary licenses while they complete an induction and preparation program run by their school districts.

Many other states are taking steps to ensure that teachers who are already in the classroom can show that they are properly qualified. Some state requirements are far more rigorous than others. According to *Education Week*, Arkansas deems teachers with five or more years in the classroom to be "highly qualified" simply on the basis of experience, while other states, including California, New Mexico, South Carolina, Ohio, and Massachusetts, are factoring in criteria such as classroom evaluations, portfolios of lesson plans, and participation in professional development activities. Only a few, including Colorado, Tennessee, and Virginia, permit or require teachers to show they are highly qualified by presenting evidence of student test performance.

Some states, however, are asking current teachers to prove they know their subjects by passing tests that weren't previously required. In

Pennsylvania, for example, an estimated 15,000 middle school teachers of math, English, science, or social studies must now begin passing tests in their subjects. That's because their teaching certificates, which have permitted them to teach any grade level from kindergarten to eighth grade, will only be valid for grades K through six by the end of the 2005–2006 school year. In middle school, the logic goes, the general knowledge that elementary school teachers possess isn't adequate for teaching subject-specific classes.

The new focus on teacher quality is having a big impact on schools of education, too. While faculty and administrators are often highly skeptical of public schools' new emphasis on testing, arguing that it's a mistake to tie high-stakes consequences to a single measure of student achievement, many are nonetheless engaged in considerable soul-searching about how to adapt their progressive tradition to an age of accountability. Arthur Levine, president of Teachers College at Columbia University (one of the schools profiled in Chapter 3), says institutions that train teachers must begin to identify quantitative measures of their graduates' effectiveness if they want public support. "We're missing an essential piece. What effect do the teachers we produce have on student achievement?" Levine says. "It's the way education schools will prove their worth." Change won't happen overnight, but the spirit of the times is already apparent at schools like Eastern Michigan University (also profiled in Chapter 3), where student teachers who try out a curriculum unit on their pupils are required to test the children before and after to see how much they have learned.

A major push to improve teacher prep is also being spearheaded by the Carnegie Corporation of New York through its "Teachers for a New Era" project. Together with the Annenberg, Ford, and Rockefeller foundations, Carnegie is spending more than $65 million on grants to 11 ed schools to "reform and reinvigorate" their teacher preparation efforts. The schools, which include the University of Texas at El Paso and Stanford University (both profiled in Chapter 3), are tasked with incorporating three principles into their program design: that it's crucial to systematically document the achievement of their students' students; that better integrating schools of education with the arts and sciences divisions of their universities makes for much better instruction of academic subjects; and that would-be teachers, like would-be doctors, need plentiful hands-on training and a period of "residency" following graduation, during which they get mentoring and support.

Many experts think that a fairly simple way to prod schools to improve is to standardize the passing score on state certification exams. The Educational Testing Service, creator of the Praxis II series of teacher-certification exams used in 23 states, is now collaborating with the National Council for Accreditation of Teacher Education (NCATE) to set a common national cutoff score. Currently, critics say, a wide variation in cutoff scores from one state to the next undercuts efforts to raise teacher quality across the board and renders meaningless a federal requirement that states report prospective teachers' passing rates on certification exams. Although no state would be forced to embrace the new benchmark, its existence would allow the public to compare how successful different states—and different ed schools—are at preparing well-qualified teachers.

Of all the efforts that are underway or on the drawing board, the most controversial would overhaul the uniform way in which teachers are compensated. It's clear that policymakers—and the teachers' unions that play a powerful role in determining salary scales—are willing to accept certain kinds of pay differentials: Several states that have had trouble attracting qualified teachers, for instance, have tried to lure new hires with signing bonuses, particularly in urban areas that often have the hardest time recruiting new hires. Similarly, teachers in subject areas where there are shortages, such as math, science, and special education, might earn extra pay.

There are also growing efforts to boost the pay of teachers who seek additional training or take on more responsibilities. In Delaware, for instance, teachers who receive certification from the National Board for Professional Teaching Standards earn a 12 percent salary boost. (A recent long-term study led by the University of Washington's Goldhaber, who has been skeptical of traditional state licensure requirements, found that teachers with the more-rigorous National Board certification had more impact on student achievement than other teachers.) Delaware teachers can also make more by completing professional-development activities and by serving on curriculum committees or mentoring other instructors, for example.

But the idea of pegging salary to performance as many propose doing—of paying teachers whose students learn the most a higher salary than teachers whose students lag—remains one of the hottest potatoes in education reform. Opponents of "merit pay" fear that it can't be implemented fairly, either because of favoritism by principals or the difficulty of determining whether a teacher is effective. Proponents insist that only when an excellent teacher can reap financial rewards based on her "outputs," or how much students learn, rather than her "inputs," or paper credentials, will the brightest college graduates be likely to go into teaching—and stay.

Several performance-pay experiments have been tried, proposed, or are underway—with varied success. Iowa's plan, which was viewed as one of the most comprehensive and innovative in the nation when it was passed in 2001, aimed to evaluate teachers every three years and give bonuses to those who met student achievement goals. But state budget troubles meant that it was never fully implemented, and in early 2004 legislators were contemplating putting an end to the program. Philadelphia also scuttled a merit pay plan on the grounds that it was too costly and hard to administer.

In Denver, by contrast, a pilot project to link pay to student performance has been well received thus far, in part because it has the joint backing of the school district and the teachers' union. In its initial phase at 16 schools, the project has aimed to attract and retain good teachers by awarding bonuses of up to $1,500 to those whose pupils make progress toward goals set by teachers and principals. Under a more complex and ambitious proposal that could ultimately affect every teacher in the district, successful veterans could see their salaries jump from $65,000 (for those holding a Ph.D.) to as much as $90,000 if they receive top marks in their evaluations, boost student achievement, and teach in underperforming schools. In Minnesota, Gov. Tim Pawlenty has proposed a pilot plan to attract better teachers to the state's most troubled schools; it would make them eligible for bonuses of $20,000 to $40,000 if they raise student scores.

Many of the new efforts to evaluate teachers' effectiveness rely on some version of the "value-added" concept pioneered in the 1990s by Tennessee researcher William Sanders. The idea is to track the performance of a teacher's pupils each year using their test results from prior years to calculate an "expected score," which can be compared to the progress actually made. A teacher whose pupils moved from the 30th to the 40th percentile would earn high marks, while a teacher whose students started at the 90th percentile and stayed there would not.

A similar approach is incorporated into the Milken Family Foundation's Teacher Advancement Program, one of the fastest-growing and most closely watched efforts to attract and retain high-quality teachers (see page 5). This initiative, which is being piloted at 70-plus schools in Arizona, Arkansas, Colorado, Florida, Indiana, Louisiana, Minnesota, and South Carolina, uses student-performance data along with detailed classroom evaluations of teachers by faculty peers and administrators to help determine who is most effective. Those teachers can receive performance bonuses and are ultimately eligible to move into more challenging and higher-paying jobs as mentor teachers, who teach a normal load while helping coach their peers, or master teachers, who teach only one class and spend most of their time evaluating and coaching their colleagues.

Value-added analysis has also helped Chattanooga, Tennessee, start turning around its struggling schools by introducing merit pay. School officials first transferred about 100 of the weakest teachers to suburban schools in the district. Then, using a $5 million grant from a local philanthropy, the district identified its most effective teachers using the value-added testing system and offered them a series of benefits for transferring to one of the nine lowest-performing schools. Each was eligible for a $5,000 bonus, tuition toward a master's degree, a $10,000 loan to buy a home near school, and a $2,000 bonus if the school's test scores rose by a certain amount. So far, teacher vacancies have decreased from 30 in 2002 to two in 2003. Most important, student pass rates on Tennessee's state tests at the nine schools have risen significantly: The average gain in the program's first year was almost twice the district average.

So what does this all mean to me?

On the one hand, the new focus on performance and accountability may seem pretty intimidating. In fact, some fear that the passion and commitment that have long drawn young people—and career switchers—to the classroom will be smothered by a blanket of new requirements. But the more optimistic reading is that higher standards can only be good news for those teachers who have what it takes. "I do think the accountability issue is really critical," says Judy Herr, a reading teacher at a suburban elementary school near Washington, D.C. "It does motivate people."

The opportunity to change young lives was a powerful draw for Herr. After spending 20 years in health care management, she decided to switch careers because she realized that "teaching really needed the teachers I had from years ago, who were well-educated, intelligent, with broad interests, who really took the worldview of trying to prepare the next generation of citizens." She wasn't thrilled with the months of ed school courses she had to take—she already had two master's degrees and didn't find her classes very useful. But she is delighted with the job she landed teaching reading in daily 90-minute blocks to mixed-ability groups of first and second graders. "I absolutely love what I do," she says.

Former USAirways executive John Long, a friend of Herr's, gave up his lucrative corporate career to teach middle school social studies. His $48,000 annual salary is about one-seventh of what he used to make, and his job can be grueling: "I feel like I'm getting up on stage giving five performances a day," he says. Yet Long, too, says his job satisfaction is high. "It was the best decision I've ever made."

With the right changes in teaching, those kind of career switches might become more common—and new college grads would be more likely to opt for teaching in the first place. If what successful teachers do can be properly measured and sufficiently rewarded, their students will learn more and their own careers will become more satisfying. In the end, teaching will finally receive—will earn, in fact—the respect that educators have long sought. And the profession will appeal to more of the talented people whose energy, expertise, and dedication American children so badly need.

Chapter Two

Alternative Routes to the Classroom

Perhaps it's already obvious to you, but it's worth saying again: Becoming a teacher isn't easy. The traditional path to a job in the public schools for anyone who already holds a bachelor's degree—a graduate education program leading to state certification—can be daunting or unappealing for any number of reasons. There's the considerable amount of classroom time required, of course, not to mention the cost of tuition—obstacles that are especially serious for career switchers who can't afford a year or more out of the work-force. Then there's the prospect of ed school classes them-selves, which can seem, well, beside the point for people who just want to get into the classroom and start teaching.

Today, however, there are more and more options for doing just that. So-called alternative certification programs have sprung up around the country, bringing some 200,000 new teachers into the field. That's still a relatively modest fraction of the 3 million teachers who hold traditionally obtained licenses, but in some districts and states the proportion is much higher: More than

---

"If education schools could make themselves more attractive to highly qualified people, then we wouldn't need alternative certification."

---

one quarter of New York City's new teachers come through alternatives routes, as do more than one in five new teachers hired in New Jersey, 16 percent of new hires in Texas, and 8 percent of California's new teachers. Nationwide, 46 states and the District of Columbia have introduced alternative pathways to teaching, up from just eight states in the early 1980s.

These programs, which typically involve a collaboration between the state departments of education that license teachers, the ed schools that have traditionally trained teachers, and the school districts that hire teachers, come in all shapes and sizes. The definition of "alternative certification" is so elastic, in fact, that some programs aimed at talented college grads who want to teach amount to no more than a slightly streamlined version of conventional ed school training, while some, like one passed recently in Texas, bypass ed school preparation entirely. Many programs consist of an intensive summer course followed by immersion in a real classroom as a full-time teacher, accompanied by mentoring and other forms of on-the-job training.

Anybody hoping to avoid ed school classes completely is, in most cases, out of luck: Most programs require that new teachers complete state certification requirements by taking education classes at night or on weekends during their first year or two of teaching.

Still, the appeal of efforts like Teach for America and New York City's Teaching Fellows program is growing, for both practical and philosophical reasons. Most alternative programs have arisen out of the need to bring new recruits into the classroom quickly, whether in hard-to-staff urban and rural schools facing severe teacher shortages or in schools with a dearth of qualified instructors in subjects such as math and science. Now, despite concerns about the uneven quality of some alternative routes, many education reformers view these programs as a healthy phenomenon in their own right. That's because they have the potential to boost the supply of highly competent teachers coming in from other professions—people who have strong content knowledge but who might not otherwise consider a career in the classroom.

"In an ideal world, every teacher would come in [to university teacher preparation programs] with very strong subject expertise and then get strong training in things like scientifically based reading instruction and classroom management," says Michael Petrilli, associate deputy under secretary in the U.S. Department of Education's new Office of Innovation and Improvement. "The problem is, we have not been successful in doing that. If education schools could reform themselves and make themselves more attractive to highly qualified people, then we wouldn't need alternative certification."

Alternative programs vary widely from state to state and district to district, which can make it tough to find the place that's right for you. Chapter 6 includes a state-by-state list of contacts for information on gaining certification, including the alternative routes. A one-stop-shopping clearinghouse of alternative certification options is now available from the National Center for Alternative Certification. The center has a comprehensive website (www.teach-now.org), toll-free number, and newsletter dedicated to providing detailed information to nontraditional teaching candidates.

In this chapter, we highlight a few of the most innovative alternative pathways into the classroom, including a new exam that gives qualified candidates the ability to start teaching right away—without going to ed school.

Teach for America

Perhaps the best known of the alternative programs is Teach for America (www.teachforamerica.org), which recruits ambitious, high-energy, recent college graduates—often from top universities—to spend two years teaching in low-income urban and rural schools. Founded by Princeton graduate Wendy Kopp in 1989, the Peace Corps–style program has grown enormously in influence and popularity. It had some 500 recruits in its first year; by the fall of 2004 it expected to place 1,700 new teachers in 21 communities, including Atlanta, Los Angeles, the Mississippi Delta, New Mexico, New York City, Phoenix, the Rio Grande Valley, South Dakota, and Washington, D.C. Despite the low pay and challenging working conditions many corps members face, TFA is immensely competitive: The nearly 16,000 applications TFA received for about 1,800 spots in its 2003 teaching corps made it harder to get into than

Harvard Law School. Last year's corps had an average grade point average of 3.5, one full point higher than school districts generally require; almost all members had held leadership positions on their undergraduate campuses.

New recruits go through an intensive summer training session at one of several sites around the country before starting their new jobs. They take courses toward certification, usually at nearby ed schools, while teaching full time, and are often placed in schools with several fellow corps members to mitigate the sense of isolation that is often the plight of new teachers. The five-week-long boot camp concentrates almost entirely on practical skills, giving corps members real classroom experience teaching summer school along with a steady diet of lectures, analysis of videotaped lessons, and one-on-one tutoring to help prepare them for the challenging schools where they'll be serving. The crash course folds in everything from how to plan reading or social studies lessons to such key classroom management techniques as sternly giving misbehaving students "the teacher look" or using physical proximity—crouching down close to a child or whispering a private reprimand—in order to regain control.

The training can be tough. In 2003, just after graduating from Georgetown University—where he'd majored in Latin American studies and interned in the White House, on Capitol Hill, and at ABC's *Nightline*—Eric Lincoln found himself struggling to keep control of a junior high summer school class in the Bronx. Despite the rules and consequences he'd carefully posted on the blackboard, and his calm efforts to keep his students focused on a graph showing how many hot dogs were sold at a baseball game, things soon degenerated. A male and a female student ended up shrieking at one another over a real or imagined slight and then scattered the contents of each other's desk on the floor. Fortunately for Lincoln, the class period soon ended. He quickly dismissed the other students before talking individually to each of the aggrieved parties. After class, he said he wished he had nipped the conflict in the bud, but chalked the incident up to experience: "This is the place to learn, to make mis-

---

"Part of our theory of change is that we need lawyers and doctors who have taught in the country's most underserved schools."

---

takes, to see things for the first time, so in the fall you're better prepared."

Six months later, midway through his first year of teaching world history and ancient civilization to sixth graders at Middle School 223 in the South Bronx, Lincoln felt that his summer coursework had prepared him pretty well for his rookie year. Still, he says, "being a first year teacher in a community with students who have so many needs is the toughest thing I have done by far." He's hoping to improve significantly by his second year, and plans to stay for at least one more after that to see his students off to high school.

To its detractors, Teach for America's premise smacks of self-righteousness and noblesse oblige; they fear that the program's bright young Ivy Leaguers, about two thirds of whom are white, hold the mistaken belief that they can parachute into ghetto classrooms and single-handedly fix the problems that ail struggling schools. Critics also fault TFA for what they view as inadequate training and a high rate of turnover. But the program's many defenders say training and mentoring has been

carefully evaluated and improved since the early days. There's a special effort made to avoid the "white knight" syndrome; instructors in the Bronx program attended by Lincoln urge corps members to tap the wisdom of veteran teachers and staff in the schools where they're assigned. Most important, boosters say, the program is helping poor kids learn: No long-term evaluations are available yet, but a recent national study by Mathematica Policy Research, Inc. found that TFA teachers outperformed a randomized control group of their non-TFA colleagues in raising student math scores and achieved about the same gains in reading. Another study in Houston found TFA teachers were disproportionately represented among the highest-performing instructors; no TFA members were in the group with the worst track record at raising student scores.

And while the program's administrators acknowledge that many graduates leave the classroom after their two-year stint is up, they note that 63 percent of TFA graduates have remained in education since the program started, whether as teachers, principals, or policymakers. In addition, says Steven Farr, TFA's vice president for program design and a former corps member in Texas's Rio Grande Valley, "Part of our theory of change is that we need lawyers and doctors who have taught in the country's most underserved schools. We need community leaders in all sectors of society who have been there."

American Board for Certification of Teacher Excellence

A new and still controversial player in the alternative movement is the American Board for Certification of Teacher Excellence (www.abcte.org). Founded in 2001, the ABCTE aims to increase the supply of highly qualified teachers by offering certification to individuals without ed school training who hold a bachelor's degree and can pass a series of tough new exams that measure subject-area mastery as well as "professional teaching knowledge."

So far, the group's tests, one for new teachers and one for those already in the classroom, are accepted in only three states: Florida, Idaho, and Pennsylvania (which also requires that those who pass the American Board's exam for new teachers complete a one-year induction period of classroom teaching in which they're mentored by a fellow teacher and supervised by the school's principal). But backers are pushing hard for approval in a dozen more states.

In the 2003 school year, ABCTE certification was available only in elementary education, mathematics (grades 6–12) and English (6–12), but several other certification tests are under development, including special education, science, history, and reading. In addition to the academic tests, candidates most take a separate pedagogy exam that asks about such matters as how to interpret student test results, how long to wait for a student answer to a tough question, and—after watching a video of a classroom interaction—how best to respond to a disruptive pupil.

The ABCTE has become a favorite of U.S. Department of Education policymakers, receiving federal grants expected to total $40 million over five years. It is lauded in a recent Education Department report on teacher quality as "an innovative way to meet the twin challenges of raising academic standards for teachers while lowering barriers to the profession." By establishing rigorous standards for passing the exams, the program aims to raise the bar for people entering the profession and at the same time "enable thousands of talented college graduates and mid-career professionals to enter teaching without having to bear the burden and expense of post-graduate training," the report says.

Yet critics of the new exam say it can't possibly measure the qualities that teachers need to succeed—in particular their mastery of the pedagogical methods taught in colleges of education. "We think it's important for people to be prepared to teach before they teach," says Arthur Wise, president of the National Council for Accreditation of Teacher Education. ABCTE, he declares, "believes in *no* teacher prep." Detractors also argue that it is a mistake to create a route to teacher certification that includes no student-teaching component or any other real-world classroom preparation.

For their part, ABCTE officials say that their certification exam is simply intended to show that nontraditional candidates have a solid professional knowledge base. The hiring process, they argue, should be used to sort out who is likely to be an effective teacher, factoring in backgrounds in and out of the classroom. "I get 100 emails a week from people who want to be teachers but can't take a year off or even 14 weeks off to go and do some kind of practice teaching experience," says the group's president, Kathleen Madigan, a former assistant dean at the University of Oregon's school of education. "Yet these are also people who have coached Little League or been Girl Scout leaders or have taught in private schools."

Profile: The suburban ESOL teacher

Thom Blain didn't become a teacher until he was 45—at which time, by his reckoning, he'd been training for the job for more than 20 years.

"What you learn in the Army is very applicable to the classroom," says Blain of his first career; he's now a teacher at Glasgow Middle School in Alexandria, Virginia, with several years' experience under his belt. Indeed, school districts often jump at hiring retired military personnel, who have interpersonal skills well honed from working with diverse groups inside a large organization. And since military retirement comes after only 20 years in the service, these retirees are men and women in the prime of their lives.

In Blain's case, as he reached his late thirties, he realized that although he was serving as a police officer in the military and had earned a master's in social work from the University of Alabama, he wanted to do something completely new. He was drawn instead to his wife's chosen field. She "was my inspiration," says Blain. He tested his interest by getting permission to observe classes in schools near his Virginia home. And though he initially hoped to draw on his seven years in Germany to teach German, he quickly changed his mind when he realized that teachers of English for Speakers of Other Languages are in such high demand. "I looked at ESOL and realized that it's closely related to teaching German as a foreign language," he says. "And it makes me much more marketable."

While still in the Army, Blain enrolled in George Washington University's alternative certification program, Transition to Teaching, and knocked out his education courses evenings and weekends. The very week he retired from the service, Blain began a semester-long student teaching assignment in high school German and middle school ESOL.

Although he works in affluent Fairfax County near Washington, D.C., where the median household income is among the top 10 in the nation, his students are overwhelmingly poor and many are new immigrants to the country. Some 65 percent qualify for

---

The key to helping qualified teachers become successful, she says, is mentoring and support once they are in the classroom. Madigan insists that there's plenty of room for both traditional and innovative approaches. "I also want to tell the colleges of education, 'We are not your enemy. If you do a good job, there are plenty of people who want to be teachers who will go through a more traditional route,'" Madigan says.

Private and charter schools

Another popular way into the classroom for college graduates or career changers is to teach in private, parochial, and some charter schools. These institutions aren't bound by state certification requirements, and may actively prefer instructors with subject-matter expertise rather than an ed school degree. "We actually eschew certification in most cases, and seek teachers who have a degree

free or reduced-price lunches, and ESOL is practically a rite of passage: Currently, 42 percent of the children in his school are enrolled in the ESOL program, and many more graduated out of the program in elementary school or sometime during middle school.

"When I first started teaching nine years ago, I was getting kids from Somalia who had not had a chance to go to school at all, and they were not literate in any language," says Blain. "You're the first reading teacher they've ever had and you're teaching them to read in a new language. You teach letters, and they don't know what letters are. I had a student who didn't know how to hold a pair of scissors, and he was in the sixth grade."

These days, most of his students are coming from Central and South America and have attended school in the past. Still, Blain can't assume any common base of knowledge. In his mixed seventh and eighth grade class, for example, some students have barely any English skills but excel in math and science; others are nearly ready to graduate from the ESOL program, but are weak in subject knowledge. To impose some order on the confusion, the school divides ESOL students into three groups: beginning, intermediate, and advanced. Beginning students take all four core classes (math, English, social studies, and science) in the ESOL department, venturing

into regular classes for gym, art, or music. Intermediate students take math and science in regular classes and return to their ESOL teachers for social studies and English. Advanced students take one ESOL language class and are otherwise fully mainstreamed into regular classes. Blain teaches social studies to the beginners, introducing new vocabulary, as he goes.

To be sure, the job Blain has set for himself requires communicating more than social studies. "The biggest challenge is convincing the kids of the value of education," he says. "My [own] kids grew up thinking that after high school you go to college, and for these kids that's not a part of their culture."

in the liberal arts in the subject which they'll be teaching" rather than a major in education and state licensure, says Patrick Bassett, a veteran private school headmaster who is now president of the National Association of Independent Schools. That's especially true of secondary school teachers, he adds, but many of the elementary schools among the 1,200 institutions in his organization also hire liberal arts grads.

Independent schools hire disproportionately from competitive colleges, most of which don't even offer education degrees. "What we use instead of formal courses in pedagogy is a mentoring system," says Bassett, "much like an apprentice system in the old guilds," with new teachers assigned to a master teacher for guidance and support. Classes in pedagogy are no substitute for hands-on experience, he says. "It's like learning to drive. You can read all the instruction manuals in the world, but until you actually do it, you don't get it."

At Phillips Academy in Andover, Massachusetts, a prestigious boarding school near Boston, "our philosophy is we're looking for people who have a real passion in their subject and who can transmit that to the kids in the classroom," says dean of faculty Stephen Carter. Most of the school's regular hires

---

Teaching is "like learning to drive. You can read all the instruction manuals in the world, but until you actually do it, you don't get it."

---

have prior teaching experience and hold master's degrees in an academic subject (some hold MAT degrees—an ed school credential that focuses primarily on content knowledge). Much as colleges hire professors who haven't been trained as teachers but who are experts in their fields, the school wants teachers "whose real interest in life is doing math, or history, or Spanish," Carter explains.

In addition, each year the school hires a dozen recent liberal arts graduates with excellent academic credentials as teaching fellows. For a $19,000 salary—plus free room and board—the fellows spend a year teaching a reduced load, living in the dorms, and coaching sports teams. They meet weekly with a department mentor to receive assistance with things like classroom management and grading. The entire group convenes every other week for seminars, led by two permanent faculty members, that cover everything from how to lead a discussion to maintaining a personal life while juggling demanding classroom and dorm responsibilities. Eight or nine of each year's fellows typically go into teach-

ing jobs afterward, Carter says, usually at other private schools.

Similarly, at the Beauvoir School in Washington, D.C., a prekindergarten through third grade elementary school that caters to the children of the city's elite, head of school Paula Carreiro likes to hire experienced teachers with a strong liberal arts background. "Most ed schools are far too narrow," she says, although she does like her teachers to have taken a class in educational psychology "so they'll understand that at age five children learn with their hands rather than their heads."

Several of the school's 37 teachers have Ph.D.s and eight have master's degrees, but only four are certified. Beauvoir also has an "associate teacher" program, similar to Andover's teaching fellows program, in which 19 graduates of top colleges spend a year or two learning the ropes while they work with a veteran teacher.

In a much poorer section of the nation's capital, teachers with nontraditional backgrounds are also plentiful at the KIPP DC: KEY Academy, a highly regarded public charter school. "Very few of my teachers have gone through the traditional schooling," says the middle school's principal, Susan Schaeffler, who has hired many Teach for America graduates—and is a former corps member herself.

Her teachers often hold a master's degree in their subject area, and she likes to see at least a couple of years' classroom experience—"I think teachers going into their third year are often in their prime," she says. They also need a willingness to dive into KIPP's demanding culture, which includes an 8 a.m. to 5 p.m. daily schedule, a high-energy work environment, and a willingness to field cell phone calls from students with homework questions at all hours. She also requires candidates to teach a practice class in front of her and a roomful of kids. "You can look great on paper, but if you get put in front of the class and you're shy or too quiet, or you don't have a good presence in the classroom, you're not going to get a job."

One major concern for some candidates considering private school teaching jobs is money. Average salaries are lower than in public schools: $42,400 in the 2003–2004 school year, according to National Association of Independent Schools statistics (which don't include even more modest parochial school salaries), compared to an estimated $46,300 in public schools. But private school jobs are nevertheless attractive to many individuals who value working in environments that are relatively free of the bureaucracy and discipline problems that characterize too many public schools—and where the lack of an ed school credential isn't a barrier to employment. Still, independent schools are making a big effort to shrink the salary gap and have already had some success, Bassett says: "We've got to be more competitive in order to attract the next generation of teachers."

Despite the lower salary scale, private schools often manage to hire strong candidates with good subject-area expertise. A study by Harvard University economist Caroline Hoxby found that private and charter schools are considerably more likely than public schools to hire teachers who attended competitive colleges: 36 percent of private and charter school teachers went to selective colleges, compared to just 20 percent of public school teachers. Hoxby also found that more than half the teachers at charter schools and 42 percent of teachers at private schools had a subject major in the arts and sciences rather than an education major, compared to 37 percent of public school teachers.

New Teacher Project

Many of the nation's best-regarded nontraditional programs for novice teachers are run in partnership with the New Teacher Project (www.tntp.org). The group bills itself as a nonprofit consulting firm and works with districts both to improve their hiring processes and to establish well-run alternative routes that help provide school systems with a better supply of high-caliber teachers. Started in 1997 as an offshoot of Teach for America, the organization set up such programs as the NYC Teaching Fellows in New York, the D.C. Teaching Fellows in the nation's capital, and Teach Baton Rouge in Louisiana's struggling East Baton Rouge Parish School System. In all, since 1997 it has established 39 programs in 18 states.

The group was started, says CEO and president Michelle Rhee, to combat the teacher shortage. But it eventually identified a key problem in the hiring practices of many poor rural and urban districts. In some cases, those schools would hire nontraditional candidates—but in the worst possible way. "They'd spend all their time and resources recruiting traditionally certified teachers, but then July and August would roll around and they wouldn't have enough," Rhee says. "Then they'd start what we affectionately refer to as the 'street sweep': If you had a pulse and could pass a criminal background check, they'd put you in the classroom" with an emergency credential. "It was giving alternative certification a bad name."

The New Teacher Project analyzed the characteristics of the best alternative routes and came up with a model that focuses on three areas:

recruitment, selectivity, and training. The project tries to make sure that its programs begin with aggressive and imaginative recruitment—not only among high-achieving recent grads but also disgruntled corporate consultants and other promising midcareer candidates—in order to create a large and top-quality applicant pool.

There's also a special effort to target a particular kind of person, Rhee says: "Not somebody who wants to come in and be a savior and think that everybody's going to love them, but somebody who has a realistic sense of the challenge they're going to face in terms of teaching in an under-resourced environment. People don't care that you were the CEO of a Fortune 500 company and that you want to have a phone in your room." The most successful recruits, she says, understand that "despite all the obstacles—the social issues students come in with, the lack of resources—their job is to help those kids succeed." To ensure the selectivity that it believes is key to program success, the Project seeks a minimum of three applications for every program vacancy and has managed to achieve an even better national average of nine to one.

Training is also key. The programs typically include at least six weeks of training—including some time teaching in a public school classroom, which Rhee calls "a pretty crucial part of what makes people feel more prepared and makes them most successful in the fall." Once they start work, most recruits enroll in a university-run certification program.

The programs founded by the project have proven extremely popular. The NYC Teaching Fellows program, for instance, which has found new recruits using catchy subway ads, at career fairs, and by visiting college campuses, attracted 20,000 applicants in 2003. It made offers to 4,000 prospects, of whom 2,700 started the seven-week summer training program. About 2,400 entered the classroom, at starting salaries of $39,000 for bachelor's degree holders and $43,800 for those with a master's. Among the program's perks: a significant subsidy—about $8,000 of the $12,000 total cost—toward the master's degrees in education that all teachers must earn to be permanently certified in New York State. The latest group of fellows made up more than one quarter of all new teachers hired in the city. For a district that has long struggled to find better teachers, this unconventional source of new talent is already making a big difference.

Chapter Three

Which Is the Right School for You?

"Who dares to teach must never cease to learn," librarian John Cotton Dana famously declared back in 1912. In light of the challenges facing educators today, this dictum has never been more relevant.

But with teacher preparation in a state of upheaval, figuring out how and where to get this schooling can be tough. Quality, to put it mildly, is uneven. On the other hand, loud and persistent calls for reform in recent years—from politicians, parents, and educators alike—are having an impact. "It's not interesting anymore to talk about whether colleges of education are under stress and not doing a good job—it's something almost everybody acknowledges," says Lisa Graham Keegan, former superintendent of public education in Arizona and chief executive of the Education Leaders Council, a Washington, D.C.–based reform organization. "But since they're under such pressure and all of these other alternatives are cropping up, I think it is pushing [ed] schools to take a look at themselves to see if they can't offer more promising and relevant programs."

The good news is that there are some excellent options out there, from yearlong certification programs for those who have yet to step into a classroom to part-time master's degrees for veteran teachers who want to upgrade their credentials— and their paychecks. The best of these incorporate the latest thinking on educational pedagogy but emphasize a thorough mastery of subject content, address the use of technology and the needs of students from different backgrounds in a comprehensive way, and provide a healthy dose of teaching practice. Here's how to ensure you get your money's worth.

For those new to teaching

Consider the basics

First things first: Before you can start teaching, you need to get certified. Someone who already has an undergraduate degree (but in a subject other than teaching) can accomplish this in two main ways: by completing a postbaccalaureate or master's program in education, or by going through a sort of boot camp alternative certification training program (see Chapter 2). In struggling districts with a desperate need for instructors, would-be teachers can also sometimes obtain emergency credentials that place novices in the classroom with little or no training and the expectation that they will get proper instruction during the next year or two.

Requirements vary considerably by state, however. In Florida, you can obtain an initial three-year teaching certification with an undergraduate degree and a major in the subject you want to teach, or with a degree and a passing score on the relevant subject area test of the Florida Teacher Certification Examination. For full licensure, instructors must complete an approved teacher-prep or alternative certification program and pass the state's professional education, general knowledge, and subject tests. In Arizona, an applicant for a provisional K–8 teaching certificate must complete an approved teacher-prep program in elementary education, or have at least forty-five hours worth of ed courses—including at least eight in field work—in addition to passing the state's professional and subject knowledge exams. It takes two years of teaching experience to upgrade to a full six-year certificate there, while those who want permanent certification in New York State must get a master's degree.

If you're confused about what, exactly, you'll need to do in your own state, check out www.title2.org, a Department of Education website. The "2003 State Reports" section provides a breakdown of information such as how to obtain certification or licensure; what an instructor should know and be able to do in the classroom; and the pass rates—by school of education—of would-be teachers on state certification exams. The latter can be an excellent indicator of an institution's quality, although some schools have tried to work the system by counting only those students who actually pass these tests as graduates, which results in an automatic—and deceptive—100 percent rate. You might want to quiz a school about its calculations if its results seem just a bit too rosy.

Bear in mind that it helps to pick a program in

the state you'd like to work in, as each school teaches to its own state's licensing exam, and transferring credentials from one state to another can be tricky. A school's location can influence your training in other ways, too. "If you want to work in a rural area, you shouldn't come to Teachers College," says Karen Zumwalt, a professor at Teachers, the education school affiliated with Columbia University in New York, where most of the student-teaching placements are in urban institutions and instruction is tailored accordingly. The University of Wisconsin–Milwaukee has a similar focus. Other schools, like the University of Connecticut in Storrs, expose students to teaching in all settings: urban, suburban, and rural.

Investigate where a program's graduates end up working: Are they taking jobs in high-needs districts, cushy suburban schools, or a mix of the two? The answer can be a good indicator of how well they're being prepared for each type of classroom environment.

In addition, you might want to examine what kind of reputation an ed school has within nearby school districts, especially for turning out teachers whose own students actually learn something, says Daniel Fallon, chair of the education division of the Carnegie Corporation of New York. The philanthropic organization is currently funding the $65 million "Teachers for a New Era" program, which is promoting reform in 11 representantive ed schools across the country. One strong focus is accountability: Schools of education, the group says, should be systematically measuring the progress made by the K–12 students of their own students.

Very few schools are actually doing this yet. East Carolina University in Greenville, North Carolina, for one, tracks the standardized test performance of the seventh and eighth grade students of teachers in its middle school program in mathematics to prove that its teaching methods work. But a good school should be moving in that direction, says Fallon: "Savvy consumers should

"If you want to work in a rural area, you shouldn't come to Teachers College."

constantly ask the question, 'Is this [education] school dominated by a culture of respect for evidence?' Are they dedicated to showing that the practices in the curriculum can be linked to data showing that those practices produce student learning growth?"

It's also a smart idea to investigate the extent to which an institution has committed resources to teacher education as opposed to more high-profile, research-based master's and Ph.D. programs. Several key questions: Does the school staff its teacher-ed courses with tenured (or tenure-track) professors, or mostly adjuncts, who may not be as experienced or qualified? Does it take the notion seriously that teachers-in-training, like doctors-in-training, need rigorous clinical practice—lots of time in K–12 classrooms, in other words? Does it have a close relationship with the local school system, so that professors get a constant stream of information about what's going on in actual classrooms and can prepare future educators accordingly? Here are a few other key questions you should ask:

What's in the curriculum?

Now it's time to focus on what, exactly, you'll be learning. Though there is plenty of debate about the proper place of pedagogy and theory in the curriculum, most experts agree that a grounding in the foundations of the field is important, says David Steiner, chairman of the department of Administration, Training, and Policy Studies at Boston University's School of Education and author of a recent study of the quality of teacher training.

So you should expect to study the philosophy, history, and psychology of education, for example—everything from Plato and Rousseau to the work of contemporary thinkers like Stanford professors David Tyack and Larry Cuban, coauthors of *Tinkering toward Utopia: A Century of Public School Reform*, and education historian Diane Ravitch, whose latest book is *The Language Police: How Pressure Groups Restrict What Students Learn*. And you should certainly be grappling with current issues in education reform, including testing and the charter school movement. Check syllabi to see if you'll cover the full range of topics.

In general, look for programs that also offer coursework in child psychology, classroom management techniques, and teaching methods that are relevant to the grades and subject area of choice. A general course such as Methods in Teaching High School and Junior High Science is probably not going to help a future tenth grade physics instructor all that much; instead, seek out more tailored offerings such as Methods in Teaching Physics.

In the end, it's not so much the number of theory courses required that's key, as whether or not or not you'll be discussing and relating the ideas learned to today's classrooms and your own professional experience. "If you're not spending more actual time working with kids in school classrooms than you are in college classrooms, then none of the theory or methods are going to matter, because you're not going to learn how to apply them," says Jon Snyder, dean of the Graduate School of Education at Bank Street College in New York City, where the ratio of time spent in K–12 schools versus graduate courses is an impressive 2 to 1.

If you truly want a *career* in teaching, it's essential to find a program that will prepare you to deal with the reality of elementary and secondary education in the twenty-first century. The reality is that states spent some $2.7 billion in federal money on educational technologies this year alone, up from a mere $81 million in 1996. Another reality: At last count, nearly 40 percent of public school students came from minority backgrounds—a figure that is only going to skyrocket in years to come. Clearly, a stand-alone course in word processing or multiculturalism just doesn't cut it anymore. The best ed schools have taken great pains to fully integrate these once trendy and now de rigueur areas of study into their curricula.

At the University of Virginia's Curry School of Education, for example, students take introductory technology courses that are differentiated by content area and grade level—computers as they apply to elementary reading, say—followed by subject-specific methods classes that also incorporate the latest innovations in hardware and software. The idea is to help would-be teachers use state-of-the-art technologies to effectively help kids learn. One science education student, for example, recently developed a research project for a high school biology class on the life cycle of the painted lady butterfly using the Intel QX3 microscope—which can produce magnified still images, movies, and time lapse photography—to capture and study the

Master of arts in teaching. Master of education. Master of arts in education. Master in teaching. Is it just us, or does deciphering ed school lingo require a course in itself? Here's a primer.

Current teachers who want to sharpen their skills or enhance their credentials to boost their pay should be on the lookout for schools that grant a **master of arts (M.A.)** or a **master of education (M.Ed.)** degree. These programs tend to focus on advanced coursework in a subject area such as math or history and typically don't require an internship. At many institutions, an M.Ed. prepares students to be better classroom instructors. By contrast, M.A.s at these schools are often research-oriented and may be a step toward a Ph.D., the principal or counselor's office, or a job with a nonprofit organization. The M.A. comes in a menu of flavors, from educational psychology and higher education administration to curriculum development, and is more of a generalist degree.

But wait! A **master of arts in teaching (M.A.T.)** or a **master in teaching (M.I.T.)** tends to be a surer ticket to the classroom than even an M.Ed. because at schools offering these programs, the M.Ed. is usually the generalist degree. Got that? Generally speaking, M.A.T.s and M.I.T.s are the degrees geared toward career switchers or new college graduates with undergraduate majors in other disciplines; they offer initial certification and emphasize courses in basic teaching skills, the history of education, and practical experience in schools.

Doctorate programs also fall into two basic categories. The **Ph.D.** is for people who want to teach at a university or work in government, forming policy, while the **Ed.D.** best suits individuals who want to work in the field, in capacities like running an elementary school or school district.

Basically, unlocking ed school code requires knowing how each institution defines its **professional degrees**, which are geared for people who intend to teach, and its **research degrees**, those most useful to nonteaching educators. Whichever you decide to pursue, compare the options in that area for all of the schools on your list—noting that some institutions focus more on one than the other—regardless of what letters will land on a diploma.

metamorphosis of the creature. Future social studies teachers work with the University's Center for Digital History, an online warehouse for primary resources such as old newspapers, maps, letters, and diaries. Then they lead children studying the battle of Gettysburg to online fighting simulations, soldiers' dossiers, and battle-day weather reports so the kids learn to interpret historical artifacts as historians do, rather than simply memorize facts.

The study of how cultural differences affect what happens in the classroom should be given similar weight, many believe, if teachers are really going to make sure no child is left behind. The worst programs still just pay lip service to issues of multiculturalism in a single lecture or class; the best, like the University of Colorado–Boulder, address racial and ethnic differences in all classes and internship experiences. Boulder's required course School and Society includes a "community mini-study" in which students investigate and report on high- and low-performing schools in a district, as well as the social, economic, and demographic conditions of the surrounding community. Would-be teachers studying how to develop children's reading skills review the literature of other cultures as well as traditionally assigned texts and discuss how to best reach students of different backgrounds. Boulder grad students complete at least one of their clinical placements in a school with a high proportion of minority students, where they also test out many of the ideas developed in class.

Is subject content stressed?

Want to teach math, but can't get a handle on advanced geometry? In the past, teacher-prep programs have emphasized pedagogical theory over mastery of a subject area, but in today's highly skilled society and test-conscious classrooms, content-lite won't do: You must know your subject matter and know it well.

Many states now require secondary-school teachers to have majors in the area in which they plan to teach, while more and more graduate schools—including Harvard, Florida Institute of Technology, and the University of Hawaii—are demanding that entering students have a major in their subject as well. "If we want to turn Americans into better mathematicians and scientists, as we should, we have to have elementary school teachers who can teach young children math with a real understanding of mathematics and its beauty," says Leon Botstein, president of

Bard College in Annandale-on-Hudson, New York. "What's wrong with teacher training today is that it has been institutionalized as a kind of separate pseudoscience, which is the science of pedagogy. There is an absolute loss of the focus on subject-matter competence."

In response, Bard is launching a new, yearlong master of arts in teaching (MAT) program that will lead to a teaching certificate in adolescent education in English, history, mathematics, or physics. Students with a liberal arts major in the subject they want to teach will take six additional content courses in their field, focusing on new knowledge as well as on relevant teaching methods. Future math instructors taking algebra, for example, will study issues like fundamental number theory and solutions of polynomials with a real mathematician—as opposed to an education professor trained in teaching math—and at the same time examine various high school textbooks and curriculum models to determine what works and what doesn't. MAT students will also take six education courses taught largely by arts and science professors trained in fields like sociology, history, and neuroscience. Current Issues in Learning and Teaching: The Adolescent in the Contemporary Classroom will be taught by a child psychologist, for example, and cover theories in learning, literacy, development, and cognitive psychology.

Other schools are making similar, if smaller, strides. At Boston College, biology teachers-to-be study the science of how urban development has influenced the Charles and Mystic rivers, along with the methods needed to engage young minds on environmental issues. The University of Pennsylvania's master's program in chemistry education requires grad students both to perform lab experiments and to take classes in teaching chemical concepts. Students in the M.A. in English Education program at the University of North Carolina–Pembroke take The Teaching of Writing alongside Shakespeare's Comedies, and Literacy and Literature in Context at the same time as Myth and Literature—so that they become proficient in their field and at communicating that knowledge to their own students.

A good indicator of a content-rich program is that at least some courses will be team-taught by faculty from the ed school and from the college of arts and sciences; research has shown that subject-specific pedagogy leads to the most student learning growth. Do professors have joint appointments in the school of education and another department like biology or history? Can you choose an advisor in your subject area, if you wish? You may want to consider the strength of the biology or history department, for that matter. It's also worthwhile to investigate whether education professors pursue research and scholarship with faculty members in other parts of the university.

Will you get plenty of supervised practice?

It's as fundamental as A, B, C: First-time teachers must spend supervised time in a classroom. "Until you do it, you don't know it," cautions one career-switcher, now a first grade instructor in Austin, Texas. Indeed, numerous studies have shown that the more practice you get and the more familiar you are with what you'll face in the classroom during your first year of teaching, the more likely you are to stay in the field.

Traditionally, grad students got only a few weeks of actual teaching experience. Ten to 12 weeks is still the standard, but a growing number of universities insist on a year or more of hands-on practice, often in several different settings. Aurora University in

Illinois, for one, has students working during the day at Harold G. Fearn Elementary School in North Aurora under the supervision of a mentor teacher while taking classes at night; the summer before students begin teaching at Fearn, many take a course in basic classroom skills that covers everything from creating lesson plans to disciplining students.

Other institutions, including Purdue University in West Lafayette, Indiana, offer extensive teaching experiences through "professional development schools." Not unlike the medical school model, where a university teams up with a hospital to train students in the trenches, a PDS program partners an ed school with one or more local public schools whose faculty work closely with university professors to train and mentor the interns. It's a way of linking pedagogy and practice, and insuring that the next generation of teachers knows how the theory applies to real-world situations.

At Purdue, for example, students might spend the morning in class learning how to use "productive questioning," a technique that encourages young students to think deeply about a topic, and then use the afternoon to practice the skill on real kids while being monitored by experienced teacher-mentors. Students get firsthand experience at managing a classroom, too. The premise: A lecture isn't going to teach you how to handle a roomful of 16-year-olds in an inner city high school who are more interested in brawling with each other than paying attention to today's math lesson. You've got to watch accomplished instructors at work and learn by doing.

In the best PDS relationships, both partners benefit, says Kevin Bolinger, an assistant professor of education at Indiana State University in Terre Haute, which has a system of 20 partner schools in neighboring communities. Teacher ed candidates

Greg Rohrer had long toyed with the idea of becoming a teacher, but he didn't want to spend a full four years in college immediately after high school. So first the Wyoming native got his associate's degree at a community college and indulged professionally in a lifetime passion: food. After working for less than a year as a manager at a Las Vegas restaurant—and feeling like he had more to offer to the world—he began studying education at the University of Wyoming, working nights in the kitchen of a nearby eatery. An alumnus of high school speech and drama clubs, Rohrer was drawn to the prospect of communicating ideas to an audience of students. Now he teaches 10 different classes in business and technology—including computer design, business math, and marketing—to high schoolers in Ekalaka, Montana.

Five years after coming to Carter County High, Rohrer is still struggling to make the transition from kitchen to classroom. "In the restaurant, if I didn't like the employees, I could get rid of them. I can't really do that with the students," he jokes. While he finds teaching to be more fulfilling than his old career—"someone's education is more important than their meals"—it is in many ways more frustrating, too. School didn't prepare him, for example, to discipline widely disparate personalities: "I have some students who will stop talking to me if [I] correct them or tell them 'no,'" he says.

His biggest challenge, though, is motivating the unmotivated. "When you've got kids who don't care or who aren't interested, you don't feel like you can accomplish your job," he says. Rohrer doesn't hesitate to mark poorly completed assignments with a zero, but he's doing his best to charge students up: In typing class, for example, he's instituted a system of clubs—the 30-word-per-minute-club, the 40-word-per-minute-club—to give students incentives to practice. In other classes, he hands out "Most Improved Player" awards in the form of gift certificates.

Of course, in a town of fewer than 500 people, the gift-certificate options are limited.

The nearest movie theater is two hours away, as is the closest Wal-Mart. When Rohrer requested a guest speaker from the Montana Public Accounting Organization for his accounting class early this year, it took the group nearly a full year to find a CPA willing to make the trek out to Ekalaka.

In addition to his teaching duties, Rohrer makes some extra money and keeps one foot in food service by overseeing all the school's extracurricular concessions, ordering and preparing food for school football games and theater productions. The job tacks on less than $1,500 to his $24,000 salary—hardly a windfall, though his monthly rent is just $200 for a two-bedroom cottage—and adds up to 15 extra hours of work a week during sports seasons. At a recent night of dinner theater that featured the high school choir, Rohrer prepared beef Wellington and chicken Kiev for more than three hundred students, parents, and locals. "A lot of them had never heard of those dishes before," he says. "It was a learning experience."

With a total student body of only 70 (more than half of whom are in Rohrer's classes each semester), Rohrer has the chance to develop strong ties with students and parents. But that sense of community, and class sizes that would make most public school teachers drool (five to 15 students, typically), may not be enough to keep him in Carter County. Recently, Rohrer's been thinking about going back to school for his master's degree. His goal: to find a post at a community college where students are more mature. "I enjoy teaching, I really do," he says. "I just wish it was a perfect situation, with students eager to learn—and wanting to be there."

complete their field work in a highly structured setting, supervised by mentor teachers who work closely with professors, and the ed school keeps its curriculum as current as possible. In return, the university provides training for partner school mentor-teachers, offers all employees in such schools fee waivers to pursue continuing education, and also gives help to struggling schools. When one elementary school with consistently low standardized test scores was having problems with low levels of parent involvement, Indiana State ran a series of seminars for parents, offering a year's worth of school supplies and three age-appropriate books for their children as incentive to come. More than 600 parents turned out.

To find out how much practical experience a program provides, ask what proportion of the total credits is devoted to student teaching. At a bare minimum, you'll want one semester of field work in a one-year program and one full year in a two-year program. (While the two-year programs may allow for considerably more time in the classroom, many would-be teachers prefer the lower cost and shorter time commitment of the one-year programs—especially given the disagreement over the value of education coursework.) Will you spend all of your time in the same suburban middle school, or will you rotate through urban or rural schools for a significant period of time—an entire trimester, say? That might leave you more prepared to work with a diverse population of students.

Also ask how much support, exactly, you'll receive from professors, professional mentors, and perhaps even alums now working as teachers in local schools. At Bank Street, grad students meet twice a month with their advisor and weekly in small advising groups of five to seven to discuss what's working in their internship classrooms and what's not; they are observed by the same advisor on-site in schools for half a day once a month. The mentor-teachers they work with daily, who also meet with this advisor, are intimately familiar with course assignments so that they can help students complete them and improve their practice.

Another important consideration is how you'll be evaluated. While traditional tests and papers remain part of the process, the best schools now require multiple sources of evidence over time and from a range of learning experiences, with particular emphasis on the student teaching. At Michigan State University, elementary and secondary education majors must produce a series of case studies that describe real situations that have occurred in their classrooms: the challenge of a child struggling

---

"We do very little to ease the transition from education to work for teachers."

---

with subtraction, say, or of one who keeps falling asleep in class. Each case involves careful analysis by the teacher in training, who might document his teaching goals and strategies and how the student reacted in the weeks that followed, integrating ideas from readings and course discussions.

"These cases invite them to build habits of disciplined observation and interpretation that will help them to analyze their own teaching," says Mary Lundeberg, chair of the school's teacher education department. Further, Michigan graduate students in a new pilot program now videotape themselves in classroom situations and then review the tape with a professor to reflect on what went well and what they'd change; the tape will then be evaluated as part of an electronic portfolio.

At the best ed schools, such analysis won't end the day you get your diploma. "One of the major criticisms of teacher preparation, and rightly so, is that we immediately put new folks into their own classroom—where they often get the hardest classes—and then close the door and let them go," says David Breneman, dean of the Curry School of

Education at Virginia. "We do very little to ease the transition from education to work for teachers." In the fall of 2004, Curry will launch a new program to track and keep in touch with both its graduates and other new teachers in local school systems. Professor-mentors in the education department and the arts and sciences will check in with these newcomers on a regular basis, either face-to-face or online. "We want to give young teachers some lifeline back to faculty in content areas and pedagogical areas, whenever they need advice or assistance, rather than washing our hands of them and turning to next crop," explains Breneman.

Will you learn to reach all kids?

Whether you face timid first graders or rambunctious teenagers—and whether you face them in inner-city schools or at the toniest private academies in the suburbs—it's almost certain you'll encounter boys and girls who can't concentrate, can't remember verbal instructions, or can't follow complex written directions. A generation ago these students would have been dismissed as lazy, slow, or worse, and left to flounder. These days they're defined by an array of acronyms—LD (learning disability), SED (severe emotional disturbance), BD (behavior disorders)—and are fully expected to master reading, writing, math, and science.

The number of "special needs" students in this country has risen exponentially in the last decade. And now that federal law mandates that students with special needs be educated whenever possible in regular classrooms, school districts expect all teachers to be able to work with all kinds of learners—in fact, sometimes certification depends on it. "It is unethical for us to graduate any student who is not prepared to engage these kids," says James Fraser, dean of Northeastern's school of education, which now has a required course called Inclusion, Equity, and Diversity in all of its degree offerings. The school also employs a professor who oversees the special needs programs at a local K–8 school and instructs would-be teachers; further, it gives students the option of getting a second licensure in special education through a program comprised of three courses and four summer workshops.

Syracuse University, which for years has demanded that all prospective secondary-school teachers take a course about adapting curricula for special-needs children, now has a mandatory class for primary teachers that covers strategies for teaching children with any of a dozen LD or special education diagnoses; in addition, the school directs all secondary-ed instructors—even music teachers—to spend time as reading tutors for children with learning disabilities. At the University of Colorado–Denver, core courses include Teaching for the Success of All Children/Adolescents, Individualizing Instruction for Diverse Learners, and Individual Instruction for Learners with Challenging Behaviors.

Developed by a professor at the University of North Carolina–Chapel Hill, the Schools Attuned program (which has influenced curricula at Bank Street and California State University–Northridge, among other schools) gives education students a grounding in brain research. The goal is to have them appreciate, say, that a child who can't seem to comprehend information projected on a screen might comprehend it better when the essential

points stand out in color. Would-be teachers study eight areas of brain function that affect learning and classroom performance, including memory and motor functions, and learn tactics to deal with special-needs children through smart classroom management: Students who don't concentrate can be moved to the front of the classroom or given frequent short breaks, for example, while a child

---

"It is unethical for us to graduate any student who is not prepared to engage these kids."

---

whose handwriting is a mess of overlapping loops might work better on a computer because typing uses different motor skills than handwriting does.

Will you be focusing on standards and testing?

Given the national trend of high-stakes testing, which ties a diploma or a school's reputation (or both) to student success on standardized assessments, it's very likely that as a teacher you're going to have to administer tests and face accountability for the results. Schools of education are just starting to respond, says Paul Reville, executive director of the Center for Education Research and Policy at MassINC, a Boston think tank. Reville recommends looking for a program that, at the very least, will allow you to observe such testing firsthand in real classrooms. State education schools, in particular, should be aligning coursework with state assessments; content classes should reflect state content standards for K–12 schools, for example, so teachers are aware of exactly what their future students will be expected to know—and what they will be tested on.

It's also important to look for instruction that focuses on how to effectively interpret and use data on student performance. "There's a lot more thinking going into how classroom teachers, principals, and coaches can utilize all of the data that diagnostic testing provides to change and improve and target their approach in the classroom," says Reville. Harvard, for one, offers a biweekly two-hour workshop in which grad students, local administrators, and teachers come together to analyze reams of actual data on student performance on the Massachusetts Comprehensive Assessment System—which may show, for instance, that all fourth graders are doing poorly on fractions. Then they formulate strategies for improvement through teaching and curriculum choices.

If you're already teaching

In teaching, as in any other profession, it makes sense to update your skills every once in a while. In fact, many states now require teachers to keep renewing even advanced teaching certification at certain intervals—in Nebraska it's every 10 years; in Ohio it's every five. A number of states, including New York and Virginia, mandate that teachers obtain a master's degree in a set number of years in order to remain employed.

If you're already a licensed teacher and are simply looking to enhance your qualifications—not to mention increase your pay—chances are that proximity, cost, and convenience are going to be major factors in selecting a master's or doctorate program. Usually, internships are no longer required because you've actually been in the classroom for a while; your practicum will come from on-the-job experiences. Otherwise, you should look for many of the same things in a program as someone just starting

out—namely, a focus on advanced content and integration of the latest theories and current issues in education into your professional practice.

You can also go on to specialize in any number of areas, such as school counseling or special education. Numerous ed schools offer flexible program options, with classes meeting in the evenings, on weekends, and occasionally for a set number of weeks over the summer. Some are specifically created in cooperation with neighboring school districts to best meet the needs of local teachers. Baker University in Baldwin, Kansas, brings its professors and graduate courses straight to instructors in the Lawrence public school district, for example; classes, which are conducted once a week and scheduled around the district's academic calendar, are held in the school buildings. It takes about 18 months to obtain a general master's of education. Ask your principal, coworkers, or the person specializing in professional development for your district if they know of such offerings.

There are also a growing number of online programs that do a credible job of delivering continuing education. The University of Wisconsin–Madison's two-year master of science in educational psychology is one such program, which many teachers pursue as a way to further improve their understanding of the field. Students spend 10 days on campus during the summer and take classes like Legal Rights and Responsibilities and Collaborative Team Work for Inclusive School Reform from home during the school year, communicating with faculty and peers via email, online discussions, file-sharing, and chat groups; audio conferencing is also used for real-time discussions and debates. If you're interested in an online degree, it goes without saying that it's important to watch out for diploma mills and to select a highly rigorous program; some districts will only accept a degree from an accredited institution for approved academic credit.

Those looking to switch gears and enter administration are wise to look at any of the growing number of dedicated programs popping up, from the Principal Leadership Institute at the University of California–Berkeley to the Principals Institute at Bank Street in New York. "There a ton of quick and dirty programs out there, where you just piece together 30 credits whenever and however you can," warns Richard Schwab, dean of the Neag School of Education at the University of Connecticut. "But in an articulated program, each course builds on the next course, which builds on the clinical experience"—shadowing current administrators—"all of which aligns with state assessments, and you end up better prepared for the real world and the job market."

In Connecticut's Administrator Preparation Program, practicing teachers take a series of courses and complete internships with practicing principals, vice principals, and the like over a two-year period using problem-based learning that often relies on real-world examples. You might receive a stack of papers documenting a specific personnel crisis, for example, as well as all of the applicable laws. The task is then to work through what you would do in the same situation, weighing all of the issues—the rights of the individual and the law, the media implications, how students will be affected and so on—in order to determine whether or not the teacher in question should be fired. The best programs accept small cohorts of students who travel through the entire process together, forming a community of learners who gain from each other's experiences.

A doctorate brings prestige along with higher pay—and getting one doesn't necessarily require a trip back into the ivory tower. Earlier this year, the University of Southern California's Rossier School of Education launched a new three-year Ed.D. program for working counselors, principals, superintendents, and teachers. It's structured like an executive M.B.A.: Classes meet at night or on weekends in several locations. The practice-based program features core courses in leadership, diversity, and accountability, as well as in research methods and various concentrations, including Leadership in Urban School Settings and Teacher Education in Multicultural Societies. In their third year, students work on individual doctoral dissertations, though teams of cohorts focus on a single educational theme or problem—Violence in Urban School Settings, say, or Principal-Led Approaches to Reducing Aggression among Boys at an Urban Middle School—resulting in a larger body of work or even a book.

The goal, again, is preparing professionals who are well-equipped to bring elementary and secondary learning into the twenty-first century. "The program is structured so that every day you're on the job, the research you have done and issues you have focused on bear directly on what you're doing, and help you work smarter," says Sharon Nordheim, assistant superintendent of human resources for the Montebello Unified School District in Los Angeles County, California, who also spent more than a decade as a teacher and counselor in local schools. One of the priorities of Nordheim's district is to figure out what kinds of tests or programs work well for kids from all ethnic backgrounds. So, she's been researching the correlation between certain teaching programs and high school GPAs. What she's learned has convinced her that the district should continue to use the "40 Developmental Assets" plan. The plan has teachers focus on providing support and promoting empowerment and a commitment to learning—say, by bringing students to museums or providing early college exposure—all of which have been shown to be crucial to teen resiliency. "Now," she says, "I have full confidence that what we're doing works."

Chapter Four

Inside Five Grad Schools

As you narrow down your search for a way into the classroom, you may find yourself deciding among schools that get you there in very distinct ways. In the pages that follow, we offer a close-up view of how five very different schools of education are responding to the challenges of training teachers today. The schools featured in this chapter include two that sit high on the *U.S. News* ranking of doctoral-degree producers (No. 1 Stanford University and No. 4 Teachers College, Columbia University) and three that are known for their prodigious output of educators for their states: the University of Texas–El Paso, Eastern Michigan University, and National University, a 26-campus school that turns out more licensed teachers than any other ed school in California. Here's a tour, from West to East.

Stanford University School of Education

Stanford, California

As teacher ed programs go, Stanford's is tiny. The elite school turns out fewer than 85 new teachers each year. All told, the master's program, which also offers degrees in Psychological Studies in

---

"We see ourselves as preparing leaders for the field who can both be expert teachers and solve social problems."

Education and Social Sciences, Policy, and Educational Practice, graduates fewer than 175, and the number of doctoral grads is no more than 40. Yet while its size may be small, Stanford's impact is anything but. "Our purpose is not to meet the need for bodies in a big way," says professor and nationally known teaching expert Linda Darling-Hammond. "We see ourselves as preparing leaders for the field who can both be expert teachers and solve social problems."

That might sound like politically correct hype, but the school's grads can be found at the forefront of some of the field's most innovative developments, including the charter school movement and the push to redesign large urban secondary schools into smaller schools where students can get more individual attention. A Stanford grad heads up the Bay Area Coalition for Equitable Schools, for example, which has opened eight small high schools in Oakland over the past few years and was recently awarded a $9.5 million grant from the Bill and Melinda Gates Foundation to create several more. Stanford's focus on tech-

nology (the university sits on more than 8,000 lush acres at the edge of Silicon Valley) has catapulted many graduates into positions where they are teaching other teachers how to use the latest software and hardware effectively in the classroom. In a charter high school that Stanford helps run in East Palo Alto, a predominantly poor African American and Latino community, researchers, teachers, and ed students work together to find new and better ways to teach low-income minority students.

Steppies, as the Stanford Teacher Education Program (STEP) students are known, arrive with an edge over many ed students: a major in the subject area they plan to teach or success on a series of tests of their subject competency. They then spend 12 jam-packed months earning a master's and preparing for the classroom. On the first day at Stanford, they are placed in a summer-school program at a "professional development school," a nearby partner school where they are supervised by mentor teachers working hand-in-hand with Stanford faculty. Stanford relies on a network of professional development schools in much the same way that medical schools use teaching hospitals—as places where students can gain clinical practice and be closely assessed every step of the way.

"We develop our own curriculum, and the program gives us the steps and the freedom to do it," says Tiffany Thomason, one of 14 Stanford students currently teaching at Hillsdale High School a few miles from campus. Thomason has recently created a curriculum for her ninth graders using Shakespeare's *Romeo and Juliet* to explore the broader issue of fate, or "what influences determine how we live our lives." She'll also devise the grading system for the unit.

Her students won't be the only ones vying for good marks. Given the growing recognition among educators that high-quality teaching is the most important factor in student achievement, Thomason, too, will be graded on her classroom performance to a degree that was almost unheard of just a few years ago. Stanford has implemented an elaborate evaluation system for student teachers that is based in part on how well their own students progress in their classes, and in part on a "scored teacher portfolio" that includes critiques in areas such as curriculum development and classroom management and videotaped teaching sessions. "This is not a bunch of touchy-feely exercises," says Darling-Hammond. "We are evaluating teacher effectiveness with a concrete set of measures."

Stanford is known for preparing its teachers not just to delve deep into a subject area—Steppies who want to teach high school algebra, for instance, take three classes on how to teach math when most schools require one—but also to manage a diverse group of learners. Every high school teacher in STEP learns how to teach reading and writing and how to work with students who are learning English as a second language. All Steppies also get a grounding in the needs of special education students. "Everything we learn is directly applicable to teaching and creating equity in the classroom," says Thomason. "By the time you graduate you just know you're going to be ready." That appears to be so: Of the STEP graduates who go into the classroom upon graduation, 85 percent stay for at least four years.

Because the STEP program is so small, Stanford students can expect a level of involvement with faculty and peers that isn't possible in many other graduate programs. Most classes consist of fewer than 20 students and often are taught by as many as four instructors. Overall, the ratio of students to teachers is 8 to 1. Master's students often work alongside faculty and doctoral students and participate in their

---

"Everything we learn is directly applicable to teaching and creating equity in the classroom."

---

research. "We get so much support here from the faculty," says Vanessa Aguayo, who student teaches ninth and eleventh graders at San Mateo High School in an innovative program where master teachers work with the same kids from ninth grade until graduation to better prepare them for college. "You never really feel alone."

The price tag for all this attention is daunting. Tuition for the 12-month program runs about $38,000, so choosing Stanford can cost over $50,000 a year. Financial aid is available, and students who elect to teach in underserved school districts upon graduation may be eligible for a loan-forgiveness program. The goods news is that you won't have trouble finding a job: The hiring rate for STEP grads is virtually 100 percent.

National University

Twenty-six locations in California

Take the Alvarado Road exit from Fletcher Parkway in eastern San Diego County, and the ramp will lead you directly into the parking lot of a nondescript

---

building. Only the sign for National University indicates that you have entered a college campus. Everything else—the plentiful parking, the blank windows—screams "office park."

But just when most office buildings start to empty, students begin streaming in through these doors. They're older than traditional college students—the average age at National is 32—and are most likely arriving straight from a long workday. They haven't enrolled to find themselves, or to explore the liberal arts. They're here to get the training needed to land the jobs they want.

Everything about National University is designed to appeal to working adults intent on career advancement. The university—which was founded in 1971 specifically for that purpose—has 26 campuses dotted throughout California, all carefully situated next to major commuting routes. The academic offerings are just as practical: Besides teacher education, National has programs in such fields as information systems, computer science, and business. Classes meet twice a week for four and a half hours at a time, and students take just one course per month. The schedule allows aspiring teachers to get their credential in a year if they are enrolled continuously, or if family or job matters require it, they can easily take a break—and then step back in again.

The school doesn't require any admissions tests, and a 2.5 undergraduate grade point average is sufficient for entry to the graduate teaching program. "The adult learner has not met with a great deal of academic success," says Lynne Anderson, associate dean of the School of Education, explaining why National's entrance requirements are minimal. But often, she adds, they've rediscovered their motivation in the working world.

Indeed, students view their classes as a second job. "I approached [school] more as a business," says National grad Jesse Schuveiller, who is now teaching eleventh and twelfth grade English at La Costa Canyon High School in Carlsbad, California. Schuveiller gravitated to teaching—and National—after a career in marketing because he realized he wanted to have a more personal impact on others. The evening classes allowed him to keep his job at a resort company until he could get one at a school. "I [wasn't] in it for the college atmosphere," he explains.

The curriculum reflects the school's emphasis on efficiency. While the state of California sets strict standards for what teacher candidates must cover, it's up to the school—and the professors—to figure out how to meet them. National does so by offering a yearlong credentialing program for college graduates as well as master's degrees for current and new teachers alike. (Californians must have a bachelor's degree in a major other than education before they can begin the credentialing process, and they must complete a postgraduate teacher-prep program and demonstrate knowledge of their subject to gain permanent certification.)

The credential candidates all take courses in health education, special education, and computer technology. Then students destined for elementary schools take courses in the foundations of education; diversity; psychology; language development; reading instruction; curriculum development in the social sciences, physical education, and the arts; and curriculum development in math and science. Those heading for middle school and high school take a similar load, with just one general class in curriculum development and a classroom management course. Although many experts see subject content expertise as the key to good teaching, it is not part of the basic curriculum at National. The school offers prep courses for the state subject-matter tests at an extra charge; still, many students end up taking the tests twice. All students finish with a semester of student teaching in a local school district.

"This is a practitioners' institution," says Thomas Reynolds, chair of the teacher education department. "Faculty are hired based on how well they function in a program driven by teacher education." Theory courses such as educational psychology require at the minimum four hours of classroom observation and practice teaching, which usually involves trying out a lesson learned in class. But how well that experience is integrated into the class discussion is up to individual professors. Most of the adjuncts—they make up about 80 percent of the instructors in the School of Education—work day jobs as teachers, principals, curriculum specialists, and even superintendents, so they tend to have firsthand practical know-how to draw on. "I was worried at first" about the quality of National University, admits Courtney Craig, who just finished up her student teaching at Oak Crest Middle School in Encinitas, California. "But lots of my professors were principals and teachers with education experience themselves."

Some students say they would gladly sacrifice all the theory coursework for more concrete tips on how to manage a class full of independent-minded kids. In the classroom management course that Nedra Crow teaches at National's Carlsbad Learning Center—one of the last before the candidates begin student teaching in middle or high school—you can feel the panic. Previously, Crow and her coteacher Bill Adams, who retired as director of curriculum at a local school district and is a former principal, assigned their students to try out teacher- and student-centered methods—a lecture

format and cooperative learning groups, for example—in the classes that they'd been observing. Then they reported back on how the different techniques affected student discipline and engagement. Now the professors are using role-playing to demonstrate the nitty-gritty of discipline. Adams plays a perpetually tardy student. Crow asks him to come out into the hall, hiding him from the class while she positions herself in the doorway to keep a watchful eye on all her charges—and to create witnesses, she quickly points out, should he hit her or claim that she hit him. The students are exceedingly grateful for the advice, but one expresses frustration: "This course is the only one that has dealt with reality. I have one course left, and I don't feel ready."

Whether candidates think they're prepared or not, National has a well-developed pipeline to get them student-teaching positions and teaching credentials. The university has student-teaching contracts with 530 districts throughout the state, and usually manages to place people exactly where they want to be. (Both Schuveiller and Craig requested and received assignments with their favorite teachers at schools that they had attended as kids.) But student teachers generally don't get a lot of faculty supervision: A professor sits in on eight lessons over a four-month period, and there's a mandatory weekly seminar that some students describe as a joke. The real help comes from the supervising teacher at the school to which they've been assigned.

When graduation at National approaches, a department with a staff of 50 makes sure that students have completed all the requirements—testing, coursework, student teaching, fingerprinting, and so forth—to put together a successful application for a teaching licensee. Not surprisingly, then,

Six years ago, when Michelle Mosher heard that a middle school near Miami was hiring a sixth-grade language arts and social studies teacher, she was initially loath to apply. "You always hear that [middle schoolers'] hormones are crazy, that they're disrespectful and unmotivated," says Mosher, who graduated from Florida International University with a special-education degree and teaching certificate in 1998. "But when you get there, you love the kids—because they're *your* kids."

Of course, it doesn't hurt that Miami Shores/Barry University Charter Middle School is a public charter school with an application process, a wait list, and a requirement that every student and parent sign a contract stating their commitment to academic achievement and good behavior. "My students' parents want them to be here, and the kids are motivated and want to be here, too," Mosher says. While some teachers from nearby public schools attribute Miami Shores' great test scores to its large contingent of gifted students, Mosher says it has

more to do with the school's size. With only 10 teachers and teacher assistants and 180 students, the school feels like a tight-knit community.

Because her school is a charter—one of thousands that are part of the public system but are run by parents, teachers, universities, or companies and are free from many of the regulations governing standard public schools—Mosher has considerable freedom in running her classroom. Unlike teachers in other Florida schools who regularly suspend their curriculum to prepare students for the state-administered Florida Comprehensive Achievement Test, or FCAT, Mosher says she feels no pressure "to cram the FCAT down my students' throats." Yet Miami Shores students regularly outperform their peers at other schools in the state. Mosher doesn't feel constrained by her textbook, either; she liberally supplements the book's lessons on ancient civilizations with novels and other materials she digs up on monthly library visits. "We're not using some curriculum we bought from

a vendor," she says. "We want our students to think freely."

While other teachers at her school treat language arts and social studies as separate subjects, Mosher combines the two in a single class that emphasizes reading and writing, which she teaches twice daily for two hours at a time. Her students read 10 books a year, mostly nonfiction about ancient civilizations, and write two or three times a week. Two recent assignments were a paper reacting to a magazine article about modern-day slavery and another about the Greek legacy in American culture. Her approach seems to be working. While nearly a third of her students began the 2002 school year at reading level 1 and 2 (the lowest on FCAT's 5-point scale) 90 percent jumped at least one reading level by year's end.

Despite the freedoms of working at a charter, Mosher sometimes yearns for the perks of the public system—like an actual bricks-and-mortar building. Miami Shores is housed in a constellation of 10 aging trailers "held together by tape and Band-Aids," as Mosher puts it, and sitting on a patch of undeveloped land near Barry University, just north of Miami. The school has no auditorium or library, and the cafeteria doubles as the gymnasium. "We're supposed to be getting a new building, but I've heard that every year for six years," she sighs.

Mosher is nearing the seven-year mark at Miami Shores, but her job security is hardly assured. The school's charter and its success in meeting the charter's goals—which include annual standards on test scores and a yearly 25-hour volunteering requirement for students—must be regularly reevaluated by the school district. While the school is in no immediate danger of losing its charter, it's a specter other public school teachers don't have to consider.

And though Mosher's salary at Miami Shores is determined by the same experience-based scale used in Miami-Dade public schools, only six years of her experience will transfer to the Miami-Dade system should she ever seek another job. For now, Mosher is supplementing her base salary by leading a special-education class during her prep period, which raises her annual pay by $3,000, to roughly $37,000. "If I had just my base salary," she says. "It would be hard to pay rent." She's currently pursuing a teaching master's at Florida Atlantic University, partly so she can get another raise. "It's a little fly-by-the-seat-of-your-pants here, a little hectic," she says. "But that's why I like it."

National credentials more teachers than any other education school in California. As one administrator puts it, "We're the workhorse of the state."

The University of Texas–El Paso

El Paso, Texas

The students of Canutillo Elementary School start their days, like most kids in America, with the Pledge of Allegiance. As they recite the words, tiny hands over hearts, the school feels like it could be anywhere in the country—until they do it all over again, this time in Spanish.

Welcome to El Paso, where more than half of the households use a language other than English.

The three largest school districts in this border town on the dusty northern bank of the Rio Grande are 85 percent Latino. The city is in the fifth poorest Congressional district in the country; 70 percent of students are eligible for free or reduced-cost lunch. Ten years ago, before education reform swept El Paso, only 55 percent of students here passed all portions of the state's math achievement tests.

This is the challenge facing the University of Texas–El Paso College of Education, a major magnet for the city's high school graduates and the chief source of its teachers. Eighty-two percent of UTEP's students come from El Paso schools, and more than 70 percent of the teachers in the surrounding districts are UTEP grads. "It's a closed loop," says Diana Natalicio, the university's president. UTEP doesn't have the luxury of prepping Ph.D.s for careers in academe or education policy. (The ed school has only one Ph.D. program—in educational leadership and administration.) Instead, the entire campus community is committed to teaching teachers to teach—and then getting them back into the schools again.

> "There's just no substitute for experience in the classroom."

"On many campuses, the college of ed is the low rung on the ladder, the one everybody feels superior to," says Natalicio, who has been president for 16 years. But talk to faculty in other departments here, and they all say the same thing: Without well-prepared teachers in the surrounding schools, you get unprepared college students who gum up the works and slow down their classes. When the majority of teachers in the area are from your own school, says Howard Daudistel, dean of the college of liberal arts, "it's kind of hard to blame [poor performance] on someone else. These teachers have all taken our classes in English and history, after all." Indeed, undergraduates who want to be secondary school teachers, for example, major in the discipline they plan to teach and minor in education; graduate students, too, take their content courses all over campus.

There are roughly 1,200 education grad students at UTEP, split more or less evenly between veteran teachers pursuing master's degrees and aspiring teachers enrolled in the school's Alternative Certification Program, a one-year crash course for college grads with degrees in other subjects. Most students are part-timers who work at local schools during the day and take classes at night; because of a teacher shortage, even students in the certification program have jobs in the local schools. The master's programs here take two years to complete, and most students are pursuing degrees as instructional specialists. Not surprisingly, the most common specialty—involving about a third of all master's students—is bilingual education. More than two dozen teachers will graduate this year with specialties in teaching "two-way dual-language classrooms," where students learn in both Spanish and English.

This campuswide concern with teacher training has only recently made its presence felt. After El Paso's test scores hit rock bottom in the early nineties, the entire city mobilized a massive reform campaign. The El Paso Collaborative for Academic Excellence was formed to get education, business, and civic leaders focused on education and working together. UTEP revamped its teacher-training curriculum, especially its undergraduate program. Before, education students spent most of their time on campus and had little contact with local kids. Now students have required courses on how to work with parents; many fourth-years take field trips into their future students' neighborhoods; and all students have to complete a whopping 650 hours of supervised teaching, most of it in local schools, before they graduate.

Ten years later, pass rates on math achievement tests citywide were up from 55 to 89 percent. Science scores too have soared, and the achievement gap between whites and minorities has closed substantially. Much of the credit obviously goes to the local schools and to community efforts, but some has come UTEP's way, too. Last summer, the university was recognized by the Carnegie Corporation of New York with a $5 million grant, which it will use to promote accountability of teachers for student achievement and further emphasize interdepartmental cooperation and clinical training.

Success has brought this culture of cooperation to the graduate school as well. Some master's classes in methodology, for example, are now team-taught by teachers from El Paso area schools and professors from UTEP. Teachers from local schools are often made adjunct professors at the university, where they teach everything from classroom management to curriculum design. "There's just no substitute for experience in the classroom," says Chris Gilmore, a former manager in the airline industry who is now getting certified to teach high school social studies through the school's Alternative Certification Program.

Teachers everywhere crave tips on how to manage diverse classrooms, how to teach classes with multiple languages, and how to reach out to kids growing up in poverty—and this UTEP does as well as anyone, according to Daniel Fallon, chair of Carnegie's education division. "What I've found in my graduate classes is a real emphasis on community, family, and really being there for the kids," says Michelle Shaw, a second-year master's student who teaches middle school reading and English. This student-centered focus seems to drive every class at UTEP, whether the subject is bringing technol-ogy to the classroom or teaching in Spanish. "What we hear over and over again," Shaw says, "is 'put everything else aside, talk to your students and actively listen to them.'"

In a predominantly Latino school system, of course, multicultural training is the coin of the realm. A class on multicultural issues is required of all teachers getting their certification, and the

"Good pedagogy means not only knowing your subject but teaching it in a way that respects the students, their backgrounds, their lives."

subject comes up in just about every other class on campus. "What I learn from a lot of these classes is what not to do," says Gilmore. If a Hispanic student hangs his head when a teacher is reprimanding him, for example, the ed students learn that confrontation isn't helpful. "You get in the face of one of these kids, and they'll never respond to you again," says Mauricio Olague, a first year master's student. "Looking down is culturally a sign of respect; they're looking down because it's polite. You can't say 'come on, look at my face.'"

Sensitivity training isn't limited only to the school of ed. In a typical literature class for teachers-in-training in the English department, for example, students talk about what changes they'd make in teaching a class about the Cinderella story, for example, if they were retelling the tale to reflect a cultural group in the El Paso area. "You can teach math to math teachers, history to history teachers—but good pedagogy means not only knowing your subject but teaching it in a way that respects the students, their backgrounds, their lives," says Daudistel. Of course, laughs Gyneth Garrison, a local teacher getting her master's at UTEP, "if you aren't aware of multicultural issues, and you're from El Paso, there's no hope for you!"

Eastern Michigan University

Ypsilanti, Michigan

By his own account, Michael Swain wasn't much of a student when he attended Eastern Michigan University as an undergrad in the 1970s. Discouraged from pursuing an education major because of slim career opportunities, he majored in biology and, after graduating in 1981, stumbled into a 20-year career running cafeterias and catering services at universities, hospitals, and corporations. He enjoyed plenty of professional success, but when it came time to give his own two daughters college and career advice, he realized that something was missing. "I talked with them about their futures, about college choices, about finding something to do that you don't mind getting up to do every day," he says. "As I listened to myself saying that, I realized that what I'd always wanted to do, what I meant to do, what would really make me happy, was to teach."

Swain returned to his alma mater in Ypsilanti for about a year of part-time coursework to earn a second bachelor's degree in earth science (graduating magna cum laude this time around). He then quit his job to enroll in Eastern Michigan's postbaccalaureate teacher certification program, 18 months of education classes and student-teaching that lead to state certification as a beginning teacher. After completing the required classes, he landed a fifth-grade student-teaching assignment at Haisley Elementary in nearby Ann Arbor. "I'm working harder now than I ever have

in my life," he says. "But I love what I do. I can't wait to get up in the morning and go back."

Home to one of the largest colleges of education in the country ("a factory," sniffs a dean at a more prestigious school), Eastern's program for beginning teachers produces 800-plus graduates each year. Of those, the majority—as at most ed schools—are traditional undergraduates earning bachelor's degrees that lead to state certification. But a growing number—about one third of the College of Education's student body in 2003—are nontraditional students like Swain who already hold bachelor's degrees and have returned to school via Eastern's postbac program. Career switchers can get through the program in as little as 16 months, but the average is a little over two years. "It's not a short program," says Christine Lancaster, who coordinates it. "This is a huge, life-changing decision."

Those who decide to take the plunge seem to find EMU a welcoming environment for nontraditional students. An emphatically unpretentious place (how many name-brand schools advertise for students with radio ads, complete with a toll-free phone number: 1-800-GOTOEMU?), the 24,000-student university attracts large numbers of undergrads who are the first in their families to go to college. Many classes are held in the evenings and on weekends to accommodate the significant number of students who hold down jobs along with their academic responsibilities. And Eastern isn't especially hard to get into. The teacher-prep program accepts any student who meets its minimum requirements: an overall 2.5 grade point average, a passing grade on the basic-skills portion of the state certification test (which covers math, reading, and writing), and a C or better in writing, speech, math, and science.

Nor, at an in-state rate of about $4,000 for 30 credit hours, is EMU particularly expensive. "We have always had a policy of being affordable and accessible," says Jerry Robbins, dean of the College of Education. "We have always been an institution for people who couldn't get into the University of Michigan, and who wouldn't have felt comfortable going to the University of Michigan even if they could."

But postbac students face a variety of challenges. "It's tough to sit next to an 18-year-old who's talking about the party they went to last night," says Alice FitzGerald, who earned an undergraduate degree in biology from the University of Michigan and enrolled in EMU's postbac program a couple of decades later, in her early forties, when the youngest of her four boys started first grade. Postbacs must also complete any of EMU's daunting general-ed course requirements that don't appear on their undergraduate transcripts. Postbac teaching candidates in elementary ed, for instance, have to pass at least one course each in literature, writing, speech, math, history, U.S. government, world geography, physics or chemistry, earth sciences, psychology, and the arts. "We expect someone who's going to be teaching English to know what laboratory science is," Lancaster says.

Some postbacs, eager to start new careers in the classroom, aren't thrilled with the prospect of jumping through extra hoops. "There was one guy who said 'You're telling me I have to take a class in art, dance, or theater? I'm not going to do that,'" Lancaster recalls. Postbacs must also work their way through a long list of required education courses before they start student teaching. Swain's classes included the Exceptional Child in the Regular

Classroom; Health Education for Elementary Teachers; Social Foundations: Schools in a Multicultural Society; Introduction to Assessment and Evaluation; Elementary Curriculum and Methods; Literacy across the Curriculum; Teaching Science in the Elementary School; and more. Some postbac students, like former engineer Jeff Marriott, say they wish EMU would create a more streamlined

"I'm working harder now than I ever have in my life. But I love what I do. I can't wait to get up in the morning and go back."

program that takes into account the experience that they bring to their new careers. Marriott has a B.A. in history from Michigan State and an M.A. in computer science from Wayne State, and he spent 19 years as an engineer before being laid off and deciding to become a teacher.

Others fault certain course requirements for being overly theoretical. Some criticize Schools in a Multicultural Society, for instance, on the grounds that it teaches more about history and court cases than about how to handle a racially diverse set of kids in the classroom. But students praise other courses for offering useful, practical assistance. "Once you get into the real meaty [classes]—the curriculum ones, the assessment ones—I thought 'Finally! That's what I'm here for,'" FitzGerald says.

On a Monday afternoon in late November, 17 students in Ethan Lowenstein's Curriculum and Methods for Secondary Education class break into small groups for a role-playing exercise designed to explore different strategies for handling a disruptive high school student who is picking on a classmate and calling him "faggot." In the first scenario, the student playing the teacher takes the bully aside privately, talks about mutual respect, and tries to accentuate the positive: "I know you're a leader—I want you to channel it in the right direction." In the second group, the teacher takes a different tack, publicly rebuking the bully and directing the entire class to an antiviolence website called www.stop-the-hate.org. Lowenstein's stu-

---

"We expect someone who's going to be teaching English to know what laboratory science is."

---

dents then discuss the pros and cons of each classroom-management approach: "It seems to me that throughout both scenarios the student was in control," observes one woman.

Lowenstein's follow-up lecture connected philosopher-educator John Dewey's belief that teachers should treat each student as they would treat their own child to a teacher's general responsibility to protect students from harassment. He suggested tools, such as a contract that spells out acceptable behavior toward fellow students; in the scenario the class acted out, he said he would have privately talked to the bully about the consequences of his actions. Drawing on his own experiences as a teacher in East Harlem, he described the need for teachers to combat everything from antigay slurs to alcohol abuse and gang violence. "As teachers," he says afterward via email, "we have a responsibility to make students feel valued and good about themselves."

Lowenstein's approach is very much in keeping with the official theme of EMU's teacher preparation program: "Caring, Professional Educators for a Diverse and Democratic Society." But if that sounds a bit like a parody of what critics consider the worst tendencies of ed schools—too much emphasis on self-esteem and the like and too little on academic rigor—Dean Robbins is quick to point to the ways in which Eastern avoids the most oft-cited deficiencies of teacher preparation programs.

An emphasis on subject-area knowledge, for example, means that prospective teachers must complete an academic major and minor in addition to their education classes. Student teaching is also a key part of EMU's program, he says: All students must complete a full semester of teaching in a local school. Before that, they must get their feet wet by logging 100 hours of observing classes, assessing students, and teaching a sample lesson. Robbins also notes that Eastern is stepping up efforts to find out how effective its student teachers are by having them test kids before and after lessons. The school is trying to assess the effectiveness of its recent graduates by asking supervisors for feedback on their classroom performance. "It's very much worthwhile," he says, "and long overdue."

Teachers College, Columbia University

New York, New York

Name-brand schools of education are often accused of neglecting the unglamorous job of preparing new teachers in favor of an emphasis on research and public policy. But Teachers College, one of the nation's oldest and best-known ed schools, is an exception to the rule. In contrast to the "boutique" teacher-prep programs favored by places like Stanford and Harvard (which together turn out fewer than 200 teachers per year), fully one-third of the 5,000-plus full- and part-time students at Teachers are enrolled in teacher-education programs—either to become first-time teachers or to bolster their credentials. The result is a rare hybrid, says TC president Arthur Levine: "I think we have a better balance of research and practice than our peers in the elites."

This big-tent approach means that academic offerings are vast at TC, which was founded in 1887 as the New York School for the Training of Teachers. Graduate students—there are no undergrads at Teachers—can choose from master's and doctoral programs in counseling and clinical psychology; health and behavior studies; human development; international and transcultural studies; and organization and leadership, to name just a few. Those who want to teach enjoy a wealth of options, too, from degrees in elementary education, technology, and physical education, to programs in English as a second language and the teaching of science, math, English, or social studies to secondary school students.

The admit rate varies by program, but TC is generally much more selective than a typical ed school. While many accept three-fourths—or more—of their applicants, TC took only 38 percent of those who applied to the elementary education program for first-time teachers for fall of 2003, for instance. A minimum undergraduate GPA of 3.0 is required for elementary education candidates, and future secondary school teachers must arrive with an undergraduate degree in their field, or the equivalent.

The eclectic collection of offerings at TC is echoed in the interlocking maze of buildings that make up its campus along the northern edge of Columbia University in Manhattan's Morningside Heights neighborhood. Because many students work or student teach during the day, the classrooms are especially crowded in the late afternoon and evening hours, and are lively with discussion

> *"I think we have a better balance of research and practice than our peers in the elites."*

among an unusually varied mix of students. "I've never been to a place that's a serious intellectual place that has so much diversity in terms of minority students, international students, students from all parts of the country," says Henry Levin, an education economist who spent three decades teaching at Stanford University before coming to Teachers in 2000 to establish its new National Center for the Study of Privatization in Education.

Ed schools are sometimes criticized for being out of touch with the gritty realities of K–12 education, but if that was ever true at Teachers College, it's no longer the case. The graduate school takes pride in its increasingly close relationships with New York City schools. Through its Center for the Professional Education of Teachers, for instance, TC helps provide ongoing staff development to teachers at 35 high schools and 20 middle schools in the Bronx, Harlem, and Washington Heights. This kind of public outreach means that those studying to become teachers are guided by professors who have an up-close-and-personal understanding of the realities of urban education. It would be a big mistake for TC to "act like an ivory tower," Levine says. "We've got to treat the city as a laboratory. In a very real sense, New York is to school reform what Mississippi was to the civil rights movement."

For Christian Carter, who is pursuing a master's in elementary education, the school's real-world focus has meant the chance to study reading

---

"In a very real sense, New York is to school reform what Mississippi was to the civil rights movement."

---

with well-known expert Lucy McCormick Calkins, who works extensively with current New York City teachers to boost student literacy. On a fall day in his second year at TC, Carter sits in Calkins's class (he is one of a handful of men among some 40 young women) listening as she reads aloud from an Australian children's book about a koala who tries to win her mother's love by competing in the bush Olympics. Calkins shows her students how to turn their pupils into thoughtful, engaged readers by stopping periodically to ask the youngsters to make predictions about what will happen next and to notice how characters in the story change. "To me, the first job of teaching is to show that words matter," she tells her students. If children are not analyzing what is being read aloud, she cautions, "the chances that they're doing it when they read by themselves are pretty small."

Carter, who previously worked as a violence-prevention coordinator at an elementary school in Alameda, California, says his TC education has helped him bridge the gap between theory and practice: His 15-week student-teaching assignment in an Upper West Side third-grade classroom has given him ample opportunity to try out what he's learned in his own classes. (Besides reading methods, his two-year elementary education certification program covered child development, health education, multicultural education, and science and math methods, among other topics.) "You learn the most when you're there," he says. "The minute you're in the classroom, you start thinking 'What did I learn in Health, what did I learn about this, how do you deal with that?'"

In addition to receiving feedback from a "cooperating teacher" at the school where they are assigned, student teachers are observed six to eight times per semester by their supervisors, experienced classroom teachers who are sometimes retirees or Teachers College doctoral students. Some student teachers are assigned to one of three public schools that participate in TC's Professional Development School program. Cooperating teachers at each participating school work alongside Teachers College faculty in mentoring students and helping guide the program.

Many professors at Teachers College see themselves as following firmly in the progressive tradition of philosopher-educator John Dewey, who taught at Columbia in the first three decades of the twentieth century. "There's an activism here. People want to change the world," says Levine. That doesn't mean they want to change the world in the manner favored by more traditionalist education reformers, of course: They're much more likely to talk about "culturally relevant pedagogy" and "student-centered learning" than to support standardized testing or merit pay for teachers.

Ed school detractors, who believe many programs focus too much on fashionable theories and too little on measurable academic results, would find plenty of ammunition at Teachers; its Peace Education Center, for instance, has a mission statement that cites the need "to address issues of security, war and peace, human rights and social justice, sustainable development and ecological balance." Calkins is a faculty star, but the reading methods she helped introduce to New York City schools have come under fire from those who would rather emphasize phonics instruction. ("I'm not a back-to-basics basal reader type," she says. "I'm more progressive.") And worthwhile subjects are often labeled with trendy jargon—as when the course catalogue refers to classes in "Learning dis/Abilities." Some students jokingly call their alma mater "PC TC," using the shorthand acronym for political correctness.

Yet Levine, who is viewed both by friends and foes as a leading light of the education establishment, points out that he is not a party-line liberal. He says he welcomes the search for ways to bring results-based accountability to ed schools. And in the late 1990s, he called publicly for school vouchers to help disadvantaged kids escape substandard schools, noting at the time that in taking this position, he was "departing from the views of most of my colleagues at Teachers

> "To me, the first job of teaching is to show that words matter."

College." He believes his stance is consistent with the grad school's mission. "When students come on the first day of orientation, what I do is go before them and say 'What we do here is probably best described in two Hebrew words—*tikkun olam,*'" he says. "And that's what we're here to do: 'repair the world.'"

Chapter Five

Finding the Money

Whether you're pursuing a teaching license or a career in academe, a graduate degree in education can cost a bundle—especially when you consider the salary track you're headed for. At Columbia University's Teachers College, the tuition for full-time students runs just under $20,000 a year. Add room, board, books, and the personal expenses of living in Manhattan, and the annual cost reaches $43,000. (Master's degree students typically spend about two years earning their degrees; doctoral candidates may spend five years or longer.) The burden can be equally heavy for out-of-state students at public institutions. A nonresident at the University of Michigan–Ann Arbor School of Education pays $26,000 a year for tuition and about $40,000 overall.

The vast majority of teacher-ed students, of course, avoid such big bills by studying in state—which makes particular sense if they plan to take a job in the area. Michigan residents pay $13,000 a year in tuition at Ann Arbor and about $26,000 when living expenses are factored in. And about three-fourths of master's students, and even many Ed.D. students, limit the damage by keeping their day jobs and funding evening, weekend, and summer classes out of their paychecks. As a result, roughly half of all graduate education students get their degrees without receiving any financial aid at all. Those who do attend school full-time, and even some part-time students, can compete for numerous scholarships, fellowships and assistantships.

Uncle Sam's largesse, in the form of tax credits for the cost of higher education, can also free up some extra cash. Work-study or summer employment can cover some of the expense, but most students borrow at least part of the cost. The average debt for master's degree students in education is $22,000.

Even if you do have to borrow, you can take comfort in the fact that, with interest rates at historic lows, education debt is as cheap as it ever has been. Through your tax deductions, Uncle Sam will chip in on the interest you do pay. And if you're willing to teach in a low-income community, you may qualify for a federal or state program that will make payments on your debt or forgive it. Here's what you need to know to pay for your degree.

Seek out fellowships and assistantships

Students who snag a university fellowship or research or teaching assistantship can often keep their student loan debt to a minimum. The opportunities are mostly for full-time students, usually those pursuing doctoral degrees. Unlike at the undergraduate level, where many grants are based on a family's demonstrated need, most awards at the graduate level are given out for academic merit or other attributes an applicant brings to the student mix. Most fellowships and many assistantships are awarded based on your application for admission; often, students interested in an assistantship land one by applying directly to a departmental advisor or faculty member.

Assistantships entail work: Some 15 hours a week of teaching, grading papers, leading discussion groups or lab sessions, and assisting faculty on a research project is typical. In exchange, the university usually waives or discounts tuition and pays a stipend of $13,000 to $20,000 to cover living expenses. Sometimes health insurance is included.

An assistantship is not a practical option for most part-timers (though there are occasionally positions that require a lesser commitment). Among full-time students, 19 percent of master's candidates in education and 32 percent of doctoral candidates finance their degrees with an assistantship, according to the National Center for Education Statistics. In some cases, students may be automatically offered an assistantship. At Trinity University in San Antonio, Texas, for example, all students in the master's school psychology program are given assistantships with a partial tuition offset and a stipend. Sometimes doctoral candidates are assigned to a research project led by a faculty mentor. Other times, students will need to seek out assistantship opportunities by talking with professors and faculty advisors.

Even more prized than an assistantship is a fellowship or scholarship with no strings attached.

Other ways and means

Be a volunteer. Students who are willing to spend a year or two honing their teaching skills in underserved communities before grad school can earn a fellowship or other financial support. For example:

• Students who have served in the Peace Corps are eligible for fellowships in education programs at a number of universities. Columbia University's Teachers College, for one, recruits 40 to 50 returned Peace Corps volunteers each year to earn master's degrees in bilingual education, English, math, science, special education, or English as a second language. Recipients of the half-tuition fellowship agree to teach for a minimum of two years, and preferably four, in New York City public schools.

• Students who complete a one-year term of service in AmeriCorps, a federal community-service program, receive an education award that can be applied to grad school expenses or used to pay off student loans.

• Fordham University's Graduate School of Education offers a scholarship worth 25 percent of tuition to students who've completed a two-year term of service in the Teach for America program, teaching in urban or rural public schools.

Live like a student. For those who attend school full-time, the student expenses budget graduate schools estimate for yearly housing, food, and personal expenses is an almost laughable $15,000 or so. (Students who have dependent children can often have their living expense budgets increased to pay for child care costs, which raises the amount you can borrow.) But you can save yourself debt by taking in roommates and brown-bagging lunch. Even part-time students can trim their debt with a little belt-tightening. Every dollar you can divert to tuition from luxuries like cable TV or high-priced lattes is a dollar you won't have to pay interest on down the road.

Build up some savings. If you're looking ahead to graduate school in the next couple of years and can set aside some savings now, consider taking advantage of the tax benefits of a state-sponsored 529 plan. While most investors use these plans to save for a child's undergraduate expenses, the plans generally allow you to open an account with yourself as the beneficiary. The primary benefit is that the earnings on your savings will be tax-free, and your state may also throw in a deduction for your contributions. All 529 plans include investments that are appropriate for adults who will need to tap the money soon, such as bonds and money market accounts.

While many of the broker-sold 529s impose up-front sales fees that would minimize or offset any tax benefits over just a year or two, many of the direct-sold plans, such as those offered by TIAA-CREF and Vanguard, do not. Several are paying a guaranteed 3 percent or so right now. Not a bad parking place for a couple of years, especially when the feds aren't claiming any of the gains.

In some programs (especially doctoral programs) virtually all students receive some fellowship support; in others, the awards go only to the best and brightest. At the University of California–Berkeley, for example, doctoral students are eligible to apply for university-wide fellowships that pay three years' tuition plus a $15,000 to $17,000 annual stipend. Students who don't earn one of those or a fellowship awarded by the School of Education usually find a teaching or research assistantship. In the sixth and seventh semesters, all Ph.D. candidates who are on schedule with their coursework and pass a qualifying exam receive a "Dean's Normative Time Fellowship" (a two-semester stipend of $14,000 plus fees) meant to fund their dissertation research.

At the master's level, students in certain specialized programs may receive fellowships, grants, or scholarships. At Vanderbilt's Peabody College of Education and Human Development, about 80 percent of the students in the master's special education program receive either a training grant (with no work obligation) or an assistantship. And at Trinity, all students in the master's school leadership program (most of whom are part-time) receive a scholarship that covers about 50 percent of tuition.

Besides the awards open to master's candidates in general, many schools reserve a handful of scholarships—typically pretty modest ones—for future teachers. At the University of Virginia's Curry School of Education, for example, master's students in the department of teaching, instruction, and special education can apply for any of about two dozen endowed scholarships ranging from $500 to $12,000. At the University of Wisconsin–Madison, more than 15 scholarships are reserved specifically for teacher ed students,

most in the $500 to $1000 range. Donors specify the eligibility criteria, which explains why there may be $1,000 set aside for a student from a certain county, or a student who plans to teach high school math, or a student who is a direct descendant of a World War I veteran. Many schools also have a limited number of scholarships that are awarded to help attract top students or students who would bring ethnic or geographic diversity to the campus. While university-wide and departmental scholarships are often based on your application for admission—plus a bit of extra paperwork in some cases—many endowed scholarships require a separate application.

Search for outside scholarships

Government agencies and private organizations also sponsor fellowships and scholarships. Many schools compile listings of such awards, either on paper or online. Two good online resources are Cornell University's free Graduate School Fellowship Notebook (at cuinfo.cornell.edu/Student/GRFN) and the listing of grants at Michigan State University's website at www.lib.msu.edu/harris23/grants/3subject.htm. (Neither is specific to education, however, so you'll have to search for awards that might apply to you.) Also check with any civic groups, religious groups, or unions you're affiliated with, and honor societies, fraternities, or sororities you belonged to as an undergraduate.

Here's a sampling of the range of scholarship opportunities available:

The Horace Mann Scholarship Program for Educators (www.horacemann.com/edscholarship) offers 36 scholarships of $500 to $5,000 to teachers with two or more years of experience. The money can be used for any kind of coursework.

The Jack Kent Cooke Foundation Graduate Scholarship program (www.jackkentcookefounda tion.org) grants 35 awards a year to college seniors or recent graduates. The scholarship pays for full tuition, fees, room, board, and books—up to $50,000 a year for up to six years of graduate study. Candidates must be nominated by their undergraduate institution.

The American Association of University Women (www.aauw.org) awards Career Development Grants of $2,000 to $8,000 to women pursuing master's degrees and about fifty Dissertation Fellowships, worth $20,000, to women pursing doctoral degrees.

The Spencer Dissertation Fellowship (www.spencer.org) is a two-year award with a $20,000 annual stipend for doctoral students who have completed their coursework and who are writing dissertations "relevant to the improvement of education." There were 30 awards in 2003–2004.

The Robert Noyce Scholarship Program makes hundreds of $10,000 awards to professionals with math, science, or technology degrees who want to become certified as K–12 teachers. Recipients must commit to teaching at least two years in a high-need school. Funded by the National Science Foundation, the awards are offered through 15 universities, including the University of Missouri–Columbia, the University of Illinois–Chicago, and the University of Texas–Austin.

The James Madison Graduate Fellowship Foundation (www.jamesmadison.com) makes grants of up to $24,000 over two years to part-time master's students who are studying American history or political science and who teach or plan to teach the American Constitution.

Get set to borrow

A financial aid advisor can counsel a law, medical, or M.B.A. student to take on huge debts because that student will eventually have the income to pay it off, says Jim Hogge, associate dean for faculty and programs at Vanderbilt's Peabody College. "We don't make representations like that to prospective teachers," he says. About two-thirds of education students borrow to finance their degrees, but whereas the typical law student ends up with more than $70,000 in debt, the average amount that education students borrow (including undergraduate debt) amounts to about $22,000 for master's degree students and $26,000 for doctoral students. So while many students borrow, they tend not to finance their degrees entirely with debt.

Government-guaranteed Stafford loans are a staple for grad students in any field. Students with financial need qualify for up to $8,500 per year in "subsidized" Stafford loans, plus up to an additional $10,000 per year in "unsubsidized" loans, for a total maximum of up to $18,500 per year. The federal government pays the interest on a subsidized loan while you're in school and for six months after you graduate or drop below half-time status. Interest accrues on the unsubsidized loan while you're in school, so the grand total mounts, but with both types of loans you can delay making payments until after graduation. All told, you can borrow up to $138,500 in Stafford loans to finance your education, including whatever you've already taken on as an undergraduate.

To qualify for a Stafford loan, you have to prove that you're going to need help paying the bills. As you'll probably remember from your undergraduate days, that means filling out the Free Application for Federal Student Aid, also known as

Becky Moore is a triple threat: She teaches ninth through twelfth grade English, coaches her school's JV rowing team, and is the live-in dorm "mom" to 36 teenage girls.

It's all in a day's work at Phillips Exeter Academy in Exeter, New Hampshire, where Moore lives with her husband and three teenage sons in a roomy apartment attached to a dormitory; students can drop in day or night to get help with homework, or homesickness, or just to say hello. All teachers are required to live in a dorm during their first 10 years on staff. "I would be disingenuous if I said it wasn't hard," says Moore. "You can potentially work from 8 in the morning to 11 o'clock at night."

But Moore says it's worth it: Aside from a highly motivated student body and a stunning 5 to 1 student-teacher ratio, by working at a top private school she also enjoys the kind of academic freedom more often accorded to college professors than to high school teachers. "I can't think of a time when somebody turned around and said, 'You can't teach that,'" she says.

Phillips Exeter, which is home to 1,000 students, has built its name on rigorous academics and elite-college prep. The admissions process is comparable to that of a highly selective college; just 27 percent of applicants were admitted last year. Fifty-minute classes run from 8:00 a.m. until 6:00 p.m. (with half-day sessions on Wednesdays and Saturdays) and are taught in a discussion-based format in which a teacher and about a dozen students sit around a circular table. "The kids have a conversation, which I'm coaching them on," says Moore. "In a class this size, every student can take a part."

Moore, who graduated from Harvard in 1979 knowing she wanted to teach but lacking the credentials needed to work in a public school, has spent her 25-year career at New England independent schools. She relishes the opportunity to interact with her students—in class, at birthday celebrations and dorm cookouts, and as they stop in to say goodnight before bed. Living on campus also allows teachers to work together outside of the weekly hour-long faculty meeting. "There's a sense of collegiality," says Moore. "People have long conversations about teaching when walking their dogs."

Fortunately for Moore, her family also relishes campus life. Having attended boarding school as a child, her husband, Marshall, understands why their family life must have a "permeable membrane" and be integrated with the life of the students. And her sons have reaped the rewards of living on a campus that features an ice skating rink, a pool, a gym, and a river. Other compensations, too, are unusually attractive. Moore makes $60,000 a year, but that's just the beginning of her pay package. She lives rent-free in school housing, utilities and cable television included. Her family can take three meals a day in the Exeter cafeteria free of charge, and she didn't have to pay the $30,000 tuition for her sons to attend Exeter. For every five years of teaching, full-time staff can take one term of paid sabbatical leave. Yearly school vacations are also generous: two weeks for spring break, more than a week for Thanksgiving, three weeks at Christmas, and two and a half months in the summer.

Positions at independent schools can be difficult to come by. A teaching credential is not generally necessary; more valued at Exeter is lots of teaching experience and a master's or Ph.D. in a teacher's field of instruction. (It also doesn't hurt to be able to coach a sport on the side.) To get a taste of the lifestyle and a leg up in the job search, Moore recommends volunteering or interning at an independent school, or applying to teach summer term at a boarding school. "I feel very lucky to have this job," she says. "There's an intensity about these schools that I've always been drawn to. They're built on the idea that we are all in this together."

the FAFSA. After all the information about your income and assets and expenses is crunched, you'll be told how much you're expected to contribute and be offered a loan to help fill any gap. If your school participates in the Federal Direct Student Loan Program, you'll borrow directly from the federal government. Otherwise you can choose your own funding source using a list of preferred lenders provided by your school. While all lenders offer the same interest rate on Stafford loans, some waive the up-front origination and guarantee fees (which can run up to 4 percent of the loan amount), some reduce the interest rate in repayment if you sign up for automatic payments or make a certain number of payments on time, and some do both. So it can pay to shop around. Rates on these variable-rate loans change every summer; they're at 3.4 percent lately. Even if rates rise, they won't exceed a cap of 8.25 percent.

Students with high financial need—the FAFSA shows that they're expected to contribute very little or nothing to their graduate education—will also qualify for a Perkins loan of up to $6,000 per year. The interest rate is a fixed 5 percent. While that's a bit higher than the 2004 rate on Stafford loans, it won't rise in future years. In addition, there are no up-front origination fees. The Perkins is a subsidized loan, so no interest accrues until nine months after you graduate or drop below half-time status.

Private loans. If the federal loan limits leave you short, private lenders stand ready to lend you up to the full cost of your education, less any financial aid. (Some schools also have their own loan programs.) Interest rates tend to be only slightly higher than the rates on Stafford loans. However, origination fees can be significantly higher—up to 6 percent of the loan amount—and interest begins accruing right away. To qualify for private loans, you need a clean credit history or a cosigner. (It's a good idea to check your credit report for errors before you apply.)

Some popular programs include Graduate Access Loan, from Access Group, Inc. (www.accessgroup.org), Signature Student Loan, from Sallie Mae (www.salliemae.com), CitiAssist Loan, from Citibank (www.studentloan.com), and Key Alternative Loan, from KeyBank (www.key.com/educate).

Home-equity loans. For students who own a home, a home-equity line of credit is another attractive choice. Rates are low, fees are minimal, and the interest on up to $100,000 in debt is tax deductible if you itemize. If you expect to graduate into a high-paying job, home-equity debt may be a better alternative than other debt because you won't qualify for tax-deductible interest on government or private student loans. Interest on student loans will be fully tax deductible only to single taxpayers whose income falls below $50,000 and to joint filers with income of less than $100,000. Remember, though, that a home-equity line of credit is secured by your home, so be certain you'll be able to make the payments after graduation.

Find help paying the money back

At 2004 rates, the payment on $25,000 in Stafford debt is about $250 a month over the standard 10-year repayment term. Those payments may be manageable on the $30,000 entry-level salary of a teacher, but if they're not, there are ways to ease the monthly burden.

Flexible repayment options. You can stretch the standard term in various ways to reduce the size of your payments. With an extended repayment plan, for example, you can lengthen the loan term to up to 30 years. Another option, a graduated repayment schedule that extends over 12 to 30 years, starts you off with lower payments than the standard plan calls for and then ratchets them up annually as your paycheck presumably grows. Income-contingent or income-sensitive repayment plans adjust your payment each year based on your income. In the end, you'll pay more interest over the longer payback periods, but you can always boost your payments as your income rises to pay down the loan more quickly than you're asked to.

Loan consolidation. You may also be able to reduce the interest you pay on Stafford loans by consolidating them when interest rates are low. That locks in current interest rates instead of allowing them to fluctuate annually. You may even be able to consolidate your undergraduate and early grad-school loans to take advantage of low rates while you're still in school. (For more details, see loanconsolidation.ed.gov, at the Department of Education's website, or www.federalconsolidation.org, a website sponsored by Access Group, Inc., a private, not-for-profit lender.)

Student loan interest deduction. If your income is modest, Uncle Sam will step in to help with the interest payments. You can deduct up to $2,500 a year in student-loan interest if you earn less than $50,000 as a single taxpayer or less than $100,000 if you are married filing jointly. (You can deduct a lesser amount with incomes of up to $65,000 and $130,000.)

Note to parents: You get to take this deduction if you're legally obligated to pay back the debt and if you claim the student as a dependent on your tax return.

Loan repayment assistance programs. Many states repay the loans of teachers who commit to subject areas with teacher shortages, such as math, science, or foreign language; to working in special education; or to teaching in low-income schools. Under California's Assumption Program of Loans for Education, for example, teachers who serve for four years in such underserved arenas in California public schools turn as much as $19,000 of their student-loan debt over to the state. Graduates of Maryland universities can take advantage of a similar program, the Janet L.

Hoffman Loan Assistance Repayment Program, which covers up to $7,500 a year in student-loan debt. Ask a financial aid officer at your school if there's a similar program in your state.

Teachers who work in schools that serve low-income students for five years can have all of their Perkins loan debt forgiven or up to $5,000 of their Stafford loan debt forgiven.

Find work

Full-time students whose FAFSA form shows financial need and who don't have an assistantship may be awarded a work-study job as part of their financial aid package. An award of $1,000 to $3,000 a year is typical, and covers the pay for 10 to 15 hours of work a week. Pay can range anywhere from $5.15 (the federal minimum wage) to $14.75 an hour, depending on the job and job market where your school is located. Most jobs are on campus, although some schools place a small percentage of students with not-for-profit organizations off campus. A job as a resident assistant in an undergraduate dorm is another option. The position usually includes tuition remission and a stipend.

Take a hand from Uncle Sam

If your income is modest, the federal government will help bear the cost of your graduate degree by giving you a tax credit or tax deduction for educational expenses. Most students will want to take advantage of the Lifetime Learning tax credit, worth $2,000 a year (20 percent of the first $10,000 you spend in tuition and fees annually). You qualify for the full credit if you file a single tax return and your income is $42,000 or less, and for a partial credit if you make up to $52,000. If you're married filing jointly, the full credit is available when income is less than $85,000, and a partial credit is available up to $105,000. A tax credit reduces your tax bill dollar for dollar.

Full-time students aren't likely to exceed those thresholds, but if you do—either because you're a part-timer or are married to a spouse with a substantial income—you may still qualify for a tax deduction for your educational expenses. In 2004 and 2005, students can take a deduction for up to $4,000 in tuition and fees if their incomes don't exceed $65,000 filing singly or $130,000 filing jointly. That's worth up to $1,000 to a taxpayer in the 25 percent tax bracket. Note: You can't take both the credit and the deduction.

Even with tax breaks and scholarship aid, your graduate degree will obviously be a major financial investment. While educators (unlike lawyers or M.B.A. grads) generally don't see big income hikes after finishing grad school, history shows that an advanced degree should increase your earning power over a lifetime.

Chapter Six

Getting Licensed in Your State

Current college students who decide to become teachers take a pretty straightforward path to the classroom: a four- or five-year accredited teacher-training program. Aspiring teachers who have already earned an undergraduate degree, on the other hand, face a wide and complex array of choices and hurdles.

Each state sets its own standards for teacher licensure, and these are often a confusing pastiche that has been added to and amended over the years. In general, most states require at least a bachelor's degree and a passing score on a basic test of reading, writing, and math skills. Many states also require teachers of specific subjects to

As an English major at the University of Arkansas back in the mid-nineties, Marcus Myers imagined himself becoming a professor and teaching big ideas to bright college students. Then, a few months before beginning a graduate program in English, Myers did something that he'd sworn he'd never do: He became a middle school teacher. All of a sudden, "teaching in public schools seemed like a much more sincere use of my time and my career," says Myers. On the cusp of graduation, he switched tracks and spent an extra three semesters at college getting the courses for certification.

Today, Myers explores big ideas with very smart 12-, 13-, 14-year-olds in an English program for the extremely gifted at Northgate Middle School in Kansas City, Missouri. "A lot of teachers are kind of scared of these kids because they're so bright," he says. For Myers, who likes to integrate psychology and philosophy into class discussions of literature, the job is a perfect fit. A unit on persecuted peoples, for example, includes *The Diary of Anne Frank*, books on the U.S. internment of Japanese civilians during World War II, and accounts of slavery. Beyond discussing the works themselves, students, who meet in tiny classes of three to 10, will examine their own biases and "why human beings, while being so loving and giving, can also be so cruel. I want them to synthesize the information into something new," says Myers.

Because his classes are so small and students often work on independent projects—his eighth graders, for example, publish their own single-topic magazines—Myers can spend much more time than the average teacher personalizing comments and designing individual

pass a test in their subject area. Some states use their own standardized tests, while others rely on the PRAXIS exams, a series of three tests administered by the Educational Testing Service, the same folks that give the SAT.

The requirements for teacher training are more complicated. Colorado, for example, requires 13 weeks of student teaching experience; Illinois demands none. Alaska does not require teachers to major in their subject areas or pass a subject-matter test. In Georgia, even a temporary provisional license requires a grade point average of at least 2.5, a subject-area major, and a passing score in both a basic skills and a subject matter test. So it's important for people considering a career in teaching to research the ins and outs of licensure in their state. For those who already have a bachelor's degree, here are the most common routes to the classroom.

Postbaccalaureate program. These one- to two-year programs offer either a master's degree in education or the necessary education courses and student teaching experience for those who have completed an undergraduate degree. Some operate as full-time graduate programs, while others offer part-time schedules for working adults.

yearlong plans. Without this intense approach, he says, these kids would get bored—which is not to say that his precocious learners never act their age. But Myers, who once thought of middle-schoolers as the "most awful" age group, now finds 12-year-olds to be "such unique, sincere little people. They want to make a good connection with me and they aren't polluted by all the attitude that older kids have."

To handle the occasional burst of hormones, he relies on a philosophy that he absorbed from his mother, a kindergarten teacher. "I learned to make the rules the enforcer," says Myers. "I put the rules and procedures on the wall, get them in their head and when the kids slip up, I point to the wall. It's much more simple and takes less energy than making every infraction a personal thing." If necessary, a warning is followed by a talk in the hall, then after-school detention and a call home, and finally, a dreaded walk to the principal's office.

With student loans, car payments, rent, and tuition for the master's degree he must complete to stay on as a teacher in his school district, Myers can't quite make ends meet on his $29,300 salary. So after school, he heads to a law firm job, where he faxes and files until 6 p.m. The modest pay is part of the reason that Myers, the son of two teachers, didn't want to go into teaching originally. A number of his male colleagues, in fact, are now preparing to make the switch from teaching to administration, where salaries are higher. But Myers has discovered that there's nothing he would rather be doing. "I want to inspire kids to read and think and write and access their world," he says.

Alternative licensure. Combining flexibility and coursework, alternative teacher training programs have become very popular in recent years. Although they vary widely, the best offer a combination of paid teaching experience, mentoring, coursework, an expedited licensing process, and in some cases a master's degree. For more information on alternative licensure, see Chapter 2.

Emergency licensure. In districts or subject areas where teachers are in short supply, emergency or temporary licensure is often a possibility—and a tempting one for people who want a job immediately without enrolling in any teaching courses. Typically, the licenses are valid for one to three years, issued by the principal of a school or superintendent of a district, and are renewable. Teachers with emergency licenses are expected, but usually not required, to complete coursework toward a regular license through evening or summer classes. To get an emergency license, prospective teachers usually must find a school or school district willing to hire them and sponsor the emergency licensee. Keep in mind, however, that most emergency teachers go to the neediest schools and receive little in the way of mentoring or on-the-job-training. Burnout is common.

The best way to investigate the regulations in your state is to go to the state's licensing website. Some sites clearly lay out the requirements and options, while others present a confusing morass of rules and links. If you can't find answers on the site, try calling or emailing with specific questions. We've provided the website addresses and contact information below. Some questions to ask:

• Do you have a list of accredited teacher training programs in my area? What about accredited alternative teacher training programs?

• Do you offer alternative licenses? Are they only available for limited grade levels, subjects, or districts?

• Do you offer emergency licenses? Are they limited to certain subjects or schools?

• In which subjects or grade levels is this state experiencing a shortage?

• Are there any partially or fully funded teacher training programs for certain subjects or for people like me?

• What are the minimum course, major, and student-teaching requirements, if any, for initial licensure?

• How many years will an initial license remain valid?

• Are there continuing education requirements to stay licensed over the years? If so, does the state support these requirements with tuition remission or time? (Depending on your state and the level of support it gives to continuing professional development, for example, you may want to finish a master's degree now, wait until you begin teaching, or not bother.)

• Which tests must I take and how can I prepare for them?

• How much will it cost to obtain a license? (With fingerprinting, testing, application fees, and license fees, the costs can run several hundred dollars).

Alabama

Alabama Department of Education–Teacher
Education and Certification
www.alsde.edu/general/general_certification_
information.pdf
tcert@alsde.edu
(334) 242-9977

Alaska

Alaska Department of Education—Teacher
Certification
www.eed.state.ak.us/TeacherCertification
tcwebmail@eed.state.ak.us
(907) 465-2831

Arizona

Arizona Department of Education—Certification
www.ade.state.az.us/certification
certification@ade.az.gov
(602) 542-4367

Arkansas

Arkansas Department of Education—Teacher
Licensure
arkedu.state.ar.us/teachers
(501) 682-4342

California

California Commission on Teacher Credentialing
www.ctc.ca.gov
credentials@ctc.ca.gov
(916) 445-7254
(888) 921-2682

Colorado

Colorado Department of Education—Educator
Licensing
www.cde.state.co.us/index_license.htm
educator.licensing@cde.state.co.us
(303) 866-6628

Connecticut

Bureau of Educator Preparation and Certification
www.ctcert.org
teacher.cert@po.state.ct.us
(860) 713-6969

Delaware

Licensure/Certification Office
deeds.doe.state.de.us
teachdelaware@usteach.com
(888) 759-9133

District of Columbia

Office of Academic Credentialing and
Accreditation
www.teachdc.org
(202) 442-5377

Florida

Bureau of Educator Certification
www.fldoe.org/edcert
edcert@fldoe.org
(850) 488-2317 out of state
(800) 445-6739 in state

Georgia

Professional Standards Commission Educator
Certification Section
www.gapsc.com
(800) 869-7775 outside the metro Atlanta area
(404) 232-2500 in the metro Atlanta area

Hawaii

Hawaii Teacher Standards Board
www.htsb.org
lhammonds@htsb.org
(808) 586-2600

Idaho

Bureau of Certification & Professional Standards
www.sde.state.id.us/certification
jjensen@sde.state.id.us
(208) 332-6880

Illinois

Illinois State Board of Education—Teacher
Certification
www.isbe.net/teachers
certification@isbe.net
not able to take phone calls; fax (217) 524-1289

Indiana

Professional Standards Board
www.in.gov/psb
helpdesk@psb.state.in.us
(866) 542-3672

Iowa

Iowa Board of Educational Examiners
www.state.ia.us/boee
(515) 281-3245

Kansas

Teacher Education and Licensure
www.ksde.org/cert/cert.html
(785) 291-3678

Kentucky

Education Professional Standards Board
www.kyepsb.net
sherry.paul@ky.gov
(888) 598-7667

Louisiana

Division of Teacher Certification and Higher
Education
www.doe.state.la.us/lde/tsac/home.html
Janet.Reed@la.gov
(877) 453-2721

Maine

Administrator and Teacher Certification
www.state.me.us/education/cert/cert.htm
Pat.Julien@maine.gov
(207) 624-6603

Maryland

Maryland State Department of Education—
Certification Branch
certification.msde.state.md.us
(410) 767-0412

Massachusetts

Massachusetts Department of Education
www.doe.mass.edu/educators/e_license.html
cert.inquiries@doe.mass.edu
(781) 338-6600

Michigan

Office of Professional Preparation Services

www.michigan.gov/mde

ciloskif@michigan.gov

(517) 373-3310

Minnesota

Minnesota Personnel Licensing

education.state.mn.us/html/intro_licensure.htm

personnel.licensing@state.mn.us

(651) 582-8691

Mississippi

Office of Educator Licensure

www.mde.k12.ms.us/license

cchester@mde.k12.ms.us

(601) 359-3483

Missouri

Division of Teacher Quality & Urban Education

dese.mo.gov/divteachqual/teachcert

webreplyteachcert@dese.mo.gov

(573) 751-0051

(573) 751-3847

Montana

Educator Licensure (Certification) Program

www.opi.state.mt.us/cert/index.html

mbowles@state.mt.us

(406) 444-3150

Nebraska

Nebraska Department of Education–Teacher Certification

www.nde.state.ne.us/tcert/tcert.html

tcertweb@nde.state.ne.us

(402) 471-2496 forms request line

(402) 471-0739

Nevada

Teacher Licensing Office

www.nde.state.nv.us/licensure

license@nsn.k12.nv.us

(702) 486-6458 Las Vegas

(775) 687-9115 Carson City

New Hampshire

Bureau of Credentialing

www.ed.state.nh.us/Certification/teacher.htm

llovering@ed.state.nh.us

(phone numbers for specific programs given on website)

New Jersey

New Jersey Department of Education–Licensing and Credentials

www.state.nj.us/njded/educators/license

(609) 292-2070

New Mexico

Professional Licensure Unit

www.sde.state.nm.us/div/ais/lic/index.html

(505) 827-6587

New York

Office of Teaching Initiatives

www.highered.nysed.gov/tcert

(518) 474-3901

North Carolina

Department of Public Instruction—Licensure Section

www.dpi.state.nc.us/licensure

(800) 577-7994 in North Carolina

(919) 807-3310 out of state

North Dakota

Education Standards and Practices Board

www.state.nd.us/espb

(701) 328-2264

diweber@state.nd.us

Ohio

Center for the Teaching Profession—The Office
of Certification/Licensure

www.ode.state.oh.us/teaching-profession/
teacher/certification_licensure

(614) 466-3593

Oklahoma

Professional Standards Section

sde.state.ok.us/pro/tcert/profstd.html

cindy_marose@sde.state.ok.us

(405) 521-3337

Oregon

Teacher Standards and Practices Commission of
Oregon

www.tspc.state.or.us

contact.tspc@state.or.us

(503) 378-3586

Pennsylvania

Bureau of Teacher Certification and Preparation

www.teaching.state.pa.us/teaching

ra-teachercert@state.pa.us

(717) 787- 3356

Rhode Island

Office of Teacher Certification and
Teacher Quality

www.ridoe.net/teacher_cert

(401) 222-4600 press 3

South Carolina

Division of Teacher Quality

www.scteachers.org

certification@scteachers.org

(877) 885-5280 toll free in state

(803) 734-8466 out of state and Columbia area

South Dakota

Office of Accreditation & Teacher Quality

www.state.sd.us/deca/OPA

gwen.rothenberger@state.sd.us

(605) 773-3553

Tennessee

Office of Teacher Licensing

www.state.tn.us/education/lic_home

sharon.henderson@state.tn.us

(615) 532-4873

(615) 532-4885 forms request line

Texas

State Board for Educator Certification

www.sbec.state.tx.us/SBECOnline

sbec@sbec.state.tx.us

(888) 863-5880

Utah

Office of Educator Licensing

www.usoe.k12.ut.us/cert

(801) 538-7740

Vermont

Educator Licensing Office

www.state.vt.us/educ/new/html/maincert.html

licensing@doe.state.vt.us

(802) 828-2445

Virginia

Division of Teacher Education & Licensure

www.pen.k12.va.us/VDOE/newvdoe/teached.html

(804) 786-7633 Career Switchers program

(804) 692-0157 licensure

Washington

The Professional Education & Certification Office

www.k12.wa.us/certification

cert@ospi.wednet.edu

(360) 725-6400

West Virginia

Department of Education, Teacher Certification

wvde.state.wv.us/certification

Mbowe@access.k12.wv.us

(800) 982-2378

Wisconsin

Teacher Education, Professional Development, & Licensing

www.dpi.state.wi.us/dpi/dlsis/tel

Tcert@dpi.state.wi.us

(800) 266-1027

Wyoming

Professional Teaching Standards Board

www.k12.wy.us/ptsb

bmarti@state.wy.us

(800) 675-6893 in state

(307) 777-7291 out of state

The U.S. News Insider's Index

How Do the Grad Schools Stack Up?

Which are the hardest and easiest education schools to get into? 78

Which are the largest and smallest education schools? 88

In which states will first-year teachers make the most money? Where will they make the least? . . 101

In which cities do teachers with master's degrees make the most and the least? 103

Whose graduates are most likely to pass the state certification test? The least? 106

Which are the hardest and easiest education schools to get into?

How much competition are you facing? Schools are ranked here within each state from most to least selective based on their acceptance rate: the proportion of applicants who made the cut into the full-time master's program. While not all graduate education programs require the Graduate Record Exam (GRE) or the Miller Analogies Test (MAT) for admittance, you'll see here which ones do—and the average scores of the fall 2003 entering class.

	Master's acceptance rate	Educational specialist acceptance rate	Doctoral acceptance rate	Required tests	Average verbal GRE score	Average quantitative GRE score	Average analytical GRE score	Average MAT score
ALABAMA								
Samford University	39%	37%	34%	GRE or MAT	441	461	N/A	48
University of Alabama–Tuscaloosa	55%	61%	42%	GRE or MAT	459	548	546	52
University of Alabama–Birmingham	63%	58%	45%	GRE or MAT	461	526	576	N/A
Spring Hill College	70%	N/A	N/A	GRE or MAT	N/A	N/A	N/A	47
Auburn University–Main Campus	72%	70%	42%	GRE	424	472	502	N/A
Troy State University–Dothan	78%	83%	N/A	GRE or MAT	375	495	N/A	41
University of North Alabama	83%	100%	N/A	GRE or MAT	N/A	N/A	N/A	40
ALASKA								
University of Alaska–Fairbanks	71%	N/A	N/A	GRE	534	512	577	N/A
University of Alaska–Southeast	81%	N/A	N/A	N/A	N/A	N/A	N/A	N/A
Alaska Pacific University	93%	N/A	N/A	GRE or MAT	530	450	455	55
ARIZONA								
Arizona State University–Main Campus	47%	N/A	22%	GRE or MAT	573	591	598	N/A
Arizona State University–West	69%	N/A	N/A	N/A	N/A	N/A	N/A	N/A
University of Arizona	73%	70%	70%	GRE or MAT	486	575	591	55
ARKANSAS								
University of Arkansas–Fayetteville	85%	75%	89%	GRE or MAT	N/A	N/A	N/A	N/A
CALIFORNIA								
University of California–Davis	26%	N/A	45%	GRE or MAT	N/A	N/A	N/A	N/A
University of California–Berkeley	32%	N/A	18%	GRE	573	626	650	N/A
California State University–Long Beach	38%	N/A	N/A	GRE	N/A	N/A	N/A	N/A
University of California–Riverside	40%	N/A	29%	N/A	500	668	N/A	N/A
San Diego State University	48%	N/A	37%	GRE	456	500	N/A	N/A
University of California–Los Angeles	51%	N/A	24%	GRE or MAT	545	604	624	N/A
Fielding Graduate Institute	53%	N/A	95%	N/A	N/A	N/A	N/A	N/A
Stanford University	54%	N/A	9%	GRE	594	678	677	N/A
Cal Poly–San Luis Obispo	57%	N/A	50%	GRE	N/A	N/A	N/A	N/A
University of La Verne	57%	N/A	46%	GRE or MAT	N/A	N/A	N/A	40
Fresno Pacific University	61%	N/A	N/A	N/A	N/A	N/A	N/A	N/A
University of California–Santa Barbara (Gevirtz)	61%	94%	29%	GRE or MAT	494	578	587	46
Alliant International University–San Diego	64%	N/A	41%	None	N/A	N/A	N/A	N/A
Holy Names College	68%	N/A	N/A	None	N/A	N/A	N/A	N/A
University of California–Irvine	68%	N/A	30%	GRE	504	577	613	N/A
University of Southern California (Rossier)	68%	N/A	47%	GRE	484	572	N/A	N/A

	Master's acceptance rate	Educational specialist acceptance rate	Doctoral acceptance rate	Required tests	Average verbal GRE score	Average quantitative GRE score	Average analytical GRE score	Average MAT score
Chapman University	69%	25%	N/A	GRE or MAT	458	548	550	N/A
University of the Pacific	69%	64%	55%	N/A	N/A	N/A	N/A	N/A
University of San Diego	70%	N/A	49%	GRE or MAT	N/A	N/A	N/A	N/A
University of California–Santa Cruz	71%	N/A	N/A	N/A	N/A	N/A	N/A	N/A
Bethany College of the Assemblies of God	73%	N/A	N/A	GRE	N/A	N/A	N/A	N/A
Claremont Graduate University	73%	N/A	63%	GRE or MAT	532	562	527	N/A
California State University–Dominguez Hills	77%	N/A	N/A	N/A	N/A	N/A	N/A	N/A
University of Judaism	78%	N/A	N/A	GRE or MAT	525	563	N/A	N/A
California State University–San Bernardino	79%	N/A	N/A	N/A	N/A	N/A	N/A	N/A
California State University–Fullerton	81%	N/A	N/A	N/A	N/A	N/A	N/A	N/A
California State University–Chico	83%	N/A	N/A	GRE or MAT	N/A	N/A	N/A	N/A
University of San Francisco	83%	N/A	78%	GRE or MAT	N/A	N/A	N/A	N/A
Concordia University	84%	N/A	N/A	GRE or MAT	N/A	N/A	N/A	N/A
Loyola Marymount University	85%	86%	N/A	GRE	462	527	440	N/A
Biola University	86%	N/A	N/A	N/A	N/A	N/A	N/A	N/A
Simpson College	88%	N/A	N/A	GRE	N/A	N/A	N/A	N/A
Hope International University	89%	N/A	N/A	None	N/A	N/A	N/A	N/A
Santa Clara University	89%	N/A	N/A	N/A	N/A	N/A	N/A	N/A
COLORADO								
Colorado State University	46%	N/A	58%	GRE	N/A	N/A	N/A	N/A
University of Colorado–Boulder	60%	N/A	38%	GRE or MAT	563	621	625	N/A
University of Northern Colorado	64%	39%	47%	GRE or MAT	482	593	558	N/A
University of Denver	77%	85%	48%	GRE	550	500	N/A	N/A
Colorado College	79%	N/A	N/A	N/A	N/A	N/A	N/A	N/A
University of Colorado–Denver	88%	60%	61%	GRE or MAT	470	546	N/A	N/A
Colorado Christian College	94%	N/A	N/A	N/A	N/A	N/A	N/A	N/A
CONNECTICUT								
Central Connecticut State University	64%	N/A	49%	GRE	N/A	N/A	N/A	N/A
Fairfield University	66%	N/A	N/A	N/A	N/A	N/A	N/A	N/A
University of Connecticut (Neag)	68%	N/A	22%	GRE or MAT	571	599	576	N/A
Quinnipiac University	74%	N/A	N/A	N/A	N/A	N/A	N/A	N/A
University of Bridgeport	76%	94%	54%	GRE or MAT	N/A	N/A	N/A	N/A
Sacred Heart University	79%	N/A	N/A	N/A	N/A	N/A	N/A	N/A
University of New Haven	89%	N/A	N/A	N/A	N/A	N/A	N/A	N/A
DELAWARE								
University of Delaware	52%	N/A	33%	GRE	535	616	N/A	N/A
Wesley College	82%	N/A	N/A	N/A	530	520	530	N/A
DISTRICT OF COLUMBIA								
Gallaudet University	38%	71%	58%	GRE or MAT	451	457	507	71
University of the District of Columbia	40%	N/A	N/A	N/A	N/A	N/A	N/A	N/A
Catholic University of America	59%	N/A	50%	GRE or MAT	518	625	538	N/A
George Washington University	69%	53%	62%	GRE or MAT	494	557	559	49
Trinity College	80%	N/A	N/A	N/A	N/A	N/A	N/A	N/A
FLORIDA								
Florida State University	49%	25%	22%	GRE	466	538	N/A	N/A
Florida International University	51%	33%	17%	GRE	422	486	N/A	N/A
St. Leo University	57%	N/A	N/A	GRE or MAT	N/A	N/A	N/A	N/A
University of South Florida	60%	20%	38%	GRE	478	531	N/A	N/A
University of Florida	62%	N/A	36%	GRE	486	589	N/A	N/A

Which are the hardest and easiest education schools to get into?

	Master's acceptance rate	Educational specialist acceptance rate	Doctoral acceptance rate	Required tests	Average verbal GRE score	Average quantitative GRE score	Average analytical GRE score	Average MAT score
University of West Florida	67%	66%	46%	N/A	N/A	N/A	N/A	N/A
University of Central Florida	70%	36%	72%	GRE	467	537	530	N/A
Jacksonville University	75%	N/A	N/A	GRE or MAT	577	662	N/A	65
University of Miami	75%	73%	17%	GRE	473	550	607	N/A
Florida Institute of Technology–Melbourne	76%	N/A	58%	N/A	N/A	N/A	N/A	N/A
Lynn University	79%	N/A	N/A	GRE	N/A	N/A	N/A	N/A
Florida Atlantic University	87%	100%	75%	GRE	460	519	N/A	N/A
Nova Southeastern University	100%	100%	99%	GRE or MAT	N/A	N/A	N/A	N/A
Trinity Baptist College	100%	N/A	N/A	GRE	550	460	N/A	N/A
GEORGIA								
University of Georgia	35%	48%	26%	GRE or MAT	488	572	581	N/A
Kennesaw State University	65%	N/A	N/A	GRE or MAT	475	497	N/A	N/A
Wesleyan College	83%	N/A	N/A	N/A	N/A	N/A	N/A	N/A
Piedmont College	87%	80%	N/A	GRE or MAT	N/A	N/A	N/A	42
Georgia College and State University	88%	80%	N/A	GRE or MAT	426	509	538	43
LaGrange College	100%	N/A	N/A	GRE or MAT	N/A	N/A	N/A	N/A
HAWAII								
University of Hawaii–Manoa	50%	N/A	39%	GRE	475	527	526	N/A
IDAHO								
Idaho State University	98%	100%	100%	GRE or MAT	446	490	N/A	43
ILLINOIS								
Southern Illinois University–Carbondale	48%	N/A	17%	GRE or MAT	482	501	561	62
University of Illinois–Urbana-Champaign	60%	N/A	37%	GRE	545	642	601	N/A
Bradley University	61%	N/A	N/A	GRE or MAT	438	495	607	49
University of St. Francis	64%	N/A	N/A	N/A	N/A	N/A	N/A	N/A
Northern Illinois University	65%	65%	46%	GRE or MAT	452	528	N/A	N/A
Illinois State University	69%	26%	63%	GRE	458	547	547	N/A
Chicago State University	71%	N/A	N/A	N/A	N/A	N/A	N/A	N/A
North Central College	75%	N/A	N/A	N/A	N/A	N/A	N/A	N/A
Northwestern University	76%	N/A	18%	GRE	598	666	675	N/A
Roosevelt University	80%	N/A	55%	GRE or MAT	N/A	N/A	N/A	N/A
Aurora University	81%	N/A	87%	N/A	N/A	N/A	N/A	N/A
DePaul University	82%	81%	N/A	N/A	N/A	N/A	N/A	N/A
University of Illinois–Chicago	82%	N/A	67%	GRE	496	553	N/A	N/A
Loyola University Chicago	83%	73%	86%	GRE or MAT	465	541	538	44
Governors State University	84%	N/A	N/A	GRE	N/A	N/A	N/A	N/A
University of Illinois–Springfield	95%	N/A	N/A	N/A	N/A	N/A	N/A	N/A
National-Louis University	96%	94%	78%	GRE or MAT	456	N/A	N/A	40
Eastern Illinois University	100%	100%	N/A	GRE or MAT	N/A	N/A	N/A	N/A
INDIANA								
Butler University	41%	N/A	N/A	N/A	N/A	N/A	N/A	N/A
Indiana University–Bloomington	54%	16%	35%	GRE	503	570	620	N/A
Purdue University–West Lafayette	60%	100%	61%	GRE	525	621	596	N/A
Ball State University	65%	31%	39%	GRE	496	565	610	N/A
University of Southern Indiana	77%	N/A	N/A	None	N/A	N/A	N/A	N/A
Valparaiso University	87%	83%	N/A	GRE or MAT	489	609	N/A	N/A

	Master's acceptance rate	Educational specialist acceptance rate	Doctoral acceptance rate	Required tests	Average verbal GRE score	Average quantitative GRE score	Average analytical GRE score	Average MAT score
Purdue University–Calumet	92%	N/A	N/A	N/A	N/A	N/A	N/A	N/A
Indiana University-Purdue University–Indianapolis	93%	N/A	N/A	GRE	N/A	N/A	N/A	N/A
Earlham College	94%	N/A	N/A	GRE	536	598	N/A	N/A
Indiana University–Southeast	97%	N/A	N/A	N/A	N/A	N/A	N/A	N/A
IOWA								
Drake University	54%	76%	N/A	GRE or MAT	487	554	586	48
University of Iowa	61%	50%	47%	GRE	535	629	627	N/A
Loras College	73%	N/A	N/A	N/A	N/A	N/A	N/A	N/A
Iowa State University	76%	N/A	66%	GRE or MAT	459	557	524	N/A
Buena Vista University	84%	N/A	N/A	GRE	N/A	N/A	600	N/A
KANSAS								
University of Kansas	72%	17%	24%	GRE or MAT	520	560	570	59
Washburn University	79%	N/A	N/A	GRE or MAT	520	563	553	46
Benedictine College	100%	N/A	N/A	MAT	N/A	N/A	N/A	N/A
KENTUCKY								
Western Kentucky University	56%	100%	N/A	GRE	430	488	521	N/A
University of Kentucky	56%	78%	45%	GRE	449	516	564	N/A
Northern Kentucky University	57%	N/A	N/A	GRE	448	502	485	N/A
Brescia University	60%	N/A	N/A	GRE	N/A	N/A	N/A	N/A
Union College	70%	N/A	N/A	N/A	N/A	N/A	N/A	N/A
Bellarmine University	79%	N/A	N/A	GRE or MAT	499	514	529	N/A
University of Louisville	81%	50%	73%	GRE or MAT	448	503	551	N/A
Murray State University	88%	88%	N/A	GRE	435	492	N/A	N/A
LOUISIANA								
University of Louisiana–Lafayette	54%	N/A	N/A	GRE	421	501	454	N/A
Louisiana State University–Baton Rouge	64%	85%	41%	GRE	461	565	576	N/A
Southeastern Louisiana University	98%	N/A	N/A	GRE	388	399	N/A	N/A
Northwestern State University of Louisiana	99%	97%	N/A	N/A	401	421	438	N/A
Louisiana State University–Shreveport	100%	100%	N/A	N/A	N/A	N/A	N/A	N/A
Louisiana Tech University	100%	N/A	100%	GRE	450	465	N/A	N/A
MAINE								
University of Maine–Orono	84%	93%	72%	GRE or MAT	485	535	592	49
MARYLAND								
University of Maryland–College Park	41%	20%	35%	GRE or MAT	534	612	633	50
University of Maryland–Baltimore County	59%	N/A	N/A	N/A	N/A	N/A	N/A	N/A
Towson University	60%	N/A	40%	GRE or MAT	N/A	N/A	N/A	N/A
Loyola College in Maryland	81%	N/A	N/A	N/A	N/A	N/A	N/A	N/A
College of Notre Dame of Maryland	90%	N/A	N/A	N/A	N/A	N/A	N/A	N/A
Goucher College	95%	N/A	N/A	N/A	N/A	N/A	N/A	N/A
MASSACHUSETTS								
University of Massachusetts–Amherst	55%	N/A	42%	None	519	566	585	N/A
Boston College (Lynch)	61%	56%	25%	GRE or MAT	522	600	618	47
Harvard University	65%	N/A	14%	GRE or MAT	579	642	614	64
Northeastern University	69%	N/A	N/A	GRE or MAT	488	585	N/A	21
University of Massachusetts–Lowell	70%	N/A	67%	GRE	506	547	552	55
Boston University	74%	80%	46%	GRE or MAT	516	598	616	54
Wheelock College	78%	N/A	N/A	None	N/A	N/A	N/A	N/A

Which are the hardest and easiest education schools to get into?

	Master's acceptance rate	Educational Specialist acceptance rate	Doctoral acceptance rate	Required tests	Average verbal GRE score	Average quantitative GRE score	Average analytical GRE score	Average MAT score
University of Massachusetts–Dartmouth	88%	N/A	N/A	GRE or MAT	N/A	N/A	N/A	N/A
Lesley University	95%	100%	39%	GRE or MAT	N/A	N/A	N/A	47
Assumption College	96%	N/A	N/A	N/A	N/A	N/A	N/A	N/A
MICHIGAN								
Michigan State University	55%	38%	46%	GRE	547	624	630	N/A
Wayne State University	68%	70%	28%	GRE or MAT	409	434	316	N/A
Andrews University	70%	80%	72%	GRE	424	443	491	N/A
Ferris State University	71%	N/A	N/A	N/A	N/A	N/A	N/A	N/A
Western Michigan University	72%	N/A	59%	N/A	427	517	509	N/A
University of Michigan–Ann Arbor	73%	N/A	39%	GRE	543	621	642	N/A
Oakland University	85%	100%	59%	GRE or MAT	N/A	N/A	N/A	N/A
Grand Valley State University	94%	N/A	N/A	GRE	506	664	717	N/A
MINNESOTA								
University of Minnesota–Twin Cities	71%	45%	48%	GRE	500	588	585	N/A
Bethel College	79%	N/A	N/A	N/A	N/A	N/A	N/A	N/A
College of St. Catherine	84%	N/A	N/A	N/A	N/A	N/A	N/A	N/A
Hamline University	86%	N/A	83%	N/A	N/A	N/A	N/A	N/A
Winona State University	89%	100%	N/A	N/A	N/A	N/A	N/A	N/A
University of Minnesota–Duluth	90%	N/A	N/A	N/A	N/A	N/A	N/A	N/A
Augsburg College	98%	N/A	N/A	N/A	N/A	N/A	N/A	N/A
Southwest Minnesota State University	100%	N/A	N/A	N/A	N/A	N/A	N/A	N/A
University of St. Thomas	100%	100%	N/A	GRE or MAT	550	554	590	46
MISSOURI								
University of Missouri–Columbia	63%	81%	51%	GRE or MAT	493	555	566	80
Columbia College	64%	N/A	N/A	None	N/A	N/A	N/A	N/A
Northwest Missouri State University	71%	100%	N/A	GRE	370	320	420	N/A
University of Missouri–Kansas City	71%	63%	9%	GRE	462	546	592	36
Central Missouri State University	73%	86%	N/A	GRE or MAT	426	490	535	N/A
University of Missouri–St. Louis	76%	N/A	60%	GRE	467	492	479	N/A
Washington University in St. Louis	77%	N/A	41%	GRE or MAT	568	649	638	34
St. Louis University	79%	100%	80%	GRE or MAT	N/A	N/A	N/A	N/A
Rockhurst University	88%	N/A	N/A	N/A	N/A	N/A	N/A	N/A
Truman State University	88%	N/A	N/A	GRE	497	584	N/A	N/A
Southeast Missouri State University	90%	100%	N/A	GRE	422	468	505	N/A
Webster University	97%	100%	N/A	N/A	N/A	N/A	N/A	N/A
Lindenwood University	100%	100%	N/A	N/A	N/A	N/A	N/A	N/A
MONTANA								
Montana State University–Billings	100%	100%	N/A	GRE	380	420	N/A	N/A
NEBRASKA								
Chadron State College	51%	N/A	N/A	GRE or MAT	N/A	N/A	N/A	N/A
University of Nebraska–Omaha	78%	100%	20%	GRE or MAT	446	549	584	48
NEVADA								
University of Nevada–Las Vegas	93%	N/A	67%	GRE or MAT	N/A	N/A	N/A	N/A

	Master's acceptance rate	Educational specialist acceptance rate	Doctoral acceptance rate	Required tests	Average verbal GRE score	Average quantitative GRE score	Average analytical GRE score	Average MAT score
NEW HAMPSHIRE								
Plymouth State University	86%	N/A	N/A	GRE or MAT	N/A	N/A	N/A	N/A
NEW JERSEY								
Caldwell College	53%	N/A	N/A	GRE or MAT	N/A	N/A	N/A	41
Kean University	53%	N/A	N/A	GRE or MAT	427	501	519	39
William Paterson University	55%	N/A	N/A	N/A	443	518	N/A	41
Rutgers State University–New Brunswick	60%	N/A	29%	GRE	488	576	579	N/A
College of St. Elizabeth	70%	N/A	N/A	N/A	N/A	N/A	N/A	N/A
Montclair State University	75%	N/A	64%	GRE or MAT	437	497	501	42
Georgian Court College	85%	86%	N/A	GRE or MAT	N/A	N/A	N/A	N/A
St. Peter's College	91%	N/A	N/A	GRE or MAT	N/A	N/A	N/A	N/A
Seton Hall University	94%	93%	47%	GRE or MAT	451	489	603	41
NEW MEXICO								
New Mexico State University	50%	50%	50%	GRE or MAT	495	480	465	N/A
Eastern New Mexico University	51%	N/A	N/A	N/A	N/A	N/A	N/A	N/A
University of New Mexico	67%	94%	39%	GRE or MAT	525	517	N/A	48
NEW YORK								
CUNY–Hunter College	44%	N/A	N/A	N/A	N/A	N/A	N/A	N/A
Cornell University	46%	N/A	24%	GRE	541	640	648	N/A
Binghamton University	48%	N/A	39%	GRE	492	543	565	N/A
Graduate College of Union University	50%	N/A	N/A	N/A	N/A	N/A	N/A	N/A
New York University	50%	N/A	17%	GRE	563	609	N/A	N/A
D'Youville College	52%	N/A	N/A	N/A	N/A	N/A	N/A	N/A
Pratt Institute	56%	N/A	N/A	N/A	N/A	N/A	N/A	N/A
SUNY–Albany	57%	53%	24%	GRE	520	586	587	N/A
Teachers College, Columbia University	57%	N/A	27%	GRE or MAT	541	619	634	N/A
Hofstra University	58%	N/A	39%	GRE or MAT	N/A	N/A	N/A	N/A
Alfred University	66%	N/A	N/A	N/A	N/A	N/A	N/A	N/A
Utica College of Syracuse University	67%	N/A	N/A	N/A	450	450	450	N/A
SUNY–New Paltz	68%	N/A	N/A	GRE or MAT	457	530	525	N/A
Syracuse University	68%	N/A	34%	GRE	499	584	578	N/A
University at Buffalo–SUNY	68%	N/A	47%	GRE or MAT	514	597	598	53
Long Island Univeristy–C.W. Post Campus	73%	68%	N/A	GRE or MAT	N/A	N/A	N/A	N/A
Wagner College	74%	N/A	N/A	N/A	N/A	N/A	N/A	N/A
Collge of St. Rose	75%	N/A	N/A	N/A	N/A	N/A	N/A	N/A
Iona College	76%	N/A	N/A	N/A	N/A	N/A	N/A	N/A
Bank Street College of Education	78%	N/A	N/A	None	N/A	N/A	N/A	N/A
Molloy College	79%	N/A	N/A	N/A	N/A	N/A	N/A	N/A
SUNY College–Geneseo	79%	N/A	N/A	GRE	454	544	N/A	N/A
Mount St. Mary College	80%	N/A	N/A	N/A	N/A	N/A	N/A	N/A
Pace University	81%	N/A	N/A	N/A	N/A	N/A	N/A	N/A
SUNY College–Oswego	82%	N/A	N/A	GRE	N/A	N/A	N/A	N/A
CUNY–City College	84%	N/A	N/A	N/A	N/A	N/A	N/A	N/A
St. John's University	84%	93%	60%	GRE	524	564	N/A	N/A
CUNY–College of Staten Island	85%	N/A	N/A	N/A	N/A	N/A	N/A	N/A
SUNY–Potsdam	86%	N/A	N/A	N/A	N/A	N/A	N/A	N/A
Fordham University	87%	60%	32%	GRE or MAT	532	594	593	46
Sarah Lawrence College	88%	N/A	N/A	N/A	N/A	N/A	N/A	N/A
Dominican College of Blauvelt	89%	N/A	N/A	N/A	N/A	N/A	N/A	N/A
SUNY College–Fredonia	89%	23%	N/A	GRE or MAT	N/A	N/A	N/A	N/A
Daemen College	90%	N/A	N/A	GRE	N/A	N/A	N/A	N/A
Nazareth College of Rochester	94%	N/A	N/A	N/A	N/A	N/A	N/A	N/A

Which are the hardest and easiest education schools to get into?

	Master's acceptance rate	Educational specialist acceptance rate	Doctoral acceptance rate	Required tests	Average verbal GRE score	Average quantitative GRE score	Average analytical GRE score	Average MAT score
Nyack College	100%	N/A	N/A	GRE	N/A	N/A	N/A	N/A
Touro College	100%	N/A	N/A	None	N/A	N/A	N/A	N/A
NORTH CAROLINA								
Wake Forest University	41%	N/A	N/A	GRE	581	662	642	N/A
Duke University	52%	N/A	N/A	GRE	612	671	N/A	N/A
Winston-Salem State University	52%	N/A	N/A	GRE or MAT	N/A	N/A	N/A	N/A
Queens University of Charlotte	54%	N/A	N/A	GRE	N/A	N/A	N/A	N/A
North Carolina State University–Raleigh	55%	N/A	42%	GRE or MAT	484	559	600	N/A
University of North Carolina–Chapel Hill	56%	N/A	46%	GRE or MAT	524	608	N/A	40
University of North Carolina–Greensboro	67%	100%	40%	GRE	495	558	531	N/A
Appalachian State University	71%	93%	71%	GRE or MAT	N/A	N/A	N/A	N/A
Meredith College	71%	N/A	N/A	GRE or MAT	555	510	N/A	55
NORTH DAKOTA								
North Dakota State University	87%	100%	82%	N/A	N/A	N/A	N/A	N/A
University of North Dakota	93%	100%	56%	GRE or MAT	437	528	608	N/A
OHIO								
John Carroll University	50%	N/A	N/A	GRE or MAT	N/A	N/A	N/A	N/A
University of Cincinnati	51%	N/A	25%	GRE	461	521	557	N/A
Ohio State University–Columbus	54%	N/A	37%	GRE	468	576	574	N/A
Xavier University	56%	N/A	N/A	GRE or MAT	N/A	N/A	N/A	N/A
University of Dayton	65%	83%	36%	GRE or MAT	364	N/A	456	45
University of Toledo	67%	80%	46%	GRE	461	570	467	N/A
Kent State University	75%	57%	49%	GRE	488	524	568	N/A
Mount Vernon Nazarene University	85%	N/A	N/A	N/A	N/A	N/A	N/A	N/A
Baldwin-Wallace College	89%	N/A	N/A	MAT	N/A	N/A	N/A	44
Ohio University	91%	N/A	83%	GRE or MAT	496	571	N/A	47
University of Akron	92%	N/A	59%	GRE or MAT	487	528	462	59
Franciscan University of Steubenville	95%	N/A	N/A	N/A	N/A	N/A	N/A	N/A
Malone College	100%	N/A	N/A	N/A	N/A	N/A	N/A	N/A
Ohio Northern University	100%	N/A	N/A	N/A	N/A	N/A	N/A	N/A
University of Findlay	100%	N/A	N/A	N/A	N/A	N/A	N/A	N/A
Ursuline College	100%	N/A	N/A	N/A	N/A	N/A	N/A	N/A
OKLAHOMA								
University of Oklahoma	23%	N/A	13%	GRE or MAT	500	550	570	N/A
University of Tulsa	52%	N/A	N/A	GRE	410	460	570	N/A
Oklahoma State University	58%	44%	49%	GRE or MAT	446	511	543	52
University of Central Oklahoma	71%	N/A	N/A	GRE	N/A	N/A	N/A	N/A
Southeastern Oklahoma State University	98%	N/A	N/A	None	N/A	N/A	N/A	N/A
OREGON								
University of Oregon	60%	N/A	21%	GRE or MAT	547	594	578	N/A
Western Oregon University	75%	N/A	N/A	N/A	N/A	N/A	N/A	N/A
Willamette University	77%	N/A	N/A	N/A	N/A	N/A	N/A	N/A
Southern Oregon University	87%	N/A	N/A	N/A	N/A	N/A	N/A	N/A
Lewis and Clark College	92%	N/A	N/A	GRE or MAT	497	523	568	N/A
Portland State University	93%	N/A	54%	GRE or MAT	508	527	583	N/A

	Master's acceptance rate	Educational specialist acceptance rate	Doctoral acceptance rate	Required tests	Average verbal GRE score	Average quantitative GRE score	Average analytical GRE score	Average MAT score
PENNSYLVANIA								
Arcadia University	32%	N/A	N/A	GRE	N/A	N/A	N/A	N/A
Slippery Rock University of Pennsylvania	49%	82%	N/A	GRE or MAT	424	507	552	N/A
Shippensburg University of Pennsylvania	50%	N/A	N/A	GRE or MAT	436	537	603	N/A
Temple University	50%	N/A	36%	GRE or MAT	534	544	570	50
Edinboro University of Pennsylvania	57%	62%	N/A	GRE or MAT	444	491	537	N/A
Cheyney University of Pennsylvania	60%	N/A	N/A	N/A	N/A	N/A	N/A	N/A
Penn State University–University Park	60%	N/A	43%	GRE or MAT	488	575	563	53
Widener University	61%	N/A	73%	GRE or MAT	510	517	512	49
Cabrini College	64%	N/A	N/A	N/A	N/A	N/A	N/A	N/A
University of Pennsylvania	64%	N/A	17%	GRE	548	621	641	N/A
Kutztown University of Pennsylvania	67%	67%	N/A	GRE	442	493	544	N/A
Lehigh University	69%	22%	17%	GRE or MAT	543	632	647	N/A
University of Pittsburgh	73%	N/A	51%	GRE	500	539	587	N/A
Clarion University of Pennsylvania	76%	89%	N/A	GRE or MAT	N/A	N/A	N/A	N/A
Millersville University of Pennsylvania	79%	N/A	N/A	N/A	N/A	N/A	N/A	N/A
Pennsylvania State University–Harrisburg	87%	N/A	50%	N/A	535	532	N/A	N/A
La Salle University	90%	N/A	N/A	GRE or MAT	N/A	N/A	N/A	47
University of Scranton	90%	N/A	N/A	N/A	N/A	N/A	N/A	N/A
Seton Hill College	92%	N/A	N/A	N/A	N/A	N/A	N/A	N/A
Neumann College	96%	N/A	N/A	N/A	N/A	N/A	N/A	N/A
Drexel University	97%	86%	44%	GRE	N/A	N/A	N/A	N/A
Lock Haven University of Pennsylvania	97%	N/A	N/A	N/A	N/A	N/A	N/A	N/A
Mercyhurst College	97%	N/A	N/A	N/A	N/A	N/A	N/A	N/A
Robert Morris University	98%	N/A	N/A	N/A	N/A	N/A	N/A	N/A
Delaware Valley College	100%	N/A	N/A	GRE or MAT	320	690	N/A	N/A
Lebanon Valley College	100%	N/A	N/A	N/A	N/A	N/A	N/A	N/A
St. Francis University	100%	N/A	N/A	GRE or MAT	N/A	N/A	N/A	N/A
RHODE ISLAND								
Roger Williams University	100%	100%	N/A	GRE or MAT	446	486	N/A	40
SOUTH CAROLINA								
University of South Carolina–Columbia	56%	35%	49%	GRE or MAT	463	540	508	47
University of South Carolina–Aiken	69%	N/A	N/A	GRE or MAT	N/A	N/A	N/A	N/A
College of Charleston	70%	N/A	N/A	GRE	504	538	601	43
Francis Marion University	83%	N/A	N/A	N/A	N/A	N/A	N/A	N/A
Clemson University	95%	100%	81%	GRE or MAT	446	512	483	N/A
SOUTH DAKOTA								
Northern State University	66%	N/A	N/A	GRE or MAT	N/A	N/A	N/A	N/A
Black Hills State University	80%	N/A	N/A	N/A	N/A	N/A	N/A	N/A
South Dakota State University	92%	N/A	N/A	N/A	N/A	N/A	N/A	N/A
University of South Dakota	96%	90%	96%	GRE or MAT	451	525	546	49
TENNESSEE								
Vanderbilt University (Peabody)	68%	N/A	15%	GRE or MAT	561	645	668	57
East Tennessee State University	69%	N/A	31%	GRE	424	479	570	N/A
Southern Adventist University	69%	N/A	N/A	GRE	450	470	500	N/A
Trevecca Nazarene University	83%	N/A	25%	GRE or MAT	430	468	437	38
University of Tennessee–Knoxville	86%	90%	68%	GRE	518	578	570	N/A
Milligan College	89%	N/A	N/A	GRE or MAT	N/A	N/A	N/A	N/A
Lee University	91%	N/A	N/A	GRE or MAT	419	575	519	40
Carson-Newman College	92%	N/A	N/A	N/A	N/A	N/A	N/A	N/A

Which are the hardest and easiest education schools to get into?

	Master's acceptance rate	Educational specialist acceptance rate	Doctoral acceptance rate	Required tests	Average verbal GRE score	Average quantitative GRE score	Average analytical GRE score	Average MAT score
University of Tennessee–Chattanooga	97%	100%	N/A	MAT	N/A	N/A	N/A	38
Tennessee State University	100%	100%	100%	GRE or MAT	400	433	N/A	36
TEXAS								
Texas Tech University	49%	N/A	63%	GRE	467	481	482	N/A
Texas A&M University–College Station	59%	N/A	54%	GRE	465	567	550	N/A
University of Houston–Main Campus	61%	N/A	42%	GRE or MAT	487	583	593	47
University of Texas–Austin	61%	N/A	44%	GRE	535	601	561	N/A
Lamar University	70%	N/A	N/A	GRE	469	512	500	N/A
Texas A&M University–Kingsville	74%	N/A	78%	N/A	N/A	N/A	N/A	N/A
Texas Woman's University	74%	N/A	67%	GRE	417	476	468	N/A
Baylor University	76%	100%	36%	GRE or MAT	474	582	457	N/A
West Texas A&M University	76%	N/A	N/A	GRE	N/A	N/A	N/A	N/A
Our Lady of the Lake University	80%	N/A	50%	N/A	N/A	N/A	N/A	N/A
Texas State University–San Marcos	84%	N/A	56%	GRE	463	516	528	N/A
Hardin-Simmons University	86%	N/A	N/A	GRE	463	513	N/A	N/A
Sam Houston State University	88%	97%	33%	GRE or MAT	N/A	N/A	N/A	N/A
Southern Methodist University	89%	N/A	N/A	GRE	460	760	670	N/A
Tarleton State University	89%	N/A	65%	N/A	N/A	N/A	N/A	N/A
University of North Texas	97%	N/A	96%	GRE or MAT	N/A	N/A	N/A	N/A
Angelo State University	100%	N/A	N/A	N/A	N/A	N/A	N/A	N/A
Dallas Baptist University	100%	N/A	N/A	N/A	N/A	N/A	N/A	N/A
Texas Wesleyan University	100%	N/A	N/A	N/A	N/A	N/A	N/A	N/A
University of Houston–Victoria	100%	N/A	N/A	GRE or MAT	428	473	441	39
University of St. Thomas	100%	N/A	N/A	GRE	N/A	N/A	N/A	N/A
UTAH								
University of Utah	53%	N/A	43%	GRE	485	539	570	45
Utah State University	65%	N/A	35%	GRE or MAT	519	620	N/A	52
Weber State University	96%	N/A	N/A	GRE or MAT	N/A	N/A	N/A	53
VERMONT								
University of Vermont	61%	N/A	51%	GRE	526	493	587	N/A
School for International Training	73%	N/A	N/A	N/A	N/A	N/A	N/A	N/A
VIRGINIA								
Liberty University	37%	47%	33%	GRE	538	492	533	N/A
College of William and Mary	49%	83%	52%	GRE or MAT	538	586	634	53
Old Dominion University	49%	58%	38%	GRE or MAT	460	500	N/A	46
University of Virginia (Curry)	61%	91%	60%	GRE	528	583	588	N/A
Virginia Tech	68%	100%	62%	GRE	N/A	N/A	N/A	N/A
George Mason University	69%	N/A	51%	GRE	515	538	N/A	N/A
Virginia Commonwealth University	78%	N/A	56%	GRE or MAT	453	511	N/A	38
Regent University	86%	N/A	32%	GRE or MAT	477	476	N/A	N/A
Shenandoah University	91%	N/A	100%	N/A	N/A	N/A	N/A	N/A
Averett University	93%	N/A	N/A	GRE or MAT	N/A	N/A	N/A	N/A
Hampton University	93%	N/A	N/A	GRE	374	401	407	N/A
Mary Baldwin College	93%	N/A	N/A	N/A	N/A	N/A	N/A	N/A

	Master's acceptance rate	Educational specialist acceptance rate	Doctoral acceptance rate	Required tests	Average verbal GRE score	Average quantitative GRE score	Average analytical GRE score	Average MAT score
WASHINGTON								
University of Washington	43%	N/A	37%	GRE	530	580	615	N/A
Evergreen State College	51%	N/A	N/A	N/A	N/A	N/A	N/A	N/A
Western Washington University	64%	N/A	N/A	GRE or MAT	N/A	N/A	N/A	N/A
Central Washington University	80%	N/A	N/A	GRE	497	555	576	N/A
Heritage College	92%	N/A	N/A	N/A	N/A	N/A	N/A	N/A
St. Martin's College	100%	N/A	N/A	GRE or MAT	506	536	480	54
WEST VIRGINIA								
Marshall University	94%	86%	53%	GRE or MAT	401	457	421	41
West Virginia University	82%	N/A	52%	GRE or MAT	512	556	558	54
WISCONSIN								
University of Wisconsin–Madison	42%	N/A	34%	GRE	542	651	588	N/A
University of Wisconsin–Stout	56%	50%	N/A	None	N/A	N/A	N/A	N/A
University of Wisconsin–Milwaukee	66%	N/A	59%	GRE	458	506	556	N/A
University of Wisconsin–Stevens Point	67%	N/A	N/A	N/A	N/A	N/A	N/A	N/A
Marquette University	75%	N/A	34%	GRE or MAT	500	550	590	N/A
University of Wisconsin–La Crosse	80%	32%	N/A	GRE	N/A	N/A	N/A	N/A
University of Wisconsin–Superior	81%	64%	N/A	N/A	400	552	306	38
University of Wisconsin–Whitewater	85%	100%	N/A	None	N/A	N/A	N/A	N/A
University of Wisconsin–Eau Claire	86%	65%	N/A	N/A	N/A	N/A	N/A	N/A
Alverno College	100%	N/A	N/A	N/A	N/A	N/A	N/A	N/A
Carthage College	100%	N/A	N/A	MAT	N/A	N/A	N/A	N/A
WYOMING								
University of Wyoming	92%	N/A	90%	GRE	486	562	577	N/A

Which are the largest and smallest education schools?

As you compare schools, you'll want to pay attention to each one's personality, which may be greatly influenced by its size: Smaller schools typically feel more intimate and allow for more faculty contact, while large schools may offer considerably more extracurricular excitement and a broader curriculum, for example. Universities that offer a doctoral program in education, as well as teaching credentials, tend to be more research-focused. Here, education schools are organized by total enrollment within each state.

	Total graduate enrollment	Master's enrollment	Master's enrollment in teacher education programs	Education specialist enrollment	Doctoral enrollment
ALABAMA					
Jacksonville State University	1,050	793	474	257	0
Alabama State University	966	899	518	37	30
University of Alabama–Birmingham	948	755	575	125	68
Troy State University–Main Campus	928	684	319	244	N/A
University of Alabama–Tuscaloosa	897	407	261	164	326
Auburn University–Main Campus	696	394	196	27	275
University of West Alabama	680	680	310	N/A	N/A
University of Montevallo	401	N/A	N/A	N/A	N/A
Auburn University–Montgomery	338	N/A	N/A	N/A	N/A
University of North Alabama	325	295	231	30	N/A
Troy State University–Montgomery	218	209	50	9	N/A
Troy State University–Dothan	202	178	87	24	N/A
Samford University	164	48	39	42	74
Spring Hill College	61	61	61	N/A	N/A
University of Mobile	59	59	59	N/A	N/A
ALASKA					
University of Alaska–Fairbanks	126	126	98	N/A	N/A
University of Alaska–Southeast	99	99	99	N/A	N/A
Alaska Pacific University	18	18	18	N/A	N/A
ARIZONA					
Northern Arizona University	3,188	2,995	1,388	N/A	193
Arizona State University–Main Campus	1,259	697	430	N/A	562
University of Arizona	933	484	297	32	417
Arizona State University–West	207	207	107	N/A	N/A
ARKANSAS					
University of Arkansas–Fayetteville	659	456	378	7	196
Arkansas Tech University	223	223	135	0	N/A
Southern Arkansas University	194	194	29	0	0
CALIFORNIA					
California State University–Dominguez Hills	2,129	2,129	1,071	N/A	N/A
University of La Verne	1,112	781	295	N/A	331
California State University–San Bernardino	1,072	1,072	592	N/A	N/A
University of Southern California (Rossier)	1,045	359	162	N/A	686

	Total graduate enrollment	Total master's enrollment	Master's enrollment in teacher education programs	Education specialist enrollment	Doctoral enrollment
University of San Francisco	998	739	433	N/A	259
Fresno Pacific University	902	902	522	N/A	N/A
University of California–Los Angeles	830	452	358	0	378
San Diego State University	809	706	290	0	103
Loyola Marymount University	702	623	435	79	0
California State University–Fullerton	628	624	390	N/A	4
California State University–Long Beach	601	601	256	N/A	N/A
University of California–Berkeley	475	202	111	0	273
University of San Diego	419	291	126	N/A	128
University of California–Santa Barbara (Gevirtz)	413	153	118	16	244
Chapman University	408	354	296	54	0
Santa Clara University	403	403	252	N/A	N/A
Stanford University	358	158	71	N/A	200
Alliant International University–San Diego	349	210	68	0	139
Fielding Graduate Institute	317	39	N/A	N/A	278
California State University–Stanislaus	273	273	N/A	N/A	N/A
Claremont Graduate University	261	141	131	N/A	120
Biola University	237	237	237	N/A	N/A
Hope International University	233	233	68	0	0
Concordia University	226	226	217	0	0
Mount St. Mary's College	220	220	200	N/A	N/A
Simpson College	204	67	66	137	N/A
Mills College	190	146	128	N/A	44
University of California–Riverside	158	33	N/A	N/A	125
University of California–Irvine	144	66	66	N/A	78
University of the Pacific	143	55	35	11	77
University of California–Davis	140	75	66	N/A	65
Cal Poly–San Luis Obispo	137	130	79	0	7
University of California–Santa Cruz	137	128	128	0	9
California State University–Chico	119	119	63	N/A	N/A
Bethany College of the Assemblies of God	63	63	63	N/A	N/A
Holy Names College	51	51	33	0	0
University of Judaism	38	38	N/A	N/A	N/A
Humboldt State University	28	28	28	N/A	N/A
COLORADO					
University of Colorado–Denver	1,310	1,112	803	103	95
University of Northern Colorado	756	566	414	29	161
Colorado State University	496	267	59	N/A	229
University of Colorado–Boulder	466	387	369	N/A	79
University of Denver	422	223	76	29	170
Colorado Christian College	85	85	85	N/A	N/A
Colorado College	26	26	26	N/A	N/A
CONNECTICUT					
Sacred Heart University	973	973	N/A	N/A	N/A
St. Joseph College	910	641	355	269	N/A
Central Connecticut State University	899	856	565	N/A	43
University of Bridgeport	744	673	592	36	35
University of Connecticut (Neag)	657	411	286	N/A	246
Fairfield University	476	476	129	N/A	N/A
Western Connecticut State University	390	364	311	0	26
Eastern Connecticut State University	254	254	223	N/A	N/A

Which are the largest and smallest education schools?

	Total graduate enrollment	Total master's enrollment	Master's enrollment in teacher education programs	Education specialist enrollment	Doctoral enrollment
University of New Haven	248	248	248	N/A	N/A
Quinnipiac University	137	137	137	N/A	N/A
DELAWARE					
Wilmington College	1,732	1,513	947	0	219
University of Delaware	526	321	216	0	205
Wesley College	57	57	57	N/A	N/A
DISTRICT OF COLUMBIA					
George Washington University	1,675	990	405	75	610
Trinity College	405	405	188	N/A	N/A
University of the District of Columbia	235	235	15	0	0
Howard University	221	123	25	N/A	98
Gallaudet University	159	99	61	26	34
Catholic University of America	62	32	25	N/A	30
FLORIDA					
Nova Southeastern University	8,600	4,254	3,536	594	3,752
University of South Florida	1,786	1,292	693	60	434
University of Central Florida	1,343	979	571	65	299
Florida State University	1,053	601	248	26	426
University of Florida	914	407	283	154	353
Florida Atlantic University	905	696	438	40	169
Florida International University	870	558	508	62	250
University of West Florida	625	339	N/A	60	226
University of North Florida	615	523	217	N/A	92
University of Miami	559	465	184	18	76
Stetson University	173	154	26	19	N/A
Jacksonville University	126	126	122	0	0
Lynn University	119	62	53	N/A	57
St. Leo University	107	107	22	N/A	N/A
Rollins College	88	88	70	N/A	N/A
Palm Beach Atlantic College	78	78	32	N/A	N/A
Florida Institute of Technology–Melbourne	37	21	8	N/A	16
Trinity Baptist College	14	14	14	0	0
GEORGIA					
University of Georgia	2,234	1,155	685	229	850
State University of West Georgia	1,835	1,540	409	247	48
Georgia State University	1,618	1,147	472	127	344
Piedmont College	1,137	940	940	197	N/A
Georgia College and State University	443	360	282	83	N/A
Kennesaw State University	422	422	257	N/A	N/A
Armstrong Atlantic State University	421	421	421	N/A	N/A
Augusta State University	236	177	N/A	59	N/A
Georgia Southwestern State University	211	N/A	N/A	N/A	N/A
Brenau University	197	171	171	26	N/A
LaGrange College	48	48	37	0	0
Oglethorpe University	40	40	40	N/A	N/A
Wesleyan College	32	32	32	N/A	N/A
Agnes Scott College	21	21	21	N/A	N/A

	Total graduate enrollment	Total master's enrollment	Master's enrollment in teacher education programs	Education specialist enrollment	Doctoral enrollment
HAWAII					
University of Hawaii–Manoa	856	700	245	0	156
IDAHO					
Idaho State University	425	325	298	28	72
Northwest Nazarene University	141	141	106	N/A	N/A
ILLINOIS					
National-Louis University	3,671	3,326	2,994	231	114
Northern Illinois University	2,130	1,547	479	36	547
DePaul University	1,770	1,700	1,403	N/A	70
Eastern Illinois University	1,464	1,329	149	135	N/A
Southern Illinois University–Carbondale	1,345	1,002	551	N/A	343
Aurora University	1,212	1,134	287	N/A	78
Loyola University Chicago	1,212	614	249	61	537
University of Illinois–Urbana-Champaign	1,000	469	54	N/A	531
Illinois State University	958	629	450	24	305
Western Illinois University	868	791	538	77	0
University of Illinois–Chicago	844	626	356	N/A	218
Chicago State University	753	753	386	N/A	N/A
Rockford College	685	685	685	0	0
University of St. Francis	566	566	198	N/A	N/A
University of Illinois–Springfield	302	302	N/A	N/A	N/A
Bradley University	226	226	25	0	0
Roosevelt University	191	N/A	N/A	N/A	N/A
Northwestern University	147	73	26	N/A	74
North Central College	111	111	59	N/A	N/A
INDIANA					
Indiana University–Bloomington	1,136	457	203	28	651
Indiana Wesleyan University	1,000	1,000	1,000	N/A	N/A
Indiana University–South Bend	924	924	863	N/A	N/A
Ball State University	671	463	244	29	179
Indiana University-Purdue University–Indianapolis	649	649	404	0	0
Indiana State University	605	380	138	44	181
Purdue University–West Lafayette	444	197	72	2	245
Indiana University–Southeast	429	429	372	N/A	N/A
Purdue University–Calumet	327	327	19	N/A	N/A
Butler University	157	157	35	N/A	N/A
University of Southern Indiana	91	91	91	0	0
Valparaiso University	56	38	37	18	N/A
Earlham College	16	16	16	N/A	N/A
Indiana University–Kokomo	14	14	14	N/A	N/A
IOWA					
University of Northern Iowa	2,969	2,798	2,327	0	171
University of Iowa	953	457	267	20	476
Drake University	592	500	191	60	32
Iowa State University	478	290	68	0	188
Morningside College	355	355	355	N/A	N/A
Buena Vista University	85	85	N/A	0	0
Dordt College	60	60	60	N/A	N/A
St. Ambrose University	39	39	12	N/A	N/A
Loras College	27	27	3	N/A	N/A

Which are the largest and smallest education schools?

	Total graduate enrollment	Total master's enrollment	Master's enrollment in teacher education programs	Education specialist enrollment	Doctoral enrollment
KANSAS					
University of Kansas	1,340	895	N/A	26	419
Newman University	60	60	29	N/A	N/A
Washburn University	60	60	49	N/A	N/A
Benedictine College	31	31	N/A	N/A	N/A
KENTUCKY					
University of Louisville	1,358	1,088	639	24	246
Western Kentucky University	1,162	1,118	515	44	N/A
University of Kentucky	912	576	259	3	333
Murray State University	683	635	323	48	N/A
Northern Kentucky University	417	417	252	N/A	N/A
Bellarmine University	228	228	N/A	0	0
Asbury College	66	66	61	N/A	N/A
Union College	43	43	43	N/A	N/A
Brescia University	12	12	12	N/A	N/A
LOUISIANA					
Louisiana Tech University	1,240	1,174	183	N/A	66
University of New Orleans	1,209	1,022	199	N/A	187
Southeastern Louisiana University	841	841	606	N/A	N/A
Northwestern State University of Louisiana	593	519	383	74	N/A
Louisiana State University–Baton Rouge	458	225	N/A	61	172
University of Louisiana–Monroe	353	278	155	26	49
Nicholls State University	300	282	66	18	0
University of Louisiana–Lafayette	216	216	93	0	0
Louisiana State University–Shreveport	215	194	129	21	N/A
Our Lady of Holy Cross College	127	127	19	N/A	N/A
MAINE					
University of Southern Maine	720	720	270	N/A	N/A
University of Maine–Orono	636	485	183	90	61
St. Joseph's College	255	255	29	N/A	N/A
MARYLAND					
University of Maryland–College Park	1,110	510	N/A	2	598
Loyola College in Maryland	706	706	164	N/A	N/A
Morgan State University	634	N/A	N/A	N/A	N/A
Salisbury University	617	617	118	N/A	N/A
College of Notre Dame of Maryland	603	603	179	0	0
University of Maryland–Baltimore County	438	438	16	N/A	N/A
Frostburg State University	415	415	199	N/A	N/A
Goucher College	270	270	100	N/A	N/A
MASSACHUSETTS					
Lesley University	4,433	4,387	4,306	4	42
Harvard University	1,077	659	109	N/A	418
Boston College (Lynch)	1,059	764	388	19	276
University of Massachusetts–Amherst	866	501	346	N/A	365
Fitchburg State College	789	789	N/A	N/A	N/A
Boston University	510	377	187	6	127

	Total graduate enrollment	Total master's enrollment	Master's enrollment in teacher education programs	Education specialist enrollment	Doctoral enrollment
University of Massachusetts–Lowell	452	252	190	0	200
Wheelock College	355	355	229	0	0
College of Our Lady of the Elms	125	106	106	19	N/A
Eastern Nazarene College	99	99	41	N/A	N/A
Northeastern University	92	92	80	N/A	N/A
Gordon College	60	60	60	N/A	N/A
University of Massachusetts–Dartmouth	38	38	38	N/A	N/A
Assumption College	29	29	29	N/A	N/A
MICHIGAN					
Marygrove College	4,590	4,590	4,582	N/A	N/A
Wayne State University	2,876	2,465	1,633	148	263
Western Michigan University	1,791	1,525	544	4	262
Oakland University	1,683	1,465	824	105	113
Michigan State University	1,376	881	487	23	472
Grand Valley State University	1,278	1,278	1,024	N/A	N/A
Eastern Michigan University	1,054	937	591	36	81
University of Michigan–Dearborn	777	777	355	0	0
University of Michigan–Flint	568	284	284	284	N/A
University of Michigan–Ann Arbor	507	201	103	N/A	306
Aquinas College	407	407	407	N/A	N/A
Andrews University	380	145	44	23	212
Ferris State University	211	211	N/A	N/A	N/A
Cornerstone University	15	15	N/A	N/A	N/A
MINNESOTA					
University of Minnesota–Twin Cities	2,240	1,321	960	19	900
University of St. Thomas	1,458	1,243	565	89	126
Hamline University	808	759	759	N/A	49
Southwest Minnesota State University	358	358	358	N/A	N/A
Winona State University	302	272	141	30	0
College of St. Catherine	260	260	260	N/A	N/A
Bethel College	196	196	196	N/A	N/A
University of Minnesota–Duluth	75	75	N/A	N/A	N/A
Augsburg College	65	65	65	N/A	N/A
MISSISSIPPI					
Mississippi State University	754	374	227	50	330
Delta State University	336	251	144	36	49
MISSOURI					
Lindenwood University	2,211	2,100	500	111	0
University of Missouri–Columbia	1,991	1,288	N/A	95	608
William Woods University	1,169	1,097	313	72	N/A
Webster University	1,156	1,120	1,120	36	N/A
University of Missouri–St. Louis	976	805	478	N/A	171
Central Missouri State University	908	787	352	105	16
University of Missouri–Kansas City	837	668	406	116	53
Missouri Baptist College	709	N/A	N/A	N/A	N/A
St. Louis University	428	117	1	6	305
Southeast Missouri State University	327	259	2	68	N/A
Northwest Missouri State University	301	272	161	29	N/A
Truman State University	142	142	102	N/A	N/A

Which are the largest and smallest education schools?

	Total graduate enrollment	Total master's enrollment	Master's enrollment in teacher education programs	Education specialist enrollment	Doctoral enrollment
Rockhurst University	139	139	139	N/A	N/A
Park University	80	80	80	N/A	N/A
Columbia College	60	60	60	0	0
Washington University in St. Louis	49	37	37	N/A	12
Evangel University	41	41	38	N/A	N/A
MONTANA					
Montana State University	295	170	59	5	120
Montana State University–Billings	266	266	176	N/A	N/A
NEBRASKA					
University of Nebraska–Lincoln	995	452	262	14	529
University of Nebraska–Omaha	725	646	334	34	45
Wayne State College	373	354	213	19	N/A
Concordia University	216	216	55	N/A	N/A
Chadron State College	96	73	29	23	N/A
Creighton University	58	58	21	N/A	N/A
NEVADA					
University of Nevada–Las Vegas	1,240	1,011	715	43	186
University of Nevada–Reno	652	516	339	17	119
NEW HAMPHIRE					
Rivier College	304	304	166	N/A	N/A
Plymouth State University	252	252	180	0	0
NEW JERSEY					
Kean University	1,138	1,138	676	N/A	N/A
Montclair State University	1,093	1,061	500	N/A	32
Seton Hall University	987	619	144	93	275
Rutgers State University–New Brunswick	827	575	401	N/A	252
College of New Jersey	726	608	344	118	N/A
Fairleigh Dickinson University	670	670	490	N/A	N/A
William Paterson University	484	484	372	N/A	N/A
Georgian Court College	457	430	187	27	N/A
Rider University	425	383	87	42	0
Centenary College	416	416	N/A	N/A	N/A
St. Peter's College	322	322	60	N/A	N/A
College of St. Elizabeth	178	178	61	N/A	N/A
Caldwell College	109	109	60	N/A	N/A
NEW MEXICO					
University of New Mexico	1,290	880	708	43	367
New Mexico State University	971	677	514	49	245
Eastern New Mexico University	402	402	131	N/A	N/A
New Mexico Highlands University	328	328	N/A	N/A	N/A
College of Santa Fe	285	285	N/A	N/A	N/A
College of the Southwest	198	198	46	N/A	N/A
NEW YORK					
Teachers College, Columbia University	4,676	2,932	1,488	0	1,744

	Total graduate enrollment	Total master's enrollment	Master's enrollment in teacher education programs	Education specialist enrollment	Doctoral enrollment
New York University	4,074	3,370	566	N/A	704
Touro College	3,044	3,044	2,401	N/A	N/A
Mercy College	2,162	2,162	1,934	N/A	N/A
Long Island Univeristy–C.W. Post Campus	2,086	2,009	N/A	77	N/A
CUNY–Hunter College	1,699	1,699	1,573	N/A	N/A
CUNY–City College	1,636	1,636	1,559	N/A	N/A
Fordham University	1,593	1,168	776	96	329
Hofstra University	1,559	1,466	1,202	N/A	93
SUNY–Cortland	1,534	1,534	1,160	N/A	N/A
St. John's University	1,382	1,102	893	129	151
Collge of St. Rose	1,362	1,362	770	N/A	N/A
SUNY–Albany	1,338	904	558	114	320
SUNY College–Oswego	1,284	1,284	618	N/A	N/A
University at Buffalo–SUNY	1,269	899	650	N/A	370
D'Youville College	1,093	1,093	1,093	N/A	N/A
Pace University	1,066	1,066	1,029	N/A	N/A
Bank Street College of Education	853	853	660	N/A	N/A
CUNY–Lehman College	848	848	809	N/A	N/A
SUNY–Potsdam	825	825	743	N/A	N/A
Nazareth College of Rochester	745	745	745	N/A	N/A
CUNY–College of Staten Island	740	673	673	67	N/A
Niagara University	715	715	538	N/A	N/A
Syracuse University	703	469	239	N/A	234
SUNY–New Paltz	688	688	681	N/A	N/A
Binghamton University	422	337	337	N/A	85
Molloy College	414	414	414	N/A	N/A
Mount St. Mary College	357	357	357	N/A	N/A
SUNY College–Fredonia	347	324	295	23	0
Utica College of Syracuse University	294	294	148	N/A	N/A
Roberts Wesleyan College	288	288	288	N/A	N/A
Iona College	235	235	128	N/A	N/A
SUNY–Stony Brook	198	198	198	N/A	N/A
SUNY College–Geneseo	161	161	161	N/A	N/A
Marist College	140	140	N/A	N/A	N/A
St. Lawrence University	129	N/A	N/A	N/A	N/A
CUNY–Graduate Center	99	N/A	N/A	N/A	99
Wagner College	99	99	54	N/A	N/A
Cornell University	80	45	36	N/A	35
Graduate College of Union University	71	71	71	N/A	N/A
Alfred University	70	70	30	N/A	N/A
Sunbridge College	65	65	49	0	0
Dominican College of Blauvelt	47	47	47	N/A	N/A
Daemen College	44	44	44	N/A	N/A
Pratt Institute	40	40	40	N/A	N/A
Sarah Lawrence College	22	22	22	N/A	N/A
Nyack College	8	8	8	N/A	N/A
NORTH CAROLINA					
Appalachian State University	980	898	185	28	54
North Carolina State University–Raleigh	932	556	310	0	376
University of North Carolina–Greensboro	907	682	N/A	2	223
University of North Carolina–Chapel Hill	566	345	197	0	221
Gardner-Webb University	481	466	84	N/A	15

Which are the largest and smallest education schools?

	Total graduate enrollment	Total master's enrollment	Master's enrollment in teacher education programs	Education specialist enrollment	Doctoral enrollment
University of North Carolina–Pembroke	367	367	140	N/A	N/A
Queens University of Charlotte	132	132	96	0	0
Pfeiffer University	110	110	110	0	0
Wake Forest University	52	52	52	0	0
Winston-Salem State University	39	39	39	N/A	N/A
Elon University	20	20	20	N/A	N/A
Duke University	16	16	16	N/A	N/A
Meredith College	15	15	15	N/A	N/A
NORTH DAKOTA					
University of North Dakota	461	263	N/A	10	188
North Dakota State University	323	235	41	50	38
Minot State University	55	40	40	15	N/A
OHIO					
Ashland University	3,838	3,780	N/A	N/A	58
Kent State University	1,339	922	449	71	346
Ohio State University–Columbus	1,231	849	384	N/A	382
University of Akron	1,130	935	573	0	195
University of Cincinnati	1,121	860	256	0	261
University of Dayton	1,060	1,004	298	20	36
Xavier University	924	924	487	N/A	N/A
Wright State University	858	858	N/A	N/A	N/A
University of Toledo	713	613	482	22	78
Ohio University	483	348	133	1	134
Miami University–Oxford	462	381	125	33	48
Baldwin-Wallace College	453	453	81	N/A	N/A
University of Findlay	272	272	230	N/A	N/A
University of Rio Grande	231	231	231	N/A	N/A
Heidelberg College	203	203	88	N/A	N/A
Franciscan University of Steubenville	173	173	123	N/A	N/A
John Carroll University	164	164	44	0	0
College of Mount St. Joseph	163	163	N/A	N/A	N/A
Mount Vernon Nazarene University	146	146	146	N/A	N/A
Ursuline College	123	123	71	N/A	N/A
Urbana University	110	110	110	N/A	N/A
Malone College	98	98	62	0	0
Otterbein College	88	88	88	N/A	N/A
Walsh University	56	56	N/A	N/A	N/A
Marietta College	54	54	54	N/A	N/A
Ohio Northern University	9	9	9	N/A	N/A
OKLAHOMA					
University of Central Oklahoma	3,154	3,154	1,571	N/A	N/A
Oklahoma State University	849	496	237	15	338
University of Oklahoma	660	372	174	N/A	288
Southeastern Oklahoma State University	180	180	87	N/A	N/A
University of Tulsa	46	46	N/A	N/A	N/A
OREGON					
Portland State University	899	807	529	N/A	92

	Total graduate enrollment	Total master's enrollment	Master's enrollment in teacher education programs	Education specialist enrollment	Doctoral enrollment
University of Oregon	713	507	126	0	206
Lewis and Clark College	561	561	148	N/A	N/A
Western Oregon University	400	400	400	N/A	N/A
University of Portland	309	309	N/A	N/A	N/A
Oregon State University	290	198	51	N/A	92
Southern Oregon University	169	169	169	N/A	N/A
Concordia University	100	100	90	0	0
Willamette University	70	70	70	N/A	N/A
Northwest Christian College	62	62	N/A	N/A	N/A
PENNSYLVANIA					
Temple University	1,497	931	664	0	566
West Chester University of Pennsylvania	1,458	1,458	268	N/A	N/A
University of Pittsburgh	1,066	692	520	0	374
Penn State University–University Park	897	293	154	0	604
University of Pennsylvania	787	428	219	N/A	359
Pennsylvania State University–Harrisburg	767	713	713	N/A	54
Kutztown University of Pennsylvania	740	673	405	67	N/A
Arcadia University	663	642	608	N/A	21
Edinboro University of Pennsylvania	649	482	283	167	N/A
Lehigh University	550	390	90	20	140
Widener University	528	259	146	0	269
Shippensburg University of Pennsylvania	467	467	202	0	0
Cabrini College	417	417	398	N/A	N/A
Slippery Rock University of Pennsylvania	414	381	217	33	N/A
Clarion University of Pennsylvania	391	391	73	N/A	N/A
Mansfield University of Pennsylvania	352	N/A	N/A	N/A	N/A
Bloomsburg University of Pennsylvania	328	328	283	N/A	N/A
Millersville University of Pennsylvania	325	325	236	0	0
Drexel University	310	222	214	45	43
Gwynedd-Mercy College	296	296	86	N/A	N/A
Cheyney University of Pennsylvania	285	285	164	N/A	N/A
La Salle University	208	208	208	N/A	N/A
Neumann College	199	199	199	N/A	N/A
DeSales University	156	156	156	N/A	N/A
St. Francis University	145	145	128	N/A	N/A
Lebanon Valley College	140	140	140	N/A	N/A
Robert Morris University	112	112	112	0	0
Seton Hill College	97	97	97	N/A	N/A
Lock Haven University of Pennsylvania	85	85	14	N/A	N/A
University of Scranton	85	75	66	10	0
Lincoln University	84	84	80	N/A	N/A
Mercyhurst College	83	83	83	N/A	N/A
Delaware Valley College	79	70	N/A	9	N/A
Waynesburg College	68	68	17	N/A	N/A
King's College	49	49	49	N/A	N/A
York College of Pennsylvania	26	19	9	7	N/A
RHODE ISLAND					
Roger Williams University	137	137	116	N/A	N/A
SOUTH CAROLINA					
Coastal Carolina University	1,170	1,170	89	N/A	N/A

Which are the largest and smallest education schools?

	Total graduate enrollment	Total master's enrollment	Master's enrollment in teacher education programs	Education specialist enrollment	Doctoral enrollment
University of South Carolina–Columbia	1,085	663	396	146	276
Clemson University	550	454	128	20	76
The Citadel	440	329	281	111	N/A
Francis Marion University	403	403	403	N/A	N/A
College of Charleston	263	263	263	N/A	N/A
Columbia College	263	263	N/A	N/A	N/A
Southern Wesleyan University	211	211	211	0	0
University of South Carolina–Spartanburg	54	54	54	N/A	N/A
University of South Carolina–Aiken	27	27	27	N/A	N/A
SOUTH DAKOTA					
University of South Dakota	515	248	151	75	192
South Dakota State University	371	371	73	N/A	N/A
Black Hills State University	98	98	98	N/A	N/A
Northern State University	93	93	46	N/A	N/A
TENNESSEE					
Tennessee State University	1,000	684	338	81	235
Tennessee Technological University	921	608	N/A	286	27
University of Tennessee–Knoxville	795	508	383	32	255
East Tennessee State University	623	469	341	13	141
Vanderbilt University (Peabody)	609	308	153	N/A	301
University of Tennessee–Chattanooga	412	378	311	34	0
Union University	404	274	274	69	61
Freed-Hardeman University	368	368	N/A	N/A	N/A
Cumberland University	365	365	365	N/A	N/A
Trevecca Nazarene University	250	179	24	N/A	71
University of Tennessee–Martin	229	229	153	N/A	N/A
Carson-Newman College	173	173	85	N/A	N/A
Tusculum College	161	161	161	N/A	N/A
Lee University	150	150	100	N/A	N/A
Milligan College	66	66	66	N/A	N/A
Southern Adventist University	30	30	N/A	0	0
TEXAS					
University of North Texas	1,709	1,258	189	N/A	451
Texas A&M University–Corpus Christi	1,590	1,500	750	N/A	90
University of Texas–Austin	1,351	484	139	0	867
Texas State University–San Marcos	1,179	1,125	653	N/A	54
Texas A&M University–College Station	1,110	435	83	N/A	675
University of Houston–Main Campus	1,040	678	352	0	362
University of Texas–Pan American	1,022	982	214	N/A	40
Tarleton State University	975	877	260	83	15
Texas Woman's University	924	876	75	N/A	48
St. Mary's University of San Antonio	807	741	38	0	66
Sam Houston State University	746	714	258	N/A	32
University of Houston–Victoria	605	605	89	N/A	N/A
Our Lady of the Lake University	587	476	258	N/A	111
Texas A&M University–Kingsville	580	452	60	N/A	128
Texas Tech University	558	331	142	0	227
Lamar University	347	347	89	N/A	N/A

	Total graduate enrollment	Total master's enrollment	Master's enrollment in teacher education programs	Education specialist enrollment	Doctoral enrollment
Baylor University	303	167	37	9	127
Texas Christian University	292	292	103	N/A	N/A
University of Texas–Tyler	286	N/A	N/A	N/A	N/A
Midwestern State University	284	284	81	0	0
University of the Incarnate Word	250	90	33	N/A	160
West Texas A&M University	248	248	N/A	N/A	N/A
Dallas Baptist University	217	184	N/A	33	N/A
University of Texas–Permian Basin	171	171	94	N/A	N/A
University of St. Thomas	166	166	101	N/A	N/A
Hardin-Simmons University	151	151	44	N/A	N/A
Southern Methodist University	144	144	30	0	0
Angelo State University	113	113	19	N/A	N/A
University of Mary Hardin-Baylor	76	76	26	N/A	N/A
Texas Wesleyan University	49	49	49	N/A	N/A
Schreiner College	48	48	38	N/A	N/A
Austin College	38	38	38	N/A	N/A
UTAH					
Utah State University	924	679	524	N/A	245
University of Utah	551	336	87	N/A	215
Weber State University	146	146	146	N/A	N/A
VERMONT					
University of Vermont	441	373	136	N/A	68
Johnson State College	212	212	183	N/A	N/A
School for International Training	126	126	126	N/A	N/A
Castleton State College	57	57	N/A	N/A	N/A
VIRGINIA					
George Mason University	2,211	2,045	1,593	N/A	166
Old Dominion University	1,364	1,246	1,028	55	63
Virginia Tech	1,115	639	469	48	428
University of Virginia (Curry)	899	456	368	12	431
Liberty University	784	591	488	16	177
Virginia Commonwealth University	747	658	487	N/A	89
Regent University	681	575	46	0	106
College of William and Mary	378	244	109	19	115
Radford University	375	350	N/A	25	N/A
Shenandoah University	279	244	46	N/A	35
James Madison University	250	207	135	43	N/A
Mary Baldwin College	125	125	125	N/A	N/A
Averett University	77	77	77	0	0
Eastern Mennonite University	75	75	N/A	N/A	N/A
Hampton University	73	73	39	0	0
WASHINGTON					
University of Washington	768	528	205	N/A	240
Heritage College	732	732	286	N/A	N/A
Antioch University–Seattle	400	400	N/A	0	0
Western Washington University	375	375	167	N/A	N/A
Whitworth College	169	169	52	N/A	N/A
Central Washington University	168	168	115	N/A	N/A
Evergreen State College	83	83	83	N/A	N/A

Which are the largest and smallest education schools?

	Total graduate enrollment	Total master's enrollment	Master's enrollment in teacher education programs	Education specialist enrollment	Doctoral enrollment
St. Martin's College	56	56	42	N/A	N/A
WEST VIRGINIA					
Marshall University	1,999	1,839	1,385	119	41
West Virginia University	1,486	1,194	733	N/A	292
WISCONSIN					
University of Wisconsin–Madison	1,024	492	N/A	N/A	532
University of Wisconsin–Milwaukee	725	557	214	N/A	168
University of Wisconsin–Whitewater	631	607	385	24	0
University of Wisconsin–Platteville	562	562	154	0	0
Concordia University Wisconsin	515	515	205	N/A	N/A
University of Wisconsin–River Falls	322	316	176	6	0
Marquette University	233	145	78	0	88
University of Wisconsin–Superior	223	195	73	28	0
Alverno College	209	209	N/A	N/A	N/A
University of Wisconsin–Stout	184	161	N/A	23	N/A
University of Wisconsin–La Crosse	174	150	150	24	N/A
Edgewood College	162	126	43	N/A	36
University of Wisconsin–Eau Claire	152	131	127	21	N/A
Carthage College	120	120	120	N/A	N/A
University of Wisconsin–Stevens Point	106	106	106	N/A	N/A
WYOMING					
University of Wyoming	375	239	145	N/A	136

In which states will first-year teachers make the most money? Where will they make the least?

You probably didn't go into teaching for the money, but where you end up can make a big difference in your take-home pay. Some states have fixed salary scales, while others let individual districts decide what starting teachers will earn. In some high-demand areas, school districts offer signing bonuses to get qualified instructors into the classroom. Here's what teachers were making in each state, from highest to lowest, in 2002, according to the latest survey by the American Federation of Teachers.

	Average first-year salary	Average salary	Average salary as a percentage of U.S. average teacher's salary	Total number of teachers
Alaska	$36,035	$49,028	110.5%	8,025
New Jersey	$35,311	$50,115 [a, d]	113.0%	105,750
New York	$34,577	$51,020 [d]	115.0%	215,500
Connecticut	$34,551	$52,376	118.1%	41,263
California	$34,180	$54,348	122.5%	304,598
Delaware	$32,868	$49,011	110.5%	7,511
Massachusetts	$32,746	$48,732 [a]	109.8%	69,000
Michigan	$32,649	$52,497 [a]	118.3%	96,900
Georgia	$32,283	$43,933	99.0%	97,563
District of Columbia	$31,982	$51,000 [a]	115.0%	5,235
Pennsylvania	$31,866	$50,599	114.0%	116,900
Maryland	$31,828	$48,251 [c]	108.8%	54,360
Illinois	$31,761	$49,679 [e]	112.0%	125,130
Hawaii	$31,340	$44,306 [a]	99.9%	10,943
Virginia	$31,238	$41,752	94.1%	87,823
Oregon	$31,026	$46,033 [b]	103.8%	30,895
Texas	$30,938	$39,230	88.4%	281,427
Rhode Island	$30,272	$51,619 [a]	116.3%	10,455
Florida	$30,096	$39,275	88.5%	135,866
Minnesota	$29,998	$42,175	95.1%	53,450
Ohio	$29,953	$44,266	99.8%	118,000
Alabama	$29,938	$37,206	83.9%	47,201
North Carolina	$29,359	$42,118 [a, c]	94.9%	83,526
Tennessee	$28,857	$38,515	86.8%	58,059
Nevada	$28,734	$44,621 [b]	100.6%	19,255
Indiana	$28,440	$44,609 [a]	100.5%	59,832
Washington	$28,348	$43,470	98.0%	51,584
Louisiana	$28,229	$36,328 [c]	81.9%	49,915
Colorado	$28,001	$40,659	91.6%	43,282
Arizona	$27,648	$38,510 [a]	86.8%	45,959
New Mexico	$27,579	$36,716	82.8%	20,000
Arkansas	$27,565	$36,026 [c]	81.2%	31,097
Missouri	$27,554	$36,053	81.3%	64,000
Iowa	$27,553	$38,230 [c]	86.2%	34,702
Oklahoma	$27,547	$32,870 [f]	74.1%	41,452
Wisconsin	$27,397	$41,056 [c]	92.5%	59,783
South Carolina	$27,268	$39,923	90.0%	46,000

In which states will first-year teachers make the most money? Where will they make the least?

	Average first-year salary	Average salary	Average salary as a percentage of U.S. average teacher's salary	Total number of teachers
Kentucky	$26,813	$37,951	85.5%	40,374
Utah	$26,806	$38,153	86.0%	21,900
Wyoming	$26,773	$37,853	85.3%	6,730
Kansas	$26,596	$37,059 [b]	83.5%	32,519
Nebraska	$26,010	$36,236	81.7%	21,004
West Virginia	$25,633	$36,775	82.9%	19,970
New Hampshire	$25,611	$39,915	90.0%	13,990
Idaho	$25,316	$39,194	88.3%	13,800
Vermont	$25,229	$39,771	89.6%	8,250
Mississippi	$24,567	$33,295	75.0%	32,757
Maine	$24,054	$37,300	84.1%	17,040
South Dakota	$23,938	$31,383	70.7%	9,089
Montana	$22,344	$34,379	77.5%	10,212
North Dakota	$20,988	$32,468	73.2%	8,503
U.S. AVERAGE	**$30,719**	**$44,367**	**100.00%**	**58,596**

a=AFT estimate
b=includes employer pick-up of employee pension contribution where applicable
c=includes extra-duty pay
d=median
e=includes pension pick-up and extra-duty pay where applicable
f=estimated to exclude fringe benefits
g=figures for 2000-01

In which cities do teachers with master's degrees make the most and the least?

While a master's degree will increase the size of your paycheck, some urban school districts will pay more for teachers who have a graduate credential than others. Cost-of-living expenses have not been factored into these data, which come from a 2002 survey of salaries in the country's 100 largest cities published by the American Federation of Teachers. But it's safe to say that a cup of coffee will probably cost more on New York City's 5th Avenue than it will in downtown Milwaukee.

	Maximum salary with a master's	Starting salary with a bachelor's	Maximum salary
Yonkers, NY	$84,310	$41,671	$93,785
Jersey City, NJ	$79,850	$36,010	$85,250
Newark, NJ	$69,277	$38,500	$72,058
Anaheim, CA	$68,989	$40,346	$74,262
Pittsburgh, PA	$67,400	$34,800	$69,000
Santa Ana, CA	$66,398	$37,586	$66,898
New York, NY	$65,865 [c]	$31,910	$70,000 [c, b]
Detroit, MI	$64,636	$34,211	$65,635
Long Beach, CA	$63,097	$37,387	$73,778
Fremont, CA	$63,054	$45,609	$74,878
Boston, MA	$62,996	$37,437	$69,821
Huntington Beach, CA	$61,604	$37,851	N/A
Riverside, CA	$61,137	$34,362	$68,153
Miami, FL	$60,775	$32,425	$64,755
Rochester, NY	$60,500	$34,100	$75,968 [e]
Columbus, OH	$60,069	$33,739	$65,161
Cleveland, OH	$59,809	$31,081	$61,260
Chicago, IL	$59,445 [d]	$36,231 [d]	$64,464 [d]
Washington, DC	$59,176	$31,982	$62,715
Baltimore, MD	$58,923	$33,308	$65,270
Charlotte, NC	$58,157	$28,533	$60,687
Philadelphia, PA	$57,830	$32,794	$65,585
Raleigh, NC	$57,204	$27,750	$59,734
Indianapolis, IN	$57,055	$30,374	$60,891
Grand Rapids, MI	$56,880	$31,975	$58,490
Fort Worth, TX	$56,421	$36,250	$59,541
Cincinnati, OH	$56,404	$31,337	$61,415
Atlanta, GA	$56,206	$35,090	$69,250
Dallas, TX	$55,821 [e]	$34,100	$57,821 [e]
Glendale, CA	$55,739 [a]	$36,816	$66,154
Houston, TX	$55,729	$34,588	$58,578
San Antonio, TX	$55,699	$34,000	$55,699
St. Paul, MN	$55,376	$29,363	$62,997
Richmond, VA	$55,241	$31,824	$59,003
Virginia Beach, VA	$54,954	$30,835	$56,554
Greensboro, NC	$54,890	$28,480	$57,670
Minneapolis, MN	$54,603	$28,942	$63,186
Worcester, MA	$54,582	$31,258	$60,324
Buffalo, NY	$54,432	$30,387	$59,403

In which cities do teachers with master's degrees make the most and the least?

	Maximum salary with a master's	Starting salary with a bachelor's	Maximum salary
Garland, TX	$54,423	$34,502	$57,898
San Jose, CA	$54,167	$36,735	$65,062
Fort Wayne, IN	$54,054	$28,752	$58,367
Oakland, CA	$53,937	$38,646	$66,497
Milwaukee, WI	$53,488	$27,948	$59,638
Tampa, FL	$53,452	$30,001	$56,366
Akron, OH	$53,416	$28,654	$56,173
San Diego, CA	$53,143	$33,904	$65,469
Portland, OR	$52,905	$30,712	$61,431
Newport News, VA	$52,786	$30,000	$56,545
Honolulu, HI	$52,344	$31,340	$62,413
Anchorage, AK	$52,334	$32,600	$63,266
Norfolk, VA	$52,250	$30,750	$55,030
El Paso, TX	$52,217	$30,000	$53,217
Stockton, CA	$52,059	$36,495	$65,387
San Francisco, CA	$51,915 [a]	$39,520	$58,387 [a]
St. Louis, MO	$51,601	$30,000	$56,342 [e]
Jacksonville, FL	$51,600	$28,155	$54,647
Louisville, KY	$51,365	$27,765	$57,336
Columbus, GA	$51,132	$31,225	$63,433
Dayton, OH	$51,100	$29,496	$54,602
Arlington, TX	$50,985	$33,500	$52,485
Austin, TX	$50,820	$32,000	$50,820
Denver, CO	$50,727	$31,320	$61,668
Bakersfield, CA	$50,694	$35,865	$64,673
Aurora, CO	$50,679	$29,000	$57,667
Spokane, WA	$50,506	$27,467	$56,571
Memphis, TN	$50,505	$33,306	$57,707
Sacramento, CA	$50,092	$35,379	$67,210
Phoenix, AZ	$50,072	$28,455	N/A
Lincoln, NE	$49,744	$25,811	$54,132
St. Petersburg, FL	$49,600	$29,400	$51,800
Tucson, AZ	$49,314	$27,000	$50,094
Madison, WI	$49,279	$28,419	$57,975
Des Moines, IA	$48,946	$28,710	$53,614
Lubbock, TX	$48,890	$30,500	$49,890
Nashville, TN	$48,881	$27,734	$57,687
Corpus Christi, TX	$48,700	$29,499	$50,200
Los Angeles, CA	$48,674	$34,853	$63,801
Omaha, NE	$48,620	$27,729	$53,122
Kansas City, MO	$48,125	$28,430	$54,155
Colorado Springs, CO	$47,575	$28,000	$59,532
Mesa, AZ	$46,737	$30,379	$59,589
Lexington, KY	$46,620	$27,001	$54,092
Shreveport, LA	$45,957	$30,380	$48,772
Little Rock, AR	$45,578	$25,804	$51,768
New Orleans, LA	$44,288	$28,249	$45,875
Toledo, OH	$44,156	$29,098	$47,688
Jackson, MS	$44,077	$25,409	$50,888
Albuquerque, NM	$43,850	$28,332	$49,728
Fresno, CA	$43,845	$32,000 [a]	$60,297

	Maximum salary with a master's	Starting salary with a bachelor's	Maximum salary
Las Vegas, NV	$43,841	$26,847	$54,194
Tacoma, WA	$43,242	$27,467	$50,253
Birmingham, AL	$42,542	$29,502	$49,217
Seattle, WA	$41,715	$27,467	$56,340
Mobile, AL	$41,195	$28,678	$47,611
Montgomery, AL	$40,781	$28,649	$47,163
Wichita, KS	$39,907	$28,229	$44,508
Baton Rouge, LA	$39,853	$25,716	$44,287
Oklahoma City, OK	$39,500	$26,700	$40,900
Tulsa, OK	$39,450	$26,000	$45,300
U.S AVERAGE	**$54,582**	**$31,567**	**$59,356**

a=AFT estimate
b=includes employer pick-up of employee pension contribution where applicable
c=includes extra-duty pay
d=median
e=includes pension pick-up and extra-duty pay where applicable
f=estimated to exclude fringe benefits
g=figures for 2000-01

Whose graduates are most likely to pass the state certification test? The least?

Almost every state requires teachers to pass a test before they enter a classroom. While some exams focus only on basic skills, most cover pedagogy and subject-matter knowledge. This list, which is compiled by the U.S. Department of Education and organized by state, shows how well each school's graduates fared on their licensure exams. Remember: Some teacher education programs require students to pass the exams before they graduate—and thus automatically have 100 percent pass rates. Schools with a very small number of graduates taking the test do not appear.

	School's pass rate	State average pass rate
ALASKA		
University of Alaska–Fairbanks	100%	99%
University of Alaska–Southeast	100%	99%
Alaska Pacific University	100%	99%
University of Alaska–Anchorage	99%	99%
ARIZONA		
University of Arizona	96%	95%
Arizona State University–Main Campus	95%	95%
Arizona State University–West	95%	95%
Grand Canyon University	94%	95%
Northern Arizona University	93%	95%
Prescott College	89%	95%
ARKANSAS		
University of Arkansas–Fayetteville	100%	100%
University of Arkansas–Little Rock	100%	100%
University of Arkansas–Monticello	100%	100%
Arkansas State University	100%	100%
Arkansas Tech University	100%	100%
University of Central Arkansas	100%	100%
Harding University	100%	100%
Henderson State University	100%	100%
Southern Arkansas University	100%	100%
CALIFORNIA		
Azusa Pacific University	100%	98%
Bethany College of the Assemblies of God	100%	98%
Biola University	100%	98%
Cal Poly–San Luis Obispo	100%	98%
University of California–Berkeley	100%	98%
University of California–Los Angeles	100%	98%
University of California–San Diego	100%	98%
University of California–Santa Barbara (Gevirtz)	100%	98%
University of California–Santa Cruz	100%	98%
California State University–Fullerton	100%	98%
California State University–Hayward	100%	98%

	School's pass rate	State average pass rate
California State University–Long Beach	100%	98%
Holy Names College	100%	98%
Hope International University	100%	98%
Mount St. Mary's College	100%	98%
College of Notre Dame	100%	98%
Occidental College	100%	98%
University of the Pacific	100%	98%
Pepperdine University	100%	98%
University of Redlands	100%	98%
University of San Diego	100%	98%
Simpson College	100%	98%
St. Mary's College of California	100%	98%
Stanford University	100%	98%
Whittier College	100%	98%
University of California–Riverside	99%	98%
California State University–Chico	99%	98%
California State University–San Marcos	99%	98%
University of La Verne	99%	98%
Point Loma Nazarene University	99%	98%
San Diego State University	99%	98%
University of San Francisco	99%	98%
University of California–Irvine	98%	98%
California Baptist University	98%	98%
California State Polytechnic University–Pomona	98%	98%
California State University–Dominguez Hills	98%	98%
California State University–Northridge	98%	98%
California State University–San Bernardino	98%	98%
Chapman University	98%	98%
Concordia University	98%	98%
Dominican College of San Rafael	98%	98%
Humboldt State University	98%	98%
Loyola Marymount University	98%	98%
California State University–Bakersfield	97%	98%
California State University–Los Angeles	97%	98%
California State University–Stanislaus	97%	98%
Fresno Pacific University	97%	98%
National University	97%	98%
Sonoma State University	97%	98%
University of Southern California (Rossier)	97%	98%
University of California–Davis	96%	98%
California State University–Fresno	96%	98%
California State University–Sacramento	96%	98%
San Jose State University	96%	98%
Santa Clara University	96%	98%
La Sierra University	95%	98%
San Francisco State University	95%	98%
Mills College	93%	98%

COLORADO

University of Colorado–Boulder	100%	94%
University of Colorado–Colorado Springs	100%	94%
Adams State College	82%	94%
University of Colorado–Denver	100%	94%
Colorado College	100%	94%
Colorado State University	95%	94%
Colorado Christian College	90%	94%

Whose graduates are most likely to pass the state certification test? The least?

	School's pass rate	State average pass rate
University of Denver	82%	94%
University of Northern Colorado	89%	94%
Regis University	87%	94%
CONNECTICUT		
University of Connecticut (Neag)	100%	97%
Eastern Connecticut State University	100%	97%
Fairfield University	100%	97%
University of New Haven	100%	97%
Quinnipiac University	100%	97%
Sacred Heart University	100%	97%
St. Joseph College	100%	97%
Western Connecticut State University	100%	97%
University of Bridgeport	98%	97%
University of Hartford	95%	97%
Central Connecticut State University	94%	97%
Southern Connecticut State University	92%	97%
DELAWARE		
Wilmington College	100%	95%
University of Delaware	96%	95%
Wesley College	86%	95%
Delaware State University	77%	95%
DISTRICT OF COLUMBIA		
George Washington University	91%	82%
American University	89%	82%
Catholic University of America	87%	82%
Trinity College	73%	82%
Howard University	68%	82%
Gallaudet University	44%	82%
FLORIDA		
Barry University	100%	96%
Florida Atlantic University	100%	96%
University of Miami	100%	96%
Lynn University	100%	96%
Palm Beach Atlantic College	100%	96%
University of South Florida	100%	96%
St. Leo University	100%	96%
University of Florida	97%	96%
University of Central Florida	96%	96%
Rollins College	96%	96%
Stetson University	95%	96%
University of West Florida	95%	96%
Florida State University	94%	96%
University of North Florida	94%	96%
Florida International University	90%	96%
Nova Southeastern University	84%	96%
Florida A&M University	81%	96%

	School's pass rate	State average pass rate
GEORGIA		
Emory University	100%	93%
Armstrong Atlantic State University	99%	93%
State University of West Georgia	98%	93%
Georgia State University	96%	93%
Albany State University	95%	93%
Brenau University	95%	93%
Columbus State University	95%	93%
Covenant College	95%	93%
University of Georgia	95%	93%
Georgia Southwestern State University	95%	93%
North Georgia College and State University	95%	93%
Valdosta State University	95%	93%
Fort Valley State University	94%	93%
Georgia College and State University	93%	93%
Georgia Southern University	93%	93%
Kennesaw State University	93%	93%
Mercer University	92%	93%
Berry College	91%	93%
Wesleyan College	90%	93%
LaGrange College	89%	93%
Augusta State University	88%	93%
Clark Atlanta University	49%	93%
HAWAII		
University of Hawaii–Manoa	90%	82%
Chaminade University of Honolulu	76%	82%
University of Hawaii–Hilo	74%	82%
ILLINOIS		
DePaul University	100%	98%
University of Illinois–Springfield	100%	98%
North Central College	100%	98%
Northwestern University	100%	98%
St. Xavier University	100%	98%
Benedictine University	99%	98%
Eastern Illinois University	99%	98%
Elmhurst College	99%	98%
University of Illinois–Urbana-Champaign	99%	98%
Northern Illinois University	99%	98%
Western Illinois University	99%	98%
Wheaton College	99%	98%
Aurora University	98%	98%
University of Illinois–Chicago	98%	98%
Loyola University Chicago	98%	98%
North Park University	98%	98%
Olivet Nazarene University	98%	98%
Southern Illinois University–Carbondale	98%	98%
University of St. Francis	98%	98%
Dominican University	97%	98%
Governors State University	97%	98%
Greenville College	97%	98%
Illinois State University	97%	98%
National-Louis University	97%	98%
Bradley University	96%	98%
Columbia College Chicago	96%	98%

Whose graduates are most likely to pass the state certification test? The least?

	School's pass rate	State average pass rate
Concordia University	96%	98%
Southern Illinois University–Edwardsville	96%	98%
Northeastern Illinois University	96%	98%
Rockford College	96%	98%
Roosevelt University	95%	98%
Chicago State University	94%	98%
Lewis University	94%	98%
Quincy University	92%	98%
INDIANA		
Indiana Wesleyan University	100%	94%
Valparaiso University	99%	94%
Indiana University–Bloomington	98%	94%
Indiana University–Kokomo	98%	94%
Indiana University–Northwest	98%	94%
Indiana University-Purdue University–Indianapolis	97%	94%
Ball State University	96%	94%
Butler University	96%	94%
Indiana University–South Bend	96%	94%
Indiana State University	95%	94%
Purdue University–West Lafayette	95%	94%
University of St. Francis	95%	94%
Indiana University–Southeast	93%	94%
Indiana University-Purdue University–Fort Wayne	91%	94%
University of Southern Indiana	91%	94%
Anderson University	90%	94%
University of Indianapolis	90%	94%
Oakland City University	86%	94%
Purdue University–Calumet	84%	94%
KANSAS		
Baker University College of Arts and Sciences	100%	97%
Benedictine College	100%	97%
Emporia State University	100%	97%
University of Kansas	100%	97%
Kansas State University	99%	97%
Washburn University	98%	97%
Wichita State University	97%	97%
Fort Hays State University	96%	97%
Southwestern College	96%	97%
MidAmerica Nazarene University	95%	97%
Pittsburg State University	94%	97%
Newman University	93%	97%
Friends University	91%	97%
KENTUCKY		
Asbury College	100%	94%
Cumberland College	100%	94%
Western Kentucky University	99%	94%
University of Louisville	98%	94%
Spalding University	98%	94%

	School's pass rate	State average pass rate
Georgetown College	97%	94%
University of Kentucky	96%	94%
Brescia University	95%	94%
Eastern Kentucky University	95%	94%
Northern Kentucky University	93%	94%
Murray State University	92%	94%
Campbellsville University	91%	94%
Morehead State University	90%	94%
Bellarmine University	89%	94%
Lindsey Wilson College	87%	94%
Union College	64%	94%
Kentucky State University	52%	94%
LOUISIANA		
Grambling State University	100%	95%
University of Louisiana–Monroe	100%	95%
Louisiana Tech University	100%	95%
Our Lady of Holy Cross College	100%	95%
Northwestern State University of Louisiana	99%	95%
Louisiana State University–Shreveport	97%	95%
Southern University and A&M College	97%	95%
University of Louisiana–Lafayette	96%	95%
Nicholls State University	95%	95%
Southeastern Louisiana University	94%	95%
Louisiana State University–Baton Rouge	93%	95%
McNeese State University	93%	95%
Loyola University New Orleans	91%	95%
University of New Orleans	91%	95%
MAINE		
University of Southern Maine	96%	89%
University of New England	86%	89%
University of Maine–Orono	80%	89%
St. Joseph's College	61%	89%
MARYLAND		
Coppin State College	100%	91%
Hood College	100%	91%
Mount St. Mary's College	100%	91%
Frostburg State University	98%	91%
Johns Hopkins University	97%	91%
Salisbury University	92%	91%
Towson University	92%	91%
Bowie State University	91%	91%
University of Maryland–College Park	91%	91%
College of Notre Dame of Maryland	91%	91%
Loyola College in Maryland	90%	91%
Goucher College	88%	91%
University of Maryland–Baltimore County	86%	91%
Morgan State University	63%	91%
University of Maryland–Eastern Shore	31%	91%
MASSACHUSETTS		
Bridgewater State College	100%	91%
College of Our Lady of the Elms	100%	91%
Endicott College	100%	91%

Whose graduates are most likely to pass the state certification test? The least?

	School's pass rate	State average pass rate
Framingham State College	100%	91%
University of Massachusetts–Lowell	100%	91%
Smith College	100%	91%
Worcester State College	99%	91%
Fitchburg State College	98%	91%
Springfield College	98%	91%
Westfield State College	98%	91%
University of Massachusetts–Amherst	97%	91%
Northeastern University	97%	91%
Simmons College	96%	91%
Boston University	95%	91%
University of Massachusetts–Boston	95%	91%
Mount Holyoke College	94%	91%
Harvard University	93%	91%
Salem State College	93%	91%
Assumption College	92%	91%
Tufts University	91%	91%
Lesley University	90%	91%
Boston College (Lynch)	89%	91%
Gordon College	89%	91%
Clark University	81%	91%
University of Massachusetts–Dartmouth	79%	91%
Anna Maria College	78%	91%
Cambridge College	78%	91%
American International College	76%	91%
Emmanuel College	67%	91%
Wheelock College	66%	91%
Eastern Nazarene College	65%	91%
Curry College	23%	91%
MICHIGAN		
Andrews University	100%	100%
Aquinas College	100%	100%
Central Michigan University	100%	100%
Cornerstone University	100%	100%
Eastern Michigan University	100%	100%
Ferris State University	100%	100%
Grand Valley State University	100%	100%
Madonna University	100%	100%
Marygrove College	100%	100%
University of Michigan–Ann Arbor	100%	100%
University of Michigan–Dearborn	100%	100%
University of Michigan–Flint	100%	100%
Michigan State University	100%	100%
Northern Michigan University	100%	100%
Oakland University	100%	100%
Saginaw Valley State University	100%	100%
Siena Heights College	100%	100%
Spring Arbor College	100%	100%
University of Detroit Mercy	100%	100%
Wayne State University	100%	100%
Western Michigan University	100%	100%

	School's pass rate	State average pass rate
MINNESOTA		
Augsburg College	100%	98%
Bethel College	100%	98%
College of St. Scholastica	100%	98%
Hamline University	100%	98%
St. Mary's University of Minnesota	100%	98%
University of St. Thomas	100%	98%
University of Minnesota–Duluth	100%	98%
University of Minnesota–Twin Cities	100%	98%
Winona State University	100%	98%
Southwest Minnesota State University	98%	98%
St. Cloud State University	97%	98%
Bemidji State University	95%	98%
Minnesota State University–Mankato	95%	98%
Minnesota State University–Moorhead	95%	98%
College of St. Catherine	94%	98%
MISSISSIPPI		
Alcorn State University	100%	95%
Belhaven College	100%	95%
Delta State University	100%	95%
Mississippi University for Women	100%	95%
Mississippi Valley State University	100%	95%
William Carey College	100%	95%
Mississippi College	99%	95%
Jackson State University	97%	95%
University of Mississippi	95%	95%
University of Southern Mississippi	95%	95%
Mississippi State University	90%	95%
MISSOURI		
Columbia College	100%	96%
Fontbonne University	100%	96%
Lindenwood University	100%	96%
University of Missouri–Columbia	100%	96%
University of Missouri–St. Louis	100%	96%
Missouri Baptist College	100%	96%
Truman State University	100%	96%
Washington University in St. Louis	100%	96%
Drury College	99%	96%
Avila College	98%	96%
Maryville University of St. Louis	98%	96%
Evangel University	97%	96%
Southwest Missouri State University	97%	96%
Webster University	96%	96%
Central Missouri State University	95%	96%
Southeast Missouri State University	95%	96%
Northwest Missouri State University	94%	96%
Southwest Baptist University	94%	96%
Rockhurst University	92%	96%
St. Louis University	91%	96%
Stephens College	91%	96%
University of Missouri–Kansas City	91%	96%
Park University	88%	96%
Central Methodist College	87%	96%
Lincoln University	84%	96%
William Woods University	55%	96%

Whose graduates are most likely to pass the state certification test? The least?

	School's pass rate	State average pass rate
MONTANA		
University of Great Falls	100%	99%
Montana State University	100%	99%
Montana State University–Billings	100%	99%
Montana State University–Northern	100%	99%
University of Montana	98%	99%
NEVADA		
University of Nevada–Las Vegas	97%	96%
University of Nevada–Reno	96%	96%
NEW HAMPSHIRE		
Rivier College	99%	93%
Plymouth State University	97%	93%
Keene State College	93%	93%
University of New Hampshire	92%	93%
Antioch New England Graduate School	90%	93%
NEW JERSEY		
Centenary College	100%	98%
College of New Jersey	100%	98%
College of St. Elizabeth	100%	98%
Rider University	100%	98%
Rutgers State University–New Brunswick	100%	98%
Georgian Court College	99%	98%
Rowan University	99%	98%
Fairleigh Dickinson University	98%	98%
Montclair State University	98%	98%
Kean University	97%	98%
Monmouth University	97%	98%
Seton Hall University	97%	98%
William Paterson University	97%	98%
Caldwell College	95%	98%
New Jersey City University	95%	98%
St. Peter's College	94%	98%
NEW MEXICO		
Eastern New Mexico University	100%	94%
College of Santa Fe	100%	94%
Western New Mexico University	100%	94%
New Mexico State University	96%	94%
University of New Mexico	93%	94%
College of the Southwest	90%	94%
New Mexico Highlands University	83%	94%
NEW YORK		
Binghamton University	100%	94%
University at Buffalo–SUNY	100%	94%
Cornell University	100%	94%
Graduate College of Union University	100%	94%
Long Island University–Brooklyn	100%	94%
University of Rochester (Warner)	100%	94%

	School's pass rate	State average pass rate
SUNY–Albany	100%	94%
Yeshiva University (Azrieli)	100%	94%
SUNY College–Geneseo	99%	94%
Syracuse University	99%	94%
Teachers College, Columbia University	99%	94%
CUNY–College of Staten Island	98%	94%
D'Youville College	98%	94%
Daemen College	98%	94%
Ithaca College	98%	94%
Le Moyne College	98%	94%
Marist College	98%	94%
New York University	98%	94%
Niagara University	98%	94%
Pace University	98%	94%
SUNY College–Fredonia	98%	94%
Utica College of Syracuse University	98%	94%
Bank Street College of Education	97%	94%
Hofstra University	97%	94%
Long Island University–Brentwood	97%	94%
Manhattanville College	97%	94%
Medaille College	97%	94%
Mount St. Mary College	97%	94%
Nazareth College of Rochester	97%	94%
New York Institute of Technology–Manhattan	97%	94%
St. Bonaventure University	97%	94%
St. Lawrence University	97%	94%
Alfred University	96%	94%
Canisius College	96%	94%
CUNY–Hunter College	96%	94%
Roberts Wesleyan College	96%	94%
SUNY–New Paltz	96%	94%
SUNY–Oneonta	96%	94%
SUNY–Potsdam	96%	94%
SUNY–Stony Brook	96%	94%
Elmira College	95%	94%
Fordham University	95%	94%
St. Joseph's College–Suffolk	95%	94%
St. Thomas Aquinas College	95%	94%
Buffalo State College–SUNY	94%	94%
Iona College	94%	94%
Molloy College	94%	94%
College of St. Rose	94%	94%
SUNY–Cortland	94%	94%
SUNY–Plattsburgh	94%	94%
CUNY–Queens College	93%	94%
Long Island University–Southampton	93%	94%
Adelphi University	92%	94%
CUNY–Lehman College	92%	94%
College of New Rochelle	92%	94%
SUNY College–Oswego	92%	94%
SUNY–Brockport	92%	94%
Long Island Univeristy–C.W. Post Campus	90%	94%
College of Mount St. Vincent	90%	94%
Wagner College	90%	94%
Manhattan College	89%	94%
Rochester Institute of Technology	89%	94%

Whose graduates are most likely to pass the state certification test? The least?

	School's pass rate	State average pass rate
Touro College	89%	94%
St. John's University	88%	94%
CUNY–Brooklyn College	87%	94%
CUNY–City College	87%	94%
Dowling College	86%	94%
Mercy College	85%	94%
Dominican College of Blauvelt	83%	94%
Nyack College	83%	94%
Pratt Institute	77%	94%
NORTH CAROLINA		
Catawba College	100%	92%
Duke University	100%	92%
University of North Carolina–Chapel Hill	100%	92%
North Carolina A&T State University	100%	92%
Wake Forest University	100%	92%
Meredith College	99%	92%
University of North Carolina–Wilmington	98%	92%
University of North Carolina–Greensboro	97%	92%
Campbell University	96%	92%
Salem College	95%	92%
Lenoir-Rhyne College	94%	92%
North Carolina State University–Raleigh	94%	92%
Appalachian State University	93%	92%
Elon University	93%	92%
University of North Carolina–Charlotte	93%	92%
Queens University of Charlotte	93%	92%
Western Carolina University	92%	92%
East Carolina University	90%	92%
Elizabeth City State University	88%	92%
University of North Carolina–Pembroke	87%	92%
North Carolina Central University	87%	92%
Pfeiffer University	85%	92%
Gardner-Webb University	82%	92%
Fayetteville State University	74%	92%
Winston-Salem State University	67%	92%
OHIO		
Antioch University (McGregor)	100%	91%
University of Cincinnati	100%	91%
Lake Erie College	100%	91%
Marietta College	100%	91%
University of Findlay	99%	91%
Xavier University	99%	91%
University of Dayton	98%	91%
Malone College	98%	91%
Baldwin-Wallace College	96%	91%
John Carroll University	96%	91%
Ohio Northern University	96%	91%
Mount Vernon Nazarene University	95%	91%
Notre Dame College of Ohio	95%	91%
Ohio State University–Columbus	95%	91%

	School's pass rate	State average pass rate
Otterbein College	95%	91%
Ursuline College	94%	91%
Franciscan University of Steubenville	92%	91%
Ashland University	91%	91%
Bluffton College	91%	91%
Cedarville College	91%	91%
Cleveland State University	91%	91%
Kent State University	91%	91%
College of Mount St. Joseph	91%	91%
Walsh University	91%	91%
University of Akron	90%	91%
Miami University–Oxford	90%	91%
Ohio University	90%	91%
Wright State University	90%	91%
Capital University	89%	91%
Bowling Green State University	87%	91%
University of Toledo	87%	91%
Defiance College	85%	91%
Urbana University	84%	91%
University of Rio Grande	83%	91%
Muskingum College	81%	91%
Youngstown State University	80%	91%
Heidelberg College	77%	91%
Central State University	43%	91%

OKLAHOMA

	School's pass rate	State average pass rate
University of Central Oklahoma	99%	94%
University of Oklahoma	99%	94%
Cameron University	97%	94%
Oklahoma State University	97%	94%
Oral Roberts University	97%	94%
Southern Nazarene University	97%	94%
Northeastern State University	93%	94%
Oklahoma City University	93%	94%
Southeastern Oklahoma State University	91%	94%
East Central University	89%	94%
Northwestern Oklahoma State University	89%	94%
Southwestern Oklahoma State University	89%	94%
University of Tulsa	86%	94%
Langston University	73%	94%

OREGON

	School's pass rate	State average pass rate
Concordia University	100%	100%
Eastern Oregon University	100%	100%
George Fox University	100%	100%
Lewis and Clark College	100%	100%
Northwest Christian College	100%	100%
University of Oregon	100%	100%
Oregon State University	100%	100%
Pacific University	100%	100%
University of Portland	100%	100%
Portland State University	100%	100%
Southern Oregon University	100%	100%
Western Oregon University	100%	100%
Willamette University	100%	100%

Whose graduates are most likely to pass the state certification test? The least?

	School's pass rate	State average pass rate
PENNSYLVANIA		
Bucknell University	100%	85%
Lock Haven University of Pennsylvania	100%	85%
University of Pittsburgh	100%	85%
Villanova University	100%	85%
Widener University	100%	85%
Westminster College	99%	85%
Drexel University	97%	85%
Gwynedd-Mercy College	96%	85%
Lehigh University	96%	85%
Cabrini College	95%	85%
Chatham College	95%	85%
Duquesne University	94%	85%
University of Pennsylvania	94%	85%
Rosemont College	93%	85%
Penn State University–University Park	91%	85%
St. Francis University	91%	85%
Arcadia University	90%	85%
Millersville University of Pennsylvania	90%	85%
Shippensburg University of Pennsylvania	89%	85%
Lebanon Valley College	88%	85%
Robert Morris University	88%	85%
East Stroudsburg University of Pennsylvania	87%	85%
Marywood University	87%	85%
Slippery Rock University of Pennsylvania	87%	85%
Geneva College	86%	85%
Mercyhurst College	86%	85%
Moravian College	86%	85%
Pennsylvania State University–Harrisburg	86%	85%
University of Scranton	86%	85%
York College of Pennsylvania	86%	85%
Edinboro University of Pennsylvania	85%	85%
La Salle University	85%	85%
King's College	83%	85%
California University of Pennsylvania	82%	85%
West Chester University of Pennsylvania	82%	85%
Alvernia College	81%	85%
Bloomsburg University of Pennsylvania	81%	85%
Clarion University of Pennsylvania	81%	85%
Eastern University	81%	85%
Indiana University of Pennsylvania	81%	85%
Kutztown University of Pennsylvania	81%	85%
Seton Hill College	79%	85%
Mansfield University of Pennsylvania	76%	85%
Lincoln University	75%	85%
Gannon University	74%	85%
Holy Family University	74%	85%
St. Joseph's University	72%	85%
Wilkes University	71%	85%
Temple University	70%	85%
Chestnut Hill College	67%	85%
Carlow College	62%	85%

	School's pass rate	State average pass rate
Point Park College	62%	85%
Neumann College	55%	85%
Cheyney University of Pennsylvania	51%	85%
Waynesburg College	47%	85%
RHODE ISLAND		
Brown University	95%	87%
Providence College	95%	87%
University of Rhode Island/Rhode Island College	83%	87%
Roger Williams University	82%	87%
SOUTH CAROLINA		
Charleston Southern University	100%	94%
Columbia College	100%	94%
Francis Marion University	100%	94%
University of South Carolina–Aiken	100%	94%
Southern Wesleyan University	100%	94%
South Carolina State University	99%	94%
University of South Carolina–Columbia	98%	94%
Winthrop Univeristy	97%	94%
College of Charleston	95%	94%
Clemson University	95%	94%
Coastal Carolina University	95%	94%
Lander University	94%	94%
University of South Carolina–Spartanburg	88%	94%
The Citadel	84%	94%
TENNESSEE		
Bethel College	100%	94%
East Tennessee State University	100%	94%
Lincoln Memorial University	100%	94%
Southern Adventist University	100%	94%
University of Tennessee–Martin	100%	94%
Union University	100%	94%
Vanderbilt University (Peabody)	100%	94%
Austin Peay State University	99%	94%
Carson-Newman College	99%	94%
University of Tennessee–Chattanooga	99%	94%
Milligan College	98%	94%
Tennessee State University	98%	94%
Lee University	97%	94%
University of Tennessee–Knoxville	97%	94%
Belmont University	95%	94%
Tennessee Technological University	92%	94%
Cumberland University	91%	94%
David Lipscomb University	91%	94%
University of Memphis	91%	94%
Trevecca Nazarene University	90%	94%
Middle Tennessee State University	89%	94%
Christian Brothers University	81%	94%
Tusculum College	76%	94%
Freed-Hardeman University	75%	94%
TEXAS		
Austin College	100%	92%
Houston Baptist University	100%	92%

Whose graduates are most likely to pass the state certification test? The least?

	School's pass rate	State average pass rate
University of the Incarnate Word	100%	92%
Sam Houston State University	100%	92%
Schreiner College	100%	92%
Southwestern Adventist University	100%	92%
University of Texas–Arlington	100%	92%
University of Texas–Austin	100%	92%
Texas Southern University	100%	92%
Texas Wesleyan University	100%	92%
Trinity University	100%	92%
University of Texas–Tyler	99%	92%
Lamar University	98%	92%
Stephen F. Austin State University	98%	92%
Texas A&M University–College Station	98%	92%
Texas A&M University–Corpus Christi	98%	92%
Wayland Baptist University	98%	92%
University of Texas–San Antonio	97%	92%
Dallas Baptist University	96%	92%
University of St. Thomas	96%	92%
Tarleton State University	96%	92%
Texas Woman's University	96%	92%
Angelo State University	95%	92%
University of North Texas	95%	92%
St. Mary's University of San Antonio	95%	92%
Concordia University–Austin	94%	92%
Texas Christian University	94%	92%
University of Houston–Main Campus	94%	92%
Hardin-Simmons University	93%	92%
Texas A&M University–Texarkana	93%	92%
Baylor University	92%	92%
University of Houston–Victoria	92%	92%
Midwestern State University	92%	92%
Texas State University–San Marcos	92%	92%
Texas A&M University–Commerce	92%	92%
Texas Tech University	91%	92%
University of Houston–Clear Lake	90%	92%
Southern Methodist University	90%	92%
Abilene Christian University	89%	92%
University of Texas–Permian Basin	89%	92%
University of Mary Hardin-Baylor	88%	92%
Texas A&M International University	86%	92%
West Texas A&M University	86%	92%
Lubbock Christian University	83%	92%
Prarie View A&M University	81%	92%
Our Lady of the Lake University	80%	92%
University of Texas–El Paso	80%	92%
University of Texas–Brownsville	79%	92%
Texas A&M University–Kingsville	72%	92%
University of Texas–Pan American	70%	92%
Sul Ross State University	68%	92%

	School's pass rate	State average pass rate
VERMONT		
Goddard College	100%	97%
Lyndon State College	100%	97%
School for International Training	100%	97%
St. Michael's College	100%	97%
College of St. Joseph	97%	97%
University of Vermont	96%	97%
Castleton State College	93%	97%
Johnson State College	92%	97%
VIRGINIA		
Averett University	100%	94%
Christopher Newport University	100%	94%
Eastern Mennonite University	100%	94%
Hampton University	100%	94%
James Madison University	100%	94%
Liberty University	100%	94%
Mary Baldwin College	100%	94%
Marymount University	100%	94%
Radford University	100%	94%
University of Virginia (Curry)	99%	94%
Old Dominion University	96%	94%
Virginia Tech	94%	94%
Lynchburg College	91%	94%
Norfolk State University	91%	94%
Longwood University	89%	94%
College of William and Mary	89%	94%
George Mason University	84%	94%
Virginia Commonwealth University	84%	94%
Shenandoah University	81%	94%
Virginia State University	80%	94%
WEST VIRGINIA		
Marshall University	100%	100%
West Virginia University	100%	100%

U.S. News
& World Report

Schools of Education Offering Graduate Degrees

How to use the directory

In the following pages, you'll find detailed profiles of more than 600 schools of education that offer graduate programs based on a survey that *U.S. News* conducted in late 2003 and early 2004. Schools are organized alphabetically by state; those that did not return the questionnaire are listed with basic contact information. You may also want to consult the online version of this directory (www.usnews.com), which allows you to do a customized search of our database.

As you browse for routes to the classroom in your state, you may want to refer to information leading each state section on what type of teacher licensure exams are required. That information comes from the 2004 *Quality Counts* report put out by *Education Week*, and is republished here with permission.

Essential Stats

In addition to the education school's address and the year the school was founded, you'll find the following key facts and figures here:

Total first-year graduate student enrollment: the number of full-time first-year students enrolled during the 2003–2004 academic year.

Total number of graduates of master's teaching program: the number of full-time master's students who graduated with a teaching specialization between July 1, 2002 and June 30, 2003.

U.S. News **ranking:** A school's overall rank indicates where it sits among its peers in *U.S News*'s 2005 ranking of education schools granting doctoral degrees. The top 77 education schools are ranked numerically. Schools below that top half are listed as "unranked," as are institutions that grant only master's degrees. If a school has been ranked in a specialty area (administration/supervision, counseling/personnel services, curriculum/instruction, educational psychology, education policy, elementary education, higher education administration, secondary education, special education, and vocational/technical education), you'll find that information here as well.

Admissions

Application deadline and fee: for fall 2005 admission.

Acceptance rate: The percentage of applicants accepted is provided for the class entering in fall 2003 and is broken down by those pursuing master's degrees, educational specialist degrees, and the Ph.D or Ed.D.

Test requirements: Here you will find whether the GRE or MAT is required for admission (and, for international students, the Test of English as a Foreign Language, or TOEFL). The average test scores listed are for students who enrolled in the class that entered in 2003. The minimum TOEFL score required on the paper- and computer-based exams is also provided.

Enrollment

You can get a sense of an education school's emphases by examining the breakdown of students enrolled in the different types of programs (master's, teacher prep, education specialist, and doctoral). All figures are for the 2003–2004 academic year.

Financial Information

Tuition and other expenses: The cost figures are for the 2003–2004 academic year. You'll find both the full-time and part-time tuition and the estimated cost of books, room and board, fees, and other miscellaneous living expenses. You'll also find the number of fellowships awarded to graduate students during the 2003–2004 academic year, as well as the number of teaching assistant and research assistant positions.

Academic Programs

Faculty profile: the total number of full-time tenure-track faculty and part-time faculty.

Teacher preparation: The teacher preparation programs schools offer are listed here, including, for example, master's degrees aimed at initial licensure and alternative certification programs for college graduates interested in changing careers. Some key attributes are noted where applicable: whether the institution has relationships with professional development schools; whether peer groups of ed students meet regularly to discuss instructional techniques during their internships; whether students in the practice teaching programs have official mentors; and whether courses that prepare teachers for certification by the National Board of Professional Teaching Standards are offered.

Accreditation: whether a school is accredited by the National Council for Accreditation of Teacher Education or the Teacher Education Accreditation Council.

Licensing Test

How good a job did the school do at preparing future teachers for the state licensing exam? The overall, or "summary," pass rate on the state exam is reported for 2002–2003 compared to the average pass rate of everyone tested in the state. Pass rates were obtained from the U.S. Department of Education, and a further breakdown of graduates' performance on the parts of the test—basic skills, professional knowledge, academic content areas, for example—can be found on the Web at www.title2.org/title2dr/default.asp. Pass rates on assessments taken by nine or fewer people at an institution are not reported. But take note: Some education schools require students to have a passing score on the state's teacher licensure exam *before* they graduate, making their pass rate automatically 100 percent.

ALABAMA

Alabama A&M University

■ PO Box 1357, Normal, AL 35762
■ Website: http://www.aamu.edu/
■ Public

Alabama State University

■ 915 S. Jackson Street, Montgomery, AL 36101
■ Website: http://www.alasu.edu/home/default.aspx
■ Public
■ **Degrees offered:** bachelor's, master's, education specialist, Ed.D.

ADMISSIONS
Admissions phone number: **(334) 229-4275**
Application fee: **$10**
Test of English as Foreign Language (TOEFL) is required for international students.
Minimum TOEFL score required for paper test: **500**

Fall 2003
Total 2003 enrollment: **966**
Master's degree enrollment: **899**
    Teacher preparation program enrollment (master's): **518**
Education specialist degree enrollment: **37**
Doctoral degree enrollment: **30**

FINANCIAL INFORMATION
Financial aid phone number: **(334) 229-6994**
Tuition, 2003-2004 academic year: Full-time in-state: **$150/credit hour**; out-of-state: **$300/credit hour**
Room and board: **$3,600**, Books and supplies: **$800**, Miscellaneous expenses: **$1,380**

ACADEMIC PROGRAMS
Areas of specialization: education administration and supervision, elementary teacher education, secondary

teacher education, special education, student counseling and personnel services.
Courses that prepare teachers to pass the National Board of Professional Teaching Standards are not offered.
The education program is currently accredited by the National Council for Accreditation of Teacher Education.

Auburn University– Main Campus

■ 3084 Haley Center, Auburn University, AL 36849
■ Website: http://www.auburn.edu/
■ Public
■ **Degrees offered:** bachelor's, master's, education specialist, Ph.D., Ed.D.

ADMISSIONS
Admissions phone number: **(334) 844-4700**
Admissions email address: *gradadm@mail.auburn.edu*
Application website: *http://gradweb.duc.auburn.edu/*
Application fee: **$25**
Fall 2005 application deadline: **8/1**
Test requirements: **GRE**
Test of English as Foreign Language (TOEFL) is required for international students.
Minimum TOEFL score required for paper test: **550**
Minimum TOEFL score required for computer test: **213**

Fall 2003
Acceptance rate for master's degree programs: **72%**
Acceptance rate for education specialist degree programs: **70%**
Acceptance rate for doctoral programs: **42%**
Average GRE verbal: **424**, Average GRE quantitative: **472**, Average GRE analytical: **502**
Total 2003 enrollment: **696**
Master's degree enrollment: **394**
    Teacher preparation program enrollment (master's): **196**
Education specialist degree enrollment: **27**
Doctoral degree enrollment: **275**

FINANCIAL INFORMATION

Financial aid phone number: **(334) 844-4723**
Tuition, 2003-2004 academic year: Full-time in-state:
$4,230; out-of-state: **$12,690**, Part-time in-state:
$175/credit hour; out-of-state: **$525/credit hour**
Fees: **$196**, Room and board: **$5,970**, Books and supplies:
$900, Miscellaneous expenses: **$1,689**
Number of teaching assistant positions: **77**
Number of research assistant positions: **15**
Number of other paid appointments: **8**

ACADEMIC PROGRAMS

Total full-time tenured or tenure-track faculty (fall 2003): **81**
Total part-time faculty (fall 2003): **9**
Areas of specialization: education administration and
supervision, educational psychology, elementary teacher
education, higher education administration, secondary
teacher education, special education, student counseling
and personnel services.
Professional development/partnership school(s) are used
by students in all of the teaching programs.
During their internships, peer groups of students meet
regularly to discuss instructional techniques in some of
the teaching programs.
All of the students in their internships are mentored.
Courses that prepare teachers to pass the National Board of
Professional Teaching Standards are not offered.
Teacher preparation programs: Four-year baccalaureate-
degree program leading to initial licensure that includes
either a major or minor in education and practice teaching. Five-year program leading to initial licensure that
results in a baccalaureate degree (with a major or minor
in education) plus a master's degree and includes practice teaching. Master's program preparing college graduates for initial licensure; includes practice teaching.
Alternative program for college graduates leading to provisional licensure.
The education program is currently accredited by the
National Council for Accreditation of Teacher Education.

Auburn University–Montgomery

- **7051 Senators Drive, Montgomery, AL 36117**
- **Website:** http://www.aum.edu
- **Public**
- **Degrees offered:** bachelor's, master's, education
specialist, Ed.D.

ADMISSIONS

Admissions phone number: **(334) 244-3611**
Admissions email address: *auminfo@mail.aum.edu*
Application fee: **$25**
Fall 2005 application deadline: **rolling**

Fall 2003
Total 2003 enrollment: **338**

FINANCIAL INFORMATION

Financial aid phone number: **(334) 244-3571**
Tuition, 2003-2004 academic year: Full-time in-state:
$1,872; out-of-state: **$11,232**, Part-time in-state:
$156/credit hour; out-of-state: **$468/credit hour**
Fees: **$230**, Room and board: **$4,890**, Books and supplies:
$600, Miscellaneous expenses: **$1,910**

ACADEMIC PROGRAMS

Total full-time tenured or tenure-track faculty (fall 2003): **190**
Total part-time faculty (fall 2003): **360**
Professional development/partnership school(s) are used
by students in none of the teaching programs.
During their internships, peer groups of students meet
regularly to discuss instructional techniques in some of
the teaching programs.
Some of the students in their internships are mentored.
Courses that prepare teachers to pass the National Board of
Professional Teaching Standards are offered.
The education program is currently accredited by the
National Council for Accreditation of Teacher Education.
The education program is currently accredited by the
Teacher Education Accreditation Council.

Jacksonville State University

- **700 Pelham Road North, Jacksonville, AL 36265**
- **Website:** http://www.jsu.edu/depart/graduate
- **Public**
- **Degrees offered:** bachelor's, master's, education
specialist

ADMISSIONS

Admissions phone number: **(256) 782-5329**
Admissions email address: *graduate@jsucc.jsu.edu*
Application website: *http://www.jsu.edu/depart/graduate*
Application fee: **$20**
Fall 2005 application deadline: **rolling**
Test requirements: **GRE or MAT**
Test of English as Foreign Language (TOEFL) is required
for international students.
Minimum TOEFL score required for paper test: **500**
Minimum TOEFL score required for computer test: **173**

Fall 2003
Average GRE verbal: **386**, Average GRE quantitative: **416**,
Average GRE analytical: **369**, Average MAT: **35**
Total 2003 enrollment: **1,050**
Master's degree enrollment: **793**
Teacher preparation program enrollment (master's): **474**
Education specialist degree enrollment: **257**

FINANCIAL INFORMATION

Financial aid phone number: **(256) 782-8399**

Tuition, 2003-2004 academic year: Full-time in-state: $3,540; out-of-state: $7,080, Part-time in-state: $177/credit hour; out-of-state: $354/credit hour
Room and board: $2,876, Books and supplies: $900, Miscellaneous expenses: $2,400
Number of other paid appointments: 54

ACADEMIC PROGRAMS

Total full-time tenured or tenure-track faculty (fall 2003): 211, Total part-time faculty (fall 2003): 132
Areas of specialization: education administration and supervision, elementary teacher education, secondary teacher education, special education.
Professional development/partnership school(s) are used by students in all of the teaching programs.
During their internships, peer groups of students meet regularly to discuss instructional techniques in all of the teaching programs.
All of the students in their internships are mentored.
Courses that prepare teachers to pass the National Board of Professional Teaching Standards are not offered.
Teacher preparation programs: Four-year baccalaureate-degree program leading to initial licensure that includes either a major or minor in education and practice teaching. Five-year program leading to initial licensure that results in a baccalaureate degree (with a major or minor in education) plus graduate credit and includes practice teaching. Master's program preparing college graduates for initial licensure; includes practice teaching.
The education program is currently accredited by the National Council for Accreditation of Teacher Education.

Samford University

- 800 Lakeshore Drive, Birmingham, AL 35229
- **Website:** http://www.samford.edu
- Private
- **Degrees offered:** bachelor's, master's, education specialist, Ed.D.

ADMISSIONS

Admissions phone number: (205) 726-2019
Admissions email address: *jmpersal@samford.edu*
Application fee: $25
Fall 2005 application deadline: rolling
Test requirements: **GRE or MAT**
Test of English as Foreign Language (TOEFL) is required for international students.
Minimum TOEFL score required for paper test: 550
Minimum TOEFL score required for computer test: 213

Fall 2003
Acceptance rate for master's degree programs: 39%
Acceptance rate for education specialist degree programs: 37%
Acceptance rate for doctoral programs: 34%
Average GRE verbal: 441, Average GRE quantitative: 461, Average MAT: 48

Total 2003 enrollment: 164
Master's degree enrollment: 48
  Teacher preparation program enrollment (master's): 39
Education specialist degree enrollment: 42
Doctoral degree enrollment: 74

FINANCIAL INFORMATION

Financial aid phone number: (205) 726-2905
Tuition, 2003-2004 academic year: Full-time: $352/credit hour; Part-time: $352/credit hour
Books and supplies: $150
Number of fellowships awarded to graduate students during the 2003-2004 academic year: 0
Number of teaching assistant positions: 0
Number of research assistant positions: 0
Number of other paid appointments: 2

ACADEMIC PROGRAMS

Total full-time tenured or tenure-track faculty (fall 2003): 3
  Total part-time faculty (fall 2003): 15
Areas of specialization: curriculum and instruction, education administration and supervision, education policy, elementary teacher education, special education.
Professional development/partnership school(s) are used by students in all of the teaching programs.
During their internships, peer groups of students meet regularly to discuss instructional techniques in all of the teaching programs.
All of the students in their internships are mentored.
Courses that prepare teachers to pass the National Board of Professional Teaching Standards are offered.
Teacher preparation programs: Four-year baccalaureate-degree program leading to initial licensure that includes either a major or minor in education and practice teaching. Master's program preparing college graduates for initial licensure; includes practice teaching. Alternative program for college graduates leading to provisional licensure.
The education program is currently accredited by the National Council for Accreditation of Teacher Education.

Spring Hill College

- 4000 Dauphin Street, Mobile, AL 36608
- **Website:** http://www.shc.edu/graduate
- Private
- **Degrees offered:** bachelor's, master's

ADMISSIONS

Admissions phone number: (251) 380-3094
Admissions email address: *grad@shc.edu*
Application website: *http://www.shc.edu/graduate/apply*
Application fee: $25
Fall 2005 application deadline: 7/15
Test requirements: **GRE or MAT**
Test of English as Foreign Language (TOEFL) is required for international students.
Minimum TOEFL score required for paper test: 550
Minimum TOEFL score required for computer test: 213

Fall 2003
Acceptance rate for master's degree programs: 70%
Average MAT: 47
Total 2003 enrollment: 61
Master's degree enrollment: 61
   Teacher preparation program enrollment (master's): 61

FINANCIAL INFORMATION
Financial aid phone number: (251) 380-3460
Tuition, 2003-2004 academic year: Full-time: $239/credit
   hour; Part-time: $239/credit hour
Fees: $256, Room and board: $5,406, Books and supplies:
   $450, Miscellaneous expenses: $2,240
Number of fellowships awarded to graduate students dur-
   ing the 2003-2004 academic year: 0
Number of teaching assistant positions: 0
Number of research assistant positions: 0

ACADEMIC PROGRAMS
Total full-time tenured or tenure-track faculty (fall 2003): 4
   Total part-time faculty (fall 2003): 11
Areas of specialization: elementary teacher education, sec-
   ondary teacher education.
Professional development/partnership school(s) are used
   by students in all of the teaching programs.
During their internships, peer groups of students meet
   regularly to discuss instructional techniques in all of the
   teaching programs.
All of the students in their internships are mentored.
Courses that prepare teachers to pass the National Board of
   Professional Teaching Standards are not offered.
Teacher preparation programs: Four-year baccalaureate-
   degree program leading to initial licensure that includes
   either a major or minor in education and practice teaching. Master's program preparing college graduates for
   initial licensure; includes practice teaching.

Troy State University –Dothan

■ 500 University Drive, Dothan, AL 36304
■ **Website:** http://www.tsud.edu
■ **Public**
■ **Degrees offered:** bachelor's, master's, education specialist

ADMISSIONS
Admissions phone number: (334) 983-6556
Admissions email address: *rcordell@troyst.edu*
Application website:
   http://www.tsud.edu/graduate_school/default.htm
Application fee: $20
Fall 2005 application deadline: 7/15
Test requirements: GRE or MAT
Test of English as Foreign Language (TOEFL) is required
   for international students.
Minimum TOEFL score required for paper test: 550
Minimum TOEFL score required for computer test: 213

Fall 2003
Acceptance rate for master's degree programs: 78%
Acceptance rate for education specialist degree programs:
   83%
Average GRE verbal: 375, Average GRE quantitative: 495,
   Average MAT: 41
Total 2003 enrollment: 202
Master's degree enrollment: 178
   Teacher preparation program enrollment (master's): 87
Education specialist degree enrollment: 24

FINANCIAL INFORMATION
Financial aid phone number: (334) 983-6556
Tuition, 2003-2004 academic year: Full-time in-state:
   $2,898; out-of-state: $5,796, Part-time in-state:
   $161/credit hour; out-of-state: $322/credit hour
Fees: $312, Books and supplies: $600, Miscellaneous
   expenses: $3,204
Number of other paid appointments: 3

ACADEMIC PROGRAMS
Total full-time tenured or tenure-track faculty (fall 2003):
   15, Total part-time faculty (fall 2003): 21
Areas of specialization: education administration and
   supervision, elementary teacher education, secondary
   teacher education, special education.
Professional development/partnership school(s) are used
   by students in some of the teaching programs.
During their internships, peer groups of students meet
   regularly to discuss instructional techniques in all of the
   teaching programs.
All of the students in their internships are mentored.
Courses that prepare teachers to pass the National Board of
   Professional Teaching Standards are not offered.
Teacher preparation programs: Four-year baccalaureate-
   degree program leading to initial licensure that includes
   either a major or minor in education and practice teaching. Master's program preparing college graduates for
   initial licensure; includes practice teaching. Alternative
   program for college graduates leading to provisional
   licensure.
The education program is currently accredited by the
   National Council for Accreditation of Teacher Education.

Troy State University– Main Campus

■ 206 McCartha Hall, Troy, AL 36082
■ **Website:** http://www.troyst.edu
■ **Public**
■ **Degrees offered:** master's, education specialist

ADMISSIONS
Admissions phone number: (334) 670-3179
Admissions email address: *admit@trojan.troyst.edu*
Application website:
   http://www.troyst.edu/graduateschool/application.html

Application fee: $40

Test of English as Foreign Language (TOEFL) is required for international students.

Minimum TOEFL score required for paper test: 525

Minimum TOEFL score required for computer test: 197

Fall 2003

Total 2003 enrollment: 928

Master's degree enrollment: 684

Teacher preparation program enrollment (master's): 319

Education specialist degree enrollment: 244

FINANCIAL INFORMATION

Financial aid phone number: (334) 670-3186

Tuition, 2003-2004 academic year: Full-time in-state: **$161/credit hour**; out-of-state: **$322/credit hour**, Part-time in-state: **$166/credit hour**; out-of-state: **$322/credit hour**

Fees: **$13**, Room and board: **$1,120**, Books and supplies: **$220**

Number of fellowships awarded to graduate students during the 2003-2004 academic year: 0

Number of teaching assistant positions: 2

Number of research assistant positions: 0

Number of other paid appointments: 0

ACADEMIC PROGRAMS

Total full-time tenured or tenure-track faculty (fall 2003): 29, Total part-time faculty (fall 2003): 35

Areas of specialization: education administration and supervision, educational psychology, elementary teacher education, secondary teacher education.

Professional development/partnership school(s) are used by students in all of the teaching programs.

During their internships, peer groups of students meet regularly to discuss instructional techniques in some of the teaching programs.

Some of the students in their internships are mentored.

Courses that prepare teachers to pass the National Board of Professional Teaching Standards are not offered.

Teacher preparation programs: Four-year baccalaureate-degree program leading to initial licensure that includes either a major or minor in education and practice teaching. Five-year program leading to initial licensure that results in a baccalaureate degree (with a major or minor in education) plus graduate credit and includes practice teaching. Master's program preparing college graduates for initial licensure; includes practice teaching. Alternative program for college graduates leading to provisional licensure.

The education program is currently accredited by the National Council for Accreditation of Teacher Education.

Troy State University–Montgomery

■ PO Drawer 4419, Montgomery, AL 36103
■ Website: http://www.tsum.edu

■ Public
■ **Degrees offered:** bachelor's, master's, education specialist

ADMISSIONS

Admissions phone number: (334) 241-5425

Admissions email address: *m01admissions@troyst.edu*

Application website: *http://www.tsum.edu*

Application fee: **$20**

Fall 2005 application deadline: **rolling**

Fall 2003

Total 2003 enrollment: 218

Master's degree enrollment: 209

Teacher preparation program enrollment (master's): 50

Education specialist degree enrollment: 9

FINANCIAL INFORMATION

Financial aid phone number: (334) 241-9520

Tuition, 2003-2004 academic year: Full-time in-state: **$161/credit hour**; out-of-state: **$322/credit hour**, Part-time in-state: **$161/credit hour**; out-of-state: **$322/credit hour**

Fees: **$70**

ACADEMIC PROGRAMS

Total full-time tenured or tenure-track faculty (fall 2003): 8

Areas of specialization: education administration and supervision, elementary teacher education, student counseling and personnel services.

Courses that prepare teachers to pass the National Board of Professional Teaching Standards are not offered.

University of Alabama–Birmingham

■ 1530 Third Avenue S, EB 217, Birmingham, AL 35294-1250
■ **Website:** http://www.uab.edu/graduate
■ Public
■ **Degrees offered:** bachelor's, master's, education specialist, Ph.D., Ed.D.

ADMISSIONS

Admissions phone number: (205) 934-8227

Admissions email address: *gradschool@uab.edu*

Application website: *http://www.uab.edu/graduate/apply/frame.htm*

Application fee: **$60**

Fall 2005 application deadline: 7/2

Test requirements: **GRE or MAT**

Test of English as Foreign Language (TOEFL) is required for international students.

Minimum TOEFL score required for paper test: 550

Minimum TOEFL score required for computer test: 220

Fall 2003

Acceptance rate for master's degree programs: 63%

Acceptance rate for education specialist degree programs: 58%

Acceptance rate for doctoral programs: 45%

Average GRE verbal: 461, Average GRE quantitative: 526, Average GRE analytical: 576

Total 2003 enrollment: 948

Master's degree enrollment: 755

Teacher preparation program enrollment (master's): 575

Education specialist degree enrollment: 125

Doctoral degree enrollment: 68

FINANCIAL INFORMATION

Financial aid phone number: (205) 934-8223

Tuition, 2003-2004 academic year: Full-time in-state: **$3,384**; out-of-state: **$8,472**, Part-time in-state: **$141/credit hour**; out-of-state: **$353/credit hour**

Fees: **$662**, Room and board: **$8,823**, Books and supplies: **$900**, Miscellaneous expenses: **$3,375**

Number of fellowships awarded to graduate students during the 2003-2004 academic year: 3

ACADEMIC PROGRAMS

Total full-time tenured or tenure-track faculty (fall 2003): 42, Total part-time faculty (fall 2003): 50

Areas of specialization: curriculum and instruction, education administration and supervision, educational psychology, elementary teacher education, higher education administration, secondary teacher education, special education, student counseling and personnel services.

Professional development/partnership school(s) are used by students in some of the teaching programs.

During their internships, peer groups of students meet regularly to discuss instructional techniques in some of the teaching programs.

All of the students in their internships are mentored.

Courses that prepare teachers to pass the National Board of Professional Teaching Standards are offered.

Teacher preparation programs: Four-year baccalaureate-degree program leading to initial licensure that includes either a major or minor in education and practice teaching. Five-year program leading to initial licensure that results in a baccalaureate degree (with a major or minor in education) plus a master's degree and includes practice teaching. Master's program preparing college graduates for initial licensure; includes practice teaching.

The education program is currently accredited by the National Council for Accreditation of Teacher Education.

University of Alabama– Tuscaloosa

- Box 870231, Tuscaloosa, AL 35487-0231
- **Website:** http://graduate.ua.edu
- Public
- **Degrees offered:** bachelor's, master's, education specialist, Ph.D., Ed.D.

ADMISSIONS

Admissions phone number: (205) 348-5921

Admissions email address: *usgradapply@aalan.ua.edu*

Application website: *http://graduate.ua.edu/application/index.html*

Application fee: **$25**

Fall 2005 application deadline: **rolling**

Test requirements: **GRE or MAT**

Test of English as Foreign Language (TOEFL) is required for international students.

Minimum TOEFL score required for paper test: **550**

Minimum TOEFL score required for computer test: **213**

Fall 2003

Acceptance rate for master's degree programs: 55%

Acceptance rate for education specialist degree programs: 61%

Acceptance rate for doctoral programs: 42%

Average GRE verbal: 459, Average GRE quantitative: 548, Average GRE analytical: 546, Average MAT: 52

Total 2003 enrollment: 897

Master's degree enrollment: 407

Teacher preparation program enrollment (master's): 261

Education specialist degree enrollment: 164

Doctoral degree enrollment: 326

FINANCIAL INFORMATION

Financial aid phone number: (205) 348-6756

Tuition, 2003-2004 academic year: Full-time in-state: **$4,134**; out-of-state: **$11,294**

Room and board: **$4,456**, Books and supplies: **$1,116**, Miscellaneous expenses: **$1,690**

Number of fellowships awarded to graduate students during the 2003-2004 academic year: 1

Number of teaching assistant positions: 38

Number of research assistant positions: 67

Number of other paid appointments: 7

ACADEMIC PROGRAMS

Total full-time tenured or tenure-track faculty (fall 2003): 66, Total part-time faculty (fall 2003): 43

Areas of specialization: curriculum and instruction, education administration and supervision, education policy, educational psychology, elementary teacher education, higher education administration, secondary teacher education, special education, student counseling and personnel services.

Professional development/partnership school(s) are used by students in some of the teaching programs.

During their internships, peer groups of students meet regularly to discuss instructional techniques in some of the teaching programs.

All of the students in their internships are mentored.

Courses that prepare teachers to pass the National Board of Professional Teaching Standards are offered.

Teacher preparation programs: Four-year baccalaureate-degree program leading to initial licensure that includes either a major or minor in education and practice teaching. Five-year program leading to initial licensure that results in a baccalaureate degree (with a major or minor in education) plus graduate credit and includes practice teaching. Five-year program leading to initial licensure that results in a baccalaureate degree (with a major or minor in education) plus a master's degree and includes practice teaching. Master's program preparing college graduates for initial licensure; includes practice teaching. Alternative program for college graduates leading to provisional licensure.

The education program is currently accredited by the National Council for Accreditation of Teacher Education.

University of Mobile

■ P.O. Box 13220, Mobile, AL 36663-0220
■ Website: http://www.umobile.edu
■ Private
■ Degrees offered: bachelor's, master's

ADMISSIONS

Admissions phone number: (251) 442-2270
Admissions email address: kayebrown@free.umobile.edu
Application fee: $40
Fall 2005 application deadline: rolling
Test requirements: GRE
Test of English as Foreign Language (TOEFL) is required for international students.
Minimum TOEFL score required for paper test: 550
Minimum TOEFL score required for computer test: 175

Fall 2003
Total 2003 enrollment: 59
Master's degree enrollment: 59
    Teacher preparation program enrollment (master's): 59

FINANCIAL INFORMATION

Financial aid phone number: (251) 442-2370
Tuition, 2003-2004 academic year: Full-time: $227/credit hour; Part-time: $227/credit hour
Fees: $200, Room and board: $5,440, Books and supplies: $500

ACADEMIC PROGRAMS

Total full-time tenured or tenure-track faculty (fall 2003): 11, Total part-time faculty (fall 2003): 7
Areas of specialization: elementary teacher education, secondary teacher education.
Professional development/partnership school(s) are used by students in all of the teaching programs.
During their internships, peer groups of students meet regularly to discuss instructional techniques in all of the teaching programs.
All of the students in their internships are mentored.
Courses that prepare teachers to pass the National Board of Professional Teaching Standards are not offered.
Teacher preparation programs: Four-year baccalaureate-degree program leading to initial licensure that includes either a major or minor in education and practice teach-

ing. Master's program preparing college graduates for initial licensure; includes practice teaching.

University of Montevallo

■ 460 Shoshone Drive, Montevallo, AL 35115
■ Website: http://www.montevallo.edu/grad/
■ Public
■ Degrees offered: bachelor's, master's, education specialist

ADMISSIONS

Admissions phone number: (205) 665-6350
Admissions email address: wyattce@montevallo.edu
Application website: http://www.montevallo.edu/grad/current_students_apps.shtm
Application fee: $25
Fall 2005 application deadline: 7/15
Test of English as Foreign Language (TOEFL) is required for international students.
Minimum TOEFL score required for paper test: 550
Minimum TOEFL score required for computer test: 213

Fall 2003
Total 2003 enrollment: 401

FINANCIAL INFORMATION

Financial aid phone number: (205) 665-6050
Tuition, 2003-2004 academic year: Full-time in-state: $160/credit hour; out-of-state: $155/credit hour, Part-time in-state: $160/credit hour; out-of-state: $160/credit hour
Fees: $133

ACADEMIC PROGRAMS

The education program is currently accredited by the National Council for Accreditation of Teacher Education

University of North Alabama

■ Box 5031 UNA, Florence, AL 35632-0001
■ Website: http://www.una.edu
■ Public
■ Degrees offered: bachelor's, master's, education specialist

ADMISSIONS

Admissions phone number: (256) 765-4608
Admissions email address: admissions@una.edu
Application website: http://www.applyweb.com
Application fee: $25
Fall 2005 application deadline: 8/1
Test requirements: GRE or MAT

Test of English as Foreign Language (TOEFL) is required for international students.
Minimum TOEFL score required for paper test: 550
Minimum TOEFL score required for computer test: 213

Fall 2003
Acceptance rate for master's degree programs: 83%
Acceptance rate for education specialist degree programs: 100%
Average MAT: 40
Total 2003 enrollment: 325
Master's degree enrollment: 295
   Teacher preparation program enrollment (master's): 231
Education specialist degree enrollment: 30

FINANCIAL INFORMATION
Financial aid phone number: (256) 765-4279
Tuition, 2003-2004 academic year: Full-time in-state: **$135/credit hour**; out-of-state: **$270/credit hour**, Part-time in-state: **$135/credit hour**; out-of-state: **$270/credit hour**
Fees: **$384**, Room and board: **$4,972**, Books and supplies: **$830**, Miscellaneous expenses: **$350**

ACADEMIC PROGRAMS
Total full-time tenured or tenure-track faculty (fall 2003): 28, Total part-time faculty (fall 2003): 1
Areas of specialization: education administration and supervision, elementary teacher education, secondary teacher education, special education, student counseling and personnel services, teacher education.
Professional development/partnership school(s) are used by students in some of the teaching programs.
During their internships, peer groups of students meet regularly to discuss instructional techniques in all of the teaching programs.
All of the students in their internships are mentored.
Courses that prepare teachers to pass the National Board of Professional Teaching Standards are not offered.
Teacher preparation programs: Four-year baccalaureate-degree program leading to initial licensure that includes either a major or minor in education and practice teaching. Master's program preparing college graduates for initial licensure; includes practice teaching. Alternative program for college graduates leading to provisional licensure.
The education program is currently accredited by the National Council for Accreditation of Teacher Education.

University of South Alabama

■ UCOM 3600, Mobile, AL 36688
■ **Website:** http://www.southalabama.edu/
■ **Public**

ADMISSIONS
Admissions phone number: **(251) 460-6141**
Admissions email address: *admiss@usouthal.edu*
Application website: *http://www.southalabama.edu/admissions/*
Test of English as Foreign Language (TOEFL) is required for international students.
Minimum TOEFL score required for paper test: **500**
Minimum TOEFL score required for computer test: **173**

FINANCIAL INFORMATION
Financial aid phone number: **(251) 460-6231**

ACADEMIC PROGRAMS
The education program is currently accredited by the National Council for Accreditation of Teacher Education.

University of West Alabama

■ Station 4, Livingston, AL 35470
■ **Website:** http://www.uwa.edu
■ **Public**
■ **Degrees offered:** bachelor's, master's

ADMISSIONS
Admissions phone number: **(205) 652-3647**
Admissions email address: *jbw@uwa.edu*
Application website: *http://graduate.uwa.edu*
Application fee: **$20**
Fall 2005 application deadline: **rolling**
Test requirements: **GRE or MAT**
Test of English as Foreign Language (TOEFL) is required for international students.
Minimum TOEFL score required for paper test: **550**

Fall 2003
Total 2003 enrollment: **680**
Master's degree enrollment: **680**
   Teacher preparation program enrollment (master's): **310**

FINANCIAL INFORMATION
Financial aid phone number: **(205) 652-3576**
Tuition, 2003-2004 academic year: Full-time in-state: **$170/credit hour**; out-of-state: **$340/credit hour**, Part-time in-state: **$170/credit hour**; out-of-state: **$340/credit hour**
Fees: **$120**, Room and board: **$3,009**, Books and supplies: **$700**, Miscellaneous expenses: **$1,200**
Number of teaching assistant positions: **20**
Number of other paid appointments: **34**

ACADEMIC PROGRAMS
Total full-time tenured or tenure-track faculty (fall 2003): 70, Total part-time faculty (fall 2003): 9
Areas of specialization: education administration and supervision, elementary teacher education, secondary

teacher education, special education, student counseling and personnel services.

Professional development/partnership school(s) are used by students in all of the teaching programs.

During their internships, peer groups of students meet regularly to discuss instructional techniques in none of the teaching programs.

All of the students in their internships are mentored.

Courses that prepare teachers to pass the National Board of Professional Teaching Standards are not offered.

Teacher preparation programs: Four-year baccalaureate-degree program leading to initial licensure that includes either a major or minor in education and practice teaching. Five-year program leading to initial licensure that results in a baccalaureate degree (with a major or minor in education) plus a master's degree and includes practice teaching.

The education program is currently accredited by the National Council for Accreditation of Teacher Education.

ALASKA

Alaska Pacific University

- 4101 University Drive, Anchorage, AK 99508-3051
- **Website:** http://www.alaskapacific.edu
- **Private**
- **Degrees offered:** bachelor's, master's

ADMISSIONS

Admissions phone number: **(907) 564-8248**
Admissions email address: *admissions@alaskapacific.edu*
Application fee: **$25**
Fall 2005 application deadline: **8/1**
Test requirements: **GRE or MAT**
Test of English as Foreign Language (TOEFL) is required for international students.
Minimum TOEFL score required for paper test: **550**
Minimum TOEFL score required for computer test: **213**

Fall 2003
Acceptance rate for master's degree programs: **93%**
Average GRE verbal: **530**, Average GRE quantitative: **450**, Average GRE analytical: **455**, Average MAT: **55**
Total 2003 enrollment: **18**
Master's degree enrollment: **18**
  Teacher preparation program enrollment (master's): **18**

FINANCIAL INFORMATION

Financial aid phone number: **(907) 564-8342**
Tuition, 2003-2004 academic year: Full-time: **$475/credit hour**; Part-time: **$475/credit hour**
Fees: **$110**, Room and board: **$6,300**, Books and supplies: **$900**, Miscellaneous expenses: **$1,400**

ACADEMIC PROGRAMS

Total full-time tenured or tenure-track faculty (fall 2003): **4**
  Total part-time faculty (fall 2003): **4**
Areas of specialization: curriculum and instruction, educational psychology, elementary teacher education.
Professional development/partnership school(s) are used by students in some of the teaching programs.

During their internships, peer groups of students meet regularly to discuss instructional techniques in all of the teaching programs.
All of the students in their internships are mentored.
Courses that prepare teachers to pass the National Board of Professional Teaching Standards are not offered.
Teacher preparation programs: Four-year baccalaureate-degree program leading to initial licensure that includes either a major or minor in education and practice teaching. Master's program preparing college graduates for initial licensure; includes practice teaching.
The education program is currently accredited by the National Council for Accreditation of Teacher Education.

LICENSING TEST

Pass rate on state's teacher licensing test for 2002-2003: **100%**
State average pass rate: **99%**

University of Alaska–Anchorage

- 3211 Providence Drive, Anchorage, AK 99508-8211
- **Website:** http://www.uaa.alaska.edu/
- **Public**

LICENSING TEST

Pass rate on state's teacher licensing test for 2002-2003: **99%**
State average pass rate: **99%**

University of Alaska–Fairbanks

- PO Box 756480, Fairbanks, AK 99775-6480
- **Website:** http://www.uaf.edu
- **Public**
- **Degrees offered:** bachelor's, master's

ADMISSIONS

Admissions phone number: **(907) 474-7500**
Admissions email address: *admissions@uaf.edu*
Application website:
   http://www.uaf.edu/admissions/apply/index.html
Application fee: **$50**
Fall 2005 application deadline: **8/1**
Test requirements: **GRE**
Test of English as Foreign Language (TOEFL) is required
   for international students.
Minimum TOEFL score required for paper test: **550**
Minimum TOEFL score required for computer test: **213**

Fall 2003

Acceptance rate for master's degree programs: **71%**
Average GRE verbal: **534**, Average GRE quantitative: **512**,
   Average GRE analytical: **577**
Total 2003 enrollment: **126**
Master's degree enrollment: **126**
   Teacher preparation program enrollment (master's): **98**

FINANCIAL INFORMATION

Financial aid phone number: **(907) 474-7256**
Tuition, 2003-2004 academic year: Full-time in-state:
   $202/credit hour; out-of-state: **$393/credit hour**, Part-
   time in-state: **$202/credit hour**; out-of-state: **$393/credit
   hour**
Fees: **$970**, Room and board: **$5,130**, Books and supplies:
   $700, Miscellaneous expenses: **$300**
Number of fellowships awarded to graduate students dur-
   ing the 2003-2004 academic year: **0**
Number of teaching assistant positions: **5**
Number of research assistant positions: **11**
Number of other paid appointments: **0**

ACADEMIC PROGRAMS

Total full-time tenured or tenure-track faculty (fall 2003):
   23, Total part-time faculty (fall 2003): **5**
Areas of specialization: curriculum and instruction, education administration and supervision, education policy,
   elementary teacher education, secondary teacher education, special education, student counseling and personnel services.
Professional development/partnership school(s) are used
   by students in all of the teaching programs.
During their internships, peer groups of students meet
   regularly to discuss instructional techniques in all of the
   teaching programs.
All of the students in their internships are mentored.
Courses that prepare teachers to pass the National Board of
   Professional Teaching Standards are not offered.
Teacher preparation programs: Four-year baccalaureate-
   degree program leading to initial licensure that includes
   either a major or minor in education and practice teaching.

LICENSING TEST

Pass rate on state's teacher licensing test for 2002-2003:
   100%
State average pass rate: **99%**

University of Alaska–Southeast

- **11120 Glacier Highway, Juneau, AK 99801**
- **Website:** http://www.uas.alaska.edu/education
- **Public**
- **Degrees offered:** bachelor's, master's

ADMISSIONS

Admissions phone number: **(907) 465-8585**
Admissions email address: *bill.stenberg@uas.alaska.edu*
Application website: *http://www.uas.alaska.edu/forms/
   documents/graduate.pdf*
Application fee: **$40**
Fall 2005 application deadline: **3/1**
Test of English as Foreign Language (TOEFL) is required
   for international students.
Minimum TOEFL score required for paper test: **550**
Minimum TOEFL score required for computer test: **213**

Fall 2003

Acceptance rate for master's degree programs: **81%**
Total 2003 enrollment: **99**
Master's degree enrollment: **99**
   Teacher preparation program enrollment (master's): **99**

FINANCIAL INFORMATION

Financial aid phone number: **(907) 465-6255**
Tuition, 2003-2004 academic year: Full-time in-state:
   $3,636; out-of-state: **$7,074**
Fees: **$383**, Room and board: **$5,930**, Books and supplies:
   $310, Miscellaneous expenses: **$1,232**

ACADEMIC PROGRAMS

Total full-time tenured or tenure-track faculty (fall 2003): **8**
   Total part-time faculty (fall 2003): **45**
Areas of specialization: curriculum and instruction, educa-
   tional psychology, elementary teacher education, second-
   ary teacher education, special education.
Professional development/partnership school(s) are used
   by students in all of the teaching programs.
During their internships, peer groups of students meet
   regularly to discuss instructional techniques in all of the
   teaching programs.
All of the students in their internships are mentored.
Courses that prepare teachers to pass the National Board of
   Professional Teaching Standards are not offered.
Teacher preparation programs: Four-year baccalaureate-
   degree program leading to initial licensure that includes
   either a major or minor in education and practice teaching. Master's program preparing college graduates for
   initial licensure; includes practice teaching.

LICENSING TEST

Pass rate on state's teacher licensing test for 2002-2003:
   100%
State average pass rate: **99%**

ARIZONA

Arizona State University—Main Campus

- Box 870211, Tempe, AZ 85287-0211
- **Website:** http://www.asu.edu/graduate
- Public
- **Degrees offered:** bachelor's, master's, Ph.D., Ed.D.
- **Overall rank in the 2005 U.S. News education schools with doctoral programs:** 22
- **Overall rank in the 2005 U.S. News education school specialty rankings:** administration/supervision: 22, counseling/personnel: 11, curriculum/instruction: 19, education policy: 15, educational psychology: 19, elementary education: 17, special education: 17

ADMISSIONS
Admissions phone number: **(480) 965-6113**
Admissions email address: *asugrad@asu.edu*
Application website: *http://www.asu.edu/graduate/forms/*
Application fee: **$50**
Fall 2005 application deadline: **rolling**
Test requirements: **GRE or MAT**
Test of English as Foreign Language (TOEFL) is required for international students.
Minimum TOEFL score required for paper test: **550**
Minimum TOEFL score required for computer test: **213**

Fall 2003
Acceptance rate for master's degree programs: **47%**
Acceptance rate for doctoral programs: **22%**
Average GRE verbal: **573**, Average GRE quantitative: **591**, Average GRE analytical: **598**
Total 2003 enrollment: **1,259**
Master's degree enrollment: **697**
 Teacher preparation program enrollment (master's): **430**
Doctoral degree enrollment: **562**

FINANCIAL INFORMATION
Financial aid phone number: **(480) 965-3521**

Tuition, 2003-2004 academic year: Full-time in-state: **$3,708**; out-of-state: **$12,228**, Part-time in-state: **$194/credit hour**; out-of-state: **$510/credit hour**
Fees: **$88**, Room and board: **$7,219**, Books and supplies: **$1,089**, Miscellaneous expenses: **$2,328**
Number of fellowships awarded to graduate students during the 2003-2004 academic year: **34**
Number of teaching assistant positions: **86**
Number of research assistant positions: **102**
Number of other paid appointments: **30**

ACADEMIC PROGRAMS
Total full-time tenured or tenure-track faculty (fall 2003): **88**
 Total part-time faculty (fall 2003): **98**
Areas of specialization: curriculum and instruction, education administration and supervision, education policy, educational psychology, elementary teacher education, higher education administration, secondary teacher education, special education, student counseling and personnel services.
Professional development/partnership school(s) are used by students in all of the teaching programs.
During their internships, peer groups of students meet regularly to discuss instructional techniques in all of the teaching programs.
All of the students in their internships are mentored.
Courses that prepare teachers to pass the National Board of Professional Teaching Standards are offered.
Teacher preparation programs: Four-year baccalaureate-degree program leading to initial licensure that includes either a major or minor in education and practice teaching. Master's program preparing college graduates for initial licensure; includes practice teaching.

LICENSING TEST
Pass rate on state's teacher licensing test for 2002-2003: **95%**
State average pass rate: **95%**

Arizona State University–West

- PO Box 37100, Phoenix, AZ 85069-7100
- Website:
  http://westcgi.west.asu.edu/acadaffairs/gradstudies/
- Public
- Degrees offered: bachelor's, master's

ADMISSIONS

Admissions phone number: (602) 543-4567
Admissions email address: *margaret.williams@asu.edu*
Application website:
  http://westcgi.west.asu.edu/acadaffairs/gradstudies/
Application fee: $50
Fall 2005 application deadline: rolling
Test of English as Foreign Language (TOEFL) is required
  for international students.
Minimum TOEFL score required for paper test: 500
Minimum TOEFL score required for computer test: 173

Fall 2003
Acceptance rate for master's degree programs: 69%
Total 2003 enrollment: 207
Master's degree enrollment: 207
   Teacher preparation program enrollment (master's): 107

FINANCIAL INFORMATION

Financial aid phone number: (602) 543-8176
Tuition, 2003-2004 academic year: Full-time in-state:
  $3,708; out-of-state: $12,228, Part-time in-state:
  $183/credit hour; out-of-state: $501/credit hour
Fees: $35, Room and board: $7,960, Books and supplies:
  $823, Miscellaneous expenses: $4,593
Number of fellowships awarded to graduate students dur-
  ing the 2003-2004 academic year: 0
Number of teaching assistant positions: 0
Number of research assistant positions: 3
Number of other paid appointments: 3

ACADEMIC PROGRAMS

Total full-time tenured or tenure-track faculty (fall 2003):
  34, Total part-time faculty (fall 2003): 66
Areas of specialization: education administration and
  supervision, elementary teacher education, secondary
  teacher education, special education.
Professional development/partnership school(s) are used
  by students in some of the teaching programs.
During their internships, peer groups of students meet
  regularly to discuss instructional techniques in all of the
  teaching programs.
Some of the students in their internships are mentored.
Courses that prepare teachers to pass the National Board of
  Professional Teaching Standards are not offered.

LICENSING TEST
Pass rate on state's teacher licensing test for 2002-2003: 95%
State average pass rate: 95%

Grand Canyon University

- 3300 W. Camelback Road, Phoenix, AZ 85017
- Website: http://www.grand-canyon.edu/coe/
- Private

LICENSING TEST
Pass rate on state's teacher licensing test for 2002-2003:
  94%
State average pass rate: 95%

Northern Arizona University

- College of Education, PO Box 5774, Flagstaff, AZ 86011-5774
- Website: http://www.nau.edu/gradcol/
- Public
- Degrees offered: bachelor's, master's, Ed.D.

ADMISSIONS

Admissions phone number: (928) 523-6728
Admissions email address: *Graduate.College@nau.edu*
Application website: *http://www.nau.edu/gradcol/*
  appoptions.htm
Application fee: $45
Test requirements: GRE or MAT
Test of English as Foreign Language (TOEFL) is required
  for international students.
Minimum TOEFL score required for paper test: 550
Minimum TOEFL score required for computer test: 213

Fall 2003
Average GRE verbal: 453, Average GRE quantitative: 472,
  Average GRE analytical: 502
Total 2003 enrollment: 3,188
Master's degree enrollment: 2,995
   Teacher preparation program enrollment (master's):
   1,388
Doctoral degree enrollment: 193

FINANCIAL INFORMATION
Financial aid phone number: (928) 523-4951
Tuition, 2003-2004 academic year: Full-time in-state:
  $3,508; out-of-state: $12,028, Part-time in-state:
  $183/credit hour; out-of-state: $501/credit hour
Fees: $120, Room and board: $7,374, Books and supplies:
  $750, Miscellaneous expenses: $3,212

ACADEMIC PROGRAMS

Total full-time tenured or tenure-track faculty (fall 2003): 71, Total part-time faculty (fall 2003): 409

Areas of specialization: curriculum and instruction, education administration and supervision, educational psychology, elementary teacher education, higher education administration, secondary teacher education, special education, student counseling and personnel services.

Professional development/partnership school(s) are used by students in some of the teaching programs.

During their internships, peer groups of students meet regularly to discuss instructional techniques in some of the teaching programs.

All of the students in their internships are mentored.

Courses that prepare teachers to pass the National Board of Professional Teaching Standards are not offered.

Teacher preparation programs: Four-year baccalaureate-degree program leading to initial licensure that includes either a major or minor in education and practice teaching. Master's program preparing college graduates for initial licensure; includes practice teaching. Alternative program for college graduates leading to provisional licensure.

LICENSING TEST

Pass rate on state's teacher licensing test for 2002-2003: 93%

State average pass rate: 95%

Prescott College

- 220 Grove Ave., Prescott, AZ 86301
- **Website:** http://www.prescott.edu
- **Private**
- **Degrees offered:** bachelor's, master's

ADMISSIONS

Admissions phone number: (800) 628-6364
Admissions email address: *admissions@prescott.edu*
Application website:
 http://www.applyweb.com/apply/prescott/menu.html
Application fee: **$40**
Fall 2005 application deadline: 2/15
Test of English as Foreign Language (TOEFL) is required for international students.
Minimum TOEFL score required for paper test: 550
Minimum TOEFL score required for computer test: 213

FINANCIAL INFORMATION

Financial aid phone number: (800) 628-6365

LICENSING TEST

Pass rate on state's teacher licensing test for 2002-2003: 89%

State average pass rate: 95%

University of Arizona

- **Box 210069, 1430 E. Second Street, Tucson, AZ 85721-0069**
- **Website:** http://www.ed.arizona.edu
- **Public**
- **Degrees offered:** bachelor's, master's, education specialist, Ph.D., Ed.D.
- **Overall rank in the 2005 U.S. News education schools with doctoral programs:** 61
- **Overall rank in the 2005 U.S. News education school specialty rankings:** curriculum/instruction: 21, elementary education: 23, higher education administration: 15, special education: 19

ADMISSIONS

Admissions phone number: (520) 621-3132
Admissions email address:
 gradadm@lorax.admin.arizona.edu
Application website:
 http://www.ed.arizona.edu/html/grad.html
Application fee: **$50**
Fall 2005 application deadline: 2/11
Test requirements: **GRE or MAT**
Test of English as Foreign Language (TOEFL) is required for international students.
Minimum TOEFL score required for paper test: 550
Minimum TOEFL score required for computer test: 213

Fall 2003
Acceptance rate for master's degree programs: 73%
Acceptance rate for education specialist degree programs: 70%
Acceptance rate for doctoral programs: 70%
Average GRE verbal: 486, Average GRE quantitative: 575, Average GRE analytical: 591, Average MAT: 55
Total 2003 enrollment: 933
Master's degree enrollment: 484
 Teacher preparation program enrollment (master's): 297
Education specialist degree enrollment: 32
Doctoral degree enrollment: 417

FINANCIAL INFORMATION

Financial aid phone number: (520) 621-1858
Tuition, 2003-2004 academic year: Full-time in-state: **$3,854**; out-of-state: **$12,624**, Part-time in-state: **$196/credit hour**; out-of-state: **$326/credit hour**
Fees: **$94**, Room and board: **$6,810**, Books and supplies: **$750**, Miscellaneous expenses: **$2,330**
Number of fellowships awarded to graduate students during the 2003-2004 academic year: 297
Number of teaching assistant positions: 20
Number of research assistant positions: 20
Number of other paid appointments: 13

ACADEMIC PROGRAMS

Total full-time tenured or tenure-track faculty (fall 2003): 64, Total part-time faculty (fall 2003): 53

Areas of specialization: curriculum and instruction, education administration and supervision, education policy, educational psychology, elementary teacher education, higher education administration, secondary teacher education, special education, student counseling and personnel services.

Professional development/partnership school(s) are used by students in all of the teaching programs.

During their internships, peer groups of students meet regularly to discuss instructional techniques in some of the teaching programs.

Courses that prepare teachers to pass the National Board of Professional Teaching Standards are offered.

Teacher preparation programs: Four-year baccalaureate-degree program leading to initial licensure that includes either a major or minor in education and practice teaching. Master's program preparing college graduates for initial licensure; includes practice teaching.

LICENSING TEST

Pass rate on state's teacher licensing test for 2002-2003: **96%**
State average pass rate: **95%**

ARKANSAS

Arkansas State University

- PO Box 10, State University, AR 72467
- Website: http://www.astate.edu/
- Public

LICENSING TEST

Pass rate on state's teacher licensing test for 2002-2003: 100%

State average pass rate: 100%

Arkansas Tech University

- Administration Building #200, Russellville, AR 72801-2222
- Website: http://graduate.atu.edu/
- Public
- Degrees offered: bachelor's, master's, education specialist

ADMISSIONS

Admissions phone number: (479) 968-0398
Admissions email address: *anna.schumacher@mail.atu.edu*
Application website: *http://graduate.atu.edu/online_application_1.htm*
Application fee: $0
Fall 2005 application deadline: rolling
Test requirements: GRE or MAT
Minimum TOEFL score required for paper test: 500
Minimum TOEFL score required for computer test: 173

Fall 2003
Total 2003 enrollment: 223
Master's degree enrollment: 223
   Teacher preparation program enrollment (master's): 135
Education specialist degree enrollment: 0

FINANCIAL INFORMATION

Financial aid phone number: (479) 968-0399
Tuition, 2003-2004 academic year: Full-time in-state: $1,314; out-of-state: $2,628, Part-time in-state: $146/credit hour; out-of-state: $292/credit hour
Fees: $97, Room and board: $3,725, Books and supplies: $990, Miscellaneous expenses: $2,100
Number of teaching assistant positions: 3
Number of research assistant positions: 5

ACADEMIC PROGRAMS

Total full-time tenured or tenure-track faculty (fall 2003): 20, Total part-time faculty (fall 2003): 48
Areas of specialization: curriculum and instruction, education administration and supervision, elementary teacher education, higher education administration, secondary teacher education, special education, student counseling and personnel services.
Professional development/partnership school(s) are used by students in some of the teaching programs.
During their internships, peer groups of students meet regularly to discuss instructional techniques in some of the teaching programs.
Some of the students in their internships are mentored.
Courses that prepare teachers to pass the National Board of Professional Teaching Standards are not offered.
The education program is currently accredited by the National Council for Accreditation of Teacher Education.

LICENSING TEST

Pass rate on state's teacher licensing test for 2002-2003: 100%
State average pass rate: 100%

Harding University

- Box 12234, Searcy, AR 72149
- Website: http://www.harding.edu/
- Private

LICENSING TEST

Pass rate on state's teacher licensing test for 2002-2003: **100%**

State average pass rate: **100%**

Henderson State University

- **1100 Henderson Street, Arkadelphia, AR 71999-0001**
- **Website:** http://www.hsu.edu/
- **Public**

LICENSING TEST

Pass rate on state's teacher licensing test for 2002-2003: **100%**

State average pass rate: **100%**

Southern Arkansas University

- **P.O. Box 9302, Magnolia, AR 71754-9302**
- **Website:** http://www.saumag.edu
- **Public**
- **Degrees offered:** master's

ADMISSIONS

Admissions phone number: **(870) 235-4055**

Admissions email address: *jrjones@saumag.edu*

Application website: *http://www.saumag.edu*

Application fee: **$0**

Fall 2005 application deadline: **8/5**

Test of English as Foreign Language (TOEFL) is required for international students.

Minimum TOEFL score required for paper test: **500**

Minimum TOEFL score required for computer test: **173**

Fall 2003

Total 2003 enrollment: **194**

Master's degree enrollment: **194**

   Teacher preparation program enrollment (master's): **29**

FINANCIAL INFORMATION

Financial aid phone number: **(870) 235-4026**

Tuition, 2003-2004 academic year: Full-time in-state: **$155/credit hour**; out-of-state: **$220/credit hour**, Part-time in-state: **$155/credit hour**; out-of-state: **$220/credit hour**

Fees: **$77**, Room and board: **$1,700**, Books and supplies: **$50**

Number of fellowships awarded to graduate students during the 2003-2004 academic year: **22**

Number of teaching assistant positions: **0**

Number of research assistant positions: **0**

Number of other paid appointments: **0**

ACADEMIC PROGRAMS

Total full-time tenured or tenure-track faculty (fall 2003): **39**

Areas of specialization: education administration and supervision, elementary teacher education, secondary teacher education, student counseling and personnel services.

Professional development/partnership school(s) are used by students in all of the teaching programs.

During their internships, peer groups of students meet regularly to discuss instructional techniques in all of the teaching programs.

All of the students in their internships are mentored.

Courses that prepare teachers to pass the National Board of Professional Teaching Standards are not offered.

Teacher preparation programs: Four-year baccalaureate-degree program leading to initial licensure that includes either a major or minor in education and practice teaching. Master's program preparing college graduates for initial licensure; includes practice teaching. Alternative program for college graduates leading to provisional licensure.

The education program is currently accredited by the National Council for Accreditation of Teacher Education.

LICENSING TEST

Pass rate on state's teacher licensing test for 2002-2003: **100%**

State average pass rate: **100%**

University of Arkansas– Fayetteville

- **324 Graduate Education Building, Fayetteville, AR 72701**
- **Website:** http://www.uark.edu
- **Public**
- **Degrees offered:** bachelor's, master's, education specialist, Ph.D., Ed.D.

ADMISSIONS

Admissions phone number: **(479) 575-4401**

Admissions email address: *gradinfo@cavern.uark.edu*

Application website: *http://www.uark.edu/depts/gradinfo/*

Application fee: **$40**

Fall 2005 application deadline: **8/1**

Test requirements: **GRE or MAT**

Test of English as Foreign Language (TOEFL) is required for international students.

Minimum TOEFL score required for paper test: **550**

Minimum TOEFL score required for computer test: **213**

Fall 2003

Acceptance rate for master's degree programs: **85%**

Acceptance rate for education specialist degree programs: **75%**

Acceptance rate for doctoral programs: **89%**

Total 2003 enrollment: **659**

Master's degree enrollment: 456
   Teacher preparation program enrollment (master's): 378
Education specialist degree enrollment: 7
Doctoral degree enrollment: 196

FINANCIAL INFORMATION
Financial aid phone number: **(479) 575-3806**
Tuition, 2003-2004 academic year: Full-time in-state: **$224/credit hour**; out-of-state: **$530/credit hour**, Part-time in-state: **$224/credit hour**; out-of-state: **$530/credit hour**
Fees: **$29/credit hour**, Room and board: **$5,087**, Books and supplies: **$851**, Miscellaneous expenses: **$1,171**
Number of fellowships awarded to graduate students during the 2003-2004 academic year: 21
Number of teaching assistant positions: 19
Number of research assistant positions: 13
Number of other paid appointments: 66

ACADEMIC PROGRAMS
Total full-time tenured or tenure-track faculty (fall 2003): 85, Total part-time faculty (fall 2003): 6
Areas of specialization: curriculum and instruction, education administration and supervision, education policy, educational psychology, elementary teacher education, higher education administration, secondary teacher education, special education, student counseling and personnel services.
Professional development/partnership school(s) are used by students in all of the teaching programs.
During their internships, peer groups of students meet regularly to discuss instructional techniques in all of the teaching programs.
All of the students in their internships are mentored.
Courses that prepare teachers to pass the National Board of Professional Teaching Standards are offered.
Teacher preparation programs: Five-year program leading to initial licensure that results in a baccalaureate degree (with a major or minor in education) plus a master's degree and includes practice teaching. Master's program preparing college graduates for initial licensure; includes practice teaching.
The education program is currently accredited by the National Council for Accreditation of Teacher Education.

LICENSING TEST
Pass rate on state's teacher licensing test for 2002-2003: **100%**
State average pass rate: **100%**

University of Arkansas– Little Rock

■ **2801 S. University Avenue, Little Rock, AR 72204**
■ **Website:**
   http://www.ualr.edu/%7Egraddept/gsprodegs.html
■ **Public**

ADMISSIONS
Admissions phone number: **(501) 569-3127**
Admissions email address: *gradinfo@ualr.edu*
Application website:
   http://www.ualr.edu/%7Egraddept/forms.html

FINANCIAL INFORMATION
Financial aid phone number: **(501) 569-3450**

LICENSING TEST
Pass rate on state's teacher licensing test for 2002-2003: **100%**
State average pass rate: **100%**

University of Arkansas– Monticello

■ **UAM Box 3478, Monticello, AR 71656**
■ **Website:** http://www.uamont.edu/education/
■ **Public**

LICENSING TEST
Pass rate on state's teacher licensing test for 2002-2003: **100%**
State average pass rate: **100%**

University of Central Arkansas

■ **201 Donaghey Avenue, Conway, AR 72035**
■ **Website:** http://www.uca.edu/academicandresearch/ graduatestudies
■ **Public**
■ **Degrees offered:** bachelor's, master's, education specialist, Ph.D.

ADMISSIONS
Admissions phone number: **(501) 450-3124**
Admissions email address: *elainem@uca.edu*
Application fee: **$25**
Fall 2005 application deadline: **3/1**
Test of English as Foreign Language (TOEFL) is required for international students.
Minimum TOEFL score required for paper test: **550**
Minimum TOEFL score required for computer test: **213**

FINANCIAL INFORMATION
Financial aid phone number: **(501) 450-3140**
Tuition, 2003-2004 academic year: Full-time in-state: **$3,770**; out-of-state: **$7,082**, Part-time in-state: **$145/credit hour**; out-of-state: **$283/credit hour**
Fees: **$735**, Room and board: **$3,796**, Books and supplies: **$1,000**, Miscellaneous expenses: **$40**

ACADEMIC PROGRAMS

Areas of specialization: curriculum and instruction, education administration and supervision, educational psychology, secondary teacher education, special education, student counseling and personnel services, teacher education.

Professional development/partnership school(s) are used by students in all of the teaching programs.

During their internships, peer groups of students meet regularly to discuss instructional techniques in some of the teaching programs.

All of the students in their internships are mentored.

Courses that prepare teachers to pass the National Board of Professional Teaching Standards are offered.

Teacher preparation programs: Four-year baccalaureate-degree program leading to initial licensure that includes either a major or minor in education and practice teaching. Master's program preparing college graduates for initial licensure; includes practice teaching.

The education program is currently accredited by the National Council for Accreditation of Teacher Education.

LICENSING TEST

Pass rate on state's teacher licensing test for 2002-2003: **100%**

State average pass rate: **100%**

CALIFORNIA

Alliant International University—San Diego

■ 10455 Pomerado Road, San Diego, CA 92131
■ **Website:** http://www.alliant.edu/
■ **Private**
■ **Degrees offered:** master's, Ed.D.

ADMISSIONS
Admissions phone number: **(866) 825-5426**
Admissions email address: *admissions@alliant.edu*
Application website: *http://www.alliant.edu/apply/*
Application fee: **$50**
Fall 2005 application deadline: **6/1**
Test requirements: **None**
Test of English as Foreign Language (TOEFL) is required for international students.
Minimum TOEFL score required for paper test: **550**
Minimum TOEFL score required for computer test: **229**

Fall 2003
Acceptance rate for master's degree programs: **64%**
Acceptance rate for doctoral programs: **41%**
Total 2003 enrollment: **349**
Master's degree enrollment: **210**
    Teacher preparation program enrollment (master's): **68**
Doctoral degree enrollment: **139**

FINANCIAL INFORMATION
Financial aid phone number: **(858) 635-4559**
Tuition, 2003-2004 academic year: Full-time: **$380/credit hour**; Part-time: **$380/credit hour**
Fees: **$240**, Room and board: **$11,440**, Books and supplies: **$1,500**, Miscellaneous expenses: **$4,300**

Number of fellowships awarded to graduate students during the 2003-2004 academic year: **1**
Number of teaching assistant positions: **6**
Number of research assistant positions: **2**
Number of other paid appointments: **2**

ACADEMIC PROGRAMS
Total full-time tenured or tenure-track faculty (fall 2003): **17**, Total part-time faculty (fall 2003): **81**
Areas of specialization: education administration and supervision, educational psychology, elementary teacher education, higher education administration, secondary teacher education, student counseling and personnel services.
Professional development/partnership school(s) are used by students in all of the teaching programs.
During their internships, peer groups of students meet regularly to discuss instructional techniques in all of the teaching programs.
All of the students in their internships are mentored.
Courses that prepare teachers to pass the National Board of Professional Teaching Standards are offered.
Teacher preparation programs: Master's degree in education, including internship/practice teaching and preparation for initial licensure.

Azusa Pacific University

■ PO Box 7000, Azusa, CA 91702
■ **Website:** http://www.apu.edu/educabs/?
■ **Private**

LICENSING TEST
Pass rate on state's teacher licensing test for 2002-2003: **100%**
State average pass rate: **98%**

Bethany College of the Assemblies of God

■ 800 Bethany Drive, Scotts Valley, CA 95066
■ **Website:** http://www.bethany.edu
■ **Private**
■ **Degrees offered:** bachelor's, master's

ADMISSIONS

Admissions phone number: **(831) 438-3800**
Admissions email address: *info@bethany.edu*
Application fee: **$35**
Fall 2005 application deadline: **rolling**
Test requirements: **GRE**
Test of English as Foreign Language (TOEFL) is required
    for international students.
Minimum TOEFL score required for paper test: **500**

Fall 2003
Acceptance rate for master's degree programs: **73%**
Total 2003 enrollment: **63**
Master's degree enrollment: **63**
    Teacher preparation program enrollment (master's): **63**

FINANCIAL INFORMATION

Financial aid phone number: **(831) 438-3800**
Tuition, 2003-2004 academic year: Full-time: **$360/credit
    hour; Part-time $360/credit hour**
Fees: **$435**, Room and board: **$5,380**, Books and supplies:
    $1,224, Miscellaneous expenses: **$1,872**
Number of fellowships awarded to graduate students dur-
    ing the 2003-2004 academic year: **0**
Number of teaching assistant positions: **0**
Number of research assistant positions: **0**
Number of other paid appointments: **0**

ACADEMIC PROGRAMS

Total full-time tenured or tenure-track faculty (fall 2003): **4**
    Total part-time faculty (fall 2003): **3**
Areas of specialization: curriculum and instruction, education
    administration and supervision, educational psychology,
    elementary teacher education, secondary teacher education.
Professional development/partnership school(s) are used
    by students in all of the teaching programs.
During their internships, peer groups of students meet
    regularly to discuss instructional techniques in all of the
    teaching programs.
All of the students in their internships are mentored.
Courses that prepare teachers to pass the National Board of
    Professional Teaching Standards are not offered.
Teacher preparation programs: Master's program prepar-
    ing college graduates for initial licensure; includes prac-
    tice teaching.

LICENSING TEST

Pass rate on state's teacher licensing test for 2002-2003: **100%**
State average pass rate: **98%**

Biola University

■ 13800 Biola Avenue, La Mirada, CA 90639
■ **Website:** http://www.biola.edu
■ **Private**
■ **Degrees offered:** bachelor's, master's

ADMISSIONS

Admissions phone number: **(562) 903-4752**
Admissions email address:
    http://www.biola.edu/grad/index.cfm
Application website:
    http://www.biola.edu/grad/admissions/applications.cfm
Application fee: **$45**
Fall 2005 application deadline: **3/1**
Test of English as Foreign Language (TOEFL) is required
    for international students.
Minimum TOEFL score required for paper test: **600**
Minimum TOEFL score required for computer test: **250**

Fall 2003
Acceptance rate for master's degree programs: **86%**
Total 2003 enrollment: **237**
Master's degree enrollment: **237**
    Teacher preparation program enrollment (master's): **237**

FINANCIAL INFORMATION

Financial aid phone number: **(562) 903-4742**
Tuition, 2003-2004 academic year: Full-time: **$341/credit
    hour**; Part-time: **$341/credit hour**
Fees: **$50**, Room and board: **$6,400**, Books and supplies:
    $900, Miscellaneous expenses: **$1,476**
Number of teaching assistant positions: **8**
Number of research assistant positions: **1**

ACADEMIC PROGRAMS

Total full-time tenured or tenure-track faculty (fall 2003): **9**
    Total part-time faculty (fall 2003): **20**
Areas of specialization: curriculum and instruction, educa-
    tional psychology, elementary teacher education, secondary
    teacher education, special education, teacher education.
Professional development/partnership school(s) are used
    by students in some of the teaching programs.
During their internships, peer groups of students meet
    regularly to discuss instructional techniques in some of
    the teaching programs.
All of the students in their internships are mentored.
Courses that prepare teachers to pass the National Board of
    Professional Teaching Standards are not offered.
Teacher preparation programs: Five-year program leading
    to initial licensure that results in a baccalaureate degree
    (with a major or minor in education) plus graduate
    credit and includes practice teaching.

LICENSING TEST

Pass rate on state's teacher licensing test for 2002-2003: **100%**
State average pass rate: **98%**

California Baptist University

- 8432 Magnolia Avenue, Riverside, CA 92504
- **Website:** http://www.calbaptist.edu
- Private

ADMISSIONS
Admissions phone number: **(909) 343-4249**
Admissions email address: *gradservice@calbaptist.edu*
Application website:
   http://www.calbaptist.edu/education/msmaedapp.htm
Application fee: **$45**
Fall 2005 application deadline: **rolling**
Test of English as Foreign Language (TOEFL) is required
   for international students.
Minimum TOEFL score required for paper test: **650**
Minimum TOEFL score required for computer test: **280**

FINANCIAL INFORMATION
Financial aid phone number: **(800) 228-8877**

LICENSING TEST
Pass rate on state's teacher licensing test for 2002-2003: **98%**
State average pass rate: **98%**

California State Polytechnic University–Pomona

- 3801 W. Temple Avenue, Pomona, CA 91768-2557
- **Website:** http://www.csupomona.edu/%7Eceis/
- Public

LICENSING TEST
Pass rate on state's teacher licensing test for 2002-2003: **98%**
State average pass rate: **98%**

California State University–Bakersfield

- 9001 Stockdale Highway, Bakersfield, CA 93311
- **Website:** http://www.csub.edu/SOE/
- Public

LICENSING TEST
Pass rate on state's teacher licensing test for 2002-2003: **97%**
State average pass rate: **98%**

California State University–Chico

- 400 West First Street, Chico, CA 95929-0145
- **Website:** http://www.csuchico.edu/gisp
- Public
- **Degrees offered:** master's

ADMISSIONS
Admissions phone number: **(530) 898-6880**
Admissions email address: *grin@csuchico.edu*
Application website:
   http://www.csumentor.edu/AdmissionApp
Application fee: **$55**
Fall 2005 application deadline: **3/1**
Test requirements: **GRE or MAT**
Test of English as Foreign Language (TOEFL) is required
   for international students.
Minimum TOEFL score required for paper test: **550**
Minimum TOEFL score required for computer test: **213**

Fall 2003
Acceptance rate for master's degree programs: **83%**
Total 2003 enrollment: **119**
Master's degree enrollment: **119**
   Teacher preparation program enrollment (master's): **63**

FINANCIAL INFORMATION
Financial aid phone number: **(530) 898-6451**
Tuition, 2003-2004 academic year: Full-time in-state:
   $2,256; out-of-state: **$7,332**, Part-time in-state: **$1,308**;
   out-of-state: **$4,692**
Fees: **$750**, Room and board: **$7,245**, Books and supplies:
   $1,132, Miscellaneous expenses: **$1,803**

ACADEMIC PROGRAMS
Total full-time tenured or tenure-track faculty (fall 2003):
   27, Total part-time faculty (fall 2003): **22**
Areas of specialization: curriculum and instruction, education administration and supervision, education policy,
   educational psychology, higher education administration,
   special education, student counseling and personnel
   services, teacher education.
Professional development/partnership school(s) are used
   by students in all of the teaching programs.
During their internships, peer groups of students meet
   regularly to discuss instructional techniques in some of
   the teaching programs.
All of the students in their internships are mentored.
Courses that prepare teachers to pass the National Board of
   Professional Teaching Standards are not offered.
Teacher preparation programs: Education minor for under-
   graduate students. Alternative program for college graduates leading to provisional licensure.

LICENSING TEST

Pass rate on state's teacher licensing test for 2002-2003: 99%

State average pass rate: 98%

California State University–Dominguez Hills

■ 1000 E. Victoria Street, Carson, CA 90747
■ **Website:** http://www.csudh.edu/
■ **Public**
■ **Degrees offered:** bachelor's, master's, education specialist

ADMISSIONS

Admissions phone number: **(310) 243-3465**
Admissions email address: *info@csudh.edu*
Application website:
  http://www.csudh.edu/csudh/ar2000/apply.htm
Application fee: **$55**
Fall 2005 application deadline: **6/1**
Test of English as Foreign Language (TOEFL) is required for international students.
Minimum TOEFL score required for paper test: **550**
Minimum TOEFL score required for computer test: **213**

Fall 2003
Acceptance rate for master's degree programs: **77%**
Total 2003 enrollment: **2,129**
Master's degree enrollment: **2,129**
  Teacher preparation program enrollment (master's): **1,071**

FINANCIAL INFORMATION

Financial aid phone number: **(310) 243-3647**
Tuition, 2003-2004 academic year: Full-time: **$2,256**; Part-time: **$1,308**
Fees: **$432**, Room and board: **$8,061**, Books and supplies: **$1,195**, Miscellaneous expenses: **$2,055**

ACADEMIC PROGRAMS

Total full-time tenured or tenure-track faculty (fall 2003): **64**, Total part-time faculty (fall 2003): **281**
Areas of specialization: curriculum and instruction, education administration and supervision, educational psychology, elementary teacher education, secondary teacher education, special education, student counseling and personnel services.
Professional development/partnership school(s) are used by students in some of the teaching programs.
During their internships, peer groups of students meet regularly to discuss instructional techniques in some of the teaching programs.
Some of the students in their internships are mentored.

Courses that prepare teachers to pass the National Board of Professional Teaching Standards are not offered.
Teacher preparation programs: Master's degree in education, including internship/practice teaching and preparation for initial licensure. Alternative program for college graduates leading to provisional licensure.
The education program is currently accredited by the National Council for Accreditation of Teacher Education.

LICENSING TEST

Pass rate on state's teacher licensing test for 2002-2003: 98%

State average pass rate: 98%

California State University–Fresno

■ 5150 N. Maple, Fresno, CA 93740
■ **Website:** http://education.csufresno.edu/
■ **Public**

LICENSING TEST

Pass rate on state's teacher licensing test for 2002-2003: 96%

State average pass rate: 98%

California State University–Fullerton

■ 800 N. State College Blvd., Fullerton, CA 92831-3599
■ **Website:** http://hdcs.fullerton.edu/education/
■ **Public**
■ **Degrees offered:** master's, Ed.D.

ADMISSIONS

Admissions phone number: **(714) 278-3352**
Admissions email address: *schofedgrad@fullerton.edu*
Application website:
  http://hdcs.fullerton.edu/adtep/default.htm
Application fee: **$50**
Fall 2005 application deadline: **2/28**
Test of English as Foreign Language (TOEFL) is required for international students.
Minimum TOEFL score required for paper test: **550**
Minimum TOEFL score required for computer test: **213**

Fall 2003
Acceptance rate for master's degree programs: **81%**
Total 2003 enrollment: **628**
Master's degree enrollment: **624**
  Teacher preparation program enrollment (master's): **390**
Doctoral degree enrollment: **4**

FINANCIAL INFORMATION

Financial aid phone number: **(714) 278-3128**

Tuition, 2003-2004 academic year: Full-time in-state:
$2,726; out-of-state: **$415/credit hour**, Part-time in-state:
$1,778; out-of-state: **$504/credit hour**

Room and board: **$4,700**, Books and supplies: **$500**,
Miscellaneous expenses: **$300**

ACADEMIC PROGRAMS

Total full-time tenured or tenure-track faculty (fall 2003):
53, Total part-time faculty (fall 2003): **172**

Areas of specialization: curriculum and instruction, education administration and supervision, education policy,
elementary teacher education, secondary teacher education, special education.

Professional development/partnership school(s) are used
by students in all of the teaching programs.

During their internships, peer groups of students meet
regularly to discuss instructional techniques in all of the
teaching programs.

All of the students in their internships are mentored.

Courses that prepare teachers to pass the National Board of
Professional Teaching Standards are offered.

The education program is currently accredited by the
National Council for Accreditation of Teacher Education.

LICENSING TEST

Pass rate on state's teacher licensing test for 2002-2003:
100%

State average pass rate: **98%**

California State University–Hayward

- **25800 Carlos Bee Boulevard, Hayward, CA 94542**
- **Website:** http://edschool.csuhayward.edu/
- **Public**

LICENSING TEST

Pass rate on state's teacher licensing test for 2002-2003:
100%

State average pass rate: **98%**

California State University–Long Beach

- **1250 Bellflower Blvd., Long Beach, CA 90840**
- **Website:** http://www.ced.csulb.edu
- **Public**
- **Degrees offered:** master's, Ed.D.

ADMISSIONS

Admissions phone number: **(562) 985-4547**

Admissions email address: *peverett@csulb.edu*

Application website: *http://www.csumentor.edu*

Application fee: **$55**

Fall 2005 application deadline: **7/1**

Test requirements: **GRE**

Test of English as Foreign Language (TOEFL) is required
for international students.

Minimum TOEFL score required for paper test: **550**

Minimum TOEFL score required for computer test: **213**

Fall 2003

Acceptance rate for master's degree programs: **38%**

Total 2003 enrollment: **601**

Master's degree enrollment: **601**

Teacher preparation program enrollment (master's): **256**

FINANCIAL INFORMATION

Financial aid phone number: **(562) 985-7497**

Tuition, 2003-2004 academic year: Full-time in-state:
$2,256; out-of-state: **$9,024**, Part-time in-state: **$1,308**;
out-of-state: **$4,692**

Fees: **$316**, Room and board: **$6,100**, Books and supplies:
$1,000, Miscellaneous expenses: **$2,500**

Number of research assistant positions: **3**

Number of other paid appointments: **21**

ACADEMIC PROGRAMS

Total full-time tenured or tenure-track faculty (fall 2003):
58, Total part-time faculty (fall 2003): **118**

Areas of specialization: curriculum and instruction, education administration and supervision, educational psychology, elementary teacher education, higher education
administration, secondary teacher education, special
education, student counseling and personnel services.

Professional development/partnership school(s) are used
by students in all of the teaching programs.

During their internships, peer groups of students meet
regularly to discuss instructional techniques in some of
the teaching programs.

All of the students in their internships are mentored.

Courses that prepare teachers to pass the National Board of
Professional Teaching Standards are not offered.

Teacher preparation programs: Five-year program leading
to initial licensure that results in a baccalaureate degree
(with a major or minor in education) plus graduate
credit and includes practice teaching. Five-year program
leading to initial licensure that results in a baccalaureate
degree (with a major or minor in education) plus a master's degree and includes practice teaching. Master's program preparing college graduates for initial licensure;
includes practice teaching.

The education program is currently accredited by the
National Council for Accreditation of Teacher Education.

LICENSING TEST

Pass rate on state's teacher licensing test for 2002-2003:
100%

State average pass rate: **98%**

California State University–Los Angeles

■ 5151 State University Drive, Los Angeles, CA 90032
■ Website: http://www.calstatela.edu/academic/ccoe/
■ Public

LICENSING TEST
Pass rate on state's teacher licensing test for 2002-2003: 97%
State average pass rate: 98%

California State University–Northridge

■ 18111 Nordhoff Street, Northridge, CA 91330
■ Website: http://www.csun.edu
■ Public
■ Degrees offered: bachelor's, master's

ADMISSIONS
Admissions phone number: (818) 677-3774
Admissions email address: *lorraine.newlon@csun.edu*
Fall 2005 application deadline: **rolling**
Test of English as Foreign Language (TOEFL) is required
  for international students.

FINANCIAL INFORMATION
Financial aid phone number: (818) 677-2085

ACADEMIC PROGRAMS
Professional development/partnership school(s) are used
  by students in some of the teaching programs.
During their internships, peer groups of students meet
  regularly to discuss instructional techniques in some of
  the teaching programs.
All of the students in their internships are mentored.
Courses that prepare teachers to pass the National Board of
  Professional Teaching Standards are not offered.
The education program is currently accredited by the
  National Council for Accreditation of Teacher Education.

LICENSING TEST
Pass rate on state's teacher licensing test for 2002-2003: 98%
State average pass rate: 98%

California State University–Sacramento

■ 6000 J Street, Sacramento, CA 95819-2694
■ Website: http://edweb.csus.edu/
■ Public

LICENSING TEST
Pass rate on state's teacher licensing test for 2002-2003: 96%
State average pass rate: 98%

California State University– San Bernardino

■ 5500 University Parkway, San Bernardino, CA 92407
■ Website: http://www.csusb.edu
■ Public
■ Degrees offered: bachelor's, master's

ADMISSIONS
Admissions phone number: (909) 880-5188
Admissions email address: *moreinfo@csusb.edu*
Application fee: $55
Fall 2005 application deadline: **rolling**
Test of English as Foreign Language (TOEFL) is required
  for international students.

Fall 2003
Acceptance rate for master's degree programs: 79%
Total 2003 enrollment: 1,072
Master's degree enrollment: 1,072
  Teacher preparation program enrollment (master's): 592

FINANCIAL INFORMATION
Financial aid phone number: (909) 880-7800
Tuition, 2003-2004 academic year: Full-time in-state: **N/A**;
  out-of-state: **$6,768**, Part-time in-state: **N/A**; out-of-state:
  $6,768
Fees: $3,087, Room and board: $5,383, Books and supplies:
  $1,215

ACADEMIC PROGRAMS
Total full-time tenured or tenure-track faculty (fall 2003):
  80, Total part-time faculty (fall 2003): 153
Areas of specialization: curriculum and instruction, education administration and supervision, educational psychology, elementary teacher education, secondary
  teacher education, special education, teacher education.
The education program is currently accredited by the
  National Council for Accreditation of Teacher Education.

LICENSING TEST

Pass rate on state's teacher licensing test for 2002-2003: 98%

State average pass rate: 98%

California State University–San Marcos

- 333 S. Twin Oaks Valley Road, San Marcos, CA 92096-0001
- **Website:** http://lynx.csusm.edu/coe/
- **Public**

LICENSING TEST

Pass rate on state's teacher licensing test for 2002-2003: 99%

State average pass rate: 98%

California State University–Stanislaus

- 801 W. Monte Vista Avenue, Turlock, CA 95382
- **Website:** http://www.csustan.edu
- **Public**
- **Degrees offered:** bachelor's, master's

ADMISSIONS

Admissions phone number: **(209) 667-3152**

Admissions email address:
Outreach_Help_Desk@csustan.edu

Application website:
http://www.csumentor.edu/AdmissionApp/

Application fee: **$55**

Fall 2005 application deadline: **7/1**

Test of English as Foreign Language (TOEFL) is required for international students.

Minimum TOEFL score required for paper test: **550**

Minimum TOEFL score required for computer test: **213**

Fall 2003

Total 2003 enrollment: **273**

Master's degree enrollment: **273**

FINANCIAL INFORMATION

Financial aid phone number: **(209) 667-3336**

Tuition, 2003-2004 academic year: Full-time in-state: **N/A**; out-of-state: **$282/credit hour**, Part-time in-state: **N/A**; out-of-state: **$282/credit hour**

Fees: **$2,634**, Room and board: **$7,101**, Books and supplies: **$1,224**, Miscellaneous expenses: **$2,646**

ACADEMIC PROGRAMS

Total full-time tenured or tenure-track faculty (fall 2003): **36**, Total part-time faculty (fall 2003): **135**

Areas of specialization: curriculum and instruction, education administration and supervision, elementary teacher education, secondary teacher education, special education, student counseling and personnel services, teacher education.

Professional development/partnership school(s) are used by students in all of the teaching programs.

During their internships, peer groups of students meet regularly to discuss instructional techniques in all of the teaching programs.

All of the students in their internships are mentored.

Courses that prepare teachers to pass the National Board of Professional Teaching Standards are not offered.

The education program is currently accredited by the National Council for Accreditation of Teacher Education.

LICENSING TEST

Pass rate on state's teacher licensing test for 2002-2003: 97%

State average pass rate: 98%

Cal Poly–San Luis Obispo

- UCTE, 1 Grand Ave., San Luis Obispo, CA 93407
- **Website:** http://www.calpoly.edu
- **Public**
- **Degrees offered:** master's, Ed.D.

ADMISSIONS

Admissions phone number: **(805) 756-2913**

Admissions email address: *admissions@calpoly.edu*

Application website: *http://www.csumentor.edu/*

Application fee: **$55**

Fall 2005 application deadline: **11/30**

Test requirements: **GRE**

Test of English as Foreign Language (TOEFL) is required for international students.

Minimum TOEFL score required for paper test: **550**

Minimum TOEFL score required for computer test: **213**

Fall 2003

Acceptance rate for master's degree programs: **57%**

Acceptance rate for doctoral programs: **50%**

Total 2003 enrollment: **137**

Master's degree enrollment: **130**

    Teacher preparation program enrollment (master's): **79**

Doctoral degree enrollment: **7**

FINANCIAL INFORMATION

Financial aid phone number: **(805) 756-2927**

Tuition, 2003-2004 academic year: Full-time in-state: **$3,108**; out-of-state: **$188/credit hour**, Part-time in-state: **$2,161**; out-of-state: **$188/credit hour**

Room and board: **$7,479**, Books and supplies: **$1,224**, Miscellaneous expenses: **$2,640**

Number of fellowships awarded to graduate students during the 2003-2004 academic year: 0
Number of teaching assistant positions: 0
Number of research assistant positions: 0
Number of other paid appointments: 0

ACADEMIC PROGRAMS

Total full-time tenured or tenure-track faculty (fall 2003): 15, Total part-time faculty (fall 2003): 78
Areas of specialization: curriculum and instruction, education administration and supervision, special education, student counseling and personnel services.
Professional development/partnership school(s) are used by students in some of the teaching programs.
During their internships, peer groups of students meet regularly to discuss instructional techniques in some of the teaching programs.
All of the students in their internships are mentored.
Courses that prepare teachers to pass the National Board of Professional Teaching Standards are not offered.

LICENSING TEST

Pass rate on state's teacher licensing test for 2002-2003: 100%
State average pass rate: 98%

Chapman University

- One University Drive, Orange, CA 92866
- **Website:** http://www.chapman.edu/soe
- **Private**
- **Degrees offered:** bachelor's, master's, education specialist

ADMISSIONS

Admissions phone number: **(714) 997-6714**
Admissions email address: *amiemw@chapman.edu*
Application website: *http://www.chapman.edu/soe*
Application fee: **$40**
Fall 2005 application deadline: **rolling**
Test requirements: **GRE or MAT**
Test of English as Foreign Language (TOEFL) is required for international students.
Minimum TOEFL score required for paper test: **550**

Fall 2003
Acceptance rate for master's degree programs: **69%**
Acceptance rate for education specialist degree programs: 25%
Average GRE verbal: 458, Average GRE quantitative: 548, Average GRE analytical: 550
Total 2003 enrollment: 408
Master's degree enrollment: 354
　Teacher preparation program enrollment (master's): 296
Education specialist degree enrollment: 54

FINANCIAL INFORMATION

Financial aid phone number: **(714) 997-6741**

Tuition, 2003-2004 academic year: Full-time: **$460/credit hour; Part time: $460/credit hour**
Number of fellowships awarded to graduate students during the 2003-2004 academic year: 0
Number of teaching assistant positions: 0
Number of research assistant positions: 0
Number of other paid appointments: 0

ACADEMIC PROGRAMS

Total full-time tenured or tenure-track faculty (fall 2003): 15
Total part-time faculty (fall 2003): 31
Areas of specialization: curriculum and instruction, education administration and supervision, educational psychology, elementary teacher education, secondary teacher education, special education, student counseling and personnel services.
Professional development/partnership school(s) are used by students in all of the teaching programs.
During their internships, peer groups of students meet regularly to discuss instructional techniques in some of the teaching programs.
All of the students in their internships are mentored.
Courses that prepare teachers to pass the National Board of Professional Teaching Standards are not offered.
Teacher preparation programs: Master's degree in education, including internship/practice teaching and preparation for initial licensure.

LICENSING TEST

Pass rate on state's teacher licensing test for 2002-2003: 98%
State average pass rate: 98%

Claremont Graduate University

- 150 E. 10th Street, Claremont, CA 91711
- **Website:** http://www.cgu.edu/ses
- **Private**
- **Degrees offered:** master's, Ph.D.
- **Overall rank in the 2005 U.S. News education schools with doctoral programs:** 58

ADMISSIONS

Admissions phone number: **(909) 621-8263**
Admissions email address: *admiss@cgu.edu*
Application website: *http://www.cgu.edu/admissions/main.asp*
Application fee: **$55**
Fall 2005 application deadline: **2/1**
Test requirements: **GRE or MAT**
Test of English as Foreign Language (TOEFL) is required for international students.
Minimum TOEFL score required for paper test: **550**
Minimum TOEFL score required for computer test: **213**

Fall 2003
Acceptance rate for master's degree programs: **73%**

Acceptance rate for doctoral programs: 63%
Average GRE verbal: 532, Average GRE quantitative: 562, Average GRE analytical: 527
Total 2003 enrollment: 261
Master's degree enrollment: 141
  Teacher preparation program enrollment (master's): 131
Doctoral degree enrollment: 120

FINANCIAL INFORMATION

Financial aid phone number: (909) 621-8337
Tuition, 2003-2004 academic year: Full-time: $25,250; Part-time: $1,099/credit hour
Fees: $220
Number of fellowships awarded to graduate students during the 2003-2004 academic year: 184
Number of teaching assistant positions: 4
Number of research assistant positions: 17
Number of other paid appointments: 11

ACADEMIC PROGRAMS

Total full-time tenured or tenure-track faculty (fall 2003): 12, Total part-time faculty (fall 2003): 42
Areas of specialization: curriculum and instruction, education administration and supervision, education policy, elementary teacher education, higher education administration, secondary teacher education.
Professional development/partnership school(s) are used by students in none of the teaching programs.
During their internships, peer groups of students meet regularly to discuss instructional techniques in all of the teaching programs.
All of the students in their internships are mentored.
Courses that prepare teachers to pass the National Board of Professional Teaching Standards are not offered.
Teacher preparation programs: Master's degree in education, including internship/practice teaching and preparation for initial licensure.

College of Notre Dame

■ 1500 Ralston Avenue, Belmont, CA 94002
■ **Website:** http://www.ndm.edu/
■ **Private**

LICENSING TEST

Pass rate on state's teacher licensing test for 2002-2003: **100%**
State average pass rate: **98%**

Concordia University

■ 1530 Concordia West, Irvine, CA 92612
■ **Website:** http://www.cui.edu
■ **Private**
■ **Degrees offered:** bachelor's, master's

ADMISSIONS

Admissions phone number: **(949) 854-8002**
Admissions email address: *lindsay.anderson@cui.edu*
Application website: *http://www.cui.edu*
Application fee: **$50**
Fall 2005 application deadline: 7/30
Test requirements: **GRE or MAT**
Test of English as Foreign Language (TOEFL) is required for international students.
Minimum TOEFL score required for paper test: 550
Minimum TOEFL score required for computer test: 213

Fall 2003
Acceptance rate for master's degree programs: 84%
Total 2003 enrollment: 226
Master's degree enrollment: 226
  Teacher preparation program enrollment (master's): 217

FINANCIAL INFORMATION

Financial aid phone number: **(949) 854-8002**
Tuition, 2003-2004 academic year: Full-time: **$365/credit hour**; Part-time: **$365/credit hour**
Number of fellowships awarded to graduate students during the 2003-2004 academic year: 0
Number of teaching assistant positions: 0
Number of research assistant positions: 0
Number of other paid appointments: 0

ACADEMIC PROGRAMS

Total full-time tenured or tenure-track faculty (fall 2003): 2 Total part-time faculty (fall 2003): 26
Areas of specialization: curriculum and instruction, education administration and supervision, elementary teacher education, secondary teacher education.
Professional development/partnership school(s) are used by students in some of the teaching programs.
During their internships, peer groups of students meet regularly to discuss instructional techniques in all of the teaching programs.
All of the students in their internships are mentored.
Courses that prepare teachers to pass the National Board of Professional Teaching Standards are not offered.
Teacher preparation programs: Four-year baccalaureate-degree program leading to initial licensure that includes either a major or minor in education and practice teaching. Master's program preparing college graduates for initial licensure; includes practice teaching.

LICENSING TEST

Pass rate on state's teacher licensing test for 2002-2003: 98%
State average pass rate: 98%

Dominican College of San Rafael

- 50 Acacia Avenue, San Rafael, CA 94901
- Website: http://www.dominican.edu/
- Private

LICENSING TEST
Pass rate on state's teacher licensing test for 2002-2003: 98%
State average pass rate: 98%

Fielding Graduate Institute

- 2112 Santa Barbara Street, Santa Barbara, CA 93105
- Website: http://www.fielding.edu
- Private
- Degrees offered: master's, Ed.D.

ADMISSIONS
Admissions phone number: (800) 340-1099
Admissions email address: *admissions@fielding.edu*
Application fee: $75
Fall 2005 application deadline: 8/30

Fall 2003
Acceptance rate for master's degree programs: 53%
Acceptance rate for doctoral programs: 95%
Total 2003 enrollment: 317
Master's degree enrollment: 39
Doctoral degree enrollment: 278

FINANCIAL INFORMATION
Financial aid phone number: (805) 898-4008
Tuition, 2003-2004 academic year: $14,560
Room and board: $13,354, Books and supplies: $2,000,
   Miscellaneous expenses: $7,177
Number of fellowships awarded to graduate students dur-
   ing the 2003-2004 academic year: 3
Number of teaching assistant positions: 0
Number of research assistant positions: 0
Number of other paid appointments: 4

ACADEMIC PROGRAMS
Total full-time tenured or tenure-track faculty (fall 2003):
   13, Total part-time faculty (fall 2003): 5
Courses that prepare teachers to pass the National Board of
   Professional Teaching Standards are not offered.

Fresno Pacific University

- 1717 S Chestnut Avenue, Fresno, CA 93702
- Website: http://www.fresno.edu
- Private
- Degrees offered: master's

ADMISSIONS
Admissions phone number: (559) 453-2016
Admissions email address: *grdadmis@fresno.edu*
Application website: *http://www.fresno.edu*
Application fee: $90
Fall 2005 application deadline: rolling
Test of English as Foreign Language (TOEFL) is required
   for international students.
Minimum TOEFL score required for paper test: 550
Minimum TOEFL score required for computer test: 213

Fall 2003
Acceptance rate for master's degree programs: 61%
Total 2003 enrollment: 902
Master's degree enrollment: 902
   Teacher preparation program enrollment (master's): 522

FINANCIAL INFORMATION
Financial aid phone number: (559) 453-2041
Tuition, 2003-2004 academic year: Full-time: $445/credit
   hour; Part-time: $445/credit hour

ACADEMIC PROGRAMS
Total full-time tenured or tenure-track faculty (fall 2003): 24
   Total part-time faculty (fall 2003): 7
Areas of specialization: curriculum and instruction, education administration and supervision, educational psy-
   chology, elementary teacher education, secondary
   teacher education, special education, student counseling
   and personnel services.
Professional development/partnership school(s) are used
   by students in none of the teaching programs.
During their internships, peer groups of students meet
   regularly to discuss instructional techniques in all of the
   teaching programs.
All of the students in their internships are mentored.
Courses that prepare teachers to pass the National Board of
   Professional Teaching Standards are not offered.

LICENSING TEST
Pass rate on state's teacher licensing test for 2002-2003:
   97%
State average pass rate: 98%

Holy Names College

- 3500 Mountain Blvd., Oakland, CA 94619
- **Website:** http://www.hnc.edu
- Private
- **Degrees offered:** master's

ADMISSIONS
Admissions phone number: **(510) 436-1351**
Admissions email address: *adulted@hnc.edu*
Application fee: **$50**
Fall 2005 application deadline: **8/1**
Test requirements: **None**
Test of English as Foreign Language (TOEFL) is required for international students.
Minimum TOEFL score required for paper test: **550**
Minimum TOEFL score required for computer test: **213**

Fall 2003
Acceptance rate for master's degree programs: **68%**
Total 2003 enrollment: **51**
Master's degree enrollment: **51**
  Teacher preparation program enrollment (master's): **33**

FINANCIAL INFORMATION
Financial aid phone number: **(510) 436-1315**
Tuition, 2003-2004 academic year: Full-time: **$520/credit hour**; Part-time: **$520/credit hour**
Fees: **$210**, Room and board: **$7,800**, Books and supplies: **$946**, Miscellaneous expenses: **$1,800**

ACADEMIC PROGRAMS
Total full-time tenured or tenure-track faculty (fall 2003): **5**
  Total part-time faculty (fall 2003): **13**
Areas of specialization: curriculum and instruction, education policy, educational psychology, elementary teacher education, secondary teacher education, special education, student counseling and personnel services.
Professional development/partnership school(s) are used by students in some of the teaching programs.
During their internships, peer groups of students meet regularly to discuss instructional techniques in none of the teaching programs.
All of the students in their internships are mentored.
Courses that prepare teachers to pass the National Board of Professional Teaching Standards are not offered.
Teacher preparation programs: Master's degree in education, including internship/practice teaching and preparation for initial licensure. Alternative program for college graduates leading to provisional licensure.

LICENSING TEST
Pass rate on state's teacher licensing test for 2002-2003: **100%**
State average pass rate: **98%**

Hope International University

- 2500 E. Nutwood Ave., Fullerton, CA 92831
- **Website:** http://www.hiu.edu
- Private
- **Degrees offered:** bachelor's, master's

ADMISSIONS
Admissions phone number: **(800) 762-1294**
Admissions email address: *grad-admissions@hiu.edu*
Application website: *http://www.hiu.edu/prospective_students/admission/graduate/forms/SGS_Gen_Appl.pdf*
Application fee: **$75**
Fall 2005 application deadline: **8/1**
Test requirements: **None**
Test of English as Foreign Language (TOEFL) is required for international students.
Minimum TOEFL score required for paper test: **550**

Fall 2003
Acceptance rate for master's degree programs: **89%**
Total 2003 enrollment: **233**
Master's degree enrollment: **233**
  Teacher preparation program enrollment (master's): **68**

FINANCIAL INFORMATION
Financial aid phone number: **(800) 762-1294**
Tuition, 2003-2004 academic year: Full-time: **$370/credit hour**; Part time: **$370/credit hour**
Fees: **$370/credit hour**
Number of fellowships awarded to graduate students during the 2003-2004 academic year: **0**
Number of teaching assistant positions: **0**
Number of research assistant positions: **0**
Number of other paid appointments: **0**

ACADEMIC PROGRAMS
Total full-time tenured or tenure-track faculty (fall 2003): **1**
  Total part-time faculty (fall 2003): **13**
Areas of specialization: curriculum and instruction, education administration and supervision, education policy, elementary teacher education.
Professional development/partnership school(s) are used by students in all of the teaching programs.
During their internships, peer groups of students meet regularly to discuss instructional techniques in all of the teaching programs.
All of the students in their internships are mentored.
Courses that prepare teachers to pass the National Board of Professional Teaching Standards are not offered.
Teacher preparation programs: Four-year baccalaureate-degree program leading to initial licensure that includes either a major or minor in education and practice teaching. Master's program preparing college graduates for initial licensure; includes practice teaching.

LICENSING TEST

Pass rate on state's teacher licensing test for 2002-2003: 100%
State average pass rate: 98%

Humboldt State University

- 1 Harpst Street, Arcata, CA 95521
- Website: http://www.humboldt.edu
- Public
- Degrees offered: master's

ADMISSIONS

Admissions phone number: (707) 826-4101
Application website: http://csumentor.com
Application fee: $55
Fall 2005 application deadline: 2/1
Test of English as Foreign Language (TOEFL) is required for international students.
Minimum TOEFL score required for paper test: 550
Minimum TOEFL score required for computer test: 213

Fall 2003

Total 2003 enrollment: 28
Master's degree enrollment: 28
　　Teacher preparation program enrollment (master's): 28

FINANCIAL INFORMATION

Financial aid phone number: (707) 826-4321
Tuition, 2003-2004 academic year: Full-time in-state: $2,256; out-of-state: $9,024, Part-time in-state: $1,308; out-of-state: $4,692
Fees: $490

ACADEMIC PROGRAMS

Total full-time tenured or tenure-track faculty (fall 2003): 7
Professional development/partnership school(s) are used by students in all of the teaching programs.
All of the students in their internships are mentored.
Courses that prepare teachers to pass the National Board of Professional Teaching Standards are offered.

LICENSING TEST

Pass rate on state's teacher licensing test for 2002-2003: 98%
State average pass rate: 98%

John F. Kennedy University

- 12 Altarinda Road, Orinda, CA 94563
- Website: http://www.jfku.edu/
- Private

La Sierra University

- 4700 Pierce Street, Riverside, CA 92515
- Website: http://www.lasierra.edu/
- Private

LICENSING TEST

Pass rate on state's teacher licensing test for 2002-2003: 95%
State average pass rate: 98%

Loyola Marymount University

- One LMU Drive, Los Angeles, CA 90045
- Website: http://www.lmu.edu
- Private
- Degrees offered: master's, education specialist

ADMISSIONS

Admissions phone number: (310) 338-2721
Admissions email address: graduate@lmu.edu
Application website:
　　https://apply.embark.com/Grad/LMU/87/
Application fee: $50
Fall 2005 application deadline: 7/15
Test requirements: GRE
Test of English as Foreign Language (TOEFL) is required for international students.
Minimum TOEFL score required for paper test: 600
Minimum TOEFL score required for computer test: 250

Fall 2003

Acceptance rate for master's degree programs: 85%
Acceptance rate for education specialist degree programs: 86%
Average GRE verbal: 462, Average GRE quantitative: 527, Average GRE analytical: 440
Total 2003 enrollment: 702
Master's degree enrollment: 623
　　Teacher preparation program enrollment (master's): 435
Education specialist degree enrollment: 79

FINANCIAL INFORMATION

Financial aid phone number: (310) 338-2753
Tuition, 2003-2004 academic year: Full-time: $664/credit hour; Part-time: $664/credit hour
Fees: $150, Room and board: $6,640, Books and supplies: $500
Number of fellowships awarded to graduate students during the 2003-2004 academic year: 0
Number of teaching assistant positions: 12
Number of research assistant positions: 5
Number of other paid appointments: 16

ACADEMIC PROGRAMS

Total full-time tenured or tenure-track faculty (fall 2003): 16, Total part-time faculty (fall 2003): 70

Areas of specialization: curriculum and instruction, education administration and supervision, education policy, educational psychology, elementary teacher education, secondary teacher education, special education, student counseling and personnel services.

Professional development/partnership school(s) are used by students in some of the teaching programs.

During their internships, peer groups of students meet regularly to discuss instructional techniques in all of the teaching programs.

All of the students in their internships are mentored.

Courses that prepare teachers to pass the National Board of Professional Teaching Standards are not offered.

Teacher preparation programs: Master's degree in education, including internship/practice teaching and preparation for initial licensure. Education minor for undergraduate students.

The education program is currently accredited by the National Council for Accreditation of Teacher Education.

LICENSING TEST

Pass rate on state's teacher licensing test for 2002-2003: 98%

State average pass rate: 98%

Mills College

- 5000 MacArthur Blvd., Oakland, CA 94613
- Website: http://www.mills.edu/
- Private
- Degrees offered: master's, Ed.D.

ADMISSIONS

Admissions phone number: (510) 430-3309
Admissions email address: *grad-studies@mills.edu*
Application website: *http://www.mills.edu/GRST/gra.applications.html*
Application fee: $50
Fall 2005 application deadline: 2/1

Fall 2003

Total 2003 enrollment: 190
Master's degree enrollment: 146
    Teacher preparation program enrollment (master's): 128
Doctoral degree enrollment: 44

FINANCIAL INFORMATION

Financial aid phone number: (510) 430-2000
Tuition, 2003-2004 academic year: Full-time: $15,000; Part-time: $3,827/credit hour
Fees: $1,305, Room and board: $9,955

ACADEMIC PROGRAMS

Total full-time tenured or tenure-track faculty (fall 2003): 10, Total part-time faculty (fall 2003): 11

Areas of specialization: curriculum and instruction, education administration and supervision, elementary teacher education, higher education administration, secondary teacher education, special education.

Teacher preparation programs: Master's degree in education, including internship/practice teaching and preparation for initial licensure.

LICENSING TEST

Pass rate on state's teacher licensing test for 2002-2003: 93%

State average pass rate: 98%

Mount St. Mary's College

- 10 Chester Place, Los Angeles, CA 90007
- Website: http://www.msmary.edu/
- Private
- Degrees offered: master's, education specialist

ADMISSIONS

Admissions phone number: (213) 477-2800
Admissions email address: *thoener@msmc.la.edu*
Application fee: $50
Fall 2005 application deadline: 6/1
Test of English as Foreign Language (TOEFL) is required for international students.
Minimum TOEFL score required for paper test: 550
Minimum TOEFL score required for computer test: 213

Fall 2003

Acceptance rate for education specialist degree programs: 75%
Total 2003 enrollment: 220
Master's degree enrollment: 220
    Teacher preparation program enrollment (master's): 200

FINANCIAL INFORMATION

Financial aid phone number: (213) 477-2562
Tuition, 2003-2004 academic year: Full-time: $530/credit hour; Part-time: $530/credit hour
Fees: $530, Books and supplies: $150
Number of fellowships awarded to graduate students during the 2003-2004 academic year: 3
Number of teaching assistant positions: 50

ACADEMIC PROGRAMS

Total full-time tenured or tenure-track faculty (fall 2003): 6
    Total part-time faculty (fall 2003): 12

Teacher preparation programs: Master's program preparing college graduates for initial licensure; includes practice teaching.

LICENSING TEST

Pass rate on state's teacher licensing test for 2002-2003: 100%

State average pass rate: 98%

National University

- 11255 N. Torrey Pines Road, La Jolla, CA 92037
- Website: http://www.nu.edu/
- Private

LICENSING TEST
Pass rate on state's teacher licensing test for 2002-2003: 97%
State average pass rate: 98%

Occidental College

- 1600 Campus Rd, Los Angeles, CA 90041
- Website: http://www.oxy.edu/
- Private

ADMISSIONS
Admissions phone number: (800) 825-5262
Admissions email address: admission@oxy.edu
Application fee: $50
Fall 2005 application deadline: 1/10
Test of English as Foreign Language (TOEFL) is required for international students.

FINANCIAL INFORMATION
Financial aid phone number: (323) 259-2548

LICENSING TEST
Pass rate on state's teacher licensing test for 2002-2003: 100%
State average pass rate: 98%

Patten College

- 2433 Coolidge Avenue, Oakland, CA 94601
- Website: http://www.patten.edu/
- Private

Pepperdine University

- 24255 Pacific Coast Highway, Malibu, CA 90263-4301
- Website: http://gsep.pepperdine.edu/
- Private

ADMISSIONS
Admissions phone number: (310) 568-5600
Admissions email address: gsep@pepperdine.edu
Application website:
    http://gsep.pepperdine.edu/programs/application/

FINANCIAL INFORMATION
Financial aid phone number: (310) 258-2848

LICENSING TEST
Pass rate on state's teacher licensing test for 2002-2003: 100%
State average pass rate: 98%

Point Loma Nazarene University

- 4007 Camino Del Rio South, San Diego, CA 92108
- Website: http://www.ptloma.edu
- Private
- Degrees offered: bachelor's, master's, education specialist

ADMISSIONS
Admissions phone number: (619) 563-2846
Admissions email address: gradinfo@ptloma.edu
Application website: http://www.ptloma.edu/grad
Application fee: $25
Fall 2005 application deadline: rolling
Test of English as Foreign Language (TOEFL) is required for international students.
Minimum TOEFL score required for paper test: 550
Minimum TOEFL score required for computer test: 216

FINANCIAL INFORMATION
Financial aid phone number: (619) 563-2845

LICENSING TEST
Pass rate on state's teacher licensing test for 2002-2003: 99%
State average pass rate: 98%

San Diego State University

- College of Education, San Diego, CA 92812
- Website: http://www.sdsu.edu
- Public
- Degrees offered: master's, Ph.D., Ed.D.
- Overall rank in the 2005 U.S. News education schools with doctoral programs: 67

ADMISSIONS
Admissions phone number: (619) 594-6544
Admissions email address: cnecoechea@mail.sdsu.edu
Application website: http://www.csumentor.edu/admissionapp/
Application fee: $55
Test requirements: GRE

Test of English as Foreign Language (TOEFL) is required
   for international students.
Minimum TOEFL score required for paper test: 550
Minimum TOEFL score required for computer test: 213

Fall 2003
Acceptance rate for master's degree programs: 48%
Acceptance rate for doctoral programs: 37%
Average GRE verbal: 456, Average GRE quantitative: 500
Total 2003 enrollment: 809
Master's degree enrollment: 706
   Teacher preparation program enrollment (master's): 290
Doctoral degree enrollment: 103

FINANCIAL INFORMATION
Financial aid phone number: (619) 594-6323
Tuition, 2003-2004 academic year: Full-time in-state:
   $2,256; out-of-state: $9,024, Part-time in-state: $1,308;
   out-of-state: $4,692
Fees: $442, Room and board: $8,385, Books and supplies:
   $1,224, Miscellaneous expenses: $2,875

ACADEMIC PROGRAMS
Total full-time tenured or tenure-track faculty (fall 2003):
   91
Areas of specialization: curriculum and instruction, education administration and supervision, educational psychology, elementary teacher education, higher education
   administration, secondary teacher education, special
   education, student counseling and personnel services.
Professional development/partnership school(s) are used
   by students in all of the teaching programs.
During their internships, peer groups of students meet
   regularly to discuss instructional techniques in all of the
   teaching programs.
All of the students in their internships are mentored.
Courses that prepare teachers to pass the National Board of
   Professional Teaching Standards are not offered.
The education program is currently accredited by the
   National Council for Accreditation of Teacher Education.

LICENSING TEST
Pass rate on state's teacher licensing test for 2002-2003:
   99%
State average pass rate: 98%

San Francisco State University

■ 1600 Holloway Avenue, San Francisco, CA 94132
■ **Website:** http://www.sfsu.edu/
■ **Public**

LICENSING TEST
Pass rate on state's teacher licensing test for 2002-2003: 95%
State average pass rate: 98%

San Jose State University

■ One Washington Square, San Jose, CA 95192-0071
■ **Website:** http://www.sjsu.edu/
■ **Public**
■ **Degrees offered:** bachelor's, master's

ADMISSIONS
Admissions phone number: (408) 924-2550
Admissions email address: *marshall.rose@sjsu.edu*
Test of English as Foreign Language (TOEFL) is required
   for international students.
Minimum TOEFL score required for paper test: 500
Minimum TOEFL score required for computer test: 173

FINANCIAL INFORMATION
Financial aid phone number: (408) 924-6070
Tuition, 2003-2004 academic year: Full-time in-state:
   $1,809; out-of-state: $282/credit hour, Part-time in-state:
   $1,050; out-of-state: $282/credit hour
Fees: $516, Room and board: $7,174, Books and supplies:
   $700, Miscellaneous expenses: $200

LICENSING TEST
Pass rate on state's teacher licensing test for 2002-2003: 96%
State average pass rate: 98%

Santa Clara University

■ 500 El Camino Real, Santa Clara, CA 95053
■ **Website:** http://www.scu.edu/ecppm
■ **Private**
■ **Degrees offered:** master's, education specialist

ADMISSIONS
Admissions phone number: (408) 554-7884
Admissions email address: *jcallahan@scu.edu*
Application fee: $50
Fall 2005 application deadline: 4/1
Test of English as Foreign Language (TOEFL) is required
   for international students.
Minimum TOEFL score required for paper test: 570
Minimum TOEFL score required for computer test: 250

Fall 2003
Acceptance rate for master's degree programs: 89%
Total 2003 enrollment: 403
Master's degree enrollment: 403
   Teacher preparation program enrollment (master's): 252

FINANCIAL INFORMATION
Financial aid phone number: (408) 554-4656
Tuition, 2003-2004 academic year: Full-time: $383/credit
   hour; Part-time: $383/credit hour
Number of fellowships awarded to graduate students dur-
   ing the 2003-2004 academic year: 0

Number of teaching assistant positions: 0
Number of research assistant positions: 0
Number of other paid appointments: 3

ACADEMIC PROGRAMS

Total full-time tenured or tenure-track faculty (fall 2003): 9
   Total part-time faculty (fall 2003): 29
Areas of specialization: education administration and supervision, elementary teacher education, higher education administration, secondary teacher education, special education.
Professional development/partnership school(s) are used by students in some of the teaching programs.
During their internships, peer groups of students meet regularly to discuss instructional techniques in all of the teaching programs.
All of the students in their internships are mentored.
Courses that prepare teachers to pass the National Board of Professional Teaching Standards are not offered.
Teacher preparation programs: Master's degree in education, including internship/practice teaching and preparation for initial licensure. Alternative program for college graduates leading to provisional licensure.

LICENSING TEST

Pass rate on state's teacher licensing test for 2002-2003: **96%**
State average pass rate: **98%**

Simpson College

■ **2211 College View Drive, Redding, CA 96003**
■ **Website:** http://www.simpsonca.edu
■ **Private**
■ **Degrees offered:** bachelor's, master's, education specialist

ADMISSIONS

Admissions phone number: **(530) 226-4606**
Admissions email address: *admissions@simpsonca.edu*
Application website: *http://www.simpsonca.edu*
Application fee: **$20**
Test requirements: **GRE**
Test of English as Foreign Language (TOEFL) is required for international students.
Minimum TOEFL score required for paper test: **500**

Fall 2003
Acceptance rate for master's degree programs: **88%**
Total 2003 enrollment: **204**
Master's degree enrollment: **67**
   Teacher preparation program enrollment (master's): **66**
Education specialist degree enrollment: **137**

FINANCIAL INFORMATION

Financial aid phone number: **(530) 224-5600**
Tuition, 2003-2004 academic year: Full-time: **$13,800**;
   Part-time: **$580/credit hour**

Number of fellowships awarded to graduate students during the 2003-2004 academic year: 0
Number of teaching assistant positions: 0
Number of research assistant positions: 0
Number of other paid appointments: 0

ACADEMIC PROGRAMS

Total full-time tenured or tenure-track faculty (fall 2003): 6
   Total part-time faculty (fall 2003): 6
Areas of specialization: curriculum and instruction, education administration and supervision, education policy, educational psychology, elementary teacher education, secondary teacher education, special education.
Professional development/partnership school(s) are used by students in all of the teaching programs.
During their internships, peer groups of students meet regularly to discuss instructional techniques in none of the teaching programs.
All of the students in their internships are mentored.
Courses that prepare teachers to pass the National Board of Professional Teaching Standards are offered.
Teacher preparation programs: Five-year program leading to initial licensure that results in a baccalaureate degree (with a major or minor in education) plus a master's degree and includes practice teaching.

LICENSING TEST

Pass rate on state's teacher licensing test for 2002-2003: **100%**
State average pass rate: **98%**

Sonoma State University

■ **1801 E. Cotati Avenue, Rohnert Park, CA 94928**
■ **Website:** http://www.sonoma.edu/
■ **Public**

LICENSING TEST

Pass rate on state's teacher licensing test for 2002-2003: **97%**
State average pass rate: **98%**

Stanford University

■ **School of Education, 485 Lasuen Mall, Stanford, CA 94305-3096**
■ **Website:** http://ed.stanford.edu/suse/index.html
■ **Private**
■ **Degrees offered:** master's, Ph.D.
■ **Overall rank in the 2005 U.S. News education schools with doctoral programs:** 1
■ **Overall rank in the 2005 U.S. News education school specialty rankings:** administration/supervision: 6, counseling/personnel: 18, curriculum/instruction: 4, education policy: 1, educational psychology: 2, elementary education: 13, higher education administration: 6, secondary education: 4

ADMISSIONS

Admissions phone number: **(650) 723-4794**
Admissions email address: *info@suse.stanford.edu*
Application website: *http://gradadmissions.stanford.edu*
Application fee: **$95**
Fall 2005 application deadline: 1/2
Test requirements: **GRE**
Test of English as Foreign Language (TOEFL) is required for international students.
Minimum TOEFL score required for paper test: **600**
Minimum TOEFL score required for computer test: **250**

Fall 2003

Acceptance rate for master's degree programs: **54%**
Acceptance rate for doctoral programs: **9%**
Average GRE verbal: **594**, Average GRE quantitative: **678**, Average GRE analytical: **677**
Total 2003 enrollment: **358**
Master's degree enrollment: **158**
    Teacher preparation program enrollment (master's): **71**
Doctoral degree enrollment: **200**

FINANCIAL INFORMATION

Financial aid phone number: **(650) 723-4794**
Tuition, 2003-2004 academic year: **$28,563**
Fees: **$200**, Room and board: **$13,900**, Books and supplies: **$1,470**, Miscellaneous expenses: **$2,665**
Number of fellowships awarded to graduate students during the 2003-2004 academic year: **108**
Number of teaching assistant positions: **49**
Number of research assistant positions: **107**

ACADEMIC PROGRAMS

Total full-time tenured or tenure-track faculty (fall 2003): **44**, Total part-time faculty (fall 2003): **0**
Areas of specialization: curriculum and instruction, education policy, educational psychology, higher education administration, secondary teacher education.
Professional development/partnership school(s) are used by students in all of the teaching programs.
During their internships, peer groups of students meet regularly to discuss instructional techniques in all of the teaching programs.
All of the students in their internships are mentored.
Courses that prepare teachers to pass the National Board of Professional Teaching Standards are offered.
Teacher preparation programs: Master's degree in education, including internship/practice teaching and preparation for initial licensure.
The education program is currently accredited by the National Council for Accreditation of Teacher Education.

LICENSING TEST

Pass rate on state's teacher licensing test for 2002-2003: **100%**
State average pass rate: **98%**

St. Mary's College of California

- **1928 St. Mary's Road, Moraga, CA 94556**
- **Website:** http://www.stmarys-ca.edu/
- **Private**

LICENSING TEST

Pass rate on state's teacher licensing test for 2002-2003: **100%**
State average pass rate: **98%**

University of California–Berkeley

- **1600 Tolman Hall, MC #1670, Berkeley, CA 94720-1670**
- **Website:** http://gse.berkeley.edu
- **Public**
- **Degrees offered:** master's, Ph.D., Ed.D.
- **Overall rank in the 2005 U.S. News education schools with doctoral programs: 6**
- **Overall rank in the 2005 U.S. News education school specialty rankings:** administration/supervision: 19, curriculum/instruction: 16, education policy: 5, educational psychology: 7, elementary education: 13, higher education administration: 22, secondary education: 15, vocational/technical: 12

ADMISSIONS

Admissions phone number: **(510) 642-0841**
Admissions email address: *gse_info@uclink4.berkeley.edu*
Application website: *http://gse.berkeley.edu*
Application fee: **$60**
Fall 2005 application deadline: 12/1
Test requirements: **GRE**
Test of English as Foreign Language (TOEFL) is required for international students.
Minimum TOEFL score required for paper test: **570**
Minimum TOEFL score required for computer test: **230**

Fall 2003

Acceptance rate for master's degree programs: **32%**
Acceptance rate for doctoral programs: **18%**
Average GRE verbal: **573**, Average GRE quantitative: **626**, Average GRE analytical: **650**
Total 2003 enrollment: **475**
Master's degree enrollment: **202**
    Teacher preparation program enrollment (master's): **111**
Education specialist degree enrollment: **0**
Doctoral degree enrollment: **273**

FINANCIAL INFORMATION

Financial aid phone number: **(510) 643-1720**

Tuition, 2003-2004 academic year: Full-time in-state: **N/A**; out-of-state: **$12,491**

Fees: **$6,168**, Room and board: **$12,966**, Books and supplies: **$1,158**, Miscellaneous expenses: **$4,036**

Number of fellowships awarded to graduate students during the 2003-2004 academic year: **369**

Number of teaching assistant positions: **51**

Number of research assistant positions: **195**

Number of other paid appointments: **18**

ACADEMIC PROGRAMS

Total full-time tenured or tenure-track faculty (fall 2003): **35**, Total part-time faculty (fall 2003): **41**

Areas of specialization: education administration and supervision, education policy, educational psychology, elementary teacher education, secondary teacher education, special education.

Professional development/partnership school(s) are used by students in all of the teaching programs.

During their internships, peer groups of students meet regularly to discuss instructional techniques in all of the teaching programs.

All of the students in their internships are mentored.

Courses that prepare teachers to pass the National Board of Professional Teaching Standards are not offered.

Teacher preparation programs: Master's degree in education, including internship/practice teaching and preparation for initial licensure. Education minor for undergraduate students.

LICENSING TEST

Pass rate on state's teacher licensing test for 2002-2003: **100%**

State average pass rate: **98%**

University of California–Davis

- ■ **2078 Academic Surge, 1 Shields Avenue, Davis, CA 95616**
- ■ **Website:** http://education.ucdavis.edu
- ■ **Public**
- ■ **Degrees offered:** master's, Ph.D., Ed.D.

ADMISSIONS

Admissions phone number: **(530) 752-0761**

Admissions email address: *kbray@ucdavis.edu*

Application website: *http://gradstudies.ucdavis.edu*

Application fee: **$60**

Fall 2005 application deadline: **12/15**

Test requirements: **GRE or MAT**

Test of English as Foreign Language (TOEFL) is required for international students.

Minimum TOEFL score required for paper test: **550**

Minimum TOEFL score required for computer test: **213**

Fall 2003

Acceptance rate for master's degree programs: **26%**

Acceptance rate for doctoral programs: **45%**

Total 2003 enrollment: **140**

Master's degree enrollment: **75**

Teacher preparation program enrollment (master's): **66**

Doctoral degree enrollment: **65**

FINANCIAL INFORMATION

Financial aid phone number: **(530) 752-9246**

Tuition, 2003-2004 academic year: Full-time in-state: **N/A**; out-of-state: **$12,245**, Part-time in-state: **N/A**; out-of-state: **$6,122**

Fees: **$7,062**

Number of fellowships awarded to graduate students during the 2003-2004 academic year: **23**

Number of teaching assistant positions: **15**

Number of research assistant positions: **14**

ACADEMIC PROGRAMS

Total full-time tenured or tenure-track faculty (fall 2003): **34**, Total part-time faculty (fall 2003): **0**

Areas of specialization: curriculum and instruction, education policy, educational psychology, elementary teacher education, secondary teacher education.

Professional development/partnership school(s) are used by students in all of the teaching programs.

During their internships, peer groups of students meet regularly to discuss instructional techniques in all of the teaching programs.

All of the students in their internships are mentored.

Teacher preparation programs: Master's degree in education, including internship/practice teaching and preparation for initial licensure. Education minor for undergraduate students.

LICENSING TEST

Pass rate on state's teacher licensing test for 2002-2003: **96%**

State average pass rate: **98%**

University of California–Irvine

- ■ **2001 Berkeley Place, Irvine, CA 92697-5500**
- ■ **Website:** http://www.admissions.uci.edu/
- ■ **Public**
- ■ **Degrees offered:** master's, Ed.D.

ADMISSIONS

Admissions phone number: **(949) 824-6703**

Admissions email address: *admissions@uci.edu*

Application website: *http://www.rgs.uci.edu/grad/*

Application fee: **$60**

Fall 2005 application deadline: **1/15**

Test requirements: **GRE**

Test of English as Foreign Language (TOEFL) is required for international students.

Minimum TOEFL score required for paper test: **550**

Minimum TOEFL score required for computer test: **213**

Fall 2003
Acceptance rate for master's degree programs: **68%**
Acceptance rate for doctoral programs: **30%**
Average GRE verbal: **504**, Average GRE quantitative: **577**,
    Average GRE analytical: **613**
Total 2003 enrollment: **144**
Master's degree enrollment: **66**
    Teacher preparation program enrollment (master's): **66**
Doctoral degree enrollment: **78**

FINANCIAL INFORMATION
Financial aid phone number: **(949) 824-6261**
Tuition, 2003-2004 academic year: Full-time in-state:
    $4,506; out-of-state: **$12,490**, Part-time in-state: **$2,253**;
    out-of-state: **$8,498**
Fees: **$2,812**, Room and board: **$8,605**, Books and sup-
    plies: **$2,300**, Miscellaneous expenses: **$2,560**
Number of fellowships awarded to graduate students dur-
    ing the 2003-2004 academic year: **96**
Number of teaching assistant positions: **10**

ACADEMIC PROGRAMS
Total full-time tenured or tenure-track faculty (fall 2003): **9**
    Total part-time faculty (fall 2003): **68**
Areas of specialization: curriculum and instruction, educa-
    tion administration and supervision, education policy,
    elementary teacher education, higher education adminis-
    tration, secondary teacher education.
Professional development/partnership school(s) are used
    by students in all of the teaching programs.
During their internships, peer groups of students meet
    regularly to discuss instructional techniques in all of the
    teaching programs.
All of the students in their internships are mentored.
Courses that prepare teachers to pass the National Board of
    Professional Teaching Standards are not offered.
Teacher preparation programs: Master's degree in educa-
    tion, including internship/practice teaching and prepara-
    tion for initial licensure. Education minor for
    undergraduate students.

LICENSING TEST
Pass rate on state's teacher licensing test for 2002-2003:
    98%
State average pass rate: **98%**

University of California– Los Angeles

- **1009 Moore Hall, MB 951521, Los Angeles, CA 90095-1521**
- **Website:** http://www.gseis.ucla.edu
- **Public**
- **Degrees offered:** master's, Ph.D., Ed.D.
- **Overall rank in the 2005 U.S. News education schools with doctoral programs: 3**

- **Overall rank in the 2005 U.S. News education school specialty rankings:** administration/supervision: 15, curriculum/instruction: 18, education policy: 8, educational psychology: 8, elementary education: 21, higher education administration: 2, secondary education: 17

ADMISSIONS
Admissions phone number: **(310) 825-8326**
Admissions email address: *info@gseis.ucla.edu*
Application website: *http://www.gdnet.ucla.edu/*
Application fee: **$60**
Fall 2005 application deadline: **12/15**
Test requirements: **GRE or MAT**
Test of English as Foreign Language (TOEFL) is required
    for international students.
Minimum TOEFL score required for paper test: **560**
Minimum TOEFL score required for computer test: **220**

Fall 2003
Acceptance rate for master's degree programs: **51%**
Acceptance rate for doctoral programs: **24%**
Average GRE verbal: **545**, Average GRE quantitative: **604**,
    Average GRE analytical: **624**
Total 2003 enrollment: **830**
Master's degree enrollment: **452**
    Teacher preparation program enrollment (master's): **358**
Education specialist degree enrollment: **0**
Doctoral degree enrollment: **378**

FINANCIAL INFORMATION
Financial aid phone number: **(310) 206-0400**
Tuition, 2003-2004 academic year: Full-time in-state: **N/A**;
    out-of-state: **$12,245**, Part-time in-state: **N/A**; out-of-state:
    $12,245
Fees: **$6,318**, Room and board: **$18,808**, Books and sup-
    plies: **$1,533**
Number of fellowships awarded to graduate students dur-
    ing the 2003-2004 academic year: **414**
Number of teaching assistant positions: **12**
Number of research assistant positions: **185**
Number of other paid appointments: **9**

ACADEMIC PROGRAMS
Total full-time tenured or tenure-track faculty (fall 2003):
    54, Total part-time faculty (fall 2003): **42**
Areas of specialization: curriculum and instruction, educa-
    tion administration and supervision, education policy,
    educational psychology, elementary teacher education,
    higher education administration, secondary teacher edu-
    cation, special education, student counseling and per-
    sonnel services.
Professional development/partnership school(s) are used
    by students in all of the teaching programs.
During their internships, peer groups of students meet
    regularly to discuss instructional techniques in all of the
    teaching programs.
All of the students in their internships are mentored.
Courses that prepare teachers to pass the National Board of
    Professional Teaching Standards are offered.

Teacher preparation programs: Master's degree in education, including internship/practice teaching and preparation for initial licensure. Education minor for undergraduate students. Alternative program for college graduates leading to provisional licensure.

LICENSING TEST
Pass rate on state's teacher licensing test for 2002-2003: 100%
State average pass rate: 98%

University of California–Riverside

- Graduate School of Education, Riverside, CA 92521
- Website: http://www.education.ucr.edu
- Public
- Degrees offered: master's, Ph.D.

ADMISSIONS
Admissions phone number: (909) 787-5990
Admissions email address: *edgrad@citrus.ucr.edu*
Application fee: $60
Test of English as Foreign Language (TOEFL) is required for international students.
Minimum TOEFL score required for paper test: 550
Minimum TOEFL score required for computer test: 213

Fall 2003
Acceptance rate for master's degree programs: 40%
Acceptance rate for doctoral programs: 29%
Average GRE verbal: 500, Average GRE quantitative: 668
Total 2003 enrollment: 158
Master's degree enrollment: 33
Doctoral degree enrollment: 125

FINANCIAL INFORMATION
Financial aid phone number: (909) 787-6362
Tuition, 2003-2004 academic year: Full-time in-state: $6,890; out-of-state: $19,381

ACADEMIC PROGRAMS
Total full-time tenured or tenure-track faculty (fall 2003): 21
Areas of specialization: curriculum and instruction, education administration and supervision, educational psychology, special education.

LICENSING TEST
Pass rate on state's teacher licensing test for 2002-2003: 99%
State average pass rate: 98%

University of California–San Diego

- 9500 Gilman Drive, La Jolla, CA 92093
- Website: http://www.ucsd.edu/
- Public

LICENSING TEST
Pass rate on state's teacher licensing test for 2002-2003: 100%
State average pass rate: 98%

University of California–Santa Barbara (Gevirtz)

- Gevirtz Graduate School of Education, Santa Barbara, CA 93106-9490
- Website: http://www.education.ucsb.edu
- Public
- Degrees offered: master's, education specialist, Ph.D., Ed.D.
- Overall rank in the 2005 U.S. News education schools with doctoral programs: 51
- Overall rank in the 2005 U.S. News education school specialty rankings: counseling/personnel: 15

ADMISSIONS
Admissions phone number: (805) 893-2137
Admissions email address: *vzumdahl@education.ucsb.edu*
Application website: *http://www.graddiv.ucsb.edu/eapp/*
Application fee: $60
Test requirements: GRE or MAT
Test of English as Foreign Language (TOEFL) is required for international students.
Minimum TOEFL score required for paper test: 550
Minimum TOEFL score required for computer test: 213

Fall 2003
Acceptance rate for master's degree programs: 61%
Acceptance rate for education specialist degree programs: 94%
Acceptance rate for doctoral programs: 29%
Average GRE verbal: 494, Average GRE quantitative: 578, Average GRE analytical: 587, Average MAT: 46
Total 2003 enrollment: 413
Master's degree enrollment: 153
    Teacher preparation program enrollment (master's): 118
Education specialist degree enrollment: 16
Doctoral degree enrollment: 244

FINANCIAL INFORMATION
Financial aid phone number: (805) 893-2432
Tuition, 2003-2004 academic year: Full-time in-state: $5,699; out-of-state: $12,246

Fees: **$1,419**, Room and board: **$13,152**, Books and supplies: **$1,279**, Miscellaneous expenses: **$2,982**
Number of fellowships awarded to graduate students during the 2003-2004 academic year: **545**
Number of teaching assistant positions: **123**
Number of research assistant positions: **64**
Number of other paid appointments: **86**

ACADEMIC PROGRAMS

Total full-time tenured or tenure-track faculty (fall 2003): **48**, Total part-time faculty (fall 2003): **29**

Areas of specialization: curriculum and instruction, education administration and supervision, education policy, elementary teacher education, higher education administration, secondary teacher education, special education, student counseling and personnel services.

Professional development/partnership school(s) are used by students in all of the teaching programs.

During their internships, peer groups of students meet regularly to discuss instructional techniques in all of the teaching programs.

All of the students in their internships are mentored.

Courses that prepare teachers to pass the National Board of Professional Teaching Standards are not offered.

Teacher preparation programs: Master's degree in education, including internship/practice teaching and preparation for initial licensure. Education minor for undergraduate students.

LICENSING TEST

Pass rate on state's teacher licensing test for 2002-2003: **100%**
State average pass rate: **98%**

University of California–Santa Cruz

■ **1156 High Street, Santa Cruz, CA 95064**
■ **Website:** http://www.graddiv.ucsc.edu/
■ **Public**
■ **Degrees offered:** master's, Ph.D.

ADMISSIONS

Admissions phone number: **(831) 459-2301**
Admissions email address: *gradadm@ucsc.edu*
Application website:
http://www.graddiv.ucsc.edu/PSapplicationfiling.html
Application fee: **$60**
Fall 2005 application deadline: **12/15**
Test of English as Foreign Language (TOEFL) is required for international students.

Fall 2003

Acceptance rate for master's degree programs: **71%**
Total 2003 enrollment: **137**
Master's degree enrollment: **128**
  Teacher preparation program enrollment (master's): **128**

Education specialist degree enrollment: **0**
Doctoral degree enrollment: **9**

FINANCIAL INFORMATION

Financial aid phone number: **(831) 459-2963**
Tuition, 2003-2004 academic year: Full-time in-state: **$6,731**; out-of-state: **$12,245**, Part-time in-state: **$3,600**; out-of-state: **$6,122**
Fees: **$682**, Room and board: **$11,265**, Books and supplies: **$1,203**, Miscellaneous expenses: **$3,624**

ACADEMIC PROGRAMS

Total full-time tenured or tenure-track faculty (fall 2003): **13**, Total part-time faculty (fall 2003): **23**

Areas of specialization: elementary teacher education, secondary teacher education.

Professional development/partnership school(s) are used by students in some of the teaching programs.

During their internships, peer groups of students meet regularly to discuss instructional techniques in all of the teaching programs.

All of the students in their internships are mentored.

Courses that prepare teachers to pass the National Board of Professional Teaching Standards are not offered.

Teacher preparation programs: Master's degree in education, including internship/practice teaching and preparation for initial licensure. Education minor for undergraduate students.

LICENSING TEST

Pass rate on state's teacher licensing test for 2002-2003: **100%**
State average pass rate: **98%**

University of Judaism

■ **15600 Mulholland Drive, Los Angeles, CA 91436**
■ **Website:** http://www.uj.edu/
■ **Private**
■ **Degrees offered:** master's

ADMISSIONS

Admissions phone number: **(310) 440-1586**
Admissions email address: *SKORIN@UJ.EDU*
Fall 2005 application deadline: **rolling**
Test requirements: **GRE or MAT**

Fall 2003

Acceptance rate for master's degree programs: **78%**
Average GRE verbal: **525**, Average GRE quantitative: **563**
Total 2003 enrollment: **38**
Master's degree enrollment: **38**

FINANCIAL INFORMATION

Financial aid phone number: **(310) 440-1252**

University of La Verne

■ 1950 Third Street, La Verne, CA 91750
■ **Website:** http://www.ulv.edu
■ **Private**
■ **Degrees offered:** bachelor's, master's, Ed.D.

ADMISSIONS

Admissions phone number: **(909) 593-3511**
Admissions email address: *gradadmt@ulv.edu*
Application fee: **$50**
Fall 2005 application deadline: **rolling**
Test requirements: **GRE or MAT**
Test of English as Foreign Language (TOEFL) is required
    for international students.
Minimum TOEFL score required for paper test: **550**
Minimum TOEFL score required for computer test: **213**

Fall 2003

Acceptance rate for master's degree programs: **57%**
Acceptance rate for doctoral programs: **46%**
Average MAT: **40**
Total 2003 enrollment: **1,112**
Master's degree enrollment: **781**
    Teacher preparation program enrollment (master's): **295**
Doctoral degree enrollment: **331**

FINANCIAL INFORMATION

Financial aid phone number: **(909) 593-3511**
Tuition, 2003-2004 academic year: Full-time: **$550/credit
    hour**; Part-time: **$550/credit hour**
Fees: **$90**

ACADEMIC PROGRAMS

Total full-time tenured or tenure-track faculty (fall 2003):
    28, Total part-time faculty (fall 2003): **86**
Areas of specialization: curriculum and instruction, educa-
    tion administration and supervision, elementary teacher
    education, secondary teacher education, special educa-
    tion, student counseling and personnel services.
Professional development/partnership school(s) are used
    by students in all of the teaching programs.
During their internships, peer groups of students meet
    regularly to discuss instructional techniques in all of the
    teaching programs.
All of the students in their internships are mentored.

LICENSING TEST

Pass rate on state's teacher licensing test for 2002-2003: **99%**
State average pass rate: **98%**

University of the Pacific

■ 3601 Pacific Avenue, Stockton, CA 95211
■ **Website:** http://www.pacific.edu
■ **Private**

■ **Degrees offered:** bachelor's, master's, education
    specialist, Ph.D., Ed.D.

ADMISSIONS

Admissions phone number: **(209) 946-2683**
Admissions email address: *gradschool@pacific.edu*
Application fee: **$50**
Fall 2005 application deadline: **1/15**
Test of English as Foreign Language (TOEFL) is required
    for international students.
Minimum TOEFL score required for paper test: **475**
Minimum TOEFL score required for computer test: **150**

Fall 2003

Acceptance rate for master's degree programs: **69%**
Acceptance rate for education specialist degree programs: **64%**
Acceptance rate for doctoral programs: **55%**
Total 2003 enrollment: **143**
Master's degree enrollment: **55**
    Teacher preparation program enrollment (master's): **35**
Education specialist degree enrollment: **11**
Doctoral degree enrollment: **77**

FINANCIAL INFORMATION

Financial aid phone number: **(209) 946-2421**
Tuition, 2003-2004 academic year: Full-time: **$725/credit
    hour**; Part-time: **$725/credit hour**
Fees: **$270**, Room and board: **$7,490**, Books and supplies:
    $612, Miscellaneous expenses: **$936**
Number of research assistant positions: **17**

ACADEMIC PROGRAMS

Total full-time tenured or tenure-track faculty (fall 2003):
    16, Total part-time faculty (fall 2003): **9**
Areas of specialization: curriculum and instruction, education
    administration and supervision, educational psychology,
    elementary teacher education, higher education adminis-
    tration, secondary teacher education, special education.
All of the students in their internships are mentored.
Courses that prepare teachers to pass the National Board of
    Professional Teaching Standards are not offered.
Teacher preparation programs: Four-year baccalaureate-
    degree program leading to initial licensure that includes
    either a major or minor in education and practice teaching.
    Five-year program leading to initial licensure that results in
    a baccalaureate degree (with a major or minor in educa-
    tion) plus graduate credit and includes practice teaching.
    Five-year program leading to initial licensure that results in
    a baccalaureate degree (with a major or minor in educa-
    tion) plus a master's degree and includes practice teaching.
    Master's program preparing college graduates for initial
    licensure; includes practice teaching. Alternative program
    for college graduates leading to provisional licensure.
The education program is currently accredited by the
    National Council for Accreditation of Teacher Education.

LICENSING TEST

Pass rate on state's teacher licensing test for 2002-2003:
    100%
State average pass rate: **98%**

University of Redlands

- PO Box 3080, Redlands, CA 92373
- Website: http://www.redlands.edu/
- Private

LICENSING TEST
Pass rate on state's teacher licensing test for 2002-2003: 100%
State average pass rate: 98%

University of San Diego

- 5998 Alcala Park, San Diego, CA 92110-2492
- Website: http://www.sandiego.edu/soe
- Private
- Degrees offered: bachelor's, master's, Ed.D.

ADMISSIONS
Admissions phone number: (619) 260-4506
Admissions email address: *grads@sandiego.edu*
Application website: *http://www.sandiego.edu/gradmiss/application.html*
Application fee: $45
Test requirements: GRE or MAT
Test of English as Foreign Language (TOEFL) is required for international students.
Minimum TOEFL score required for paper test: 580
Minimum TOEFL score required for computer test: 237

Fall 2003
Acceptance rate for master's degree programs: 70%
Acceptance rate for doctoral programs: 49%
Total 2003 enrollment: 419
Master's degree enrollment: 291
   Teacher preparation program enrollment (master's): 126
Doctoral degree enrollment: 128

FINANCIAL INFORMATION
Financial aid phone number: (619) 260-4514
Tuition, 2003-2004 academic year: Full-time: $825/credit hour; Part-time: $825/credit hour
Fees: $50/credit hour, Room and board: $8,290, Books and supplies: $1,298, Miscellaneous expenses: $3,486
Number of teaching assistant positions: 5
Number of research assistant positions: 4
Number of other paid appointments: 96

ACADEMIC PROGRAMS
Total full-time tenured or tenure-track faculty (fall 2003): 32, Total part-time faculty (fall 2003): 70
Areas of specialization: curriculum and instruction, education administration and supervision, elementary teacher education, higher education administration, secondary teacher education, special education, student counseling and personnel services.

Professional development/partnership school(s) are used by students in none of the teaching programs.
During their internships, peer groups of students meet regularly to discuss instructional techniques in some of the teaching programs.
All of the students in their internships are mentored.
Courses that prepare teachers to pass the National Board of Professional Teaching Standards are not offered.
Teacher preparation programs: Master's degree in education, including internship/practice teaching and preparation for initial licensure.

LICENSING TEST
Pass rate on state's teacher licensing test for 2002-2003: 100%
State average pass rate: 98%

University of San Francisco

- 2130 Fulton Street, San Francisco, CA 94117-1080
- Website: http://www.usfca.edu
- Private
- Degrees offered: master's, Ed.D.

ADMISSIONS
Admissions phone number: (415) 422-6563
Admissions email address: *admissions@usfca.edu*
Application website: *http://www.usfca.edu/acadserv/admission/gradandadult/apply.html*
Application fee: $55
Test requirements: GRE or MAT
Test of English as Foreign Language (TOEFL) is required for international students.
Minimum TOEFL score required for paper test: 570
Minimum TOEFL score required for computer test: 230

Fall 2003
Acceptance rate for master's degree programs: 83%
Acceptance rate for doctoral programs: 78%
Total 2003 enrollment: 998
Master's degree enrollment: 739
   Teacher preparation program enrollment (master's): 433
Doctoral degree enrollment: 259

FINANCIAL INFORMATION
Financial aid phone number: (415) 422-6303
Tuition, 2003-2004 academic year: full-time: $800/credit hour; Part-time: $800/credit hour
Fees: $800/credit hour, Room and board: $10,860, Books and supplies: $900
Number of teaching assistant positions: 16
Number of research assistant positions: 10

ACADEMIC PROGRAMS
Total full-time tenured or tenure-track faculty (fall 2003): 32, Total part-time faculty (fall 2003): 94
Areas of specialization: curriculum and instruction, education administration and supervision, educational psy-

chology, elementary teacher education, higher education administration, secondary teacher education, special education, student counseling and personnel services.

Professional development/partnership school(s) are used by students in some of the teaching programs.

During their internships, peer groups of students meet regularly to discuss instructional techniques in all of the teaching programs.

All of the students in their internships are mentored.

Courses that prepare teachers to pass the National Board of Professional Teaching Standards are not offered.

Teacher preparation programs: Master's degree in education, including internship/practice teaching and preparation for initial licensure.

LICENSING TEST
Pass rate on state's teacher licensing test for 2002-2003: 99%
State average pass rate: 98%

University of Southern California (Rossier)

- 3470 Trousdale Parkway, Waite Phillips Hall, Los Angeles, CA 90089-0031
- **Website:** http://www.usc.edu/dept/education/
- **Private**
- **Degrees offered:** bachelor's, master's, Ph.D., Ed.D.
- **Overall rank in the 2005 U.S. News education schools with doctoral programs:** 22
- **Overall rank in the 2005 U.S. News education school specialty rankings:** administration/supervision: 18, education policy: 15, higher education administration: 5

ADMISSIONS
Admissions phone number: **(213) 740-2606**
Admissions email address: *soeinfo@usc.edu*
Application website: *http://www.usc.edu/dept/education/admission_graduate.html*
Application fee: **$65**
Fall 2005 application deadline: **3/15**
Test requirements: **GRE**

Fall 2003
Acceptance rate for master's degree programs: **68%**
Acceptance rate for doctoral programs: **47%**
Average GRE verbal: **484**, Average GRE quantitative: **572**
Total 2003 enrollment: **1,045**
Master's degree enrollment: **359**
    Teacher preparation program enrollment (master's): **162**
Doctoral degree enrollment: **686**

FINANCIAL INFORMATION
Financial aid phone number: **(213) 740-2157**
Tuition, 2003-2004 academic year: Full-time: **$949/credit hour**; Part-time: **$949/credit hour**

Fees: **$855**, Room and board: **$9,258**, Books and supplies: **$962**, Miscellaneous expenses: **$1,728**
Number of fellowships awarded to graduate students during the 2003-2004 academic year: **12**
Number of teaching assistant positions: **14**
Number of research assistant positions: **16**
Number of other paid appointments: **24**

ACADEMIC PROGRAMS
Total full-time tenured or tenure-track faculty (fall 2003): **29**, Total part-time faculty (fall 2003): **47**
Areas of specialization: curriculum and instruction, education administration and supervision, education policy, educational psychology, elementary teacher education, higher education administration, secondary teacher education, special education, student counseling and personnel services.

Professional development/partnership school(s) are used by students in all of the teaching programs.

During their internships, peer groups of students meet regularly to discuss instructional techniques in all of the teaching programs.

All of the students in their internships are mentored.

Courses that prepare teachers to pass the National Board of Professional Teaching Standards are not offered.

Teacher preparation programs: Four-year baccalaureate-degree program leading to initial licensure that includes either a major or minor in education and practice teaching.

LICENSING TEST
Pass rate on state's teacher licensing test for 2002-2003: 97%
State average pass rate: 98%

Whittier College

- 13406 Philadelphia Street, PO Box 634, Whittier, CA 90608
- **Website:** http://www.whittier.edu/
- **Private**

ADMISSIONS
Admissions phone number: **(562) 907-4248**
Admissions email address: *cgeorge@whittier.edu*
Application fee: **$60**
Fall 2005 application deadline: **3/1**
Test of English as Foreign Language (TOEFL) is required for international students.

FINANCIAL INFORMATION
Financial aid phone number: **(562) 907-4285**

LICENSING TEST
Pass rate on state's teacher licensing test for 2002-2003: **100%**
State average pass rate: 98%

COLORADO

Adams State College

- **208 Edgemont Boulevard, Alamosa, CO 81102**
- **Website:** http://www.adams.edu/
- **Public**

LICENSING TEST
Pass rate on state's teacher licensing test for 2002-2003: 82%
State average pass rate: 94%

Colorado Christian College

- **180 S. Garrison Street, Lakewood, CO 80226**
- **Website:** http://www.ccu.edu/
- **Private**
- **Degrees offered:** master's

ADMISSIONS
Admissions phone number: (303) 963-3150
Admissions email address: *smountjoy@ccu.edu*
Application fee: $40
Fall 2005 application deadline: 8/15
Test of English as Foreign Language (TOEFL) is required for international students.
Minimum TOEFL score required for paper test: 650

Fall 2003
Acceptance rate for master's degree programs: 94%
Total 2003 enrollment: 85
Master's degree enrollment: 85
   Teacher preparation program enrollment (master's): 85

FINANCIAL INFORMATION
Financial aid phone number: (303) 963-3230
Tuition, 2003-2004 academic year: Full-time: **$342/credit hour**; Part-time: **$342/credit hour**

Books and supplies: **$1,100**

ACADEMIC PROGRAMS
Areas of specialization: curriculum and instruction.
Professional development/partnership school(s) are used by students in none of the teaching programs.
During their internships, peer groups of students meet regularly to discuss instructional techniques in none of the teaching programs.
All of the students in their internships are mentored.
Courses that prepare teachers to pass the National Board of Professional Teaching Standards are not offered.
Teacher preparation programs: Four-year baccalaureate-degree program leading to initial licensure that includes either a major or minor in education and practice teaching. Five-year program leading to initial licensure that results in a baccalaureate degree (with a major or minor in education) plus a master's degree and includes practice teaching. Alternative program for college graduates leading to provisional licensure.

LICENSING TEST
Pass rate on state's teacher licensing test for 2002-2003: 90%
State average pass rate: 94%

Colorado College

- **14 East Cache La Poudre, Colorado Springs, CO 80903**
- **Website:** http://www.ColoradoCollege.edu/Dept/ED/
- **Private**
- **Degrees offered:** master's

ADMISSIONS
Admissions phone number: (719) 389-6472
Admissions email address: *munruh@ColoradoCollege.edu*
Application fee: $50
Fall 2005 application deadline: 2/1

Fall 2003
Acceptance rate for master's degree programs: 79%

Total 2003 enrollment: 26
Master's degree enrollment: 26
   Teacher preparation program enrollment (master's): 26

FINANCIAL INFORMATION
Financial aid phone number: **(719) 389-6651**
Tuition, 2003-2004 academic year: **$19,775**
Books and supplies: **$800**, Miscellaneous expenses: **$1,145**
Number of other paid appointments: **26**

ACADEMIC PROGRAMS
Total full-time tenured or tenure-track faculty (fall 2003): **3**,
   Total part-time faculty (fall 2003): **23**
Areas of specialization: elementary teacher education, secondary teacher education.
Professional development/partnership school(s) are used by students in all of the teaching programs.
During their internships, peer groups of students meet regularly to discuss instructional techniques in all of the teaching programs.
All of the students in their internships are mentored.
Courses that prepare teachers to pass the National Board of Professional Teaching Standards are not offered.
Teacher preparation programs: Master's program preparing college graduates for initial licensure; includes practice teaching.

LICENSING TEST
Pass rate on state's teacher licensing test for 2002-2003: **100%**
State average pass rate: **94%**

Colorado State University

- ■ Graduate School, Fort Collins, CO 80523-2015
- ■ **Website:** http://www.colostate.edu/
- ■ **Public**
- ■ **Degrees offered:** master's, Ph.D.
- ■ **Overall rank in the 2005 U.S. News education school specialty rankings:** vocational/technical: 7

ADMISSIONS
Admissions phone number: **(970) 491-6909**
Admissions email address: *gschool@grad.colostate.edu*
Application website: *http://www.colostate.edu/Depts/Grad*
Application fee: **$50**
Fall 2005 application deadline: **3/15**
Test requirements: **GRE**
Test of English as Foreign Language (TOEFL) is required for international students.
Minimum TOEFL score required for paper test: **550**
Minimum TOEFL score required for computer test: **213**

Fall 2003
Acceptance rate for master's degree programs: **46%**
Acceptance rate for doctoral programs: **58%**
Total 2003 enrollment: **496**
Master's degree enrollment: **267**

   Teacher preparation program enrollment (master's): **59**
Doctoral degree enrollment: **229**

FINANCIAL INFORMATION
Financial aid phone number: **(970) 491-6321**
Tuition, 2003-2004 academic year: Full-time in-state: **$3,347**; out-of-state: **$13,955**, Part-time in-state: **$186/credit hour**; out-of-state: **$775/credit hour**
Fees: **$806**, Room and board: **$6,045**, Books and supplies: **$900**, Miscellaneous expenses: **$2,700**
Number of fellowships awarded to graduate students during the 2003-2004 academic year: **1**
Number of teaching assistant positions: **8**
Number of research assistant positions: **9**
Number of other paid appointments: **4**

ACADEMIC PROGRAMS
Total full-time tenured or tenure-track faculty (fall 2003): **25**, Total part-time faculty (fall 2003): **1**
Areas of specialization: curriculum and instruction, education administration and supervision, education policy, higher education administration, secondary teacher education, student counseling and personnel services.
The education program is currently accredited by the National Council for Accreditation of Teacher Education.

LICENSING TEST
Pass rate on state's teacher licensing test for 2002-2003: **95%**
State average pass rate: **94%**

Regis University

- ■ 3333 Regis Boulevard, Denver, CO 80221
- ■ **Website:** http://www.regis.edu/default.asp
- ■ **Private**

LICENSING TEST
Pass rate on state's teacher licensing test for 2002-2003: **87%**
State average pass rate: **94%**

University of Colorado– Boulder

- ■ Campus Box 249, Boulder, CO 80309-0249
- ■ **Website:** http://www.colorado.edu/education
- ■ **Public**
- ■ **Degrees offered:** master's, Ph.D.
- ■ **Overall rank in the 2005 U.S. News education schools with doctoral programs:** 44

ADMISSIONS
Admissions phone number: **(303) 492-6555**
Admissions email address: *edadvise@colorado.edu*

Application website:
http://www.colorado.edu/education/admissions/index.html
Application fee: $50
Fall 2005 application deadline: 2/1
Test requirements: **GRE or MAT**
Test of English as Foreign Language (TOEFL) is required
for international students.
Minimum TOEFL score required for paper test: 650
Minimum TOEFL score required for computer test: 280

Fall 2003
Acceptance rate for master's degree programs: 60%
Acceptance rate for doctoral programs: 38%
Average GRE verbal: 563, Average GRE quantitative: 621,
Average GRE analytical: 625
Total 2003 enrollment: 466
Master's degree enrollment: 387
Teacher preparation program enrollment (master's): 369
Doctoral degree enrollment: 79

FINANCIAL INFORMATION
Financial aid phone number: (303) 492-5091
Tuition, 2003-2004 academic year: Full-time in-state:
$2,484; out-of-state: $11,042, Part-time in-state:
$711/credit hour; out-of-state: $3,278/credit hour
Fees: $419, Room and board: $6,272, Books and supplies:
$1,142, Miscellaneous expenses: $3,294
Number of fellowships awarded to graduate students dur-
ing the 2003-2004 academic year: 11
Number of teaching assistant positions: 52
Number of research assistant positions: 62

ACADEMIC PROGRAMS
Total full-time tenured or tenure-track faculty (fall 2003):
31, Total part-time faculty (fall 2003): 41
Areas of specialization: curriculum and instruction, education
policy, educational psychology, elementary teacher educa-
tion, secondary teacher education, special education.
Professional development/partnership school(s) are used
by students in some of the teaching programs.
During their internships, peer groups of students meet
regularly to discuss instructional techniques in all of the
teaching programs.
All of the students in their internships are mentored.
Courses that prepare teachers to pass the National Board of
Professional Teaching Standards are not offered.
Teacher preparation programs: Master's degree in educa-
tion, including internship/practice teaching and prepara-
tion for initial licensure.
The education program is currently accredited by the
National Council for Accreditation of Teacher Education.

LICENSING TEST
Pass rate on state's teacher licensing test for 2002-2003:
100%
State average pass rate: 94%

University of Colorado–Colorado Springs

■ PO Box 7150, Colorado Springs, CO 80933-3383
■ **Website:** http://www.uccs.edu/
■ Public

LICENSING TEST
Pass rate on state's teacher licensing test for 2002-2003:
100%
State average pass rate: 94%

University of Colorado–Denver

■ Campus Box 106, PO Box 173364, Denver, CO 80217-3364
■ **Website:** http://www.cudenver.edu
■ Public
■ **Degrees offered:** master's, education specialist, Ph.D.

ADMISSIONS
Admissions phone number: (303) 556-8854
Admissions email address: *lori.sisneros@cudenver.edu*
Application website:
*http://www.cudenver.edu/admissions/graduate+
admissions/default.htm*
Application fee: $50
Fall 2005 application deadline: 4/15
Test requirements: **GRE or MAT**
Test of English as Foreign Language (TOEFL) is required
for international students.
Minimum TOEFL score required for paper test: 500
Minimum TOEFL score required for computer test: 173

Fall 2003
Acceptance rate for master's degree programs: 88%
Acceptance rate for education specialist degree programs:
60%
Acceptance rate for doctoral programs: 61%
Average GRE verbal: 470, Average GRE quantitative: 546
Total 2003 enrollment: 1,310
Master's degree enrollment: 1,112
Teacher preparation program enrollment (master's): 803
Education specialist degree enrollment: 103
Doctoral degree enrollment: 95

FINANCIAL INFORMATION
Financial aid phone number: (303) 556-2886
Tuition, 2003-2004 academic year: Full-time in-state:
$4,516; out-of-state: $16,074, Part-time in-state: $2,895;
out-of-state: $6,750
Fees: $600, Room and board: $6,184, Books and supplies:
$820, Miscellaneous expenses: $1,323
Number of research assistant positions: 12

ACADEMIC PROGRAMS

Total full-time tenured or tenure-track faculty (fall 2003): 35, Total part-time faculty (fall 2003): 79

Areas of specialization: curriculum and instruction, education administration and supervision, education policy, educational psychology, elementary teacher education, secondary teacher education, special education, student counseling and personnel services.

Professional development/partnership school(s) are used by students in all of the teaching programs.

During their internships, peer groups of students meet regularly to discuss instructional techniques in all of the teaching programs.

All of the students in their internships are mentored.

Courses that prepare teachers to pass the National Board of Professional Teaching Standards are offered.

Teacher preparation programs: Master's degree in education, including internship/practice teaching and preparation for initial licensure. Education minor for undergraduate students.

The education program is currently accredited by the National Council for Accreditation of Teacher Education.

LICENSING TEST

Pass rate on state's teacher licensing test for 2002-2003: 100%

State average pass rate: 94%

University of Denver

- **■** Graduate Office, A. Hyde Building, Denver, CO 80208
- **■** **Website:** http://www.du.edu/education/
- **■** **Private**
- **■** **Degrees offered:** master's, education specialist, Ph.D.

ADMISSIONS

Admissions phone number: **(303) 871-2509**

Admissions email address: *educo3@denver.du.edu*

Application fee: **$50**

Test requirements: **GRE**

Minimum TOEFL score required for paper test: **550**

Minimum TOEFL score required for computer test: **213**

Fall 2003

Acceptance rate for master's degree programs: **77%**

Acceptance rate for education specialist degree programs: **85%**

Acceptance rate for doctoral programs: **48%**

Average GRE verbal: **550**, Average GRE quantitative: **500**

Total 2003 enrollment: **422**

Master's degree enrollment: **223**

　Teacher preparation program enrollment (master's): **76**

Education specialist degree enrollment: **29**

Doctoral degree enrollment: **170**

FINANCIAL INFORMATION

Financial aid phone number: **(303) 871-4020**

Tuition, 2003-2004 academic year: Full-time: **$674/credit hour**; Part-time: **$674/credit hour**

Fees: **$4/credit hour**

Number of fellowships awarded to graduate students during the 2003-2004 academic year: **15**

Number of teaching assistant positions: **5**

Number of research assistant positions: **18**

Number of other paid appointments: **7**

ACADEMIC PROGRAMS

Total full-time tenured or tenure-track faculty (fall 2003): 18, Total part-time faculty (fall 2003): 0

Areas of specialization: curriculum and instruction, education administration and supervision, educational psychology, elementary teacher education, higher education administration, secondary teacher education, student counseling and personnel services.

Professional development/partnership school(s) are used by students in none of the teaching programs.

During their internships, peer groups of students meet regularly to discuss instructional techniques in all of the teaching programs.

Courses that prepare teachers to pass the National Board of Professional Teaching Standards are not offered.

LICENSING TEST

Pass rate on state's teacher licensing test for 2002-2003: 82%

State average pass rate: 94%

University of Northern Colorado

- **■** College of Education, Greeley, CO 80639
- **■** **Website:** http://www.unco.edu/grad/general/home.htm
- **■** **Public**
- **■** **Degrees offered:** master's, education specialist, Ph.D., Ed.D.
- **■** **Overall rank in the 2005 U.S. News education school specialty rankings:** special education: 19

ADMISSIONS

Admissions phone number: **(970) 351-2831**

Admissions email address: *gradsch@unco.edu*

Application website: *http://www.unco.edu/grad/admissions/home.htm*

Application fee: **$35**

Fall 2005 application deadline: **rolling**

Test requirements: **GRE or MAT**

Test of English as Foreign Language (TOEFL) is required for international students.

Minimum TOEFL score required for paper test: **550**

Fall 2003

Acceptance rate for master's degree programs: **64%**

Acceptance rate for education specialist degree programs: **39%**

Acceptance rate for doctoral programs: **47%**

Average GRE verbal: **482**, Average GRE quantitative: **593**, Average GRE analytical: **558**
Total 2003 enrollment: **756**
Master's degree enrollment: **566**
    Teacher preparation program enrollment (master's): **414**
Education specialist degree enrollment: **29**
Doctoral degree enrollment: **161**

FINANCIAL INFORMATION
Financial aid phone number: **(970) 351-2502**
Tuition, 2003-2004 academic year: Full-time in-state: **$2,980**; out-of-state: **$12,396**, Part-time in-state: **$166/credit hour**; out-of-state: **$689**
Fees: **$627**, Room and board: **$5,782**, Books and supplies: **$892**, Miscellaneous expenses: **$2,249**
Number of teaching assistant positions: **26**
Number of other paid appointments: **33**

ACADEMIC PROGRAMS
Total full-time tenured or tenure-track faculty (fall 2003): **71**, Total part-time faculty (fall 2003): **12**

Areas of specialization: education administration and supervision, education policy, educational psychology, elementary teacher education, higher education administration, secondary teacher education, special education, student counseling and personnel services.
Professional development/partnership school(s) are used by students in all of the teaching programs.
During their internships, peer groups of students meet regularly to discuss instructional techniques in all of the teaching programs.
All of the students in their internships are mentored.
Teacher preparation programs: Master's degree in education, including internship/practice teaching and preparation for initial licensure.
The education program is currently accredited by the National Council for Accreditation of Teacher Education.

LICENSING TEST
Pass rate on state's teacher licensing test for 2002-2003: **89%**
State average pass rate: **94%**

CONNECTICUT

Central Connecticut State University

■ **1615 Stanley Street, New Britain, CT 06050**
■ **Website:** http://www.ccsu.edu/grad/
■ **Public**
■ **Degrees offered:** bachelor's, master's, Ed.D.

ADMISSIONS

Admissions phone number: **(860) 832-2350**
Admissions email address: *oliva@ccsu.edu*
Application website:
   http://www.ccsu.edu/grad/admissions.htm
Application fee: **$50**
Test requirements: **GRE**
Fall 2005 application deadline: **7/1**
Test of English as Foreign Language (TOEFL) is required for international students.
Minimum TOEFL score required for paper test: **550**
Minimum TOEFL score required for computer test: **213**

Fall 2003
Acceptance rate for master's degree programs: **64%**
Acceptance rate for doctoral programs: **49%**
Total 2003 enrollment: **899**
Master's degree enrollment: **856**
   Teacher preparation program enrollment (master's): **565**
Doctoral degree enrollment: **43**

FINANCIAL INFORMATION

Financial aid phone number: **(860) 832-2200**
Tuition, 2003-2004 academic year: Full-time in-state: **$3,298**; out-of-state: **$9,190**, Part-time in-state: **$300/credit hour**; out-of-state: **$300/credit hour**
Fees: **$2,670**, Room and board: **$6,576**, Books and supplies: **$750**, Miscellaneous expenses: **$1,744**
Number of paid appointments: **29**

ACADEMIC PROGRAMS

Total full-time tenured or tenure-track faculty (fall 2003): **64**, Total part-time faculty (fall 2003): **76**
Areas of specialization: education administration and supervision, elementary teacher education, secondary teacher education, special education, student counseling and personnel services.
Professional development/partnership school(s) are used by students in some of the teaching programs.
During their internships, peer groups of students meet regularly to discuss instructional techniques in some of the teaching programs.
All of the students in their internships are mentored.
Courses that prepare teachers to pass the National Board of Professional Teaching Standards are not offered.
The education program is currently accredited by the National Council for Accreditation of Teacher Education.

LICENSING TEST

Pass rate on state's teacher licensing test for 2002-2003: **94%**
State average pass rate: **97%**

Eastern Connecticut State University

■ **83 Windham Street, Willimantic, CT 06226**
■ **Website:** http://www.easternct.edu
■ **Public**
■ **Degrees offered:** bachelor's, master's

ADMISSIONS

Admissions phone number: **(860) 465-5292**
Admissions email address:
   graduateadmissions@easternct.edu
Application website: *http://www.onlinecsu.net*
Application fee: **$40**
Fall 2005 application deadline: **rolling**
Test of English as Foreign Language (TOEFL) is required for international students.
Minimum TOEFL score required for paper test: **550**

Fall 2003

Total 2003 enrollment: 254

Master's degree enrollment: 254

   Teacher preparation program enrollment (master's): 223

FINANCIAL INFORMATION

Financial aid phone number: **(860) 465-5205**

Tuition, 2003-2004 academic year: Full-time in-state: **$3,298**; out-of-state: **$9,190**, Part-time in-state: **$265/credit hour**; out-of-state: **$265/credit hour**

Fees: **$2,773**

Number of teaching assistant positions: 2

ACADEMIC PROGRAMS

Total full-time tenured or tenure-track faculty (fall 2003): **9** Total part-time faculty (fall 2003): **17**

Areas of specialization: elementary teacher education, secondary teacher education.

Professional development/partnership school(s) are used by students in all of the teaching programs.

During their internships, peer groups of students meet regularly to discuss instructional techniques in all of the teaching programs.

All of the students in their internships are mentored.

Courses that prepare teachers to pass the National Board of Professional Teaching Standards are not offered.

Teacher preparation programs: Four-year baccalaureate-degree program leading to initial licensure that includes either a major or minor in education and practice teaching. Master's program preparing college graduates for initial licensure; includes practice teaching.

LICENSING TEST

Pass rate on state's teacher licensing test for 2002-2003: **100%**

State average pass rate: **97%**

Fairfield University

■ **1073 North Benson Road, Fairfield, CT 06824-5195**
■ **Website:** http://www.fairfield.edu
■ **Private**
■ **Degrees offered:** master's

ADMISSIONS

Admissions phone number: **(203) 254-4184**

Admissions email address: *gradadmis@mail.fairfield.edu*

Application fee: **$55**

Fall 2005 application deadline: **rolling**

Test of English as Foreign Language (TOEFL) is required for international students.

Minimum TOEFL score required for paper test: **550**

Minimum TOEFL score required for computer test: **213**

Fall 2003

Acceptance rate for master's degree programs: **66%**

Total 2003 enrollment: **476**

Master's degree enrollment: **476**

   Teacher preparation program enrollment (master's): **129**

FINANCIAL INFORMATION

Financial aid phone number: **(203) 254-4125**

Tuition, 2003-2004 academic year: Full-time: **$410/credit hour**; Part-time: **$410/credit hour**

Fees: **$85**, Room and board: **$8,920**, Books and supplies: **$500**, Miscellaneous expenses: **$1,900**

Number of other paid appointments: **13**

ACADEMIC PROGRAMS

Total full-time tenured or tenure-track faculty (fall 2003): **17**, Total part-time faculty (fall 2003): **28**

Areas of specialization: curriculum and instruction, educational psychology, elementary teacher education, secondary teacher education, special education, student counseling and personnel services.

Professional development/partnership school(s) are used by students in all of the teaching programs.

During their internships, peer groups of students meet regularly to discuss instructional techniques in all of the teaching programs.

All of the students in their internships are mentored.

Courses that prepare teachers to pass the National Board of Professional Teaching Standards are not offered.

Teacher preparation programs: Master's degree in education, including internship/practice teaching and preparation for initial licensure. Education minor for undergraduate students.

LICENSING TEST

Pass rate on state's teacher licensing test for 2002-2003: **100%**

State average pass rate: **97%**

Quinnipiac University

■ **275 Mt. Carmel Avenue, Hamden, CT 06518**
■ **Website:** http://www.quinnipiac.edu
■ **Private**
■ **Degrees offered:** master's

ADMISSIONS

Admissions phone number: **(203) 582-8795**

Admissions email address: *graduate@quinnipiac.edu*

Application fee: **$45**

Fall 2005 application deadline: **rolling**

Test of English as Foreign Language (TOEFL) is required for international students.

Minimum TOEFL score required for paper test: **575**

Minimum TOEFL score required for computer test: **233**

Fall 2003

Acceptance rate for master's degree programs: **74%**

Total 2003 enrollment: **137**

Master's degree enrollment: **137**

   Teacher preparation program enrollment (master's): **137**

FINANCIAL INFORMATION

Financial aid phone number: **(203) 582-8588**

Tuition, 2003-2004 academic year: **$500/credit hour**
Fees: **$500**
Number of paid appointments: **1**

ACADEMIC PROGRAMS

Total full-time tenured or tenure-track faculty (fall 2003): **6**
Total part-time faculty (fall 2003): **36**
Areas of specialization: elementary teacher education, secondary teacher education.
Professional development/partnership school(s) are used by students in all of the teaching programs.
During their internships, peer groups of students meet regularly to discuss instructional techniques in all of the teaching programs.
All of the students in their internships are mentored.
Courses that prepare teachers to pass the National Board of Professional Teaching Standards are not offered.
Teacher preparation programs: Master's degree in education, including internship/practice teaching and preparation for initial licensure.

LICENSING TEST

Pass rate on state's teacher licensing test for 2002-2003: **100%**
State average pass rate: **97%**

Sacred Heart University

■ **5151 Park Avenue, Fairfield, CT 06825**
■ **Website:** http://www.sacredheart.edu/graduate
■ **Private**
■ **Degrees offered:** bachelor's, master's, education specialist

ADMISSIONS

Admissions phone number: **(203) 365-7619**
Admissions email address: *gradstudies@sacredheart.edu*
Application website:
http://www.sacredheart.edu/graduate/applyonline
Application fee: **$50**
Fall 2005 application deadline: **rolling**
Test of English as Foreign Language (TOEFL) is required for international students.
Minimum TOEFL score required for paper test: **550**
Minimum TOEFL score required for computer test: **213**

Fall 2003
Acceptance rate for master's degree programs: **79%**
Total 2003 enrollment: **973**
Master's degree enrollment: **973**

FINANCIAL INFORMATION

Financial aid phone number: **(203) 371-7980**
Tuition, 2003-2004 academic year: Full-time: **$405/credit hour**; Part-time: **$405/credit hour**

ACADEMIC PROGRAMS

Areas of specialization: education administration and supervision, elementary teacher education, secondary teacher education.
Professional development/partnership school(s) are used by students in all of the teaching programs.
During their internships, peer groups of students meet regularly to discuss instructional techniques in all of the teaching programs.
All of the students in their internships are mentored.
Courses that prepare teachers to pass the National Board of Professional Teaching Standards are not offered.
Teacher preparation programs: Four-year baccalaureate-degree program leading to initial licensure that includes either a major or minor in education and practice teaching. Five-year program leading to initial licensure that results in a baccalaureate degree (with a major or minor in education) plus graduate credit and includes practice teaching. Five-year program leading to initial licensure that results in a baccalaureate degree (with a major or minor in education) plus a master's degree and includes practice teaching. Master's program preparing college graduates for initial licensure; includes practice teaching.

LICENSING TEST

Pass rate on state's teacher licensing test for 2002-2003: **100%**
State average pass rate: **97%**

Southern Connecticut State University

■ **501 Crescent Street, New Haven, CT 06515**
■ **Website:** http://www.southernct.edu/
■ **Public**

ADMISSIONS

Admissions email address: *GradInfo@southernCT.edu*
Application website: *https://www.southernct.edu/admissions/applications/gradapp/?file=app.php*
Application fee: **$40**
Test of English as Foreign Language (TOEFL) is required for international students.

FINANCIAL INFORMATION

Financial aid phone number: **(203) 392-5222**

LICENSING TEST

Pass rate on state's teacher licensing test for 2002-2003: **92%**
State average pass rate: **97%**

St. Joseph College

- 1678 Asylum Avenue, West Hartford, CT 06117
- **Website:** http://www.sjc.edu
- Private
- **Degrees offered:** bachelor's, master's, education specialist

ADMISSIONS

Admissions phone number: **(860) 231-5261**
Admissions email address: *cerik@sjc.edu*
Application website: *http://www.sjc.edu/graduate*
Application fee: **$25**
Fall 2005 application deadline: **rolling**
Test requirements: **GRE or MAT**
Test of English as Foreign Language (TOEFL) is required for international students.

Fall 2003
Acceptance rate for education specialist degree programs: **44%**
Total 2003 enrollment: **910**
Master's degree enrollment: **641**
 Teacher preparation program enrollment (master's): **355**
Education specialist degree enrollment: **269**

FINANCIAL INFORMATION

Financial aid phone number: **(860) 231-5223**
Tuition, 2003-2004 academic year: Full-time: **$540/credit hour**; Part-time: **$540/credit hour**
Fees: **$55/credit hour**, Books and supplies: **$90**, Miscellaneous expenses: **$30**
Number of research assistant positions: **4**

ACADEMIC PROGRAMS

Total full-time tenured or tenure-track faculty (fall 2003): **81**, Total part-time faculty (fall 2003): **116**
Areas of specialization: curriculum and instruction, education policy, educational psychology, elementary teacher education, secondary teacher education, special education.
Professional development/partnership school(s) are used by students in some of the teaching programs.
During their internships, peer groups of students meet regularly to discuss instructional techniques in all of the teaching programs.
All of the students in their internships are mentored.
Courses that prepare teachers to pass the National Board of Professional Teaching Standards are not offered.
Teacher preparation programs: Four-year baccalaureate-degree program leading to initial licensure that includes either a major or minor in education and practice teaching. Master's program preparing college graduates for initial licensure; includes practice teaching.

LICENSING TEST

Pass rate on state's teacher licensing test for 2002-2003: **100%**
State average pass rate: **97%**

University of Bridgeport

- 126 Park Avenue, Bridgeport, CT 06604
- **Website:** http://www.bridgeport.edu/
- Private
- **Degrees offered:** bachelor's, master's, education specialist, Ed.D.

ADMISSIONS

Admissions phone number: **(203) 576-4552**
Admissions email address: *admit@bridgeport.edu*
Application fee: **$25**
Fall 2005 application deadline: **rolling**
Test requirements: **GRE or MAT**
Test of English as Foreign Language (TOEFL) is required for international students.
Minimum TOEFL score required for paper test: **550**

Fall 2003
Acceptance rate for master's degree programs: **76%**
Acceptance rate for education specialist degree programs: **94%**
Acceptance rate for doctoral programs: **54%**
Total 2003 enrollment: **744**
Master's degree enrollment: **673**
 Teacher preparation program enrollment (master's): **592**
Education specialist degree enrollment: **36**
Doctoral degree enrollment: **35**

FINANCIAL INFORMATION

Financial aid phone number: **(203) 576-4568**
Tuition, 2003-2004 academic year: Full-time: **$433/credit hour**; Part-time: **$433/credit hour**
Fees: **$110**, Room and board: **$4,400**, Books and supplies: **$500**, Miscellaneous expenses: **$500**
Number of paid appointments: **256**

ACADEMIC PROGRAMS

Total full-time tenured or tenure-track faculty (fall 2003): **18**, Total part-time faculty (fall 2003): **33**
Areas of specialization: curriculum and instruction, elementary teacher education, secondary teacher education, student counseling and personnel services.
Professional development/partnership school(s) are used by students in all of the teaching programs.
During their internships, peer groups of students meet regularly to discuss instructional techniques in all of the teaching programs.
All of the students in their internships are mentored.
Courses that prepare teachers to pass the National Board of Professional Teaching Standards are offered.
Teacher preparation programs: Four-year baccalaureate-degree program leading to initial licensure that includes either a major or minor in education and practice teaching. Five-year program leading to initial licensure that results in a baccalaureate degree (with a major or minor in education) plus graduate credit and includes practice teaching. Five-year program leading to initial licensure

that results in a baccalaureate degree (with a major or minor in education) plus a master's degree and includes practice teaching. Master's program preparing college graduates for initial licensure; includes practice teaching.

LICENSING TEST

Pass rate on state's teacher licensing test for 2002-2003: **98%**
State average pass rate: **97%**

University of Connecticut (Neag)

■ **249 Glenbrook Road, Storrs, CT 06269-2064**
■ **Website:** http://www.grad.uconn.edu
■ **Public**
■ **Degrees offered:** bachelor's, master's, Ph.D., Ed.D.
■ **Overall rank in the 2005 U.S. News education schools with doctoral programs:** 31
■ **Overall rank in the 2005 U.S. News education school specialty rankings:** elementary education: 17

ADMISSIONS

Admissions phone number: **(860) 486-3617**
Admissions email address: *gradschool@uconn.edu*
Application website: *http://www.grad.uconn.edu/ applications.html*
Application fee: **$55**
Fall 2005 application deadline: **2/1**
Test requirements: **GRE or MAT**
Test of English as Foreign Language (TOEFL) is required for international students.
Minimum TOEFL score required for paper test: **550**
Minimum TOEFL score required for computer test: **213**

Fall 2003

Acceptance rate for master's degree programs: **68%**
Acceptance rate for doctoral programs: **22%**
Average GRE verbal: **571**, Average GRE quantitative: **599**, Average GRE analytical: **576**
Total 2003 enrollment: **657**
Master's degree enrollment: **411**
    Teacher preparation program enrollment (master's): **286**
Doctoral degree enrollment: **246**

FINANCIAL INFORMATION

Financial aid phone number: **(860) 486-2819**
Tuition, 2003-2004 academic year: Full-time in-state: **$6,538**; out-of-state: **$16,830**, Part-time in-state: **$360/credit hour**; out-of-state: **$935/credit hour**
Fees: **$1,202**, Room and board: **$9,000**, Books and supplies: **$1,250**
Number of fellowships awarded to graduate students during the 2003-2004 academic year: **4**
Number of teaching assistant positions: **47**
Number of research assistant positions: **71**
Number of other paid appointments: **6**

ACADEMIC PROGRAMS

Total full-time tenured or tenure-track faculty (fall 2003): **44**, Total part-time faculty (fall 2003): **38**
Areas of specialization: curriculum and instruction, education administration and supervision, education policy, educational psychology, elementary teacher education, higher education administration, secondary teacher education, special education, student counseling and personnel services.
Professional development/partnership school(s) are used by students in all of the teaching programs.
During their internships, peer groups of students meet regularly to discuss instructional techniques in all of the teaching programs.
All of the students in their internships are mentored.
Courses that prepare teachers to pass the National Board of Professional Teaching Standards are not offered.
Teacher preparation programs: Five-year program leading to initial licensure that results in a baccalaureate degree (with a major or minor in education) plus a master's degree and includes practice teaching. Master's program preparing college graduates for initial licensure; includes practice teaching.
The education program is currently accredited by the National Council for Accreditation of Teacher Education.

LICENSING TEST

Pass rate on state's teacher licensing test for 2002-2003: **100%**
State average pass rate: **97%**

University of Hartford

■ **200 Bloomfield Avenue, Room 200, West Hartford, CT 06117**
■ **Website:** http://www.hartford.edu/
■ **Private**

ADMISSIONS

Admissions phone number: **(860) 768-4371**
Admissions email address: *gettoknow@mail.hartford.edu*
Application website: *http://www.hartford.edu/admission/graduate/gradform.htm*
Minimum TOEFL score required for paper test: **550**

FINANCIAL INFORMATION

Financial aid phone number: **(860) 768-4296**

LICENSING TEST

Pass rate on state's teacher licensing test for 2002-2003: **95%**
State average pass rate: **97%**

University of New Haven

- 300 Boston Post Rd., West Haven, CT 06516
- **Website:** http://www.newhaven.edu
- Private
- **Degrees offered:** master's

ADMISSIONS
Admissions phone number: **(203) 932-7133**
Admissions email address: *gradinfo@newhaven.edu*
Application website: *http://www.newhaven.edu/unh/gradappinfo.html*
Application fee: **$50**
Test of English as Foreign Language (TOEFL) is required for international students.
Minimum TOEFL score required for paper test: **520**
Minimum TOEFL score required for computer test: **190**

Fall 2003
Acceptance rate for master's degree programs: **89%**
Total 2003 enrollment: **248**
Master's degree enrollment: **248**
   Teacher preparation program enrollment (master's): **248**

FINANCIAL INFORMATION
Financial aid phone number: **(203) 932-7315**
Tuition, 2003-2004 academic year: Full-time: **$20,130**; Part-time: **$495/credit hour**
Fees: **$530**, Room and board: **$8,500**, Books and supplies: **$450**
Number of teaching assistant positions: **2**

ACADEMIC PROGRAMS
Total full-time tenured or tenure-track faculty (fall 2003): **10**, Total part-time faculty (fall 2003): **30**
Areas of specialization: curriculum and instruction, educational psychology, elementary teacher education, secondary teacher education, special education.
During their internships, peer groups of students meet regularly to discuss instructional techniques in all of the teaching programs.
All of the students in their internships are mentored.
Courses that prepare teachers to pass the National Board of Professional Teaching Standards are not offered.

LICENSING TEST
Pass rate on state's teacher licensing test for 2002-2003: **100%**
State average pass rate: **97%**

Western Connecticut State University

- 181 White Street, Danbury, CT 06810
- **Website:** http:/www.wcsu.edu
- Public
- **Degrees offered:** bachelor's, master's, Ed.D.

ADMISSIONS
Admissions phone number: **(203) 837-9000**
Application website: *http:/www.wcsu.edu/admissions*
Application fee: **$40**
Fall 2005 application deadline: **rolling**
Test requirements: **MAT**
Test of English as Foreign Language (TOEFL) is required for international students.
Minimum TOEFL score required for paper test: **550**
Minimum TOEFL score required for computer test: **213**

Fall 2003
Total 2003 enrollment: **390**
Master's degree enrollment: **364**
   Teacher preparation program enrollment (master's): **311**
Doctoral degree enrollment: **26**

FINANCIAL INFORMATION
Financial aid phone number: **(203) 837-8528**
Tuition, 2003-2004 academic year: Full-time in-state: **$3,298**; out-of-state: **$9,190**, Part-time in-state: **$285/credit hour**; out-of-state: **$285/credit hour**
Fees: **$2,392**, Room and board: **$6,390**

ACADEMIC PROGRAMS
Total full-time tenured or tenure-track faculty (fall 2003): **14**, Total part-time faculty (fall 2003): **11**
Areas of specialization: curriculum and instruction, educational psychology, elementary teacher education, higher education administration, secondary teacher education, special education, student counseling and personnel services.
Professional development/partnership school(s) are used by students in all of the teaching programs.
During their internships, peer groups of students meet regularly to discuss instructional techniques in some of the teaching programs.
Some of the students in their internships are mentored.
Courses that prepare teachers to pass the National Board of Professional Teaching Standards are not offered.
Teacher preparation programs: Four-year baccalaureate-degree program leading to initial licensure that includes either a major or minor in education and practice teaching. Master's program preparing college graduates for initial licensure; includes practice teaching.

LICENSING TEST
Pass rate on state's teacher licensing test for 2002-2003: **100%**
State average pass rate: **97%**

DELAWARE

Delaware State University

- 1200N. DuPont Highway, Dover, DE 19901
- Website: http://www.dsc.edu/
- Public
- Degrees offered: master's

FINANCIAL INFORMATION
Financial aid phone number: (302) 857-6250

LICENSING TEST
Pass rate on state's teacher licensing test for 2002-2003: 77%
State average pass rate: 95%

University of Delaware

- 113 Willard Hall Education Building, Newark, DE 19716
- Website: http://www.udel.edu/gradoffice/applicants/ degreesmajors.html
- Public
- Degrees offered: bachelor's, master's, Ph.D., Ed.D.
- Overall rank in the 2005 U.S. News education schools with doctoral programs: 55
- Overall rank in the 2005 U.S. News education school specialty rankings: elementary education: 23

ADMISSIONS
Admissions phone number: (302) 831-2129
Admissions email address: *marym@udel.edu*
Application website: *http://www.udel.edu/gradoffice/ applicants/indexhtml*
Application fee: $60
Fall 2005 application deadline: 2/1
Test requirements: GRE
Test of English as Foreign Language (TOEFL) is required for international students.

Minimum TOEFL score required for paper test: 600
Minimum TOEFL score required for computer test: 250

Fall 2003
Acceptance rate for master's degree programs: 52%
Acceptance rate for doctoral programs: 33%
Average GRE verbal: 535, Average GRE quantitative: 616
Total 2003 enrollment: 526
Master's degree enrollment: 321
   Teacher preparation program enrollment (master's): 216
Doctoral degree enrollment: 205

FINANCIAL INFORMATION
Financial aid phone number: (302) 831-2129
Tuition, 2003-2004 academic year: Full-time in-state: $5,890; out-of-state: $15,420, Part-time in-state: $327/credit hour; out-of-state: $857/credit hour
Fees: $484, Room and board: $6,100, Books and supplies: $1,000, Miscellaneous expenses: $1,700
Number of fellowships awarded to graduate students during the 2003-2004 academic year: 11
Number of teaching assistant positions: 22
Number of research assistant positions: 35
Number of other paid appointments: 39

ACADEMIC PROGRAMS
Total full-time tenured or tenure-track faculty (fall 2003): 48, Total part-time faculty (fall 2003): 1
Areas of specialization: curriculum and instruction, education administration and supervision, educational psychology, higher education administration, secondary teacher education, special education, student counseling and personnel services.
Professional development/partnership school(s) are used by students in some of the teaching programs.
During their internships, peer groups of students meet regularly to discuss instructional techniques in some of the teaching programs.
All of the students in their internships are mentored.
Courses that prepare teachers to pass the National Board of Professional Teaching Standards are offered.
Teacher preparation programs: Four-year baccalaureate-degree program leading to initial licensure that includes

either a major or minor in education and practice teaching. Master's program preparing college graduates for initial licensure; includes practice teaching.
The education program is currently accredited by the National Council for Accreditation of Teacher Education.

LICENSING TEST
Pass rate on state's teacher licensing test for 2002-2003: **96%**
State average pass rate: **95%**

Wesley College

■ 120 N State St, Dover, DE 19901
■ **Website:** http://www.wesley.edu
■ **Private**
■ **Degrees offered:** bachelor's, master's

ADMISSIONS
Admissions phone number: **(302) 736-2400**
Admissions email address: *admissions@wesley.edu*
Application fee: **$25**
Fall 2005 application deadline: **rolling**
Test of English as Foreign Language (TOEFL) is required for international students.
Minimum TOEFL score required for paper test: **500**
Minimum TOEFL score required for computer test: **200**

Fall 2003
Acceptance rate for master's degree programs: **82%**
Average GRE verbal: **530**, Average GRE quantitative: **520**, Average GRE analytical: **530**
Total 2003 enrollment: **57**
Master's degree enrollment: **57**
    Teacher preparation program enrollment (master's): **57**

FINANCIAL INFORMATION
Financial aid phone number: **(302) 736-2334**
Tuition, 2003-2004 academic year: Full-time: **$280/credit hour**; Part-time: **$280/credit hour**
Fees: **$35**, Books and supplies: **$300**
Number of fellowships awarded to graduate students during the 2003-2004 academic year: **0**
Number of teaching assistant positions: **0**
Number of research assistant positions: **0**
Number of other paid appointments: **6**

ACADEMIC PROGRAMS
Total full-time tenured or tenure-track faculty (fall 2003): **12**, Total part-time faculty (fall 2003): **0**
Areas of specialization: elementary teacher education.
Professional development/partnership school(s) are used by students in all of the teaching programs.
During their internships, peer groups of students meet regularly to discuss instructional techniques in all of the teaching programs.
All of the students in their internships are mentored.
Courses that prepare teachers to pass the National Board of Professional Teaching Standards are offered.

Teacher preparation programs: Four-year baccalaureate-degree program leading to initial licensure that includes either a major or minor in education and practice teaching. Master's program preparing college graduates for initial licensure; includes practice teaching.
The education program is currently accredited by the National Council for Accreditation of Teacher Education.

LICENSING TEST
Pass rate on state's teacher licensing test for 2002-2003: **86%**
State average pass rate: **95%**

Wilmington College

■ 320 DuPont Highway, Wilmington, DE 19720
■ **Website:** http://www.wilmcoll.edu/education/
■ **Private**
■ **Degrees offered:** bachelor's, master's, Ed.D.

ADMISSIONS
Admissions phone number: **(302) 328-9407**
Admissions email address: *inquire@wilmcoll.edu*
Application website:
    http://www.wilmcoll.edu/admission/applications.html
Application fee: **$25**
Test requirements: **None**
Test of English as Foreign Language (TOEFL) is required for international students.

Fall 2003
Total 2003 enrollment: **1,732**
Master's degree enrollment: **1,513**
    Teacher preparation program enrollment (master's): **947**
Doctoral degree enrollment: **219**

FINANCIAL INFORMATION
Financial aid phone number: **(302) 328-9437**
Tuition, 2003-2004 academic year: Full-time: **$284/credit hour**; Part-time: **$284/credit hour**
Fees: **$50**, Books and supplies: **$750**

ACADEMIC PROGRAMS
Areas of specialization: curriculum and instruction, education administration and supervision, elementary teacher education, special education, student counseling and personnel services.
Professional development/partnership school(s) are used by students in some of the teaching programs.
During their internships, peer groups of students meet regularly to discuss instructional techniques in some of the teaching programs.
All of the students in their internships are mentored.
Courses that prepare teachers to pass the National Board of Professional Teaching Standards are offered.

LICENSING TEST
Pass rate on state's teacher licensing test for 2002-2003: **100%**
State average pass rate: **95%**

DISTRICT OF COLUMBIA

American University

- 4400 Massachusetts Avenue NW, Washington, DC 20016-8030
- Website: http://www.american.edu/cas/department_education .shtml
- Private

ADMISSIONS

Admissions phone number: **(202) 885-3720**
Admissions email address: *casgrad@american.edu*
Application website: *http://app.applyyourself.com/?id=au-cas*

FINANCIAL INFORMATION

Financial aid phone number: **(202) 885-6100**

LICENSING TEST

Pass rate on state's teacher licensing test for 2002-2003: 89%
State average pass rate: 82%

Catholic University of America

- Department of Education Cardinal Station, Washington, DC 20064
- Website: http://www.cua.edu
- Private
- Degrees offered: bachelor's, master's, Ph.D.
- Overall rank in the 2005 U.S. News education schools with doctoral programs: 73

ADMISSIONS

Admissions phone number: **(202) 319-5305**
Admissions email address: *cua-admissions@cua.edu*
Application website: *http://admissions.cua.edu/graduate/*
Application fee: **$55**

Test requirements: **GRE or MAT**
Test of English as Foreign Language (TOEFL) is required for international students.
Minimum TOEFL score required for paper test: 580
Minimum TOEFL score required for computer test: 237

Fall 2003

Acceptance rate for master's degree programs: 59%
Acceptance rate for doctoral programs: 50%
Average GRE verbal: 518, Average GRE quantitative: 625, Average GRE analytical: 538
Total 2003 enrollment: 62
Master's degree enrollment: 32
    Teacher preparation program enrollment (master's): 25
Doctoral degree enrollment: 30

FINANCIAL INFORMATION

Financial aid phone number: **(202) 319-5307**
Tuition, 2003-2004 academic year: Full-time: **$22,200**; Part-time: **$850/credit hour**
Fees: **$940**, Room and board: **$11,357**, Books and supplies: **$1,300**, Miscellaneous expenses: **$2,800**
Number of teaching assistant positions: 2

ACADEMIC PROGRAMS

Total full-time tenured or tenure-track faculty (fall 2003): 11, Total part-time faculty (fall 2003): 4
Areas of specialization: curriculum and instruction, education administration and supervision, education policy, educational psychology, elementary teacher education, higher education administration, secondary teacher education, special education, student counseling and personnel services.
Professional development/partnership school(s) are used by students in all of the teaching programs.
During their internships, peer groups of students meet regularly to discuss instructional techniques in all of the teaching programs.
All of the students in their internships are mentored.
Courses that prepare teachers to pass the National Board of Professional Teaching Standards are not offered.
Teacher preparation programs: Four-year baccalaureate-degree program leading to initial licensure that includes

either a major or minor in education and practice teaching. Five-year program leading to initial licensure that results in a baccalaureate degree (with a major or minor in education) plus a master's degree and includes practice teaching. Master's program preparing college graduates for initial licensure; includes practice teaching. Alternative program for college graduates leading to provisional licensure.

The education program is currently accredited by the National Council for Accreditation of Teacher Education.

LICENSING TEST
Pass rate on state's teacher licensing test for 2002-2003: 87%
State average pass rate: 82%

Gallaudet University

- GSPP-HM S-450, 800 Florida Avenue NE, Washington, DC 20002-3695
- Website: http://gradschool.gallaudet.edu
- Private
- Degrees offered: bachelor's, master's, education specialist, Ph.D.

ADMISSIONS
Admissions phone number: (202) 651-5717
Admissions email address: *graduate.school@gallaudet.edu*
Application website: *http://gradschool.gallaudet.edu/gradschool/prospective/application.html*
Application fee: $50
Fall 2005 application deadline: rolling
Test requirements: GRE or MAT
Test of English as Foreign Language (TOEFL) is required for international students.

Fall 2003
Acceptance rate for master's degree programs: 38%
Acceptance rate for education specialist degree programs: 71%
Acceptance rate for doctoral programs: 58%
Average GRE verbal: 451, Average GRE quantitative: 457, Average GRE analytical: 507, Average MAT: 71
Total 2003 enrollment: 159
Master's degree enrollment: 99
    Teacher preparation program enrollment (master's): 61
Education specialist degree enrollment: 26
Doctoral degree enrollment: 34

FINANCIAL INFORMATION
Financial aid phone number: (202) 651-5290
Tuition, 2003-2004 academic year: Full-time: $9,910 Part-time: $551/credit hour
Fees: $1,275, Room and board: $8,030, Books and supplies: $1,000
Number of fellowships awarded to graduate students during the 2003-2004 academic year: 50
Number of teaching assistant positions: 1

Number of research assistant positions: 4
Number of other paid appointments: 30

ACADEMIC PROGRAMS
Total full-time tenured or tenure-track faculty (fall 2003): 35, Total part-time faculty (fall 2003): 10
Areas of specialization: curriculum and instruction, education administration and supervision, education policy, educational psychology, elementary teacher education, higher education administration, secondary teacher education, special education, student counseling and personnel services.
Professional development/partnership school(s) are used by students in all of the teaching programs.
During their internships, peer groups of students meet regularly to discuss instructional techniques in all of the teaching programs.
None of the students in their internships are mentored.
Courses that prepare teachers to pass the National Board of Professional Teaching Standards are offered.
Teacher preparation programs: Four-year baccalaureate-degree program leading to initial licensure that includes either a major or minor in education and practice teaching. Master's program preparing college graduates for initial licensure; includes practice teaching.
The education program is currently accredited by the National Council for Accreditation of Teacher Education.

LICENSING TEST
Pass rate on state's teacher licensing test for 2002-2003: 44%
State average pass rate: 82%

George Washington University

- 2134 G Street NW, Washington, DC 20052
- Website: http://www.gwu.edu/~gsehd
- Private
- Degrees offered: master's, education specialist, Ph.D., Ed.D.
- Overall rank in the 2005 U.S. News education schools with doctoral programs: 24

ADMISSIONS
Admissions phone number: (202) 994-9283
Admissions email address: *gsehdapp@gwu.edu*
Application website: *http://www.gwu.edu/~gradinfo*
Application fee: $60
Fall 2005 application deadline: 1/15
Test requirements: GRE or MAT
Test of English as Foreign Language (TOEFL) is required for international students.
Minimum TOEFL score required for paper test: 550
Minimum TOEFL score required for computer test: 213

Fall 2003
Acceptance rate for master's degree programs: 69%

Acceptance rate for education specialist degree programs: 53%

Acceptance rate for doctoral programs: 62%

Average GRE verbal: 494, Average GRE quantitative: 557, Average GRE analytical: 559, Average MAT: 49

Total 2003 enrollment: 1,675

Master's degree enrollment: 990

Teacher preparation program enrollment (master's): 405

Education specialist degree enrollment: 75

Doctoral degree enrollment: 610

FINANCIAL INFORMATION

Financial aid phone number: (202) 994-6822

Tuition, 2003-2004 academic year: Full-time: **$834/credit hour**; Part-time: **$834/credit hour**

Fees: **$1/credit hour**, Room and board: **$15,600**, Books and supplies: **$2,480**

Number of fellowships awarded to graduate students during the 2003-2004 academic year: **104**

Number of teaching assistant positions: **0**

Number of research assistant positions: **14**

Number of other paid appointments: **0**

ACADEMIC PROGRAMS

Total full-time tenured or tenure-track faculty (fall 2003): 40, Total part-time faculty (fall 2003): **144**

Areas of specialization: curriculum and instruction, education administration and supervision, education policy, elementary teacher education, higher education administration, secondary teacher education, special education, student counseling and personnel services.

Professional development/partnership school(s) are used by students in some of the teaching programs.

During their internships, peer groups of students meet regularly to discuss instructional techniques in some of the teaching programs.

All of the students in their internships are mentored.

Courses that prepare teachers to pass the National Board of Professional Teaching Standards are offered.

Teacher preparation programs: Master's degree in education, including internship/practice teaching and preparation for initial licensure.

The education program is currently accredited by the National Council for Accreditation of Teacher Education.

LICENSING TEST

Pass rate on state's teacher licensing test for 2002-2003: 91%

State average pass rate: **82%**

Howard University

■ **2441 Fourth Street NW, Washington, DC 20059**
■ **Website:** http://www.gs.howard.edu/ gp-educationproginfo.htm
■ **Private**
■ **Degrees offered:** bachelor's, master's, Ph.D., Ed.D.

ADMISSIONS

Admissions phone number: **(202) 806-7340**

Admissions email address: *hugsadmission@howard.edu*

Application website: *http://www.howard.edu/banner/ applyonline.asp*

Fall 2003

Total 2003 enrollment: **221**

Master's degree enrollment: **123**

Teacher preparation program enrollment (master's): **25**

Doctoral degree enrollment: **98**

FINANCIAL INFORMATION

Financial aid phone number: **(202) 806-2820**

ACADEMIC PROGRAMS

Total full-time tenured or tenure-track faculty (fall 2003): 30, Total part-time faculty (fall 2003): **17**

Areas of specialization: curriculum and instruction, education administration and supervision, educational psychology, elementary teacher education, higher education administration, secondary teacher education, special education, student counseling and personnel services.

Professional development/partnership school(s) are used by students in all of the teaching programs.

During their internships, peer groups of students meet regularly to discuss instructional techniques in some of the teaching programs.

All of the students in their internships are mentored.

The education program is currently accredited by the National Council for Accreditation of Teacher Education.

LICENSING TEST

Pass rate on state's teacher licensing test for 2002-2003: 68%

State average pass rate: **82%**

Trinity College

■ **125 Michigan Avenue, NE, Washington, DC 20017**
■ **Website:** http://www.trinitydc.edu
■ **Private**
■ **Degrees offered:** bachelor's, master's

ADMISSIONS

Admissions phone number: **(800) 492-6882**

Admissions email address: *admissions@trinitydc.edu*

Application website: *http://www.trinitydc.edu/admissions/apply/ EDUappJuly03.pdf*

Application fee: **$35**

Fall 2005 application deadline: **rolling**

Test of English as Foreign Language (TOEFL) is required for international students.

Minimum TOEFL score required for paper test: **550**

Minimum TOEFL score required for computer test: **213**

Fall 2003
Acceptance rate for master's degree programs: 80%
Total 2003 enrollment: 405
Master's degree enrollment: 405
    Teacher preparation program enrollment (master's): 188

FINANCIAL INFORMATION
Financial aid phone number: (202) 884-9535
Tuition, 2003-2004 academic year: $535/credit hour
Room and board: $10,300, Books and supplies: $600,
    Miscellaneous expenses: $2,000
Number of fellowships awarded to graduate students dur-
    ing the 2003-2004 academic year: 0
Number of teaching assistant positions: 0
Number of research assistant positions: 0
Number of other paid appointments: 0

ACADEMIC PROGRAMS
Total full-time tenured or tenure-track faculty (fall 2003): 9
    Total part-time faculty (fall 2003): 30
Areas of specialization: curriculum and instruction, educa-
    tion administration and supervision, education policy,
    educational psychology, elementary teacher education,
    secondary teacher education, special education, student
    counseling and personnel services.
Professional development/partnership school(s) are used
    by students in some of the teaching programs.
During their internships, peer groups of students meet
    regularly to discuss instructional techniques in all of the
    teaching programs.
All of the students in their internships are mentored.
Courses that prepare teachers to pass the National Board of
    Professional Teaching Standards are not offered.
Teacher preparation programs: Four-year baccalaureate-
    degree program leading to initial licensure that includes
    either a major or minor in education and practice teach-
    ing. Five-year program leading to initial licensure that
    results in a baccalaureate degree (with a major or minor
    in education) plus a master's degree and includes prac-
    tice teaching. Master's program preparing college gradu-
    ates for initial licensure; includes practice teaching.
    Alternative program for college graduates leading to pro-
    visional licensure.

LICENSING TEST
Pass rate on state's teacher licensing test for 2002-2003:
    73%
State average pass rate: 82%

University of the District of Columbia

- 4200 Connecticut Avenue N.W., Washington, DC 20008
- **Website:** http://www.universityofdc.org/
- **Public**
- **Degrees offered:** bachelor's, master's

ADMISSIONS
Admissions phone number: (202) 274-6110
Application fee: $20
Fall 2005 application deadline: 6/15
Test of English as Foreign Language (TOEFL) is required
    for international students.
Minimum TOEFL score required for paper test: 500
Minimum TOEFL score required for computer test: 300

Fall 2003
Acceptance rate for master's degree programs: 40%
Total 2003 enrollment: 235
Master's degree enrollment: 235
    Teacher preparation program enrollment (master's): 15

FINANCIAL INFORMATION
Financial aid phone number: (202) 274-5060
Tuition, 2003-2004 academic year: Full-time in-state:
    $1,800; out-of-state: $4,440, Part-time in-state:
    $75/credit hour; out-of-state: $185/credit hour
Fees: $270, Books and supplies: $800

ACADEMIC PROGRAMS
Areas of specialization: educational psychology, elementary
    teacher education, special education.
Professional development/partnership school(s) are used
    by students in all of the teaching programs.
During their internships, peer groups of students meet
    regularly to discuss instructional techniques in all of the
    teaching programs.
All of the students in their internships are mentored.
Courses that prepare teachers to pass the National Board of
    Professional Teaching Standards are offered.
Teacher preparation programs: Four-year baccalaureate-
    degree program leading to initial licensure that includes
    either a major or minor in education and practice teaching.

FLORIDA

Barry University

■ 11300 N.E. Second Avenue, Miami Shores, FL 33161-6695
■ **Website:** http://www.barry.edu/ed/
■ Private

ADMISSIONS
Admissions phone number: (305) 899-3100
Admissions email address: *admissions@mail.barry.edu*

FINANCIAL INFORMATION
Financial aid phone number: (305) 899-3673

LICENSING TEST
Pass rate on state's teacher licensing test for 2002-2003: 100%
State average pass rate: 96%

Florida A&M University

■ College of Education, Tallahassee, FL 32307
■ Website:
http://www.famu.edu/acad/colleges/ced/index.php
■ Public

ADMISSIONS
Admissions phone number: (850) 599-3482
Admissions email address: *adm@famu.edu*

FINANCIAL INFORMATION
Financial aid phone number: (850) 599-3730

LICENSING TEST
Pass rate on state's teacher licensing test for 2002-2003: 81%
State average pass rate: 96%

Florida Atlantic University

■ 777 Glades Road, PO Box 3091, Boca Raton, FL 33431-0991
■ **Website:** http://www.fau.edu
■ **Public**
■ **Degrees offered:** bachelor's, master's, education specialist, Ed.D.

ADMISSIONS
Admissions phone number: (561) 297-3624
Admissions email address: *gradadm@fau.edu*
Application website: *http://www.fau.edu/academic/gradstud/online.htm*
Application fee: $20
Fall 2005 application deadline: 7/1
Test requirements: GRE
Test of English as Foreign Language (TOEFL) is required for international students.
Minimum TOEFL score required for paper test: 550
Minimum TOEFL score required for computer test: 213

Fall 2003
Acceptance rate for master's degree programs: 87%
Acceptance rate for education specialist degree programs: 100%
Acceptance rate for doctoral programs: 75%
Average GRE verbal: 460, Average GRE quantitative: 519
Total 2003 enrollment: 905
Master's degree enrollment: 696
  Teacher preparation program enrollment (master's): 438
Education specialist degree enrollment: 40
Doctoral degree enrollment: 169

FINANCIAL INFORMATION
Financial aid phone number: (561) 297-3131
Tuition, 2003-2004 academic year: Full-time in-state: $210/credit hour; out-of-state: $775/credit hour, Part-

time in-state: **$210/credit hour**; out-of-state: **$775/credit hour**

Room and board: **$5,600**, Books and supplies: **$660**, Miscellaneous expenses: **$2,816**

Number of fellowships awarded to graduate students during the 2003-2004 academic year: **0**

Number of teaching assistant positions: **12**

Number of research assistant positions: **0**

Number of other paid appointments: **28**

ACADEMIC PROGRAMS

Total full-time tenured or tenure-track faculty (fall 2003): **98**, Total part-time faculty (fall 2003): **230**

Areas of specialization: curriculum and instruction, education administration and supervision, educational psychology, elementary teacher education, higher education administration, secondary teacher education, special education, student counseling and personnel services.

Professional development/partnership school(s) are used by students in some of the teaching programs.

During their internships, peer groups of students meet regularly to discuss instructional techniques in some of the teaching programs.

Some of the students in their internships are mentored.

Courses that prepare teachers to pass the National Board of Professional Teaching Standards are not offered.

Teacher preparation programs: Four-year baccalaureate-degree program leading to initial licensure that includes either a major or minor in education and practice teaching. Master's program preparing college graduates for initial licensure; includes practice teaching. Alternative program for college graduates leading to provisional licensure.

The education program is currently accredited by the National Council for Accreditation of Teacher Education.

LICENSING TEST

Pass rate on state's teacher licensing test for 2002-2003: **100%**

State average pass rate: **96%**

Florida Institute of Technology–Melbourne

■ **150 W. University Boulevard, Melbourne, FL 32901**
■ **Website:**
http://hyper.fit.edu/education/grad/graduate.html
■ **Private**
■ **Degrees offered:** bachelor's, master's, education specialist, Ph.D., Ed.D.

ADMISSIONS

Admissions phone number: **(321) 674-7578**
Admissions email address: *GRAD-Admissions@fit.edu*
Application website: *https://inq.applyyourself.com/ ?id=fit-g&pid=509*
Application fee: **$50**

Fall 2005 application deadline: **rolling**

Test of English as Foreign Language (TOEFL) is required for international students.

Minimum TOEFL score required for paper test: **550**

Minimum TOEFL score required for computer test: **213**

Fall 2003

Acceptance rate for master's degree programs: **76%**

Acceptance rate for doctoral programs: **58%**

Total 2003 enrollment: **37**

Master's degree enrollment: **21**

Teacher preparation program enrollment (master's): **8**

Doctoral degree enrollment: **16**

FINANCIAL INFORMATION

Financial aid phone number: **(321) 674-8070**

Tuition, 2003-2004 academic year: Full-time: **$745/credit hour**; Part-time: **$745/credit hour**

Room and board: **$6,140**, Books and supplies: **$1,000**, Miscellaneous expenses: **$1,600**

Number of teaching assistant positions: **1**

ACADEMIC PROGRAMS

Total full-time tenured or tenure-track faculty (fall 2003): **5** Total part-time faculty (fall 2003): **2**

Professional development/partnership school(s) are used by students in some of the teaching programs.

During their internships, peer groups of students meet regularly to discuss instructional techniques in some of the teaching programs.

Some of the students in their internships are mentored.

Courses that prepare teachers to pass the National Board of Professional Teaching Standards are not offered.

Teacher preparation programs: Four-year baccalaureate-degree program leading to initial licensure that includes either a major or minor in education and practice teaching. Alternative program for college graduates leading to provisional licensure.

Florida International University

■ **11200 S.W. Eighth Street, Miami, FL 33199**
■ **Website:** http://www.fiu.edu
■ **Public**
■ **Degrees offered:** bachelor's, master's, education specialist, Ph.D., Ed.D.

ADMISSIONS

Admissions phone number: **(305) 348-2363**
Admissions email address: *admiss@fiu.edu*
Application website: *http://www.fiu.edu/gradadm/ instructions-apply-online.htm*
Application fee: **$25**
Test requirements: **GRE**
Test of English as Foreign Language (TOEFL) is required for international students.

Minimum TOEFL score required for paper test: 550
Minimum TOEFL score required for computer test: 213

Fall 2003
Acceptance rate for master's degree programs: 51%
Acceptance rate for education specialist degree programs: 33%
Acceptance rate for doctoral programs: 17%
Average GRE verbal: 422, Average GRE quantitative: 486
Total 2003 enrollment: 870
Master's degree enrollment: 558
    Teacher preparation program enrollment (master's): 508
Education specialist degree enrollment: 62
Doctoral degree enrollment: 250

FINANCIAL INFORMATION
Financial aid phone number: (305) 348-2489
Tuition, 2003-2004 academic year: Full-time in-state: **$202/credit hour**; out-of-state: **$771/credit hour**, Part-time in-state: **$202/credit hour**; out-of-state: **$771/credit hour**
Fees: **$221**, Room and board: **$7,465**, Books and supplies: **$1,110**, Miscellaneous expenses: **$2,196**

ACADEMIC PROGRAMS
Total full-time tenured or tenure-track faculty (fall 2003): **76**, Total part-time faculty (fall 2003): **108**
Areas of specialization: curriculum and instruction, education administration and supervision, education policy, elementary teacher education, higher education administration, secondary teacher education, special education, student counseling and personnel services.
Professional development/partnership school(s) are used by students in some of the teaching programs.
During their internships, peer groups of students meet regularly to discuss instructional techniques in some of the teaching programs.
All of the students in their internships are mentored.
Courses that prepare teachers to pass the National Board of Professional Teaching Standards are offered.
Teacher preparation programs: Four-year baccalaureate-degree program leading to initial licensure that includes either a major or minor in education and practice teaching. Master's program preparing college graduates for initial licensure; includes practice teaching. Alternative program for college graduates leading to provisional licensure.
The education program is currently accredited by the National Council for Accreditation of Teacher Education.

LICENSING TEST
Pass rate on state's teacher licensing test for 2002-2003: 90%
State average pass rate: 96%

Florida State University

- **236 Stone Building, Tallahassee, FL 32306-4450**
- **Website:** http://admissions.fsu.edu
- **Public**
- **Degrees offered:** bachelor's, master's, education specialist, Ph.D., Ed.D.
- **Overall rank in the 2005 U.S. News education schools with doctoral programs:** 55
- **Overall rank in the 2005 U.S. News education school specialty rankings:** curriculum/instruction: 21, elementary education: 23, secondary education: 18

ADMISSIONS
Admissions phone number: (850) 644-3760
Admissions email address: *admissions@admin.fsu.edu*
Application website: *http://admissions.fsu.edu/online.html*
Application fee: **$20**
Fall 2005 application deadline: 7/1
Test requirements: **GRE**
Test of English as Foreign Language (TOEFL) is required for international students.
Minimum TOEFL score required for paper test: 550
Minimum TOEFL score required for computer test: 213

Fall 2003
Acceptance rate for master's degree programs: 49%
Acceptance rate for education specialist degree programs: 25%
Acceptance rate for doctoral programs: 22%
Average GRE verbal: 466, Average GRE quantitative: 538
Total 2003 enrollment: 1,053
Master's degree enrollment: 601
    Teacher preparation program enrollment (master's): 248
Education specialist degree enrollment: 26
Doctoral degree enrollment: 426

FINANCIAL INFORMATION
Financial aid phone number: (850) 644-0539
Tuition, 2003-2004 academic year: Full-time in-state: **$196/credit hour**; out-of-state: **$731/credit hour**, Part-time in-state: **$196/credit hour**; out-of-state: **$731/credit hour**
Fees: **$5/credit hour**, Room and board: **$8,352**, Books and supplies: **$725**, Miscellaneous expenses: **$2,000**
Number of fellowships awarded to graduate students during the 2003-2004 academic year: 16
Number of teaching assistant positions: 246
Number of research assistant positions: 384
Number of other paid appointments: 0

ACADEMIC PROGRAMS
Total full-time tenured or tenure-track faculty (fall 2003): **100**, Total part-time faculty (fall 2003): **9**
Areas of specialization: curriculum and instruction, education administration and supervision, education policy, educational psychology, elementary teacher education, higher education administration, secondary teacher edu-

cation, special education, student counseling and personnel services, teacher education.

Professional development/partnership school(s) are used by students in some of the teaching programs.

During their internships, peer groups of students meet regularly to discuss instructional techniques in some of the teaching programs.

Some of the students in their internships are mentored.

Courses that prepare teachers to pass the National Board of Professional Teaching Standards are not offered.

Teacher preparation programs: Four-year baccalaureate-degree program leading to initial licensure that includes either a major or minor in education and practice teaching. Five-year program leading to initial licensure that results in a baccalaureate degree (with a major or minor in education) plus a master's degree and includes practice teaching. Master's program preparing college graduates for initial licensure; includes practice teaching.

The education program is currently accredited by the National Council for Accreditation of Teacher Education.

LICENSING TEST

Pass rate on state's teacher licensing test for 2002-2003: 94%

State average pass rate: 96%

Jacksonville University

- **2800 University Blvd. N., Jacksonville, FL 32211**
- **Website:** http://www.ju.edu
- **Private**
- **Degrees offered:** bachelor's, master's

ADMISSIONS

Admissions phone number: (904) 256-7155
Admissions email address: *admissions@ju.edu*
Application fee: $30
Fall 2005 application deadline: **rolling**
Test requirements: **GRE or MAT**
Test of English as Foreign Language (TOEFL) is required for international students.
Minimum TOEFL score required for paper test: 540
Minimum TOEFL score required for computer test: 207

Fall 2003

Acceptance rate for master's degree programs: 75%
Average GRE verbal: 577, Average GRE quantitative: 662, Average MAT: 65
Total 2003 enrollment: 126
Master's degree enrollment: 126
    Teacher preparation program enrollment (master's): 122

FINANCIAL INFORMATION

Financial aid phone number: (904) 256-7060
Tuition, 2003-2004 academic year: Full-time: $17,700; Part-time: $590/credit hour
Fees: $240, Room and board: $5,620, Books and supplies: $1,800, Miscellaneous expenses: $300

Number of fellowships awarded to graduate students during the 2003-2004 academic year: 0
Number of teaching assistant positions: 0
Number of research assistant positions: 0
Number of other paid appointments: 0

ACADEMIC PROGRAMS

Total full-time tenured or tenure-track faculty (fall 2003): 4
    Total part-time faculty (fall 2003): 0
Areas of specialization: education administration and supervision, elementary teacher education, secondary teacher education.

Professional development/partnership school(s) are used by students in all of the teaching programs.

During their internships, peer groups of students meet regularly to discuss instructional techniques in all of the teaching programs.

All of the students in their internships are mentored.

Courses that prepare teachers to pass the National Board of Professional Teaching Standards are not offered.

Teacher preparation programs: Four-year baccalaureate-degree program leading to initial licensure that includes either a major or minor in education and practice teaching. Five-year program leading to initial licensure that results in a baccalaureate degree (with a major or minor in education) plus graduate credit and includes practice teaching. Five-year program leading to initial licensure that results in a baccalaureate degree (with a major or minor in education) plus a master's degree and includes practice teaching. Master's program preparing college graduates for initial licensure; includes practice teaching. Alternative program for college graduates leading to provisional licensure.

Lynn University

- **3601 North Military Trail, Boca Raton, FL 33431**
- **Website:** http://www.lynn.edu
- **Private**
- **Degrees offered:** bachelor's, master's, education specialist, Ph.D., Ed.D.

ADMISSIONS

Admissions phone number: (561) 237-7900
Admissions email address: *admission@lynn.edu*
Application website: *http://www.lynn.edu/index.php? submenu=Admissions&src=forms&id=Online%20Verification*
Application fee: $30
Fall 2005 application deadline: **rolling**
Test requirements: **GRE**
Test of English as Foreign Language (TOEFL) is required for international students.
Minimum TOEFL score required for paper test: 550
Minimum TOEFL score required for computer test: 137

Fall 2003

Acceptance rate for master's degree programs: 79%
Total 2003 enrollment: 119

Master's degree enrollment: 62
  Teacher preparation program enrollment (master's): 53
Doctoral degree enrollment: 57

FINANCIAL INFORMATION
Financial aid phone number: (561) 237-7816
Tuition, 2003-2004 academic year: Full-time: **$460/credit hour**; Part-time: **$460/credit hour**
Fees: **$750**, Room and board: **$8,000**, Books and supplies: **$800**, Miscellaneous expenses: **$2,260**

ACADEMIC PROGRAMS
Areas of specialization: education administration and supervision, elementary teacher education.
Professional development/partnership school(s) are used by students in all of the teaching programs.
During their internships, peer groups of students meet regularly to discuss instructional techniques in all of the teaching programs.
All of the students in their internships are mentored.
Courses that prepare teachers to pass the National Board of Professional Teaching Standards are not offered.
Teacher preparation programs: Four-year baccalaureate-degree program leading to initial licensure that includes either a major or minor in education and practice teaching. Master's program preparing college graduates for initial licensure; includes practice teaching.

LICENSING TEST
Pass rate on state's teacher licensing test for 2002-2003: **100%**
State average pass rate: **96%**

Nova Southeastern University

- 3301 College Avenue, Fort Lauderdale, FL 33314
- **Website:** http://www.fgse.nova.edu
- **Private**
- **Degrees offered:** master's, education specialist, Ed.D.

ADMISSIONS
Admissions phone number: (954) 262-8500
Admissions email address: *http://www.nova.edu/cwis/nsuinforequest.html*
Application fee: **$50**
Fall 2005 application deadline: **rolling**
Test requirements: **GRE or MAT**
Test of English as Foreign Language (TOEFL) is required for international students.
Minimum TOEFL score required for paper test: **550**

Fall 2003
Acceptance rate for master's degree programs: **100%**
Acceptance rate for education specialist degree programs: **100%**
Acceptance rate for doctoral programs: **99%**

Total 2003 enrollment: **8,600**
Master's degree enrollment: **4,254**
  Teacher preparation program enrollment (master's): **3,536**
Education specialist degree enrollment: **594**
Doctoral degree enrollment: **3,752**

FINANCIAL INFORMATION
Financial aid phone number: (954) 262-3380
Tuition, 2003-2004 academic year: Full-time: **$340/credit hour**; Part-time: **$340/credit hour**
Fees: **$195**, Room and board: **$10,431**, Books and supplies: **$1,141**, Miscellaneous expenses: **$4,655**
Number of fellowships awarded to graduate students during the 2003-2004 academic year: 4
Number of teaching assistant positions: 2
Number of research assistant positions: 3
Number of other paid appointments: 0

ACADEMIC PROGRAMS
Total full-time tenured or tenure-track faculty (fall 2003): **58**, Total part-time faculty (fall 2003): **369**
Areas of specialization: curriculum and instruction, education administration and supervision, education policy, educational psychology, elementary teacher education, higher education administration, secondary teacher education, special education, student counseling and personnel services, teacher education.
Professional development/partnership school(s) are used by students in some of the teaching programs.
During their internships, peer groups of students meet regularly to discuss instructional techniques in all of the teaching programs.
Courses that prepare teachers to pass the National Board of Professional Teaching Standards are offered.
Teacher preparation programs: Master's degree in education, including internship/practice teaching and preparation for initial licensure.

LICENSING TEST
Pass rate on state's teacher licensing test for 2002-2003: **84%**
State average pass rate: **96%**

Palm Beach Atlantic College

- 901 South Flagler Drive, West Palm Beach, FL 33401
- **Website:**
  http://www.pba.edu/admissions/Graduate/graduate.htm
- **Private**
- **Degrees offered:** bachelor's, master's

ADMISSIONS
Admissions phone number: (888) 468-6722
Admissions email address: *grad@pba.edu*
Application fee: **$35**

Fall 2005 application deadline: **rolling**
Test requirements: **GRE**
Test of English as Foreign Language (TOEFL) is required
for international students.
Minimum TOEFL score required for paper test: **550**

Fall 2003
Total 2003 enrollment: 78
Master's degree enrollment: 78
    Teacher preparation program enrollment (master's): 32

FINANCIAL INFORMATION
Financial aid phone number: (888) 468-6722
Tuition, 2003-2004 academic year: Full-time: **$5,800**; Part-
time: **$320/credit hour**
Fees: **$160**, Room and board: **$10,200**, Books and supplies:
$700, Miscellaneous expenses: **$3,700**

ACADEMIC PROGRAMS
Total full-time tenured or tenure-track faculty (fall 2003):
17, Total part-time faculty (fall 2003): 12
Areas of specialization: curriculum and instruction, educa-
tional psychology, elementary teacher education, special
education, student counseling and personnel services.
Professional development/partnership school(s) are used
by students in some of the teaching programs.
During their internships, peer groups of students meet
regularly to discuss instructional techniques in all of the
teaching programs.
All of the students in their internships are mentored.
Courses that prepare teachers to pass the National Board of
Professional Teaching Standards are not offered.
Teacher preparation programs: Four-year baccalaureate-
degree program leading to initial licensure that includes
either a major or minor in education and practice teaching. Master's program preparing college graduates for
initial licensure; includes practice teaching.

LICENSING TEST
Pass rate on state's teacher licensing test for 2002-2003:
100%
State average pass rate: 96%

Rollins College

■ **1000 Holt Avenue, Winter Park, FL 32789**
■ **Website:** http://www.rollins.edu/
■ **Private**
■ **Degrees offered:** bachelor's, master's

ADMISSIONS
Admissions phone number: **(407) 646-1568**
Admissions email address: *jhewit@rollins.edu*
Application website: *http://www.rollins.edu/holt/*
Application fee: **$50**
Fall 2005 application deadline: **rolling**
Test of English as Foreign Language (TOEFL) is required
for international students.

Minimum TOEFL score required for paper test: **550**
Minimum TOEFL score required for computer test: **213**

Fall 2003
Total 2003 enrollment: **88**
Master's degree enrollment: **88**
    Teacher preparation program enrollment (master's): **70**

FINANCIAL INFORMATION
Financial aid phone number: **(407) 646-2395**
Tuition, 2003-2004 academic year: Full-time: **$265/credit
hour**; Part-time: **$265/credit hour**
Fees: **$265/credit hour**, Books and supplies: **$450**,
Miscellaneous expenses: **$60**

LICENSING TEST
Pass rate on state's teacher licensing test for 2002-2003:
96%
State average pass rate: 96%

Stetson University

■ **421 N. Woodland Boulevard, Deland, FL 32723**
■ **Website:** http://www.stetson.edu/education
■ **Private**
■ **Degrees offered:** bachelor's, master's, education
specialist

ADMISSIONS
Admissions phone number: **(386) 822-7075**
Admissions email address: *pleclair@stetson.edu*
Application fee: **$25**
Fall 2005 application deadline: **rolling**

Fall 2003
Total 2003 enrollment: **173**
Master's degree enrollment: **154**
    Teacher preparation program enrollment (master's): **26**
Education specialist degree enrollment: **19**

FINANCIAL INFORMATION
Financial aid phone number: **(386) 822-7120**
Tuition, 2003-2004 academic year: **$450/credit hour**
Room and board: **$6,855**

ACADEMIC PROGRAMS
Areas of specialization: education administration and
supervision, special education, student counseling and
personnel services.
The education program is currently accredited by the
National Council for Accreditation of Teacher Education.

LICENSING TEST
Pass rate on state's teacher licensing test for 2002-2003:
95%
State average pass rate: 96%

St. Leo University

■ PO Box 6665, Saint Leo, FL 33574-6665
■ Website: http://www.saintleo.edu
■ Private
■ Degrees offered: bachelor's, master's

ADMISSIONS

Admissions phone number: (352) 588-8236
Admissions email address: joy.bryan@saintleo.edu
Application website:
  http://www.saintleo.edu/SaintLeo/Templates/Inner.aspx?
  pid=407&durki=407
Application fee: $45
Fall 2005 application deadline: 7/1
Test requirements: GRE or MAT

Fall 2003

Acceptance rate for master's degree programs: 57%
Total 2003 enrollment: 107
Master's degree enrollment: 107
  Teacher preparation program enrollment (master's): 22

FINANCIAL INFORMATION

Financial aid phone number: (352) 588-8270
Tuition, 2003-2004 academic year: Full-time: $300/credit
  hour; Part-time: $300/credit hour
Books and supplies: $1,200

ACADEMIC PROGRAMS

Total full-time tenured or tenure-track faculty (fall 2003): 5
  Total part-time faculty (fall 2003): 6
Areas of specialization: curriculum and instruction, educa-
  tion administration and supervision.
Professional development/partnership school(s) are used
  by students in some of the teaching programs.
During their internships, peer groups of students meet
  regularly to discuss instructional techniques in all of the
  teaching programs.
All of the students in their internships are mentored.
Courses that prepare teachers to pass the National Board of
  Professional Teaching Standards are not offered.
Teacher preparation programs: Four-year baccalaureate-
  degree program leading to initial licensure that includes
  either a major or minor in education and practice teaching.

LICENSING TEST

Pass rate on state's teacher licensing test for 2002-2003:
  100%
State average pass rate: 96%

St. Thomas University

■ 16400 NW 32nd Avenue, Maimi, FL 33054
■ Website: http://www.stu.edu/admission/graduate/
■ Private

Trinity Baptist College

■ 800 Hammond Blvd., Jacksonville, FL 32221
■ Website: http://www.tbc.edu
■ Private
■ Degrees offered: master's

ADMISSIONS

Admissions phone number: (904) 596-2449
Admissions email address: jvadnal@tbc.edu
Application website: http://www.tbc.edu
Application fee: $35
Fall 2005 application deadline: rolling
Test requirements: GRE
Test of English as Foreign Language (TOEFL) is required
  for international students.

Fall 2003

Acceptance rate for master's degree programs: 100%
Average GRE verbal: 550, Average GRE quantitative: 460
Total 2003 enrollment: 14
Master's degree enrollment: 14
  Teacher preparation program enrollment (master's): 14

FINANCIAL INFORMATION

Financial aid phone number: (904) 596-2445
Tuition, 2003-2004 academic year: Full-time: $210/credit
  hour; Part-time: $210/credit hour
Books and supplies: $600
Number of fellowships awarded to graduate students dur-
  ing the 2003-2004 academic year: 0
Number of teaching assistant positions: 0
Number of research assistant positions: 0
Number of other paid appointments: 0

ACADEMIC PROGRAMS

Total full-time tenured or tenure-track faculty (fall 2003): 0
  Total part-time faculty (fall 2003): 13
Professional development/partnership school(s) are used
  by students in all of the teaching programs.
During their internships, peer groups of students meet
  regularly to discuss instructional techniques in all of the
  teaching programs.
All of the students in their internships are mentored.
Courses that prepare teachers to pass the National Board of
  Professional Teaching Standards are not offered.
Teacher preparation programs: Alternative program for col-
  lege graduates leading to provisional licensure.

Trinity International University

- 111 NW 183rd Street, Suite 500, Miami, FL 33169
- **Website:** http://www.tiu.edu/
- Private

University of Central Florida

- 4000 Central Florida Boulevard, Orlando, FL 32816-1250
- **Website:** http://www.graduate.ucf.edu
- Public
- **Degrees offered:** bachelor's, master's, education specialist, Ph.D., Ed.D.

ADMISSIONS

Admissions phone number: **(407) 823-2766**
Admissions email address: *graduate@mail.ucf.edu*
Application website: *http://www.ucf.edu/gradonlineapp/*
Application fee: **$30**
Fall 2005 application deadline: **7/15**
Test requirements: **GRE**
Test of English as Foreign Language (TOEFL) is required for international students.
Minimum TOEFL score required for paper test: **500**
Minimum TOEFL score required for computer test: **220**

Fall 2003
Acceptance rate for master's degree programs: **70%**
Acceptance rate for education specialist degree programs: **36%**
Acceptance rate for doctoral programs: **72%**
Average GRE verbal: **467**, Average GRE quantitative: **537**, Average GRE analytical: **530**
Total 2003 enrollment: **1,343**
Master's degree enrollment: **979**
    Teacher preparation program enrollment (master's): **571**
Education specialist degree enrollment: **65**
Doctoral degree enrollment: **299**

FINANCIAL INFORMATION

Financial aid phone number: **(407) 823-2827**
Tuition, 2003-2004 academic year: Full-time in-state: **$207/credit hour**; out-of-state: **$776/credit hour**, Part-time in-state: **$207/credit hour**; out-of-state: **$776/credit hour**
Fees: **$6/credit hour**, Room and board: **$7,191**, Books and supplies: **$800**, Miscellaneous expenses: **$4,000**
Number of fellowships awarded to graduate students during the 2003-2004 academic year: **109**
Number of teaching assistant positions: **9**
Number of research assistant positions: **96**

Number of other paid appointments: **4**

ACADEMIC PROGRAMS

Total full-time tenured or tenure-track faculty (fall 2003): **86**, Total part-time faculty (fall 2003): **121**
Areas of specialization: curriculum and instruction, education administration and supervision, elementary teacher education, secondary teacher education, special education, student counseling and personnel services.
Professional development/partnership school(s) are used by students in some of the teaching programs.
During their internships, peer groups of students meet regularly to discuss instructional techniques in some of the teaching programs.
All of the students in their internships are mentored.
Courses that prepare teachers to pass the National Board of Professional Teaching Standards are offered.
Teacher preparation programs: Four-year baccalaureate-degree program leading to initial licensure that includes either a major or minor in education and practice teaching. Master's program preparing college graduates for initial licensure; includes practice teaching.
The education program is currently accredited by the National Council for Accreditation of Teacher Education.

LICENSING TEST

Pass rate on state's teacher licensing test for 2002-2003: **96%**
State average pass rate: **96%**

University of Florida

- 125 Norman Hall, PO Box 117043, Gainesville, FL 32611-7043
- **Website:** http://www.coe.ufl.edu
- Public
- **Degrees offered:** bachelor's, master's, education specialist, Ph.D., Ed.D.
- **Overall rank in the 2005 U.S. News education schools with doctoral programs: 24**
- **Overall rank in the 2005 U.S. News education school specialty rankings:** counseling/personnel: 3, curriculum/instruction: 19, elementary education: 23, special education: 9

ADMISSIONS

Admissions phone number: **(352) 392-1275**
Admissions email address: *edugrad@coe.ufl.edu*
Application website:
    http://gradschool.rgp.ufl.edu/education/toapply.html
Application fee: **$30**
Fall 2005 application deadline: **rolling**
Test requirements: **GRE**
Test of English as Foreign Language (TOEFL) is required for international students.
Minimum TOEFL score required for paper test: **550**
Minimum TOEFL score required for computer test: **213**

Fall 2003

Fall 2003

Acceptance rate for master's degree programs: 62%
Acceptance rate for doctoral programs: 36%
Average GRE verbal: 486, Average GRE quantitative: 589
Total 2003 enrollment: 914
Master's degree enrollment: 407
    Teacher preparation program enrollment (master's): 283
Education specialist degree enrollment: 154
Doctoral degree enrollment: 353

FINANCIAL INFORMATION

Financial aid phone number: (352) 392-0728
Tuition, 2003-2004 academic year: Full-time in-state: **$184/credit hour**; out-of-state: **$774/credit hour**, Part-time in-state: **$184/credit hour**; out-of-state: **$774/credit hour**
Fees: **$21/credit hour**, Room and board: **$6,730**, Books and supplies: **$1,540**, Miscellaneous expenses: **$2,620**
Number of fellowships awarded to graduate students during the 2003-2004 academic year: **68**
Number of teaching assistant positions: 60
Number of research assistant positions: 63
Number of other paid appointments: 2

ACADEMIC PROGRAMS

Total full-time tenured or tenure-track faculty (fall 2003): 80, Total part-time faculty (fall 2003): 0
Areas of specialization: curriculum and instruction, education administration and supervision, education policy, educational psychology, elementary teacher education, higher education administration, secondary teacher education, special education, student counseling and personnel services.
Professional development/partnership school(s) are used by students in some of the teaching programs.
During their internships, peer groups of students meet regularly to discuss instructional techniques in some of the teaching programs.
All of the students in their internships are mentored.
Courses that prepare teachers to pass the National Board of Professional Teaching Standards are not offered.
The education program is currently accredited by the National Council for Accreditation of Teacher Education.

LICENSING TEST

Pass rate on state's teacher licensing test for 2002-2003: 97%
State average pass rate: 96%

University of Miami

- PO Box 248065, Coral Gables, FL 33124
- **Website:** http://www.education.miami.edu
- **Private**
- **Degrees offered:** bachelor's, master's, education specialist, Ph.D.
- **Overall rank in the 2005 U.S. News education schools with doctoral programs:** 47

ADMISSIONS

Admissions phone number: (305) 284-3711
Admissions email address: *soe@umiami.ir.miami.edu*
Fall 2005 application deadline: **rolling**
Test requirements: **GRE**
Test of English as Foreign Language (TOEFL) is required for international students.
Minimum TOEFL score required for paper test: 550
Minimum TOEFL score required for computer test: 213

Fall 2003

Acceptance rate for master's degree programs: 75%
Acceptance rate for education specialist degree programs: 73%
Acceptance rate for doctoral programs: 17%
Average GRE verbal: 473, Average GRE quantitative: 550, Average GRE analytical: 607
Total 2003 enrollment: 559
Master's degree enrollment: 465
    Teacher preparation program enrollment (master's): 184
Education specialist degree enrollment: 18
Doctoral degree enrollment: 76

FINANCIAL INFORMATION

Financial aid phone number: (305) 284-5212
Tuition, 2003-2004 academic year: Full-time: **$25,838**; Part-time: **$1,074/credit hour**
Fees: **$442**, Room and board: **$8,328**, Books and supplies: **$2,040**, Miscellaneous expenses: **$1,148**
Number of fellowships awarded to graduate students during the 2003-2004 academic year: 1
Number of teaching assistant positions: 17
Number of research assistant positions: 54
Number of other paid appointments: 0

ACADEMIC PROGRAMS

Total full-time tenured or tenure-track faculty (fall 2003): 35, Total part-time faculty (fall 2003): 56
Areas of specialization: curriculum and instruction, elementary teacher education, higher education administration, secondary teacher education, special education, student counseling and personnel services.
Professional development/partnership school(s) are used by students in all of the teaching programs.
During their internships, peer groups of students meet regularly to discuss instructional techniques in some of the teaching programs.
Some of the students in their internships are mentored.

Courses that prepare teachers to pass the National Board of Professional Teaching Standards are not offered.

Teacher preparation programs: Four-year baccalaureate-degree program leading to initial licensure that includes either a major or minor in education and practice teaching. Master's program preparing college graduates for initial licensure; includes practice teaching.

The education program is currently accredited by the National Council for Accreditation of Teacher Education.

LICENSING TEST

Pass rate on state's teacher licensing test for 2002-2003: 100%

State average pass rate: 96%

University of North Florida

- 4567 St. Johns Bluff Road, S., Jacksonville, FL 32224
- **Website:** http://www.unf.edu/admissions/
- Public
- **Degrees offered:** bachelor's, master's, Ed.D.

ADMISSIONS

Admissions phone number: **(904) 620-2624**
Admissions email address: *admissions@unf.edu*
Application website: *http://www.unf.edu/admissions/ applying/download/app-grad.pdf*
Application fee: **$20**
Fall 2005 application deadline: **7/1**
Test requirements: **GRE**
Test of English as Foreign Language (TOEFL) is required for international students.
Minimum TOEFL score required for paper test: **500**
Minimum TOEFL score required for computer test: **173**

Fall 2003

Total 2003 enrollment: **615**
Master's degree enrollment: **523**
    Teacher preparation program enrollment (master's): **217**
Doctoral degree enrollment: **92**

FINANCIAL INFORMATION

Financial aid phone number: **(904) 620-2604**
Tuition, 2003-2004 academic year: Full-time in-state: **$208/credit hour**; out-of-state: **$743/credit hour**, Part-time in-state: **$208/credit hour**; out-of-state: **$743/credit hour**
Fees: **$35**, Room and board: **$2,700**, Books and supplies: **$300**, Miscellaneous expenses: **$751**
Number of fellowships awarded to graduate students during the 2003-2004 academic year: **18**

ACADEMIC PROGRAMS

Areas of specialization: curriculum and instruction, education administration and supervision, elementary teacher

education, secondary teacher education, special education, student counseling and personnel services.

Professional development/partnership school(s) are used by students in some of the teaching programs.

During their internships, peer groups of students meet regularly to discuss instructional techniques in all of the teaching programs.

All of the students in their internships are mentored.

Courses that prepare teachers to pass the National Board of Professional Teaching Standards are offered.

Teacher preparation programs: Four-year baccalaureate-degree program leading to initial licensure that includes either a major or minor in education and practice teaching. Master's program preparing college graduates for initial licensure; includes practice teaching. Alternative program for college graduates leading to provisional licensure.

The education program is currently accredited by the National Council for Accreditation of Teacher Education.

LICENSING TEST

Pass rate on state's teacher licensing test for 2002-2003: 94%

State average pass rate: 96%

University of South Florida

- 4202 E. Fowler Avenue, EDU 162, Tampa, FL 33620
- **Website:** http://www.grad.usf.edu
- Public
- **Degrees offered:** bachelor's, master's, education specialist, Ph.D., Ed.D.
- **Overall rank in the 2005 U.S. News education schools with doctoral programs:** 60

ADMISSIONS

Admissions phone number: **(813) 974-8800**
Admissions email address: *admissions@grad.usf.edu*
Application website: *http://www.usf.edu/apply.html*
Application fee: **$20**
Fall 2005 application deadline: **rolling**
Test requirements: **GRE**
Test of English as Foreign Language (TOEFL) is required for international students.
Minimum TOEFL score required for paper test: **550**
Minimum TOEFL score required for computer test: **213**

Fall 2003

Acceptance rate for master's degree programs: **60%**
Acceptance rate for education specialist degree programs: **20%**
Acceptance rate for doctoral programs: **38%**
Average GRE verbal: **478**, Average GRE quantitative: **531**
Total 2003 enrollment: **1,786**
Master's degree enrollment: **1,292**
    Teacher preparation program enrollment (master's): **693**

Education specialist degree enrollment: 60
Doctoral degree enrollment: 434

FINANCIAL INFORMATION
Financial aid phone number: **(813) 974-4700**
Tuition, 2003-2004 academic year: Full-time in-state: **$209/credit hour**; out-of-state: **$778/credit hour**, Part-time in-state: **$209/credit hour**; out-of-state: **$778/credit hour**
Fees: **$32/credit hour**, Room and board: **$6,450**, Books and supplies: **$800**, Miscellaneous expenses: **$3,600**
Number of fellowships awarded to graduate students during the 2003-2004 academic year: **7**
Number of teaching assistant positions: **53**
Number of research assistant positions: **48**
Number of other paid appointments: **23**

ACADEMIC PROGRAMS
Total full-time tenured or tenure-track faculty (fall 2003): **122**, Total part-time faculty (fall 2003): **8**
Areas of specialization: education administration and supervision, educational psychology, elementary teacher education, higher education administration, secondary teacher education, special education, student counseling and personnel services, teacher education.
Professional development/partnership school(s) are used by students in all of the teaching programs.
During their internships, peer groups of students meet regularly to discuss instructional techniques in all of the teaching programs.
All of the students in their internships are mentored.
Courses that prepare teachers to pass the National Board of Professional Teaching Standards are offered.
Teacher preparation programs: Four-year baccalaureate-degree program leading to initial licensure that includes either a major or minor in education and practice teaching. Master's program preparing college graduates for initial licensure; includes practice teaching.
The education program is currently accredited by the National Council for Accreditation of Teacher Education.

LICENSING TEST
Pass rate on state's teacher licensing test for 2002-2003: **100%**
State average pass rate: **96%**

University of West Florida

■ **11000 University Parkway, Pensacola, FL 32514-5750**
■ **Website:** http://uwf.edu
■ **Public**
■ **Degrees offered:** bachelor's, master's, education specialist, Ed.D.

ADMISSIONS
Admissions phone number: **(850) 474-2230**
Admissions email address: *admissions@uwf.edu*
Application website: *http://uwf.edu/survey/enrollment/*
Application fee: **$20**
Fall 2005 application deadline: **6/30**
Test of English as Foreign Language (TOEFL) is required for international students.
Minimum TOEFL score required for paper test: **550**
Minimum TOEFL score required for computer test: **213**

Fall 2003
Acceptance rate for master's degree programs: **67%**
Acceptance rate for education specialist degree programs: **66%**
Acceptance rate for doctoral programs: **46%**
Total 2003 enrollment: **625**
Master's degree enrollment: **339**
Education specialist degree enrollment: **60**
Doctoral degree enrollment: **226**

FINANCIAL INFORMATION
Financial aid phone number: **(850) 474-2400**
Tuition, 2003-2004 academic year: Full-time in-state: **$208/credit hour**; out-of-state: **$777/credit hour**, Part-time in-state: **$208/credit hour**; out-of-state: **$777/credit hour**
Fees: **$20**, Room and board: **$3,000**, Books and supplies: **$800**, Miscellaneous expenses: **$2,950**

ACADEMIC PROGRAMS
Areas of specialization: curriculum and instruction, education administration and supervision, elementary teacher education, secondary teacher education, special education, student counseling and personnel services.
Professional development/partnership school(s) are used by students in some of the teaching programs.
During their internships, peer groups of students meet regularly to discuss instructional techniques in some of the teaching programs.
All of the students in their internships are mentored.
Courses that prepare teachers to pass the National Board of Professional Teaching Standards are not offered.
Teacher preparation programs: Four-year baccalaureate-degree program leading to initial licensure that includes either a major or minor in education and practice teaching. Master's program preparing college graduates for initial licensure; includes practice teaching. Alternative program for college graduates leading to provisional licensure.
The education program is currently accredited by the National Council for Accreditation of Teacher Education.

LICENSING TEST
Pass rate on state's teacher licensing test for 2002-2003: **95%**
State average pass rate: **96%**

GEORGIA

TEACHER TESTING IN GEORGIA
Teacher licensure rules vary widely from state to state, but almost all states require tests. The exams typically cover the basics of reading, writing and math, although some states mandate in-depth, subject-specific teacher tests. For information on where to go in your state for specific academic requirements, see Chapter 6 on page 67. Note: Some schools require students to pass exams by graduation, and thus automatically report pass rates of 100 percent.

- This state **does** require a basic skills test in order to obtain a teaching license.
- This state **does** require a subject-knowledge test in order to obtain a middle school teaching license.
- This state **does** require a subject-knowledge test in order to obtain a high school teaching license.
- This state **does** require a subject-specific pedagogy test in order to obtain a teaching license.

Agnes Scott College

- **141 E. College Avenue, Decatur, GA 30030**
- **Website:** http://www.agnesscott.edu
- **Private**
- **Degrees offered:** master's

ADMISSIONS
Admissions phone number: **(404) 471-6252**
Admissions email address: *graduatestudies@agnesscott.edu*
Application website: *http://www.agnesscott.edu/academics*
Application fee: **$35**
Fall 2005 application deadline: 4/1

Fall 2003
Total 2003 enrollment: 21
Master's degree enrollment: 21
   Teacher preparation program enrollment (master's): 21

FINANCIAL INFORMATION
Financial aid phone number: **(404) 471-6396**
Tuition, 2003-2004 academic year: Full-time: **$15,000**; Part-time: **$425/credit hour**
Fees: **$150**

Albany State University

- **504 College Drive, Albany, GA 31705**
- **Website:** http://asuweb.asurams.edu/asu/
- **Public**
- **Degrees offered:** bachelor's, master's, education specialist

ADMISSIONS
Admissions phone number: **(229) 430-4646**
Admissions email address: *robinm@asurams.edu*
Application fee: **$20**
Fall 2005 application deadline: 7/1

FINANCIAL INFORMATION
Financial aid phone number: **(229) 430-4650**
Tuition, 2003-2004 academic year: Full-time in-state: **$2,654**; out-of-state: **$10,616**, Part-time in-state: **$111/credit hour**; out-of-state: **$443/credit hour**
Fees: **$562**, Room and board: **$3,550**, Books and supplies: **$1,000**, Miscellaneous expenses: **$1,593**

LICENSING TEST
Pass rate on state's teacher licensing test for 2002-2003: 95%
State average pass rate: 93%

Armstrong Atlantic State University

- **11935 Abercorn Street, Savannah, GA 31419**
- **Website:** http://www.admissions.armstrong.edu/
- **Public**
- **Degrees offered:** bachelor's, master's

ADMISSIONS
Admissions phone number: **(912) 927-5277**
Admissions email address: *admissions@mail.armstrong.edu*
Application website: *http://www.gs.armstrong.edu/formlinks.html*
Application fee: **$25**
Fall 2005 application deadline: 7/1
Test requirements: **GRE or MAT**
Test of English as Foreign Language (TOEFL) is required for international students.
Minimum TOEFL score required for paper test: 523
Minimum TOEFL score required for computer test: 193

Fall 2003
Average GRE verbal: 465, Average GRE quantitative: 500, Average GRE analytical: 498, Average MAT: 45
Total 2003 enrollment: 421
Master's degree enrollment: 421
   Teacher preparation program enrollment (master's): 421

FINANCIAL INFORMATION

Financial aid phone number: **(912) 927-5272**
Tuition, 2003-2004 academic year: Full-time in-state:
$1,998; out-of-state: **$7,974**, Part-time in-state:
$111/credit hour; out-of-state: **$443/credit hour**
Fees: **$390**

ACADEMIC PROGRAMS

Total full-time tenured or tenure-track faculty (fall 2003):
30
Areas of specialization: elementary teacher education, secondary teacher education, special education.
Professional development/partnership school(s) are used by students in some of the teaching programs.
During their internships, peer groups of students meet regularly to discuss instructional techniques in some of the teaching programs.
All of the students in their internships are mentored.
Courses that prepare teachers to pass the National Board of Professional Teaching Standards are not offered.
Teacher preparation programs: Four-year baccalaureate-degree program leading to initial licensure that includes either a major or minor in education and practice teaching. Master's program preparing college graduates for initial licensure; includes practice teaching. Alternative program for college graduates leading to provisional licensure.
The education program is currently accredited by the National Council for Accreditation of Teacher Education.

LICENSING TEST

Pass rate on state's teacher licensing test for 2002-2003:
99%
State average pass rate: 93%

Augusta State University

■ **2500 Walton Way, Augusta, GA 30904**
■ **Website:** http://www.aug.edu/school_of_education
■ **Public**
■ **Degrees offered:** bachelor's, master's, education specialist

ADMISSIONS

Admissions phone number: **(706) 737-1632**
Admissions email address: *admissio@aug.edu*
Application website: *http://www.aug.edu/school_of_education/pages/admissions.htm*
Application fee: **$20**
Fall 2005 application deadline: **rolling**
Test requirements: **GRE or MAT**
Test of English as Foreign Language (TOEFL) is required for international students.
Minimum TOEFL score required for paper test: **500**
Minimum TOEFL score required for computer test: **250**

Fall 2003
Average GRE verbal: **486**, Average GRE quantitative: **512**, Average GRE analytical: **581**, Average MAT: **48**
Total 2003 enrollment: **236**
Master's degree enrollment: **177**
Education specialist degree enrollment: **59**

FINANCIAL INFORMATION

Financial aid phone number: **(706) 737-1431**
Tuition, 2003-2004 academic year: Full-time in-state:
$2,654; out-of-state: **$10,616**, Part-time in-state:
$111/credit hour; out-of-state: **$443/credit hour**
Fees: **$380**, Room and board: **$7,266**, Books and supplies:
$900, Miscellaneous expenses: **$3,130**

ACADEMIC PROGRAMS

Total full-time tenured or tenure-track faculty (fall 2003): **28**
Total part-time faculty (fall 2003): **10**
Areas of specialization: curriculum and instruction, education administration and supervision, education policy, educational psychology, elementary teacher education, higher education administration, secondary teacher education, special education, student counseling and personnel services.
Professional development/partnership school(s) are used by students in all of the teaching programs.
During their internships, peer groups of students meet regularly to discuss instructional techniques in all of the teaching programs.
All of the students in their internships are mentored.
Courses that prepare teachers to pass the National Board of Professional Teaching Standards are offered.
The education program is currently accredited by the National Council for Accreditation of Teacher Education.

LICENSING TEST

Pass rate on state's teacher licensing test for 2002-2003:
88%
State average pass rate: 93%

Berry College

■ **Po Box 490279, Mount Berry, GA 30149**
■ **Website:** http://www.berry.edu/
■ **Private**

LICENSING TEST

Pass rate on state's teacher licensing test for 2002-2003:
91%
State average pass rate: 93%

Brenau University

- One Centennial Circle, Gainesville, GA 30501
- **Website:** http://www.brenau.edu
- Private
- **Degrees offered:** bachelor's, master's, education specialist

ADMISSIONS
Admissions phone number: **(770) 534-6162**
Admissions email address: *EWC_grad@lib.brenau.edu*
Application website: *http://www.brenau.edu*
Application fee: **$30**
Fall 2005 application deadline: **rolling**
Test requirements: **GRE or MAT**
Test of English as Foreign Language (TOEFL) is required for international students.
Minimum TOEFL score required for paper test: **550**
Minimum TOEFL score required for computer test: **213**

Fall 2003
Total 2003 enrollment: **197**
Master's degree enrollment: **171**
    Teacher preparation program enrollment (master's): **171**
Education specialist degree enrollment: **26**

FINANCIAL INFORMATION
Financial aid phone number: **(770) 534-6152**
Tuition, 2003-2004 academic year: Full-time: **$260/credit hour**; Part-time: **$260/credit hour**
Fees: **$100**, Books and supplies: **$600**, Miscellaneous expenses: **$1,400**
Number of fellowships awarded to graduate students during the 2003-2004 academic year: **0**
Number of teaching assistant positions: **0**
Number of research assistant positions: **0**
Number of other paid appointments: **0**

ACADEMIC PROGRAMS
Areas of specialization: curriculum and instruction, educational psychology, elementary teacher education, secondary teacher education, special education.
Professional development/partnership school(s) are used by students in some of the teaching programs.
During their internships, peer groups of students meet regularly to discuss instructional techniques in all of the teaching programs.
All of the students in their internships are mentored.
Courses that prepare teachers to pass the National Board of Professional Teaching Standards are not offered.
Teacher preparation programs: Four-year baccalaureate-degree program leading to initial licensure that includes either a major or minor in education and practice teaching. Master's program preparing college graduates for initial licensure; includes practice teaching. Alternative program for college graduates leading to provisional licensure.

LICENSING TEST
Pass rate on state's teacher licensing test for 2002-2003: **95%**
State average pass rate: **93%**

Clark Atlanta University

- 223 James P. Brawley Drive, SW, Atlanta, GA 30314
- **Website:** http://www.cau.edu/
- Private

LICENSING TEST
Pass rate on state's teacher licensing test for 2002-2003: **49%**
State average pass rate: **93%**

Columbus State University

- 4225 University Ave., Columbus, GA 31907
- **Website:** http://www.colstate.edu/
- Public

LICENSING TEST
Pass rate on state's teacher licensing test for 2002-2003: **95%**
State average pass rate: **93%**

Covenant College

- 14049 Scenic Highway, Lookout Mountain, GA 30750
- **Website:** http://www.covenant.edu/
- Private

LICENSING TEST
Pass rate on state's teacher licensing test for 2002-2003: **95%**
State average pass rate: **93%**

Emory University

- North Decatur Building, Suite 240, Atlanta, GA 30322
- **Website:** http://www.emory.edu/EDUCATION/
- Private

ADMISSIONS
Admissions phone number: **(404) 727-6468**
Admissions email address: *gavant@emory.edu*
Application website: *http://www.emory.edu/gsoas/ application.html*

FINANCIAL INFORMATION

Financial aid phone number: **(404) 727-6039**

LICENSING TEST

Pass rate on state's teacher licensing test for 2002-2003: **100%**

State average pass rate: **93%**

Fort Valley State University

- ■ **1005 State University Drive, Fort Valley, GA 31030-4313**
- ■ **Website:** http://www.fvsu.edu/
- ■ **Public**
- ■ **Degrees offered:** bachelor's, master's

ADMISSIONS

Admissions phone number: **(478) 825-5307**

Admissions email address: *admissap@fvsu.edu*

Application fee: **$20**

FINANCIAL INFORMATION

Financial aid phone number: **(478) 825-6351**

Tuition, 2003-2004 academic year: Full-time in-state: **$1,998**; out-of-state: **$7,404**, Part-time in-state: **$1,332**; out-of-state: **$4,746**

Fees: **$570**, Room and board: **$2,089**, Books and supplies: **$250**

LICENSING TEST

Pass rate on state's teacher licensing test for 2002-2003: **94%**

State average pass rate: **93%**

Georgia College and State University

- ■ **Campus PO Box 52, Milledgeville, GA 31061**
- ■ **Website:** http://www.gcsu.edu
- ■ **Public**
- ■ **Degrees offered:** bachelor's, master's, education specialist

ADMISSIONS

Admissions phone number: **(478) 445-4056**

Admissions email address: *b.crews@gcsu.edu*

Application website: *http://www.gcsu.edu*

Application fee: **$25**

Fall 2005 application deadline: **4/1**

Test requirements: **GRE or MAT**

Test of English as Foreign Language (TOEFL) is required for international students.

Minimum TOEFL score required for paper test: **500**

Minimum TOEFL score required for computer test: **173**

Fall 2003

Acceptance rate for master's degree programs: **88%**

Acceptance rate for education specialist degree programs: **80%**

Average GRE verbal: **426**, Average GRE quantitative: **509**, Average GRE analytical: **538**, Average MAT: **43**

Total 2003 enrollment: **443**

Master's degree enrollment: **360**

Teacher preparation program enrollment (master's): **282**

Education specialist degree enrollment: **83**

FINANCIAL INFORMATION

Financial aid phone number: **(478) 445-5149**

Tuition, 2003-2004 academic year: Full-time in-state: **$151/credit hour**; out-of-state: **$601/credit hour**, Part-time in-state: **$151/credit hour**; out-of-state: **$601/credit hour**

Fees: **$339**, Room and board: **$3,094**, Books and supplies: **$350**

Number of paid appointments: **24**

ACADEMIC PROGRAMS

Total full-time tenured or tenure-track faculty (fall 2003): **35**, Total part-time faculty (fall 2003): **14**

Areas of specialization: curriculum and instruction, education administration and supervision, elementary teacher education, secondary teacher education, special education.

Professional development/partnership school(s) are used by students in some of the teaching programs.

During their internships, peer groups of students meet regularly to discuss instructional techniques in all of the teaching programs.

All of the students in their internships are mentored.

Courses that prepare teachers to pass the National Board of Professional Teaching Standards are offered.

Teacher preparation programs: Four-year baccalaureate-degree program leading to initial licensure that includes either a major or minor in education and practice teaching. Five-year program leading to initial licensure that results in a baccalaureate degree (with a major or minor in education) plus a master's degree and includes practice teaching. Master's program preparing college graduates for initial licensure; includes practice teaching.

The education program is currently accredited by the National Council for Accreditation of Teacher Education.

LICENSING TEST

Pass rate on state's teacher licensing test for 2002-2003: **93%**

State average pass rate: **93%**

Georgia Southern University

- U.S. Highway 301, S, P.O. Box 8033, Statesboro, GA 30460
- Website: http://www.gasou.edu/
- Public

LICENSING TEST
Pass rate on state's teacher licensing test for 2002-2003: 93%
State average pass rate: 93%

Georgia Southwestern State University

- 800 Wheatley Street, Americus, GA 31709
- Website: http://www.gsw.edu
- Public
- Degrees offered: bachelor's, master's, education specialist

ADMISSIONS
Admissions phone number: (229) 931-2002
Admissions email address: loliver@gsw.edu
Application website: http://www.gsw.edu/admissions/graduate.html
Application fee: $20
Fall 2005 application deadline: 6/30
Test requirements: GRE or MAT
Test of English as Foreign Language (TOEFL) is required for international students.
Minimum TOEFL score required for paper test: 523
Minimum TOEFL score required for computer test: 193

Fall 2003
Total 2003 enrollment: 211

FINANCIAL INFORMATION
Financial aid phone number: (229) 928-1378
Tuition, 2003-2004 academic year: Full-time in-state: $1,327; out-of-state: $5,308, Part-time in-state: $111/credit hour; out-of-state: $443/credit hour
Fees: $282

ACADEMIC PROGRAMS
Total full-time tenured or tenure-track faculty (fall 2003): 46, Total part-time faculty (fall 2003): 10
Areas of specialization: elementary teacher education, secondary teacher education, special education.
Professional development/partnership school(s) are used by students in none of the teaching programs.

During their internships, peer groups of students meet regularly to discuss instructional techniques in some of the teaching programs.
Some of the students in their internships are mentored.
Courses that prepare teachers to pass the National Board of Professional Teaching Standards are not offered.
Teacher preparation programs: Four-year baccalaureate-degree program leading to initial licensure that includes either a major or minor in education and practice teaching. Master's program preparing college graduates for initial licensure; includes practice teaching. Alternative program for college graduates leading to provisional licensure.
The education program is currently accredited by the National Council for Accreditation of Teacher Education.

LICENSING TEST
Pass rate on state's teacher licensing test for 2002-2003: 95%
State average pass rate: 93%

Georgia State University

- MSC6A1005, 33 Gilmer St SE, Unit 6, Atlanta, GA 30303-3086
- Website: http://education.gsu.edu/coe/
- Public
- Degrees offered: bachelor's, master's, education specialist, Ph.D.

ADMISSIONS
Admissions phone number: (404) 651-2525
Admissions email address: educadmissions@gsu.edu
Application fee: $25
Test requirements: GRE or MAT
Test of English as Foreign Language (TOEFL) is required for international students.
Minimum TOEFL score required for paper test: 550
Minimum TOEFL score required for computer test: 213

Fall 2003
Total 2003 enrollment: 1,618
Master's degree enrollment: 1,147
  Teacher preparation program enrollment (master's): 472
Education specialist degree enrollment: 127
Doctoral degree enrollment: 344

FINANCIAL INFORMATION
Financial aid phone number: (404) 651-2227
Tuition, 2003-2004 academic year: Full-time in-state: $161/credit hour; out-of-state: $642/credit hour, Part-time in-state: $161/credit hour; out-of-state: $642/credit hour
Fees: $712, Room and board: $8,976, Books and supplies: $780
Number of fellowships awarded to graduate students during the 2003-2004 academic year: 0
Number of teaching assistant positions: 33
Number of research assistant positions: 206
Number of other paid appointments: 35

ACADEMIC PROGRAMS

Total full-time tenured or tenure-track faculty (fall 2003): 104, Total part-time faculty (fall 2003): 72

Areas of specialization: curriculum and instruction, education administration and supervision, education policy, educational psychology, elementary teacher education, higher education administration, secondary teacher education, special education, student counseling and personnel services.

Professional development/partnership school(s) are used by students in none of the teaching programs.

During their internships, peer groups of students meet regularly to discuss instructional techniques in some of the teaching programs.

Courses that prepare teachers to pass the National Board of Professional Teaching Standards are offered.

Teacher preparation programs: Four-year baccalaureate-degree program leading to initial licensure that includes either a major or minor in education and practice teaching. Master's program preparing college graduates for initial licensure; includes practice teaching. Alternative program for college graduates leading to provisional licensure.

The education program is currently accredited by the National Council for Accreditation of Teacher Education.

LICENSING TEST

Pass rate on state's teacher licensing test for 2002-2003: 96%
State average pass rate: 93%

Kennesaw State University

■ 1000 Chastain Road; Campus Box 0123, Kennesaw, GA 30144
■ **Website:** http://www.kennesaw.edu
■ **Public**
■ **Degrees offered:** bachelor's, master's

ADMISSIONS

Admissions phone number: **(770) 420-4377**
Admissions email address: *ksuadmit@kennesaw.edu*
Application website: *http://www.kennesaw.edu*
Application fee: **$40**
Fall 2005 application deadline: **7/8**
Test requirements: **GRE or MAT**
Test of English as Foreign Language (TOEFL) is required for international students.
Minimum TOEFL score required for paper test: **550**
Minimum TOEFL score required for computer test: **213**

Fall 2003
Acceptance rate for master's degree programs: **65%**
Average GRE verbal: **475**, Average GRE quantitative: **497**
Total 2003 enrollment: **422**
Master's degree enrollment: **422**
    Teacher preparation program enrollment (master's): **257**

FINANCIAL INFORMATION

Financial aid phone number: **(770) 423-6074**
Tuition, 2003-2004 academic year: Full-time in-state: **$2,654**; out-of-state: **$10,616**, Part-time in-state: **$111/credit hour**; out-of-state: **$443/credit hour**
Fees: **$566**, Room and board: **$8,600**, Books and supplies: **$1,000**, Miscellaneous expenses: **$3,260**
Number of research assistant positions: **4**

ACADEMIC PROGRAMS

Total full-time tenured or tenure-track faculty (fall 2003): 27, Total part-time faculty (fall 2003): 42

Areas of specialization: education administration and supervision, elementary teacher education, secondary teacher education, special education.

Professional development/partnership school(s) are used by students in some of the teaching programs.

During their internships, peer groups of students meet regularly to discuss instructional techniques in some of the teaching programs.

All of the students in their internships are mentored.

Courses that prepare teachers to pass the National Board of Professional Teaching Standards are not offered.

Teacher preparation programs: Four-year baccalaureate-degree program leading to initial licensure that includes either a major or minor in education and practice teaching.

The education program is currently accredited by the National Council for Accreditation of Teacher Education.

LICENSING TEST

Pass rate on state's teacher licensing test for 2002-2003: 93%
State average pass rate: 93%

LaGrange College

■ 601 Broad Street, LaGrange, GA 30240
■ **Website:** http://www.lagrange.edu
■ **Private**
■ **Degrees offered:** bachelor's, master's

ADMISSIONS

Admissions phone number: **(706) 880-8005**
Admissions email address: *admis@lagrange.edu*
Application fee: **$20**
Fall 2005 application deadline: **rolling**
Test requirements: **GRE or MAT**
Test of English as Foreign Language (TOEFL) is required for international students.
Minimum TOEFL score required for paper test: **550**

Fall 2003
Acceptance rate for master's degree programs: **100%**
Total 2003 enrollment: **48**
Master's degree enrollment: **48**
    Teacher preparation program enrollment (master's): **37**

FINANCIAL INFORMATION

Financial aid phone number: **(706) 880-8241**
Tuition, 2003-2004 academic year: Full-time: **$591/credit hour**; Part-time: **$591/credit hour**
Room and board: **$6,018**, Books and supplies: **$1,000**
Number of fellowships awarded to graduate students during the 2003-2004 academic year: **0**
Number of teaching assistant positions: **0**
Number of research assistant positions: **0**
Number of other paid appointments: **0**

ACADEMIC PROGRAMS

Total full-time tenured or tenure-track faculty (fall 2003): **5**
    Total part-time faculty (fall 2003): **4**
Areas of specialization: curriculum and instruction, educational psychology, secondary teacher education, special education.
Professional development/partnership school(s) are used by students in all of the teaching programs.
During their internships, peer groups of students meet regularly to discuss instructional techniques in all of the teaching programs.
All of the students in their internships are mentored.
Courses that prepare teachers to pass the National Board of Professional Teaching Standards are not offered.
Teacher preparation programs: Four-year baccalaureate-degree program leading to initial licensure that includes either a major or minor in education and practice teaching. Master's program preparing college graduates for initial licensure; includes practice teaching.

LICENSING TEST

Pass rate on state's teacher licensing test for 2002-2003: **89%**
State average pass rate: **93%**

Mercer University

- **1400 Coleman Avenue, Macon, GA 31207**
- **Website:** http://www2.mercer.edu/default.htm
- **Private**
- **Degrees offered:** bachelor's, master's, education specialist

LICENSING TEST

Pass rate on state's teacher licensing test for 2002-2003: **92%**
State average pass rate: **93%**

North Georgia College and State University

- **College Circle, Dahlonega, GA 30597**
- **Website:** http://www.ngcsu.edu/
- **Public**

LICENSING TEST

Pass rate on state's teacher licensing test for 2002-2003: **95%**
State average pass rate: **93%**

Oglethorpe University

- **4484 Peachtree Road, Atlanta, GA 30319**
- **Website:** http://www.oglethorpe.edu/academics/graduate/mat
- **Private**
- **Degrees offered:** master's

ADMISSIONS

Admissions phone number: **(404) 364-8376**
Admissions email address: *khwakins@oglethorpe.edu*
Application fee: **$35**
Fall 2005 application deadline: **7/15**
Test of English as Foreign Language (TOEFL) is required for international students.

Fall 2003
Total 2003 enrollment: **40**
Master's degree enrollment: **40**
    Teacher preparation program enrollment (master's): **40**

FINANCIAL INFORMATION

Financial aid phone number: **(404) 364-8534**

ACADEMIC PROGRAMS

Total full-time tenured or tenure-track faculty (fall 2003): **4**
    Total part-time faculty (fall 2003): **5**
Areas of specialization: elementary teacher education.
Professional development/partnership school(s) are used by students in some of the teaching programs.
During their internships, peer groups of students meet regularly to discuss instructional techniques in all of the teaching programs.
All of the students in their internships are mentored.
Courses that prepare teachers to pass the National Board of Professional Teaching Standards are not offered.
Teacher preparation programs: Master's degree in education, including internship/practice teaching and preparation for initial licensure.

Piedmont College

- 165 Central Avenue, PO Box 10, Demorest, GA 30535
- **Website:** http://www.piedmont.edu
- **Private**
- **Degrees offered:** bachelor's, master's, education specialist

ADMISSIONS

Admissions phone number: **(800) 277-7020**
Admissions email address: *ckokesh@piedmont.edu*
Application fee: **$30**
Fall 2005 application deadline: **7/15**
Test requirements: **GRE or MAT**
Test of English as Foreign Language (TOEFL) is required for international students.
Minimum TOEFL score required for paper test: **550**
Minimum TOEFL score required for computer test: **213**

Fall 2003

Acceptance rate for master's degree programs: **87%**
Acceptance rate for education specialist degree programs: **80%**
Average MAT: **42**
Total 2003 enrollment: **1,137**
Master's degree enrollment: **940**
  Teacher preparation program enrollment (master's): **940**
Education specialist degree enrollment: **197**

FINANCIAL INFORMATION

Financial aid phone number: **(800) 277-7020**
Tuition, 2003-2004 academic year: Full-time: **$270/credit hour**; Part-time: **$270/credit hour**
Room and board: **$4,700**, Books and supplies: **$1,175**, Miscellaneous expenses: **$4,040**
Number of fellowships awarded to graduate students during the 2003-2004 academic year: **0**
Number of teaching assistant positions: **0**
Number of research assistant positions: **0**
Number of other paid appointments: **4**

ACADEMIC PROGRAMS

Total full-time tenured or tenure-track faculty (fall 2003): **20**, Total part-time faculty (fall 2003): **43**
Areas of specialization: curriculum and instruction, educational psychology, elementary teacher education, secondary teacher education, special education.
Professional development/partnership school(s) are used by students in some of the teaching programs.
During their internships, peer groups of students meet regularly to discuss instructional techniques in all of the teaching programs.
All of the students in their internships are mentored.
Courses that prepare teachers to pass the National Board of Professional Teaching Standards are offered.
Teacher preparation programs: Four-year baccalaureate-degree program leading to initial licensure that includes either a major or minor in education and practice teaching. Master's program preparing college graduates for initial licensure; includes practice teaching.

State University of West Georgia

- 1600 Maple Street, Carrollton, GA 30118
- **Website:** http://coe.westga.edu
- **Public**
- **Degrees offered:** bachelor's, master's, education specialist, Ed.D.

ADMISSIONS

Admissions phone number: **(770) 836-6419**
Admissions email address: *jjenkins@westga.edu*
Application website: *http://www.westga.edu*
Application fee: **$20**
Fall 2005 application deadline: **rolling**
Test of English as Foreign Language (TOEFL) is required for international students.
Minimum TOEFL score required for paper test: **550**
Minimum TOEFL score required for computer test: **213**

Fall 2003

Total 2003 enrollment: **1,835**
Master's degree enrollment: **1,540**
  Teacher preparation program enrollment (master's): **409**
Education specialist degree enrollment: **247**
Doctoral degree enrollment: **48**

FINANCIAL INFORMATION

Financial aid phone number: **(770) 836-6421**
Tuition, 2003-2004 academic year: Full-time in-state: **$1,998**; out-of-state: **$7,974**, Part-time in-state: **$111/credit hour**; out-of-state: **$443/credit hour**
Fees: **$472**, Room and board: **$5,006**, Books and supplies: **$600**

ACADEMIC PROGRAMS

Total full-time tenured or tenure-track faculty (fall 2003): **68**, Total part-time faculty (fall 2003): **17**
Areas of specialization: curriculum and instruction, education administration and supervision, educational psychology, elementary teacher education, secondary teacher education, special education, student counseling and personnel services, teacher education.
Professional development/partnership school(s) are used by students in all of the teaching programs.
During their internships, peer groups of students meet regularly to discuss instructional techniques in all of the teaching programs.
All of the students in their internships are mentored.
Courses that prepare teachers to pass the National Board of Professional Teaching Standards are not offered.

Teacher preparation programs: Four-year baccalaureate-degree program leading to initial licensure that includes either a major or minor in education and practice teaching. Master's program preparing college graduates for initial licensure; includes practice teaching.

The education program is currently accredited by the National Council for Accreditation of Teacher Education.

The education program is currently accredited by the Teacher Education Accreditation Council.

LICENSING TEST
Pass rate on state's teacher licensing test for 2002-2003: 98%
State average pass rate: 93%

University of Georgia

■ College of Education, G-3 Aderhold Hall, Athens, GA 30602
■ Website: http://www.gradsch.uga.edu
■ Public
■ Degrees offered: bachelor's, master's, education specialist, Ph.D., Ed.D.
■ Overall rank in the 2005 U.S. News education schools with doctoral programs: 24
■ Overall rank in the 2005 U.S. News education school specialty rankings: administration/supervision: 19, counseling/personnel: 5, curriculum/instruction: 6, educational psychology: 13, elementary education: 3, higher education administration: 18, secondary education: 3, vocational/technical: 4

ADMISSIONS
Admissions phone number: (706) 542-1739
Admissions email address: gradadm@uga.edu
Application website: http://www.gradsch.uga.edu/admissions
Application fee: $50
Fall 2005 application deadline: 7/1
Test requirements: GRE or MAT
Test of English as Foreign Language (TOEFL) is required for international students.
Minimum TOEFL score required for paper test: 550
Minimum TOEFL score required for computer test: 213

Fall 2003
Acceptance rate for master's degree programs: 35%
Acceptance rate for education specialist degree programs: 48%
Acceptance rate for doctoral programs: 26%
Average GRE verbal: 488, Average GRE quantitative: 572, Average GRE analytical: 581
Total 2003 enrollment: 2,234
Master's degree enrollment: 1,155
   Teacher preparation program enrollment (master's): 685
Education specialist degree enrollment: 229
Doctoral degree enrollment: 850

FINANCIAL INFORMATION
Financial aid phone number: (706) 542-3476
Tuition, 2003-2004 academic year: Full-time in-state: $3,850; out-of-state: $16,550, Part-time in-state: $161/credit hour; out-of-state: $690/credit hour
Fees: $870, Room and board: $5,560, Books and supplies: $850, Miscellaneous expenses: $2,600
Number of fellowships awarded to graduate students during the 2003-2004 academic year: 51
Number of teaching assistant positions: 131
Number of research assistant positions: 42
Number of other paid appointments: 175

ACADEMIC PROGRAMS
Total full-time tenured or tenure-track faculty (fall 2003): 201, Total part-time faculty (fall 2003): 61
Areas of specialization: education administration and supervision, educational psychology, elementary teacher education, higher education administration, secondary teacher education, special education, student counseling and personnel services.
Professional development/partnership school(s) are used by students in some of the teaching programs.
During their internships, peer groups of students meet regularly to discuss instructional techniques in some of the teaching programs.
All of the students in their internships are mentored.
Courses that prepare teachers to pass the National Board of Professional Teaching Standards are offered.
Teacher preparation programs: Four-year baccalaureate-degree program leading to initial licensure that includes either a major or minor in education and practice teaching. Master's program preparing college graduates for initial licensure; includes practice teaching. Alternative program for college graduates leading to provisional licensure.
The education program is currently accredited by the National Council for Accreditation of Teacher Education.

LICENSING TEST
Pass rate on state's teacher licensing test for 2002-2003: 95%
State average pass rate: 93%

Valdosta State University

■ 1500 N. Patterson Street, Valdosta, GA 31698
■ Website: http://www.valdosta.edu/
■ Public

LICENSING TEST
Pass rate on state's teacher licensing test for 2002-2003: 95%
State average pass rate: 93%

Wesleyan College

- 4760 Forsyth Road, Macon, GA 31204
- **Website:** http://www.wesleyancollege.edu/
- **Private**
- **Degrees offered:** master's

ADMISSIONS

Admissions phone number: **(478) 757-2480**
Admissions email address: *jcarson@wesleyancollege.edu*
Application fee: **$25**
Fall 2005 application deadline: **8/1**
Test of English as Foreign Language (TOEFL) is required for international students.
Minimum TOEFL score required for paper test: **550**
Minimum TOEFL score required for computer test: **250**

Fall 2003
Acceptance rate for master's degree programs: **83%**
Total 2003 enrollment: **32**
Master's degree enrollment: **32**
    Teacher preparation program enrollment (master's): **32**

FINANCIAL INFORMATION

Financial aid phone number: **(478) 757-5161**

Tuition, 2003-2004 academic year: Full-time: **$200/credit hour**; Part-time: **$200/credit hour**
Books and supplies: **$400**

ACADEMIC PROGRAMS

Total full-time tenured or tenure-track faculty (fall 2003): **3**
Areas of specialization: elementary teacher education.
Professional development/partnership school(s) are used by students in all of the teaching programs.
During their internships, peer groups of students meet regularly to discuss instructional techniques in all of the teaching programs.
All of the students in their internships are mentored.
Courses that prepare teachers to pass the National Board of Professional Teaching Standards are not offered.
Teacher preparation programs: Four-year baccalaureate-degree program leading to initial licensure that includes either a major or minor in education and practice teaching. Alternative program for college graduates leading to provisional licensure.

LICENSING TEST

Pass rate on state's teacher licensing test for 2002-2003: **90%**
State average pass rate: **93%**

HAWAII

Chaminade University of Honolulu

- 3140 Waialae Ave., Honolulu, HI 96816
- **Website:** http://www.chaminade.edu/
- **Private**
- **Degrees offered:** bachelor's, master's, education specialist

ADMISSIONS
Admissions phone number: (808) 739-4663
Admissions email address: *gradserv@chaminade.edu*
Application fee: **$50**
Fall 2005 application deadline: **rolling**
Test of English as Foreign Language (TOEFL) is required for international students.
Minimum TOEFL score required for paper test: **550**
Minimum TOEFL score required for computer test: **230**

FINANCIAL INFORMATION
Financial aid phone number: (808) 735-4780
Tuition, 2003-2004 academic year: Full-time: **$415/credit hour**; Part-time: **$415/credit hour**
Fees: **$415/credit hour**, Books and supplies: **$1,200**

LICENSING TEST
Pass rate on state's teacher licensing test for 2002-2003: 76%
State average pass rate: 82%

University of Hawaii– Hilo

- 200 W. Kawili Street, Hilo, HI 96720
- **Website:** http://www.uhh.hawaii.edu/
- **Public**

LICENSING TEST
Pass rate on state's teacher licensing test for 2002-2003: 74%
State average pass rate: 82%

University of Hawaii– Manoa

- 1776 University Avenue, Wist Annex 2-128, Honolulu, HI 96822
- **Website:** http://www.hawaii.edu/graduate/
- **Public**
- **Degrees offered:** bachelor's, master's, Ph.D.
- **Overall rank in the 2005 U.S. News education schools with doctoral programs:** 73

ADMISSIONS
Admissions phone number: (808) 956-8544
Admissions email address: *admissions@grad.hawaii.edu*
Application fee: **$50**
Fall 2005 application deadline: **2/1**
Test requirements: **GRE**
Test of English as Foreign Language (TOEFL) is required for international students.
Minimum TOEFL score required for paper test: **500**
Minimum TOEFL score required for computer test: **173**

Fall 2003
Acceptance rate for master's degree programs: **50%**
Acceptance rate for doctoral programs: **39%**
Average GRE verbal: **475**, Average GRE quantitative: **527**, Average GRE analytical: **526**
Total 2003 enrollment: **856**
Master's degree enrollment: **700**
    Teacher preparation program enrollment (master's): **245**
Doctoral degree enrollment: **156**

FINANCIAL INFORMATION
Financial aid phone number: (808) 956-7251

Tuition, 2003-2004 academic year: Full-time in-state: $4,464; out-of-state: $10,608, Part-time in-state: $186/credit hour; out-of-state: $442/credit hour

Fees: $152, Room and board: $6,101, Books and supplies: $1,049, Miscellaneous expenses: $1,409

Number of fellowships awarded to graduate students during the 2003-2004 academic year: 0

Number of teaching assistant positions: 20

Number of research assistant positions: 20

Number of other paid appointments: 18

ACADEMIC PROGRAMS

Total full-time tenured or tenure-track faculty (fall 2003): 101, Total part-time faculty (fall 2003): 0

Areas of specialization: curriculum and instruction, education administration and supervision, educational psychology, elementary teacher education, higher education administration, secondary teacher education, special education, student counseling and personnel services.

Professional development/partnership school(s) are used by students in some of the teaching programs.

During their internships, peer groups of students meet regularly to discuss instructional techniques in some of the teaching programs.

Courses that prepare teachers to pass the National Board of Professional Teaching Standards are offered.

Teacher preparation programs: Four-year baccalaureate-degree program leading to initial licensure that includes either a major or minor in education and practice teaching. Master's program preparing college graduates for initial licensure; includes practice teaching. Alternative program for college graduates leading to provisional licensure.

The education program is currently accredited by the National Council for Accreditation of Teacher Education.

LICENSING TEST

Pass rate on state's teacher licensing test for 2002-2003: 90%

State average pass rate: 82%

IDAHO

TEACHER TESTING IN IDAHO
The state is currently developing teacher licensure exams. For information on where to go in your state for specific academic requirements, see Chapter 6 on page 67.

Boise State University

- 1910 University Drive, Boise, ID 83725-1700
- Website:
  http://www.boisestate.edu/gradcoll/3admis.html
- Public
- **Degrees offered:** bachelor's, master's, Ed.D.

ADMISSIONS

Admissions phone number: **(208) 426-1337**
Admissions email address: *gradcoll@boisestate.edu,*
Application website:
  http://www.boisestate.edu/gradcoll/2apply.html
Application fee: **$30**
Fall 2005 application deadline: 7/16
Test of English as Foreign Language (TOEFL) is required
  for international students.

FINANCIAL INFORMATION

Financial aid phone number: **(208) 426-1664**
Tuition, 2003-2004 academic year: Full-time in-state:
  $4,668; out-of-state: **$11,388**, Part-time in-state:
  $199/credit hour; out-of-state: **$199/credit hour**
Room and board: **$5,126**, Books and supplies: **$500**,
  Miscellaneous expenses: **$1,000**

ACADEMIC PROGRAMS

Total full-time tenured or tenure-track faculty (fall 2003): **60**
Professional development/partnership school(s) are used
  by students in some of the teaching programs.
During their internships, peer groups of students meet
  regularly to discuss instructional techniques in some of
  the teaching programs.
All of the students in their internships are mentored.
Courses that prepare teachers to pass the National Board of
  Professional Teaching Standards are offered.
Teacher preparation programs: Four-year baccalaureate-
  degree program leading to initial licensure that includes
  either a major or minor in education and practice teach-
  ing. Alternative program for college graduates leading to
  provisional licensure.
The education program is currently accredited by the
  National Council for Accreditation of Teacher Education.

Idaho State University

- 921 S. 8th, Pocatello, ID 83209
- **Website:** http://www.isu.edu/departments/graduate
- **Public**
- **Degrees offered:** bachelor's, master's, education
  specialist, Ed.D.

ADMISSIONS

Admissions phone number: **(208) 282-2150**
Admissions email address: *graddean@isu.edu*
Application website: *http://www.isu.edu/departments/*
  graduate/graduate-application.html
Application fee: **$35**
Fall 2005 application deadline: 7/1
Test requirements: **GRE or MAT**
Test of English as Foreign Language (TOEFL) is required
  for international students.
Minimum TOEFL score required for paper test: 550
Minimum TOEFL score required for computer test: 213

Fall 2003
Acceptance rate for master's degree programs: 98%
Acceptance rate for education specialist degree programs: 100%
Acceptance rate for doctoral programs: 100%
Average GRE verbal: 446, Average GRE quantitative: 490,
  Average MAT: 43
Total 2003 enrollment: 425
Master's degree enrollment: 325
  Teacher preparation program enrollment (master's): 298
Education specialist degree enrollment: 28
Doctoral degree enrollment: 72

FINANCIAL INFORMATION

Financial aid phone number: **(208) 282-2756**
Tuition, 2003-2004 academic year: Full-time in-state: **N/A**;
  out-of-state: **$6,600**, Part-time in-state: **$205/credit**
  hour; out-of-state: **$300/credit hour**
Fees: **$4,976**, Room and board: **$6,848**, Books and sup-
  plies: **$800**, Miscellaneous expenses: **$3,150**
Number of fellowships awarded to graduate students dur-
  ing the 2003-2004 academic year: 1
Number of teaching assistant positions: 22
Number of research assistant positions: 0
Number of other paid appointments: 0

ACADEMIC PROGRAMS

Total full-time tenured or tenure-track faculty (fall 2003): 29, Total part-time faculty (fall 2003): 120

Areas of specialization: curriculum and instruction, education administration and supervision, elementary teacher education, higher education administration, secondary teacher education, special education, student counseling and personnel services.

Professional development/partnership school(s) are used by students in all of the teaching programs.

During their internships, peer groups of students meet regularly to discuss instructional techniques in all of the teaching programs.

All of the students in their internships are mentored.

Courses that prepare teachers to pass the National Board of Professional Teaching Standards are offered.

Teacher preparation programs: Four-year baccalaureate-degree program leading to initial licensure that includes either a major or minor in education and practice teaching. Master's program preparing college graduates for initial licensure; includes practice teaching. Alternative program for college graduates leading to provisional licensure.

The education program is currently accredited by the National Council for Accreditation of Teacher Education.

Northwest Nazarene University

- **623 Holly Street, Nampa, ID 83686**
- **Website:** http://www.nnu.edu
- **Private**
- **Degrees offered:** bachelor's, master's

ADMISSIONS

Admissions phone number: **(208) 467-8341**
Admissions email address: *empoe@nnu.edu*
Application fee: **$25**

Fall 2003
Total 2003 enrollment: **141**
Master's degree enrollment: **141**
    Teacher preparation program enrollment (master's): **106**

FINANCIAL INFORMATION

Financial aid phone number: **(208) 467-8774**
Tuition, 2003-2004 academic year: Full-time: **$315/credit hour**; Part-time: **$315/credit hour**

ACADEMIC PROGRAMS

Total full-time tenured or tenure-track faculty (fall 2003): **9**
Areas of specialization: curriculum and instruction, education administration and supervision, education policy,

educational psychology, elementary teacher education, secondary teacher education, special education, student counseling and personnel services.

Professional development/partnership school(s) are used by students in some of the teaching programs.

During their internships, peer groups of students meet regularly to discuss instructional techniques in some of the teaching programs.

Some of the students in their internships are mentored.

Courses that prepare teachers to pass the National Board of Professional Teaching Standards are offered.

Teacher preparation programs: Four-year baccalaureate-degree program leading to initial licensure that includes either a major or minor in education and practice teaching.

The education program is currently accredited by the National Council for Accreditation of Teacher Education.

University of Idaho

- **College of Education, Moscow, ID 83844-3080**
- **Website:** http://www.uidaho.edu/
- **Public**
- **Degrees offered:** bachelor's, master's, education specialist, Ph.D., Ed.D.

ADMISSIONS

Admissions phone number: **(208) 885-4001**
Admissions email address: *gadms@uidaho.edu*
Application website: *http://www.uidaho.edu/cogs/*
Application fee: **$55**
Test requirements: **GRE**
Test of English as Foreign Language (TOEFL) is required for international students.
Minimum TOEFL score required for paper test: **525**
Minimum TOEFL score required for computer test: **193**

FINANCIAL INFORMATION

Financial aid phone number: **(208) 885-6312**
Tuition, 2003-2004 academic year: Full-time in-state: **N/A**; out-of-state: **$7,392**, Part-time in-state: **N/A/credit hour**; out-of-state: **$309/credit hour**
Fees: **$3,880**, Room and board: **$6,714**, Books and supplies: **$1,248**, Miscellaneous expenses: **$2,964**

ACADEMIC PROGRAMS

Areas of specialization: curriculum and instruction, education administration and supervision, elementary teacher education, higher education administration, secondary teacher education, special education, student counseling and personnel services.

The education program is currently accredited by the National Council for Accreditation of Teacher Education.

ILLINOIS

Aurora University

■ **347 S. Gladstone Avenue, Aurora, IL 60506-4892**
■ **Website:** http://www.aurora.edu
■ **Private**
■ **Degrees offered:** bachelor's, master's, Ed.D.

ADMISSIONS
Admissions phone number: **(630) 844-5533**
Admissions email address: *admissions@aurora.edu*
Application website: *http://www.aurora.edu*
Application fee: **$25**
Fall 2005 application deadline: **rolling**
Test of English as Foreign Language (TOEFL) is required for international students.
Minimum TOEFL score required for paper test: **550**
Minimum TOEFL score required for computer test: **213**

Fall 2003
Acceptance rate for master's degree programs: **81%**
Acceptance rate for doctoral programs: **87%**
Total 2003 enrollment: **1,212**
Master's degree enrollment: **1,134**
    Teacher preparation program enrollment (master's): **287**
Doctoral degree enrollment: **78**

FINANCIAL INFORMATION
Financial aid phone number: **(630) 844-5149**
Tuition, 2003-2004 academic year: Full-time: **$490/credit hour**; Part-time: **$490/credit hour**
Room and board: **$7,169**, Books and supplies: **$750**, Miscellaneous expenses: **$3,073**
Number of fellowships awarded to graduate students during the 2003-2004 academic year: **0**
Number of teaching assistant positions: **0**
Number of research assistant positions: **0**
Number of other paid appointments: **0**

ACADEMIC PROGRAMS
Areas of specialization: curriculum and instruction, education administration and supervision, elementary teacher education, secondary teacher education.
Professional development/partnership school(s) are used by students in some of the teaching programs.
During their internships, peer groups of students meet regularly to discuss instructional techniques in all of the teaching programs.
All of the students in their internships are mentored.
Courses that prepare teachers to pass the National Board of Professional Teaching Standards are offered.
Teacher preparation programs: Four-year baccalaureate-degree program leading to initial licensure that includes either a major or minor in education and practice teaching. Master's program preparing college graduates for initial licensure; includes practice teaching. Alternative program for college graduates leading to provisional licensure.

LICENSING TEST
Pass rate on state's teacher licensing test for 2002-2003: **98%**
State average pass rate: **98%**

Benedictine University

■ **5700 College Road, Lisle, IL 60532**
■ **Website:** http://www.ben.edu/
■ **Private**
■ **Degrees offered:** bachelor's, master's

ADMISSIONS
Admissions phone number: **(630) 829-6300**
Admissions email address: *admissions@ben.edu*
Application website: *http://www.ben.edu/admissions/graduate/applications.asp*
Application fee: **$40**
Fall 2005 application deadline: **8/22**
Test of English as Foreign Language (TOEFL) is required for international students.

Minimum TOEFL score required for paper test: 550
Minimum TOEFL score required for computer test: 213

FINANCIAL INFORMATION

Financial aid phone number: (630) 829-6108
Tuition, 2003-2004 academic year: Full-time: $570/credit hour; Part-time: $570/credit hour
Fees: $250, Books and supplies: $900

LICENSING TEST

Pass rate on state's teacher licensing test for 2002-2003: 99%
State average pass rate: 98%

Bradley University

- 1501 W. Bradley Avenue, Peoria, IL 61625
- **Website:** http://www.bradley.edu
- **Private**
- **Degrees offered:** bachelor's, master's, education specialist

ADMISSIONS

Admissions phone number: (309) 677-1000
Admissions email address: *nickie@bradley.edu*
Application website: *http://www.bradley.edu*
Application fee: $35
Fall 2005 application deadline: 5/1
Test requirements: **GRE or MAT**
Test of English as Foreign Language (TOEFL) is required for international students.
Minimum TOEFL score required for paper test: 550
Minimum TOEFL score required for computer test: 213

Fall 2003

Acceptance rate for master's degree programs: 61%
Average GRE verbal: 438, Average GRE quantitative: 495, Average GRE analytical: 607, Average MAT: 49
Total 2003 enrollment: 226
Master's degree enrollment: 226
    Teacher preparation program enrollment (master's): 25
Education specialist degree enrollment: 0

FINANCIAL INFORMATION

Financial aid phone number: (309) 677-3089
Tuition, 2003-2004 academic year: Full-time: $16,800; Part-time: $460/credit hour
Fees: $130, Room and board: $5,980

ACADEMIC PROGRAMS

Total full-time tenured or tenure-track faculty (fall 2003): 53, Total part-time faculty (fall 2003): 68
Areas of specialization: curriculum and instruction, education administration and supervision, student counseling and personnel services.
Professional development/partnership school(s) are used by students in all of the teaching programs.

During their internships, peer groups of students meet regularly to discuss instructional techniques in all of the teaching programs.
All of the students in their internships are mentored.
Courses that prepare teachers to pass the National Board of Professional Teaching Standards are not offered.
Teacher preparation programs: Four-year baccalaureate-degree program leading to initial licensure that includes either a major or minor in education and practice teaching.
The education program is currently accredited by the National Council for Accreditation of Teacher Education.
The education program is currently accredited by the Teacher Education Accreditation Council.

LICENSING TEST

Pass rate on state's teacher licensing test for 2002-2003: 96%
State average pass rate: 98%

Chicago State University

- 9501 S. King Drive - ED 320, Chicago, IL 60628
- **Website:** http://www.csu.edu/
- **Public**
- **Degrees offered:** bachelor's, master's

ADMISSIONS

Admissions phone number: (773) 995-2404
Admissions email address: *G-studies1@csu.edu*
Application website: *http://www.csu.edu/*
Application fee: $25
Fall 2005 application deadline: 3/15
Test of English as Foreign Language (TOEFL) is required for international students.
Minimum TOEFL score required for paper test: 550
Minimum TOEFL score required for computer test: 213

Fall 2003

Acceptance rate for master's degree programs: 71%
Total 2003 enrollment: 753
Master's degree enrollment: 753
    Teacher preparation program enrollment (master's): 386

FINANCIAL INFORMATION

Financial aid phone number: (773) 995-2304
Tuition, 2003-2004 academic year: Full-time in-state: $147/credit hour; out-of-state: $420/credit hour
Fees: $608, Room and board: $5,856, Books and supplies: $450, Miscellaneous expenses: $100

ACADEMIC PROGRAMS

Areas of specialization: curriculum and instruction, education administration and supervision, education policy, educational psychology, elementary teacher education, higher education administration, secondary teacher education, special education, student counseling and personnel services, teacher education.

Professional development/partnership school(s) are used by students in all of the teaching programs.

During their internships, peer groups of students meet regularly to discuss instructional techniques in all of the teaching programs.

All of the students in their internships are mentored.

Teacher preparation programs: Four-year baccalaureate-degree program leading to initial licensure that includes either a major or minor in education and practice teaching. Master's program preparing college graduates for initial licensure; includes practice teaching. Alternative program for college graduates leading to provisional licensure.

The education program is currently accredited by the National Council for Accreditation of Teacher Education.

LICENSING TEST
Pass rate on state's teacher licensing test for 2002-2003: 94%
State average pass rate: 98%

Columbia College Chicago

■ 600 S. Michigan Avenue, Chicago, IL 60605-1996
■ Website: http://www.colum.edu/
■ Private

LICENSING TEST
Pass rate on state's teacher licensing test for 2002-2003: 96%
State average pass rate: 98%

Concordia University

■ 7400 Augusta Street, River Forest, IL 60305-1499
■ Website: http://www.curf.edu/
■ Private

LICENSING TEST
Pass rate on state's teacher licensing test for 2002-2003: 96%
State average pass rate: 98%

DePaul University

■ 1 E. Jackson Boulevard, Chicago, IL 60604-2287
■ Website: http://education.depaul.edu
■ Private
■ **Degrees offered:** bachelor's, master's, Ed.D.

ADMISSIONS
Admissions phone number: **(773) 325-4405**

Admissions email address: *edgradadmissions@depaul.edu*
Application website:
https://robin.depaul.edu/onlineapps/webapp/edupass.asp
Application fee: **$40**
Fall 2005 application deadline: **7/15**
Test of English as Foreign Language (TOEFL) is required for international students.
Minimum TOEFL score required for paper test: **550**
Minimum TOEFL score required for computer test: **210**

Fall 2003
Acceptance rate for master's degree programs: **82%**
Acceptance rate for education specialist degree programs: **81%**
Total 2003 enrollment: **1,770**
Master's degree enrollment: **1,700**
    Teacher preparation program enrollment (master's): **1,403**
Doctoral degree enrollment: **70**

FINANCIAL INFORMATION
Tuition, 2003-2004 academic year: Full-time: **$395/credit hour**; Part-time: **$395/credit hour**
Number of fellowships awarded to graduate students during the 2003-2004 academic year: **0**
Number of teaching assistant positions: **0**
Number of research assistant positions: **10**
Number of other paid appointments: **0**

ACADEMIC PROGRAMS
Total full-time tenured or tenure-track faculty (fall 2003): **55**, Total part-time faculty (fall 2003): **113**
Areas of specialization: curriculum and instruction, education administration and supervision, elementary teacher education, higher education administration, secondary teacher education, special education, student counseling and personnel services.

Professional development/partnership school(s) are used by students in all of the teaching programs.

During their internships, peer groups of students meet regularly to discuss instructional techniques in all of the teaching programs.

All of the students in their internships are mentored.

Courses that prepare teachers to pass the National Board of Professional Teaching Standards are not offered.

Teacher preparation programs: Four-year baccalaureate-degree program leading to initial licensure that includes either a major or minor in education and practice teaching. Master's program preparing college graduates for initial licensure; includes practice teaching.

The education program is currently accredited by the National Council for Accreditation of Teacher Education.

LICENSING TEST
Pass rate on state's teacher licensing test for 2002-2003: 100%
State average pass rate: 98%

Dominican University

- **7900 West Division Street, River Forest, IL 60305**
- **Website:** http://www.dom.edu
- **Private**
- **Degrees offered:** bachelor's, master's

ADMISSIONS

Admissions phone number: **(708) 524-6921**
Admissions email address: *708-524-6665*
Application website: *http://www.dom.edu*
Application fee: **$25**
Fall 2005 application deadline: **7/15**
Test of English as Foreign Language (TOEFL) is required for international students.
Minimum TOEFL score required for paper test: **550**
Minimum TOEFL score required for computer test: **213**

FINANCIAL INFORMATION

Financial aid phone number: **(708) 524-6809**
Tuition, 2003-2004 academic year: Full-time: **$445/credit hour**; Part-time: **$445/credit hour**
Fees: **$10/credit hour**, Room and board: **$6,810**, Books and supplies: **$300**, Miscellaneous expenses: **$100**

LICENSING TEST

Pass rate on state's teacher licensing test for 2002-2003: **97%**
State average pass rate: **98%**

Eastern Illinois University

- **600 Lincoln, Charleston, IL 61920**
- **Website:** http://www.eiu.edu/~graduate/
- **Public**
- **Degrees offered:** bachelor's, master's, education specialist

ADMISSIONS

Admissions phone number: **(217) 581-7489**
Admissions email address: *cscas@eiu.edu*
Application website: *http://www.shopeiu.eiu.edu/grad-index.htm*
Application fee: **$30**
Fall 2005 application deadline: **8/1**
Test requirements: **GRE or MAT**
Test of English as Foreign Language (TOEFL) is required for international students.
Minimum TOEFL score required for paper test: **550**
Minimum TOEFL score required for computer test: **213**

Fall 2003
Acceptance rate for master's degree programs: **100%**

Acceptance rate for education specialist degree programs: **100%**
Total 2003 enrollment: **1,464**
Master's degree enrollment: **1,329**
  Teacher preparation program enrollment (master's): **149**
Education specialist degree enrollment: **135**

FINANCIAL INFORMATION

Financial aid phone number: **(217) 581-3713**
Tuition, 2003-2004 academic year: Full-time in-state: **$125/credit hour**; out-of-state: **$375/credit hour**, Part-time in-state: **$125/credit hour**; out-of-state: **$375/credit hour**
Fees: **$4,376**, Room and board: **$6,210**, Books and supplies: **$120**, Miscellaneous expenses: **$3,043**
Number of teaching assistant positions: **168**
Number of research assistant positions: **21**
Number of other paid appointments: **100**

ACADEMIC PROGRAMS

The education program is currently accredited by the National Council for Accreditation of Teacher Education.

LICENSING TEST

Pass rate on state's teacher licensing test for 2002-2003: **99%**
State average pass rate: **98%**

Elmhurst College

- **190 Prospect Avenue, Elmhurst, IL 60126**
- **Website:** http://elmhurst.edu/
- **Private**

LICENSING TEST

Pass rate on state's teacher licensing test for 2002-2003: **99%**
State average pass rate: **98%**

Governors State University

- **One University Parkway, University Park, IL 60466**
- **Website:** http://www.govst.edu
- **Public**
- **Degrees offered:** bachelor's, master's

ADMISSIONS

Admissions phone number: **(708) 534-4490**
Admissions email address: *gsunow@govst.edu*
Application website:
  http://www.govst.edu/users/gapply/app.htm
Application fee: **$25**
Fall 2005 application deadline: **rolling**
Test requirements: **GRE**

Test of English as Foreign Language (TOEFL) is required
for international students.
Minimum TOEFL score required for paper test: 550
Minimum TOEFL score required for computer test: 213

Fall 2003
Acceptance rate for master's degree programs: 84%

FINANCIAL INFORMATION
Financial aid phone number: (708) 534-4590
Tuition, 2003-2004 academic year: Full-time in-state:
$130/credit hour; out-of-state: **$390/credit hour,** Part-
time in-state: **$130/credit hour**; out-of-state: **$390/credit
hour**
Fees: **$242**, Books and supplies: **$500**, Miscellaneous
expenses: **$100**
Number of fellowships awarded to graduate students dur-
ing the 2003-2004 academic year: **0**
Number of teaching assistant positions: **0**
Number of research assistant positions: **0**
Number of other paid appointments: **10**

ACADEMIC PROGRAMS
Total full-time tenured or tenure-track faculty (fall 2003):
66, Total part-time faculty (fall 2003): 120
Areas of specialization: education administration and
supervision, elementary teacher education, special edu-
cation, student counseling and personnel services.
Professional development/partnership school(s) are used
by students in none of the teaching programs.
During their internships, peer groups of students meet
regularly to discuss instructional techniques in some of
the teaching programs.
Some of the students in their internships are mentored.
Courses that prepare teachers to pass the National Board of
Professional Teaching Standards are not offered.
Teacher preparation programs: Master's program prepar-
ing college graduates for initial licensure; includes prac-
tice teaching. Alternative program for college graduates
leading to provisional licensure.
The education program is currently accredited by the
National Council for Accreditation of Teacher Education.

LICENSING TEST
Pass rate on state's teacher licensing test for 2002-2003:
97%
State average pass rate: 98%

Greenville College

- 315 E. College Avenue, Greenville, IL 62246-0159
- **Website:** http://www.greenville.edu/
- **Private**

LICENSING TEST
Pass rate on state's teacher licensing test for 2002-2003: 97%
State average pass rate: 98%

Illinois State University

- **Campus Box 5300, Normal, IL 61790-5300**
- **Website:** http://www.ilstu.edu
- **Public**
- **Degrees offered:** master's, Ph.D., Ed.D.
- **Overall rank in the 2005 U.S. News education schools
  with doctoral programs:** 62

ADMISSIONS
Admissions phone number: (309) 438-2181
Admissions email address: *gradinfo@ilstu.edu*
Application website:
  https://www.arr.ilstu.edu/OnApp/GradApp/
Application fee: **$30**
Fall 2005 application deadline: **rolling**
Test requirements: **GRE**
Test of English as Foreign Language (TOEFL) is required
for international students.
Minimum TOEFL score required for paper test: 550
Minimum TOEFL score required for computer test: 213

Fall 2003
Acceptance rate for master's degree programs: 69%
Acceptance rate for education specialist degree programs:
26%
Acceptance rate for doctoral programs: 63%
Average GRE verbal: 458, Average GRE quantitative: 547,
Average GRE analytical: 547
Total 2003 enrollment: 958
Master's degree enrollment: 629
  Teacher preparation program enrollment (master's): 450
Education specialist degree enrollment: 24
Doctoral degree enrollment: 305

FINANCIAL INFORMATION
Financial aid phone number: (309) 438-2231
Tuition, 2003-2004 academic year: Full-time in-state:
$3,322; out-of-state: **$6,922,** Part-time in-state:
$138/credit hour; out-of-state: **$288/credit hour**
Fees: **$1,164**, Room and board: **$5,414**, Books and supplies:
$786, Miscellaneous expenses: **$2,304**
Number of teaching assistant positions: **60**
Number of research assistant positions: **24**
Number of other paid appointments: **106**

ACADEMIC PROGRAMS
Total full-time tenured or tenure-track faculty (fall 2003):
112, Total part-time faculty (fall 2003): 131
Areas of specialization: curriculum and instruction, education administration and supervision, education policy,
educational psychology, higher education administration,
secondary teacher education, special education, student
counseling and personnel services.
Professional development/partnership school(s) are used
by students in all of the teaching programs.

During their internships, peer groups of students meet regularly to discuss instructional techniques in some of the teaching programs.

All of the students in their internships are mentored.

Courses that prepare teachers to pass the National Board of Professional Teaching Standards are offered.

Teacher preparation programs: Four-year baccalaureate-degree program leading to initial licensure that includes either a major or minor in education and practice teaching. Alternative program for college graduates leading to provisional licensure.

The education program is currently accredited by the National Council for Accreditation of Teacher Education.

LICENSING TEST

Pass rate on state's teacher licensing test for 2002-2003: 97%

State average pass rate: 98%

Lewis University

- One University Parkway, Romeoville, IL 60446
- Website: http://www.lewisu.edu/
- Private
- Degrees offered: bachelor's, master's, education specialist

ADMISSIONS

Admissions phone number: (815) 836-5570
Admissions email address: *admissions@lewisu.edu*
Application fee: $40
Fall 2005 application deadline: 8/15
Test of English as Foreign Language (TOEFL) is required for international students.

FINANCIAL INFORMATION

Financial aid phone number: (815) 836-5263
Tuition, 2003-2004 academic year: Full-time: $540/credit hour; Part-time: $540/credit hour

LICENSING TEST

Pass rate on state's teacher licensing test for 2002-2003: 94%

State average pass rate: 98%

Loyola University Chicago

- 820 N. Michigan Avenue, Chicago, IL 60611
- Website: http://www.luc.edu/
- Private
- Degrees offered: bachelor's, master's, education specialist, Ph.D., Ed.D.

ADMISSIONS

Admissions phone number: (312) 915-6880
Admissions email address: *schleduc@luc.edu*
Application website: *http://www.luc.edu/schools/education*
Application fee: $40
Fall 2005 application deadline: 7/1
Test requirements: **GRE or MAT**
Test of English as Foreign Language (TOEFL) is required for international students.
Minimum TOEFL score required for paper test: 550
Minimum TOEFL score required for computer test: 213

Fall 2003

Acceptance rate for master's degree programs: 83%
Acceptance rate for education specialist degree programs: 73%
Acceptance rate for doctoral programs: 86%
Average GRE verbal: 465, Average GRE quantitative: 541, Average GRE analytical: 538, Average MAT: 44
Total 2003 enrollment: 1,212
Master's degree enrollment: 614
   Teacher preparation program enrollment (master's): 249
Education specialist degree enrollment: 61
Doctoral degree enrollment: 537

FINANCIAL INFORMATION

Financial aid phone number: (773) 508-3155
Tuition, 2003-2004 academic year: Full-time: $578/credit hour; Part-time: $578/credit hour
Fees: $578/credit hour
Number of fellowships awarded to graduate students during the 2003-2004 academic year: 12
Number of research assistant positions: 15
Number of other paid appointments: 1

ACADEMIC PROGRAMS

Total full-time tenured or tenure-track faculty (fall 2003): 37, Total part-time faculty (fall 2003): 38

Areas of specialization: curriculum and instruction, education administration and supervision, education policy, educational psychology, elementary teacher education, higher education administration, secondary teacher education, special education, student counseling and personnel services.

Professional development/partnership school(s) are used by students in all of the teaching programs.

During their internships, peer groups of students meet regularly to discuss instructional techniques in all of the teaching programs.

All of the students in their internships are mentored.

Courses that prepare teachers to pass the National Board of Professional Teaching Standards are not offered.

Teacher preparation programs: Four-year baccalaureate-degree program leading to initial licensure that includes either a major or minor in education and practice teaching. Master's program preparing college graduates for initial licensure; includes practice teaching.

The education program is currently accredited by the National Council for Accreditation of Teacher Education.

LICENSING TEST

Pass rate on state's teacher licensing test for 2002-2003: **98%**

State average pass rate: **98%**

National-Louis University

- **122 South Michigan Avenue, Chicago, IL 60603**
- **Website:** http://www.nl.edu
- **Private**
- **Degrees offered:** bachelor's, master's, education specialist, Ed.D.

ADMISSIONS

Admissions phone number: **(888) 658-8632**

Admissions email address: *nluinfo@nl.edu*

Application website: *http://www3.nl.edu/enroll/applying.cfm*

Application fee: **$95**

Fall 2005 application deadline: **rolling**

Test requirements: **GRE or MAT**

Minimum TOEFL score required for paper test: **550**

Minimum TOEFL score required for computer test: **213**

Fall 2003

Acceptance rate for master's degree programs: **96%**

Acceptance rate for education specialist degree programs: **94%**

Acceptance rate for doctoral programs: **78%**

Average GRE verbal: **456**, Average MAT: **40**

Total 2003 enrollment: **3,671**

Master's degree enrollment: **3,326**

   Teacher preparation program enrollment (master's): **2,994**

Education specialist degree enrollment: **231**

Doctoral degree enrollment: **114**

FINANCIAL INFORMATION

Financial aid phone number: **(888) 658-8632**

Tuition, 2003-2004 academic year: Full-time: **$513/credit hour**; Part-time: **$513/credit hour**

Fees: **$40**

ACADEMIC PROGRAMS

Total full-time tenured or tenure-track faculty (fall 2003): **105**, Total part-time faculty (fall 2003): **430**

Areas of specialization: curriculum and instruction, education administration and supervision, educational psychology, elementary teacher education, higher education administration, secondary teacher education, special education, student counseling and personnel services, teacher education.

Professional development/partnership school(s) are used by students in all of the teaching programs.

During their internships, peer groups of students meet regularly to discuss instructional techniques in some of the teaching programs.

All of the students in their internships are mentored.

Courses that prepare teachers to pass the National Board of Professional Teaching Standards are offered.

Teacher preparation programs: Four-year baccalaureate-degree program leading to initial licensure that includes either a major or minor in education and practice teaching. Master's program preparing college graduates for initial licensure; includes practice teaching. Alternative program for college graduates leading to provisional licensure.

The education program is currently accredited by the National Council for Accreditation of Teacher Education.

LICENSING TEST

Pass rate on state's teacher licensing test for 2002-2003: **97%**

State average pass rate: **98%**

North Central College

- **30 N. Brainard Street, Naperville, IL 60540**
- **Website:** http://www.northcentralcollegeedu
- **Private**
- **Degrees offered:** bachelor's, master's

ADMISSIONS

Admissions phone number: **(888) 595-4723**

Admissions email address: *grad@noctrl.edu*

Application fee: **$25**

Fall 2005 application deadline: **8/1**

Test of English as Foreign Language (TOEFL) is required for international students.

Minimum TOEFL score required for paper test: **600**

Minimum TOEFL score required for computer test: **250**

Fall 2003

Acceptance rate for master's degree programs: **75%**

Total 2003 enrollment: **111**

Master's degree enrollment: **111**

   Teacher preparation program enrollment (master's): **59**

FINANCIAL INFORMATION

Financial aid phone number: **(630) 637-5600**

Tuition, 2003-2004 academic year: Full-time: **$284/credit hour**; Part-time: **$284/credit hour**

Fees: **$60**, Room and board: **$7,413**, Books and supplies: **$1,000**, Miscellaneous expenses: **$500**

Number of fellowships awarded to graduate students during the 2003-2004 academic year: **0**

Number of teaching assistant positions: **0**

Number of research assistant positions: **0**

Number of other paid appointments: **0**

ACADEMIC PROGRAMS

Total full-time tenured or tenure-track faculty (fall 2003): **7**

Areas of specialization: curriculum and instruction, education administration and supervision.

Professional development/partnership school(s) are used by students in none of the teaching programs.

During their internships, peer groups of students meet regularly to discuss instructional techniques in all of the teaching programs.

Courses that prepare teachers to pass the National Board of Professional Teaching Standards are not offered.

Teacher preparation programs: Four-year baccalaureate-degree program leading to initial licensure that includes either a major or minor in education and practice teaching.

LICENSING TEST

Pass rate on state's teacher licensing test for 2002-2003: 100%

State average pass rate: 98%

Northeastern Illinois University

- 5500 N. St. Louis Avenue, Chicago, IL 60625
- Website: http://www.neiu.edu/Grad.htm
- Public
- Degrees offered: bachelor's, master's

ADMISSIONS

Admissions phone number: **(773) 442-6008**
Admissions email address: *GRADCOLL@NEIU.EDU*
Application website: *http://www.neiu.edu/Grad.htm*
Application fee: **$25**
Fall 2005 application deadline: **2/28**
Test requirements: **GRE**
Test of English as Foreign Language (TOEFL) is required for international students.
Minimum TOEFL score required for paper test: **550**
Minimum TOEFL score required for computer test: **213**

FINANCIAL INFORMATION

Financial aid phone number: **(773) 442-5010**
Tuition, 2003-2004 academic year: Full-time in-state: **$2,644**; out-of-state: **$5,438**, Part-time in-state: **$147/credit hour**; out-of-state: **$272/credit hour**
Fees: **$294**

ACADEMIC PROGRAMS

Areas of specialization: curriculum and instruction, education administration and supervision, elementary teacher education, higher education administration, secondary teacher education, special education, student counseling and personnel services.

Professional development/partnership school(s) are used by students in all of the teaching programs.

During their internships, peer groups of students meet regularly to discuss instructional techniques in all of the teaching programs.

All of the students in their internships are mentored.

Courses that prepare teachers to pass the National Board of Professional Teaching Standards are not offered.

Teacher preparation programs: Four-year baccalaureate-degree program leading to initial licensure that includes

either a major or minor in education and practice teaching. Master's program preparing college graduates for initial licensure; includes practice teaching.

The education program is currently accredited by the National Council for Accreditation of Teacher Education.

LICENSING TEST

Pass rate on state's teacher licensing test for 2002-2003: 96%

State average pass rate: 98%

Northern Illinois University

- College of Education, DeKalb, IL 60115
- Website: http://www.cedu.niu.edu
- Public
- Degrees offered: bachelor's, master's, education specialist, Ed.D.

ADMISSIONS

Admissions phone number: **(815) 753-0395**
Admissions email address: *gradsch@niu.edu*
Application website: *http://www.grad.niu.edu/apply.htm*
Application fee: **$30**
Fall 2005 application deadline: **6/1**
Test requirements: **GRE or MAT**
Test of English as Foreign Language (TOEFL) is required for international students.
Minimum TOEFL score required for paper test: **550**
Minimum TOEFL score required for computer test: **213**

Fall 2003

Acceptance rate for master's degree programs: **65%**
Acceptance rate for education specialist degree programs: **65%**
Acceptance rate for doctoral programs: **46%**
Average GRE verbal: **452**, Average GRE quantitative: **528**
Total 2003 enrollment: **2,130**
Master's degree enrollment: **1,547**
  Teacher preparation program enrollment (master's): **479**
Education specialist degree enrollment: **36**
Doctoral degree enrollment: **547**

FINANCIAL INFORMATION

Financial aid phone number: **(815) 753-1395**
Tuition, 2003-2004 academic year: Full-time in-state: **$3,968**; out-of-state: **$7,937**, Part-time in-state: **$165/credit hour**; out-of-state: **$331/credit hour**
Fees: **$52/credit hour**, Room and board: **$4,510**, Books and supplies: **$750**, Miscellaneous expenses: **$750**
Number of fellowships awarded to graduate students during the 2003-2004 academic year: **8**
Number of teaching assistant positions: **65**
Number of research assistant positions: **53**
Number of other paid appointments: **20**

ACADEMIC PROGRAMS

Total full-time tenured or tenure-track faculty (fall 2003): 117, Total part-time faculty (fall 2003): 120

Areas of specialization: curriculum and instruction, education administration and supervision, education policy, educational psychology, elementary teacher education, higher education administration, secondary teacher education, special education, student counseling and personnel services.

Professional development/partnership school(s) are used by students in some of the teaching programs.

During their internships, peer groups of students meet regularly to discuss instructional techniques in some of the teaching programs.

All of the students in their internships are mentored.

Courses that prepare teachers to pass the National Board of Professional Teaching Standards are offered.

Teacher preparation programs: Four-year baccalaureate-degree program leading to initial licensure that includes either a major or minor in education and practice teaching. Master's program preparing college graduates for initial licensure; includes practice teaching.

The education program is currently accredited by the National Council for Accreditation of Teacher Education.

LICENSING TEST

Pass rate on state's teacher licensing test for 2002-2003: 99%

State average pass rate: 98%

North Park University

■ 3225 W. Foster Avenue, Chicago, IL 60625-4895
■ **Website:** http://www.northpark.edu/
■ **Private**

LICENSING TEST

Pass rate on state's teacher licensing test for 2002-2003: 98%

State average pass rate: 98%

Northwestern University

■ 2120 Campus Drive, Evanston, IL 60208
■ **Website:** http://www.sesp.northwestern.edu
■ **Private**
■ **Degrees offered:** bachelor's, master's, Ph.D.
■ **Overall rank in the 2005 U.S. News education schools with doctoral programs:** 11
■ **Overall rank in the 2005 U.S. News education school specialty rankings:** educational psychology: 16

ADMISSIONS

Admissions phone number: **(847) 491-3790**
Admissions email address: *sesp@northwestern.edu*
Application website: *http://www.northwestern.edu/graduate/*

Application fee: **$60**
Fall 2005 application deadline: **12/31**
Test requirements: **GRE**
Test of English as Foreign Language (TOEFL) is required for international students.
Minimum TOEFL score required for paper test: **560**
Minimum TOEFL score required for computer test: **220**

Fall 2003

Acceptance rate for master's degree programs: **76%**
Acceptance rate for doctoral programs: **18%**
Average GRE verbal: **598**, Average GRE quantitative: **666**, Average GRE analytical: **675**
Total 2003 enrollment: **147**
Master's degree enrollment: **73**
   Teacher preparation program enrollment (master's): **26**
Doctoral degree enrollment: **74**

FINANCIAL INFORMATION

Financial aid phone number: **(847) 491-3790**
Tuition, 2003-2004 academic year: Full-time: **$28,404**; Part-time: **$3,370/credit hour**
Number of fellowships awarded to graduate students during the 2003-2004 academic year: **16**
Number of teaching assistant positions: **15**
Number of research assistant positions: **43**
Number of other paid appointments: **3**

ACADEMIC PROGRAMS

Total full-time tenured or tenure-track faculty (fall 2003): 23, Total part-time faculty (fall 2003): 55

Areas of specialization: elementary teacher education, higher education administration, secondary teacher education.

Professional development/partnership school(s) are used by students in all of the teaching programs.

During their internships, peer groups of students meet regularly to discuss instructional techniques in all of the teaching programs.

All of the students in their internships are mentored.

Courses that prepare teachers to pass the National Board of Professional Teaching Standards are not offered.

Teacher preparation programs: Four-year baccalaureate-degree program leading to initial licensure that includes either a major or minor in education and practice teaching. Master's program preparing college graduates for initial licensure; includes practice teaching. Alternative program for college graduates leading to provisional licensure.

LICENSING TEST

Pass rate on state's teacher licensing test for 2002-2003: 100%

State average pass rate: 98%

Olivet Nazarene University

■ 1 University Avenue, Bourbonnais, IL 60914
■ **Website:** http://www.olivet.edu/
■ **Private**

LICENSING TEST

Pass rate on state's teacher licensing test for 2002-2003: 98%
State average pass rate: 98%

Quincy University

■ 1800 College Avenue, Quincy, IL 62301
■ **Website:** http://www.quincy.edu/
■ **Private**

LICENSING TEST

Pass rate on state's teacher licensing test for 2002-2003: 92%
State average pass rate: 98%

Rockford College

■ 5050 East State St., Rockford, IL 61103
■ **Website:** http://www.rockford.edu
■ **Private**
■ **Degrees offered:** bachelor's, master's

ADMISSIONS

Admissions phone number: **(815) 226-4041**
Admissions email address: *Andrea_Freeman@rockford.edu*
Application website: *http://www.rockford.edu/forms/graduate/gradapplform.htm*
Application fee: **$50**
Fall 2005 application deadline: **rolling**
Test requirements: **GRE**
Test of English as Foreign Language (TOEFL) is required for international students.
Minimum TOEFL score required for paper test: **550**
Minimum TOEFL score required for computer test: **213**

Fall 2003

Average GRE verbal: **520**, Average GRE quantitative: **460**
Total 2003 enrollment: **685**
Master's degree enrollment: **685**
    Teacher preparation program enrollment (master's): **685**

FINANCIAL INFORMATION

Financial aid phone number: **(815) 226-3396**
Tuition, 2003-2004 academic year: Full-time: **$20,210;**
    Part-time: **$530/credit hour**

Fees: **$60**, Room and board: **$7,000**, Books and supplies: **$920**, Miscellaneous expenses: **$50**

ACADEMIC PROGRAMS

Areas of specialization: educational psychology, elementary teacher education, secondary teacher education, special education.
Professional development/partnership school(s) are used by students in none of the teaching programs.
During their internships, peer groups of students meet regularly to discuss instructional techniques in none of the teaching programs.
All of the students in their internships are mentored.
Courses that prepare teachers to pass the National Board of Professional Teaching Standards are not offered.
Teacher preparation programs: Master's program preparing college graduates for initial licensure; includes practice teaching. Alternative program for college graduates leading to provisional licensure.

LICENSING TEST

Pass rate on state's teacher licensing test for 2002-2003: 96%
State average pass rate: 98%

Roosevelt University

■ 430 S. Michigan Avenue, Chicago, IL 60605
■ **Website:** http://www.roosevelt.edu
■ **Private**
■ **Degrees offered:** bachelor's, master's, Ed.D.

ADMISSIONS

Admissions phone number: **(312) 341-3523**
Admissions email address: *applyRU@roosevelt.edu*
Application website:
    http://www.roosevelt.edu/admission/howtohtm
Application fee: **$25**
Fall 2005 application deadline: **rolling**
Test requirements: **GRE or MAT**
Test of English as Foreign Language (TOEFL) is required for international students.
Minimum TOEFL score required for paper test: **525**
Minimum TOEFL score required for computer test: **213**

Fall 2003

Acceptance rate for master's degree programs: **80%**
Acceptance rate for doctoral programs: **55%**
Total 2003 enrollment: **191**

FINANCIAL INFORMATION

Financial aid phone number: **(312) 341-2195**
Tuition, 2003-2004 academic year: Full-time: **$624/credit hour**; Part-time: **$624/credit hour**
Fees: **$300**, Room and board: **$3,575**
Number of fellowships awarded to graduate students during the 2003-2004 academic year: **0**
Number of teaching assistant positions: **0**

Number of research assistant positions: 11
Number of other paid appointments: 0

ACADEMIC PROGRAMS

Total full-time tenured or tenure-track faculty (fall 2003):
23

Areas of specialization: curriculum and instruction, education administration and supervision, elementary teacher education, secondary teacher education, special education, student counseling and personnel services.

Professional development/partnership school(s) are used by students in some of the teaching programs.

During their internships, peer groups of students meet regularly to discuss instructional techniques in all of the teaching programs.

All of the students in their internships are mentored.

Courses that prepare teachers to pass the National Board of Professional Teaching Standards are offered.

Teacher preparation programs: Four-year baccalaureate-degree program leading to initial licensure that includes either a major or minor in education and practice teaching. Master's program preparing college graduates for initial licensure; includes practice teaching.

The education program is currently accredited by the National Council for Accreditation of Teacher Education.

LICENSING TEST

Pass rate on state's teacher licensing test for 2002-2003:
95%
State average pass rate: 98%

Southern Illinois University–Carbondale

- ■ Wham Building 115, Carbondale, IL 62901-4624
- ■ **Website:** http://web.coehs.siu.edu/Public/
- ■ **Public**
- ■ **Degrees offered:** bachelor's, master's, Ph.D.

ADMISSIONS

Admissions phone number: **(618) 536-7791**
Admissions email address: *gradschl@siu.edu*
Application website: *http://www.siu.edu/gradschl/admissions.htm*
Application fee: **$35**
Fall 2005 application deadline: **5/23**
Test requirements: **GRE or MAT**
Test of English as Foreign Language (TOEFL) is required for international students.
Minimum TOEFL score required for paper test: **550**
Minimum TOEFL score required for computer test: **220**

Fall 2003
Acceptance rate for master's degree programs: **48%**
Acceptance rate for doctoral programs: **17%**
Average GRE verbal: **482**, Average GRE quantitative: **501**, Average GRE analytical: **561**, Average MAT: **62**

Total 2003 enrollment: 1,345
Master's degree enrollment: 1,002
    Teacher preparation program enrollment (master's): 551
Doctoral degree enrollment: 343

FINANCIAL INFORMATION

Financial aid phone number: **(618) 453-4334**
Tuition, 2003-2004 academic year: Full-time in-state: **$179/credit hour**; out-of-state: **$358/credit hour**, Part-time in-state: **$90/credit hour**; out-of-state: **$179/credit hour**
Fees: **$299/credit hour**, Room and board: **$6,323**
Number of fellowships awarded to graduate students during the 2003-2004 academic year: **8**
Number of teaching assistant positions: **97**
Number of research assistant positions: **121**
Number of other paid appointments: **9**

ACADEMIC PROGRAMS

Total full-time tenured or tenure-track faculty (fall 2003): **93**, Total part-time faculty (fall 2003): **78**
Areas of specialization: curriculum and instruction, education administration and supervision, educational psychology, elementary teacher education, higher education administration, secondary teacher education, special education, student counseling and personnel services, teacher education.

Professional development/partnership school(s) are used by students in some of the teaching programs.

During their internships, peer groups of students meet regularly to discuss instructional techniques in some of the teaching programs.

All of the students in their internships are mentored.

Courses that prepare teachers to pass the National Board of Professional Teaching Standards are offered.

Teacher preparation programs: Four-year baccalaureate-degree program leading to initial licensure that includes either a major or minor in education and practice teaching. Master's program preparing college graduates for initial licensure; includes practice teaching. Alternative program for college graduates leading to provisional licensure.

The education program is currently accredited by the National Council for Accreditation of Teacher Education.

LICENSING TEST

Pass rate on state's teacher licensing test for 2002-2003:
98%
State average pass rate: 98%

Southern Illinois University–Edwardsville

- ■ Campus Box 1049, Edwardsville, IL 62026
- ■ **Website:** http://www.siue.edu/
- ■ **Public**

ADMISSIONS

Admissions phone number: **(618) 650-3705**
Admissions email address: *admis@siue.edu*
Application website:
  http://www.admis.siue.edu/prospective/apply/index.html
Application fee: **$30**
Fall 2005 application deadline: 7/23
Test of English as Foreign Language (TOEFL) is required for international students.
Minimum TOEFL score required for paper test: 550
Minimum TOEFL score required for computer test: 213

FINANCIAL INFORMATION

Financial aid phone number: **(618) 650-3880**

LICENSING TEST

Pass rate on state's teacher licensing test for 2002-2003: 96%
State average pass rate: 98%

St. Xavier University

- ■ 3700 W. 103rd Street, Chicago, IL 60655
- ■ **Website:** http://www.sxu.edu
- ■ **Private**
- ■ **Degrees offered:** bachelor's, master's, education specialist

ADMISSIONS

Admissions phone number: **(773) 298-3053**
Admissions email address: *graduateadmission@sxu.edu*
Application website: *http://www.sxu.edu*
Application fee: **$0**
Fall 2005 application deadline: 8/1
Test requirements: **None**
Test of English as Foreign Language (TOEFL) is required for international students.
Minimum TOEFL score required for paper test: 550
Minimum TOEFL score required for computer test: 213

FINANCIAL INFORMATION

Financial aid phone number: **(773) 298-3070**
Tuition, 2003-2004 academic year: Full-time: **$16,500**; Part-time: **$550/credit hour**
Fees: **$170**, Room and board: **$6,484**, Books and supplies: **$900**, Miscellaneous expenses: **$1,268**
Number of fellowships awarded to graduate students during the 2003-2004 academic year: 0

Number of teaching assistant positions: **14**
Number of research assistant positions: **0**
Number of other paid appointments: **2**

ACADEMIC PROGRAMS

Total full-time tenured or tenure-track faculty (fall 2003): 30, Total part-time faculty (fall 2003): 2
Areas of specialization: curriculum and instruction, education administration and supervision, elementary teacher education, secondary teacher education, special education, student counseling and personnel services.
Professional development/partnership school(s) are used by students in all of the teaching programs.
During their internships, peer groups of students meet regularly to discuss instructional techniques in some of the teaching programs.
All of the students in their internships are mentored.
Courses that prepare teachers to pass the National Board of Professional Teaching Standards are not offered.
The education program is currently accredited by the National Council for Accreditation of Teacher Education.

LICENSING TEST

Pass rate on state's teacher licensing test for 2002-2003: 100%
State average pass rate: 98%

University of Illinois–Chicago

- ■ 1040 W. Harrison Street, Chicago, IL 60607-7133
- ■ **Website:** http://www.uic.edu/educ/indexhtml/admissions/index.html
- ■ **Public**
- ■ **Degrees offered:** bachelor's, master's, Ph.D.
- ■ **Overall rank in the 2005 U.S. News education schools with doctoral programs:** 44
- ■ **Overall rank in the 2005 U.S. News education school specialty rankings:** elementary education: 23

ADMISSIONS

Admissions phone number: **(312) 996-4532**
Admissions email address: *scoleman@uic.edu*
Application website: *http://www.uic.edu/depts/ims/uiconline/uic_appl_strt.htm*
Application fee: **$40**
Fall 2005 application deadline: 1/1
Test requirements: **GRE**
Test of English as Foreign Language (TOEFL) is required for international students.
Minimum TOEFL score required for paper test: 550
Minimum TOEFL score required for computer test: 213

Fall 2003
Acceptance rate for master's degree programs: 82%
Acceptance rate for doctoral programs: 67%
Average GRE verbal: 496, Average GRE quantitative: 553

Total 2003 enrollment: **844**
Master's degree enrollment: **626**
   Teacher preparation program enrollment (master's): **356**
Doctoral degree enrollment: **218**

FINANCIAL INFORMATION
Financial aid phone number: **(312) 996-3126**
Tuition, 2003-2004 academic year: Full-time in-state:
   $5,648; out-of-state: **$16,030**, Part-time in-state: **$3,766**;
   out-of-state: **$10,688**
Fees: **$1,900**, Room and board: **$7,270**, Books and sup-
   plies: **$850**, Miscellaneous expenses: **$1,200**
Number of fellowships awarded to graduate students dur-
   ing the 2003-2004 academic year: **2**
Number of teaching assistant positions: **29**
Number of research assistant positions: **219**
Number of other paid appointments: **20**

ACADEMIC PROGRAMS
Total full-time tenured or tenure-track faculty (fall 2003):
   50, Total part-time faculty (fall 2003): **8**
Areas of specialization: curriculum and instruction, education administration and supervision, education policy,
   educational psychology, elementary teacher education,
   higher education administration, secondary teacher education, special education.
Professional development/partnership school(s) are used
   by students in none of the teaching programs.
During their internships, peer groups of students meet
   regularly to discuss instructional techniques in all of the
   teaching programs.
All of the students in their internships are mentored.
Courses that prepare teachers to pass the National Board of
   Professional Teaching Standards are not offered.
Teacher preparation programs: Four-year baccalaureate-
   degree program leading to initial licensure that includes
   either a major or minor in education and practice teaching. Master's program preparing college graduates for
   initial licensure; includes practice teaching.

LICENSING TEST
Pass rate on state's teacher licensing test for 2002-2003:
   98%
State average pass rate: **98%**

University of Illinois– Springfield

- **One University Plaza, MS PAC 522, Springfield, IL 62703**
- **Website:** http://www.uis.edu
- **Public**
- **Degrees offered:** bachelor's, master's

ADMISSIONS
Admissions phone number: **(217) 206-6729**
Admissions email address: *admissions@uis.edu*
Application fee: **$40**

Fall 2005 application deadline: **rolling**
Test of English as Foreign Language (TOEFL) is required
   for international students.
Minimum TOEFL score required for paper test: **500**
Minimum TOEFL score required for computer test: **173**

Fall 2003
Acceptance rate for master's degree programs: **95%**
Total 2003 enrollment: **302**
Master's degree enrollment: **302**

FINANCIAL INFORMATION
Financial aid phone number: **(217) 206-6724**
Tuition, 2003-2004 academic year: Full-time in-state:
   $130/credit hour; out-of-state: **$389/credit hour**, Part-
   time in-state: **$130/credit hour**; out-of-state: **$389/credit
   hour**
Fees: **$860**, Room and board: **$7,000**, Books and supplies:
   $1,000, Miscellaneous expenses: **$1,800**
Number of paid appointments: **2**

ACADEMIC PROGRAMS
Total full-time tenured or tenure-track faculty (fall 2003): **4**
   Total part-time faculty (fall 2003): **14**
Professional development/partnership school(s) are used
   by students in some of the teaching programs.
During their internships, peer groups of students meet
   regularly to discuss instructional techniques in all of the
   teaching programs.
All of the students in their internships are mentored.
Courses that prepare teachers to pass the National Board of
   Professional Teaching Standards are offered.
Teacher preparation programs: Four-year baccalaureate-
   degree program leading to initial licensure that includes
   either a major or minor in education and practice teaching.

LICENSING TEST
Pass rate on state's teacher licensing test for 2002-2003: **100%**
State average pass rate: **98%**

University of Illinois– Urbana-Champaign

- **1310 S. Sixth Street, Champaign, IL 61820**
- **Website:** http://www.ed.uiuc.edu/ipo
- **Public**
- **Degrees offered:** bachelor's, master's, Ph.D., Ed.D.
- **Overall rank in the 2005 U.S. News education schools
  with doctoral programs: 27**
- **Overall rank in the 2005 U.S. News education school
  specialty rankings:** administration/supervision: 12,
  counseling/personnel: 10, curriculum/instruction: 7,
  education policy: 12, educational psychology: 5,
  elementary education: 5, higher education
  administration: 16, secondary education: 7, special
  education: 5, vocational/technical: 6

ADMISSIONS

Admissions phone number: **(217) 333-2267**
Admissions email address: *admissions@mail.ed.uiuc.edu*
Application website:
http://www.oar.uiuc.edu/prospective/grad/applygr.html
Application fee: **$40**
Test requirements: **GRE**
Test of English as Foreign Language (TOEFL) is required
for international students.
Minimum TOEFL score required for paper test: **590**
Minimum TOEFL score required for computer test: **243**

Fall 2003
Acceptance rate for master's degree programs: **60%**
Acceptance rate for doctoral programs: **37%**
Average GRE verbal: **545**, Average GRE quantitative: **642**,
Average GRE analytical: **601**
Total 2003 enrollment: **1,000**
Master's degree enrollment: **469**
  Teacher preparation program enrollment (master's): **54**
Doctoral degree enrollment: **531**

FINANCIAL INFORMATION

Financial aid phone number: **(217) 333-2267**
Tuition, 2003-2004 academic year: Full-time in-state:
$6,196; out-of-state: **$17,306**, Part-time in-state: **$4,132**;
out-of-state: **$11,538**
Fees: **$1,560**, Room and board: **$8,532**, Books and supplies:
$1,004, Miscellaneous expenses: **$2,786**
Number of fellowships awarded to graduate students dur-
ing the 2003-2004 academic year: **81**
Number of teaching assistant positions: **144**
Number of research assistant positions: **204**
Number of other paid appointments: **128**

ACADEMIC PROGRAMS

Total full-time tenured or tenure-track faculty (fall 2003):
  94, Total part-time faculty (fall 2003): **0**
Areas of specialization: curriculum and instruction, education administration and supervision, education policy,
educational psychology, elementary teacher education,
higher education administration, secondary teacher education, special education, student counseling and personnel services.
Professional development/partnership school(s) are used
by students in some of the teaching programs.
During their internships, peer groups of students meet
regularly to discuss instructional techniques in some of
the teaching programs.
All of the students in their internships are mentored.
Courses that prepare teachers to pass the National Board of
Professional Teaching Standards are not offered.
Teacher preparation programs: Four-year baccalaureate-
degree program leading to initial licensure that includes
either a major or minor in education and practice teaching. Master's program preparing college graduates for
initial licensure; includes practice teaching.

LICENSING TEST

Pass rate on state's teacher licensing test for 2002-2003:
  99%
State average pass rate: **98%**

University of St. Francis

■ **500 Wilcox Street, Joliet, IL 60435**
■ **Website:** http://www.stfrancis.edu
■ **Private**
■ **Degrees offered:** bachelor's, master's

ADMISSIONS

Admissions phone number: **(800) 735-7500**
Admissions email address: *admissions@stfrancis.edu*
Application website:
http://www.stfrancis.edu/admissions/apply.htm
Application fee: **$25**
Fall 2005 application deadline: **rolling**
Test of English as Foreign Language (TOEFL) is required
for international students.
Minimum TOEFL score required for paper test: **550**
Minimum TOEFL score required for computer test: **213**

Fall 2003
Acceptance rate for master's degree programs: **64%**
Total 2003 enrollment: **566**
Master's degree enrollment: **566**
  Teacher preparation program enrollment (master's): **198**

FINANCIAL INFORMATION

Financial aid phone number: **(866) 890-8331**
Tuition, 2003-2004 academic year: **$455/credit hour**
Number of fellowships awarded to graduate students dur-
ing the 2003-2004 academic year: **0**
Number of teaching assistant positions: **0**
Number of research assistant positions: **0**
Number of other paid appointments: **3**

ACADEMIC PROGRAMS

Total full-time tenured or tenure-track faculty (fall 2003): **7**,
  Total part-time faculty (fall 2003): **33**
Areas of specialization: curriculum and instruction, educa-
tion administration and supervision, educational psy-
chology, elementary teacher education, secondary
teacher education, special education.
Professional development/partnership school(s) are used
by students in some of the teaching programs.
During their internships, peer groups of students meet
regularly to discuss instructional techniques in all of the
teaching programs.
All of the students in their internships are mentored.
Courses that prepare teachers to pass the National Board of
Professional Teaching Standards are offered.
Teacher preparation programs: Four-year baccalaureate-
degree program leading to initial licensure that includes
either a major or minor in education and practice teach-

ing. Master's program preparing college graduates for initial licensure; includes practice teaching.

LICENSING TEST
Pass rate on state's teacher licensing test for 2002-2003: 98%
State average pass rate: 98%

Western Illinois University

- 1 University Circle, Macomb, IL 61455
- **Website:** http://www.wiu.edu
- Public
- **Degrees offered:** bachelor's, master's, education specialist

ADMISSIONS
Admissions phone number: (309) 298-1806
Admissions email address: *grad-office@wiu.edu*
Application website: *http://www.wiu.edu/grad*
Application fee: **$30**
Fall 2005 application deadline: **rolling**
Test of English as Foreign Language (TOEFL) is required for international students.
Minimum TOEFL score required for paper test: 550
Minimum TOEFL score required for computer test: 213

Fall 2003
Total 2003 enrollment: 868
Master's degree enrollment: 791
    Teacher preparation program enrollment (master's): 538
Education specialist degree enrollment: 77

FINANCIAL INFORMATION
Financial aid phone number: (309) 298-2446
Tuition, 2003-2004 academic year: Full-time in-state: $3,450; out-of-state: $6,900, Part-time in-state: $144/credit hour; out-of-state: $288/credit hour

Fees: **$1,270**, Room and board: **$2,683**, Books and supplies: **$510**, Miscellaneous expenses: **$3,366**

ACADEMIC PROGRAMS
Areas of specialization: curriculum and instruction, education administration and supervision, educational psychology, elementary teacher education, higher education administration, secondary teacher education, special education, student counseling and personnel services.
Professional development/partnership school(s) are used by students in some of the teaching programs.
During their internships, peer groups of students meet regularly to discuss instructional techniques in all of the teaching programs.
All of the students in their internships are mentored.
Courses that prepare teachers to pass the National Board of Professional Teaching Standards are offered.
Teacher preparation programs: Four-year baccalaureate-degree program leading to initial licensure that includes either a major or minor in education and practice teaching.
The education program is currently accredited by the National Council for Accreditation of Teacher Education.

LICENSING TEST
Pass rate on state's teacher licensing test for 2002-2003: 99%
State average pass rate: 98%

Wheaton College

- 501 College Avenue, Wheaton, IL 60187
- **Website:** http://www.wheaton.edu/
- Private
- **Degrees offered:** bachelor's, master's

LICENSING TEST
Pass rate on state's teacher licensing test for 2002-2003: 99%
State average pass rate: 98%

INDIANA

Anderson University

■ 1100 E. Fifth Street, Anderson, IN 46012
■ Website: http://www.anderson.edu/
■ Private

LICENSING TEST

Pass rate on state's teacher licensing test for 2002-2003: **90%**
State average pass rate: **94%**

Ball State University

■ Teachers College, Muncie, IN 47306
■ Website: http://www.bsu.edu/gradschool/
■ Public
■ Degrees offered: bachelor's, master's, education specialist, Ph.D., Ed.D.

ADMISSIONS

Admissions phone number: **(765) 285-1297**
Admissions email address: *whitena@bsu.edu*
Application website: *http://www.bsu.edu/gradschool/graduation*
Application fee: **$35**
Fall 2005 application deadline: **rolling**
Test requirements: **GRE**
Test of English as Foreign Language (TOEFL) is required for international students.
Minimum TOEFL score required for paper test: **550**
Minimum TOEFL score required for computer test: **213**

Fall 2003
Acceptance rate for master's degree programs: **65%**
Acceptance rate for education specialist degree programs: **31%**
Acceptance rate for doctoral programs: **39%**
Average GRE verbal: **496**, Average GRE quantitative: **565**, Average GRE analytical: **610**
Total 2003 enrollment: **671**

Master's degree enrollment: **463**
    Teacher preparation program enrollment (master's): **244**
Education specialist degree enrollment: **29**
Doctoral degree enrollment: **179**

FINANCIAL INFORMATION

Financial aid phone number: **(765) 295-5600**
Tuition, 2003-2004 academic year: Full-time in-state: **$4,536**; out-of-state: **$12,316**, Part-time in-state: **$2,828**; out-of-state: **$7,268**
Fees: **$1,100**, Room and board: **$6,061**, Books and supplies: **$1,000**, Miscellaneous expenses: **$2,000**
Number of teaching assistant positions: **122**
Number of research assistant positions: **14**

ACADEMIC PROGRAMS

Total full-time tenured or tenure-track faculty (fall 2003): **85**, Total part-time faculty (fall 2003): **0**
Areas of specialization: curriculum and instruction, education administration and supervision, educational psychology, elementary teacher education, secondary teacher education, special education, student counseling and personnel services.
The education program is currently accredited by the National Council for Accreditation of Teacher Education.

LICENSING TEST

Pass rate on state's teacher licensing test for 2002-2003: **96%**
State average pass rate: **94%**

Butler University

■ 4600 Sunset Avenue, Indianapolis, IN 46208
■ Website: http://www.butler.edu/
■ Private
■ Degrees offered: bachelor's, master's

ADMISSIONS

Admissions phone number: **(317) 940-8124**
Admissions email address: *wpreble@butler.edu*

Application website: *http://www.butler.edu/admission*
Application fee: **$35**
Fall 2005 application deadline: **7/15**
Test of English as Foreign Language (TOEFL) is required for international students.
Minimum TOEFL score required for paper test: **550**
Minimum TOEFL score required for computer test: **213**

Fall 2003
Acceptance rate for master's degree programs: **41%**
Total 2003 enrollment: **157**
Master's degree enrollment: **157**
   Teacher preparation program enrollment (master's): **35**

FINANCIAL INFORMATION
Financial aid phone number: **(317) 940-8200**
Tuition, 2003-2004 academic year: Full-time: **$270/credit hour**; Part-time: **$270/credit hour**

ACADEMIC PROGRAMS
Total full-time tenured or tenure-track faculty (fall 2003): **10**, Total part-time faculty (fall 2003): **13**
Areas of specialization: curriculum and instruction, education administration and supervision, elementary teacher education, secondary teacher education, special education, student counseling and personnel services.
Teacher preparation programs: Four-year baccalaureate-degree program leading to initial licensure that includes either a major or minor in education and practice teaching. Master's program preparing college graduates for initial licensure; includes practice teaching. Alternative program for college graduates leading to provisional licensure.
The education program is currently accredited by the National Council for Accreditation of Teacher Education.

LICENSING TEST
Pass rate on state's teacher licensing test for 2002-2003: **96%**
State average pass rate: **94%**

Earlham College

■ **801 National Road West, Richmond, IN 47374**
■ **Website:** http://www.earlham.edu/mat
■ **Private**
■ **Degrees offered:** master's

ADMISSIONS
Admissions phone number: **(765) 983-1871**
Admissions email address: *hillst@earlham.edu*
Application website: *http://www.earlham.edu/mat*
Application fee: **$35**
Fall 2005 application deadline: **2/1**
Fall 2005 application deadline: **2/1**
Test requirements: **GRE**
Test of English as Foreign Language (TOEFL) is required for international students.

Fall 2003
Acceptance rate for master's degree programs: **94%**
Average GRE verbal: **536**, Average GRE quantitative: **598**
Total 2003 enrollment: **16**
Master's degree enrollment: **16**
   Teacher preparation program enrollment (master's): **16**

FINANCIAL INFORMATION
Financial aid phone number: **(765) 983-1217**
Tuition, 2003-2004 academic year: **$20,000**
Number of fellowships awarded to graduate students during the 2003-2004 academic year: **0**
Number of teaching assistant positions: **0**
Number of research assistant positions: **0**
Number of other paid appointments: **0**

ACADEMIC PROGRAMS
Total full-time tenured or tenure-track faculty (fall 2003): **2**, Total part-time faculty (fall 2003): **1**
Areas of specialization: secondary teacher education.
Professional development/partnership school(s) are used by students in all of the teaching programs.
During their internships, peer groups of students meet regularly to discuss instructional techniques in all of the teaching programs.
All of the students in their internships are mentored.
Courses that prepare teachers to pass the National Board of Professional Teaching Standards are not offered.
Teacher preparation programs: Master's degree in education, including internship/practice teaching and preparation for initial licensure.

Indiana State University

■ **School of Education, Terre Haute, IN 47809**
■ **Website:** http://web.indstate.edu/sogs/
■ **Public**
■ **Degrees offered:** bachelor's, master's, education specialist, Ph.D.

ADMISSIONS
Admissions phone number: **(812) 237-3111**
Admissions email address: *grdstudies@indstate.edu*
Application website:
   http://web.indstate.edu/sogs/GradNewtemp/usform.html
Application fee: **$35**
Test requirements: **GRE or MAT**
Test of English as Foreign Language (TOEFL) is required for international students.
Minimum TOEFL score required for paper test: **550**
Minimum TOEFL score required for computer test: **213**

Fall 2003
Average GRE verbal: **464**, Average GRE quantitative: **513**, Average GRE analytical: **503**
Total 2003 enrollment: **605**
Master's degree enrollment: **380**
   Teacher preparation program enrollment (master's): **138**

Education specialist degree enrollment: 44
Doctoral degree enrollment: 181

FINANCIAL INFORMATION
Financial aid phone number: (800) 841-4744
Tuition, 2003-2004 academic year: Full-time in-state:
$242/credit hour; out-of-state: **$481/credit hour**, Part-
time in-state: **$242/credit hour**; out-of-state: **$481/credit
hour**
Fees: **$100**, Room and board: **$5,580**, Books and supplies:
$630
Number of fellowships awarded to graduate students dur-
ing the 2003-2004 academic year: 29
Number of research assistant positions: 38

ACADEMIC PROGRAMS
Total full-time tenured or tenure-track faculty (fall 2003):
67, Total part-time faculty (fall 2003): 29
Areas of specialization: curriculum and instruction, education administration and supervision, educational psychology, elementary teacher education, higher education
administration, secondary teacher education, special
education, student counseling and personnel services,
teacher education.
Professional development/partnership school(s) are used
by students in all of the teaching programs.
During their internships, peer groups of students meet
regularly to discuss instructional techniques in some of
the teaching programs.
All of the students in their internships are mentored.
Courses that prepare teachers to pass the National Board of
Professional Teaching Standards are not offered.
Teacher preparation programs: Four-year baccalaureate-
degree program leading to initial licensure that includes
either a major or minor in education and practice teach-
ing. Alternative program for college graduates leading to
provisional licensure.
The education program is currently accredited by the
National Council for Accreditation of Teacher Education.

LICENSING TEST
Pass rate on state's teacher licensing test for 2002-2003:
95%
State average pass rate: 94%

Indiana University–Bloomington

■ 201 N. Rose Avenue, Bloomington, IN 47405-1006
■ **Website:** http://education.indiana.edu/
■ **Public**
■ **Degrees offered:** bachelor's, master's, education
specialist, Ph.D., Ed.D.
■ **Overall rank in the 2005 U.S. News education schools
with doctoral programs:** 18
■ **Overall rank in the 2005 U.S. News education school
specialty rankings:** administration/supervision: 11,

counseling/personnel: 8, curriculum/instruction: 8,
education policy: 15, elementary education: 9, higher
education administration: 7, secondary education: 8

ADMISSIONS
Admissions phone number: (812) 856-8543
Admissions email address: *educate@indiana.edu*
Application website:
http://www.indiana.edu/~educate/appadvice.html
Application fee: **$45**
Fall 2005 application deadline: 1/15
Test requirements: **GRE**
Test of English as Foreign Language (TOEFL) is required
for international students.
Minimum TOEFL score required for paper test: 550
Minimum TOEFL score required for computer test: 213

Fall 2003
Acceptance rate for master's degree programs: 54%
Acceptance rate for education specialist degree programs:
16%
Acceptance rate for doctoral programs: 35%
Average GRE verbal: 503, Average GRE quantitative: 570,
Average GRE analytical: 620
Total 2003 enrollment: 1,136
Master's degree enrollment: 457
    Teacher preparation program enrollment (master's): 203
Education specialist degree enrollment: 28
Doctoral degree enrollment: 651

FINANCIAL INFORMATION
Financial aid phone number: (812) 855-3278
Tuition, 2003-2004 academic year: Full-time in-state:
$205/credit hour; out-of-state: **$596/credit hour**, Part-
time in-state: **$205/credit hour**; out-of-state: **$596/credit
hour**
Fees: **$661**, Room and board: **$8,266**, Books and supplies:
$550, Miscellaneous expenses: **$2,895**
Number of fellowships awarded to graduate students dur-
ing the 2003-2004 academic year: 157
Number of teaching assistant positions: 181
Number of research assistant positions: 51
Number of other paid appointments: 91

ACADEMIC PROGRAMS
Total full-time tenured or tenure-track faculty (fall 2003):
113, Total part-time faculty (fall 2003): 46
Areas of specialization: curriculum and instruction, education administration and supervision, education policy,
educational psychology, elementary teacher education,
higher education administration, secondary teacher education, special education, student counseling and personnel services.
Professional development/partnership school(s) are used
by students in some of the teaching programs.
During their internships, peer groups of students meet
regularly to discuss instructional techniques in some of
the teaching programs.
All of the students in their internships are mentored.

Courses that prepare teachers to pass the National Board of Professional Teaching Standards are not offered.

Teacher preparation programs: Four-year baccalaureate-degree program leading to initial licensure that includes either a major or minor in education and practice teaching. Five-year program leading to initial licensure that results in a baccalaureate degree (with a major or minor in education) plus graduate credit and includes practice teaching. Master's program preparing college graduates for initial licensure; includes practice teaching. Alternative program for college graduates leading to provisional licensure.

The education program is currently accredited by the National Council for Accreditation of Teacher Education.

LICENSING TEST

Pass rate on state's teacher licensing test for 2002-2003: **98%**

State average pass rate: **94%**

Indiana University–Kokomo

- 2300 S. Washington Street, PO Box 9003, Kokomo, IN 46904
- **Website:** http://www.iuk.edu
- **Public**
- **Degrees offered:** bachelor's, master's

ADMISSIONS

Admissions phone number: **(765) 455-9287**
Admissions email address: *lhenry@iuk.edu*
Application website: *http://www.iuk.edu*
Application fee: **$40**
Fall 2005 application deadline: **rolling**
Test requirements: **GRE**
Test of English as Foreign Language (TOEFL) is required for international students.

Fall 2003

Total 2003 enrollment: **14**
Master's degree enrollment: **14**
  Teacher preparation program enrollment (master's): **14**

FINANCIAL INFORMATION

Financial aid phone number: **(765) 455-9214**
Tuition, 2003-2004 academic year: Full-time in-state: **$157/credit hour**; out-of-state: **$360/credit hour**, Part-time in-state: **$157/credit hour**; out-of-state: **$360/credit hour**
Fees: **$345**
Number of fellowships awarded to graduate students during the 2003-2004 academic year: **0**
Number of teaching assistant positions: **0**
Number of research assistant positions: **0**
Number of other paid appointments: **0**

ACADEMIC PROGRAMS

Total full-time tenured or tenure-track faculty (fall 2003): **6**
Areas of specialization: curriculum and instruction, educational psychology, elementary teacher education, secondary teacher education, special education.
Professional development/partnership school(s) are used by students in some of the teaching programs.
During their internships, peer groups of students meet regularly to discuss instructional techniques in some of the teaching programs.
All of the students in their internships are mentored.
Courses that prepare teachers to pass the National Board of Professional Teaching Standards are offered.

Teacher preparation programs: Four-year baccalaureate-degree program leading to initial licensure that includes either a major or minor in education and practice teaching. Alternative program for college graduates leading to provisional licensure.

The education program is currently accredited by the National Council for Accreditation of Teacher Education.

LICENSING TEST

Pass rate on state's teacher licensing test for 2002-2003: **98%**

State average pass rate: **94%**

Indiana University–Northwest

- 3400 Broadway, HH 354, Gary, IN 46408
- **Website:** http://www.iun.edu/~edu
- **Public**
- **Degrees offered:** bachelor's, master's

ADMISSIONS

Admissions phone number: **(219) 980-6510**
Admissions email address: *ccatecle@iun.edu*
Application fee: **$25**
Fall 2005 application deadline: **8/1**

FINANCIAL INFORMATION

Financial aid phone number: **(219) 980-6779**
Tuition, 2003-2004 academic year: Full-time in-state: **$155/credit hour**; out-of-state: **$360/credit hour**, Part-time in-state: **$155/credit hour**; out-of-state: **$360/credit hour**
Fees: **$66/credit hour**
Number of fellowships awarded to graduate students during the 2003-2004 academic year: **0**
Number of teaching assistant positions: **0**
Number of research assistant positions: **0**
Number of other paid appointments: **2**

ACADEMIC PROGRAMS

Areas of specialization: education administration and supervision, elementary teacher education, secondary teacher education, special education.

Courses that prepare teachers to pass the National Board of Professional Teaching Standards are offered.

Teacher preparation programs: Four-year baccalaureate-degree program leading to initial licensure that includes either a major or minor in education and practice teaching. Alternative program for college graduates leading to provisional licensure.

The education program is currently accredited by the National Council for Accreditation of Teacher Education.

LICENSING TEST
Pass rate on state's teacher licensing test for 2002-2003: 98%
State average pass rate: 94%

Indiana University-Purdue University–Fort Wayne

- 2101 E. Coliseum Boulevard, Fort Wayne, IN 46805
- **Website:** http://www.ipfw.edu/
- **Public**

LICENSING TEST
Pass rate on state's teacher licensing test for 2002-2003: 91%
State average pass rate: 94%

Indiana University-Purdue University–Indianapolis

- School of Education, 902 W New York St, Indianapolis, IN 46202-5155
- **Website:** http://education.iupui.edu
- **Public**
- **Degrees offered:** bachelor's, master's

ADMISSIONS
Admissions phone number: (317) 278-5739
Admissions email address: *educgrad@iupui.edu*
Application website: *http://education.iupui.edu/forms/forms/graduate-application.htm*
Application fee: $45
Fall 2005 application deadline: 5/1
Test requirements: GRE
Test of English as Foreign Language (TOEFL) is required for international students.
Minimum TOEFL score required for paper test: 550
Minimum TOEFL score required for computer test: 213

Fall 2003
Acceptance rate for master's degree programs: 93%
Total 2003 enrollment: 649
Master's degree enrollment: 649
    Teacher preparation program enrollment (master's): 404

FINANCIAL INFORMATION
Financial aid phone number: (317) 274-4162
Tuition, 2003-2004 academic year: Full-time in-state: **$194/credit hour**; out-of-state: **$560/credit hour**, Part-time in-state: **$194/credit hour**; out-of-state: **$560/credit hour**
Fees: **$534**, Books and supplies: **$1,000**
Number of fellowships awarded to graduate students during the 2003-2004 academic year: 0
Number of teaching assistant positions: 0
Number of research assistant positions: 1
Number of other paid appointments: 0

ACADEMIC PROGRAMS
Total full-time tenured or tenure-track faculty (fall 2003): 21, Total part-time faculty (fall 2003): 19
Areas of specialization: curriculum and instruction, education administration and supervision, educational psychology, elementary teacher education, secondary teacher education, special education, student counseling and personnel services.
Professional development/partnership school(s) are used by students in all of the teaching programs.
During their internships, peer groups of students meet regularly to discuss instructional techniques in all of the teaching programs.
All of the students in their internships are mentored.
Courses that prepare teachers to pass the National Board of Professional Teaching Standards are not offered.
Teacher preparation programs: Four-year baccalaureate-degree program leading to initial licensure that includes either a major or minor in education and practice teaching. Alternative program for college graduates leading to provisional licensure.
The education program is currently accredited by the National Council for Accreditation of Teacher Education.

LICENSING TEST
Pass rate on state's teacher licensing test for 2002-2003: 97%
State average pass rate: 94%

Indiana University–South Bend

- 1700 Mishawaka Avenue, PO Box 7111, South Bend, IN 46634
- **Website:** http://www.iusb.edu/~edud/
- **Public**
- **Degrees offered:** bachelor's, master's

ADMISSIONS

Admissions phone number: **(574) 237-4845**
Admissions email address: *aslane@iusb.edu*
Application website: *http://www.iusb.edu*
Application fee: **$40**
Fall 2005 application deadline: **8/22**
Test of English as Foreign Language (TOEFL) is required for international students.
Minimum TOEFL score required for paper test: **550**
Minimum TOEFL score required for computer test: **213**

Fall 2003

Total 2003 enrollment: **924**
Master's degree enrollment: **924**
Teacher preparation program enrollment (master's): **863**

FINANCIAL INFORMATION

Financial aid phone number: **(574) 237-4357**
Tuition, 2003-2004 academic year: Full-time in-state: **$159/credit hour**; out-of-state: **$387/credit hour**, Part-time in-state: **$159/credit hour**; out-of-state: **$387/credit hour**
Fees: **$30/credit hour**

ACADEMIC PROGRAMS

Total full-time tenured or tenure-track faculty (fall 2003): **45**, Total part-time faculty (fall 2003): **114**
Areas of specialization: curriculum and instruction, education administration and supervision, education policy, educational psychology, elementary teacher education, higher education administration, secondary teacher education, special education, student counseling and personnel services.
Professional development/partnership school(s) are used by students in some of the teaching programs.
During their internships, peer groups of students meet regularly to discuss instructional techniques in all of the teaching programs.
All of the students in their internships are mentored.
Courses that prepare teachers to pass the National Board of Professional Teaching Standards are not offered.
The education program is currently accredited by the National Council for Accreditation of Teacher Education.

LICENSING TEST

Pass rate on state's teacher licensing test for 2002-2003: **96%**
State average pass rate: **94%**

Indiana University– Southeast

- **4201 Grant Line Rd., New Albany, IN 47150**
- **Website:** http://www.ius.edu/Education/
- **Public**
- **Degrees offered:** bachelor's, master's

ADMISSIONS

Admissions phone number: **(812) 941-2169**

Admissions email address: *http://www.ius.edu/Admissions/*
Application fee: **$30**
Fall 2005 application deadline: **3/1**

Fall 2003

Acceptance rate for master's degree programs: **97%**
Total 2003 enrollment: **429**
Master's degree enrollment: **429**
Teacher preparation program enrollment (master's): **372**

FINANCIAL INFORMATION

Financial aid phone number: **(812) 941-2246**
Tuition, 2003-2004 academic year: Full-time in-state: **$157/credit hour**; out-of-state: **$360/credit hour**, Part-time in-state: **$157/credit hour**; out-of-state: **$360/credit hour**
Fees: **$16/credit hour**, Books and supplies: **$250**
Number of fellowships awarded to graduate students during the 2003-2004 academic year: **0**
Number of teaching assistant positions: **0**
Number of research assistant positions: **0**
Number of other paid appointments: **0**

ACADEMIC PROGRAMS

Total full-time tenured or tenure-track faculty (fall 2003): **21**, Total part-time faculty (fall 2003): **40**
Areas of specialization: curriculum and instruction, education administration and supervision, educational psychology, elementary teacher education, secondary teacher education, special education, student counseling and personnel services.
Professional development/partnership school(s) are used by students in all of the teaching programs.
During their internships, peer groups of students meet regularly to discuss instructional techniques in all of the teaching programs.
All of the students in their internships are mentored.
Courses that prepare teachers to pass the National Board of Professional Teaching Standards are offered.
Teacher preparation programs: Four-year baccalaureate-degree program leading to initial licensure that includes either a major or minor in education and practice teaching. Alternative program for college graduates leading to provisional licensure.
The education program is currently accredited by the National Council for Accreditation of Teacher Education.

LICENSING TEST

Pass rate on state's teacher licensing test for 2002-2003: **93%**
State average pass rate: **94%**

Indiana Wesleyan University

■ 4301 S. Washington St, Marion, IN 46953
■ **Website:** http://caps.indwes.edu/
■ **Private**
■ **Degrees offered:** bachelor's, master's

ADMISSIONS

Admissions phone number: **(765) 677-2860**
Admissions email address: *aes@indwes.edu*
Application fee: **$0**
Fall 2005 application deadline: **rolling**

Fall 2003
Total 2003 enrollment: **1,000**
Master's degree enrollment: **1,000**
    Teacher preparation program enrollment (master's): **1,000**

FINANCIAL INFORMATION

Financial aid phone number: **(765) 677-2404**
Tuition, 2003-2004 academic year: Full-time: **$4,275**; Part-time: **$285/credit hour**
Fees: **$300**
Number of fellowships awarded to graduate students during the 2003-2004 academic year: **0**
Number of teaching assistant positions: **0**
Number of research assistant positions: **0**
Number of other paid appointments: **0**

ACADEMIC PROGRAMS

Areas of specialization: curriculum and instruction, education administration and supervision.
Professional development/partnership school(s) are used by students in none of the teaching programs.
During their internships, peer groups of students meet regularly to discuss instructional techniques in some of the teaching programs.
All of the students in their internships are mentored.
Courses that prepare teachers to pass the National Board of Professional Teaching Standards are not offered.
Teacher preparation programs: Alternative program for college graduates leading to provisional licensure.
The education program is currently accredited by the National Council for Accreditation of Teacher Education.

LICENSING TEST

Pass rate on state's teacher licensing test for 2002-2003: **100%**
State average pass rate: **94%**

Oakland City University

■ 143 N. Lucretia Street, Oakland City, IN 47660
■ **Website:** http://www.oak.edu/
■ **Private**

LICENSING TEST

Pass rate on state's teacher licensing test for 2002-2003: **86%**
State average pass rate: **94%**

Purdue University– Calumet

■ 2200 169th Street, Hammond, IN 46323
■ **Website:**
    http://www.calumet.purdue.edu/education/grad/
■ **Public**
■ **Degrees offered:** bachelor's, master's

ADMISSIONS

Admissions phone number: **(219) 989-2326**
Admissions email address: *robinsdd@calumet.purdue.edu*
Application website: *http://www.calumet.purdue.edu/gradschool/*
Application fee: **$55**
Fall 2005 application deadline: **rolling**
Test of English as Foreign Language (TOEFL) is required for international students.
Minimum TOEFL score required for paper test: **550**
Minimum TOEFL score required for computer test: **213**

Fall 2003
Acceptance rate for master's degree programs: **92%**
Total 2003 enrollment: **327**
Master's degree enrollment: **327**
    Teacher preparation program enrollment (master's): **19**

FINANCIAL INFORMATION

Financial aid phone number: **(219) 989-2301**
Tuition, 2003-2004 academic year: Full-time in-state: **$180/credit hour**; out-of-state: **$388/credit hour**
Books and supplies: **$800**
Number of teaching assistant positions: **1**
Number of research assistant positions: **5**

ACADEMIC PROGRAMS

Total full-time tenured or tenure-track faculty (fall 2003): **14**, Total part-time faculty (fall 2003): **4**
Areas of specialization: curriculum and instruction, education administration and supervision, educational psychology, elementary teacher education, secondary teacher education, special education, student counseling and personnel services.

Professional development/partnership school(s) are used by students in all of the teaching programs.

During their internships, peer groups of students meet regularly to discuss instructional techniques in all of the teaching programs.

All of the students in their internships are mentored.

Courses that prepare teachers to pass the National Board of Professional Teaching Standards are not offered.

Teacher preparation programs: Four-year baccalaureate-degree program leading to initial licensure that includes either a major or minor in education and practice teaching. Alternative program for college graduates leading to provisional licensure.

The education program is currently accredited by the National Council for Accreditation of Teacher Education.

LICENSING TEST

Pass rate on state's teacher licensing test for 2002-2003: 84%

State average pass rate: 94%

Purdue University—West Lafayette

■ 100 N. University Street, West Lafayette, IN 47907-2098
■ **Website:** http://www.soe.purdue.edu/
■ **Public**
■ **Degrees offered:** bachelor's, master's, education specialist, Ph.D.
■ **Overall rank in the 2005 U.S. News education schools with doctoral programs:** 47

ADMISSIONS

Admissions phone number: **(765) 494-2345**
Admissions email address: *gradoffice@soe.purdue.edu*
Application website:
   http://www.purdue.edu/GradSchool/Admissions/admissions.html
Application fee: **$55**
Test requirements: **GRE**
Test of English as Foreign Language (TOEFL) is required for international students.
Minimum TOEFL score required for paper test: **550**
Minimum TOEFL score required for computer test: **213**

Fall 2003
Acceptance rate for master's degree programs: **60%**
Acceptance rate for education specialist degree programs: **100%**
Acceptance rate for doctoral programs: **61%**
Average GRE verbal: **525**, Average GRE quantitative: **621**, Average GRE analytical: **596**
Total 2003 enrollment: **444**
Master's degree enrollment: **197**
   Teacher preparation program enrollment (master's): **72**
Education specialist degree enrollment: **2**
Doctoral degree enrollment: **245**

FINANCIAL INFORMATION

Financial aid phone number: **(765) 494-5050**
Tuition, 2003-2004 academic year: Full-time in-state: **$5,860**; out-of-state: **$17,640**, Part-time in-state: **$210/credit hour**; out-of-state: **$586/credit hour**
Fees: **$100**, Room and board: **$6,700**, Books and supplies: **$890**, Miscellaneous expenses: **$1,340**
Number of fellowships awarded to graduate students during the 2003-2004 academic year: **14**
Number of teaching assistant positions: **72**
Number of research assistant positions: **45**
Number of other paid appointments: **7**

ACADEMIC PROGRAMS

Total full-time tenured or tenure-track faculty (fall 2003): **65**, Total part-time faculty (fall 2003): **5**
Areas of specialization: curriculum and instruction, education administration and supervision, education policy, educational psychology, elementary teacher education, higher education administration, secondary teacher education, special education, student counseling and personnel services, teacher education.
Professional development/partnership school(s) are used by students in some of the teaching programs.
During their internships, peer groups of students meet regularly to discuss instructional techniques in some of the teaching programs.
All of the students in their internships are mentored.
Courses that prepare teachers to pass the National Board of Professional Teaching Standards are not offered.
Teacher preparation programs: Four-year baccalaureate-degree program leading to initial licensure that includes either a major or minor in education and practice teaching. Master's program preparing college graduates for initial licensure; includes practice teaching. Alternative program for college graduates leading to provisional licensure.
The education program is currently accredited by the National Council for Accreditation of Teacher Education.

LICENSING TEST

Pass rate on state's teacher licensing test for 2002-2003: 95%

State average pass rate: 94%

University of Indianapolis

■ 1400 E. Hanna Avenue, Indianapolis, IN 46227-3697
■ **Website:** http://www.uindy.edu
■ **Private**
■ **Degrees offered:** bachelor's, master's

ADMISSIONS

Admissions phone number: **(317) 788-3365**
Admissions email address: *jrose@uindy.edu*
Application website: *http://www.uindy.edu*

Application fee: **$30**
Fall 2005 application deadline: **8/25**
Test of English as Foreign Language (TOEFL) is required for international students.
Minimum TOEFL score required for paper test: **550**

FINANCIAL INFORMATION
Financial aid phone number: **(317) 788-3217**
Tuition, 2003-2004 academic year: **$285/credit hour**
Books and supplies: **$100**
Number of research assistant positions: **1**

ACADEMIC PROGRAMS
Total full-time tenured or tenure-track faculty (fall 2003): **4**
    Total part-time faculty (fall 2003): **20**
Areas of specialization: curriculum and instruction.
Professional development/partnership school(s) are used by students in all of the teaching programs.
During their internships, peer groups of students meet regularly to discuss instructional techniques in none of the teaching programs.
Some of the students in their internships are mentored.
Courses that prepare teachers to pass the National Board of Professional Teaching Standards are offered.
Teacher preparation programs: Four-year baccalaureate-degree program leading to initial licensure that includes either a major or minor in education and practice teaching.
The education program is currently accredited by the National Council for Accreditation of Teacher Education.

LICENSING TEST
Pass rate on state's teacher licensing test for 2002-2003: **90%**
State average pass rate: **94%**

University of Southern Indiana

■ **8600 University Boulevard, Evansville, IN 47712**
■ **Website:** http://www.usi.edu/gradstud
■ **Public**
■ **Degrees offered:** bachelor's, master's

ADMISSIONS
Admissions phone number: **(812) 465-7015**
Admissions email address: *gssr@usi.edu*
Application website: *http://www.usi.edu/gradstud/appl.asp*
Application fee: **$25**
Fall 2005 application deadline: **rolling**
Test requirements: **None**
Test of English as Foreign Language (TOEFL) is required for international students.
Minimum TOEFL score required for paper test: **500**
Minimum TOEFL score required for computer test: **173**

Fall 2003
Acceptance rate for master's degree programs: **77%**

Total 2003 enrollment: **91**
Master's degree enrollment: **91**
    Teacher preparation program enrollment (master's): **91**

FINANCIAL INFORMATION
Financial aid phone number: **(812) 464-1767**
Tuition, 2003-2004 academic year: Full-time in-state: **$185/credit hour**; out-of-state: **$366/credit hour**, Part-time in-state: **$185/credit hour**; out-of-state: **$366/credit hour**
Fees: **$120**, Room and board: **$5,140**, Books and supplies: **$850**, Miscellaneous expenses: **$1,822**
Number of fellowships awarded to graduate students during the 2003-2004 academic year: **0**
Number of teaching assistant positions: **0**
Number of research assistant positions: **0**
Number of other paid appointments: **0**

ACADEMIC PROGRAMS
Total full-time tenured or tenure-track faculty (fall 2003): **12**, Total part-time faculty (fall 2003): **0**
Areas of specialization: elementary teacher education, secondary teacher education.
Professional development/partnership school(s) are used by students in all of the teaching programs.
During their internships, peer groups of students meet regularly to discuss instructional techniques in some of the teaching programs.
All of the students in their internships are mentored.
Courses that prepare teachers to pass the National Board of Professional Teaching Standards are not offered.
Teacher preparation programs: Four-year baccalaureate-degree program leading to initial licensure that includes either a major or minor in education and practice teaching. Alternative program for college graduates leading to provisional licensure.
The education program is currently accredited by the National Council for Accreditation of Teacher Education.

LICENSING TEST
Pass rate on state's teacher licensing test for 2002-2003: **91%**
State average pass rate: **94%**

University of St. Francis

■ **2701 Spring Street, Fort Wayne, IN 46808**
■ **Website:** http://www.sfc.edu/
■ **Private**

LICENSING TEST
Pass rate on state's teacher licensing test for 2002-2003: **95%**
State average pass rate: **94%**

Valparaiso University

- ■ **Miller Hall, 824 LaPorte Avenue, Valparaiso, IN 46383**
- ■ **Website:** http://www.valpo.edu/gce/graduate/
- ■ **Private**
- ■ **Degrees offered:** bachelor's, master's, education specialist

ADMISSIONS

Admissions phone number: **(219) 464-5313**
Admissions email address: *graduate.studies@valpo.edu*
Application website:
https://www.valpo.edu/gce/forms/main.htm
Application fee: **$30**
Fall 2005 application deadline: **rolling**
Test requirements: **GRE or MAT**
Test of English as Foreign Language (TOEFL) is required for international students.
Minimum TOEFL score required for paper test: **550**
Minimum TOEFL score required for computer test: **213**

Fall 2003

Acceptance rate for master's degree programs: **87%**
Acceptance rate for education specialist degree programs: **83%**
Average GRE verbal: **489**, Average GRE quantitative: **609**
Total 2003 enrollment: **56**
Master's degree enrollment: **38**
   Teacher preparation program enrollment (master's): **37**
Education specialist degree enrollment: **18**

FINANCIAL INFORMATION

Financial aid phone number: **(219) 464-5015**
Tuition, 2003-2004 academic year: Full-time: **$335/credit hour**; Part-time: **$335/credit hour**

Fees: **$50**, Room and board: **$6,600**, Books and supplies: **$540**, Miscellaneous expenses: **$2,510**
Number of fellowships awarded to graduate students during the 2003-2004 academic year: **0**
Number of teaching assistant positions: **0**
Number of research assistant positions: **0**
Number of other paid appointments: **0**

ACADEMIC PROGRAMS

Total full-time tenured or tenure-track faculty (fall 2003): **10**, Total part-time faculty (fall 2003): **9**
Areas of specialization: curriculum and instruction, educational psychology, elementary teacher education, secondary teacher education, special education.
Professional development/partnership school(s) are used by students in some of the teaching programs.
During their internships, peer groups of students meet regularly to discuss instructional techniques in all of the teaching programs.
All of the students in their internships are mentored.
Courses that prepare teachers to pass the National Board of Professional Teaching Standards are not offered.
Teacher preparation programs: Four-year baccalaureate-degree program leading to initial licensure that includes either a major or minor in education and practice teaching. Master's program preparing college graduates for initial licensure; includes practice teaching. Alternative program for college graduates leading to provisional licensure.
The education program is currently accredited by the National Council for Accreditation of Teacher Education.

LICENSING TEST

Pass rate on state's teacher licensing test for 2002-2003: **99%**
State average pass rate: **94%**

IOWA

TEACHER TESTING IN IOWA
The state is currently considering teacher licensure exams. For information on where to go in your state for specific academic requirements, see Chapter 6 on page 67.

Buena Vista University

- **610 W. Fourth Street, Storm Lake, IA 50588**
- **Website:** http://www.grad.bvu.edu
- **Private**
- **Degrees offered:** bachelor's, master's

ADMISSIONS
Admissions phone number: **(712) 749-2162**
Admissions email address: *grad@bvu.edu*
Application website:
   http://www.bvu.edu/academics/grad/applynow.asp
Application fee: **$0**
Test requirements: **GRE**

Fall 2003
Acceptance rate for master's degree programs: **84%**
Average GRE analytical: **600**
Total 2003 enrollment: **85**
Master's degree enrollment: **85**

FINANCIAL INFORMATION
Financial aid phone number: **(712) 749-2164**
Tuition, 2003-2004 academic year: Full-time: **$233/credit hour**; Part-time: **$233/credit hour**
Room and board: **$200**, Books and supplies: **$400**, Miscellaneous expenses: **$300**
Number of teaching assistant positions: **1**
Number of other paid appointments: **3**

ACADEMIC PROGRAMS
Total full-time tenured or tenure-track faculty (fall 2003): **3**
   Total part-time faculty (fall 2003): **6**
Areas of specialization: education administration and supervision, student counseling and personnel services.
Professional development/partnership school(s) are used by students in some of the teaching programs.
During their internships, peer groups of students meet regularly to discuss instructional techniques in some of the teaching programs.
All of the students in their internships are mentored.
Courses that prepare teachers to pass the National Board of Professional Teaching Standards are not offered.

Clarke College

- **1550 Clarke Drive, Dubuque, IA 52001**
- **Website:** http://www.clarke.edu/
- **Private**

Dordt College

- **498 4th Ave NE, Sioux Center, IA 51250**
- **Website:** http://www.dordt.edu/academics/departments/education/med/
- **Private**
- **Degrees offered:** bachelor's, master's

ADMISSIONS
Admissions phone number: **(800) 343-6738**
Admissions email address: *kdeboom@dordt.edu*
Application fee: **$35**
Fall 2005 application deadline: **6/1**
Fall 2005 application deadline: **6/1**
Test requirements: **GRE or MAT**
Test of English as Foreign Language (TOEFL) is required for international students.
Minimum TOEFL score required for paper test: **550**

Fall 2003
Total 2003 enrollment: **60**
Master's degree enrollment: **60**
   Teacher preparation program enrollment (master's): **60**

FINANCIAL INFORMATION
Financial aid phone number: **(712) 722-6087**
Tuition, 2003-2004 academic year: Full-time: **$215/credit hour**; Part-time: **$215/credit hour**

ACADEMIC PROGRAMS
Total full-time tenured or tenure-track faculty (fall 2003): **8**
   Total part-time faculty (fall 2003): **4**
Areas of specialization: curriculum and instruction, educational psychology, elementary teacher education, secondary teacher education.

Teacher preparation programs: Four-year baccalaureate-degree program leading to initial licensure that includes either a major or minor in education and practice teaching.

Drake University

- 3206 University Avenue, Des Moines, IA 50311
- Website: http://www.educ.drake.edu/
- Private
- Degrees offered: bachelor's, master's, education specialist, Ed.D.
- Overall rank in the 2005 U.S. News education schools with doctoral programs: 62

ADMISSIONS
Admissions phone number: (515) 271-3871
Admissions email address: *gradadmission@drake.edu*
Application website: *https://www.applyweb.com/aw?drakeg*
Application fee: $25
Fall 2005 application deadline: rolling
Test requirements: GRE or MAT
Test of English as Foreign Language (TOEFL) is required for international students.
Minimum TOEFL score required for paper test: 550
Minimum TOEFL score required for computer test: 213

Fall 2003
Acceptance rate for master's degree programs: 54%
Acceptance rate for education specialist degree programs: 76%
Average GRE verbal: 487, Average GRE quantitative: 554, Average GRE analytical: 586, Average MAT: 48
Total 2003 enrollment: 592
Master's degree enrollment: 500
   Teacher preparation program enrollment (master's): 191
Education specialist degree enrollment: 60
Doctoral degree enrollment: 32

FINANCIAL INFORMATION
Financial aid phone number: (515) 271-2905
Tuition, 2003-2004 academic year: Full-time: $19,100; Part-time: $312/credit hour
Fees: $320, Room and board: $7,190, Books and supplies: $800, Miscellaneous expenses: $3,100
Number of fellowships awarded to graduate students during the 2003-2004 academic year: 0
Number of teaching assistant positions: 0
Number of research assistant positions: 0
Number of other paid appointments: 7

ACADEMIC PROGRAMS
Total full-time tenured or tenure-track faculty (fall 2003): 17, Total part-time faculty (fall 2003): 2
Areas of specialization: education administration and supervision, elementary teacher education, secondary teacher education, special education, student counseling and personnel services.

Professional development/partnership school(s) are used by students in none of the teaching programs.
During their internships, peer groups of students meet regularly to discuss instructional techniques in all of the teaching programs.
All of the students in their internships are mentored.
Courses that prepare teachers to pass the National Board of Professional Teaching Standards are offered.
Teacher preparation programs: Four-year baccalaureate-degree program leading to initial licensure that includes either a major or minor in education and practice teaching. Master's program preparing college graduates for initial licensure; includes practice teaching.

Graceland College

- 1 University Place, Lamoni, IA 50140-1698
- Website: http://www.graceland.edu/edgrad
- Private

ADMISSIONS
Admissions phone number: (641) 784-5493
Admissions email address: *soegrad@graceland.edu*
Application fee: $50

Iowa State University

- E262 Lagomarcino Hall, Ames, IA 50011
- Website: http://www.grad-college.iastate.edu/
- Public
- Degrees offered: bachelor's, master's, Ph.D.
- Overall rank in the 2005 U.S. News education schools with doctoral programs: 69
- Overall rank in the 2005 U.S. News education school specialty rankings: administration/supervision: 26, counseling/personnel: 18, higher education administration: 20, vocational/technical: 13

ADMISSIONS
Admissions phone number: (515) 294-5836
Admissions email address: *admissions@iastate.edu*
Application website:
   http://www.public.iastate.edu/~adm_info/
Application fee: $20
Fall 2005 application deadline: rolling
Test requirements: GRE or MAT
Test of English as Foreign Language (TOEFL) is required for international students.
Minimum TOEFL score required for paper test: 560
Minimum TOEFL score required for computer test: 220

Fall 2003
Acceptance rate for master's degree programs: 76%
Acceptance rate for doctoral programs: 66%
Average GRE verbal: 459, Average GRE quantitative: 557, Average GRE analytical: 524

Total 2003 enrollment: 478
Master's degree enrollment: 290
    Teacher preparation program enrollment (master's): 68
Doctoral degree enrollment: 188

FINANCIAL INFORMATION
Financial aid phone number: (515) 294-2223
Tuition, 2003-2004 academic year: Full-time in-state:
    $5,038; out-of-state: $14,214, Part-time in-state:
    $280/credit hour; out-of-state: $790/credit hour
Fees: $396, Room and board: $6,957, Books and supplies:
    $820, Miscellaneous expenses: $2,054
Number of fellowships awarded to graduate students dur-
    ing the 2003-2004 academic year: 2
Number of teaching assistant positions: 58
Number of research assistant positions: 58
Number of other paid appointments: 64

ACADEMIC PROGRAMS
Total full-time tenured or tenure-track faculty (fall 2003): 70
    Total part-time faculty (fall 2003): 17
Areas of specialization: curriculum and instruction, educa-
    tion administration and supervision, education policy,
    educational psychology, elementary teacher education,
    higher education administration, secondary teacher edu-
    cation, special education, student counseling and per-
    sonnel services.
Professional development/partnership school(s) are used
    by students in some of the teaching programs.
During their internships, peer groups of students meet
    regularly to discuss instructional techniques in some of
    the teaching programs.
All of the students in their internships are mentored.
Courses that prepare teachers to pass the National Board of
    Professional Teaching Standards are not offered.
Teacher preparation programs: Four-year baccalaureate-
    degree program leading to initial licensure that includes
    either a major or minor in education and practice teach-
    ing. Master's program preparing college graduates for
    initial licensure; includes practice teaching.

Loras College

■ 1450 Alta Vista, Dubuque, IA 52004-0176
■ Website: http://www.loras.edu
■ Private
■ Degrees offered: bachelor's, master's

ADMISSIONS
Admissions phone number: (563) 588-7236
Admissions email address: admissions@loras.edu
Application website: http://www.loras.edu
Application fee: $25
Test of English as Foreign Language (TOEFL) is required
    for international students.
Minimum TOEFL score required for paper test: 500

Fall 2003
Acceptance rate for master's degree programs: 73%
Total 2003 enrollment: 27
Master's degree enrollment: 27
    Teacher preparation program enrollment (master's): 3

FINANCIAL INFORMATION
Financial aid phone number: (563) 588-7136
Tuition, 2003-2004 academic year: Full-time: $400/credit
    hour; Part-time: $400/credit hour
Number of fellowships awarded to graduate students dur-
    ing the 2003-2004 academic year: 0
Number of teaching assistant positions: 0
Number of research assistant positions: 0
Number of other paid appointments: 0

ACADEMIC PROGRAMS
Total full-time tenured or tenure-track faculty (fall 2003): 8
    Total part-time faculty (fall 2003): 15
Areas of specialization: education administration and
    supervision.
Professional development/partnership school(s) are used
    by students in none of the teaching programs.
During their internships, peer groups of students meet
    regularly to discuss instructional techniques in none of
    the teaching programs.
All of the students in their internships are mentored.
Courses that prepare teachers to pass the National Board of
    Professional Teaching Standards are not offered.

Maharishi University of Management

■ 1000 N. 4th Street, Fairfield, IA 52557
■ Website: http://www.mum.edu
■ Private
■ Degrees offered: bachelor's, master's

ADMISSIONS
Admissions phone number: (800) 369-6480
Admissions email address: admissions@mum.edu
Application fee: $40
Fall 2005 application deadline: rolling
Test of English as Foreign Language (TOEFL) is required
    for international students.
Minimum TOEFL score required for paper test: 550
Minimum TOEFL score required for computer test: 213

FINANCIAL INFORMATION
Financial aid phone number: (641) 472-1156

Morningside College

- 1501 Morningside Avenue, Sioux City, IA 51106
- **Website:** http://www.morningside.edu
- **Private**
- **Degrees offered:** bachelor's, master's

ADMISSIONS
Admissions phone number: **(712) 274-5375**
Application fee: **$25**
Fall 2005 application deadline: **rolling**

Fall 2003
Total 2003 enrollment: **355**
Master's degree enrollment: **355**
Teacher preparation program enrollment (master's): **355**

FINANCIAL INFORMATION
Financial aid phone number: **(712) 274-5159**
Tuition, 2003-2004 academic year: **$140/credit hour**

ACADEMIC PROGRAMS
Total full-time tenured or tenure-track faculty (fall 2003): **6**
Total part-time faculty (fall 2003): **50**
Areas of specialization: curriculum and instruction, elementary teacher education, special education.
Professional development/partnership school(s) are used by students in none of the teaching programs.
During their internships, peer groups of students meet regularly to discuss instructional techniques in all of the teaching programs.
All of the students in their internships are mentored.
Courses that prepare teachers to pass the National Board of Professional Teaching Standards are not offered.
Teacher preparation programs: Four-year baccalaureate-degree program leading to initial licensure that includes either a major or minor in education and practice teaching. The education program is currently accredited by the National Council for Accreditation of Teacher Education.

St. Ambrose University

- 518 W. Locust Street, Davenport, IA 52803
- **Website:** http://www.sau.edu/
- **Private**
- **Degrees offered:** master's

ADMISSIONS
Admissions phone number: **(563) 333-6435**
Admissions email address: *TiceCindyR@sau.edu*
Application fee: **$25**
Fall 2005 application deadline: **rolling**
Test of English as Foreign Language (TOEFL) is required for international students.
Minimum TOEFL score required for paper test: **550**
Minimum TOEFL score required for computer test: **213**

Fall 2003
Total 2003 enrollment: **39**
Master's degree enrollment: **39**
Teacher preparation program enrollment (master's): **12**

FINANCIAL INFORMATION
Financial aid phone number: **(563) 333-6314**
Tuition, 2003-2004 academic year: Full-time: **$518/credit hour; Part-time: $518/credit hour**
Room and board: **$3,065**, Books and supplies: **$500**
Number of other paid appointments: **1**

ACADEMIC PROGRAMS
Total full-time tenured or tenure-track faculty (fall 2003): **1**
Total part-time faculty (fall 2003): **4**
Areas of specialization: special education.
Professional development/partnership school(s) are used by students in none of the teaching programs.
During their internships, peer groups of students meet regularly to discuss instructional techniques in all of the teaching programs.
All of the students in their internships are mentored.
Courses that prepare teachers to pass the National Board of Professional Teaching Standards are not offered.
Teacher preparation programs: Four-year baccalaureate-degree program leading to initial licensure that includes either a major or minor in education and practice teaching. Master's program preparing college graduates for initial licensure; includes practice teaching.

University of Iowa

- Lindquist Center, Iowa City, IA 52242
- **Website:** http://www.education.uiowa.edu
- **Public**
- **Degrees offered:** master's, education specialist, Ph.D.
- **Overall rank in the 2005 U.S. News education schools with doctoral programs:** 11
- **Overall rank in the 2005 U.S. News education school specialty rankings:** counseling/personnel: 13, educational psychology: 16, higher education administration: 17, secondary education: 15

ADMISSIONS
Admissions phone number: **(319) 335-5359**
Admissions email address: *coe-tess@uiowa.edu*
Application website:
http://www.uiowa.edu/admissions/apply.html
Application fee: **$30**
Fall 2005 application deadline: **7/15**
Test requirements: **GRE**
Test of English as Foreign Language (TOEFL) is required for international students.
Minimum TOEFL score required for paper test: **550**
Minimum TOEFL score required for computer test: **213**

Fall 2003
Acceptance rate for master's degree programs: **61%**

Acceptance rate for education specialist degree programs:
50%
Acceptance rate for doctoral programs: 47%
Average GRE verbal: 535, Average GRE quantitative: 629,
Average GRE analytical: 627
Total 2003 enrollment: 953
Master's degree enrollment: 457
Teacher preparation program enrollment (master's): 267
Education specialist degree enrollment: 20
Doctoral degree enrollment: 476

FINANCIAL INFORMATION
Financial aid phone number: (319) 335-1450
Tuition, 2003-2004 academic year: Full-time in-state:
$5,038; out-of-state: $15,072, Part-time in-state:
$280/credit hour; out-of-state: $838/credit hour
Fees: $651/credit hour, Room and board: $6,515, Books and
supplies: $800, Miscellaneous expenses: $950
Number of fellowships awarded to graduate students dur-
ing the 2003-2004 academic year: 12
Number of teaching assistant positions: 96
Number of research assistant positions: 115
Number of other paid appointments: 78

ACADEMIC PROGRAMS
Total full-time tenured or tenure-track faculty (fall 2003): 88
Total part-time faculty (fall 2003): 0
Areas of specialization: curriculum and instruction, education administration and supervision, education policy,
educational psychology, elementary teacher education,
higher education administration, secondary teacher education, special education, student counseling and personnel services.
Professional development/partnership school(s) are used
by students in none of the teaching programs.
During their internships, peer groups of students meet
regularly to discuss instructional techniques in some of
the teaching programs.
All of the students in their internships are mentored.
Courses that prepare teachers to pass the National Board of
Professional Teaching Standards are offered.

University of Northern Iowa

- **159A Schindler Center, Cedar Falls, IA 50614-0610**
- **Website:** http://www.uni.edu/coe
- **Public**
- **Degrees offered:** bachelor's, master's, education
  specialist, Ed.D.

ADMISSIONS
Admissions phone number: (800) 772-2037
Admissions email address: *admissions@uni.edu*
Application website: *http://access.uni.edu/stdt/ugapinst.htm*
Application fee: $50
Fall 2005 application deadline: 4/1
Test requirements: GRE
Test of English as Foreign Language (TOEFL) is required
for international students.
Minimum TOEFL score required for paper test: 500

Fall 2003
Total 2003 enrollment: 2,969
Master's degree enrollment: 2,798
Teacher preparation program enrollment (master's):
2,327
Education specialist degree enrollment: 0
Doctoral degree enrollment: 171

FINANCIAL INFORMATION
Financial aid phone number: (800) 772-2736
Tuition, 2003-2004 academic year: Full-time in-state:
$5,612; out-of-state: $12,686, Part-time in-state:
$617/credit hour; out-of-state: $617/credit hour
Fees: $574, Room and board: $4,930, Books and supplies:
$804, Miscellaneous expenses: $2,976
Number of other paid appointments: 22

ACADEMIC PROGRAMS
Total full-time tenured or tenure-track faculty (fall 2003):
876
Areas of specialization: curriculum and instruction, educa-
tion administration and supervision, special education.
Professional development/partnership school(s) are used
by students in all of the teaching programs.
During their internships, peer groups of students meet
regularly to discuss instructional techniques in all of the
teaching programs.
Some of the students in their internships are mentored.
Courses that prepare teachers to pass the National Board of
Professional Teaching Standards are offered.
Teacher preparation programs: Four-year baccalaureate-
degree program leading to initial licensure that includes
either a major or minor in education and practice teaching. Master's program preparing college graduates for
initial licensure; includes practice teaching.

KANSAS

Baker University College of Arts and Sciences

- PO Box 65, Baldwin City, KS 66006
- Website: http://www.bakeru.edu/
- Private

LICENSING TEST
Pass rate on state's teacher licensing test for 2002-2003: 100%
State average pass rate: 97%

Benedictine College

- 1020 N 2nd Street, Atchison, KS 66002
- Website: http://www.benedictine.edu
- Private
- Degrees offered: bachelor's, master's

ADMISSIONS
Admissions phone number: (913) 367-5340
Admissions email address: *diannah@benedictine.edu*
Application fee: $25
Fall 2005 application deadline: rolling
Test requirements: MAT

Fall 2003
Acceptance rate for master's degree programs: 100%
Total 2003 enrollment: 31
Master's degree enrollment: 31

FINANCIAL INFORMATION
Financial aid phone number: (913) 360-7484
Tuition, 2003-2004 academic year: Full-time: $210/credit hour; Part-time: $210/credit hour
Books and supplies: $1,100, Miscellaneous expenses: $100

ACADEMIC PROGRAMS
Total full-time tenured or tenure-track faculty (fall 2003): 1
  Total part-time faculty (fall 2003): 1
Areas of specialization: education administration and supervision.

Professional development/partnership school(s) are used by students in all of the teaching programs.
During their internships, peer groups of students meet regularly to discuss instructional techniques in all of the teaching programs.
All of the students in their internships are mentored.
Courses that prepare teachers to pass the National Board of Professional Teaching Standards are not offered.
Teacher preparation programs: Four-year baccalaureate-degree program leading to initial licensure that includes either a major or minor in education and practice teaching.
The education program is currently accredited by the National Council for Accreditation of Teacher Education.

LICENSING TEST
Pass rate on state's teacher licensing test for 2002-2003: 100%
State average pass rate: 97%

Emporia State University

- 1200 Commercial, Emporia, KS 66801
- Website: http://www.emporia.edu/
- Public

LICENSING TEST
Pass rate on state's teacher licensing test for 2002-2003: 100%
State average pass rate: 97%

Fort Hays State University

- 600 Park Street, Hays, KS 67601
- Website: http://www.fhsu.edu/
- Public

LICENSING TEST
Pass rate on state's teacher licensing test for 2002-2003: 96%
State average pass rate: 97%

Friends University

- 2100 W. University Street, Wichita, KS 67213
- **Website:** http://www.friends.edu/
- **Private**

LICENSING TEST

Pass rate on state's teacher licensing test for 2002-2003: 91%

State average pass rate: 97%

Kansas State University

- 2 Bluemont Hall, Manhattan, KS 66506
- **Website:** http://www.ksu.edu/
- **Public**
- **Overall rank in the 2005 U.S. News education school specialty rankings:** special education: 17

ADMISSIONS

Admissions phone number: (785) 532-5595
Admissions email address: *gradstudy@mail.educ.ksu.edu*
Minimum TOEFL score required for paper test: 550
Minimum TOEFL score required for computer test: 213

FINANCIAL INFORMATION

Financial aid phone number: (785) 532-6420

LICENSING TEST

Pass rate on state's teacher licensing test for 2002-2003: 99%

State average pass rate: 97%

MidAmerica Nazarene University

- 2030 E. College Way, Olathe, KS 66062
- **Website:** http://www.manc.edu/
- **Private**

LICENSING TEST

Pass rate on state's teacher licensing test for 2002-2003: 95%

State average pass rate: 97%

Newman University

- 3100 McCormick Avenue, Wichita, KS 67213-2097
- **Website:** http://www.newmanu.edu
- **Private**
- **Degrees offered:** bachelor's, master's

ADMISSIONS

Admissions phone number: (316) 942-4291
Admissions email address: *sexsonm@newmanu.edu*
Application website: *http://www.newmanu.edu/graduateapp.html*
Application fee: $25
Fall 2005 application deadline: **rolling**
Test of English as Foreign Language (TOEFL) is required for international students.
Minimum TOEFL score required for paper test: 600
Minimum TOEFL score required for computer test: 250

Fall 2003

Total 2003 enrollment: 60
Master's degree enrollment: 60
    Teacher preparation program enrollment (master's): 29

FINANCIAL INFORMATION

Financial aid phone number: (316) 942-4291
Tuition, 2003-2004 academic year: Full-time: **$327/credit hour**; Part-time: **$327/credit hour**
Fees: **$5/credit hour**, Room and board: **$5,976**, Books and supplies: **$1,200**, Miscellaneous expenses: **$75**
Number of fellowships awarded to graduate students during the 2003-2004 academic year: 0
Number of teaching assistant positions: 0
Number of research assistant positions: 0
Number of other paid appointments: 0

ACADEMIC PROGRAMS

Total full-time tenured or tenure-track faculty (fall 2003): **4**
    Total part-time faculty (fall 2003): **0**
Areas of specialization: curriculum and instruction, education administration and supervision.
Professional development/partnership school(s) are used by students in some of the teaching programs.
During their internships, peer groups of students meet regularly to discuss instructional techniques in all of the teaching programs.
All of the students in their internships are mentored.
Courses that prepare teachers to pass the National Board of Professional Teaching Standards are not offered.
Teacher preparation programs: Four-year baccalaureate-degree program leading to initial licensure that includes either a major or minor in education and practice teaching. Alternative program for college graduates leading to provisional licensure.

LICENSING TEST

Pass rate on state's teacher licensing test for 2002-2003: **93%**
State average pass rate: **97%**

Pittsburg State University

■ 1701 S. Broadway, Pittsburg, KS 66762
■ Website: http://www.pittstate.edu/
■ Public

LICENSING TEST
Pass rate on state's teacher licensing test for 2002-2003: 94%
State average pass rate: 97%

Southwestern College

■ 100 College Street, Winfield, KS 67156-2499
■ Website: http://www.sckans.edu/
■ Private

LICENSING TEST
Pass rate on state's teacher licensing test for 2002-2003: 96%
State average pass rate: 97%

University of Kansas

■ 217 Joseph R. Pearson Hall, Lawrence, KS 66045
■ Website: http://www.soe.ukans.edu
■ Public
■ Degrees offered: bachelor's, master's, education specialist, Ph.D., Ed.D.
■ Overall rank in the 2005 U.S. News education schools with doctoral programs: 36
■ Overall rank in the 2005 U.S. News education school specialty rankings: special education: 2

ADMISSIONS
Admissions phone number: (785) 864-4510
Admissions email address: fredrod@ku.edu
Test requirements: GRE or MAT
Test of English as Foreign Language (TOEFL) is required for international students.
Minimum TOEFL score required for paper test: 570
Minimum TOEFL score required for computer test: 23

Fall 2003
Acceptance rate for master's degree programs: 72%
Acceptance rate for education specialist degree programs: 17%
Acceptance rate for doctoral programs: 24%
Average GRE verbal: 520, Average GRE quantitative: 560, Average GRE analytical: 570, Average MAT: 59
Total 2003 enrollment: 1,340
Master's degree enrollment: 895

Education specialist degree enrollment: 26
Doctoral degree enrollment: 419

FINANCIAL INFORMATION
Financial aid phone number: (785) 864-4700
Tuition, 2003-2004 academic year: Full-time in-state: $156/credit hour; out-of-state: $420/credit hour, Part-time in-state: $156/credit hour; out-of-state: $420/credit hour
Fees: $48/credit hour
Number of teaching assistant positions: 53
Number of research assistant positions: 29

ACADEMIC PROGRAMS
Total full-time tenured or tenure-track faculty (fall 2003): 85, Total part-time faculty (fall 2003): 0
Areas of specialization: curriculum and instruction, education administration and supervision, education policy, educational psychology, elementary teacher education, higher education administration, secondary teacher education, special education, student counseling and personnel services.
Professional development/partnership school(s) are used by students in some of the teaching programs.
During their internships, peer groups of students meet regularly to discuss instructional techniques in some of the teaching programs.
All of the students in their internships are mentored.
Courses that prepare teachers to pass the National Board of Professional Teaching Standards are not offered.
Teacher preparation programs: Five-year program leading to initial licensure that results in a baccalaureate degree (with a major or minor in education) plus graduate credit and includes practice teaching.
The education program is currently accredited by the National Council for Accreditation of Teacher Education.

LICENSING TEST
Pass rate on state's teacher licensing test for 2002-2003: 100%
State average pass rate: 97%

Washburn University

■ 1700 S.W. College, Topeka, KS 66621
■ Website: http://www.washburn.edu
■ Public
■ Degrees offered: bachelor's, master's

ADMISSIONS
Admissions phone number: (800) 332-0291
Admissions email address: admissions@washburn.edu
Application website: http://my.washburn.edu/cp/tn/fs
Application fee: $30
Fall 2005 application deadline: 3/1
Test requirements: GRE or MAT
Test of English as Foreign Language (TOEFL) is required for international students.

Minimum TOEFL score required for paper test: 520
Minimum TOEFL score required for computer test: 193

Fall 2003
Acceptance rate for master's degree programs: 79%
Average GRE verbal: 520, Average GRE quantitative: 563,
   Average GRE analytical: 553, Average MAT: 46
Total 2003 enrollment: 60
Master's degree enrollment: 60
   Teacher preparation program enrollment (master's): 49

FINANCIAL INFORMATION
Financial aid phone number: (800) 524-8447
Tuition, 2003-2004 academic year: Full-time in-state:
   $3,330; out-of-state: $6,786, Part-time in-state:
   $185/credit hour; out-of-state: $377/credit hour
Fees: $62, Room and board: $4,872, Books and supplies:
   $760, Miscellaneous expenses: $3,955

ACADEMIC PROGRAMS
Total full-time tenured or tenure-track faculty (fall 2003):
   10, Total part-time faculty (fall 2003): 10
Areas of specialization: curriculum and instruction, education administration and supervision, education policy,
   educational psychology, special education.
Professional development/partnership school(s) are used
   by students in all of the teaching programs.
During their internships, peer groups of students meet
   regularly to discuss instructional techniques in all of the
   teaching programs.

All of the students in their internships are mentored.
Courses that prepare teachers to pass the National Board of
   Professional Teaching Standards are offered.
Teacher preparation programs: Four-year baccalaureate-
   degree program leading to initial licensure that includes
   either a major or minor in education and practice teaching.
The education program is currently accredited by the
   National Council for Accreditation of Teacher Education.

LICENSING TEST
Pass rate on state's teacher licensing test for 2002-2003:
   98%
State average pass rate: 97%

Wichita State University

■ **1845 Fairmont, Wichita, KS 67260**
■ **Website:** http://www.wichita.edu/my/visitors/
■ **Public**

LICENSING TEST
Pass rate on state's teacher licensing test for 2002-2003:
   97%
State average pass rate: 97%

KENTUCKY

Asbury College

- 1 Macklem Drive, Wilmore, KY 40390
- **Website:** http://www.asbury.edu
- **Private**
- **Degrees offered:** bachelor's, master's

ADMISSIONS
Admissions phone number: **(859) 858-3511**
Admissions email address: *GradEd@asbury.edu*
Application fee: **$25**
Fall 2005 application deadline: **rolling**

Fall 2003
Total 2003 enrollment: **66**
Master's degree enrollment: **66**
    Teacher preparation program enrollment (master's): **61**

FINANCIAL INFORMATION
Financial aid phone number: **(859) 858-3511**
Tuition, 2003-2004 academic year: Full-time: **$274/credit hour**; Part-time: **$274/credit hour**

ACADEMIC PROGRAMS
Total full-time tenured or tenure-track faculty (fall 2003): **8**
    Total part-time faculty (fall 2003): **5**
Areas of specialization: special education.
Professional development/partnership school(s) are used by students in all of the teaching programs.
During their internships, peer groups of students meet regularly to discuss instructional techniques in all of the teaching programs.
Some of the students in their internships are mentored.
Courses that prepare teachers to pass the National Board of Professional Teaching Standards are not offered.
Teacher preparation programs: Four-year baccalaureate-degree program leading to initial licensure that includes either a major or minor in education and practice teaching. Master's program preparing college graduates for initial licensure; includes practice teaching.

The education program is currently accredited by the National Council for Accreditation of Teacher Education.

LICENSING TEST
Pass rate on state's teacher licensing test for 2002-2003: **100%**
State average pass rate: **94%**

Bellarmine University

- 2001 Newburg Road, Louisville, KY 40205
- **Website:** http://www.bellarmine.edu
- **Private**
- **Degrees offered:** bachelor's, master's

ADMISSIONS
Admissions phone number: **(502) 452-8037**
Admissions email address: *admissions@bellarmine.edu*
Application website:
    http://www.bellarmine.edu/admissions/graduate/frazierthornton.asp#
Application fee: **$25**
Fall 2005 application deadline: **8/1**
Test requirements: **GRE or MAT**
Test of English as Foreign Language (TOEFL) is required for international students.
Minimum TOEFL score required for paper test: **550**
Minimum TOEFL score required for computer test: **213**

Fall 2003
Acceptance rate for master's degree programs: **79%**
Average GRE verbal: **499**, Average GRE quantitative: **514**, Average GRE analytical: **529**
Total 2003 enrollment: **228**
Master's degree enrollment: **228**

FINANCIAL INFORMATION
Financial aid phone number: **(502) 452-8124**
Tuition, 2003-2004 academic year: Full-time: **$5,100**; Part-time: **$2,550**
Books and supplies: **$600**, Miscellaneous expenses: **$3,194**

Number of fellowships awarded to graduate students during the 2003-2004 academic year: o
Number of teaching assistant positions: o
Number of research assistant positions: o
Number of other paid appointments: o

ACADEMIC PROGRAMS

Total full-time tenured or tenure-track faculty (fall 2003): 9
Total part-time faculty (fall 2003): 20
Areas of specialization: curriculum and instruction, elementary teacher education, secondary teacher education, special education.
Professional development/partnership school(s) are used by students in some of the teaching programs.
During their internships, peer groups of students meet regularly to discuss instructional techniques in all of the teaching programs.
All of the students in their internships are mentored.
Courses that prepare teachers to pass the National Board of Professional Teaching Standards are not offered.
Teacher preparation programs: Four-year baccalaureate-degree program leading to initial licensure that includes either a major or minor in education and practice teaching. Master's program preparing college graduates for initial licensure; includes practice teaching. Alternative program for college graduates leading to provisional licensure.
The education program is currently accredited by the National Council for Accreditation of Teacher Education.

LICENSING TEST

Pass rate on state's teacher licensing test for 2002-2003: 89%
State average pass rate: 94%

Brescia University

■ 717 Frederica Street, Owensboro, KY 42301
■ **Website:** http://www.brescia.edu
■ **Private**
■ **Degrees offered:** bachelor's, master's

ADMISSIONS

Admissions phone number: (270) 685-3131
Admissions email address: *hollyc@brescia.edu*
Application fee: $50
Fall 2005 application deadline: **rolling**
Test requirements: **GRE**

Fall 2003
Acceptance rate for master's degree programs: 60%
Total 2003 enrollment: 12
Master's degree enrollment: 12
Teacher preparation program enrollment (master's): 12

FINANCIAL INFORMATION

Financial aid phone number: (270) 685-3131

Tuition, 2003-2004 academic year: Full-time: **$290/credit hour**; Part-time: **$290/credit hour**
Books and supplies: **$200**, Miscellaneous expenses: **$80**

ACADEMIC PROGRAMS

Total full-time tenured or tenure-track faculty (fall 2003): 5
Total part-time faculty (fall 2003): o
Areas of specialization: curriculum and instruction.
Professional development/partnership school(s) are used by students in none of the teaching programs.
During their internships, peer groups of students meet regularly to discuss instructional techniques in all of the teaching programs.
All of the students in their internships are mentored.
Courses that prepare teachers to pass the National Board of Professional Teaching Standards are not offered.
Teacher preparation programs: Four-year baccalaureate-degree program leading to initial licensure that includes either a major or minor in education and practice teaching.

LICENSING TEST

Pass rate on state's teacher licensing test for 2002-2003: 95%
State average pass rate: 94%

Campbellsville University

■ 1 University Drive, Campbellsville, KY 42718
■ **Website:** http://www.campbellsville.edu/
■ **Private**

LICENSING TEST

Pass rate on state's teacher licensing test for 2002-2003: 91%
State average pass rate: 94%

Cumberland College

■ 6178 College Station Drive, Williamsburg, KY 40769
■ **Website:** http://www.cumberlandcollege.edu/
■ **Private**

LICENSING TEST

Pass rate on state's teacher licensing test for 2002-2003: 100%
State average pass rate: 94%

Eastern Kentucky University

■ 521 Lancaster Avenue, Richmond, KY 40475
■ **Website:** http://www.eku.edu/
■ **Public**

LICENSING TEST

Pass rate on state's teacher licensing test for 2002-2003: **95%**
State average pass rate: **94%**

Georgetown College

- 400 E. College Street, Georgetown, KY 40324
- Website: http://www.georgetowncollege.edu/
- Private

LICENSING TEST

Pass rate on state's teacher licensing test for 2002-2003: **97%**
State average pass rate: **94%**

Kentucky State University

- 400 E. Main Street, Frankfort, KY 40601
- Website: http://www.kysu.edu/
- Public

LICENSING TEST

Pass rate on state's teacher licensing test for 2002-2003: **52%**
State average pass rate: **94%**

Lindsey Wilson College

- 210 Lindsey Wilson Street, Columbia, KY 42728
- Website: http://www.lindsey.edu/
- Private

LICENSING TEST

Pass rate on state's teacher licensing test for 2002-2003: **87%**
State average pass rate: **94%**

Morehead State University

- Ginger Hall 100, Morehead, KY 40351
- Website: http://www.moreheadstate.edu/units/graduate
- Public
- Degrees offered: bachelor's, master's, education specialist

ADMISSIONS

Admissions phone number: **(606) 783-2039**

Admissions email address: *graduate@moreheadstate.edu*
Application fee: **$65**
Fall 2005 application deadline: **7/1**
Test requirements: **GRE**
Test of English as Foreign Language (TOEFL) is required for international students.
Minimum TOEFL score required for paper test: **500**
Minimum TOEFL score required for computer test: **173**

FINANCIAL INFORMATION

Financial aid phone number: **(606) 783-2011**
Tuition, 2003-2004 academic year: Full-time in-state: **$203/credit hour**; out-of-state: **$544/credit hour**, Part-time in-state: **$203/credit hour**; out-of-state: **$544/credit hour**
Number of fellowships awarded to graduate students during the 2003-2004 academic year: **94**
Number of teaching assistant positions: **50**
Number of research assistant positions: **44**
Number of other paid appointments: **0**

ACADEMIC PROGRAMS

Total full-time tenured or tenure-track faculty (fall 2003): **367**, Total part-time faculty (fall 2003): **123**
Areas of specialization: curriculum and instruction, education administration and supervision, elementary teacher education, secondary teacher education, special education, student counseling and personnel services, teacher education.
Professional development/partnership school(s) are used by students in some of the teaching programs.
During their internships, peer groups of students meet regularly to discuss instructional techniques in all of the teaching programs.
All of the students in their internships are mentored.
Courses that prepare teachers to pass the National Board of Professional Teaching Standards are not offered.
The education program is currently accredited by the National Council for Accreditation of Teacher Education.

LICENSING TEST

Pass rate on state's teacher licensing test for 2002-2003: **90%**
State average pass rate: **94%**

Murray State University

- 3101 Alexander Hall, Murray, KY 42071
- Website: http://www.murraystate.edu
- Public
- Degrees offered: bachelor's, master's, education specialist

ADMISSIONS

Admissions phone number: **(270) 762-3779**
Admissions email address: *Admissions@murraystate.edu*
Application fee: **$25**
Fall 2005 application deadline: **rolling**

Test requirements: **GRE**

Test of English as Foreign Language (TOEFL) is required for international students.

Minimum TOEFL score required for paper test: **525**

Minimum TOEFL score required for computer test: **197**

Fall 2003

Acceptance rate for master's degree programs: **88%**

Acceptance rate for education specialist degree programs: **88%**

Average GRE verbal: **435**, Average GRE quantitative: **492**

Total 2003 enrollment: **683**

Master's degree enrollment: **635**

   Teacher preparation program enrollment (master's): **323**

Education specialist degree enrollment: **48**

FINANCIAL INFORMATION

Financial aid phone number: **(270) 762-2596**

Tuition, 2003-2004 academic year: Full-time in-state: **$3,602**; out-of-state: **$5,200**, Part-time in-state: **$143/credit hour**; out-of-state: **$288/credit hour**

Fees: **$368**, Room and board: **$4,380**, Books and supplies: **$800**, Miscellaneous expenses: **$800**

Number of fellowships awarded to graduate students during the 2003-2004 academic year: **0**

Number of teaching assistant positions: **0**

Number of research assistant positions: **15**

Number of other paid appointments: **0**

ACADEMIC PROGRAMS

Total full-time tenured or tenure-track faculty (fall 2003): **35**, Total part-time faculty (fall 2003): **4**

Areas of specialization: curriculum and instruction, education administration and supervision, education policy, educational psychology, elementary teacher education, higher education administration, secondary teacher education, special education, student counseling and personnel services, teacher education.

Professional development/partnership school(s) are used by students in none of the teaching programs.

During their internships, peer groups of students meet regularly to discuss instructional techniques in some of the teaching programs.

All of the students in their internships are mentored.

Courses that prepare teachers to pass the National Board of Professional Teaching Standards are not offered.

Teacher preparation programs: Alternative program for college graduates leading to provisional licensure.

The education program is currently accredited by the National Council for Accreditation of Teacher Education.

LICENSING TEST

Pass rate on state's teacher licensing test for 2002-2003: **92%**

State average pass rate: **94%**

Northern Kentucky University

- **Nunn Drive, Highland Heights, KY 41099**
- **Website:** http://www.nku.edu/~graduate/2002
- **Public**
- **Degrees offered:** bachelor's, master's

ADMISSIONS

Admissions phone number: **(859) 572-1555**

Admissions email address: *gradschool@nku.edu*

Application website: *http://gradschool.nku.edu/applications.html*

Application fee: **$30**

Fall 2005 application deadline: **8/1**

Test requirements: **GRE**

Test of English as Foreign Language (TOEFL) is required for international students.

Minimum TOEFL score required for paper test: **550**

Minimum TOEFL score required for computer test: **213**

Fall 2003

Acceptance rate for master's degree programs: **57%**

Average GRE verbal: **448**, Average GRE quantitative: **502**, Average GRE analytical: **485**

Total 2003 enrollment: **417**

Master's degree enrollment: **417**

   Teacher preparation program enrollment (master's): **252**

FINANCIAL INFORMATION

Financial aid phone number: **(859) 572-6437**

Tuition, 2003-2004 academic year: Full-time in-state: **$3,780**; out-of-state: **$8,694**, Part-time in-state: **$210/credit hour**; out-of-state: **$483/credit hour**

Fees: **$102**, Room and board: **$5,376**, Books and supplies: **$800**, Miscellaneous expenses: **$1,756**

Number of teaching assistant positions: **3**

ACADEMIC PROGRAMS

Total full-time tenured or tenure-track faculty (fall 2003): **15**, Total part-time faculty (fall 2003): **16**

Areas of specialization: education administration and supervision, elementary teacher education, secondary teacher education.

Professional development/partnership school(s) are used by students in some of the teaching programs.

During their internships, peer groups of students meet regularly to discuss instructional techniques in some of the teaching programs.

All of the students in their internships are mentored.

Courses that prepare teachers to pass the National Board of Professional Teaching Standards are offered.

Teacher preparation programs: Four-year baccalaureate-degree program leading to initial licensure that includes either a major or minor in education and practice teaching. Master's program preparing college graduates for initial licensure; includes practice teaching. Alternative program for college graduates leading to provisional licensure.

The education program is currently accredited by the National Council for Accreditation of Teacher Education.

LICENSING TEST

Pass rate on state's teacher licensing test for 2002-2003: 93%

State average pass rate: 94%

Spalding University

- 851 South Fourth Street, Louisville, KY 40203
- Website: http://www.spalding.edu/
- Private
- Degrees offered: bachelor's, master's, Ed.D.

ADMISSIONS

Admissions phone number: (502) 585-9911

Admissions email address: *chouk@spalding.edu*

Application fee: $35

Fall 2005 application deadline: rolling

Test of English as Foreign Language (TOEFL) is required for international students.

Minimum TOEFL score required for paper test: 535

Minimum TOEFL score required for computer test: 203

FINANCIAL INFORMATION

Financial aid phone number: (502) 585-9911

LICENSING TEST

Pass rate on state's teacher licensing test for 2002-2003: 98%

State average pass rate: 94%

Union College

- Lamont Graduate Center, Schenectady, KY 12308
- Website: http://www.graduatecollege.union.edu
- Private
- Degrees offered: master's

ADMISSIONS

Admissions phone number: (518) 388-6238

Admissions email address: *sheehanr@union.edu*

Application website:
  http://www.graduatecollege.union.edu/gradadmin/index.htm

Application fee: $60

Fall 2005 application deadline: 3/1

Test of English as Foreign Language (TOEFL) is required for international students.

Fall 2003

Acceptance rate for master's degree programs: 70%

Total 2003 enrollment: 43

Master's degree enrollment: 43

  Teacher preparation program enrollment (master's): 43

FINANCIAL INFORMATION

Financial aid phone number: (518) 388-6238

Tuition, 2003-2004 academic year: Full-time: $329/credit hour; Part-time: $329/credit hour

Fees: $150, Room and board: $7,500, Books and supplies: $1,540, Miscellaneous expenses: $700

Number of other paid appointments: 10

ACADEMIC PROGRAMS

Total full-time tenured or tenure-track faculty (fall 2003): 3

  Total part-time faculty (fall 2003): 15

Areas of specialization: secondary teacher education, teacher education.

Professional development/partnership school(s) are used by students in all of the teaching programs.

During their internships, peer groups of students meet regularly to discuss instructional techniques in all of the teaching programs.

All of the students in their internships are mentored.

Courses that prepare teachers to pass the National Board of Professional Teaching Standards are offered.

Teacher preparation programs: Master's degree in education, including internship/practice teaching and preparation for initial licensure.

The education program is currently accredited by the Teacher Education Accreditation Council.

LICENSING TEST

Pass rate on state's teacher licensing test for 2002-2003: 64%

State average pass rate: 94%

University of Kentucky

- 351 Patterson Office Tower, Lexington, KY 40506-0027
- Website: http://www.rgs.uky.edu/gs
- Public
- Degrees offered: bachelor's, master's, education specialist, Ph.D., Ed.D.
- Overall rank in the 2005 U.S. News education schools with doctoral programs: 62

ADMISSIONS

Admissions phone number: (859) 257-4905

Admissions email address: *Brian.Jackson@uky.edu*

Application website: *http://www.rgs.uky.edu/gs/ gsapplication.html*

Application fee: $35

Fall 2005 application deadline: 3/1

Test requirements: GRE

Test of English as Foreign Language (TOEFL) is required for international students.

Minimum TOEFL score required for paper test: 550

Minimum TOEFL score required for computer test: 213

Fall 2003

Acceptance rate for master's degree programs: 56%

Acceptance rate for education specialist degree programs: 78%

Acceptance rate for doctoral programs: 45%
Average GRE verbal: 449, Average GRE quantitative: 516,
   Average GRE analytical: 564
Total 2003 enrollment: 912
Master's degree enrollment: 576
   Teacher preparation program enrollment (master's): 259
Education specialist degree enrollment: 3
Doctoral degree enrollment: 333

FINANCIAL INFORMATION
Financial aid phone number: (859) 257-3172
Tuition, 2003-2004 academic year: Full-time in-state:
   $4,974; out-of-state: **$12,314**, Part-time in-state:
   $261/credit hour; out-of-state: **$668/credit hour**
Room and board: **$8,300**, Books and supplies: **$1,200**,
   Miscellaneous expenses: **$500**
Number of fellowships awarded to graduate students dur-
   ing the 2003-2004 academic year: 17
Number of teaching assistant positions: 39
Number of research assistant positions: 39
Number of other paid appointments: 24

ACADEMIC PROGRAMS
Total full-time tenured or tenure-track faculty (fall 2003):
   90, Total part-time faculty (fall 2003): 47
Areas of specialization: curriculum and instruction, education administration and supervision, education policy,
   educational psychology, elementary teacher education,
   higher education administration, secondary teacher education, special education, student counseling and personnel services.
Professional development/partnership school(s) are used
   by students in some of the teaching programs.
During their internships, peer groups of students meet
   regularly to discuss instructional techniques in some of
   the teaching programs.
All of the students in their internships are mentored.
Courses that prepare teachers to pass the National Board of
   Professional Teaching Standards are not offered.
Teacher preparation programs: Four-year baccalaureate-
   degree program leading to initial licensure that includes
   either a major or minor in education and practice teach-
   ing. Alternative program for college graduates leading to
   provisional licensure.
The education program is currently accredited by the
   National Council for Accreditation of Teacher Education.

LICENSING TEST
Pass rate on state's teacher licensing test for 2002-2003: **96%**
State average pass rate: **94%**

University of Louisville

- ■ **College of Education & Human Development, Louisville, KY 40292**
- ■ **Website:** http://www.louisville.edu
- ■ **Public**
- ■ **Degrees offered:** bachelor's, master's, education specialist, Ph.D.

ADMISSIONS
Admissions phone number: (502) 852-3101
Admissions email address: *gradadm@louisville.edu*
Application website: *http://graduate.louisville.edu/app/*
Application fee: $25
Fall 2005 application deadline: **rolling**
Test requirements: **GRE or MAT**
Test of English as Foreign Language (TOEFL) is required
   for international students.
Minimum TOEFL score required for paper test: 550
Minimum TOEFL score required for computer test: 213

Fall 2003
Acceptance rate for master's degree programs: 81%
Acceptance rate for education specialist degree programs:
   50%
Acceptance rate for doctoral programs: 73%
Average GRE verbal: 448, Average GRE quantitative: 503,
   Average GRE analytical: 551
Total 2003 enrollment: 1,358
Master's degree enrollment: 1,088
   Teacher preparation program enrollment (master's): 639
Education specialist degree enrollment: 24
Doctoral degree enrollment: 246

FINANCIAL INFORMATION
Financial aid phone number: (502) 852-5511
Tuition, 2003-2004 academic year: Full-time in-state:
   $4,842; out-of-state: **$13,338**, Part-time in-state:
   $269/credit hour; out-of-state: **$741/credit hour**
Room and board: **$5,766**, Books and supplies: **$700**,
   Miscellaneous expenses: **$4,824**
Number of fellowships awarded to graduate students dur-
   ing the 2003-2004 academic year: 2
Number of teaching assistant positions: 9
Number of research assistant positions: 45
Number of other paid appointments: 0

ACADEMIC PROGRAMS
Total full-time tenured or tenure-track faculty (fall 2003):
   59, Total part-time faculty (fall 2003): 84
Areas of specialization: curriculum and instruction, education administration and supervision, educational psychology, elementary teacher education, higher education
   administration, secondary teacher education, special
   education, student counseling and personnel services,
   teacher education.
Professional development/partnership school(s) are used
   by students in some of the teaching programs.

During their internships, peer groups of students meet regularly to discuss instructional techniques in some of the teaching programs.

Some of the students in their internships are mentored.

Courses that prepare teachers to pass the National Board of Professional Teaching Standards are not offered.

Teacher preparation programs: Four-year baccalaureate-degree program leading to initial licensure that includes either a major or minor in education and practice teaching. Master's program preparing college graduates for initial licensure; includes practice teaching. Alternative program for college graduates leading to provisional licensure.

The education program is currently accredited by the National Council for Accreditation of Teacher Education.

LICENSING TEST

Pass rate on state's teacher licensing test for 2002-2003: 98%

State average pass rate: 94%

Western Kentucky University

- 1 Big Red Way, Bowling Green, KY 42101
- **Website:** http://www.wku.edu/graduate/
- Public
- **Degrees offered:** bachelor's, master's, education specialist

ADMISSIONS

Admissions phone number: **(270) 745-2446**
Admissions email address: *graduate.studies@wku.edu*
Application website: *http://www.wku.edu/graduate/app.htm*
Application fee: **$35**
Fall 2005 application deadline: **6/15**
Test requirements: **GRE**
Test of English as Foreign Language (TOEFL) is required for international students.
Minimum TOEFL score required for paper test: **550**
Minimum TOEFL score required for computer test: **213**

Fall 2003
Acceptance rate for master's degree programs: **56%**
Acceptance rate for education specialist degree programs: **100%**

Average GRE verbal: **430**, Average GRE quantitative: **488**, Average GRE analytical: **521**
Total 2003 enrollment: **1,162**
Master's degree enrollment: **1,118**
    Teacher preparation program enrollment (master's): **515**
Education specialist degree enrollment: **44**

FINANCIAL INFORMATION

Financial aid phone number: **(270) 745-2755**
Tuition, 2003-2004 academic year: Full-time in-state: **$3,998**; out-of-state: **$4,358**, Part-time in-state: **$222/credit hour**; out-of-state: **$242/credit hour**
Fees: **$418**
Number of fellowships awarded to graduate students during the 2003-2004 academic year: **0**
Number of teaching assistant positions: **0**
Number of research assistant positions: **0**
Number of other paid appointments: **58**

ACADEMIC PROGRAMS

Total full-time tenured or tenure-track faculty (fall 2003): 35, Total part-time faculty (fall 2003): **76**
Areas of specialization: curriculum and instruction, education administration and supervision, educational psychology, elementary teacher education, higher education administration, secondary teacher education, special education, student counseling and personnel services, teacher education.

Professional development/partnership school(s) are used by students in some of the teaching programs.

During their internships, peer groups of students meet regularly to discuss instructional techniques in all of the teaching programs.

All of the students in their internships are mentored.

Courses that prepare teachers to pass the National Board of Professional Teaching Standards are not offered.

Teacher preparation programs: Four-year baccalaureate-degree program leading to initial licensure that includes either a major or minor in education and practice teaching. Master's program preparing college graduates for initial licensure; includes practice teaching. Alternative program for college graduates leading to provisional licensure.

The education program is currently accredited by the National Council for Accreditation of Teacher Education.

LICENSING TEST

Pass rate on state's teacher licensing test for 2002-2003: 99%

State average pass rate: 94%

LOUISIANA

Centenary College of Louisiana

- PO Box 41188, Shreveport, LA 71134-1188
- Website: http://www.centenary.edu/
- Private

Grambling State University

- PO Box 805, Grambling, LA 71245
- Website: http://www.gram.edu/
- Public

ADMISSIONS
Admissions phone number: (318) 274-2457
Admissions email address: *admissions@gram.edu*
Minimum TOEFL score required for paper test: 550
Minimum TOEFL score required for computer test: 250

FINANCIAL INFORMATION
Financial aid phone number: (318) 274-6056

LICENSING TEST
Pass rate on state's teacher licensing test for 2002-2003: 100%
State average pass rate: 95%

Louisiana State University–Baton Rouge

- 221 Peabody Hall, Baton Rouge, LA 70803
- Website: http://appl003.lsu.edu/educ/coe.nsf/index

- Public
- **Degrees offered:** bachelor's, master's, education specialist, Ph.D.
- **Overall rank in the 2005 U.S. News education schools with doctoral programs:** 69

ADMISSIONS
Admissions phone number: **(225) 578-1641**
Admissions email address: *graddeanoffice@lsu.edu*
Application website: *http://appl003.lsu.edu/grad/gradschool.nsf/index*
Application fee: **$25**
Fall 2005 application deadline: **5/15**
Test requirements: **GRE**
Test of English as Foreign Language (TOEFL) is required for international students.
Minimum TOEFL score required for paper test: 550
Minimum TOEFL score required for computer test: 213

Fall 2003
Acceptance rate for master's degree programs: **64%**
Acceptance rate for education specialist degree programs: 85%
Acceptance rate for doctoral programs: **41%**
Average GRE verbal: **461**, Average GRE quantitative: **565**, Average GRE analytical: **576**
Total 2003 enrollment: **458**
Master's degree enrollment: **225**
Education specialist degree enrollment: **61**
Doctoral degree enrollment: **172**

FINANCIAL INFORMATION
Financial aid phone number: **(225) 578-3103**
Tuition, 2003-2004 academic year: Full-time in-state: **$2,739**; out-of-state: **$8,039**, Part-time in-state: **$1,218**; out-of-state: **$3,468**
Fees: **$1,060**, Room and board: **$5,216**, Books and supplies: **$1,000**, Miscellaneous expenses: **$2,975**
Number of fellowships awarded to graduate students during the 2003-2004 academic year: **4**
Number of teaching assistant positions: **55**
Number of research assistant positions: **27**
Number of other paid appointments: **72**

ACADEMIC PROGRAMS

Total full-time tenured or tenure-track faculty (fall 2003): 48, Total part-time faculty (fall 2003): 22

Areas of specialization: curriculum and instruction, education administration and supervision, educational psychology, elementary teacher education, higher education administration, secondary teacher education, student counseling and personnel services, teacher education.

Professional development/partnership school(s) are used by students in some of the teaching programs.

During their internships, peer groups of students meet regularly to discuss instructional techniques in all of the teaching programs.

All of the students in their internships are mentored.

Courses that prepare teachers to pass the National Board of Professional Teaching Standards are not offered.

Teacher preparation programs: Four-year baccalaureate-degree program leading to initial licensure that includes either a major or minor in education and practice teaching. Five-year program leading to initial licensure that results in a baccalaureate degree (with a major or minor in education) plus a master's degree and includes practice teaching. The education program is currently accredited by the National Council for Accreditation of Teacher Education.

LICENSING TEST

Pass rate on state's teacher licensing test for 2002-2003: 93%

State average pass rate: 95%

Louisiana State University–Shreveport

- One University Place, Shreveport, LA 71115
- **Website:** http://www.lsus.edu
- **Public**
- **Degrees offered:** bachelor's, master's, education specialist

ADMISSIONS

Admissions phone number: (318) 797-5061

Admissions email address: *admissions@pilot.lsus.edu*

Application website: *http://www.lsus.edu/admissions/graduate.htm*

Application fee: **$10**

Fall 2005 application deadline: 8/1

Test of English as Foreign Language (TOEFL) is required for international students.

Minimum TOEFL score required for paper test: 550

Minimum TOEFL score required for computer test: 213

Fall 2003

Acceptance rate for master's degree programs: 100%

Acceptance rate for education specialist degree programs: 100%

Total 2003 enrollment: 215

Master's degree enrollment: 194

Teacher preparation program enrollment (master's): 129

Education specialist degree enrollment: 21

FINANCIAL INFORMATION

Financial aid phone number: (318) 797-5363

Tuition, 2003-2004 academic year: Full-time in-state: **$2,022**; out-of-state: **$6,132**, Part-time in-state: **$2,022**; out-of-state: **$6,132**

Fees: **$580**

ACADEMIC PROGRAMS

Total full-time tenured or tenure-track faculty (fall 2003): 18

Areas of specialization: education administration and supervision, elementary teacher education, secondary teacher education.

Professional development/partnership school(s) are used by students in some of the teaching programs.

During their internships, peer groups of students meet regularly to discuss instructional techniques in none of the teaching programs.

All of the students in their internships are mentored.

Courses that prepare teachers to pass the National Board of Professional Teaching Standards are not offered.

The education program is currently accredited by the National Council for Accreditation of Teacher Education.

LICENSING TEST

Pass rate on state's teacher licensing test for 2002-2003: 97%

State average pass rate: 95%

Louisiana Tech University

- PO Box 3163, Ruston, LA 71272-0001
- **Website:** http://www.latech.edu/tech/education/
- **Public**
- **Degrees offered:** bachelor's, master's, Ph.D., Ed.D.

ADMISSIONS

Admissions phone number: (318) 257-3036

Admissions email address: *gschool@latech.edu*

Application website: *http://www.latech.edu/tech/gradschool/admithtml*

Fall 2005 application deadline: **rolling**

Test requirements: **GRE**

Test of English as Foreign Language (TOEFL) is required for international students.

Minimum TOEFL score required for paper test: 550

Minimum TOEFL score required for computer test: 213

Fall 2003

Acceptance rate for master's degree programs: 100%

Acceptance rate for doctoral programs: 100%

Average GRE verbal: 450, Average GRE quantitative: 465

Total 2003 enrollment: 1,240

Master's degree enrollment: 1,174
  Teacher preparation program enrollment (master's): 183
Doctoral degree enrollment: 66

FINANCIAL INFORMATION
Financial aid phone number: (318) 257-2641
Tuition, 2003-2004 academic year: Full-time in-state:
  $2,148; out-of-state: $4,833, Part-time in-state: $1,674;
  out-of-state: $3,804
Fees: $333, Room and board: $3,675, Books and supplies:
  $900, Miscellaneous expenses: $1,500
Number of fellowships awarded to graduate students dur-
  ing the 2003-2004 academic year: 2
Number of teaching assistant positions: 12
Number of research assistant positions: 2
Number of other paid appointments: 39

ACADEMIC PROGRAMS
Areas of specialization: curriculum and instruction, education administration and supervision, educational psychology, elementary teacher education, higher education
  administration, secondary teacher education, special
  education, student counseling and personnel services.
During their internships, peer groups of students meet
  regularly to discuss instructional techniques in some of
  the teaching programs.
All of the students in their internships are mentored.
Courses that prepare teachers to pass the National Board of
  Professional Teaching Standards are offered.
Teacher preparation programs: Four-year baccalaureate-
  degree program leading to initial licensure that includes
  either a major or minor in education and practice teaching. Master's program preparing college graduates for
  initial licensure; includes practice teaching. Alternative
  program for college graduates leading to provisional
  licensure.
The education program is currently accredited by the
  National Council for Accreditation of Teacher Education.

LICENSING TEST
Pass rate on state's teacher licensing test for 2002-2003:
  100%
State average pass rate: 95%

Loyola University New Orleans

■ 6363 St. Charles Avenue, New Orleans, LA 70118-6195
■ **Website:** http://www.loyno.edu/
■ **Private**

ACADEMIC PROGRAMS
The education program is currently accredited by the
  National Council for Accreditation of Teacher Education.

LICENSING TEST
Pass rate on state's teacher licensing test for 2002-2003:
  91%
State average pass rate: 95%

McNeese State University

■ 4100 Ryan Street, Lake Charles, LA 70609
■ **Website:** http://www.mcneese.edu/
■ **Public**

LICENSING TEST
Pass rate on state's teacher licensing test for 2002-2003:
  93%
State average pass rate: 95%

Nicholls State University

■ PO Box 2004, University Station, Thibodaux, LA 70310
■ **Website:** http://www.nicholls.edu
■ **Public**
■ **Degrees offered:** bachelor's, master's, education
  specialist

ADMISSIONS
Admissions phone number: (985) 448-4507
Admissions email address: *nicholls@nicholls.edu*
Application website:
  http://www.nicholls.edu/admissions/applyhtml
Application fee: $20
Fall 2005 application deadline: **rolling**
Test of English as Foreign Language (TOEFL) is required
  for international students.
Minimum TOEFL score required for paper test: 550
Minimum TOEFL score required for computer test: 213

Fall 2003
Total 2003 enrollment: 300
Master's degree enrollment: 282
  Teacher preparation program enrollment (master's): 66
Education specialist degree enrollment: 18

FINANCIAL INFORMATION
Financial aid phone number: (985) 448-4048
Tuition, 2003-2004 academic year: Full-time in-state:
  $2,115; out-of-state: $7,563, Part-time in-state: $889; out-
  of-state: $3,159
Fees: $743, Room and board: $3,402, Books and supplies:
  $1,000, Miscellaneous expenses: $2,364
Number of teaching assistant positions: 8
Number of other paid appointments: 9

ACADEMIC PROGRAMS

Areas of specialization: curriculum and instruction, education administration and supervision, educational psychology, elementary teacher education, higher education administration, secondary teacher education, student counseling and personnel services.

The education program is currently accredited by the National Council for Accreditation of Teacher Education.

LICENSING TEST

Pass rate on state's teacher licensing test for 2002-2003: 95%

State average pass rate: 95%

Northwestern State University of Louisiana

- 350 Sam Sibley Drive, Natchitoches, LA 71497
- **Website:** http://www.nsula.edu
- Public
- **Degrees offered:** bachelor's, master's, education specialist

ADMISSIONS

Admissions phone number: (318) 357-4503

Admissions email address: *grad_school@nsula.edu*

Application fee: $20

Fall 2005 application deadline: 8/1

Test of English as Foreign Language (TOEFL) is required for international students.

Minimum TOEFL score required for paper test: 500

Minimum TOEFL score required for computer test: 173

Fall 2003

Acceptance rate for master's degree programs: 99%

Acceptance rate for education specialist degree programs: 97%

Average GRE verbal: 401, Average GRE quantitative: 421, Average GRE analytical: 438

Total 2003 enrollment: 593

Master's degree enrollment: 519

  Teacher preparation program enrollment (master's): 383

Education specialist degree enrollment: 74

FINANCIAL INFORMATION

Financial aid phone number: (318) 357-5961

Tuition, 2003-2004 academic year: Full-time in-state: $2,726; out-of-state: $8,800, Part-time in-state: $390/credit hour; out-of-state: $285/credit hour

Fees: $280, Room and board: $3,400, Books and supplies: $1,200

ACADEMIC PROGRAMS

Total full-time tenured or tenure-track faculty (fall 2003): 18, Total part-time faculty (fall 2003): 13

Professional development/partnership school(s) are used by students in some of the teaching programs.

During their internships, peer groups of students meet regularly to discuss instructional techniques in some of the teaching programs.

All of the students in their internships are mentored.

Courses that prepare teachers to pass the National Board of Professional Teaching Standards are offered.

Teacher preparation programs: Four-year baccalaureate-degree program leading to initial licensure that includes either a major or minor in education and practice teaching. Master's program preparing college graduates for initial licensure; includes practice teaching. Alternative program for college graduates leading to provisional licensure.

The education program is currently accredited by the National Council for Accreditation of Teacher Education.

LICENSING TEST

Pass rate on state's teacher licensing test for 2002-2003: 99%

State average pass rate: 95%

Our Lady of Holy Cross College

- 4123 Woodland Drive, New Orleans, LA 70131
- **Website:** http://www.olhcc.edu
- Private
- **Degrees offered:** bachelor's, master's

ADMISSIONS

Admissions phone number: (504) 398-2175

Admissions email address: *admissions@olhcc.edu*

Application website: *http://www.olhcc.edu/inquiry/index.cfm?formID=3*

Application fee: $15

Fall 2005 application deadline: **rolling**

Fall 2003

Average GRE verbal: 450, Average GRE quantitative: 450, Average MAT: 40

Total 2003 enrollment: 127

Master's degree enrollment: 127

  Teacher preparation program enrollment (master's): 19

FINANCIAL INFORMATION

Financial aid phone number: (504) 398-2165

Tuition, 2003-2004 academic year: Full-time: **$290/credit hour**; Part-time: **$290/credit hour**

Fees: **$245**

Number of fellowships awarded to graduate students during the 2003-2004 academic year: 0

Number of teaching assistant positions: 0

Number of research assistant positions: 0

Number of other paid appointments: 20

ACADEMIC PROGRAMS

Areas of specialization: curriculum and instruction, education administration and supervision, elementary teacher education, secondary teacher education, student counseling and personnel services.

Professional development/partnership school(s) are used by students in all of the teaching programs.

During their internships, peer groups of students meet regularly to discuss instructional techniques in all of the teaching programs.

All of the students in their internships are mentored.

Courses that prepare teachers to pass the National Board of Professional Teaching Standards are not offered.

Teacher preparation programs: Four-year baccalaureate-degree program leading to initial licensure that includes either a major or minor in education and practice teaching. Master's program preparing college graduates for initial licensure; includes practice teaching. Alternative program for college graduates leading to provisional licensure.

LICENSING TEST

Pass rate on state's teacher licensing test for 2002-2003: 100%

State average pass rate: 95%

Southeastern Louisiana University

- SLU 10752, Hammond, LA 70402
- **Website:** http://www.selu.edu/ProspectiveStudents.html
- Public
- **Degrees offered:** bachelor's, master's

ADMISSIONS

Admissions phone number: **(985) 549-2066**
Admissions email address: *admissions@selu.edu*
Application website:
http://www.selu.edu/ProspectiveStudents.html
Application fee: **$20**
Fall 2005 application deadline: **7/15**
Test requirements: **GRE**
Test of English as Foreign Language (TOEFL) is required for international students.
Minimum TOEFL score required for paper test: **500**
Minimum TOEFL score required for computer test: **173**

Fall 2003
Acceptance rate for master's degree programs: **98%**
Average GRE verbal: **388**, Average GRE quantitative: **399**
Total 2003 enrollment: **841**
Master's degree enrollment: **841**
   Teacher preparation program enrollment (master's): **606**

FINANCIAL INFORMATION

Financial aid phone number: **(985) 549-2244**
Tuition, 2003-2004 academic year: Full-time in-state: **$2,754**; out-of-state: **$6,750**, Part-time in-state: **$153/credit hour**; out-of-state: **$375/credit hour**

Room and board: **$3,840**, Books and supplies: **$1,000**, Miscellaneous expenses: **$2,500**
Number of fellowships awarded to graduate students during the 2003-2004 academic year: **0**
Number of teaching assistant positions: **0**
Number of research assistant positions: **6**
Number of other paid appointments: **35**

ACADEMIC PROGRAMS

Total full-time tenured or tenure-track faculty (fall 2003): **47**, Total part-time faculty (fall 2003): **40**

Areas of specialization: curriculum and instruction, education administration and supervision, educational psychology, elementary teacher education, secondary teacher education, special education, student counseling and personnel services.

Professional development/partnership school(s) are used by students in all of the teaching programs.

During their internships, peer groups of students meet regularly to discuss instructional techniques in all of the teaching programs.

All of the students in their internships are mentored.

Courses that prepare teachers to pass the National Board of Professional Teaching Standards are offered.

Teacher preparation programs: Four-year baccalaureate-degree program leading to initial licensure that includes either a major or minor in education and practice teaching. Master's program preparing college graduates for initial licensure; includes practice teaching.

The education program is currently accredited by the National Council for Accreditation of Teacher Education.

LICENSING TEST

Pass rate on state's teacher licensing test for 2002-2003: 94%

State average pass rate: 95%

Southern University and A&M College

- JC Clark Admin. Building, 4th Floor, Baton Rouge, LA 70813
- **Website:** http://www.subr.edu/coeducation/
- Public

ACADEMIC PROGRAMS

The education program is currently accredited by the National Council for Accreditation of Teacher Education.

LICENSING TEST

Pass rate on state's teacher licensing test for 2002-2003: 97%

State average pass rate: 95%

University of Louisiana–Lafayette

- PO Drawer 44872, Lafayette, LA 70504-4872
- **Website:** http://admissions.louisiana.edu/basics/
- **Public**
- **Degrees offered:** bachelor's, master's

ADMISSIONS

Admissions phone number: **(337) 482-6467**
Admissions email address: *enroll@louisiana.edu*
Application website:
http://gradschool.louisiana.edu/forms/indix shtml
Application fee: **$20**
Fall 2005 application deadline: **7/1**
Test requirements: **GRE**
Test of English as Foreign Language (TOEFL) is required for international students.
Minimum TOEFL score required for paper test: **550**
Minimum TOEFL score required for computer test: **213**

Fall 2003

Acceptance rate for master's degree programs: **54%**
Average GRE verbal: **421**, Average GRE quantitative: **501**, Average GRE analytical: **454**
Total 2003 enrollment: **216**
Master's degree enrollment: **216**
Teacher preparation program enrollment (master's): **93**

FINANCIAL INFORMATION

Financial aid phone number: **(337) 482-6497**
Tuition, 2003-2004 academic year: Full-time in-state: **$2,892**; out-of-state: **$9,072**, Part-time in-state: **$1,749**; out-of-state: **$4,839**
Fees: **$1,648**, Room and board: **$3,086**, Books and supplies: **$1,000**, Miscellaneous expenses: **$1,000**
Number of fellowships awarded to graduate students during the 2003-2004 academic year: **0**
Number of teaching assistant positions: **4**
Number of research assistant positions: **14**
Number of other paid appointments: **13**

ACADEMIC PROGRAMS

Total full-time tenured or tenure-track faculty (fall 2003): **33**, Total part-time faculty (fall 2003): **25**
Areas of specialization: curriculum and instruction, education administration and supervision, student counseling and personnel services.
Professional development/partnership school(s) are used by students in some of the teaching programs.
During their internships, peer groups of students meet regularly to discuss instructional techniques in all of the teaching programs.
All of the students in their internships are mentored.
Courses that prepare teachers to pass the National Board of Professional Teaching Standards are offered.

Teacher preparation programs: Four-year baccalaureate-degree program leading to initial licensure that includes either a major or minor in education and practice teaching. Alternative program for college graduates leading to provisional licensure.
The education program is currently accredited by the National Council for Accreditation of Teacher Education.

LICENSING TEST

Pass rate on state's teacher licensing test for 2002-2003: **96%**
State average pass rate: **95%**

University of Louisiana–Monroe

- Strauss Hall, Monroe, LA 71209-0001
- **Website:** http://www.ulm.edu
- **Public**
- **Degrees offered:** bachelor's, master's, education specialist, Ph.D., Ed.D.

ADMISSIONS

Admissions phone number: **(318) 342-5252**
Admissions email address: *admissions@ulm.edu*
Application website: *http://www.ulm.edu/enroll/toapply.html*
Application fee: **$20**
Fall 2005 application deadline: **7/1**
Test requirements: **GRE**
Test of English as Foreign Language (TOEFL) is required for international students.
Minimum TOEFL score required for paper test: **480**
Minimum TOEFL score required for computer test: **157**

Fall 2003

Acceptance rate for doctoral programs: **60%**
Total 2003 enrollment: **353**
Master's degree enrollment: **278**
Teacher preparation program enrollment (master's): **155**
Education specialist degree enrollment: **26**
Doctoral degree enrollment: **49**

FINANCIAL INFORMATION

Financial aid phone number: **(318) 342-5320**
Tuition, 2003-2004 academic year: Full-time in-state: **$2,620**; out-of-state: **$8,578**, Part-time in-state: **$147/credit hour**; out-of-state: **$147/credit hour**
Room and board: **$1,645**, Books and supplies: **$500**
Number of teaching assistant positions: **11**
Number of research assistant positions: **45**
Number of other paid appointments: **9**

ACADEMIC PROGRAMS

Total full-time tenured or tenure-track faculty (fall 2003): **46**, Total part-time faculty (fall 2003): **33**
Areas of specialization: curriculum and instruction, education administration and supervision, educational psy-

chology, elementary teacher education, secondary teacher education, special education, student counseling and personnel services.

Professional development/partnership school(s) are used by students in all of the teaching programs.

During their internships, peer groups of students meet regularly to discuss instructional techniques in all of the teaching programs.

All of the students in their internships are mentored.

Courses that prepare teachers to pass the National Board of Professional Teaching Standards are offered.

Teacher preparation programs: Four-year baccalaureate-degree program leading to initial licensure that includes either a major or minor in education and practice teaching. Master's program preparing college graduates for initial licensure; includes practice teaching. Alternative program for college graduates leading to provisional licensure.

The education program is currently accredited by the National Council for Accreditation of Teacher Education.

LICENSING TEST

Pass rate on state's teacher licensing test for 2002-2003: 100%

State average pass rate: 95%

University of New Orleans

- College of Education, New Orleans, LA 70148
- Website: http//www.uno.edu
- Public
- Degrees offered: bachelor's, master's, Ph.D.
- Overall rank in the 2005 U.S. News education school specialty rankings: counseling/personnel: 22

ADMISSIONS

Admissions phone number: (504) 280-6595
Admissions email address: *admissions@uno.edu*
Application website: *http://www.uno.edu/~admi/app.html*
Application fee: $20
Fall 2005 application deadline: 7/1
Test requirements: GRE
Test of English as Foreign Language (TOEFL) is required for international students.
Minimum TOEFL score required for paper test: 550
Minimum TOEFL score required for computer test: 213

Fall 2003
Average GRE verbal: 442, Average GRE quantitative: 461
Total 2003 enrollment: 1,209
Master's degree enrollment: 1,022

Teacher preparation program enrollment (master's): 199
Doctoral degree enrollment: 187

FINANCIAL INFORMATION

Financial aid phone number: (504) 280-6603
Tuition, 2003-2004 academic year: Full-time in-state: $3,084; out-of-state: $10,128, Part-time in-state: $1,918; out-of-state: $5,446
Fees: $510, Room and board: $3,520, Books and supplies: $825, Miscellaneous expenses: $1,490

ACADEMIC PROGRAMS

Total full-time tenured or tenure-track faculty (fall 2003): 59

Areas of specialization: curriculum and instruction, education administration and supervision, elementary teacher education, higher education administration, secondary teacher education, special education, student counseling and personnel services.

Professional development/partnership school(s) are used by students in all of the teaching programs.

During their internships, peer groups of students meet regularly to discuss instructional techniques in all of the teaching programs.

All of the students in their internships are mentored.

Courses that prepare teachers to pass the National Board of Professional Teaching Standards are offered.

Teacher preparation programs: Four-year baccalaureate-degree program leading to initial licensure that includes either a major or minor in education and practice teaching. Five-year program leading to initial licensure that results in a baccalaureate degree (with a major or minor in education) plus graduate credit and includes practice teaching. Five-year program leading to initial licensure that results in a baccalaureate degree (with a major or minor in education) plus a master's degree and includes practice teaching. Alternative program for college graduates leading to provisional licensure.

The education program is currently accredited by the National Council for Accreditation of Teacher Education.

LICENSING TEST

Pass rate on state's teacher licensing test for 2002-2003: 91%
State average pass rate: 95%

Xavier University of Louisiana

- 1 Drexel Drive, New Orleans, LA 70125
- Website: http://www.xula.edu/education/
- Private

MAINE

St. Joseph's College

■ 278 Whites Bridge Rd, Standish, ME 04084
■ **Website:** http://www.sjcme.edu/gps
■ **Private**
■ **Degrees offered:** bachelor's, master's

ADMISSIONS
Admissions phone number: **(800) 752-4723**
Admissions email address: *info@sjcme.edu*
Application website: *http://www.sjcme.edu/gpsapp*
Application fee: **$50**
Fall 2005 application deadline: **rolling**
Test of English as Foreign Language (TOEFL) is required for international students.
Minimum TOEFL score required for paper test: **550**
Minimum TOEFL score required for computer test: **213**

Fall 2003
Total 2003 enrollment: **255**
Master's degree enrollment: **255**
    Teacher preparation program enrollment (master's): **29**

FINANCIAL INFORMATION
Financial aid phone number: **(800) 752-1266**
Tuition, 2003-2004 academic year: Full-time: **$250/credit hour**; Part-time: **$250/credit hour**
Fees: **$250/credit hour**

ACADEMIC PROGRAMS
Total full-time tenured or tenure-track faculty (fall 2003): **0**
    Total part-time faculty (fall 2003): **14**
Areas of specialization: curriculum and instruction, education administration and supervision, secondary teacher education.
Professional development/partnership school(s) are used by students in some of the teaching programs.
During their internships, peer groups of students meet regularly to discuss instructional techniques in some of the teaching programs.
Some of the students in their internships are mentored.

Courses that prepare teachers to pass the National Board of Professional Teaching Standards are not offered.
Teacher preparation programs: Four-year baccalaureate-degree program leading to initial licensure that includes either a major or minor in education and practice teaching. Alternative program for college graduates leading to provisional licensure.

LICENSING TEST
Pass rate on state's teacher licensing test for 2002-2003: **61%**
State average pass rate: **89%**

University of Maine– Orono

■ Shibles Hall, Orono, ME 04469-5766
■ **Website:** http://www.umaine.edu/graduate/
■ **Public**
■ **Degrees offered:** bachelor's, master's, education specialist, Ed.D.

ADMISSIONS
Admissions phone number: **(207) 581-3218**
Admissions email address: *graduate@maine.maine.edu*
Application website: *http://www.umaine.edu/graduate/ onlineap.htm*
Application fee: **$50**
Fall 2005 application deadline: **rolling**
Test requirements: **GRE or MAT**
Test of English as Foreign Language (TOEFL) is required for international students.
Minimum TOEFL score required for paper test: **550**
Minimum TOEFL score required for computer test: **213**

Fall 2003
Acceptance rate for master's degree programs: **84%**
Acceptance rate for education specialist degree programs: **93%**
Acceptance rate for doctoral programs: **72%**

Average GRE verbal: 485, Average GRE quantitative: 535, Average GRE analytical: 592, Average MAT: 49
Total 2003 enrollment: 636
Master's degree enrollment: 485
   Teacher preparation program enrollment (master's): 183
Education specialist degree enrollment: 90
Doctoral degree enrollment: 61

FINANCIAL INFORMATION

Financial aid phone number: (207) 581-1324
Tuition, 2003-2004 academic year: Full-time in-state: **$235/credit hour**; out-of-state: **$670/credit hour**, Part-time in-state: **$235/credit hour**; out-of-state: **$670/credit hour**
Fees: **$486/credit hour**, Room and board: **$6,156**, Books and supplies: **$550**, Miscellaneous expenses: **$900**
Number of fellowships awarded to graduate students during the 2003-2004 academic year: 1
Number of teaching assistant positions: 19
Number of research assistant positions: 5
Number of other paid appointments: 28

ACADEMIC PROGRAMS

Total full-time tenured or tenure-track faculty (fall 2003): 39, Total part-time faculty (fall 2003): 1
Areas of specialization: curriculum and instruction, education administration and supervision, elementary teacher education, higher education administration, secondary teacher education, special education, student counseling and personnel services.
Professional development/partnership school(s) are used by students in all of the teaching programs.
During their internships, peer groups of students meet regularly to discuss instructional techniques in all of the teaching programs.
Some of the students in their internships are mentored.
Courses that prepare teachers to pass the National Board of Professional Teaching Standards are not offered.
Teacher preparation programs: Four-year baccalaureate-degree program leading to initial licensure that includes either a major or minor in education and practice teaching. Master's program preparing college graduates for initial licensure; includes practice teaching.
The education program is currently accredited by the National Council for Accreditation of Teacher Education.

LICENSING TEST

Pass rate on state's teacher licensing test for 2002-2003: 80%
State average pass rate: 89%

University of New England

- **11 Hills Beach Road, Biddeford, ME 04055**
- **Website:** http://study.une.edu.au/
- **Private**
- **Degrees offered:** bachelor's, master's

ADMISSIONS

Fall 2005 application deadline: **rolling**

LICENSING TEST

Pass rate on state's teacher licensing test for 2002-2003: 86%
State average pass rate: 89%

University of Southern Maine

- **37 College Avenue, Gorham, ME 04038**
- **Website:** http://www.usm.maine.edu/grad
- **Public**
- **Degrees offered:** master's

ADMISSIONS

Admissions phone number: (207) 780-5306
Admissions email address: *jsteeves@usm.maine.edu*
Application website: *http://www.applyweb.com/apply/usmaine/index.html*
Application fee: **$50**
Test of English as Foreign Language (TOEFL) is required for international students.
Minimum TOEFL score required for paper test: 550
Minimum TOEFL score required for computer test: 213

Fall 2003

Total 2003 enrollment: 720
Master's degree enrollment: 720
   Teacher preparation program enrollment (master's): 270

FINANCIAL INFORMATION

Financial aid phone number: (207) 780-5250
Tuition, 2003-2004 academic year: Full-time in-state: **$215/credit hour**; out-of-state: **$603/credit hour**, Part-time in-state: **$215/credit hour**; out-of-state: **$603/credit hour**
Fees: **$250**, Room and board: **$6,978**, Books and supplies: **$500**
Number of other paid appointments: 17

ACADEMIC PROGRAMS

Total full-time tenured or tenure-track faculty (fall 2003): 32, Total part-time faculty (fall 2003): 116

Areas of specialization: curriculum and instruction, education administration and supervision, education policy, educational psychology, elementary teacher education, higher education administration, secondary teacher education, special education, student counseling and personnel services, teacher education.

Professional development/partnership school(s) are used by students in all of the teaching programs.

During their internships, peer groups of students meet regularly to discuss instructional techniques in all of the teaching programs.

All of the students in their internships are mentored.

Courses that prepare teachers to pass the National Board of Professional Teaching Standards are not offered.

The education program is currently accredited by the National Council for Accreditation of Teacher Education.

LICENSING TEST

Pass rate on state's teacher licensing test for 2002-2003: **96%**

State average pass rate: **89%**

MARYLAND

Bowie State University

■ 14000 Jericho Park Road, Bowie, MD 20715-9465
■ Website: http://education.bowiestate.edu/index.php
■ Public

LICENSING TEST
Pass rate on state's teacher licensing test for 2002-2003: 91%
State average pass rate: 91%

College of Notre Dame of Maryland

■ 4701 North Charles Street, Baltimore, MD 21210
■ Website: http://www.ndm.edu
■ Private
■ Degrees offered: bachelor's, master's

ADMISSIONS
Admissions phone number: (410) 532-5317
Admissions email address: *gradadm@ndm.edu*
Application website: *https://www.cnd-md.edu/app/*
Application fee: **$25**
Fall 2005 application deadline: **rolling**
Test of English as Foreign Language (TOEFL) is required for international students.
Minimum TOEFL score required for paper test: **550**

Fall 2003
Acceptance rate for master's degree programs: **90%**
Total 2003 enrollment: **603**
Master's degree enrollment: **603**
  Teacher preparation program enrollment (master's): **179**

FINANCIAL INFORMATION
Financial aid phone number: (410) 532-5369

Tuition, 2003-2004 academic year: Full-time: **$340/credit hour**; Part-time: **$340/credit hour**
Fees: **$40**
Number of fellowships awarded to graduate students during the 2003-2004 academic year: 0
Number of teaching assistant positions: 0
Number of research assistant positions: 0
Number of other paid appointments: 0

ACADEMIC PROGRAMS
Total full-time tenured or tenure-track faculty (fall 2003): 14, Total part-time faculty (fall 2003): 43
Areas of specialization: curriculum and instruction, education administration and supervision, education policy, educational psychology, elementary teacher education, secondary teacher education, special education.
Professional development/partnership school(s) are used by students in all of the teaching programs.
During their internships, peer groups of students meet regularly to discuss instructional techniques in all of the teaching programs.
All of the students in their internships are mentored.
Courses that prepare teachers to pass the National Board of Professional Teaching Standards are not offered.
Teacher preparation programs: Four-year baccalaureate-degree program leading to initial licensure that includes either a major or minor in education and practice teaching. Five-year program leading to initial licensure that results in a baccalaureate degree (with a major or minor in education) plus a master's degree and includes practice teaching.
The education program is currently accredited by the National Council for Accreditation of Teacher Education.

LICENSING TEST
Pass rate on state's teacher licensing test for 2002-2003: 91%
State average pass rate: 91%

Coppin State College

- 2500 W. North Avenue, Baltimore, MD 21216-3698
- **Website:** http://www.coppin.edu/education/
- Public

LICENSING TEST

Pass rate on state's teacher licensing test for 2002-2003: 100%
State average pass rate: 91%

Frostburg State University

- 101 Braddock Road, Frostburg, MD 21532
- **Website:**
  http://www.frostburg.edu/dept/educ/gprograms.htm
- Public
- **Degrees offered:** bachelor's, master's

ADMISSIONS

Admissions phone number: (301) 687-7053
Admissions email address: *gradservices@frostburg.edu*
Application website:
  http://www.acaff.usmh.usmd.edu/gradapp/index.html
Application fee: $30
Fall 2005 application deadline: **rolling**
Test of English as Foreign Language (TOEFL) is required
  for international students.
Minimum TOEFL score required for paper test: 560
Minimum TOEFL score required for computer test: 220

Fall 2003

Average GRE verbal: 468, Average GRE quantitative: 503,
  Average GRE analytical: 567
Total 2003 enrollment: 415
Master's degree enrollment: 415
  Teacher preparation program enrollment (master's): 199

FINANCIAL INFORMATION

Financial aid phone number: (301) 687-4301
Tuition, 2003-2004 academic year: Full-time in-state:
  $234/credit hour; out-of-state: **$271/credit hour**, Part-
  time in-state: **$234/credit hour**; out-of-state: **$271/credit
  hour**
Fees: **$41/credit hour**, Room and board: **$5,772**, Books and
  supplies: **$500**

ACADEMIC PROGRAMS

Total full-time tenured or tenure-track faculty (fall 2003):
  26, Total part-time faculty (fall 2003): 12
Areas of specialization: curriculum and instruction, education administration and supervision, elementary teacher
  education, secondary teacher education, special education, student counseling and personnel services.

Teacher preparation programs: Four-year baccalaureate-
  degree program leading to initial licensure that includes
  either a major or minor in education and practice teaching. Master's program preparing college graduates for
  initial licensure; includes practice teaching.
The education program is currently accredited by the
  National Council for Accreditation of Teacher Education.

LICENSING TEST

Pass rate on state's teacher licensing test for 2002-2003: 98%
State average pass rate: 91%

Goucher College

- 1021 Dulaney Valley Road, Towson, MD 21204
- **Website:** http://www.goucher.edu/gpedu
- Private
- **Degrees offered:** master's

ADMISSIONS

Admissions phone number: (410) 337-6392
Admissions email address: *sgray@goucher.edu*
Application fee: $25
Fall 2005 application deadline: **rolling**
Test of English as Foreign Language (TOEFL) is required
  for international students.

Fall 2003

Acceptance rate for master's degree programs: 95%
Total 2003 enrollment: 270
Master's degree enrollment: 270
  Teacher preparation program enrollment (master's): 100

FINANCIAL INFORMATION

Financial aid phone number: (410) 337-6340
Tuition, 2003-2004 academic year: Full-time: **$310/credit
  hour**; Part-time: **$310/credit hour**
Number of paid appointments: 3

ACADEMIC PROGRAMS

Total full-time tenured or tenure-track faculty (fall 2003): 0
  Total part-time faculty (fall 2003): 98
Areas of specialization: curriculum and instruction, education
  administration and supervision, elementary teacher educa-
  tion, secondary teacher education, special education.
Professional development/partnership school(s) are used
  by students in all of the teaching programs.
During their internships, peer groups of students meet
  regularly to discuss instructional techniques in all of the
  teaching programs.
All of the students in their internships are mentored.
Courses that prepare teachers to pass the National Board of
  Professional Teaching Standards are not offered.
Teacher preparation programs: Master's degree in educa-
  tion, including internship/practice teaching and preparation for initial licensure.

LICENSING TEST

Pass rate on state's teacher licensing test for 2002-2003: 88%

State average pass rate: 91%

Hood College

- 401 Rosemont Avenue, Frederick, MD 21701
- **Website:** http://www.hood.edu/
- **Private**

LICENSING TEST

Pass rate on state's teacher licensing test for 2002-2003: 100%

State average pass rate: 91%

Johns Hopkins University

- 7150 Columbia Gateway Drive, Suite A/B, Columbia, MD 21046
- **Website:** http://www.spsbe.jhu.edu/programs/grad_edu.cfm
- **Private**
- **Degrees offered:** master's, Ed.D.
- **Overall rank in the 2005 U.S. News education school specialty rankings:** special education: 16

ADMISSIONS

Admissions phone number: (410) 872-1234
Admissions email address: *edspsbe@jhu.edu*
Application website: *http://apply.spsbe.jhu.edu/*

FINANCIAL INFORMATION

Financial aid phone number: (410) 872-1230

ACADEMIC PROGRAMS

Areas of specialization: education administration and supervision, elementary teacher education, secondary teacher education, special education, student counseling and personnel services.

The education program is currently accredited by the National Council for Accreditation of Teacher Education.

LICENSING TEST

Pass rate on state's teacher licensing test for 2002-2003: 97%

State average pass rate: 91%

Loyola College in Maryland

- 4501 North Charles Street, Baltimore, MD 21210
- **Website:** http://www.loyola.edu
- **Private**
- **Degrees offered:** bachelor's, master's

ADMISSIONS

Admissions phone number: (410) 617-5020
Admissions email address: *graduate@loyola.edu*
Application website:
   http://apply.embark.com/MBAedge/Loyola?Sellinger/100
Application fee: $50
Fall 2005 application deadline: 8/15
Test of English as Foreign Language (TOEFL) is required for international students.
Minimum TOEFL score required for paper test: 550
Minimum TOEFL score required for computer test: 213

Fall 2003
Acceptance rate for master's degree programs: 81%
Total 2003 enrollment: 706
Master's degree enrollment: 706
   Teacher preparation program enrollment (master's): 164

FINANCIAL INFORMATION

Financial aid phone number: (410) 617-2576
Tuition, 2003-2004 academic year: Full-time: $310/credit hour; Part-time: $310/credit hour
Fees: $50, Miscellaneous expenses: $12,645
Number of fellowships awarded to graduate students during the 2003-2004 academic year: 0
Number of teaching assistant positions: 0
Number of research assistant positions: 0
Number of other paid appointments: 12

ACADEMIC PROGRAMS

Total full-time tenured or tenure-track faculty (fall 2003): 16, Total part-time faculty (fall 2003): 60
Areas of specialization: curriculum and instruction, education administration and supervision, elementary teacher education, secondary teacher education, special education, student counseling and personnel services.
Professional development/partnership school(s) are used by students in all of the teaching programs.
During their internships, peer groups of students meet regularly to discuss instructional techniques in some of the teaching programs.
All of the students in their internships are mentored.
Courses that prepare teachers to pass the National Board of Professional Teaching Standards are not offered.
The education program is currently accredited by the National Council for Accreditation of Teacher Education.

LICENSING TEST

Pass rate on state's teacher licensing test for 2002-2003: 90%
State average pass rate: 91%

Morgan State University

- **1700 E. Cold Spring Lane, Baltimore, MD 21251**
- **Website:** http://www.morgan.edu/academics/
  Grad-Studies/default.asp
- **Public**
- **Degrees offered:** bachelor's, master's, Ph.D., Ed.D.

ADMISSIONS

Admissions phone number: **(443) 885-3185**
Admissions email address: *jwaller@moac.morgan.edu*
Application website:
  http://www.morgan.edu/academics/Grad-Studies/apply.asp
Application fee: **$0**
Test of English as Foreign Language (TOEFL) is required
  for international students.
Minimum TOEFL score required for paper test: **550**
Minimum TOEFL score required for computer test: **213**

Fall 2003

Total 2003 enrollment: **634**

FINANCIAL INFORMATION

Financial aid phone number: **(443) 885-3185**
Tuition, 2003-2004 academic year: Full-time in-state:
  $215/credit hour; out-of-state: **$409/credit hour**, Part-time
  in-state: **$215/credit hour**; out-of-state: **$409/credit hour**
Fees: **$48/credit hour**, Room and board: **$6,570**, Books and
  supplies: **$2,000**, Miscellaneous expenses: **$2,300**
Number of teaching assistant positions: **9**

ACADEMIC PROGRAMS

Areas of specialization: curriculum and instruction, education administration and supervision, education policy,
  elementary teacher education, higher education administration, secondary teacher education.
Professional development/partnership school(s) are used
  by students in all of the teaching programs.
Teacher preparation programs: Four-year baccalaureate-
  degree program leading to initial licensure that includes
  either a major or minor in education and practice teaching. Master's program preparing college graduates for
  initial licensure; includes practice teaching.
The education program is currently accredited by the
  National Council for Accreditation of Teacher Education.

LICENSING TEST

Pass rate on state's teacher licensing test for 2002-2003: 63%
State average pass rate: 91%

Mount St. Mary's College

- **16300 Old Emmitsburg Road, Emmitsburg, MD 21727**
- **Website:**
  http://www.msmary.edu/college/html/graduate/
  mastereducation.htm
- **Private**
- **Degrees offered:** bachelor's, master's

ADMISSIONS

Admissions phone number: **(301) 447-5371**
Admissions email address: *frazier@msmary.edu*

FINANCIAL INFORMATION

Financial aid phone number: **(301) 447-5207**

LICENSING TEST

Pass rate on state's teacher licensing test for 2002-2003:
  100%
State average pass rate: **91%**

Salisbury University

- **1101 Camden Avenue, Salisbury, MD 21801**
- **Website:** http://www.salisbury.edu/
- **Public**
- **Degrees offered:** bachelor's, master's

ADMISSIONS

Admissions phone number: **(410) 546-6161**
Admissions email address: *http://www.salisbury.edu/
  admissions/*
Application website: *http://www.salisbury.edu/apply/*
Application fee: **$45**
Fall 2005 application deadline: **1/15**
Test of English as Foreign Language (TOEFL) is required
  for international students.
Minimum TOEFL score required for paper test: **550**
Minimum TOEFL score required for computer test: **213**

Fall 2003

Total 2003 enrollment: **617**
Master's degree enrollment: **617**
  Teacher preparation program enrollment (master's): **118**

FINANCIAL INFORMATION

Financial aid phone number: **(410) 543-6165**
Tuition, 2003-2004 academic year: Full-time in-state:
  $215/credit hour; out-of-state: **$455/credit hour**, Part-time
  in-state: **$215/credit hour**; out-of-state: **$455/credit hour**
Fees: **$8/credit hour**

ACADEMIC PROGRAMS

Total full-time tenured or tenure-track faculty (fall 2003):
  299, Total part-time faculty (fall 2003): **203**

Courses that prepare teachers to pass the National Board of Professional Teaching Standards are offered.

Teacher preparation programs: Four-year baccalaureate-degree program leading to initial licensure that includes either a major or minor in education and practice teaching. Five-year program leading to initial licensure that results in a baccalaureate degree (with a major or minor in education) plus graduate credit and includes practice teaching. Five-year program leading to initial licensure that results in a baccalaureate degree (with a major or minor in education) plus a master's degree and includes practice teaching.

The education program is currently accredited by the National Council for Accreditation of Teacher Education.

LICENSING TEST

Pass rate on state's teacher licensing test for 2002-2003: 92%
State average pass rate: 91%

Towson University

- 8000 York Road, Towson, MD 21204
- **Website:** http://www.towson.edu/grad
- Public
- **Degrees offered:** bachelor's, master's, Ed.D.

ADMISSIONS

Admissions phone number: **(410) 704-2501**
Admissions email address: *grads@towson.edu*
Application website: *http://www.applyweb.com/apply/towson*
Application fee: **$40**
Fall 2005 application deadline: **rolling**
Test requirements: **GRE or MAT**
Test of English as Foreign Language (TOEFL) is required for international students.
Minimum TOEFL score required for paper test: **550**
Minimum TOEFL score required for computer test: **213**

Fall 2003

Acceptance rate for master's degree programs: **60%**
Acceptance rate for doctoral programs: **40%**

FINANCIAL INFORMATION

Financial aid phone number: **(410) 704-4236**
Tuition, 2003-2004 academic year: Full-time in-state: **$244/credit hour**; out-of-state: **$510/credit hour**, Part-time in-state: **$244/credit hour**; out-of-state: **$510/credit hour**
Fees: **$66/credit hour**, Room and board: **$6,208**, Books and supplies: **$1,624**, Miscellaneous expenses: **$3,100**
Number of fellowships awarded to graduate students during the 2003-2004 academic year: **3**
Number of teaching assistant positions: **12**
Number of research assistant positions: **7**
Number of other paid appointments: **112**

ACADEMIC PROGRAMS

Total full-time tenured or tenure-track faculty (fall 2003): **52**
Areas of specialization: curriculum and instruction, education administration and supervision, elementary teacher education, higher education administration, secondary teacher education, special education.
Professional development/partnership school(s) are used by students in all of the teaching programs.
During their internships, peer groups of students meet regularly to discuss instructional techniques in all of the teaching programs.
All of the students in their internships are mentored.
Courses that prepare teachers to pass the National Board of Professional Teaching Standards are offered.
Teacher preparation programs: Four-year baccalaureate-degree program leading to initial licensure that includes either a major or minor in education and practice teaching. Master's program preparing college graduates for initial licensure; includes practice teaching.
The education program is currently accredited by the National Council for Accreditation of Teacher Education.

LICENSING TEST

Pass rate on state's teacher licensing test for 2002-2003: 92%
State average pass rate: 91%

University of Maryland– Baltimore County

- 1000 Hilltop Circle, Baltimore, MD 21250
- **Website:** http://www.umbc.edu/education/
- Public
- **Degrees offered:** bachelor's, master's

ADMISSIONS

Admissions phone number: **(410) 455-2327**
Admissions email address: *vwilli5@umbc.edu*
Application fee: **$50**
Fall 2005 application deadline: **6/1**
Test of English as Foreign Language (TOEFL) is required for international students.
Minimum TOEFL score required for paper test: **550**
Minimum TOEFL score required for computer test: **213**

Fall 2003

Acceptance rate for master's degree programs: **59%**
Total 2003 enrollment: **438**
Master's degree enrollment: **438**
    Teacher preparation program enrollment (master's): **16**

FINANCIAL INFORMATION

Financial aid phone number: **(410) 455-2387**
Tuition, 2003-2004 academic year: Full-time in-state: **$322/credit hour**; out-of-state: **$518/credit hour**, Part-time in-state: **$322/credit hour**; out-of-state: **$518/credit hour**

Fees: **$65/credit hour,** Room and board: **$7,000,** Books and supplies: **$500,** Miscellaneous expenses: **$75**

Number of teaching assistant positions: **11**

ACADEMIC PROGRAMS

Total full-time tenured or tenure-track faculty (fall 2003): **17,** Total part-time faculty (fall 2003): **36**

Areas of specialization: curriculum and instruction, educational psychology, elementary teacher education, secondary teacher education.

Professional development/partnership school(s) are used by students in all of the teaching programs.

During their internships, peer groups of students meet regularly to discuss instructional techniques in all of the teaching programs.

All of the students in their internships are mentored.

Teacher preparation programs: Master's program preparing college graduates for initial licensure; includes practice teaching.

The education program is currently accredited by the National Council for Accreditation of Teacher Education.

LICENSING TEST

Pass rate on state's teacher licensing test for 2002-2003: **86%**

State average pass rate: **91%**

University of Maryland–College Park

- **3119 Benjamin Building, College Park, MD 20742-1121**
- **Website:** http://www.education.umd.edu
- **Public**
- **Degrees offered:** bachelor's, master's, education specialist, Ph.D., Ed.D.
- **Overall rank in the 2005 U.S. News education schools with doctoral programs:** 20
- **Overall rank in the 2005 U.S. News education school specialty rankings:** administration/supervision: 17, counseling/personnel: 1, curriculum/instruction: 11, education policy: 13, educational psychology: 9, elementary education: 17, higher education administration: 10, special education: 7

ADMISSIONS

Admissions phone number: **(301) 405-2359**

Admissions email address: *kangel@deans.umd.edu*

Application website: *http://www.gradschool.umd.edu/Admit/web.html*

Application fee: **$50**

Test requirements: **GRE or MAT**

Test of English as Foreign Language (TOEFL) is required for international students.

Minimum TOEFL score required for paper test: **575**

Minimum TOEFL score required for computer test: **233**

Fall 2003

Acceptance rate for master's degree programs: **41%**

Acceptance rate for education specialist degree programs: **20%**

Acceptance rate for doctoral programs: **35%**

Average GRE verbal: **534,** Average GRE quantitative: **612,** Average GRE analytical: **633,** Average MAT: **50**

Total 2003 enrollment: **1,110**

Master's degree enrollment: **510**

Education specialist degree enrollment: **2**

Doctoral degree enrollment: **598**

FINANCIAL INFORMATION

Financial aid phone number: **(301) 314-9000**

Tuition, 2003-2004 academic year: Full-time in-state: **$349/credit hour**; out-of-state: **$602/credit hour**, Part-time in-state: **$349/credit hour**; out-of-state: **$602/credit hour**

Fees: **$477/credit hour,** Room and board: **$7,468,** Books and supplies: **$800,** Miscellaneous expenses: **$350**

Number of fellowships awarded to graduate students during the 2003-2004 academic year: **156**

Number of teaching assistant positions: **55**

Number of research assistant positions: **111**

Number of other paid appointments: **136**

ACADEMIC PROGRAMS

Total full-time tenured or tenure-track faculty (fall 2003): **103,** Total part-time faculty (fall 2003): **15**

Areas of specialization: curriculum and instruction, education administration and supervision, education policy, educational psychology, elementary teacher education, higher education administration, secondary teacher education, special education, student counseling and personnel services.

Professional development/partnership school(s) are used by students in all of the teaching programs.

During their internships, peer groups of students meet regularly to discuss instructional techniques in some of the teaching programs.

All of the students in their internships are mentored.

Courses that prepare teachers to pass the National Board of Professional Teaching Standards are offered.

Teacher preparation programs: Four-year baccalaureate-degree program leading to initial licensure that includes either a major or minor in education and practice teaching. Five-year program leading to initial licensure that results in a baccalaureate degree (with a major or minor in education) plus graduate credit and includes practice teaching. Master's program preparing college graduates for initial licensure; includes practice teaching. Alternative program for college graduates leading to provisional licensure.

The education program is currently accredited by the National Council for Accreditation of Teacher Education.

LICENSING TEST

Pass rate on state's teacher licensing test for 2002-2003: **91%**

State average pass rate: **91%**

University of Maryland–Eastern Shore

■ 1 Backbone Road, Princess Anne, MD 21853
■ Website: http://www.umes.edu/
■ Public

LICENSING TEST
Pass rate on state's teacher licensing test for 2002-2003:
  31%
State average pass rate: 91%

MASSACHUSETTS

TEACHER TESTING IN MASSACHUSETTS
Teacher licensure rules vary widely from state to state, but almost all states require tests. The exams typically cover the basics of reading, writing and math, although some states mandate in-depth, subject-specific teacher tests. For information on where to go in your state for specific academic requirements, see Chapter 6 on page 67. Note: Some schools require students to pass exams by graduation, and thus automatically report pass rates of 100 percent.

- This state **does** require a basic skills test in order to obtain a teaching license.
- This state **does** require a subject-knowledge test in order to obtain a middle school teaching license.
- This state **does** require a subject-knowledge test in order to obtain a high school teaching license.
- This state **does** require a reading pedagogy test for elementry school teachers.

American International College

- 1000 State Street, Springfield, MA 01109
- Website: http://www.aic.edu/pages/399.html
- Private

LICENSING TEST
Pass rate on state's teacher licensing test for 2002-2003: 76%
State average pass rate: 91%

Anna Maria College

- 50 Sunset Lane, Paxton, MA 01612
- Website: http://www.annamaria.edu
- Private
- Degrees offered: bachelor's, master's, education specialist

ADMISSIONS
Admissions phone number: (508) 849-3482
Admissions email address: *dsanderson@annamaria.edu*
Application website: *http://www.annamaria.edu*
Application fee: $40
Fall 2005 application deadline: **rolling**
Test of English as Foreign Language (TOEFL) is required for international students.
Minimum TOEFL score required for paper test: 500

FINANCIAL INFORMATION
Financial aid phone number: (508) 849-3367
Tuition, 2003-2004 academic year: Full-time: **$350/credit hour**; Part-time: **$350/credit hour**

LICENSING TEST
Pass rate on state's teacher licensing test for 2002-2003: 78%
State average pass rate: 91%

Assumption College

- 500 Salisbury Street, Worcester, MA 01609
- Website: http://www.assumption.edu
- Private
- Degrees offered: master's

ADMISSIONS
Admissions phone number: (508) 767-7387
Admissions email address: *graduate@assumption.edu*
Application website: *http://www.assumption.edu/nhtml/ gradce/grad/admissions/applying.php*
Application fee: $30
Fall 2005 application deadline: **rolling**
Test of English as Foreign Language (TOEFL) is required for international students.
Minimum TOEFL score required for paper test: 540
Minimum TOEFL score required for computer test: 200

Fall 2003
Acceptance rate for master's degree programs: 96%
Total 2003 enrollment: 29
Master's degree enrollment: 29
  Teacher preparation program enrollment (master's): 29

FINANCIAL INFORMATION
Financial aid phone number: (508) 767-7158
Tuition, 2003-2004 academic year: Full-time: **$370/credit hour**; Part-time: **$370/credit hour**

ACADEMIC PROGRAMS
Total full-time tenured or tenure-track faculty (fall 2003): 1
  Total part-time faculty (fall 2003): 2
Areas of specialization: special education.
Professional development/partnership school(s) are used by students in some of the teaching programs.
During their internships, peer groups of students meet regularly to discuss instructional techniques in all of the teaching programs.
All of the students in their internships are mentored.

Courses that prepare teachers to pass the National Board of Professional Teaching Standards are not offered.

Teacher preparation programs: Four-year baccalaureate-degree program leading to initial licensure that includes either a major or minor in education and practice teaching. Five-year program leading to initial licensure that results in a baccalaureate degree (with a major or minor in education) plus a master's degree and includes practice teaching. Master's program preparing college graduates for initial licensure; includes practice teaching.

LICENSING TEST

Pass rate on state's teacher licensing test for 2002-2003: 92%

State average pass rate: 91%

Boston College (Lynch)

- Campion Hall, Chestnut Hill, MA 02467-3813
- Website: http://www.bc.edu/education
- Private
- Degrees offered: bachelor's, master's, education specialist, Ph.D., Ed.D.
- Overall rank in the 2005 U.S. News education schools with doctoral programs: 16
- Overall rank in the 2005 U.S. News education school specialty rankings: elementary education: 23

ADMISSIONS

Admissions phone number: **(617) 552-4214**
Admissions email address: *grad.ed.info@bc.edu*
Application website:
 http://www.bc.edu/bc_org/avp/soe/admissions
Application fee: **$40**
Fall 2005 application deadline: **2/15**
Test requirements: **GRE or MAT**
Test of English as Foreign Language (TOEFL) is required for international students.
Minimum TOEFL score required for paper test: **550**
Minimum TOEFL score required for computer test: **213**

Fall 2003
Acceptance rate for master's degree programs: **61%**
Acceptance rate for education specialist degree programs: **56%**
Acceptance rate for doctoral programs: **25%**
Average GRE verbal: **522**, Average GRE quantitative: **600**, Average GRE analytical: **618**, Average MAT: **47**
Total 2003 enrollment: **1,059**
Master's degree enrollment: **764**
 Teacher preparation program enrollment (master's): **388**
Education specialist degree enrollment: **19**
Doctoral degree enrollment: **276**

FINANCIAL INFORMATION

Financial aid phone number: **(617) 552-3300**
Tuition, 2003-2004 academic year: Full-time: **$796/credit hour**; Part-time: **$796/credit hour**

Fees: **$60**, Room and board: **$9,310**, Books and supplies: **$400**, Miscellaneous expenses: **$4,315**
Number of fellowships awarded to graduate students during the 2003-2004 academic year: **875**
Number of teaching assistant positions: **129**
Number of research assistant positions: **223**
Number of other paid appointments: **444**

ACADEMIC PROGRAMS

Total full-time tenured or tenure-track faculty (fall 2003): **61**, Total part-time faculty (fall 2003): **57**
Areas of specialization: curriculum and instruction, education administration and supervision, education policy, educational psychology, elementary teacher education, higher education administration, secondary teacher education, special education, student counseling and personnel services.
Professional development/partnership school(s) are used by students in all of the teaching programs.
During their internships, peer groups of students meet regularly to discuss instructional techniques in all of the teaching programs.
All of the students in their internships are mentored.
Courses that prepare teachers to pass the National Board of Professional Teaching Standards are not offered.
Teacher preparation programs: Four-year baccalaureate-degree program leading to initial licensure that includes either a major or minor in education and practice teaching. Five-year program leading to initial licensure that results in a baccalaureate degree (with a major or minor in education) plus a master's degree and includes practice teaching. Master's program preparing college graduates for initial licensure; includes practice teaching. Alternative program for college graduates leading to provisional licensure.
The education program is currently accredited by the National Council for Accreditation of Teacher Education.

LICENSING TEST

Pass rate on state's teacher licensing test for 2002-2003: 89%

State average pass rate: 91%

Boston University

- 2 Sherborn Street, Boston, MA 02215
- Website: http://www.bu.edu/education/
- Private
- Degrees offered: bachelor's, master's, education specialist, Ed.D.
- Overall rank in the 2005 U.S. News education schools with doctoral programs: 51

ADMISSIONS

Admissions phone number: **(617) 353-4237**
Admissions email address: *sedgrad@bu.edu*
Application fee: **$65**
Test requirements: **GRE or MAT**

Test of English as Foreign Language (TOEFL) is required for international students.
Minimum TOEFL score required for paper test: 550
Minimum TOEFL score required for computer test: 213

Fall 2003
Acceptance rate for master's degree programs: 74%
Acceptance rate for education specialist degree programs: 80%
Acceptance rate for doctoral programs: 46%
Average GRE verbal: 516, Average GRE quantitative: 598, Average GRE analytical: 616, Average MAT: 54
Total 2003 enrollment: 510
Master's degree enrollment: 377
    Teacher preparation program enrollment (master's): 187
Education specialist degree enrollment: 6
Doctoral degree enrollment: 127

FINANCIAL INFORMATION
Financial aid phone number: (617) 353-4238
Tuition, 2003-2004 academic year: Full-time: $28,512; Part-time: $446/credit hour
Fees: $274, Room and board: $10,312, Books and supplies: $1,045, Miscellaneous expenses: $3,088
Number of fellowships awarded to graduate students during the 2003-2004 academic year: 10
Number of teaching assistant positions: 27
Number of research assistant positions: 10
Number of other paid appointments: 8

ACADEMIC PROGRAMS
Total full-time tenured or tenure-track faculty (fall 2003): 25, Total part-time faculty (fall 2003): 51
Areas of specialization: curriculum and instruction, education administration and supervision, education policy, elementary teacher education, higher education administration, secondary teacher education, special education, student counseling and personnel services.
Professional development/partnership school(s) are used by students in all of the teaching programs.
During their internships, peer groups of students meet regularly to discuss instructional techniques in all of the teaching programs.
All of the students in their internships are mentored.
Courses that prepare teachers to pass the National Board of Professional Teaching Standards are not offered.
Teacher preparation programs: Four-year baccalaureate-degree program leading to initial licensure that includes either a major or minor in education and practice teaching. Master's program preparing college graduates for initial licensure; includes practice teaching.

LICENSING TEST
Pass rate on state's teacher licensing test for 2002-2003: 95%
State average pass rate: 91%

Bridgewater State College

- Park Avenue, Bridgewater, MA 02325
- **Website:** http://www.bridgew.edu/gce
- Public
- **Degrees offered:** bachelor's, master's, education specialist

ADMISSIONS
Admissions phone number: (508) 531-1300
Admissions email address: *gradschool@bridgew.edu*
Application fee: $50
Fall 2005 application deadline: 6/1
Test requirements: **GRE**
Test of English as Foreign Language (TOEFL) is required for international students.
Minimum TOEFL score required for paper test: 550
Minimum TOEFL score required for computer test: 213

FINANCIAL INFORMATION
Financial aid phone number: (508) 531-2685
Tuition, 2003-2004 academic year: Full-time in-state: $227/credit hour; out-of-state: $451/credit hour, Part-time in-state: $227/credit hour; out-of-state: $227/credit hour

ACADEMIC PROGRAMS
Areas of specialization: curriculum and instruction, education administration and supervision, education policy, educational psychology, elementary teacher education, higher education administration, secondary teacher education, special education, student counseling and personnel services.
Professional development/partnership school(s) are used by students in some of the teaching programs.
During their internships, peer groups of students meet regularly to discuss instructional techniques in all of the teaching programs.
All of the students in their internships are mentored.
Courses that prepare teachers to pass the National Board of Professional Teaching Standards are offered.
Teacher preparation programs: Four-year baccalaureate-degree program leading to initial licensure that includes either a major or minor in education and practice teaching. Five-year program leading to initial licensure that results in a baccalaureate degree (with a major or minor in education) plus graduate credit and includes practice teaching. Five-year program leading to initial licensure that results in a baccalaureate degree (with a major or minor in education) plus a master's degree and includes practice teaching. Master's program preparing college graduates for initial licensure; includes practice teaching.
The education program is currently accredited by the National Council for Accreditation of Teacher Education.

LICENSING TEST

Pass rate on state's teacher licensing test for 2002-2003: 100%
State average pass rate: 91%

Cambridge College

- 1000 Massachusetts Avenue, Cambridge, MA 02138
- **Website:** http://www.cambridgecollege.edu/
- **Private**

LICENSING TEST

Pass rate on state's teacher licensing test for 2002-2003: **78%**
State average pass rate: 91%

Clark University

- 950 Maine Street, Worcester, MA 01610-1477
- **Website:** http://www.clarku.edu/
- **Private**

LICENSING TEST

Pass rate on state's teacher licensing test for 2002-2003: **81%**
State average pass rate: 91%

College of Our Lady of the Elms

- 291 Springfield Street, Chicopee, MA 01013
- **Website:** http://www.elms.edu
- **Private**
- **Degrees offered:** bachelor's, master's

ADMISSIONS

Admissions phone number: **(800) 255-3567**
Admissions email address: *admissions@elms.edu*
Application fee: **$30**
Fall 2005 application deadline: **rolling**
Test of English as Foreign Language (TOEFL) is required for international students.
Minimum TOEFL score required for paper test: **550**

Fall 2003

Total 2003 enrollment: **125**
Master's degree enrollment: **106**
  Teacher preparation program enrollment (master's): **106**
Education specialist degree enrollment: **19**

FINANCIAL INFORMATION

Financial aid phone number: **(413) 265-2340**
Tuition, 2003-2004 academic year: Full-time: **$450/credit hour**; Part-time: **$450/credit hour**
Fees: **$40**

ACADEMIC PROGRAMS

Total full-time tenured or tenure-track faculty (fall 2003): **7**
Areas of specialization: curriculum and instruction, elementary teacher education, secondary teacher education, special education.
Professional development/partnership school(s) are used by students in none of the teaching programs.
During their internships, peer groups of students meet regularly to discuss instructional techniques in all of the teaching programs.
All of the students in their internships are mentored.
Courses that prepare teachers to pass the National Board of Professional Teaching Standards are not offered.
Teacher preparation programs: Four-year baccalaureate-degree program leading to initial licensure that includes either a major or minor in education and practice teaching. Master's program preparing college graduates for initial licensure; includes practice teaching.

LICENSING TEST

Pass rate on state's teacher licensing test for 2002-2003: 100%
State average pass rate: 91%

Curry College

- 1071 Blue Hill Avenue, Milton, MA 02186-2395
- **Website:** http://www.curry.edu
- **Private**
- **Degrees offered:** master's

ADMISSIONS

Admissions phone number: **(617) 333-2243**
Application website: *http://www.curry.edu/continuing_education*
Application fee: **$50**
Fall 2005 application deadline: **rolling**
Test of English as Foreign Language (TOEFL) is required for international students.

FINANCIAL INFORMATION

Financial aid phone number: **(617) 333-2146**
Tuition, 2003-2004 academic year: **$365/credit hour**
Number of fellowships awarded to graduate students during the 2003-2004 academic year: **0**
Number of teaching assistant positions: **0**
Number of research assistant positions: **0**
Number of other paid appointments: **0**

ACADEMIC PROGRAMS

Areas of specialization: education administration and supervision, elementary teacher education, special education.

LICENSING TEST

Pass rate on state's teacher licensing test for 2002-2003: 23%
State average pass rate: 91%

Eastern Nazarene College

- 23 E. Elm Avenue, Quincy, MA 02170
- **Website:** http://www.enc.edu
- **Private**
- **Degrees offered:** bachelor's, master's

ADMISSIONS
Admissions phone number: **(617) 745-6826**
Admissions email address: *cakridac@enc.edu*
Application website:
  http://www.enc.edu/grad/admission.html#app
Application fee: **$35**
Fall 2005 application deadline: **rolling**
Test of English as Foreign Language (TOEFL) is required
  for international students.
Minimum TOEFL score required for paper test: **500**

Fall 2003
Total 2003 enrollment: **99**
Master's degree enrollment: **99**
  Teacher preparation program enrollment (master's): **41**

FINANCIAL INFORMATION
Financial aid phone number: **(617) 745-3869**
Tuition, 2003-2004 academic year: **$6,750**
Fees: **$125**

ACADEMIC PROGRAMS
Total full-time tenured or tenure-track faculty (fall 2003):.5
  Total part-time faculty (fall 2003): **0**
Areas of specialization: curriculum and instruction, ele-
  mentary teacher education, higher education administra-
  tion, secondary teacher education, special education.
Professional development/partnership school(s) are used
  by students in some of the teaching programs.
During their internships, peer groups of students meet
  regularly to discuss instructional techniques in all of the
  teaching programs.
All of the students in their internships are mentored.
Courses that prepare teachers to pass the National Board of
  Professional Teaching Standards are offered.
Teacher preparation programs: Four-year baccalaureate-
  degree program leading to initial licensure that includes
  either a major or minor in education and practice teaching. Master's program preparing college graduates for
  initial licensure; includes practice teaching.

LICENSING TEST
Pass rate on state's teacher licensing test for 2002-2003:
  65%
State average pass rate: **91%**

Emmanuel College

- 400 The Fenway, Boston, MA 02115
- **Website:** http://www.emmanuel.edu/
- **Private**

LICENSING TEST
Pass rate on state's teacher licensing test for 2002-2003: **67%**
State average pass rate: **91%**

Endicott College

- 376 Hale Street, Beverly, MA 01915
- **Website:** http://www.endicott.edu/
- **Private**

LICENSING TEST
Pass rate on state's teacher licensing test for 2002-2003:
  100%
State average pass rate: **91%**

Framingham State College

- 100 State Street, P.O. Box 9101, Framingham, MA 01701
- **Website:** http://www.framingham.edu/
- **Public**

LICENSING TEST
Pass rate on state's teacher licensing test for 2002-2003:
  100%
State average pass rate: **91%**

Fitchburg State College

- 160 Pearl Street, Fitchburg, MA 01420-2697
- **Website:** http://www.fsc.edu
- **Public**
- **Degrees offered:** bachelor's, master's

ADMISSIONS
Admissions phone number: **(978) 665-3144**
Admissions email address: *admissions@fsc.edu*
Application website: *http://www.fsc.edu/admissions*
Application fee: **$25**
Fall 2005 application deadline: **rolling**
Test requirements: **GRE or MAT**
Test of English as Foreign Language (TOEFL) is required
  for international students.
Minimum TOEFL score required for paper test: **550**
Minimum TOEFL score required for computer test: **213**

Fall 2003
Total 2003 enrollment: 789
Master's degree enrollment: 789

FINANCIAL INFORMATION
Financial aid phone number: (978) 665-3156
Tuition, 2003-2004 academic year: Full-time in-state:
$150/credit hour; out-of-state: $150/credit hour, Part-time
in-state: $150/credit hour; out-of-state: $150/credit hour
Fees: $72/credit hour, Room and board: $5,000, Books and
supplies: $300, Miscellaneous expenses: $2,000

ACADEMIC PROGRAMS
Areas of specialization: education administration and
supervision, elementary teacher education, higher education administration, secondary teacher education, special
education, student counseling and personnel services,
teacher education.
Professional development/partnership school(s) are used
by students in some of the teaching programs.
During their internships, peer groups of students meet
regularly to discuss instructional techniques in some of
the teaching programs.
All of the students in their internships are mentored.
Courses that prepare teachers to pass the National Board of
Professional Teaching Standards are not offered.
Teacher preparation programs: Four-year baccalaureate-
degree program leading to initial licensure that includes
either a major or minor in education and practice teach-
ing. Master's program preparing college graduates for
initial licensure; includes practice teaching.
The education program is currently accredited by the
National Council for Accreditation of Teacher Education.

LICENSING TEST
Pass rate on state's teacher licensing test for 2002-2003: **98%**
State average pass rate: 91%

Gordon College

■ **255 Grapevine Road, Wenham, MA 01984**
■ **Website:** http://www.gordon.edu/med
■ **Private**
■ **Degrees offered:** bachelor's, master's

ADMISSIONS
Admissions phone number: **(978) 867-4322**
Admissions email address: *lwells@gordon.edu*
Application fee: $40
Fall 2005 application deadline: **rolling**
Test of English as Foreign Language (TOEFL) is required
for international students.
Minimum TOEFL score required for paper test: **500**

Fall 2003
Total 2003 enrollment: 60
Master's degree enrollment: 60
Teacher preparation program enrollment (master's): 60

FINANCIAL INFORMATION
Tuition, 2003-2004 academic year: $280/credit hour
Fees: $35

ACADEMIC PROGRAMS
Areas of specialization: curriculum and instruction, education administration and supervision, education policy,
special education.
Teacher preparation programs: Master's degree in education, including internship/practice teaching and preparation for initial licensure.

LICENSING TEST
Pass rate on state's teacher licensing test for 2002-2003:
89%
State average pass rate: 91%

Harvard University

■ **Appian Way, Cambridge, MA 02138**
■ **Website:** http://www.gse.harvard.edu
■ **Private**
■ **Degrees offered:** master's, Ed.D.
■ **Overall rank in the 2005 U.S. News education schools
with doctoral programs:** 1
■ **Overall rank in the 2005 U.S. News education school
specialty rankings:** administration/supervision: 1,
education policy: 2, educational psychology: 10, higher
education administration: 8

ADMISSIONS
Admissions phone number: **(617) 495-3414**
Admissions email address: *gseadmissions@harvard.edu*
Application website: *http://www.gse.harvard.edu/admissions/*
Fall 2005 application deadline: 1/3
Test requirements: **GRE or MAT**
Test of English as Foreign Language (TOEFL) is required
for international students.
Minimum TOEFL score required for paper test: 600
Minimum TOEFL score required for computer test: 250

Fall 2003
Acceptance rate for master's degree programs: 65%
Acceptance rate for doctoral programs: 14%
Average GRE verbal: 579, Average GRE quantitative: 642,
Average GRE analytical: 614, Average MAT: 64
Total 2003 enrollment: 1,077
Master's degree enrollment: 659
Teacher preparation program enrollment (master's): 109
Doctoral degree enrollment: 418

FINANCIAL INFORMATION
Financial aid phone number: (617) 495-3416
Tuition, 2003-2004 academic year: Full-time: $26,628;
Part-time: $13,314
Fees: $2,338, Room and board: $13,000, Books and sup-
plies: $1,786, Miscellaneous expenses: $4,624

Number of fellowships awarded to graduate students during the 2003-2004 academic year: 162
Number of teaching assistant positions: 151
Number of research assistant positions: 37
Number of other paid appointments: 26

ACADEMIC PROGRAMS

Total full-time tenured or tenure-track faculty (fall 2003): 40, Total part-time faculty (fall 2003): 40

Areas of specialization: curriculum and instruction, education administration and supervision, education policy, educational psychology, higher education administration, secondary teacher education.

Professional development/partnership school(s) are used by students in all of the teaching programs.

During their internships, peer groups of students meet regularly to discuss instructional techniques in all of the teaching programs.

All of the students in their internships are mentored.

Courses that prepare teachers to pass the National Board of Professional Teaching Standards are offered.

Teacher preparation programs: Master's degree in education, including internship/practice teaching and preparation for initial licensure.

LICENSING TEST

Pass rate on state's teacher licensing test for 2002-2003: 93%

State average pass rate: 91%

Lesley University

- 29 Everett Street, Cambridge, MA 02138-2790
- **Website:** http://www.lesley.edu/education
- **Private**
- **Degrees offered:** bachelor's, master's, education specialist, Ph.D.

ADMISSIONS

Admissions phone number: (888) 537-5398
Admissions email address: *learn@lesley.edu*
Application website:
   http://www.lesley.edu/grad_admiss/printapp.html
Application fee: $50
Fall 2005 application deadline: **rolling**
Test requirements: **GRE or MAT**
Test of English as Foreign Language (TOEFL) is required for international students.
Minimum TOEFL score required for paper test: 550
Minimum TOEFL score required for computer test: 213

Fall 2003
Acceptance rate for master's degree programs: 95%
Acceptance rate for education specialist degree programs: 100%
Acceptance rate for doctoral programs: 39%
Average MAT: 47
Total 2003 enrollment: 4,433

Master's degree enrollment: 4,387
   Teacher preparation program enrollment (master's): 4,306
Education specialist degree enrollment: 4
Doctoral degree enrollment: 42

FINANCIAL INFORMATION

Financial aid phone number: (617) 349-8710
Tuition, 2003-2004 academic year: Full-time: **$565/credit hour**; Part-time: **$370/credit hour**
Fees: **$100**, Books and supplies: **$585**, Miscellaneous expenses: **$2,205**
Number of research assistant positions: 6

ACADEMIC PROGRAMS

Total full-time tenured or tenure-track faculty (fall 2003): 74, Total part-time faculty (fall 2003): 365

Areas of specialization: curriculum and instruction, education administration and supervision, education policy, educational psychology, elementary teacher education, secondary teacher education, special education, student counseling and personnel services.

Professional development/partnership school(s) are used by students in some of the teaching programs.

During their internships, peer groups of students meet regularly to discuss instructional techniques in all of the teaching programs.

All of the students in their internships are mentored.

Courses that prepare teachers to pass the National Board of Professional Teaching Standards are not offered.

Teacher preparation programs: Four-year baccalaureate-degree program leading to initial licensure that includes either a major or minor in education and practice teaching. Five-year program leading to initial licensure that results in a baccalaureate degree (with a major or minor in education) plus a master's degree and includes practice teaching. Master's program preparing college graduates for initial licensure; includes practice teaching.

LICENSING TEST

Pass rate on state's teacher licensing test for 2002-2003: 90%

State average pass rate: 91%

Mount Holyoke College

- 50 College Street, South Hadley, MA 01075
- **Website:** http://www.mtholyoke.edu
- **Private**

LICENSING TEST

Pass rate on state's teacher licensing test for 2002-2003: 94%

State average pass rate: 91%

Northeastern University

- 360 Huntington Avenue - 50 Nightingale Hall, Boston, MA 02115
- Website: http://www.education.neu.edu
- Private
- Degrees offered: bachelor's, master's

ADMISSIONS

Admissions phone number: (617) 373-2630
Admissions email address: *a.irving@neu.edu*
Application website: *http://www.applyweb.com/aw?neuga*
Application fee: $50
Fall 2005 application deadline: 4/1
Test requirements: GRE or MAT
Test of English as Foreign Language (TOEFL) is required for international students.
Minimum TOEFL score required for paper test: 550
Minimum TOEFL score required for computer test: 213

Fall 2003
Acceptance rate for master's degree programs: 69%
Average GRE verbal: 488, Average GRE quantitative: 585, Average MAT: 21
Total 2003 enrollment: 92
Master's degree enrollment: 92
  Teacher preparation program enrollment (master's): 80

FINANCIAL INFORMATION

Financial aid phone number: (617) 373-4153
Tuition, 2003-2004 academic year: Full-time: $790/credit hour; Part-time: $790/credit hour
Fees: $180, Room and board: $9,500, Books and supplies: $1,000, Miscellaneous expenses: $3,700
Number of fellowships awarded to graduate students during the 2003-2004 academic year: 13

ACADEMIC PROGRAMS

Total full-time tenured or tenure-track faculty (fall 2003): 26, Total part-time faculty (fall 2003): 11
Areas of specialization: elementary teacher education, secondary teacher education, special education.
Professional development/partnership school(s) are used by students in all of the teaching programs.
During their internships, peer groups of students meet regularly to discuss instructional techniques in all of the teaching programs.
All of the students in their internships are mentored.
Teacher preparation programs: Four-year baccalaureate-degree program leading to initial licensure that includes either a major or minor in education and practice teaching. Five-year program leading to initial licensure that results in a baccalaureate degree (with a major or minor in education) plus graduate credit and includes practice teaching. Five-year program leading to initial licensure that results in a baccalaureate degree (with a major or minor in education) plus a master's degree and includes practice teaching. Master's program preparing college graduates for initial licensure; includes practice teaching. Alternative program for college graduates leading to provisional licensure.

LICENSING TEST

Pass rate on state's teacher licensing test for 2002-2003: 97%
State average pass rate: 91%

Regis College

- 235 Wellesley Street, Weston, MA 02493-1571
- Website: http://www.regiscollege.edu/
- Private

Salem State College

- 352 Lafayette Street, Salem, MA 01970
- Website: http://www.salemstate.edu/graduate
- Public
- Degrees offered: bachelor's, master's

ADMISSIONS

Admissions phone number: (978) 542-6323
Admissions email address: *graduate@salemstate.edu*
Application fee: $25
Fall 2005 application deadline: 6/1
Test of English as Foreign Language (TOEFL) is required for international students.
Minimum TOEFL score required for paper test: 500

FINANCIAL INFORMATION

Financial aid phone number: (978) 542-6319
Tuition, 2003-2004 academic year: Part-time in-state: $55/credit hour; out-of-state: $55/credit hour
Fees: $55/credit hour

ACADEMIC PROGRAMS

Areas of specialization: curriculum and instruction, education administration and supervision, education policy, educational psychology, elementary teacher education, higher education administration, secondary teacher education, special education, student counseling and personnel services, teacher education.
Professional development/partnership school(s) are used by students in all of the teaching programs.
During their internships, peer groups of students meet regularly to discuss instructional techniques in some of the teaching programs.
All of the students in their internships are mentored.
Courses that prepare teachers to pass the National Board of Professional Teaching Standards are offered.
Teacher preparation programs: Four-year baccalaureate-degree program leading to initial licensure that includes either a major or minor in education and practice teach-

ing. Master's program preparing college graduates for initial licensure; includes practice teaching. Alternative program for college graduates leading to provisional licensure.

The education program is currently accredited by the National Council for Accreditation of Teacher Education.

LICENSING TEST
Pass rate on state's teacher licensing test for 2002-2003: 93%
State average pass rate: 91%

Simmons College

- 300 The Fenway, Boston, MA 02115
- Website: http://www.simmons.edu/academics/graduate/
- Private

LICENSING TEST
Pass rate on state's teacher licensing test for 2002-2003: 96%
State average pass rate: 91%

Smith College

- 7 College Lane, Northampton, MA 01063
- Website: http://www.smith.edu/educ/
- Private

LICENSING TEST
Pass rate on state's teacher licensing test for 2002-2003: 100%
State average pass rate: 91%

Springfield College

- 263 Alden Street, Springfield, MA 01109
- Website: http://www.spfldcol.edu/
- Private

LICENSING TEST
Pass rate on state's teacher licensing test for 2002-2003: 98%
State average pass rate: 91%

Suffolk University

- 8 Ashburton Place, Boston, MA 02108
- Website: http://www.suffolk.edu/
- Private

Tufts University

- Tufts University, Medford, MA 02155
- Website: http://ase.tufts.edu/GradStudy/programs.htm
- Private

LICENSING TEST
Pass rate on state's teacher licensing test for 2002-2003: 91%
State average pass rate: 91%

University of Massachusetts–Amherst

- Furcolo Hall, 813 North Pleasant Street, Amherst, MA 01003-9308
- Website: http://www.umass.edu/education
- Public
- Degrees offered: master's, Ph.D., Ed.D.
- Overall rank in the 2005 U.S. News education schools with doctoral programs: 51
- Overall rank in the 2005 U.S. News education school specialty rankings: education policy: 21

ADMISSIONS
Admissions phone number: (413) 545-0721
Admissions email address: *gradadm@resgs.umass.edu*
Application website: *http://www.umass.edu/gradschool*
Application fee: $40
Fall 2005 application deadline: 1/15
Test requirements: None
Test of English as Foreign Language (TOEFL) is required for international students.
Minimum TOEFL score required for paper test: 550
Minimum TOEFL score required for computer test: 213

Fall 2003
Acceptance rate for master's degree programs: 55%
Acceptance rate for doctoral programs: 42%
Average GRE verbal: 519, Average GRE quantitative: 566, Average GRE analytical: 585
Total 2003 enrollment: 866
Master's degree enrollment: 501
    Teacher preparation program enrollment (master's): 346
Doctoral degree enrollment: 365

FINANCIAL INFORMATION
Financial aid phone number: (413) 577-0555
Tuition, 2003-2004 academic year: Full-time in-state: $2,640; out-of-state: $9,937, Part-time in-state: $110/credit hour; out-of-state: $414/credit hour
Fees: $5,113, Room and board: $5,300, Books and supplies: $900, Miscellaneous expenses: $2,300

Number of fellowships awarded to graduate students during the 2003-2004 academic year: 17
Number of teaching assistant positions: 166
Number of research assistant positions: 145
Number of other paid appointments: 63

ACADEMIC PROGRAMS
Total full-time tenured or tenure-track faculty (fall 2003): 50, Total part-time faculty (fall 2003): 18
Areas of specialization: curriculum and instruction, education administration and supervision, education policy, educational psychology, elementary teacher education, higher education administration, secondary teacher education, special education, student counseling and personnel services.
Professional development/partnership school(s) are used by students in some of the teaching programs.
During their internships, peer groups of students meet regularly to discuss instructional techniques in some of the teaching programs.
All of the students in their internships are mentored.
Courses that prepare teachers to pass the National Board of Professional Teaching Standards are not offered.
Teacher preparation programs: Master's degree in education, including internship/practice teaching and preparation for initial licensure. Education minor for undergraduate students. Alternative program for college graduates leading to provisional licensure.
The education program is currently accredited by the National Council for Accreditation of Teacher Education.

LICENSING TEST
Pass rate on state's teacher licensing test for 2002-2003: 97%
State average pass rate: 91%

University of Massachusetts–Boston

■ 100 Morrissey Blvd, Boston, MA 02125-3393
■ Website: http://www.umb.edu
■ Public

LICENSING TEST
Pass rate on state's teacher licensing test for 2002-2003: 95%
State average pass rate: 91%

University of Massachusetts– Dartmouth

■ 285 Old Westport Road, N Dartmouth, MA 02747-2300
■ Website: http://www.umassd.edu/graduate
■ Public
■ Degrees offered: master's

ADMISSIONS
Admissions phone number: (508) 999-8604
Admissions email address: *graduate@umassd.edu*
Application website:
   http://www.umassd.edu/graduate/prospects/waystoapply.cfm
Application fee: $35
Fall 2005 application deadline: 4/20
Test requirements: GRE or MAT
Test of English as Foreign Language (TOEFL) is required for international students.
Minimum TOEFL score required for paper test: 500
Minimum TOEFL score required for computer test: 173

Fall 2003
Acceptance rate for master's degree programs: 88%
Total 2003 enrollment: 38
Master's degree enrollment: 38
   Teacher preparation program enrollment (master's): 38

FINANCIAL INFORMATION
Financial aid phone number: (508) 999-8632
Tuition, 2003-2004 academic year: Full-time in-state: $7,267; out-of-state: $15,629, Part-time in-state: $303/credit hour; out-of-state: $651/credit hour
Room and board: $7,000, Books and supplies: $600, Miscellaneous expenses: $2,000

ACADEMIC PROGRAMS
Total full-time tenured or tenure-track faculty (fall 2003): 4
   Total part-time faculty (fall 2003): 4
Areas of specialization: elementary teacher education, secondary teacher education.
Professional development/partnership school(s) are used by students in some of the teaching programs.
During their internships, peer groups of students meet regularly to discuss instructional techniques in some of the teaching programs.
All of the students in their internships are mentored.
Courses that prepare teachers to pass the National Board of Professional Teaching Standards are not offered.

LICENSING TEST
Pass rate on state's teacher licensing test for 2002-2003: 79%
State average pass rate: 91%

University of Massachusetts–Lowell

- 510 O'Leary Library, 61 Wilder Street, Lowell, MA 01854
- **Website:** http://www.uml.edu/grad/
- **Public**
- **Degrees offered:** master's, Ed.D.

ADMISSIONS

Admissions phone number: **(978) 934-4601**
Admissions email address: *donald_pierson@uml.edu*
Application website: *http://gse.uml.edu*
Application fee: **$20**
Fall 2005 application deadline: **rolling**
Test requirements: **GRE**
Test of English as Foreign Language (TOEFL) is required for international students.
Minimum TOEFL score required for paper test: **550**
Minimum TOEFL score required for computer test: **173**

Fall 2003
Acceptance rate for master's degree programs: **70%**
Acceptance rate for doctoral programs: **67%**
Average GRE verbal: **506**, Average GRE quantitative: **547**, Average GRE analytical: **552**, Average MAT: **55**
Total 2003 enrollment: **452**
Master's degree enrollment: **252**
  Teacher preparation program enrollment (master's): **190**
Doctoral degree enrollment: **200**

FINANCIAL INFORMATION

Financial aid phone number: **(978) 934-4220**
Tuition, 2003-2004 academic year: Full-time in-state: **$91/credit hour**; out-of-state: **$357/credit hour**, Part-time in-state: **$91/credit hour**; out-of-state: **$357/credit hour**
Fees: **$244/credit hour**
Number of fellowships awarded to graduate students during the 2003-2004 academic year: **11**
Number of teaching assistant positions: **4**
Number of research assistant positions: **6**
Number of other paid appointments: **2**

ACADEMIC PROGRAMS

Total full-time tenured or tenure-track faculty (fall 2003): **17**
  Total part-time faculty (fall 2003): **7**
Areas of specialization: curriculum and instruction, education administration and supervision, elementary teacher education, higher education administration, secondary teacher education.
Professional development/partnership school(s) are used by students in some of the teaching programs.
During their internships, peer groups of students meet regularly to discuss instructional techniques in some of the teaching programs.
All of the students in their internships are mentored.
Courses that prepare teachers to pass the National Board of Professional Teaching Standards are not offered.

Teacher preparation programs: Master's degree in education, including internship/practice teaching and preparation for initial licensure.
The education program is currently accredited by the National Council for Accreditation of Teacher Education.

LICENSING TEST

Pass rate on state's teacher licensing test for 2002-2003: **100%**
State average pass rate: **91%**

Westfield State College

- Western Avenue, Westfield, MA 01086
- **Website:** http://www.wsc.ma.edu/education/
- **Public**

LICENSING TEST

Pass rate on state's teacher licensing test for 2002-2003: **98%**
State average pass rate: **91%**

Wheelock College

- 200 The Riverway, Boston, MA 02215
- **Website:** http://www.wheelock.edu
- **Private**
- **Degrees offered:** master's

ADMISSIONS

Admissions phone number: **(617) 879-2206**
Admissions email address: *graduate@wheelock.edu*
Application website: *http://www.wheelock.edu/gadm/gadm_app.htm*
Application fee: **$40**
Fall 2005 application deadline: **8/15**
Test requirements: **None**
Test of English as Foreign Language (TOEFL) is required for international students.
Minimum TOEFL score required for paper test: **550**
Minimum TOEFL score required for computer test: **173**

Fall 2003
Acceptance rate for master's degree programs: **78%**
Total 2003 enrollment: **355**
Master's degree enrollment: **355**
  Teacher preparation program enrollment (master's): **229**

FINANCIAL INFORMATION

Financial aid phone number: **(617) 879-2208**
Tuition, 2003-2004 academic year: Full-time: **$680/credit hour**; Part-time: **$680/credit hour**
Room and board: **$12,150**, Books and supplies: **$870**, Miscellaneous expenses: **$565**
Number of fellowships awarded to graduate students during the 2003-2004 academic year: **0**

Number of teaching assistant positions: o
Number of research assistant positions: o
Number of other paid appointments: 1

ACADEMIC PROGRAMS

Total full-time tenured or tenure-track faculty (fall 2003): 14, Total part-time faculty (fall 2003): 10

Areas of specialization: curriculum and instruction, education administration and supervision, education policy, educational psychology, elementary teacher education, special education.

Professional development/partnership school(s) are used by students in some of the teaching programs.

During their internships, peer groups of students meet regularly to discuss instructional techniques in some of the teaching programs.

All of the students in their internships are mentored.

Courses that prepare teachers to pass the National Board of Professional Teaching Standards are offered.

Teacher preparation programs: Four-year baccalaureate-degree program leading to initial licensure that includes either a major or minor in education and practice teaching. Master's program preparing college graduates for initial licensure; includes practice teaching. Alternative program for college graduates leading to provisional licensure.

The education program is currently accredited by the National Council for Accreditation of Teacher Education.

LICENSING TEST

Pass rate on state's teacher licensing test for 2002-2003: 66%

State average pass rate: 91%

Worcester State College

■ **486 Chandler Street, Worcester, MA 01602**
■ **Website:** http://wwwfac.worcester.edu/graduate/
■ **Public**

LICENSING TEST

Pass rate on state's teacher licensing test for 2002-2003: 99%

State average pass rate: 91%

MICHIGAN

Andrews University

- **School of Education, Berrien Springs, MI 49104-0100**
- **Website:** http://www.andrews.edu/
- **Private**
- **Degrees offered:** bachelor's, master's, education specialist, Ph.D., Ed.D.

ADMISSIONS

Admissions phone number: **(800) 253-2874**
Admissions email address: *enroll@andrews.edu*
Application website: *http://connect.andrews.edu/apply/*
Application fee: **$40**
Fall 2005 application deadline: **rolling**
Test requirements: **GRE**
Test of English as Foreign Language (TOEFL) is required for international students.
Minimum TOEFL score required for paper test: **550**
Minimum TOEFL score required for computer test: **213**

Fall 2003

Acceptance rate for master's degree programs: **70%**
Acceptance rate for education specialist degree programs: **80%**
Acceptance rate for doctoral programs: **72%**
Average GRE verbal: **424**, Average GRE quantitative: **443**, Average GRE analytical: **491**
Total 2003 enrollment: **380**
Master's degree enrollment: **145**
   Teacher preparation program enrollment (master's): **44**
Education specialist degree enrollment: **23**
Doctoral degree enrollment: **212**

FINANCIAL INFORMATION

Financial aid phone number: **(269) 471-3334**
Tuition, 2003-2004 academic year: Full-time: **$685/credit hour**; Part-time: **$685/credit hour**
Fees: **$685/credit hour**, Room and board: **$4,750**, Books and supplies: **$1,450**
Number of fellowships awarded to graduate students during the 2003-2004 academic year: **0**
Number of teaching assistant positions: **5**

Number of research assistant positions: **8**
Number of other paid appointments: **19**

ACADEMIC PROGRAMS

Total full-time tenured or tenure-track faculty (fall 2003): **25**, Total part-time faculty (fall 2003): **0**
Areas of specialization: curriculum and instruction, education administration and supervision, educational psychology, elementary teacher education, secondary teacher education, special education, student counseling and personnel services.
Professional development/partnership school(s) are used by students in all of the teaching programs.
During their internships, peer groups of students meet regularly to discuss instructional techniques in all of the teaching programs.
All of the students in their internships are mentored.
Courses that prepare teachers to pass the National Board of Professional Teaching Standards are not offered.
Teacher preparation programs: Four-year baccalaureate-degree program leading to initial licensure that includes either a major or minor in education and practice teaching. Five-year program leading to initial licensure that results in a baccalaureate degree (with a major or minor in education) plus graduate credit and includes practice teaching. Five-year program leading to initial licensure that results in a baccalaureate degree (with a major or minor in education) plus a master's degree and includes practice teaching. Master's program preparing college graduates for initial licensure; includes practice teaching.
The education program is currently accredited by the National Council for Accreditation of Teacher Education.

LICENSING TEST

Pass rate on state's teacher licensing test for 2002-2003: **100%**
State average pass rate: **100%**

Aquinas College

- 1607 Robinson Road SE, Grand Rapids, MI 49506
- Website:
  http://www.aquinas.edu/education/graduate.html
- Private
- Degrees offered: bachelor's, master's

ADMISSIONS
Admissions phone number: (616) 632-2441
Admissions email address: *rademsan@aquinas.edu*
Application website: *http://www.aquinas.edu/education/
  graduate.html*
Application fee: $35
Fall 2005 application deadline: 8/1

Fall 2003
Total 2003 enrollment: 407
Master's degree enrollment: 407
    Teacher preparation program enrollment (master's): 407

FINANCIAL INFORMATION
Financial aid phone number: (616) 632-2895
Tuition, 2003-2004 academic year: Full-time: $386/credit
  hour; Part-time: $386/credit hour
Number of fellowships awarded to graduate students dur-
  ing the 2003-2004 academic year: 0
Number of teaching assistant positions: 0
Number of research assistant positions: 0
Number of other paid appointments: 0

ACADEMIC PROGRAMS
Areas of specialization: elementary teacher education, secondary teacher education.

LICENSING TEST
Pass rate on state's teacher licensing test for 2002-2003:
  100%
State average pass rate: 100%

Central Michigan University

- 105 Warriner, Mount Pleasant, MI 48859
- Website: http://www.ehs.cmich.edu/
- Public

LICENSING TEST
Pass rate on state's teacher licensing test for 2002-2003:
  100%
State average pass rate: 100%

Cornerstone University

- 1001 E. Beltline, NE, Grand Rapids, MI 49525
- Website: http://www.cornerstone.edu
- Private
- Degrees offered: master's

ADMISSIONS
Admissions phone number: (800) 787-9778
Admissions email address: *admissions@cornerstone.edu*
Application website: *http://www.cornerstone.edu/*
Application fee: $25
Fall 2005 application deadline: rolling
Test of English as Foreign Language (TOEFL) is required
  for international students.
Minimum TOEFL score required for paper test: 500
Minimum TOEFL score required for computer test: 173

Fall 2003
Total 2003 enrollment: 15
Master's degree enrollment: 15

FINANCIAL INFORMATION
Financial aid phone number: (616) 222-1424
Tuition, 2003-2004 academic year: Full-time: $555/credit
  hour; Part-time: $555/credit hour
Room and board: $4,518, Books and supplies: $860,
  Miscellaneous expenses: $1,550

LICENSING TEST
Pass rate on state's teacher licensing test for 2002-2003:
  100%
State average pass rate: 100%

Eastern Michigan University

- 310 Porter Building, Ypsilanti, MI 48197
- Website: http://www.gradord.emich.edu
- Public
- Degrees offered: bachelor's, master's, education
  specialist, Ed.D.

ADMISSIONS
Admissions phone number: (734) 487-3400
Admissions email address: *graduate.admissions@emich.edu*
Application website: *http://www.emich.edu/admissions/forms*
Application fee: $25
Fall 2005 application deadline: rolling
Test of English as Foreign Language (TOEFL) is required
  for international students.
Minimum TOEFL score required for paper test: 550
Minimum TOEFL score required for computer test: 213

Fall 2003

Average GRE verbal: 436, Average GRE quantitative: 496, Average GRE analytical: 512

Total 2003 enrollment: 1,054

Master's degree enrollment: 937

    Teacher preparation program enrollment (master's): 591

Education specialist degree enrollment: 36

Doctoral degree enrollment: 81

FINANCIAL INFORMATION

Financial aid phone number: (734) 487-0455

Tuition, 2003-2004 academic year: Full-time in-state: **$270/credit hour**; out-of-state: **$548/credit hour**, Part-time in-state: **$270/credit hour**; out-of-state: **$548/credit hour**

Fees: **$32/credit hour**, Room and board: **$7,480**, Books and supplies: **$900**, Miscellaneous expenses: **$2,500**

Number of fellowships awarded to graduate students during the 2003-2004 academic year: 5

Number of teaching assistant positions: 38

Number of research assistant positions: 0

Number of other paid appointments: 0

ACADEMIC PROGRAMS

Total full-time tenured or tenure-track faculty (fall 2003): 81, Total part-time faculty (fall 2003): 78

Areas of specialization: curriculum and instruction, education administration and supervision, education policy, educational psychology, elementary teacher education, higher education administration, secondary teacher education, special education, student counseling and personnel services, teacher education.

Professional development/partnership school(s) are used by students in some of the teaching programs.

During their internships, peer groups of students meet regularly to discuss instructional techniques in all of the teaching programs.

All of the students in their internships are mentored.

Courses that prepare teachers to pass the National Board of Professional Teaching Standards are not offered.

The education program is currently accredited by the National Council for Accreditation of Teacher Education.

LICENSING TEST

Pass rate on state's teacher licensing test for 2002-2003: 100%

State average pass rate: 100%

Ferris State University

■ **1349 Cramer Circle, Bishop 421, Big Rapids, MI 49307**
■ **Website:** http://www.ferris.edu/education/education
■ **Public**
■ **Degrees offered:** bachelor's, master's

ADMISSIONS

Admissions phone number: (231) 591-5361

Admissions email address: *laker@ferris.edu*

Application website: *http://www.ferris.edu/education/ education/MEDgrad.htm*

Application fee: **$30**

Fall 2005 application deadline: 7/1

Fall 2003

Acceptance rate for master's degree programs: 71%

Total 2003 enrollment: 211

Master's degree enrollment: 211

FINANCIAL INFORMATION

Financial aid phone number: (800) 433-7747

Tuition, 2003-2004 academic year: Full-time in-state: **$309/credit hour**; out-of-state: **$618/credit hour**, Part-time in-state: **$309/credit hour**; out-of-state: **$618/credit hour**

Room and board: **$6,326**, Books and supplies: **$1,000**, Miscellaneous expenses: **$1,926**

ACADEMIC PROGRAMS

Total full-time tenured or tenure-track faculty (fall 2003): 14

Areas of specialization: curriculum and instruction, education administration and supervision, elementary teacher education, higher education administration, secondary teacher education, special education, teacher education.

Professional development/partnership school(s) are used by students in all of the teaching programs.

During their internships, peer groups of students meet regularly to discuss instructional techniques in all of the teaching programs.

All of the students in their internships are mentored.

Courses that prepare teachers to pass the National Board of Professional Teaching Standards are not offered.

Teacher preparation programs: Four-year baccalaureate-degree program leading to initial licensure that includes either a major or minor in education and practice teaching. Master's program preparing college graduates for initial licensure; includes practice teaching. Alternative program for college graduates leading to provisional licensure.

LICENSING TEST

Pass rate on state's teacher licensing test for 2002-2003: 100%

State average pass rate: 100%

Grand Valley State University

■ **301 W. Fulton, Grand Rapids, MI 49504**
■ **Website:** http://www.gvsu.edu
■ **Public**
■ **Degrees offered:** bachelor's, master's

ADMISSIONS

Admissions phone number: (616) 331-2025

Admissions email address: *go2gvsu@gvsu.edu*
Application website: *http://www.admissions.gvsu.edu*
Application fee: **$30**
Fall 2005 application deadline: **rolling**
Test requirements: **GRE**
Test of English as Foreign Language (TOEFL) is required for international students.
Minimum TOEFL score required for computer test: **213**

Fall 2003
Acceptance rate for master's degree programs: **94%**
Average GRE verbal: **506**, Average GRE quantitative: **664**, Average GRE analytical: **717**
Total 2003 enrollment: **1,278**
Master's degree enrollment: **1,278**
    Teacher preparation program enrollment (master's): **1,024**

FINANCIAL INFORMATION
Financial aid phone number: **(616) 331-3234**
Tuition, 2003-2004 academic year: Full-time in-state: **$270/credit hour**; out-of-state: **$520/credit hour**
Room and board: **$2,414**, Books and supplies: **$800**
Number of research assistant positions: **48**

ACADEMIC PROGRAMS
Total full-time tenured or tenure-track faculty (fall 2003): **33**, Total part-time faculty (fall 2003): **68**
Areas of specialization: education administration and supervision, elementary teacher education, secondary teacher education, special education, student counseling and personnel services.
Professional development/partnership school(s) are used by students in some of the teaching programs.
During their internships, peer groups of students meet regularly to discuss instructional techniques in some of the teaching programs.
All of the students in their internships are mentored.
Teacher preparation programs: Four-year baccalaureate-degree program leading to initial licensure that includes either a major or minor in education and practice teaching. Five-year program leading to initial licensure that results in a baccalaureate degree (with a major or minor in education) plus graduate credit and includes practice teaching. Five-year program leading to initial licensure that results in a baccalaureate degree (with a major or minor in education) plus a master's degree and includes practice teaching. Master's program preparing college graduates for initial licensure; includes practice teaching.
The education program is currently accredited by the National Council for Accreditation of Teacher Education.

LICENSING TEST
Pass rate on state's teacher licensing test for 2002-2003: **100%**
State average pass rate: **100%**

Madonna University

■ **36600 Schoolcraft Road, Livonia, MI 48150**
■ **Website:** http://www.munet.edu/
■ **Private**

LICENSING TEST
Pass rate on state's teacher licensing test for 2002-2003: **100%**
State average pass rate: **100%**

Marygrove College

■ **8425 West McNichols Road, Detroit, MI 48221**
■ **Website:** http://www.marygrove.edu
■ **Private**
■ **Degrees offered:** bachelor's, master's

ADMISSIONS
Admissions phone number: **(313) 927-1390**
Admissions email address: *info@marygrove.edu*
Application website: *http://www.marygrove.edu/graduate/gradapp.html*
Application fee: **$25**
Fall 2005 application deadline: **rolling**
Test of English as Foreign Language (TOEFL) is required for international students.
Minimum TOEFL score required for paper test: **500**

Fall 2003
Total 2003 enrollment: **4,590**
Master's degree enrollment: **4,590**
    Teacher preparation program enrollment (master's): **4,582**

FINANCIAL INFORMATION
Financial aid phone number: **(313) 927-1245**
Tuition, 2003-2004 academic year: **$446/credit hour**
Room and board: **$5,800**

ACADEMIC PROGRAMS
Total full-time tenured or tenure-track faculty (fall 2003): **14**, Total part-time faculty (fall 2003): **32**
Teacher preparation programs: Four-year baccalaureate-degree program leading to initial licensure that includes either a major or minor in education and practice teaching. Master's program preparing college graduates for initial licensure; includes practice teaching.
The education program is currently accredited by the National Council for Accreditation of Teacher Education.

LICENSING TEST
Pass rate on state's teacher licensing test for 2002-2003: **100%**
State average pass rate: **100%**

Michigan State University

- 501 Erickson Hall, East Lansing, MI 48824-1034
- Website: http://www.educ.msu.edu
- Public
- Degrees offered: bachelor's, master's, education specialist, Ph.D.
- Overall rank in the 2005 U.S. News education schools with doctoral programs: 13
- Overall rank in the 2005 U.S. News education school specialty rankings: administration/supervision: 9, counseling/personnel: 13, curriculum/instruction: 2, education policy: 9, educational psychology: 3, elementary education: 1, higher education administration: 4, secondary education: 1, special education: 19

ADMISSIONS

Admissions phone number: (517) 355-8332
Admissions email address: *admis@msu.edu*
Application website: *http://www.msu.edu/user/gradschl/ apply.htm*
Application fee: $50
Fall 2005 application deadline: 12/26
Test requirements: GRE
Test of English as Foreign Language (TOEFL) is required for international students.
Minimum TOEFL score required for paper test: 550
Minimum TOEFL score required for computer test: 213

Fall 2003
Acceptance rate for master's degree programs: 55%
Acceptance rate for education specialist degree programs: 38%
Acceptance rate for doctoral programs: 46%
Average GRE verbal: 547, Average GRE quantitative: 624, Average GRE analytical: 630
Total 2003 enrollment: 1,376
Master's degree enrollment: 881
   Teacher preparation program enrollment (master's): 487
Education specialist degree enrollment: 23
Doctoral degree enrollment: 472

FINANCIAL INFORMATION

Financial aid phone number: (517) 353-5940
Tuition, 2003-2004 academic year: Full-time in-state: $291/credit hour; out-of-state: $589/credit hour, Part-time in-state: $291/credit hour; out-of-state: $589/credit hour
Fees: $778, Room and board: $7,006, Books and supplies: $1,144, Miscellaneous expenses: $2,942
Number of fellowships awarded to graduate students during the 2003-2004 academic year: 257
Number of teaching assistant positions: 156
Number of research assistant positions: 133

ACADEMIC PROGRAMS

Total full-time tenured or tenure-track faculty (fall 2003): 126, Total part-time faculty (fall 2003): 1
Areas of specialization: curriculum and instruction, education administration and supervision, education policy, educational psychology, elementary teacher education, higher education administration, secondary teacher education, special education, student counseling and personnel services.
Professional development/partnership school(s) are used by students in all of the teaching programs.
During their internships, peer groups of students meet regularly to discuss instructional techniques in all of the teaching programs.
All of the students in their internships are mentored.
Courses that prepare teachers to pass the National Board of Professional Teaching Standards are not offered.
Teacher preparation programs: Five-year program leading to initial licensure that results in a baccalaureate degree (with a major or minor in education) plus graduate credit and includes practice teaching.

LICENSING TEST

Pass rate on state's teacher licensing test for 2002-2003: 100%
State average pass rate: 100%

Northern Michigan University

- 1401 Presque Isle Avenue, Marquette, MI 49855
- Website: http://www.nmu.edu/departments/graduate/
- Public

LICENSING TEST

Pass rate on state's teacher licensing test for 2002-2003: 100%
State average pass rate: 100%

Oakland University

- 415 Education Building, Rochester, MI 48309-4494
- Website: http://www.oakland.edu/sehs
- Public
- Degrees offered: bachelor's, master's, education specialist, Ph.D.

ADMISSIONS

Admissions phone number: (248) 370-3167
Admissions email address: *applygrad@oakland.edu*
Application fee: $30
Fall 2005 application deadline: 8/1
Test requirements: GRE or MAT
Test of English as Foreign Language (TOEFL) is required for international students.

Minimum TOEFL score required for paper test: 550
Minimum TOEFL score required for computer test: 213

Fall 2003
Acceptance rate for master's degree programs: 85%
Acceptance rate for education specialist degree programs: 100%
Acceptance rate for doctoral programs: 59%
Total 2003 enrollment: 1,683
Master's degree enrollment: 1,465
  Teacher preparation program enrollment (master's): 824
Education specialist degree enrollment: 105
Doctoral degree enrollment: 113

FINANCIAL INFORMATION
Financial aid phone number: (248) 370-2550
Tuition, 2003-2004 academic year: Full-time in-state: $7,077; out-of-state: $12,804, Part-time in-state: $295/credit hour; out-of-state: $534/credit hour
Fees: $486, Room and board: $5,515, Books and supplies: $705, Miscellaneous expenses: $1,712
Number of fellowships awarded to graduate students during the 2003-2004 academic year: 21
Number of teaching assistant positions: 3
Number of research assistant positions: 16
Number of other paid appointments: 10

ACADEMIC PROGRAMS
Total full-time tenured or tenure-track faculty (fall 2003): 64, Total part-time faculty (fall 2003): 125
Areas of specialization: curriculum and instruction, education administration and supervision, higher education administration, secondary teacher education, special education, student counseling and personnel services.
Professional development/partnership school(s) are used by students in some of the teaching programs.
During their internships, peer groups of students meet regularly to discuss instructional techniques in some of the teaching programs.
All of the students in their internships are mentored.
Courses that prepare teachers to pass the National Board of Professional Teaching Standards are not offered.
Teacher preparation programs: Four-year baccalaureate-degree program leading to initial licensure that includes either a major or minor in education and practice teaching. Master's program preparing college graduates for initial licensure; includes practice teaching. Alternative program for college graduates leading to provisional licensure.
The education program is currently accredited by the National Council for Accreditation of Teacher Education.

LICENSING TEST
Pass rate on state's teacher licensing test for 2002-2003: 100%
State average pass rate: 100%

Saginaw Valley State University

- **7400 Bay Rd., University Center, MI 48710**
- **Website:** http://www.svsu.edu/coe
- **Public**
- **Degrees offered:** bachelor's, master's, education specialist

ADMISSIONS
Admissions phone number: (989) 964-6067
Admissions email address: *barbus@svsu.edu*
Application fee: $35
Fall 2005 application deadline: 9/10

FINANCIAL INFORMATION
Financial aid phone number: (989) 964-4103
Tuition, 2003-2004 academic year: Full-time in-state: $239/credit hour; out-of-state: $473/credit hour, Part-time in-state: $239/credit hour; out-of-state: $473/credit hour
Fees: $20/credit hour

LICENSING TEST
Pass rate on state's teacher licensing test for 2002-2003: 100%
State average pass rate: 100%

Siena Heights College

- **1247 E. Siena Heights Drive, Adrian, MI 49221**
- **Website:** http://www.sienahts.edu/~grs/index.html
- **Private**

LICENSING TEST
Pass rate on state's teacher licensing test for 2002-2003: 100%
State average pass rate: 100%

Spring Arbor College

- **106 E. Main Street, Spring Arbor, MI 49283-9799**
- **Website:** http://www.arbor.edu/
- **Private**

LICENSING TEST
Pass rate on state's teacher licensing test for 2002-2003: 100%
State average pass rate: 100%

University of Detroit Mercy

- ■ PO Box 19900, Detroit, MI 48219-0900
- ■ Website: http://liberalarts.udmercy.edu/
- ■ Private

LICENSING TEST
Pass rate on state's teacher licensing test for 2002-2003: 100%
State average pass rate: 100%

University of Michigan–Ann Arbor

- ■ 610 E. University Street, Ann Arbor, MI 48109-1259
- ■ Website: http://www.soe.umich.edu/
- ■ Public
- ■ Degrees offered: bachelor's, master's, Ph.D.
- ■ Overall rank in the 2005 U.S. News education schools with doctoral programs: 10
- ■ Overall rank in the 2005 U.S. News education school specialty rankings: administration/supervision: 10, curriculum/instruction: 9, education policy: 4, educational psychology: 3, elementary education: 8, higher education administration: 1, secondary education: 11

ADMISSIONS
Admissions phone number: (734) 764-7563
Admissions email address: *ed.grad.admit@umich.edu*
Application website: *http://www.rackham.umich.edu*
Application fee: $60
Fall 2005 application deadline: 1/1
Test requirements: GRE
Test of English as Foreign Language (TOEFL) is required for international students.
Minimum TOEFL score required for paper test: 600
Minimum TOEFL score required for computer test: 220

Fall 2003
Acceptance rate for master's degree programs: 73%
Acceptance rate for doctoral programs: 39%
Average GRE verbal: 543, Average GRE quantitative: 621, Average GRE analytical: 642
Total 2003 enrollment: 507
Master's degree enrollment: 201
   Teacher preparation program enrollment (master's): 103
Doctoral degree enrollment: 306

FINANCIAL INFORMATION
Financial aid phone number: (734) 764-7563

Tuition, 2003-2004 academic year: Full-time in-state: $12,628; out-of-state: $25,964, Part-time in-state: $2,194/credit hour; out-of-state: $4,414/credit hour
Fees: $557, Room and board: $13,200, Books and supplies: $800
Number of fellowships awarded to graduate students during the 2003-2004 academic year: 781
Number of teaching assistant positions: 86
Number of research assistant positions: 260
Number of other paid appointments: 38

ACADEMIC PROGRAMS
Total full-time tenured or tenure-track faculty (fall 2003): 64, Total part-time faculty (fall 2003): 1
Areas of specialization: curriculum and instruction, education administration and supervision, education policy, educational psychology, elementary teacher education, higher education administration, secondary teacher education, special education.
Professional development/partnership school(s) are used by students in some of the teaching programs.
During their internships, peer groups of students meet regularly to discuss instructional techniques in all of the teaching programs.
All of the students in their internships are mentored.
Courses that prepare teachers to pass the National Board of Professional Teaching Standards are not offered.

LICENSING TEST
Pass rate on state's teacher licensing test for 2002-2003: 100%
State average pass rate: 100%

University of Michigan–Dearborn

- ■ 4901 Evergreen Rd., Dearborn, MI 48323
- ■ Website: http://www.soe.umd.umich.edu/
- ■ Public
- ■ Degrees offered: bachelor's, master's

ADMISSIONS
Admissions phone number: (313) 593-5006
Admissions email address: *Joanno@umd.umich.edu*
Application website: *http://www.soe.umd.umich.edu/*
Application fee: $30
Fall 2005 application deadline: 7/30
Test of English as Foreign Language (TOEFL) is required for international students.
Minimum TOEFL score required for paper test: 550
Minimum TOEFL score required for computer test: 225

Fall 2003
Total 2003 enrollment: 777
Master's degree enrollment: 777
   Teacher preparation program enrollment (master's): 355

FINANCIAL INFORMATION

Financial aid phone number: **(313) 593-5300**

Tuition, 2003-2004 academic year: Full-time in-state: **$3,119**; out-of-state: **$9,846**, Part-time in-state: **$260/credit hour**; out-of-state: **$821/credit hour**

Fees: **$107**, Books and supplies: **$640**, Miscellaneous expenses: **$2,000**

LICENSING TEST

Pass rate on state's teacher licensing test for 2002-2003: **100%**

State average pass rate: **100%**

University of Michigan–Flint

- ■ 303 E. Kearsley, Flint, MI 48502-1950
- ■ Website: http://graduateprograms.umflint.edu/education.htm
- ■ Public
- ■ **Degrees offered:** bachelor's, master's

Fall 2003

Total 2003 enrollment: **568**

Master's degree enrollment: **284**

    Teacher preparation program enrollment (master's): **284**

Education specialist degree enrollment: **284**

ACADEMIC PROGRAMS

Total full-time tenured or tenure-track faculty (fall 2003): **16**

    Total part-time faculty (fall 2003): **40**

Areas of specialization: curriculum and instruction, education administration and supervision, educational psychology, elementary teacher education, secondary teacher education, special education.

Professional development/partnership school(s) are used by students in some of the teaching programs.

During their internships, peer groups of students meet regularly to discuss instructional techniques in some of the teaching programs.

All of the students in their internships are mentored.

Courses that prepare teachers to pass the National Board of Professional Teaching Standards are offered.

Teacher preparation programs: Four-year baccalaureate-degree program leading to initial licensure that includes either a major or minor in education and practice teaching. Master's program preparing college graduates for initial licensure; includes practice teaching.

The education program is currently accredited by the National Council for Accreditation of Teacher Education.

LICENSING TEST

Pass rate on state's teacher licensing test for 2002-2003: **100%**

State average pass rate: **100%**

Wayne State University

- ■ **College of Education, Detroit, MI 48202-3489**
- ■ **Website:** http://www.coe.wayne.edu/
- ■ **Public**
- ■ **Degrees offered:** bachelor's, master's, education specialist, Ph.D., Ed.D.

ADMISSIONS

Admissions phone number: **(313) 577-1605**

Application website: *http://www.admissions.wayne.edu/*

Application fee: **$50**

Fall 2005 application deadline: **rolling**

Test requirements: **GRE or MAT**

Test of English as Foreign Language (TOEFL) is required for international students.

Minimum TOEFL score required for paper test: **550**

Minimum TOEFL score required for computer test: **213**

Fall 2003

Acceptance rate for master's degree programs: **68%**

Acceptance rate for education specialist degree programs: **70%**

Acceptance rate for doctoral programs: **28%**

Average GRE verbal: **409**, Average GRE quantitative: **434**, Average GRE analytical: **316**

Total 2003 enrollment: **2,876**

Master's degree enrollment: **2,465**

    Teacher preparation program enrollment (master's): **1,633**

Education specialist degree enrollment: **148**

Doctoral degree enrollment: **263**

FINANCIAL INFORMATION

Financial aid phone number: **(313) 577-3378**

Tuition, 2003-2004 academic year: Full-time in-state: **$262/credit hour**; out-of-state: **$579/credit hour**, Part-time in-state: **$262/credit hour**; out-of-state: **$579/credit hour**

Fees: **$553/credit hour**, Room and board: **$6,870**, Books and supplies: **$800**, Miscellaneous expenses: **$3,584**

Number of fellowships awarded to graduate students during the 2003-2004 academic year: **0**

Number of teaching assistant positions: **5**

Number of research assistant positions: **1**

Number of other paid appointments: **0**

ACADEMIC PROGRAMS

Total full-time tenured or tenure-track faculty (fall 2003): **54**, Total part-time faculty (fall 2003): **120**

Areas of specialization: curriculum and instruction, education administration and supervision, education policy, educational psychology, elementary teacher education, secondary teacher education, special education, student counseling and personnel services.

Professional development/partnership school(s) are used by students in all of the teaching programs.

During their internships, peer groups of students meet regularly to discuss instructional techniques in all of the teaching programs.

All of the students in their internships are mentored.

Courses that prepare teachers to pass the National Board of Professional Teaching Standards are not offered.

Teacher preparation programs: Four-year baccalaureate-degree program leading to initial licensure that includes either a major or minor in education and practice teaching. Master's program preparing college graduates for initial licensure; includes practice teaching.

LICENSING TEST

Pass rate on state's teacher licensing test for 2002-2003: 100%

State average pass rate: 100%

Western Michigan University

■ 1903 W. Michigan Avenue, Kalamazoo, MI 49008
■ **Website:** http://www.wmich.edu/coe
■ Public
■ **Degrees offered:** bachelor's, master's, education specialist, Ph.D., Ed.D.

ADMISSIONS

Admissions phone number: **(269) 387-2000**
Admissions email address: *ask-wmu@wmich.edu*
Application website: *http://www.wmich.edu/grad/*
Application fee: **$25**
Fall 2005 application deadline: **rolling**
Test of English as Foreign Language (TOEFL) is required for international students.
Minimum TOEFL score required for paper test: **550**

Fall 2003
Acceptance rate for master's degree programs: **72%**
Acceptance rate for doctoral programs: **59%**
Average GRE verbal: **427**, Average GRE quantitative: **517**, Average GRE analytical: **509**
Total 2003 enrollment: **1,791**

Master's degree enrollment: **1,525**
    Teacher preparation program enrollment (master's): **544**
Education specialist degree enrollment: **4**
Doctoral degree enrollment: **262**

FINANCIAL INFORMATION

Financial aid phone number: **(269) 387-6000**
Tuition, 2003-2004 academic year: Full-time in-state: **$234/credit hour**; out-of-state: **$569/credit hour**, Part-time in-state: **$234/credit hour**; out-of-state: **$569/credit hour**
Fees: **$602**, Room and board: **$6,640**, Books and supplies: **$1,370**, Miscellaneous expenses: **$4,610**
Number of fellowships awarded to graduate students during the 2003-2004 academic year: **0**
Number of teaching assistant positions: **37**
Number of research assistant positions: **25**
Number of other paid appointments: **39**

ACADEMIC PROGRAMS

Total full-time tenured or tenure-track faculty (fall 2003): **88**, Total part-time faculty (fall 2003): **105**
Areas of specialization: elementary teacher education, higher education administration, special education.
Professional development/partnership school(s) are used by students in all of the teaching programs.
During their internships, peer groups of students meet regularly to discuss instructional techniques in all of the teaching programs.
All of the students in their internships are mentored.
Courses that prepare teachers to pass the National Board of Professional Teaching Standards are not offered.
Teacher preparation programs: Four-year baccalaureate-degree program leading to initial licensure that includes either a major or minor in education and practice teaching.
The education program is currently accredited by the National Council for Accreditation of Teacher Education.

LICENSING TEST

Pass rate on state's teacher licensing test for 2002-2003: 100%

State average pass rate: 100%

MINNESOTA

Augsburg College

- **2211 Riverside Avenue, Minneapolis, MN 55454**
- **Website:** http://www.augsburg.edu/mae
- **Private**
- **Degrees offered:** bachelor's, master's

ADMISSIONS
Admissions phone number: **(612) 330-1520**
Admissions email address: *maeinfo@augsburg.edu*
Application website: *http://www.augsburg.edu/apply/m_education.html*
Application fee: **$35**
Fall 2005 application deadline: **8/15**
Test of English as Foreign Language (TOEFL) is required for international students.
Minimum TOEFL score required for paper test: **550**
Minimum TOEFL score required for computer test: **213**

Fall 2003
Acceptance rate for master's degree programs: **98%**
Total 2003 enrollment: **65**
Master's degree enrollment: **65**
   Teacher preparation program enrollment (master's): **65**

FINANCIAL INFORMATION
Financial aid phone number: **(800) 458-1721**

ACADEMIC PROGRAMS
Total full-time tenured or tenure-track faculty (fall 2003): **8**
   Total part-time faculty (fall 2003): **28**
Areas of specialization: elementary teacher education, secondary teacher education, special education.
Professional development/partnership school(s) are used by students in none of the teaching programs.
During their internships, peer groups of students meet regularly to discuss instructional techniques in all of the teaching programs.
All of the students in their internships are mentored.
Courses that prepare teachers to pass the National Board of Professional Teaching Standards are not offered.

Teacher preparation programs: Four-year baccalaureate-degree program leading to initial licensure that includes either a major or minor in education and practice teaching. Master's program preparing college graduates for initial licensure; includes practice teaching.
The education program is currently accredited by the National Council for Accreditation of Teacher Education.

LICENSING TEST
Pass rate on state's teacher licensing test for 2002-2003: **100%**
State average pass rate: **98%**

Bemidji State University

- **1500 Birchmont Drive, N.E., Bemidji, MN 56601**
- **Website:** http://bsued.bemidji.msus.edu/
- **Public**

LICENSING TEST
Pass rate on state's teacher licensing test for 2002-2003: **95%**
State average pass rate: **98%**

Bethel College

- **3900 Bethel Drive, St. Paul, MN 55112**
- **Website:** http://www.bethel.edu/cgcs
- **Private**
- **Degrees offered:** master's

ADMISSIONS
Admissions phone number: **(651) 635-8000**
Admissions email address: *cgcs@bethel.edu*
Application website: *http://www.bethel.edu/cgcs/admissions*
Application fee: **$25**
Fall 2005 application deadline: **rolling**
Test of English as Foreign Language (TOEFL) is required for international students.
Minimum TOEFL score required for paper test: **550**
Minimum TOEFL score required for computer test: **213**

Fall 2003
Acceptance rate for master's degree programs: 79%
Total 2003 enrollment: 196
Master's degree enrollment: 196
    Teacher preparation program enrollment (master's): 196

FINANCIAL INFORMATION
Financial aid phone number: (651) 638-6241
Tuition, 2003-2004 academic year: Full-time: **$340/credit hour**; Part-time: **$340/credit hour**
Fees: **$100**

ACADEMIC PROGRAMS
Areas of specialization: secondary teacher education, special education.
Professional development/partnership school(s) are used by students in some of the teaching programs.
During their internships, peer groups of students meet regularly to discuss instructional techniques in all of the teaching programs.
All of the students in their internships are mentored.
Courses that prepare teachers to pass the National Board of Professional Teaching Standards are not offered.
Teacher preparation programs: Four-year baccalaureate-degree program leading to initial licensure that includes either a major or minor in education and practice teaching. Master's program preparing college graduates for initial licensure; includes practice teaching.
The education program is currently accredited by the National Council for Accreditation of Teacher Education.
The education program is currently accredited by the Teacher Education Accreditation Council.

LICENSING TEST
Pass rate on state's teacher licensing test for 2002-2003: 100%
State average pass rate: 98%

College of St. Catherine

■ 2004 Randolph Ave. #4196, St. Paul, MN 55105
■ **Website:** http://www.stkate.edu
■ **Private**
■ **Degrees offered:** bachelor's, master's

ADMISSIONS
Admissions phone number: (651) 690-6933
Admissions email address: *graduate_study@stkate.edu*
Application website: *http://minerva.stkate.edu/offices/academic/maed.nsf/maedapp?OpenForm*
Application fee: **$25**
Fall 2005 application deadline: 6/1
Test of English as Foreign Language (TOEFL) is required for international students.
Minimum TOEFL score required for paper test: **600**
Minimum TOEFL score required for computer test: **250**

Fall 2003
Acceptance rate for master's degree programs: 84%
Total 2003 enrollment: 260
Master's degree enrollment: 260
    Teacher preparation program enrollment (master's): 260

FINANCIAL INFORMATION
Financial aid phone number: (651) 690-6540
Tuition, 2003-2004 academic year: Full-time: **$400/credit hour**; Part-time: **$400/credit hour**
Fees: **$140**, Books and supplies: **$600**, Miscellaneous expenses: **$1,000**

ACADEMIC PROGRAMS
Total full-time tenured or tenure-track faculty (fall 2003): 8
    Total part-time faculty (fall 2003): 2
Professional development/partnership school(s) are used by students in some of the teaching programs.
During their internships, peer groups of students meet regularly to discuss instructional techniques in all of the teaching programs.
All of the students in their internships are mentored.
Courses that prepare teachers to pass the National Board of Professional Teaching Standards are not offered.
Teacher preparation programs: Four-year baccalaureate-degree program leading to initial licensure that includes either a major or minor in education and practice teaching. Master's program preparing college graduates for initial licensure; includes practice teaching.

LICENSING TEST
Pass rate on state's teacher licensing test for 2002-2003: 94%
State average pass rate: 98%

College of St. Scholastica

■ 1200 Kenwood Avenue, Duluth, MN 55811
■ **Website:** http://www.css.edu
■ **Private**
■ **Degrees offered:** master's

ADMISSIONS
Admissions phone number: (218) 723-6169
Admissions email address: *ctrettel@css.edu*
Application website: *http://www.css.edu/ECI/admissions.shtml*
Application fee: **$50**
Fall 2005 application deadline: 6/30
Test of English as Foreign Language (TOEFL) is required for international students.
Minimum TOEFL score required for paper test: 550
Minimum TOEFL score required for computer test: 213

FINANCIAL INFORMATION
Financial aid phone number: (218) 723-6047
Tuition, 2003-2004 academic year: Full-time: **$323/credit hour**; Part-time: **$323/credit hour**
Fees: **$323/credit hour**

ACADEMIC PROGRAMS

Total full-time tenured or tenure-track faculty (fall 2003): 7
  Total part-time faculty (fall 2003): 10
Areas of specialization: curriculum and instruction.
Professional development/partnership school(s) are used
  by students in some of the teaching programs.
During their internships, peer groups of students meet
  regularly to discuss instructional techniques in all of the
  teaching programs.
All of the students in their internships are mentored.

LICENSING TEST

Pass rate on state's teacher licensing test for 2002-2003:
  100%
State average pass rate: 98%

Hamline University

- 1536 Hewitt Ave, St Paul, MN 55104-1284
- **Website:** http://www.hamline.edu
- **Private**
- **Degrees offered:** master's, Ed.D.

ADMISSIONS

Admissions phone number: **(651) 523-2900**
Admissions email address: *gradprog@hamline.edu*
Application website:
  http://www.hamline.edu/graduate/admission
Application fee: **$30**
Fall 2005 application deadline: **rolling**
Test of English as Foreign Language (TOEFL) is required
  for international students.
Minimum TOEFL score required for paper test: **550**
Minimum TOEFL score required for computer test: **217**

Fall 2003

Acceptance rate for master's degree programs: **86%**
Acceptance rate for doctoral programs: **83%**
Total 2003 enrollment: **808**
Master's degree enrollment: **759**
  Teacher preparation program enrollment (master's): **759**
Doctoral degree enrollment: **49**

FINANCIAL INFORMATION

Financial aid phone number: **(651) 523-3000**
Tuition, 2003-2004 academic year: **$355/credit hour**
Fees: **$150**, Room and board: **$6,770**, Books and supplies:
  $140, Miscellaneous expenses: **$200**

ACADEMIC PROGRAMS

Total full-time tenured or tenure-track faculty (fall 2003):
  24, Total part-time faculty (fall 2003): **67**
Areas of specialization: curriculum and instruction.
Professional development/partnership school(s) are used
  by students in all of the teaching programs.
During their internships, peer groups of students meet
  regularly to discuss instructional techniques in all of the
  teaching programs.

All of the students in their internships are mentored.
Courses that prepare teachers to pass the National Board of
  Professional Teaching Standards are not offered.
Teacher preparation programs: Master's degree in educa-
  tion, including internship/practice teaching and prepara-
  tion for initial licensure.
The education program is currently accredited by the
  National Council for Accreditation of Teacher Education.

LICENSING TEST

Pass rate on state's teacher licensing test for 2002-2003: **100%**
State average pass rate: **98%**

Minnesota State University–Mankato

- 118 Armstrong Hall, Mankato, MN 56001
- **Website:** http://www.coled.mnsu.edu/
- **Public**

LICENSING TEST

Pass rate on state's teacher licensing test for 2002-2003: **95%**
State average pass rate: **98%**

Minnesota State University–Moorhead

- 1104 Seventh Avenue, S, Moorhead, MN 56563
- **Website:** http://www.mnstate.edu/edhuman/
- **Public**

LICENSING TEST

Pass rate on state's teacher licensing test for 2002-2003:
  95%
State average pass rate: **98%**

Southwest Minnesota State University

- 1501 State Street, Marshall, MN 56258
- **Website:** http://www.southwestmsu.edu
- **Public**
- **Degrees offered:** bachelor's, master's

ADMISSIONS

Admissions phone number: **(507) 537-6286**
Admissions email address: *shearerr@southwestmsu.edu*
Application website: *http://www.southwestmsu.edu/*
  admission/forms.cfm
Application fee: **$20**

Test of English as Foreign Language (TOEFL) is required
for international students.
Minimum TOEFL score required for paper test: 550
Minimum TOEFL score required for computer test: 220

Fall 2003
Acceptance rate for master's degree programs: 100%
Total 2003 enrollment: 358
Master's degree enrollment: 358
　　Teacher preparation program enrollment (master's): 358

FINANCIAL INFORMATION
Financial aid phone number: (507) 537-6281
Tuition, 2003-2004 academic year: Full-time in-state:
　　$203/credit hour; out-of-state: $203/credit hour, Part-
　　time in-state: $203/credit hour; out-of-state: $203/credit
　　hour
Fees: $27, Room and board: $4,490, Books and supplies:
　　$900, Miscellaneous expenses: $1,800
Number of other paid appointments: 19

ACADEMIC PROGRAMS
Total full-time tenured or tenure-track faculty (fall 2003): 5
　　Total part-time faculty (fall 2003): 11
Areas of specialization: elementary teacher education, sec-
　　ondary teacher education, special education.
Professional development/partnership school(s) are used
　　by students in some of the teaching programs.
During their internships, peer groups of students meet
　　regularly to discuss instructional techniques in some of
　　the teaching programs.
Some of the students in their internships are mentored.
Courses that prepare teachers to pass the National Board of
　　Professional Teaching Standards are not offered.

LICENSING TEST
Pass rate on state's teacher licensing test for 2002-2003:
　　98%
State average pass rate: 98%

St. Cloud State University

■ 720 S. Fourth Avenue, St. Cloud, MN 56301
■ Website: http://www.stcloudstate.edu/coe/
■ Public

LICENSING TEST
Pass rate on state's teacher licensing test for 2002-2003:
　　97%
State average pass rate: 98%

St. Mary's University of Minnesota

■ 700 Terrace Heights, Winona, MN 55987-1700
■ Website: http://www.smumn.edu/sitepages/pid3.php
■ Private

LICENSING TEST
Pass rate on state's teacher licensing test for 2002-2003:
　　100%
State average pass rate: 98%

University of Minnesota– Duluth

■ 1207 Ordean Court, Duluth, MN 55812
■ Website: http://www.d.umn.edu/cehsp/GradProg
■ Public
■ Degrees offered: bachelor's, master's

ADMISSIONS
Admissions phone number: (218) 726-7442
Admissions email address: *lvelande@d.umn.edu*
Application fee: $30
Fall 2005 application deadline: 7/15
Test of English as Foreign Language (TOEFL) is required
　　for international students.
Minimum TOEFL score required for paper test: 550
Minimum TOEFL score required for computer test: 213

Fall 2003
Acceptance rate for master's degree programs: 90%
Total 2003 enrollment: 75
Master's degree enrollment: 75

FINANCIAL INFORMATION
Financial aid phone number: (218) 726-8794
Tuition, 2003-2004 academic year: Full-time in-state:
　　$292/credit hour; out-of-state: $584/credit hour, Part-
　　time in-state: $292/credit hour; out-of-state: $584/credit
　　hour
Fees: $1,004, Room and board: $5,800, Books and sup-
　　plies: $900, Miscellaneous expenses: $1,000

ACADEMIC PROGRAMS
Total full-time tenured or tenure-track faculty (fall 2003):
　　21, Total part-time faculty (fall 2003): 32
Areas of specialization: curriculum and instruction, special
　　education.
Professional development/partnership school(s) are used
　　by students in none of the teaching programs.
During their internships, peer groups of students meet
　　regularly to discuss instructional techniques in some of
　　the teaching programs.

None of the students in their internships are mentored. Courses that prepare teachers to pass the National Board of Professional Teaching Standards are offered.

Teacher preparation programs: Four-year baccalaureate-degree program leading to initial licensure that includes either a major or minor in education and practice teaching. The education program is currently accredited by the National Council for Accreditation of Teacher Education.

LICENSING TEST

Pass rate on state's teacher licensing test for 2002-2003: 100%
State average pass rate: 98%

University of Minnesota–Twin Cities

- 104 Burton Hall, 178 Pillsbury Drive SE, Minneapolis, MN 55455
- **Website:** http://education.umn.edu/
- **Public**
- **Degrees offered:** bachelor's, master's, education specialist, Ph.D., Ed.D.
- **Overall rank in the 2005 U.S. News education schools with doctoral programs:** 19
- **Overall rank in the 2005 U.S. News education school specialty rankings:** administration/supervision: 14, counseling/personnel: 3, curriculum/instruction: 13, education policy: 18, educational psychology: 6, elementary education: 11, higher education administration: 20, secondary education: 13, special education: 6, vocational/technical: 2

ADMISSIONS

Admissions phone number: (612) 625-6501
Admissions email address: *spsinfo@umn.edu*
Application website: *http://www.grad.umn.edu/admissions/*
Application fee: $55
Fall 2005 application deadline: 12/1
Test requirements: **GRE**
Test of English as Foreign Language (TOEFL) is required for international students.
Minimum TOEFL score required for paper test: 550
Minimum TOEFL score required for computer test: 213

Fall 2003
Acceptance rate for master's degree programs: 71%
Acceptance rate for education specialist degree programs: 45%
Acceptance rate for doctoral programs: 48%
Average GRE verbal: 500, Average GRE quantitative: 588, Average GRE analytical: 585
Total 2003 enrollment: 2,240
Master's degree enrollment: 1,321
  Teacher preparation program enrollment (master's): 960
Education specialist degree enrollment: 19
Doctoral degree enrollment: 900

FINANCIAL INFORMATION

Financial aid phone number: **(612) 624-1111**
Tuition, 2003-2004 academic year: Full-time in-state: **$7,363**; out-of-state: **$14,462**, Part-time in-state: **$614/credit hour**; out-of-state: **$1,205/credit hour**
Fees: **$714**, Room and board: **$6,302**, Books and supplies: **$850**, Miscellaneous expenses: **$2,500**
Number of fellowships awarded to graduate students during the 2003-2004 academic year: 51
Number of teaching assistant positions: 141
Number of research assistant positions: 217
Number of other paid appointments: 0

ACADEMIC PROGRAMS

Total full-time tenured or tenure-track faculty (fall 2003): 127
  Total part-time faculty (fall 2003): 2
Areas of specialization: curriculum and instruction, education administration and supervision, education policy, educational psychology, elementary teacher education, higher education administration, secondary teacher education, special education, student counseling and personnel services, teacher education.
Professional development/partnership school(s) are used by students in some of the teaching programs.
During their internships, peer groups of students meet regularly to discuss instructional techniques in all of the teaching programs.
All of the students in their internships are mentored.
Courses that prepare teachers to pass the National Board of Professional Teaching Standards are offered.
Teacher preparation programs: Four-year baccalaureate-degree program leading to initial licensure that includes either a major or minor in education and practice teaching. Master's program preparing college graduates for initial licensure; includes practice teaching.
The education program is currently accredited by the National Council for Accreditation of Teacher Education.

LICENSING TEST

Pass rate on state's teacher licensing test for 2002-2003: 100%
State average pass rate: 98%

University of St. Thomas

- 1000 LaSalle Avenue, Minneapolis, MN 55403
- **Website:** http://www.stthomas.edu/education
- **Private**
- **Degrees offered:** bachelor's, master's, education specialist, Ed.D.

ADMISSIONS

Admissions phone number: (651) 962-4550
Admissions email address: *education@stthomas.edu*
Application fee: $50
Fall 2005 application deadline: 6/1
Test requirements: **GRE or MAT**

Test of English as Foreign Language (TOEFL) is required for international students.
Minimum TOEFL score required for paper test: 550
Minimum TOEFL score required for computer test: 213

Fall 2003
Acceptance rate for master's degree programs: 100%
Acceptance rate for education specialist degree programs: 100%
Average GRE verbal: 550, Average GRE quantitative: 554, Average GRE analytical: 590, Average MAT: 46
Total 2003 enrollment: 1,458
Master's degree enrollment: 1,243
 Teacher preparation program enrollment (master's): 565
Education specialist degree enrollment: 89
Doctoral degree enrollment: 126

FINANCIAL INFORMATION
Financial aid phone number: (651) 962-6550
Tuition, 2003-2004 academic year: Full-time: **$449/credit hour**; Part-time: **$449/credit hour**
Books and supplies: $350, Miscellaneous expenses: $100
Number of fellowships awarded to graduate students during the 2003-2004 academic year: 0
Number of teaching assistant positions: 0
Number of research assistant positions: 16
Number of other paid appointments: 0

ACADEMIC PROGRAMS
Total full-time tenured or tenure-track faculty (fall 2003): 31
 Total part-time faculty (fall 2003): 71
Areas of specialization: curriculum and instruction, education administration and supervision, education policy, elementary teacher education, higher education administration, secondary teacher education, special education.
Professional development/partnership school(s) are used by students in none of the teaching programs.
During their internships, peer groups of students meet regularly to discuss instructional techniques in none of the teaching programs.
All of the students in their internships are mentored.
Courses that prepare teachers to pass the National Board of Professional Teaching Standards are offered.
Teacher preparation programs: Four-year baccalaureate-degree program leading to initial licensure that includes either a major or minor in education and practice teaching. Five-year program leading to initial licensure that results in a baccalaureate degree (with a major or minor in education) plus graduate credit and includes practice teaching. Master's program preparing college graduates for initial licensure; includes practice teaching.
The education program is currently accredited by the National Council for Accreditation of Teacher Education.

LICENSING TEST
Pass rate on state's teacher licensing test for 2002-2003: 100%
State average pass rate: 98%

Walden University

■ **155 Fifth Avenue, S, Minneapolis, MN 55401**
■ **Website:** http://www.waldenu.edu/acad-prog/index.html
■ **Private**

Winona State University

■ **PO Box 5838, Winona, MN 55987-5838**
■ **Website:** http://www.winona.edu/graduatestudy/
■ **Public**
■ **Degrees offered:** bachelor's, master's, education specialist

ADMISSIONS
Admissions phone number: (507) 457-5038
Application fee: $20
Fall 2005 application deadline: **rolling**
Test of English as Foreign Language (TOEFL) is required for international students.
Minimum TOEFL score required for paper test: 550
Minimum TOEFL score required for computer test: 173

Fall 2003
Acceptance rate for master's degree programs: 89%
Acceptance rate for education specialist degree programs: 100%
Total 2003 enrollment: 302
Master's degree enrollment: 272
 Teacher preparation program enrollment (master's): 141
Education specialist degree enrollment: 30

FINANCIAL INFORMATION
Financial aid phone number: (507) 457-5090
Tuition, 2003-2004 academic year: Full-time in-state: $3,660; out-of-state: $5,520, Part-time in-state: $1,830; out-of-state: $2,760
Fees: $480, Room and board: $4,640, Books and supplies: $860, Miscellaneous expenses: $3,020
Number of fellowships awarded to graduate students during the 2003-2004 academic year: 16
Number of teaching assistant positions: 6
Number of research assistant positions: 0
Number of other paid appointments: 0

ACADEMIC PROGRAMS
Total full-time tenured or tenure-track faculty (fall 2003): 32, Total part-time faculty (fall 2003): 28
Areas of specialization: education administration and supervision, educational psychology, elementary teacher education, secondary teacher education, special education, student counseling and personnel services.
Professional development/partnership school(s) are used by students in some of the teaching programs.

During their internships, peer groups of students meet regularly to discuss instructional techniques in all of the teaching programs.

All of the students in their internships are mentored.

Courses that prepare teachers to pass the National Board of Professional Teaching Standards are not offered.

Teacher preparation programs: Four-year baccalaureate-degree program leading to initial licensure that includes either a major or minor in education and practice teaching. Master's program preparing college graduates for initial licensure; includes practice teaching.

The education program is currently accredited by the National Council for Accreditation of Teacher Education.

LICENSING TEST

Pass rate on state's teacher licensing test for 2002-2003: 100%

State average pass rate: 98%

MISSISSIPPI

TEACHER TESTING IN MISSISSIPPI

Teacher licensure rules vary widely from state to state, but almost all states require tests. The exams typically cover the basics of reading, writing and math, although some states mandate in-depth, subject-specific teacher tests. For information on where to go in your state for specific academic requirements, see Chapter 6 on page 67. Note: Some schools require students to pass exams by graduation, and thus automatically report pass rates of 100 percent.

- This state **does** require a basic skills test in order to obtain a teaching license.
- This state **does not** require a subject-knowledge test in order to obtain a middle school teaching license.
- This state **does** require a subject-knowledge test in order to obtain a high school teaching license.
- This state **does** require a subject-specific pedagogy test in order to obtain a teaching license.

Alcorn State University

- 1000 ASU Drive #359, Alcorn State, MS 39096
- Website:
  http://www.alcorn.edu/academic/academ/grads.htm
- Public
- Degrees offered: bachelor's, master's, education specialist

ADMISSIONS
Admissions phone number: **(601) 877-6122**
Application fee: **$10**
Fall 2005 application deadline: **7/15**
Test of English as Foreign Language (TOEFL) is required for international students.

FINANCIAL INFORMATION
Financial aid phone number: **(601) 877-6190**
Tuition, 2003-2004 academic year: Full-time in-state: **$5,112**; out-of-state: **$9,618**, Part-time in-state: **$3,882**; out-of-state: **$6,886**

ACADEMIC PROGRAMS
Areas of specialization: elementary teacher education, secondary teacher education.
The education program is currently accredited by the National Council for Accreditation of Teacher Education.

LICENSING TEST
Pass rate on state's teacher licensing test for 2002-2003: **100%**
State average pass rate: **95%**

Belhaven College

- 1500 Peachtree Street, Jackson, MS 39202
- Website: http://www.belhaven.edu/Academics/Graduate/Default.htm
- Private

LICENSING TEST
Pass rate on state's teacher licensing test for 2002-2003: **100%**
State average pass rate: **95%**

Delta State University

- 1003 W. Sunflower, Cleveland, MS 38733
- Website: http://www.deltastate.edu
- Public
- Degrees offered: bachelor's, master's, education specialist, Ed.D.

ADMISSIONS
Admissions phone number: **(662) 846-4875**
Admissions email address: *grad-info@deltastate.edu*
Application website: *http://ntweb.deltastate.edu/vp_academic/coned/gradstudies_intropage.htm*
Application fee: **$25**
Test of English as Foreign Language (TOEFL) is required for international students.
Minimum TOEFL score required for paper test: **525**
Minimum TOEFL score required for computer test: **196**

Fall 2003
Total 2003 enrollment: **336**
Master's degree enrollment: **251**
  Teacher preparation program enrollment (master's): **144**
Education specialist degree enrollment: **36**
Doctoral degree enrollment: **49**

FINANCIAL INFORMATION

Financial aid phone number: **(662) 846-4670**
Tuition, 2003-2004 academic year: Full-time in-state: **$3,348**; out-of-state: **$7,965**, Part-time in-state: **$156/credit hour**; out-of-state: **$412/credit hour**
Room and board: **$3,270**, Books and supplies: **$500**

ACADEMIC PROGRAMS

Total full-time tenured or tenure-track faculty (fall 2003): 25, Total part-time faculty (fall 2003): 12
Areas of specialization: curriculum and instruction, education administration and supervision, elementary teacher education, secondary teacher education, special education, student counseling and personnel services.
Professional development/partnership school(s) are used by students in some of the teaching programs.
During their internships, peer groups of students meet regularly to discuss instructional techniques in some of the teaching programs.
All of the students in their internships are mentored.
Courses that prepare teachers to pass the National Board of Professional Teaching Standards are offered.
Teacher preparation programs: Four-year baccalaureate-degree program leading to initial licensure that includes either a major or minor in education and practice teaching. Master's program preparing college graduates for initial licensure; includes practice teaching. Alternative program for college graduates leading to provisional licensure.
The education program is currently accredited by the National Council for Accreditation of Teacher Education.

LICENSING TEST

Pass rate on state's teacher licensing test for 2002-2003: **100%**
State average pass rate: **95%**

Jackson State University

■ **1400 John R. Lynch Street Administration Tower, Jackson, MS 39217**
■ **Website:** http://ccaix.jsums.edu/~gadmappl/
■ **Public**

LICENSING TEST

Pass rate on state's teacher licensing test for 2002-2003: **97%**
State average pass rate: **95%**

Mississippi College

■ **P.O. Box 4026, Clinton, MS 39058**
■ **Website:** http://www.mc.edu
■ **Private**
■ **Degrees offered:** bachelor's, master's, education specialist

ADMISSIONS

Admissions phone number: **(601) 925-3800**
Admissions email address: *http://www.mc.edu*
Application fee: **$25**
Fall 2005 application deadline: **8/15**
Test of English as Foreign Language (TOEFL) is required for international students.
Minimum TOEFL score required for paper test: **550**
Minimum TOEFL score required for computer test: **213**

FINANCIAL INFORMATION

Financial aid phone number: **(601) 925-3319**
Tuition, 2003-2004 academic year: Full-time: **$373/credit hour**; Part-time: **$373/credit hour**
Fees: **$373/credit hour**, Room and board: **$5,246**

ACADEMIC PROGRAMS

The education program is currently accredited by the National Council for Accreditation of Teacher Education.

LICENSING TEST

Pass rate on state's teacher licensing test for 2002-2003: **99%**
State average pass rate: **95%**

Mississippi State University

■ **PO Box 9710, Mississippi State, MS 39762**
■ **Website:** http://www.msstate.edu/dept/coe/
■ **Public**
■ **Degrees offered:** bachelor's, master's, education specialist, Ph.D., Ed.D.

ADMISSIONS

Admissions phone number: **(662) 325-2224**
Admissions email address: *admit@admissions.msstate.edu*
Application fee: **$25**
Test requirements: **GRE**
Test of English as Foreign Language (TOEFL) is required for international students.
Minimum TOEFL score required for paper test: **550**
Minimum TOEFL score required for computer test: **250**

Fall 2003
Average GRE verbal: **401**, Average GRE quantitative: **459**, Average GRE analytical: **500**
Total 2003 enrollment: **754**

Master's degree enrollment: **374**
   Teacher preparation program enrollment (master's): **227**
Education specialist degree enrollment: **50**
Doctoral degree enrollment: **330**

FINANCIAL INFORMATION
Financial aid phone number: **(662) 325-2450**
Tuition, 2003-2004 academic year: Full-time in-state:
   $3,874; out-of-state: **$8,780**, Part-time in-state:
   $162/credit hour; out-of-state: **$205/credit hour**
Fees: **$388**, Room and board: **$2,540**, Books and supplies:
   $750, Miscellaneous expenses: **$1,800**
Number of fellowships awarded to graduate students dur-
   ing the 2003-2004 academic year: **2**
Number of teaching assistant positions: **25**
Number of research assistant positions: **12**
Number of other paid appointments: **20**

ACADEMIC PROGRAMS
Total full-time tenured or tenure-track faculty (fall 2003): **81**
   Total part-time faculty (fall 2003): **29**
Areas of specialization: curriculum and instruction, education administration and supervision, educational psychology, elementary teacher education, higher education
   administration, secondary teacher education, special
   education, student counseling and personnel services.
Professional development/partnership school(s) are used
   by students in all of the teaching programs.
During their internships, peer groups of students meet
   regularly to discuss instructional techniques in all of the
   teaching programs.
Courses that prepare teachers to pass the National Board of
   Professional Teaching Standards are offered.
Teacher preparation programs: Four-year baccalaureate-
   degree program leading to initial licensure that includes
   either a major or minor in education and practice teaching. Master's program preparing college graduates for
   initial licensure; includes practice teaching.
The education program is currently accredited by the
   National Council for Accreditation of Teacher Education.

LICENSING TEST
Pass rate on state's teacher licensing test for 2002-2003:
   90%
State average pass rate: **95%**

Mississippi University for Women

- **W. Box 1600, Columbus, MS 39701**
- **Website:** http://www.muw.edu/edu_hs/grad/index.html
- **Public**

LICENSING TEST
Pass rate on state's teacher licensing test for 2002-2003:
   100%
State average pass rate: **95%**

Mississippi Valley State University

- **14000 Highway 82 West, Itta Bena, MS 38930**
- **Website:** http://www.mvsu.edu
- **Public**
- **Degrees offered:** bachelor's, master's

ADMISSIONS
Admissions phone number: **(662) 254-3347**
Admissions email address: *leewilson@mvsu.edu*
Application fee: **$0**
Fall 2005 application deadline: **8/1**
Test requirements: **GRE**
Test of English as Foreign Language (TOEFL) is required
   for international students.
Minimum TOEFL score required for paper test: **400**

FINANCIAL INFORMATION
Financial aid phone number: **(662) 254-3765**
Tuition, 2003-2004 academic year: Full-time in-state:
   $3,502; out-of-state: **$8,056**
Room and board: **$3,354**, Books and supplies: **$1,000**

ACADEMIC PROGRAMS
Total full-time tenured or tenure-track faculty (fall 2003):
   110
Areas of specialization: elementary teacher education, special education.
Teacher preparation programs: Four-year baccalaureate-
   degree program leading to initial licensure that includes
   either a major or minor in education and practice teaching. Alternative program for college graduates leading to
   provisional licensure.
The education program is currently accredited by the
   National Council for Accreditation of Teacher Education.

LICENSING TEST
Pass rate on state's teacher licensing test for 2002-2003: **100%**
State average pass rate: **95%**

University of Mississippi

- **Office of the Dean, 164 Education, University, MS 38677**
- **Website:** http://www.olemiss.edu/depts/educ_school
- **Public**

ADMISSIONS
Admissions phone number: **(662) 915-7226**
Admissions email address: *bhoworth@olemiss.edu*
Application website:
   http://www.olemiss.edu/depts/graduate_school/apply.html
Test requirements: **GRE**
Test of English as Foreign Language (TOEFL) is required
   for international students.

Minimum TOEFL score required for paper test: 525
Minimum TOEFL score required for computer test: 197

FINANCIAL INFORMATION
Financial aid phone number: **(662) 915-7175**

LICENSING TEST
Pass rate on state's teacher licensing test for 2002-2003:
95%
State average pass rate: 95%

University of Southern Mississippi

- Box 5023, Hattiesburg, MS 39406
- **Website:** http://www.usm.edu
- Public

ADMISSIONS
Admissions phone number: **(601) 266-4369**
Admissions email address:
admissions@gradsch.mccain.usm.edu

Application website: *https://www.usm.edu/gradapp/*
Minimum TOEFL score required for paper test: 525

FINANCIAL INFORMATION
Financial aid phone number: **(601) 266-4774**

LICENSING TEST
Pass rate on state's teacher licensing test for 2002-2003:
95%
State average pass rate: 95%

William Carey College

- **498 Tuscan Avenue, Hattiesburg, MS 39401-5499**
- **Website:** http://www.wmcarey.edu/
- Private

LICENSING TEST
Pass rate on state's teacher licensing test for 2002-2003:
100%
State average pass rate: 95%

MISSOURI

Avila College

- 11901 Wornall Road, Kansas City, MO 64145
- **Website:** http://www.avila.edu/gradprograms/index.htm
- **Private**

LICENSING TEST
Pass rate on state's teacher licensing test for 2002-2003: 98%
State average pass rate: 96%

Central Methodist College

- Administrative Building; Room 114, Warrensburg, MO 64093
- **Website:** http://www.cmc.edu/
- **Private**

LICENSING TEST
Pass rate on state's teacher licensing test for 2002-2003: 87%
State average pass rate: 96%

Central Missouri State University

- Lov 2190, Warrensburg, MO 64093
- **Website:** http://www.cmsu.edu/graduate
- **Public**
- **Degrees offered:** bachelor's, master's, education specialist, Ed.D.

ADMISSIONS
Admissions phone number: **(660) 543-4621**
Admissions email address: *Gradinfo@cmsu1.cmsu.edu*
Application website: *http://www.cmsu.edu/graduate/adminssion/apply*
Application fee: **$30**
Fall 2005 application deadline: 7/30
Test requirements: **GRE or MAT**
Test of English as Foreign Language (TOEFL) is required for international students.
Minimum TOEFL score required for paper test: 550
Minimum TOEFL score required for computer test: 213

Fall 2003
Acceptance rate for master's degree programs: 73%
Acceptance rate for education specialist degree programs: 86%
Average GRE verbal: 426, Average GRE quantitative: 490, Average GRE analytical: 535
Total 2003 enrollment: 908
Master's degree enrollment: 787
  Teacher preparation program enrollment (master's): 352
Education specialist degree enrollment: 105
Doctoral degree enrollment: 16

FINANCIAL INFORMATION
Financial aid phone number: **(660) 543-4040**
Tuition, 2003-2004 academic year: Full-time in-state: **$198/credit hour**; out-of-state: **$396/credit hour**, Part-time in-state: **$198/credit hour**; out-of-state: **$396/credit hour**
Fees: **$12/credit hour**, Room and board: **$4,796**, Books and supplies: **$500**, Miscellaneous expenses: **$1,400**

ACADEMIC PROGRAMS
Total full-time tenured or tenure-track faculty (fall 2003): 102, Total part-time faculty (fall 2003): 43
Areas of specialization: curriculum and instruction, education administration and supervision, elementary teacher education, higher education administration, secondary teacher education, special education, student counseling and personnel services, teacher education.
Professional development/partnership school(s) are used by students in some of the teaching programs.

During their internships, peer groups of students meet regularly to discuss instructional techniques in some of the teaching programs.

All of the students in their internships are mentored.

Courses that prepare teachers to pass the National Board of Professional Teaching Standards are offered.

Teacher preparation programs: Four-year baccalaureate-degree program leading to initial licensure that includes either a major or minor in education and practice teaching. Alternative program for college graduates leading to provisional licensure.

The education program is currently accredited by the National Council for Accreditation of Teacher Education.

The education program is currently accredited by the Teacher Education Accreditation Council.

LICENSING TEST

Pass rate on state's teacher licensing test for 2002-2003: 95%

State average pass rate: 96%

Columbia College

- 1001 Rogers St., Columbia, MO 65216
- **Website:** http://www.ccis.edu/
- **Private**
- **Degrees offered:** master's

ADMISSIONS

Admissions phone number: **(573) 875-7352**
Admissions email address: *admissions@ccis.edu*
Application website: *http://www.ccis.edu/Graduate/mat/index.html*
Application fee: **$25**
Fall 2005 application deadline: **rolling**
Test requirements: **None**
Test of English as Foreign Language (TOEFL) is required for international students.
Minimum TOEFL score required for paper test: **500**
Minimum TOEFL score required for computer test: **173**

Fall 2003
Acceptance rate for master's degree programs: **64%**
Total 2003 enrollment: **60**
Master's degree enrollment: **60**
  Teacher preparation program enrollment (master's): **60**

FINANCIAL INFORMATION

Financial aid phone number: **(573) 875-7390**
Tuition, 2003-2004 academic year: Full-time: **$235/credit hour**; Part-time: **$235/credit hour**
Fees: **$235/credit hour**
Number of fellowships awarded to graduate students during the 2003-2004 academic year: **0**
Number of teaching assistant positions: **0**
Number of research assistant positions: **0**
Number of other paid appointments: **0**

ACADEMIC PROGRAMS

Total full-time tenured or tenure-track faculty (fall 2003): **6**,
  Total part-time faculty (fall 2003): **12**
Areas of specialization: curriculum and instruction, educational psychology, special education.

Professional development/partnership school(s) are used by students in none of the teaching programs.

During their internships, peer groups of students meet regularly to discuss instructional techniques in some of the teaching programs.

None of the students in their internships are mentored.

Courses that prepare teachers to pass the National Board of Professional Teaching Standards are not offered.

Teacher preparation programs: Four-year baccalaureate-degree program leading to initial licensure that includes either a major or minor in education and practice teaching. Five-year program leading to initial licensure that results in a baccalaureate degree (with a major or minor in education) plus graduate credit and includes practice teaching. Five-year program leading to initial licensure that results in a baccalaureate degree (with a major or minor in education) plus a master's degree and includes practice teaching. Master's program preparing college graduates for initial licensure; includes practice teaching. Alternative program for college graduates leading to provisional licensure.

LICENSING TEST

Pass rate on state's teacher licensing test for 2002-2003: 100%

State average pass rate: 96%

Drury College

- 900 N. Benton Ave., Springfield, MO 65802
- **Website:** http://www.drury.edu
- **Private**
- **Degrees offered:** bachelor's, master's

LICENSING TEST

Pass rate on state's teacher licensing test for 2002-2003: 99%

State average pass rate: 96%

Evangel University

- 1111 N. Glenstone, Springfield, MO 65802
- **Website:** http://www.evangel.edu
- **Private**
- **Degrees offered:** master's

ADMISSIONS

Admissions phone number: **(417) 865-2815**
Application fee: **$25**
Fall 2005 application deadline: **rolling**

Test of English as Foreign Language (TOEFL) is required
for international students.
Minimum TOEFL score required for paper test: 550
Minimum TOEFL score required for computer test: 213

Fall 2003
Total 2003 enrollment: 41
Master's degree enrollment: 41
Teacher preparation program enrollment (master's): 38

FINANCIAL INFORMATION
Financial aid phone number: **(417) 865-2815**
Tuition, 2003-2004 academic year: Full-time: **$250/credit
hour**; Part-time: **$250/credit hour**
Fees: **$40**

ACADEMIC PROGRAMS
The education program is currently accredited by the
National Council for Accreditation of Teacher Education.

LICENSING TEST
Pass rate on state's teacher licensing test for 2002-2003: **97%**
State average pass rate: **96%**

Fontbonne University

■ **6800 Wydown Blvd., St. Louis, MO 63105**
■ **Website:** http://www.fontbonne.edu
■ **Private**
■ **Degrees offered:** bachelor's, master's

ADMISSIONS
Admissions phone number: **(314) 889-1430**
Admissions email address: *cmdavis@fontbonne.edu*
Application website: *http://www.fontbonne.edu*
Application fee: **$25**
Fall 2005 application deadline: **rolling**
Test of English as Foreign Language (TOEFL) is required
for international students.
Minimum TOEFL score required for paper test: **525**

FINANCIAL INFORMATION
Financial aid phone number: **(314) 889-1414**

LICENSING TEST
Pass rate on state's teacher licensing test for 2002-2003:
100%
State average pass rate: **96%**

Lincoln University

■ **PO Box 29, Jefferson City, MO 65102-0029**
■ **Website:**
http://www.lincolnu.edu/%7Eeduc/div_of_ed/index.htm
■ **Public**

LICENSING TEST
Pass rate on state's teacher licensing test for 2002-2003:
84%
State average pass rate: **96%**

Lindenwood University

■ **209 S. Kingshighway, St. Charles, MO 63301**
■ **Website:** http://www.lindenwood.edu
■ **Private**
■ **Degrees offered:** bachelor's, master's, education
specialist

ADMISSIONS
Admissions phone number: **(636) 949-4949**
Admissions email address: *http://www.lindenwood.edu*
Application fee: **$25**
Fall 2005 application deadline: **7/30**
Test of English as Foreign Language (TOEFL) is required
for international students.
Minimum TOEFL score required for paper test: **500**
Minimum TOEFL score required for computer test: **173**

Fall 2003
Acceptance rate for master's degree programs: **100%**
Acceptance rate for education specialist degree programs:
100%
Total 2003 enrollment: **2,211**
Master's degree enrollment: **2,100**
Teacher preparation program enrollment (master's): **500**
Education specialist degree enrollment: **111**

FINANCIAL INFORMATION
Financial aid phone number: **(636) 949-4925**
Tuition, 2003-2004 academic year: Full-time: **$310/credit
hour**; Part-time: **$310/credit hour**
Room and board: **$5,600**, Books and supplies: **$800**,
Miscellaneous expenses: **$400**
Number of fellowships awarded to graduate students dur-
ing the 2003-2004 academic year: **0**
Number of teaching assistant positions: **0**
Number of research assistant positions: **0**
Number of other paid appointments: **0**

ACADEMIC PROGRAMS
Total full-time tenured or tenure-track faculty (fall 2003):
16, Total part-time faculty (fall 2003): **58**
Areas of specialization: education administration and
supervision, educational psychology, elementary teacher

education, secondary teacher education, special education, student counseling and personnel services, teacher education.

Professional development/partnership school(s) are used by students in some of the teaching programs.

During their internships, peer groups of students meet regularly to discuss instructional techniques in some of the teaching programs.

All of the students in their internships are mentored.

Courses that prepare teachers to pass the National Board of Professional Teaching Standards are not offered.

Teacher preparation programs: Four-year baccalaureate-degree program leading to initial licensure that includes either a major or minor in education and practice teaching. Master's program preparing college graduates for initial licensure; includes practice teaching. Alternative program for college graduates leading to provisional licensure.

The education program is currently accredited by the Teacher Education Accreditation Council.

LICENSING TEST
Pass rate on state's teacher licensing test for 2002-2003: 100%

State average pass rate: 96%

Maryville University of St. Louis

■ 13550 Conway Road, St. Louis, MO 63141
■ Website:
  http://www.maryville.edu/academics/home_ed.asp
■ Private

LICENSING TEST
Pass rate on state's teacher licensing test for 2002-2003: 98%
State average pass rate: 96%

Missouri Baptist College

■ 1 College Park Drive, St. Louis, MO 63141
■ Website: http://www.mobap.edu
■ Private
■ Degrees offered: bachelor's, master's

ADMISSIONS
Admissions phone number: **(314) 392-2296**
Admissions email address: *admissions@mobap.edu*
Application website: *http://www.mobap.edu/admissions/index.asp*
Application fee: **$25**
Fall 2005 application deadline: **rolling**
Test of English as Foreign Language (TOEFL) is required for international students.
Minimum TOEFL score required for paper test: **500**

Minimum TOEFL score required for computer test: 173

Fall 2003
Total 2003 enrollment: **709**

FINANCIAL INFORMATION
Financial aid phone number: **(314) 392-2366**
Tuition, 2003-2004 academic year: Full-time: **$270/credit hour**; Part-time: **$270/credit hour**
Fees: **$8/credit hour**

ACADEMIC PROGRAMS
Areas of specialization: curriculum and instruction, education administration and supervision, student counseling and personnel services.

Professional development/partnership school(s) are used by students in some of the teaching programs.

During their internships, peer groups of students meet regularly to discuss instructional techniques in all of the teaching programs.

All of the students in their internships are mentored.

Courses that prepare teachers to pass the National Board of Professional Teaching Standards are not offered.

Teacher preparation programs: Four-year baccalaureate-degree program leading to initial licensure that includes either a major or minor in education and practice teaching. Master's program preparing college graduates for initial licensure; includes practice teaching. Alternative program for college graduates leading to provisional licensure.

LICENSING TEST
Pass rate on state's teacher licensing test for 2002-2003: 100%
State average pass rate: 96%

Northwest Missouri State University

■ 800 University Drive, Maryville, MO 64468
■ Website: http://www.nwmissouri.edu
■ Public
■ Degrees offered: bachelor's, master's, education specialist

ADMISSIONS
Admissions phone number: **(660) 562-1148**
Admissions email address:
  admissions@mail.nwmissouri.edu
Application website: *http://www.nwmissouri.edu/graduate*
Application fee: **$0**
Test requirements: **GRE**
Test of English as Foreign Language (TOEFL) is required for international students.
Minimum TOEFL score required for paper test: **550**
Minimum TOEFL score required for computer test: **213**

Fall 2003

Acceptance rate for master's degree programs: 71%

Acceptance rate for education specialist degree programs: 100%

Average GRE verbal: 370, Average GRE quantitative: 320, Average GRE analytical: 420

Total 2003 enrollment: 301

Master's degree enrollment: 272

    Teacher preparation program enrollment (master's): 161

Education specialist degree enrollment: 29

FINANCIAL INFORMATION

Financial aid phone number: (660) 562-1363

Tuition, 2003-2004 academic year: Full-time in-state: **$202/credit hour**; out-of-state: **$354/credit hour**, Part-time in-state: **$202/credit hour**; out-of-state: **$354/credit hour**

Room and board: **$5,276**

Number of teaching assistant positions: 27

Number of research assistant positions: 14

Number of other paid appointments: 1

ACADEMIC PROGRAMS

Total full-time tenured or tenure-track faculty (fall 2003): 49, Total part-time faculty (fall 2003): 7

Areas of specialization: curriculum and instruction, education administration and supervision, elementary teacher education, secondary teacher education, special education, student counseling and personnel services.

Courses that prepare teachers to pass the National Board of Professional Teaching Standards are offered.

Teacher preparation programs: Four-year baccalaureate-degree program leading to initial licensure that includes either a major or minor in education and practice teaching. Master's program preparing college graduates for initial licensure; includes practice teaching. Alternative program for college graduates leading to provisional licensure.

The education program is currently accredited by the National Council for Accreditation of Teacher Education.

LICENSING TEST

Pass rate on state's teacher licensing test for 2002-2003: 94%

State average pass rate: 96%

Park University

■ **8700 N.W. River Park Drive, Parkville, MO 64152**
■ **Website:** http://www.park.edu
■ **Private**
■ **Degrees offered:** bachelor's, master's

ADMISSIONS

Admissions phone number: (800) 745-7275

Admissions email address: *admissions@park.edu*

Application fee: **$25**

Fall 2005 application deadline: **rolling**

Test of English as Foreign Language (TOEFL) is required for international students.

Minimum TOEFL score required for paper test: 500

Fall 2003

Total 2003 enrollment: 80

Master's degree enrollment: 80

    Teacher preparation program enrollment (master's): 80

FINANCIAL INFORMATION

Financial aid phone number: (816) 584-6290

Tuition, 2003-2004 academic year: Full-time: **$200/credit hour**; Part-time: **$200/credit hour**

Room and board: **$2,590**

Number of fellowships awarded to graduate students during the 2003-2004 academic year: 0

Number of teaching assistant positions: 0

Number of research assistant positions: 0

ACADEMIC PROGRAMS

Total full-time tenured or tenure-track faculty (fall 2003): 7

Areas of specialization: curriculum and instruction, education administration and supervision, special education.

Professional development/partnership school(s) are used by students in some of the teaching programs.

During their internships, peer groups of students meet regularly to discuss instructional techniques in all of the teaching programs.

Some of the students in their internships are mentored.

Courses that prepare teachers to pass the National Board of Professional Teaching Standards are not offered.

Teacher preparation programs: Four-year baccalaureate-degree program leading to initial licensure that includes either a major or minor in education and practice teaching. Master's program preparing college graduates for initial licensure; includes practice teaching. Alternative program for college graduates leading to provisional licensure.

LICENSING TEST

Pass rate on state's teacher licensing test for 2002-2003: 88%

State average pass rate: 96%

Rockhurst University

■ **1100 Rockhurst Road, Kansas City, MO 64110**
■ **Website:** http://www.rockhurst.edu
■ **Private**
■ **Degrees offered:** bachelor's, master's

ADMISSIONS

Admissions phone number: (816) 501-4100

Admissions email address: *admission@rockhurst.edu*

Application website: *http://www.rockhurst.edu/admission/ grad/med/index.asp*

Application fee: **$0**

Fall 2005 application deadline: **rolling**

Test of English as Foreign Language (TOEFL) is required for international students.
Minimum TOEFL score required for paper test: 550
Minimum TOEFL score required for computer test: 213

Fall 2003
Acceptance rate for master's degree programs: 88%
Total 2003 enrollment: 139
Master's degree enrollment: 139
    Teacher preparation program enrollment (master's): 139

FINANCIAL INFORMATION
Financial aid phone number: (816) 501-4536
Tuition, 2003-2004 academic year: Full-time: **$280/credit hour**; Part-time: **$280/credit hour**
Fees: **$50**, Room and board: **$6,111**, Books and supplies: **$1,050**, Miscellaneous expenses: **$3,090**

ACADEMIC PROGRAMS
Total full-time tenured or tenure-track faculty (fall 2003): **6**, Total part-time faculty (fall 2003): **9**
Areas of specialization: elementary teacher education, secondary teacher education.
Professional development/partnership school(s) are used by students in all of the teaching programs.
During their internships, peer groups of students meet regularly to discuss instructional techniques in some of the teaching programs.
All of the students in their internships are mentored.
Courses that prepare teachers to pass the National Board of Professional Teaching Standards are not offered.
Teacher preparation programs: Four-year baccalaureate-degree program leading to initial licensure that includes either a major or minor in education and practice teaching. Master's program preparing college graduates for initial licensure; includes practice teaching.
The education program is currently accredited by the Teacher Education Accreditation Council.

LICENSING TEST
Pass rate on state's teacher licensing test for 2002-2003: **92%**
State average pass rate: **96%**

Southeast Missouri State University

- One University Plaza, cape Girardeau, MO 63701
- **Website:** http://www.semo.edu/admissions/index.htm
- Public
- **Degrees offered:** bachelor's, master's, education specialist

ADMISSIONS
Admissions phone number: (573) 651-2590
Admissions email address: *admissions@semo.edu*

Application website: *http://www.semo.edu/admissions/apply.htm*
Application fee: **$20**
Fall 2005 application deadline: **rolling**
Test requirements: **GRE**
Test of English as Foreign Language (TOEFL) is required for international students.
Minimum TOEFL score required for paper test: 550
Minimum TOEFL score required for computer test: 213

Fall 2003
Acceptance rate for master's degree programs: 90%
Acceptance rate for education specialist degree programs: 100%
Average GRE verbal: 422, Average GRE quantitative: 468, Average GRE analytical: 505
Total 2003 enrollment: 327
Master's degree enrollment: 259
    Teacher preparation program enrollment (master's): 2
Education specialist degree enrollment: 68

FINANCIAL INFORMATION
Financial aid phone number: (573) 651-2253
Tuition, 2003-2004 academic year: Full-time in-state: **$4,061**; out-of-state: **$7,514**, Part-time in-state: **$180/credit hour**; out-of-state: **$324/credit hour**
Fees: **$257**, Room and board: **$5,092**, Books and supplies: **$350**, Miscellaneous expenses: **$3,022**
Number of fellowships awarded to graduate students during the 2003-2004 academic year: 0
Number of teaching assistant positions: 61
Number of research assistant positions: 59
Number of other paid appointments: 47

ACADEMIC PROGRAMS
Total full-time tenured or tenure-track faculty (fall 2003): **31**
Areas of specialization: education administration and supervision, elementary teacher education, higher education administration, secondary teacher education, special education, student counseling and personnel services.
Professional development/partnership school(s) are used by students in some of the teaching programs.
During their internships, peer groups of students meet regularly to discuss instructional techniques in some of the teaching programs.
All of the students in their internships are mentored.
Courses that prepare teachers to pass the National Board of Professional Teaching Standards are offered.
Teacher preparation programs: Four-year baccalaureate-degree program leading to initial licensure that includes either a major or minor in education and practice teaching. Alternative program for college graduates leading to provisional licensure.
The education program is currently accredited by the National Council for Accreditation of Teacher Education.

LICENSING TEST
Pass rate on state's teacher licensing test for 2002-2003: **95%**
State average pass rate: **96%**

Southwest Baptist University

■ 1600 University Avenue, Bolivar, MO 65613
■ Website: http://www.sbuniv.edu/mseducation/index.htm
■ Private

LICENSING TEST
Pass rate on state's teacher licensing test for 2002-2003: 94%
State average pass rate: 96%

Southwest Missouri State University

■ 901 S. National, Springfield, MO 65804-0094
■ Website: http://education.smsu.edu/
■ Public

LICENSING TEST
Pass rate on state's teacher licensing test for 2002-2003: 97%
State average pass rate: 96%

Stephens College

■ 1200 E. Broadway, Box 2121, Columbia, MO 65215
■ Website: http://www.stephens.edu/academics/graduate/
■ Private

LICENSING TEST
Pass rate on state's teacher licensing test for 2002-2003: 91%
State average pass rate: 96%

St. Louis University

■ 3750 Lindell Boulevard, St. Louis, MO 63108-3412
■ Website: http://www.slu.edu/colleges/cops/es/grad.html
■ Private
■ Degrees offered: bachelor's, master's, education specialist, Ph.D., Ed.D.

ADMISSIONS
Admissions phone number: (314) 977-2350
Admissions email address: *grequest@slu.edu*
Application fee: $40
Fall 2005 application deadline: 7/1
Test requirements: GRE or MAT
Test of English as Foreign Language (TOEFL) is required for international students.
Minimum TOEFL score required for paper test: 550

Fall 2003
Acceptance rate for master's degree programs: 79%
Acceptance rate for education specialist degree programs: 100%
Acceptance rate for doctoral programs: 80%
Total 2003 enrollment: 428
Master's degree enrollment: 117
  Teacher preparation program enrollment (master's): 1
Education specialist degree enrollment: 6
Doctoral degree enrollment: 305

FINANCIAL INFORMATION
Financial aid phone number: (314) 977-2350
Tuition, 2003-2004 academic year: Full-time: $690/credit hour; Part-time: $690/credit hour
Fees: $168/credit hour, Room and board: $8,520, Books and supplies: $1,040
Number of fellowships awarded to graduate students during the 2003-2004 academic year: 4
Number of teaching assistant positions: 3
Number of research assistant positions: 10
Number of other paid appointments: 11

ACADEMIC PROGRAMS
Total full-time tenured or tenure-track faculty (fall 2003): 29
  Total part-time faculty (fall 2003): 34
Areas of specialization: curriculum and instruction, education administration and supervision, elementary teacher education, higher education administration, secondary teacher education, special education, student counseling and personnel services.
Professional development/partnership school(s) are used by students in all of the teaching programs.
During their internships, peer groups of students meet regularly to discuss instructional techniques in all of the teaching programs.
All of the students in their internships are mentored.
Courses that prepare teachers to pass the National Board of Professional Teaching Standards are not offered.
The education program is currently accredited by the National Council for Accreditation of Teacher Education.

LICENSING TEST
Pass rate on state's teacher licensing test for 2002-2003: 91%
State average pass rate: 96%

Truman State University

■ 100 East Normal, Kirksville, MO 63501
■ Website: http://gradschool.truman.edu/
■ Public
■ Degrees offered: master's

ADMISSIONS
Admissions phone number: (660) 785-4109
Admissions email address: *cristac@truman.edu*

Application website: *http://gradschool.truman.edu/ applying.stm*
Application fee: $0
Fall 2005 application deadline: 2/15
Test requirements: GRE
Test of English as Foreign Language (TOEFL) is required for international students.
Minimum TOEFL score required for paper test: 550
Minimum TOEFL score required for computer test: 213

Fall 2003
Acceptance rate for master's degree programs: 88%
Average GRE verbal: 497, Average GRE quantitative: 584
Total 2003 enrollment: 142
Master's degree enrollment: 142
    Teacher preparation program enrollment (master's): 102

FINANCIAL INFORMATION
Financial aid phone number: (660) 785-4130
Tuition, 2003-2004 academic year: Full-time in-state: **$207/credit hour**; out-of-state: **$370/credit hour**, Part-time in-state: **$207/credit hour**; out-of-state: **$370/credit hour**
Fees: **$112**, Room and board: **$5,072**, Books and supplies: **$1,000**
Number of fellowships awarded to graduate students during the 2003-2004 academic year: 15
Number of teaching assistant positions: 6

ACADEMIC PROGRAMS
Total full-time tenured or tenure-track faculty (fall 2003): 16
    Total part-time faculty (fall 2003): 1
Areas of specialization: elementary teacher education, secondary teacher education, special education, student counseling and personnel services.
Professional development/partnership school(s) are used by students in some of the teaching programs.
During their internships, peer groups of students meet regularly to discuss instructional techniques in all of the teaching programs.
All of the students in their internships are mentored.
Courses that prepare teachers to pass the National Board of Professional Teaching Standards are not offered.
Teacher preparation programs: Master's degree in education, including internship/practice teaching and preparation for initial licensure.
The education program is currently accredited by the National Council for Accreditation of Teacher Education.

LICENSING TEST
Pass rate on state's teacher licensing test for 2002-2003: 100%
State average pass rate: 96%

University of Missouri–Columbia

■ **118 Hill Hall, Columbia, MO 65211**
■ **Website:** http://www.coe.missouri.edu
■ **Public**
■ **Degrees offered:** bachelor's, master's, education specialist, Ph.D., Ed.D.
■ **Overall rank in the 2005 U.S. News education schools with doctoral programs:** 42
■ **Overall rank in the 2005 U.S. News education school specialty rankings:** administration/supervision: 16, counseling/personnel: 9, higher education administration: 25, vocational/technical: 9

ADMISSIONS
Admissions phone number: (573) 882-2961
Admissions email address: *pullism@missouri.edu*
Application website: *http://www.missouri.edu/~gradschl/ apply/index.html*
Application fee: $45
Fall 2005 application deadline: 7/1
Test requirements: **GRE or MAT**
Test of English as Foreign Language (TOEFL) is required for international students.
Minimum TOEFL score required for paper test: 530
Minimum TOEFL score required for computer test: 197

Fall 2003
Acceptance rate for master's degree programs: 63%
Acceptance rate for education specialist degree programs: 81%
Acceptance rate for doctoral programs: 51%
Average GRE verbal: 493, Average GRE quantitative: 555, Average GRE analytical: 566, Average MAT: 80
Total 2003 enrollment: 1,991
Master's degree enrollment: 1,288
Education specialist degree enrollment: 95
Doctoral degree enrollment: 608

FINANCIAL INFORMATION
Financial aid phone number: (573) 882-7506
Tuition, 2003-2004 academic year: Full-time in-state: **$237/credit hour**; out-of-state: **$639/credit hour**, Part-time in-state: **$237/credit hour**; out-of-state: **$639/credit hour**
Fees: **$287**, Room and board: **$7,224**, Books and supplies: **$838**, Miscellaneous expenses: **$4,846**
Number of fellowships awarded to graduate students during the 2003-2004 academic year: 62
Number of teaching assistant positions: 74
Number of research assistant positions: 116

ACADEMIC PROGRAMS
Total full-time tenured or tenure-track faculty (fall 2003): 88
    Total part-time faculty (fall 2003): 52

Areas of specialization: curriculum and instruction, education administration and supervision, education policy, educational psychology, elementary teacher education, higher education administration, secondary teacher education, special education, student counseling and personnel services.

Professional development/partnership school(s) are used by students in all of the teaching programs.

During their internships, peer groups of students meet regularly to discuss instructional techniques in some of the teaching programs.

Some of the students in their internships are mentored.

Courses that prepare teachers to pass the National Board of Professional Teaching Standards are offered.

Teacher preparation programs: Four-year baccalaureate-degree program leading to initial licensure that includes either a major or minor in education and practice teaching. Master's program preparing college graduates for initial licensure; includes practice teaching. Alternative program for college graduates leading to provisional licensure.

LICENSING TEST

Pass rate on state's teacher licensing test for 2002-2003: 100%
State average pass rate: 96%

University of Missouri–Kansas City

■ 5100 Rockhill Road, Kansas City, MO 64110
■ Website: http://www.umkc.edu/
■ Public
■ Degrees offered: bachelor's, master's, education specialist, Ph.D., Ed.D.

ADMISSIONS

Admissions phone number: (816) 235-1111
Admissions email address: *admit@umkc.edu*
Application fee: $35
Fall 2005 application deadline: rolling
Test requirements: GRE
Test of English as Foreign Language (TOEFL) is required for international students.
Minimum TOEFL score required for paper test: 550
Minimum TOEFL score required for computer test: 213

Fall 2003

Acceptance rate for master's degree programs: 71%
Acceptance rate for education specialist degree programs: 63%
Acceptance rate for doctoral programs: 9%
Average GRE verbal: 462, Average GRE quantitative: 546, Average GRE analytical: 592, Average MAT: 36
Total 2003 enrollment: 837
Master's degree enrollment: 668

Teacher preparation program enrollment (master's): 406
Education specialist degree enrollment: 116
Doctoral degree enrollment: 53

FINANCIAL INFORMATION

Financial aid phone number: (816) 235-1154
Tuition, 2003-2004 academic year: Full-time in-state: $237/credit hour; out-of-state: $639/credit hour, Part-time in-state: $237/credit hour; out-of-state: $639/credit hour
Fees: $220, Room and board: $12,400, Books and supplies: $2,000, Miscellaneous expenses: $150
Number of fellowships awarded to graduate students during the 2003-2004 academic year: 1
Number of teaching assistant positions: 0
Number of research assistant positions: 12
Number of other paid appointments: 0

ACADEMIC PROGRAMS

Total full-time tenured or tenure-track faculty (fall 2003): 36
Total part-time faculty (fall 2003): 97
Areas of specialization: curriculum and instruction, education administration and supervision, educational psychology, elementary teacher education, higher education administration, secondary teacher education, special education, student counseling and personnel services.

Professional development/partnership school(s) are used by students in some of the teaching programs.

During their internships, peer groups of students meet regularly to discuss instructional techniques in some of the teaching programs.

Some of the students in their internships are mentored.

Courses that prepare teachers to pass the National Board of Professional Teaching Standards are not offered.

Teacher preparation programs: Four-year baccalaureate-degree program leading to initial licensure that includes either a major or minor in education and practice teaching. Master's program preparing college graduates for initial licensure; includes practice teaching. Alternative program for college graduates leading to provisional licensure.

The education program is currently accredited by the National Council for Accreditation of Teacher Education.

LICENSING TEST

Pass rate on state's teacher licensing test for 2002-2003: 91%
State average pass rate: 96%

University of Missouri–St. Louis

- 8001 Natural Bridge, St. Louis, MO 63121
- Website: http://www.umsl.edu
- Public
- Degrees offered: bachelor's, master's, Ph.D., Ed.D.

ADMISSIONS

Admissions phone number: (314) 516-5483
Admissions email address: *gradadm@umsl.edu*
Application website: *http://www.umsl.edu/divisions/graduate/*
Application fee: $35
Fall 2005 application deadline: 7/1
Test requirements: GRE
Test of English as Foreign Language (TOEFL) is required for international students.
Minimum TOEFL score required for paper test: 550
Minimum TOEFL score required for computer test: 213

Fall 2003

Acceptance rate for master's degree programs: 76%
Acceptance rate for doctoral programs: 60%
Average GRE verbal: 467, Average GRE quantitative: 492, Average GRE analytical: 479
Total 2003 enrollment: 976
Master's degree enrollment: 805
   Teacher preparation program enrollment (master's): 478
Doctoral degree enrollment: 171

FINANCIAL INFORMATION

Financial aid phone number: (314) 516-5508
Tuition, 2003-2004 academic year: Full-time in-state: $237/credit hour; out-of-state: $638/credit hour, Part-time in-state: $237/credit hour; out-of-state: $638/credit hour
Fees: $50/credit hour, Room and board: $8,762, Books and supplies: $618, Miscellaneous expenses: $4,859
Number of fellowships awarded to graduate students during the 2003-2004 academic year: 0
Number of teaching assistant positions: 5
Number of research assistant positions: 13
Number of other paid appointments: 0

ACADEMIC PROGRAMS

Total full-time tenured or tenure-track faculty (fall 2003): 57, Total part-time faculty (fall 2003): 59
Areas of specialization: curriculum and instruction, education administration and supervision, education policy, educational psychology, elementary teacher education, higher education administration, secondary teacher education, special education, student counseling and personnel services.
Professional development/partnership school(s) are used by students in some of the teaching programs.

During their internships, peer groups of students meet regularly to discuss instructional techniques in some of the teaching programs.
All of the students in their internships are mentored.
Courses that prepare teachers to pass the National Board of Professional Teaching Standards are not offered.
The education program is currently accredited by the National Council for Accreditation of Teacher Education.

LICENSING TEST

Pass rate on state's teacher licensing test for 2002-2003: 100%
State average pass rate: 96%

Washington University in St. Louis

- 1 Brookings Drive, Box 1187, St. Louis, MO 63130
- Website: http://www.artsci.wustl.edu/~educ/
- Private
- Degrees offered: bachelor's, master's, Ph.D.
- Overall rank in the 2005 U.S. News education schools with doctoral programs: 55

ADMISSIONS

Admissions phone number: (314) 935-6776
Admissions email address: *bcmiller@artsci.wustl.edu*
Application fee: $35
Fall 2005 application deadline: 1/15
Test requirements: GRE or MAT
Test of English as Foreign Language (TOEFL) is required for international students.
Minimum TOEFL score required for paper test: 600

Fall 2003

Acceptance rate for master's degree programs: 77%
Acceptance rate for doctoral programs: 41%
Average GRE verbal: 568, Average GRE quantitative: 649, Average GRE analytical: 638, Average MAT: 34
Total 2003 enrollment: 49
Master's degree enrollment: 37
   Teacher preparation program enrollment (master's): 37
Doctoral degree enrollment: 12

FINANCIAL INFORMATION

Financial aid phone number: (314) 935-5900
Tuition, 2003-2004 academic year: Full-time: $28,300; Part-time: $330/credit hour
Fees: $470, Room and board: $11,320, Books and supplies: $1,010, Miscellaneous expenses: $2,270
Number of fellowships awarded to graduate students during the 2003-2004 academic year: 14
Number of teaching assistant positions: 3
Number of research assistant positions: 3
Number of other paid appointments: 0

ACADEMIC PROGRAMS

Total full-time tenured or tenure-track faculty (fall 2003): **9**
Total part-time faculty (fall 2003): **11**

Areas of specialization: curriculum and instruction, education policy, educational psychology, elementary teacher education, secondary teacher education.

Professional development/partnership school(s) are used by students in some of the teaching programs.

During their internships, peer groups of students meet regularly to discuss instructional techniques in all of the teaching programs.

All of the students in their internships are mentored.

Courses that prepare teachers to pass the National Board of Professional Teaching Standards are not offered.

Teacher preparation programs: Four-year baccalaureate-degree program leading to initial licensure that includes either a major or minor in education and practice teaching. Five-year program leading to initial licensure that results in a baccalaureate degree (with a major or minor in education) plus a master's degree and includes practice teaching. Master's program preparing college graduates for initial licensure; includes practice teaching.

LICENSING TEST

Pass rate on state's teacher licensing test for 2002-2003: **100%**
State average pass rate: **96%**

Webster University

■ **470 East Lockwood, St. Louis, MO 63119**
■ **Website:** http://www.webster.edu
■ **Private**
■ **Degrees offered:** bachelor's, master's, education specialist

ADMISSIONS

Admissions phone number: **(314) 968-7089**
Admissions email address: *gadmit@webster.edu*
Application website: *http://www.webster.edu/admissions/graduate.html*
Application fee: **$25**
Fall 2005 application deadline: **rolling**
Test of English as Foreign Language (TOEFL) is required for international students.
Minimum TOEFL score required for paper test: **550**
Minimum TOEFL score required for computer test: **230**

Fall 2003
Acceptance rate for master's degree programs: **97%**
Acceptance rate for education specialist degree programs: **100%**
Total 2003 enrollment: **1,156**
Master's degree enrollment: **1,120**
    Teacher preparation program enrollment (master's): **1,120**
Education specialist degree enrollment: **36**

FINANCIAL INFORMATION

Financial aid phone number: **(800) 983-4623**
Tuition, 2003-2004 academic year: Full-time: **$15,480**; Part-time: **$370/credit hour**
Room and board: **$3,140**, Books and supplies: **$1,300**

ACADEMIC PROGRAMS

Total full-time tenured or tenure-track faculty (fall 2003): **19**
Total part-time faculty (fall 2003): **106**

Areas of specialization: curriculum and instruction, education administration and supervision, educational psychology, elementary teacher education, higher education administration, secondary teacher education, special education.

Professional development/partnership school(s) are used by students in some of the teaching programs.

During their internships, peer groups of students meet regularly to discuss instructional techniques in all of the teaching programs.

All of the students in their internships are mentored.

Courses that prepare teachers to pass the National Board of Professional Teaching Standards are offered.

LICENSING TEST

Pass rate on state's teacher licensing test for 2002-2003: **96%**
State average pass rate: **96%**

William Woods University

■ **One University Avenue, Fulton, MO 65251**
■ **Website:** http://www.williamwoods.edu
■ **Private**
■ **Degrees offered:** bachelor's, master's, education specialist

ADMISSIONS

Admissions phone number: **(573) 592-1149**
Admissions email address: *cgas@williamwoods.edu*
Application website: *http://www.williamwoods.edu/admin/gas/gradapplication.asp*
Application fee: **$25**
Fall 2005 application deadline: **rolling**
Test of English as Foreign Language (TOEFL) is required for international students.
Minimum TOEFL score required for paper test: **550**

Fall 2003
Total 2003 enrollment: **1,169**
Master's degree enrollment: **1,097**
    Teacher preparation program enrollment (master's): **313**
Education specialist degree enrollment: **72**

FINANCIAL INFORMATION

Financial aid phone number: **(573) 592-4236**

Tuition, 2003-2004 academic year: Full-time: **$245/credit hour**; Part-time: **$245/credit hour**

Books and supplies: **$1,000**

Number of fellowships awarded to graduate students during the 2003-2004 academic year: **0**

Number of teaching assistant positions: **0**

Number of research assistant positions: **0**

Number of other paid appointments: **0**

ACADEMIC PROGRAMS

Total full-time tenured or tenure-track faculty (fall 2003): **8**
Total part-time faculty (fall 2003): **268**

Areas of specialization: curriculum and instruction, education administration and supervision.

Professional development/partnership school(s) are used by students in some of the teaching programs.

During their internships, peer groups of students meet regularly to discuss instructional techniques in all of the teaching programs.

All of the students in their internships are mentored.

Courses that prepare teachers to pass the National Board of Professional Teaching Standards are offered.

Teacher preparation programs: Four-year baccalaureate-degree program leading to initial licensure that includes either a major or minor in education and practice teaching. Alternative program for college graduates leading to provisional licensure.

LICENSING TEST

Pass rate on state's teacher licensing test for 2002-2003: **55%**

State average pass rate: **96%**

MONTANA

TEACHER TESTING IN MONTANA
Teacher licensure rules vary widely from state to state, but almost all states require tests. The exams typically cover the basics of reading, writing and math, although some states mandate in-depth, subject-specific teacher tests. For information on where to go in your state for specific academic requirements, see Chapter 6 on page 67. Note: Some schools require students to pass exams by graduation, and thus automatically report pass rates of 100 percent.

- This state **does** require a basic skills test in order to obtain a teaching license.
- This state **does not** require a subject-knowledge test in order to obtain a middle school teaching license.
- This state **does not** require a subject-knowledge test in order to obtain a high school teaching license.
- This state **does not** require a subject-specific pedagogy test in order to obtain a teaching license.

Montana State University

- **215 Reid Hall, Bozeman, MT 59717**
- **Website:** http://www.montana.edu/wwwdg
- **Public**
- **Degrees offered:** bachelor's, master's, education specialist, Ed.D.

ADMISSIONS
Admissions phone number: **(406) 994-4145**
Admissions email address: *gradstudy@montana.edu*
Application website: *http://www.montana.edu/wwwdg/ apply.shtml*
Application fee: **$50**
Fall 2005 application deadline: **4/15**
Test requirements: **GRE**
Test of English as Foreign Language (TOEFL) is required for international students.
Minimum TOEFL score required for paper test: **550**
Minimum TOEFL score required for computer test: **213**

Fall 2003
Average GRE verbal: **470**, Average GRE quantitative: **450**
Total 2003 enrollment: **295**
Master's degree enrollment: **170**
    Teacher preparation program enrollment (master's): **59**
Education specialist degree enrollment: **5**
Doctoral degree enrollment: **120**

FINANCIAL INFORMATION
Financial aid phone number: **(406) 994-2845**
Tuition, 2003-2004 academic year: Full-time in-state: **$229/credit hour**; out-of-state: **$547/credit hour**, Part-time in-state: **$229/credit hour**; out-of-state: **$547/credit hour**
Number of fellowships awarded to graduate students during the 2003-2004 academic year: **0**
Number of teaching assistant positions: **16**
Number of research assistant positions: **0**

Number of other paid appointments: **0**

ACADEMIC PROGRAMS
Total full-time tenured or tenure-track faculty (fall 2003): **18**, Total part-time faculty (fall 2003): **14**
Areas of specialization: curriculum and instruction, education administration and supervision, education policy, educational psychology, elementary teacher education, higher education administration, secondary teacher education, student counseling and personnel services.
All of the students in their internships are mentored.
Courses that prepare teachers to pass the National Board of Professional Teaching Standards are offered.
Teacher preparation programs: Four-year baccalaureate-degree program leading to initial licensure that includes either a major or minor in education and practice teaching. Master's program preparing college graduates for initial licensure; includes practice teaching. Alternative program for college graduates leading to provisional licensure.
The education program is currently accredited by the National Council for Accreditation of Teacher Education.

LICENSING TEST
Pass rate on state's teacher licensing test for 2002-2003: **100%**
State average pass rate: **99%**

Montana State University–Billings

- **1500 University Drive, Billings, MT 59101**
- **Website:** http://www.msubillings.edu
- **Public**
- **Degrees offered:** bachelor's, master's

ADMISSIONS
Admissions phone number: **(406) 657-2158**
Admissions email address: *admissions@msubillings.edu*

Application website: *http://www.msubillings.edu/grad/admis-forms.htm*

Application fee: **$40**

Fall 2005 application deadline: **3/1**

Test requirements: **GRE**

Test of English as Foreign Language (TOEFL) is required for international students.

Fall 2003

Acceptance rate for master's degree programs: **100%**

Acceptance rate for education specialist degree programs: **100%**

Average GRE verbal: **380**, Average GRE quantitative: **420**

Total 2003 enrollment: **266**

Master's degree enrollment: **266**

Teacher preparation program enrollment (master's): **176**

FINANCIAL INFORMATION

Financial aid phone number: **(406) 657-2188**

Tuition, 2003-2004 academic year: Full-time in-state: **$4,789**; out-of-state: **$12,149**, Part-time in-state: **$2,459**; out-of-state: **$6,139**

Room and board: **$5,370**, Books and supplies: **$900**, Miscellaneous expenses: **$2,420**

Number of research assistant positions: **35**

ACADEMIC PROGRAMS

Total full-time tenured or tenure-track faculty (fall 2003): **156**, Total part-time faculty (fall 2003): **88**

Areas of specialization: curriculum and instruction, education policy, educational psychology, elementary teacher education, secondary teacher education, special education, student counseling and personnel services.

Professional development/partnership school(s) are used by students in all of the teaching programs.

During their internships, peer groups of students meet regularly to discuss instructional techniques in all of the teaching programs.

All of the students in their internships are mentored.

Courses that prepare teachers to pass the National Board of Professional Teaching Standards are not offered.

Teacher preparation programs: Four-year baccalaureate-degree program leading to initial licensure that includes either a major or minor in education and practice teaching. Master's program preparing college graduates for initial licensure; includes practice teaching.

The education program is currently accredited by the National Council for Accreditation of Teacher Education.

LICENSING TEST

Pass rate on state's teacher licensing test for 2002-2003: **100%**

State average pass rate: **99%**

Montana State University–Northern

- **P.O. Box 7751, Havre, MT 59501**
- **Website:** http://www.msun.edu
- **Public**
- **Degrees offered:** bachelor's, master's

ADMISSIONS

Admissions phone number: **(406) 265-3727**

Admissions email address: *admissions@msun.edu*

Application website: *http://www.msun.edu*

Application fee: **$30**

Fall 2005 application deadline: **rolling**

FINANCIAL INFORMATION

Financial aid phone number: **(406) 265-3787**

LICENSING TEST

Pass rate on state's teacher licensing test for 2002-2003: **100%**

State average pass rate: **99%**

University of Great Falls

- **1301 20th Street, S, Great Falls, MT 59405**
- **Website:** http://www.ugf.edu/academics/gradPrograms.htm
- **Private**

LICENSING TEST

Pass rate on state's teacher licensing test for 2002-2003: **100%**

State average pass rate: **99%**

University of Montana

- **Education Building, Room 108, Missoula, MT 59812**
- **Website:** http://www.soe.umt.edu
- **Public**

ADMISSIONS

Admissions phone number: **(406) 243-5304**

Admissions email address: *lisa.blank@mso.umt.edu*

FINANCIAL INFORMATION

Financial aid phone number: **(406) 243-5373**

LICENSING TEST

Pass rate on state's teacher licensing test for 2002-2003: **98%**

State average pass rate: **99%**

NEBRASKA

Chadron State College

■ **1000 Main Street, Chadron, NE 69337**
■ **Website:** http://www.csc.edu/
■ **Public**
■ **Degrees offered:** bachelor's, master's, education specialist

ADMISSIONS
Admissions phone number: **(308) 432-6263**
Application fee: **$15**
Fall 2005 application deadline: **rolling**
Test requirements: **GRE or MAT**
Test of English as Foreign Language (TOEFL) is required for international students.
Minimum TOEFL score required for paper test: **550**
Minimum TOEFL score required for computer test: **213**

Fall 2003
Acceptance rate for master's degree programs: **51%**
Total 2003 enrollment: **96**
Master's degree enrollment: **73**
   Teacher preparation program enrollment (master's): **29**
Education specialist degree enrollment: **23**

FINANCIAL INFORMATION
Financial aid phone number: **(308) 432-6230**
Tuition, 2003-2004 academic year: Full-time in-state: **$110/credit hour**; out-of-state: **$220/credit hour**, Part-time in-state: **$110/credit hour**; out-of-state: **$220/credit hour**
Fees: **$33/credit hour**, Room and board: **$3,654**, Books and supplies: **$650**, Miscellaneous expenses: **$1,075**
Number of fellowships awarded to graduate students during the 2003-2004 academic year: **2**

ACADEMIC PROGRAMS
Total full-time tenured or tenure-track faculty (fall 2003): **11**
Areas of specialization: education administration and supervision, elementary teacher education, secondary teacher education, student counseling and personnel services.

Professional development/partnership school(s) are used by students in none of the teaching programs.
During their internships, peer groups of students meet regularly to discuss instructional techniques in all of the teaching programs.
All of the students in their internships are mentored.
Courses that prepare teachers to pass the National Board of Professional Teaching Standards are not offered.
Teacher preparation programs: Four-year baccalaureate-degree program leading to initial licensure that includes either a major or minor in education and practice teaching.
The education program is currently accredited by the National Council for Accreditation of Teacher Education.

Concordia University

■ **800 N Columbia Avenue, Seward, NE 68434**
■ **Website:** http://www.cune.edu
■ **Private**
■ **Degrees offered:** bachelor's, master's, education specialist

ADMISSIONS
Admissions phone number: **(402) 643-7464**
Admissions email address: *gradadmiss@cune.edu*
Application website: *http://www.cune.edu/gradcatalog/*
Application fee: **$25**
Fall 2005 application deadline: **rolling**
Test of English as Foreign Language (TOEFL) is required for international students.
Minimum TOEFL score required for paper test: **550**
Minimum TOEFL score required for computer test: **213**

Fall 2003
Total 2003 enrollment: **216**
Master's degree enrollment: **216**
   Teacher preparation program enrollment (master's): **55**

FINANCIAL INFORMATION
Financial aid phone number: **(402) 643-7270**

Tuition, 2003-2004 academic year: Full-time: **$173/credit hour**; Part-time: **$173/credit hour**
Room and board: **$2,068**
Number of teaching assistant positions: **1**

ACADEMIC PROGRAMS
Total full-time tenured or tenure-track faculty (fall 2003): **49**, Total part-time faculty (fall 2003): **5**
Areas of specialization: curriculum and instruction, education administration and supervision, secondary teacher education, special education, teacher education.
Professional development/partnership school(s) are used by students in none of the teaching programs.
During their internships, peer groups of students meet regularly to discuss instructional techniques in some of the teaching programs.
None of the students in their internships are mentored.
Courses that prepare teachers to pass the National Board of Professional Teaching Standards are offered.
Teacher preparation programs: Master's degree in education, including internship/practice teaching and preparation for initial licensure.
The education program is currently accredited by the National Council for Accreditation of Teacher Education.

Creighton University

- **2500 California Plaza, Omaha, NE 68178**
- **Website:** http://www.creighton.edu/
- **Private**
- **Degrees offered:** bachelor's, master's

ADMISSIONS
Admissions phone number: **(402) 280-2870**
Admissions email address: *lhanson@creighton.edu*
Application fee: **$40**
Fall 2005 application deadline: **rolling**
Test requirements: **GRE**

Fall 2003
Total 2003 enrollment: **58**
Master's degree enrollment: **58**
   Teacher preparation program enrollment (master's): **21**

FINANCIAL INFORMATION
Financial aid phone number: **(402) 280-2870**
Tuition, 2003-2004 academic year: **$535/credit hour**
Room and board: **$3,800**, Books and supplies: **$500**, Miscellaneous expenses: **$300**
Number of fellowships awarded to graduate students during the 2003-2004 academic year: **0**
Number of teaching assistant positions: **0**
Number of research assistant positions: **0**
Number of other paid appointments: **0**

ACADEMIC PROGRAMS
Areas of specialization: education administration and supervision, student counseling and personnel services.

The education program is currently accredited by the National Council for Accreditation of Teacher Education.

Doane College

- **1014 Boswell Avenue, Crete, NE 68333**
- **Website:** http://www.doane.edu/
- **Private**

Hastings College

- **800 North Turner Avenue, Box 269, Hastings, NE 68902**
- **Website:** http://www.hastings.edu/
- **Private**

Peru State College

- **Box 10, Peru, NE 68421-0010**
- **Website:** http://www.hpcnet.org/cgi-bin/global/ a_bus_card.cgi?SiteID=75**
- **Public**

University of Nebraska– Kearney

- **905 W. 25th Street, Kearney, NE 68849**
- **Website:** http://www.unk.edu
- **Public**
- **Degrees offered:** bachelor's, master's, education specialist

ADMISSIONS
Admissions phone number: **(308) 865-8841**
Admissions email address: *gradstudies@unk.edu*
Application website: *http://webeasi.unk.edu*
Application fee: **$45**
Fall 2005 application deadline: **5/1**
Test of English as Foreign Language (TOEFL) is required for international students.
Minimum TOEFL score required for paper test: **550**
Minimum TOEFL score required for computer test: **213**

FINANCIAL INFORMATION
Financial aid phone number: **(308) 865-8520**
Tuition, 2003-2004 academic year: Full-time in-state: **$3,090**; out-of-state: **$6,390**, Part-time in-state: **$129/credit hour**; out-of-state: **$266/credit hour**

Fees: $676, Room and board: $4,542, Books and supplies: $738, Miscellaneous expenses: $2,138

The education program is currently accredited by the National Council for Accreditation of Teacher Education.

University of Nebraska–Lincoln

- 116 Henzlik Hall, Lincoln, NE 68588-0385
- **Website:** http://cehs.unl.edu
- **Public**
- **Degrees offered:** bachelor's, master's, education specialist, Ph.D., Ed.D.
- **Overall rank in the 2005 U.S. News education school specialty rankings:** educational psychology: 13, special education: 19

ADMISSIONS
Admissions phone number: (402) 472-5333
Admissions email address: *graduate@unl.edu*
Application website: *http://www.unl.edu/gradstudies*
Application fee: $45
Test requirements: **GRE or MAT**
Test of English as Foreign Language (TOEFL) is required for international students.
Minimum TOEFL score required for paper test: 550
Minimum TOEFL score required for computer test: 213

Fall 2003
Total 2003 enrollment: 995
Master's degree enrollment: 452
    Teacher preparation program enrollment (master's): 262
Education specialist degree enrollment: 14
Doctoral degree enrollment: 529

FINANCIAL INFORMATION
Financial aid phone number: (402) 472-2030
Tuition, 2003-2004 academic year: Full-time in-state: **$170/credit hour**; out-of-state: **$457/credit hour**, Part-time in-state: **$170/credit hour**; out-of-state: **$457/credit hour**
Fees: $852, Room and board: $5,220, Books and supplies: $600, Miscellaneous expenses: $153
Number of fellowships awarded to graduate students during the 2003-2004 academic year: 13
Number of teaching assistant positions: 71
Number of research assistant positions: 122
Number of other paid appointments: 14

ACADEMIC PROGRAMS
Total full-time tenured or tenure-track faculty (fall 2003): 107, Total part-time faculty (fall 2003): 74
Areas of specialization: curriculum and instruction, education administration and supervision, education policy, educational psychology, elementary teacher education, higher education administration, secondary teacher education, special education, student counseling and personnel services.

University of Nebraska–Omaha

- 6001 Dodge Street, Omaha, NE 68182
- **Website:** http://www.unomaha.edu
- **Public**
- **Degrees offered:** bachelor's, master's, education specialist, Ed.D.

ADMISSIONS
Admissions phone number: (402) 554-2341
Admissions email address: *graduate@unomaha.edu*
Application website: *https://ebruno.unomaha.edu/grapp.html*
Application fee: $45
Test requirements: **GRE or MAT**
Test of English as Foreign Language (TOEFL) is required for international students.
Minimum TOEFL score required for paper test: 550
Minimum TOEFL score required for computer test: 173

Fall 2003
Acceptance rate for master's degree programs: 78%
Acceptance rate for education specialist degree programs: 100%
Acceptance rate for doctoral programs: 20%
Average GRE verbal: 446, Average GRE quantitative: 549, Average GRE analytical: 584, Average MAT: 48
Total 2003 enrollment: 725
Master's degree enrollment: 646
    Teacher preparation program enrollment (master's): 334
Education specialist degree enrollment: 34
Doctoral degree enrollment: 45

FINANCIAL INFORMATION
Financial aid phone number: (402) 554-3408
Tuition, 2003-2004 academic year: Full-time in-state: **$146/credit hour**; out-of-state: **$384/credit hour**, Part-time in-state: **$146/credit hour**; out-of-state: **$384/credit hour**
Fees: $312, Room and board: $5,000, Books and supplies: $850, Miscellaneous expenses: $450
Number of fellowships awarded to graduate students during the 2003-2004 academic year: 0
Number of teaching assistant positions: 0
Number of research assistant positions: 3
Number of other paid appointments: 24

ACADEMIC PROGRAMS
Total full-time tenured or tenure-track faculty (fall 2003): 60, Total part-time faculty (fall 2003): 84
Areas of specialization: education administration and supervision, educational psychology, elementary teacher education, secondary teacher education, special education, student counseling and personnel services.

Professional development/partnership school(s) are used by students in some of the teaching programs.

During their internships, peer groups of students meet regularly to discuss instructional techniques in all of the teaching programs.

All of the students in their internships are mentored.

Courses that prepare teachers to pass the National Board of Professional Teaching Standards are not offered.

Teacher preparation programs: Five-year program leading to initial licensure that results in a baccalaureate degree (with a major or minor in education) plus graduate credit and includes practice teaching. Master's program preparing college graduates for initial licensure; includes practice teaching. Alternative program for college graduates leading to provisional licensure.

The education program is currently accredited by the National Council for Accreditation of Teacher Education.

Wayne State College

■ 1111 Main Street, Wayne, NE 68787
■ **Website:** http://www.wsc.edu
■ **Public**
■ **Degrees offered:** bachelor's, master's, education specialist

ADMISSIONS

Admissions phone number: **(402) 375-7235**
Admissions email address: *admit1@wsc.edu*
Application fee: **$30**
Fall 2005 application deadline: **8/25**
Test of English as Foreign Language (TOEFL) is required for international students.
Minimum TOEFL score required for paper test: **550**
Minimum TOEFL score required for computer test: **213**

Fall 2003
Total 2003 enrollment: **373**
Master's degree enrollment: **354**
    Teacher preparation program enrollment (master's): **213**
Education specialist degree enrollment: **19**

FINANCIAL INFORMATION

Financial aid phone number: **(402) 375-7230**
Tuition, 2003-2004 academic year: Full-time in-state: **$87/credit hour**; out-of-state: **$174/credit hour**, Part-time in-state: **$87/credit hour**; out-of-state: **$174/credit hour**
Fees: **$33/credit hour**, Room and board: **$3,920**, Books and supplies: **$800**, Miscellaneous expenses: **$903**
Number of teaching assistant positions: **4**

ACADEMIC PROGRAMS

Total full-time tenured or tenure-track faculty (fall 2003): **16**, Total part-time faculty (fall 2003): **49**
Areas of specialization: curriculum and instruction, education administration and supervision, education policy, educational psychology, elementary teacher education, secondary teacher education, special education, student counseling and personnel services, teacher education.

Professional development/partnership school(s) are used by students in all of the teaching programs.

During their internships, peer groups of students meet regularly to discuss instructional techniques in all of the teaching programs.

All of the students in their internships are mentored.

Courses that prepare teachers to pass the National Board of Professional Teaching Standards are offered.

Teacher preparation programs: Four-year baccalaureate-degree program leading to initial licensure that includes either a major or minor in education and practice teaching.

The education program is currently accredited by the National Council for Accreditation of Teacher Education.

NEVADA

University of Nevada–Las Vegas

■ 4505 Maryland Parkway Box 453001, Las Vegas, NV 89154-3001
■ **Website:** http://www.unlv.edu/colleges/graduate
■ **Public**
■ **Degrees offered:** bachelor's, master's, education specialist, Ph.D., Ed.D.

ADMISSIONS

Admissions phone number: **(702) 895-3320**
Admissions email address: *gradcollege@ccmail.nevada.edu*
Application fee: **$40**
Fall 2005 application deadline: **2/15**
Test requirements: **GRE or MAT**
Test of English as Foreign Language (TOEFL) is required for international students.
Minimum TOEFL score required for paper test: **550**

Fall 2003
Acceptance rate for master's degree programs: **93%**
Acceptance rate for doctoral programs: **67%**
Total 2003 enrollment: **1,240**
Master's degree enrollment: **1,011**
   Teacher preparation program enrollment (master's): **715**
Education specialist degree enrollment: **43**
Doctoral degree enrollment: **186**

FINANCIAL INFORMATION

Financial aid phone number: **(702) 895-3424**
Tuition, 2003-2004 academic year: Full-time in-state:
   $115/credit hour; out-of-state: **$8,487**, Part-time in-state:
   $115/credit hour; out-of-state: **$127/credit hour**
Fees: **$242**, Room and board: **$3,917**, Books and supplies:
   $275, Miscellaneous expenses: **$325**
Number of fellowships awarded to graduate students during the 2003-2004 academic year: **0**
Number of teaching assistant positions: **0**
Number of research assistant positions: **0**

Number of other paid appointments: **58**

ACADEMIC PROGRAMS

Total full-time tenured or tenure-track faculty (fall 2003):
   89, Total part-time faculty (fall 2003): **188**
Areas of specialization: curriculum and instruction, education administration and supervision, educational psychology, higher education administration, student counseling and personnel services.
Professional development/partnership school(s) are used by students in all of the teaching programs.
During their internships, peer groups of students meet regularly to discuss instructional techniques in all of the teaching programs.
Some of the students in their internships are mentored.
Courses that prepare teachers to pass the National Board of Professional Teaching Standards are not offered.
Teacher preparation programs: Four-year baccalaureate-degree program leading to initial licensure that includes either a major or minor in education and practice teaching.
The education program is currently accredited by the National Council for Accreditation of Teacher Education.
The education program is currently accredited by the Teacher Education Accreditation Council.

LICENSING TEST

Pass rate on state's teacher licensing test for 2002-2003:
   97%
State average pass rate: **96%**

University of Nevada–Reno

■ MS278, Reno, NV 89557
■ **Website:** http://www.unr.edu/grad
■ **Public**
■ **Degrees offered:** bachelor's, master's, education specialist, Ph.D., Ed.D.

ADMISSIONS

Admissions phone number: **(775) 784-6869**
Admissions email address: *gradadmissions@unr.edu*
Application website: *http://www.vpr.unr.edu/grad2/*
Application fee: **$60**
Fall 2005 application deadline: **3/1**
Test requirements: **GRE**
Test of English as Foreign Language (TOEFL) is required for international students.
Minimum TOEFL score required for paper test: **500**
Minimum TOEFL score required for computer test: **173**

Fall 2003

Total 2003 enrollment: **652**
Master's degree enrollment: **516**
  Teacher preparation program enrollment (master's): **339**
Education specialist degree enrollment: **17**
Doctoral degree enrollment: **119**

FINANCIAL INFORMATION

Financial aid phone number: **(775) 784-4666**
Tuition, 2003-2004 academic year: Full-time in-state: **$119/credit hour**; out-of-state: **$10,629**, Part-time in-state: **$119/credit hour**; out-of-state: **$246/credit hour**
Fees: **$160**, Room and board: **$3,800**

ACADEMIC PROGRAMS

Areas of specialization: curriculum and instruction, education administration and supervision, educational psychology, elementary teacher education, secondary teacher education, special education, teacher education.
During their internships, peer groups of students meet regularly to discuss instructional techniques in some of the teaching programs.
Some of the students in their internships are mentored.
Courses that prepare teachers to pass the National Board of Professional Teaching Standards are offered.
Teacher preparation programs: Four-year baccalaureate-degree program leading to initial licensure that includes either a major or minor in education and practice teaching. Master's program preparing college graduates for initial licensure; includes practice teaching. Alternative program for college graduates leading to provisional licensure.
The education program is currently accredited by the National Council for Accreditation of Teacher Education.

LICENSING TEST

Pass rate on state's teacher licensing test for 2002-2003: **96%**
State average pass rate: **96%**

NEW HAMPSHIRE

TEACHER TESTING IN NEW HAMPSHIRE

Teacher licensure rules vary widely from state to state, but almost all states require tests. The exams typically cover the basics of reading, writing and math, although some states mandate in-depth, subject-specific teacher tests. For information on where to go in your state for specific academic requirements, see Chapter 6 on page 67. Note: Some schools require students to pass exams by graduation, and thus automatically report pass rates of 100 percent.

- This state **does** require a basic skills test in order to obtain a teaching license.
- This state **does not** require a subject-knowledge test in order to obtain a middle school teaching license.
- This state **does** require a subject-knowledge test in order to obtain a high school teaching license.
- This state **does not** require a subject-specific pedagogy test in order to obtain a teaching license.

Antioch New England Graduate School

- **40 Avon Street, Keene, NH 03431**
- **Website:** http://www.antiochne.edu/
- **Private**

LICENSING TEST

Pass rate on state's teacher licensing test for 2002-2003: **90%**
State average pass rate: **93%**

Keene State College

- **229 Main Street, Keene, NH 03435**
- **Website:** http://www.keene.edu/
- **Public**

LICENSING TEST

Pass rate on state's teacher licensing test for 2002-2003: **93%**
State average pass rate: **93%**

Plymouth State University

- **17 High Street MSC 11, Plymouth, NH 03264**
- **Website:** http://www.plymouth.edu/graded
- **Public**
- **Degrees offered:** master's

ADMISSIONS

Admissions phone number: **(603) 535-2636**
Admissions email address: *forgrad@plymouth.edu*
Application fee: **$75**
Fall 2005 application deadline: **rolling**
Test requirements: **GRE or MAT**

Test of English as Foreign Language (TOEFL) is required for international students.

Fall 2003

Acceptance rate for master's degree programs: **86%**
Total 2003 enrollment: **252**
Master's degree enrollment: **252**
 Teacher preparation program enrollment (master's): **180**

FINANCIAL INFORMATION

Financial aid phone number: **(603) 535-2338**
Tuition, 2003-2004 academic year: Full-time in-state: **$320/credit hour**; out-of-state: **$352/credit hour**, Part-time in-state: **$320/credit hour**; out-of-state: **$352/credit hour**
Number of fellowships awarded to graduate students during the 2003-2004 academic year: **17**
Number of teaching assistant positions: **12**
Number of research assistant positions: **0**
Number of other paid appointments: **0**

ACADEMIC PROGRAMS

Total full-time tenured or tenure-track faculty (fall 2003): **33**
 Total part-time faculty (fall 2003): **61**
Areas of specialization: curriculum and instruction, education administration and supervision, education policy, educational psychology, elementary teacher education, secondary teacher education, special education, student counseling and personnel services.
Professional development/partnership school(s) are used by students in all of the teaching programs.
During their internships, peer groups of students meet regularly to discuss instructional techniques in some of the teaching programs.
Some of the students in their internships are mentored.
Courses that prepare teachers to pass the National Board of Professional Teaching Standards are not offered.
Teacher preparation programs: Master's degree in education, including internship/practice teaching and preparation for initial licensure. Alternative program for college graduates leading to provisional licensure.
The education program is currently accredited by the National Council for Accreditation of Teacher Education.

LICENSING TEST

Pass rate on state's teacher licensing test for 2002-2003: 97%

State average pass rate: 93%

Rivier College

- 420 Main Street, Nashua, NH 03060
- **Website:** http://www.rivier.edu
- **Private**
- **Degrees offered:** bachelor's, master's

ADMISSIONS

Admissions phone number: **(603) 897-8219**
Admissions email address: *gadmissions@rivier.edu*
Application website: *http://www.rivier.edu*
Application fee: **$25**
Fall 2005 application deadline: **rolling**
Test requirements: **GRE or MAT**
Test of English as Foreign Language (TOEFL) is required for international students.
Minimum TOEFL score required for paper test: **550**
Minimum TOEFL score required for computer test: **263**

Fall 2003

Total 2003 enrollment: **304**
Master's degree enrollment: **304**
  Teacher preparation program enrollment (master's): **166**

FINANCIAL INFORMATION

Financial aid phone number: **(603) 897-8510**
Tuition, 2003-2004 academic year: Full-time: **$393/credit hour**; Part-time: **$393/credit hour**

ACADEMIC PROGRAMS

Total full-time tenured or tenure-track faculty (fall 2003): **11**
  Total part-time faculty (fall 2003): **30**
Areas of specialization: curriculum and instruction, education administration and supervision, education policy, educational psychology, elementary teacher education, higher education administration, secondary teacher education, special education, student counseling and personnel services.
Professional development/partnership school(s) are used by students in all of the teaching programs.

During their internships, peer groups of students meet regularly to discuss instructional techniques in all of the teaching programs.
All of the students in their internships are mentored.
Courses that prepare teachers to pass the National Board of Professional Teaching Standards are not offered.
Teacher preparation programs: Four-year baccalaureate-degree program leading to initial licensure that includes either a major or minor in education and practice teaching. Five-year program leading to initial licensure that results in a baccalaureate degree (with a major or minor in education) plus a master's degree and includes practice teaching. Master's program preparing college graduates for initial licensure; includes practice teaching.

LICENSING TEST

Pass rate on state's teacher licensing test for 2002-2003: 99%

State average pass rate: 93%

University of New Hampshire

- Morrill Hall, Durham, NH 03824
- **Website:** http://www.unh.edu/education/
- **Public**

ADMISSIONS

Admissions phone number: **(603) 862-2311**
Admissions email address: *ruthe@cisunix.unh.edu*
Application website: *http://www.gradschool.unh.edu*
Test of English as Foreign Language (TOEFL) is required for international students.
Minimum TOEFL score required for paper test: **550**
Minimum TOEFL score required for computer test: **213**

FINANCIAL INFORMATION

Financial aid phone number: **(603) 862-3600**

LICENSING TEST

Pass rate on state's teacher licensing test for 2002-2003: 92%

State average pass rate: 93%

NEW JERSEY

Caldwell College

- 9 Ryerson Avenue, Caldwell, NJ 07006
- **Website:** http://www.caldwell.edu/graduate
- **Private**
- **Degrees offered:** bachelor's, master's

ADMISSIONS

Admissions phone number: **(973) 618-3384**
Admissions email address: *lcorrao@caldwell.edu*
Application website: *http://www.caldwell.edu/graduate/admissions.html*
Application fee: **$40**
Fall 2005 application deadline: **rolling**
Test requirements: **GRE or MAT**
Test of English as Foreign Language (TOEFL) is required for international students.
Minimum TOEFL score required for paper test: **550**
Minimum TOEFL score required for computer test: **213**

Fall 2003
Acceptance rate for master's degree programs: **53%**
Average MAT: **41**
Total 2003 enrollment: **109**
Master's degree enrollment: **109**
    Teacher preparation program enrollment (master's): **60**

FINANCIAL INFORMATION

Financial aid phone number: **(973) 618-3222**
Tuition, 2003-2004 academic year: Full-time: **$500/credit hour**; Part-time: **$500/credit hour**
Books and supplies: **$600**, Miscellaneous expenses: **$2,400**
Number of research assistant positions: **1**

ACADEMIC PROGRAMS

Total full-time tenured or tenure-track faculty (fall 2003): **9**
    Total part-time faculty (fall 2003): **29**
Areas of specialization: curriculum and instruction, education administration and supervision, special education, student counseling and personnel services.

Professional development/partnership school(s) are used by students in all of the teaching programs.
During their internships, peer groups of students meet regularly to discuss instructional techniques in all of the teaching programs.
All of the students in their internships are mentored.
Courses that prepare teachers to pass the National Board of Professional Teaching Standards are not offered.
Teacher preparation programs: Four-year baccalaureate-degree program leading to initial licensure that includes either a major or minor in education and practice teaching.

LICENSING TEST

Pass rate on state's teacher licensing test for 2002-2003: **95%**
State average pass rate: **98%**

Centenary College

- 400 Jefferson Street, Hackettstown, NJ 07840
- **Website:** http://www.centenarycollege.edu/
- **Private**
- **Degrees offered:** bachelor's, master's

Fall 2003
Total 2003 enrollment: **416**
Master's degree enrollment: **416**

ACADEMIC PROGRAMS

Total full-time tenured or tenure-track faculty (fall 2003): **4**
    Total part-time faculty (fall 2003): **9**

LICENSING TEST

Pass rate on state's teacher licensing test for 2002-2003: **100%**
State average pass rate: **98%**

College of New Jersey

- P.O. Box 7718, 2000 Pennington Road, Ewing, NJ 08628
- **Website:** http://www.tcnj.edu
- Public
- **Degrees offered:** bachelor's, master's, education specialist

ADMISSIONS

Admissions phone number: **(609) 771-2300**
Admissions email address: *Graduate@tcnj.edu*
Application website: *http://www.TCNJ.edu/~graduate/application.html*
Application fee: **$50**
Fall 2005 application deadline: **4/15**
Test of English as Foreign Language (TOEFL) is required for international students.

Fall 2003
Total 2003 enrollment: **726**
Master's degree enrollment: **608**
   Teacher preparation program enrollment (master's): **344**
Education specialist degree enrollment: **118**

FINANCIAL INFORMATION

Financial aid phone number: **(609) 771-2211**
Tuition, 2003-2004 academic year: Full-time in-state: **$7,610**; out-of-state: **$10,652**, Part-time in-state: **$422/credit hour**; out-of-state: **$591/credit hour**
Fees: **$1,157**, Room and board: **$7,744**, Books and supplies: **$736**, Miscellaneous expenses: **$1,685**

ACADEMIC PROGRAMS

Professional development/partnership school(s) are used by students in all of the teaching programs.
During their internships, peer groups of students meet regularly to discuss instructional techniques in some of the teaching programs.
None of the students in their internships are mentored.
Courses that prepare teachers to pass the National Board of Professional Teaching Standards are not offered.
Teacher preparation programs: Four-year baccalaureate-degree program leading to initial licensure that includes either a major or minor in education and practice teaching. Five-year program leading to initial licensure that results in a baccalaureate degree (with a major or minor in education) plus a master's degree and includes practice teaching. Master's program preparing college graduates for initial licensure; includes practice teaching. Alternative program for college graduates leading to provisional licensure.
The education program is currently accredited by the National Council for Accreditation of Teacher Education.

LICENSING TEST

Pass rate on state's teacher licensing test for 2002-2003: **100%**
State average pass rate: **98%**

College of St. Elizabeth

- 2 Convent Road, Morristown, NJ 07960-6989
- **Website:** http://www.cse.edu
- Private
- **Degrees offered:** bachelor's, master's

ADMISSIONS

Admissions phone number: **(973) 290-4600**
Admissions email address: *mszarek@cse.edu*
Application website: *http://www.cse.edu*
Application fee: **$35**
Fall 2005 application deadline: **rolling**
Test of English as Foreign Language (TOEFL) is required for international students.
Minimum TOEFL score required for paper test: **559**
Minimum TOEFL score required for computer test: **210**

Fall 2003
Acceptance rate for master's degree programs: **70%**
Total 2003 enrollment: **178**
Master's degree enrollment: **178**
   Teacher preparation program enrollment (master's): **61**

FINANCIAL INFORMATION

Financial aid phone number: **(973) 290-4492**
Tuition, 2003-2004 academic year: Full-time: **$525/credit hour**; Part-time: **$525/credit hour**
Fees: **$37/credit hour**, Books and supplies: **$200**, Miscellaneous expenses: **$100**
Number of research assistant positions: **1**

ACADEMIC PROGRAMS

Total full-time tenured or tenure-track faculty (fall 2003): **2**
Areas of specialization: curriculum and instruction, education administration and supervision, education policy, educational psychology, elementary teacher education, secondary teacher education, special education, student counseling and personnel services.
Professional development/partnership school(s) are used by students in all of the teaching programs.
During their internships, peer groups of students meet regularly to discuss instructional techniques in some of the teaching programs.
All of the students in their internships are mentored.
Courses that prepare teachers to pass the National Board of Professional Teaching Standards are not offered.

LICENSING TEST

Pass rate on state's teacher licensing test for 2002-2003: **100%**
State average pass rate: **98%**

Fairleigh Dickinson University

- **1000 River Road Mail code: T-BH2-01, Teaneck, NJ 07666**
- **Website:** http://www.fdu.edu/
- **Private**
- **Degrees offered:** master's, education specialist

ADMISSIONS

Admissions phone number: **(201) 692-2205**
Admissions email address: *thomas_shea@fdu.edu*
Application fee: **$40**
Fall 2005 application deadline: **rolling**
Test of English as Foreign Language (TOEFL) is required
  for international students.
Minimum TOEFL score required for paper test: **550**
Minimum TOEFL score required for computer test: **213**

Fall 2003
Total 2003 enrollment: **670**
Master's degree enrollment: **670**
  Teacher preparation program enrollment (master's):
    490

FINANCIAL INFORMATION

Financial aid phone number: **(201) 692-2232**
Tuition, 2003-2004 academic year: Full-time: **$700/credit
  hour**; Part-time: **$700/credit hour**
Fees: **$820**, Room and board: **$8,250**

ACADEMIC PROGRAMS

Total full-time tenured or tenure-track faculty (fall 2003): **16**
Areas of specialization: education administration and supervision, educational psychology, elementary teacher education,
  secondary teacher education, special education.
During their internships, peer groups of students meet
  regularly to discuss instructional techniques in all of the
  teaching programs.
All of the students in their internships are mentored.
Teacher preparation programs: Five-year program leading
  to initial licensure that results in a baccalaureate degree
  (with a major or minor in education) plus graduate
  credit and includes practice teaching. Master's program
  preparing college graduates for initial licensure; includes
  practice teaching.

LICENSING TEST

Pass rate on state's teacher licensing test for 2002-2003:
  98%
State average pass rate: **98%**

Georgian Court College

- **900 Lakewood Avenue, Lakewood, NJ 08701**
- **Website:** http://georgian.edu/admissions
- **Private**
- **Degrees offered:** bachelor's, master's, education
  specialist

ADMISSIONS

Admissions phone number: **(732) 364-2200**
Admissions email address: *admissions@georgian.edu*
Application website: *http://registrar.georgian.edu/IQweb/
  secure/Guest/onlineapp.asp*
Application fee: **$40**
Fall 2005 application deadline: **rolling**
Test requirements: **GRE or MAT**
Test of English as Foreign Language (TOEFL) is required
  for international students.
Minimum TOEFL score required for paper test: **550**
Minimum TOEFL score required for computer test: **213**

Fall 2003
Acceptance rate for master's degree programs: **85%**
Acceptance rate for education specialist degree programs: **86%**
Total 2003 enrollment: **457**
Master's degree enrollment: **430**
  Teacher preparation program enrollment (master's): **187**
Education specialist degree enrollment: **27**

FINANCIAL INFORMATION

Financial aid phone number: **(732) 364-2200**
Tuition, 2003-2004 academic year: Full-time: **$8,496**; Part-
  time: **$472/credit hour**
Fees: **$200**, Books and supplies: **$450**

ACADEMIC PROGRAMS

Total full-time tenured or tenure-track faculty (fall 2003): **25**
  Total part-time faculty (fall 2003): **70**
Areas of specialization: curriculum and instruction, education administration and supervision, education policy,
  educational psychology, elementary teacher education,
  secondary teacher education, special education, student
  counseling and personnel services, teacher education.
Professional development/partnership school(s) are used
  by students in some of the teaching programs.
During their internships, peer groups of students meet
  regularly to discuss instructional techniques in some of
  the teaching programs.
All of the students in their internships are mentored.
Courses that prepare teachers to pass the National Board of
  Professional Teaching Standards are offered.
Teacher preparation programs: Four-year baccalaureate-
  degree program leading to initial licensure that includes
  either a major or minor in education and practice teaching.

LICENSING TEST

Pass rate on state's teacher licensing test for 2002-2003: **99%**
State average pass rate: **98%**

Kean University

■ 1000 Morris Ave, Union, NJ 07083
■ Website: http://www.kean.edu
■ Public
■ Degrees offered: bachelor's, master's, education specialist

ADMISSIONS

Admissions phone number: (908) 737-3440
Admissions email address: *grad-adm@kean.edu*
Application website: *http://www.kean.edu/~keangrad*
Application fee: $60
Fall 2005 application deadline: 6/1
Test requirements: GRE or MAT

Fall 2003

Acceptance rate for master's degree programs: 53%
Average GRE verbal: 427, Average GRE quantitative: 501,
  Average GRE analytical: 519, Average MAT: 39
Total 2003 enrollment: 1,138
Master's degree enrollment: 1,138
  Teacher preparation program enrollment (master's): 676

FINANCIAL INFORMATION

Financial aid phone number: (908) 737-3190
Tuition, 2003-2004 academic year: Full-time in-state:
  $7,488; out-of-state: $9,528, Part-time in-state:
  $312/credit hour; out-of-state: $397/credit hour
Fees: $1,814
Number of other paid appointments: 44

ACADEMIC PROGRAMS

Total full-time tenured or tenure-track faculty (fall 2003):
  86, Total part-time faculty (fall 2003): 111
Areas of specialization: curriculum and instruction, education administration and supervision, educational psychology, elementary teacher education, secondary teacher education, special education, student counseling and personnel services, teacher education.
Professional development/partnership school(s) are used by students in all of the teaching programs.
During their internships, peer groups of students meet regularly to discuss instructional techniques in all of the teaching programs.
All of the students in their internships are mentored.
Teacher preparation programs: Four-year baccalaureate-degree program leading to initial licensure that includes either a major or minor in education and practice teaching. Master's program preparing college graduates for initial licensure; includes practice teaching. Alternative program for college graduates leading to provisional licensure.
The education program is currently accredited by the National Council for Accreditation of Teacher Education.

LICENSING TEST

Pass rate on state's teacher licensing test for 2002-2003: 97%
State average pass rate: 98%

Monmouth University

■ 400 Cedar Avenue, West Long Branch, NJ 07764
■ Website: http://www.monmouth.edu/
■ Private

LICENSING TEST

Pass rate on state's teacher licensing test for 2002-2003: 97%
State average pass rate: 98%

Montclair State University

■ 1 Normal Avenue, Upper Montclair, NJ 07043
■ Website: http://www.montclair.edu
■ Public
■ Degrees offered: bachelor's, master's, Ed.D.

ADMISSIONS

Admissions phone number: (973) 655-5147
Admissions email address: *Graduate.School@Montclair.edu*
Application website: *http://www.montclair.edu/graduate*
Application fee: $60
Fall 2005 application deadline: 2/15
Test requirements: GRE or MAT
Test of English as Foreign Language (TOEFL) is required for international students.
Minimum TOEFL score required for paper test: 550
Minimum TOEFL score required for computer test: 220

Fall 2003

Acceptance rate for master's degree programs: 75%
Acceptance rate for doctoral programs: 64%
Average GRE verbal: 437, Average GRE quantitative: 497,
  Average GRE analytical: 501, Average MAT: 42
Total 2003 enrollment: 1,093
Master's degree enrollment: 1,061
  Teacher preparation program enrollment (master's): 500
Doctoral degree enrollment: 32

FINANCIAL INFORMATION

Financial aid phone number: (973) 655-4461
Tuition, 2003-2004 academic year: Full-time in-state:
  $323/credit hour; out-of-state: $469/credit hour, Part-time in-state: $323/credit hour; out-of-state: $469/credit hour
Fees: $42/credit hour, Room and board: $8,538, Books and supplies: $800, Miscellaneous expenses: $950
Number of fellowships awarded to graduate students during the 2003-2004 academic year: 0
Number of teaching assistant positions: 6
Number of research assistant positions: 25

ACADEMIC PROGRAMS

Total full-time tenured or tenure-track faculty (fall 2003): 86, Total part-time faculty (fall 2003): **146**

Areas of specialization: education administration and supervision, educational psychology, elementary teacher education, secondary teacher education, special education, student counseling and personnel services.

Professional development/partnership school(s) are used by students in all of the teaching programs.

During their internships, peer groups of students meet regularly to discuss instructional techniques in all of the teaching programs.

All of the students in their internships are mentored.

Courses that prepare teachers to pass the National Board of Professional Teaching Standards are not offered.

Teacher preparation programs: Master's program preparing college graduates for initial licensure; includes practice teaching.

The education program is currently accredited by the National Council for Accreditation of Teacher Education.

LICENSING TEST

Pass rate on state's teacher licensing test for 2002-2003: **98%**

State average pass rate: **98%**

New Jersey City University

■ **2039 Kennedy Boulevard, Jersey City, NJ 07305**
■ **Website:** http://www.njcu.edu
■ **Public**
■ **Degrees offered:** bachelor's, master's

ADMISSIONS

Admissions phone number: **(201) 200-3409**
Admissions email address: *cshevey@njcu.edu*
Application fee: **$0**
Fall 2005 application deadline: **8/1**
Test of English as Foreign Language (TOEFL) is required for international students.

FINANCIAL INFORMATION

Financial aid phone number: **(201) 200-3173**
Tuition, 2003-2004 academic year: Full-time in-state: **$293/credit hour**; out-of-state: **$513/credit hour**, Part-time in-state: **$293/credit hour**; out-of-state: **$513/credit hour**
Fees: **$48/credit hour**, Room and board: **$6,586**, Books and supplies: **$250**, Miscellaneous expenses: **$500**

LICENSING TEST

Pass rate on state's teacher licensing test for 2002-2003: **95%**

State average pass rate: **98%**

Rider University

■ **2083 Lawrenceville Road, Lawrenceville, NJ 08648-3099**
■ **Website:** http://www.rider.edu
■ **Private**
■ **Degrees offered:** bachelor's, master's, education specialist

ADMISSIONS

Admissions phone number: **(609) 896-5036**
Admissions email address: *gradadm@rider.edu*
Application website: *http://www.rider.edu*
Application fee: **$40**
Fall 2005 application deadline: **rolling**
Test of English as Foreign Language (TOEFL) is required for international students.
Minimum TOEFL score required for paper test: **550**
Minimum TOEFL score required for computer test: **213**

Fall 2003

Total 2003 enrollment: **425**
Master's degree enrollment: **383**
  Teacher preparation program enrollment (master's): **87**
Education specialist degree enrollment: **42**

FINANCIAL INFORMATION

Financial aid phone number: **(609) 896-5360**
Tuition, 2003-2004 academic year: Full-time: **$415/credit hour**; Part-time: **$415/credit hour**
Fees: **$35**, Room and board: **$9,190**

ACADEMIC PROGRAMS

Areas of specialization: curriculum and instruction, education administration and supervision, higher education administration, special education, student counseling and personnel services.

Teacher preparation programs: Alternative program for college graduates leading to provisional licensure.

The education program is currently accredited by the National Council for Accreditation of Teacher Education.

LICENSING TEST

Pass rate on state's teacher licensing test for 2002-2003: **100%**

State average pass rate: **98%**

Rowan University

■ **201 Mullica Hill Road, Glassboro, NJ 08028**
■ **Website:** http://www.rowan.edu/
■ **Public**

LICENSING TEST

Pass rate on state's teacher licensing test for 2002-2003: **99%**

State average pass rate: **98%**

Rutgers State University –New Brunswick

- 10 Seminary Place, New Brunswick, NJ 08901-1183
- **Website:** http://www.gse.rutgers.edu
- **Public**
- **Degrees offered:** master's, Ph.D., Ed.D.
- **Overall rank in the 2005 U.S. News education schools with doctoral programs:** 35

ADMISSIONS

Admissions phone number: **(732) 932-7711**
Admissions email address: *gradadm@rutgers.edu*
Application website: *http://gradstudy.rutgers.edu*
Application fee: **$50**
Fall 2005 application deadline: **2/1**
Test requirements: **GRE**
Test of English as Foreign Language (TOEFL) is required for international students.
Minimum TOEFL score required for paper test: **550**
Minimum TOEFL score required for computer test: **213**

Fall 2003

Acceptance rate for master's degree programs: **60%**
Acceptance rate for doctoral programs: **29%**
Average GRE verbal: **488**, Average GRE quantitative: **576**, Average GRE analytical: **579**
Total 2003 enrollment: **827**
Master's degree enrollment: **575**
    Teacher preparation program enrollment (master's): **401**
Doctoral degree enrollment: **252**

FINANCIAL INFORMATION

Financial aid phone number: **(732) 932-7057**
Tuition, 2003-2004 academic year: Full-time in-state: **$8,952**; out-of-state: **$13,125**, Part-time in-state: **$373/credit hour**; out-of-state: **$547/credit hour**
Fees: **$878**, Room and board: **$9,596**, Books and supplies: **$1,025**, Miscellaneous expenses: **$925**
Number of fellowships awarded to graduate students during the 2003-2004 academic year: **3**
Number of teaching assistant positions: **15**
Number of research assistant positions: **27**
Number of other paid appointments: **0**

ACADEMIC PROGRAMS

Total full-time tenured or tenure-track faculty (fall 2003): **55**, Total part-time faculty (fall 2003): **0**
Areas of specialization: curriculum and instruction, education administration and supervision, education policy, educational psychology, elementary teacher education, secondary teacher education, special education, student counseling and personnel services.
Professional development/partnership school(s) are used by students in some of the teaching programs.

During their internships, peer groups of students meet regularly to discuss instructional techniques in all of the teaching programs.
All of the students in their internships are mentored.
Courses that prepare teachers to pass the National Board of Professional Teaching Standards are not offered.

LICENSING TEST

Pass rate on state's teacher licensing test for 2002-2003: **100%**
State average pass rate: **98%**

Seton Hall University

- 400 S. Orange Avenue, South Orange, NJ 07079
- **Website:** http://education.shu.edu
- **Private**
- **Degrees offered:** bachelor's, master's, education specialist, Ph.D., Ed.D.

ADMISSIONS

Admissions phone number: **(973) 761-9668**
Admissions email address: *educate@shu.edu*
Application website: *http://education.shu.edu/admissions/ applyonline.html*
Application fee: **$50**
Fall 2005 application deadline: **rolling**
Test requirements: **GRE or MAT**
Test of English as Foreign Language (TOEFL) is required for international students.
Minimum TOEFL score required for paper test: **550**
Minimum TOEFL score required for computer test: **213**

Fall 2003

Acceptance rate for master's degree programs: **94%**
Acceptance rate for education specialist degree programs: **93%**
Acceptance rate for doctoral programs: **47%**
Average GRE verbal: **451**, Average GRE quantitative: **489**, Average GRE analytical: **603**, Average MAT: **41**
Total 2003 enrollment: **987**
Master's degree enrollment: **619**
    Teacher preparation program enrollment (master's): **144**
Education specialist degree enrollment: **93**
Doctoral degree enrollment: **275**

FINANCIAL INFORMATION

Financial aid phone number: **(973) 761-9332**
Tuition, 2003-2004 academic year: Full-time: **$675/credit hour**; Part-time: **$675/credit hour**
Fees: **$370**, Room and board: **$8,600**, Books and supplies: **$700**, Miscellaneous expenses: **$1,650**
Number of fellowships awarded to graduate students during the 2003-2004 academic year: **12**
Number of other paid appointments: **20**

ACADEMIC PROGRAMS

Total full-time tenured or tenure-track faculty (fall 2003): 22, Total part-time faculty (fall 2003): 76

Areas of specialization: curriculum and instruction, education administration and supervision, education policy, elementary teacher education, higher education administration, secondary teacher education, student counseling and personnel services.

Professional development/partnership school(s) are used by students in all of the teaching programs.

During their internships, peer groups of students meet regularly to discuss instructional techniques in some of the teaching programs.

All of the students in their internships are mentored.

Courses that prepare teachers to pass the National Board of Professional Teaching Standards are not offered.

Teacher preparation programs: Four-year baccalaureate-degree program leading to initial licensure that includes either a major or minor in education and practice teaching. Master's program preparing college graduates for initial licensure; includes practice teaching.

LICENSING TEST

Pass rate on state's teacher licensing test for 2002-2003: 97%

State average pass rate: 98%

St. Peter's College

- 2641 Kennedy Blvd, Jersey City, NJ 07306
- **Website:** http://www.spc.edu
- Private
- **Degrees offered:** bachelor's, master's

ADMISSIONS

Admissions phone number: (201) 915-9220
Admissions email address: *gradadmit@spc.edu*
Application website: *http://grad.spc.edu/admissions*
Application fee: $0
Fall 2005 application deadline: **rolling**
Test requirements: **GRE or MAT**
Test of English as Foreign Language (TOEFL) is required for international students.
Minimum TOEFL score required for paper test: 550
Minimum TOEFL score required for computer test: 213

Fall 2003

Acceptance rate for master's degree programs: 91%
Total 2003 enrollment: 322
Master's degree enrollment: 322
   Teacher preparation program enrollment (master's): 60

FINANCIAL INFORMATION

Financial aid phone number: (201) 915-4929
Tuition, 2003-2004 academic year: Full-time: **$646/credit hour**; Part-time: **$646/credit hour**
Fees: $60

ACADEMIC PROGRAMS

Total full-time tenured or tenure-track faculty (fall 2003): 5
   Total part-time faculty (fall 2003): 18

Areas of specialization: curriculum and instruction, education administration and supervision, educational psychology, elementary teacher education, secondary teacher education.

Professional development/partnership school(s) are used by students in all of the teaching programs.

During their internships, peer groups of students meet regularly to discuss instructional techniques in all of the teaching programs.

All of the students in their internships are mentored.

Courses that prepare teachers to pass the National Board of Professional Teaching Standards are not offered.

Teacher preparation programs: Four-year baccalaureate-degree program leading to initial licensure that includes either a major or minor in education and practice teaching. Master's program preparing college graduates for initial licensure; includes practice teaching. Alternative program for college graduates leading to provisional licensure.

LICENSING TEST

Pass rate on state's teacher licensing test for 2002-2003: 94%

State average pass rate: 98%

William Paterson University

- PO Box 920, Wayne, NJ 07474-6920
- **Website:** http://www.wpunj.edu
- Public
- **Degrees offered:** bachelor's, master's

ADMISSIONS

Admissions phone number: (973) 720-3641
Admissions email address: *graduate@wpunj.edu*
Application website: *http://www.wpunj.edu/admissn/ apply_now.cfm*
Application fee: $50
Fall 2005 application deadline: **rolling**
Test of English as Foreign Language (TOEFL) is required for international students.
Minimum TOEFL score required for paper test: 550
Minimum TOEFL score required for computer test: 213

Fall 2003

Acceptance rate for master's degree programs: 55%
Average GRE verbal: 443, Average GRE quantitative: 518, Average MAT: 41
Total 2003 enrollment: 484
Master's degree enrollment: 484
   Teacher preparation program enrollment (master's): 372

FINANCIAL INFORMATION

Financial aid phone number: **(973) 720-2186**

Tuition, 2003-2004 academic year: Full-time in-state: **$395/credit hour**; out-of-state: **$602/credit hour**, Part-time in-state: **$395/credit hour**; out-of-state: **$602/credit hour**

Number of other paid appointments: **14**

ACADEMIC PROGRAMS

Total full-time tenured or tenure-track faculty (fall 2003): **30**, Total part-time faculty (fall 2003): **155**

Areas of specialization: education administration and supervision, elementary teacher education, secondary teacher education, special education, student counseling and personnel services.

Professional development/partnership school(s) are used by students in some of the teaching programs.

During their internships, peer groups of students meet regularly to discuss instructional techniques in all of the teaching programs.

All of the students in their internships are mentored.

Courses that prepare teachers to pass the National Board of Professional Teaching Standards are not offered.

Teacher preparation programs: Four-year baccalaureate-degree program leading to initial licensure that includes either a major or minor in education and practice teaching. Master's program preparing college graduates for initial licensure; includes practice teaching.

The education program is currently accredited by the National Council for Accreditation of Teacher Education.

LICENSING TEST

Pass rate on state's teacher licensing test for 2002-2003: **97%**

State average pass rate: **98%**

NEW MEXICO

College of Santa Fe

- **1600 St. Michael's Drive, Santa Fe, NM 87505**
- **Website:** http://www.csf.edu/splash/index.html
- **Private**
- **Degrees offered:** master's

ADMISSIONS
Admissions phone number: (505) 855-7269
Application fee: **$35**
Fall 2005 application deadline: **rolling**
Test of English as Foreign Language (TOEFL) is required for international students.
Minimum TOEFL score required for paper test: 550
Minimum TOEFL score required for computer test: 213

Fall 2003
Total 2003 enrollment: 285
Master's degree enrollment: 285

FINANCIAL INFORMATION
Financial aid phone number: (505) 473-6454
Tuition, 2003-2004 academic year: **$322/credit hour**
Fees: **$195**, Books and supplies: **$816**, Miscellaneous expenses: **$1,146**

ACADEMIC PROGRAMS
Total full-time tenured or tenure-track faculty (fall 2003): 8
  Total part-time faculty (fall 2003): 20
Areas of specialization: curriculum and instruction, education administration and supervision, special education, student counseling and personnel services.
Professional development/partnership school(s) are used by students in all of the teaching programs.
During their internships, peer groups of students meet regularly to discuss instructional techniques in all of the teaching programs.
All of the students in their internships are mentored.
Courses that prepare teachers to pass the National Board of Professional Teaching Standards are not offered.

Teacher preparation programs: Four-year baccalaureate-degree program leading to initial licensure that includes either a major or minor in education and practice teaching. Five-year program leading to initial licensure that results in a baccalaureate degree (with a major or minor in education) plus graduate credit and includes practice teaching. Five-year program leading to initial licensure that results in a baccalaureate degree (with a major or minor in education) plus a master's degree and includes practice teaching. Master's program preparing college graduates for initial licensure; includes practice teaching. Alternative program for college graduates leading to provisional licensure.
The education program is currently accredited by the National Council for Accreditation of Teacher Education.

LICENSING TEST
Pass rate on state's teacher licensing test for 2002-2003: 100%
State average pass rate: 94%

College of the Southwest

- **6610 Lovington Highway, Hobbs, NM 88240**
- **Website:** http://www.csw.edu
- **Private**
- **Degrees offered:** bachelor's, master's

ADMISSIONS
Admissions phone number: (505) 392-6561
Admissions email address: *lchapman@csw.edu*
Application fee: **$50**
Fall 2005 application deadline: **4/1**
Test requirements: **GRE**
Test of English as Foreign Language (TOEFL) is required for international students.
Minimum TOEFL score required for paper test: 550

Fall 2003
Total 2003 enrollment: 198
Master's degree enrollment: 198

Teacher preparation program enrollment (master's): 46

FINANCIAL INFORMATION

Financial aid phone number: (505) 392-6561

Tuition, 2003-2004 academic year: Full-time: **$220/credit hour**; Part-time: **$220/credit hour**

Fees: **$300**, Books and supplies: **$800**, Miscellaneous expenses: **$750**

Number of fellowships awarded to graduate students during the 2003-2004 academic year: 2

ACADEMIC PROGRAMS

Areas of specialization: curriculum and instruction, education administration and supervision, student counseling and personnel services.

During their internships, peer groups of students meet regularly to discuss instructional techniques in all of the teaching programs.

All of the students in their internships are mentored.

Courses that prepare teachers to pass the National Board of Professional Teaching Standards are not offered.

The education program is currently accredited by the National Council for Accreditation of Teacher Education.

LICENSING TEST

Pass rate on state's teacher licensing test for 2002-2003: **90%**

State average pass rate: **94%**

Eastern New Mexico University

- 1500 S. Av. K., Portales, NM 88130
- Website: http://www.enmu.edu/academics/graduate/index.shtml
- Public
- **Degrees offered:** bachelor's, master's

ADMISSIONS

Admissions phone number: (505) 562-2150

Admissions email address: *Phillip.Shelley@enmu.edu*

Application website: *http://www.enmu.edu/academics/graduate/admissions/Online-Application.shtml*

Application fee: **$10**

Fall 2005 application deadline: **rolling**

Test of English as Foreign Language (TOEFL) is required for international students.

Minimum TOEFL score required for paper test: **550**

Fall 2003

Acceptance rate for master's degree programs: **51%**

Total 2003 enrollment: **402**

Master's degree enrollment: **402**

Teacher preparation program enrollment (master's): **131**

FINANCIAL INFORMATION

Financial aid phone number: (505) 562-2194

Tuition, 2003-2004 academic year: Full-time in-state: **$86/credit hour**; out-of-state: **$318/credit hour**, Part-time in-state: **$86/credit hour**; out-of-state: **$86/credit hour**

Fees: **$29/credit hour**, Room and board: **$4,290**, Books and supplies: **$748**

Number of fellowships awarded to graduate students during the 2003-2004 academic year: 2

Number of teaching assistant positions: 15

ACADEMIC PROGRAMS

Total full-time tenured or tenure-track faculty (fall 2003): **21**, Total part-time faculty (fall 2003): **51**

Areas of specialization: curriculum and instruction, education administration and supervision, elementary teacher education, higher education administration, secondary teacher education, special education, student counseling and personnel services.

Professional development/partnership school(s) are used by students in some of the teaching programs.

During their internships, peer groups of students meet regularly to discuss instructional techniques in some of the teaching programs.

All of the students in their internships are mentored.

Courses that prepare teachers to pass the National Board of Professional Teaching Standards are not offered.

Teacher preparation programs: Four-year baccalaureate-degree program leading to initial licensure that includes either a major or minor in education and practice teaching. Master's program preparing college graduates for initial licensure; includes practice teaching. Alternative program for college graduates leading to provisional licensure.

The education program is currently accredited by the National Council for Accreditation of Teacher Education.

LICENSING TEST

Pass rate on state's teacher licensing test for 2002-2003: **100%**

State average pass rate: **94%**

New Mexico Highlands University

- Box 9000, Las Vegas, NM 87701
- Website: http://www.nmhu.edu
- Public
- **Degrees offered:** bachelor's, master's

ADMISSIONS

Admissions phone number: (800) 338-6648

Application fee: **$15**

Fall 2005 application deadline: **rolling**

Test of English as Foreign Language (TOEFL) is required for international students.

Minimum TOEFL score required for paper test: **500**

Fall 2003
Total 2003 enrollment: 328
Master's degree enrollment: 328

FINANCIAL INFORMATION
Financial aid phone number: (800) 379-4038
Tuition, 2003-2004 academic year: Full-time in-state:
$2,328; out-of-state: $9,672
Fees: $50, Room and board: $2,362

ACADEMIC PROGRAMS
Areas of specialization: curriculum and instruction, educational psychology, higher education administration, special education.
Professional development/partnership school(s) are used by students in some of the teaching programs.
During their internships, peer groups of students meet regularly to discuss instructional techniques in some of the teaching programs.
Some of the students in their internships are mentored.
Courses that prepare teachers to pass the National Board of Professional Teaching Standards are offered.
The education program is currently accredited by the National Council for Accreditation of Teacher Education.

LICENSING TEST
Pass rate on state's teacher licensing test for 2002-2003: 83%
State average pass rate: 94%

New Mexico State University

■ **College of Education, Las Cruces, NM 88003-8001**
■ **Website:** http://www.nmsu.edu/~gradcolg
■ **Public**
■ **Degrees offered:** bachelor's, master's, education specialist, Ph.D., Ed.D.

ADMISSIONS
Admissions phone number: (505) 646-2736
Admissions email address: *gradinfo@nmsu.edu*
Application fee: $15
Test requirements: **GRE or MAT**
Test of English as Foreign Language (TOEFL) is required for international students.
Minimum TOEFL score required for paper test: 530
Minimum TOEFL score required for computer test: 197

Fall 2003
Acceptance rate for master's degree programs: 50%
Acceptance rate for education specialist degree programs: 50%
Acceptance rate for doctoral programs: 50%
Average GRE verbal: 495, Average GRE quantitative: 480, Average GRE analytical: 465
Total 2003 enrollment: 971

Master's degree enrollment: 677
Teacher preparation program enrollment (master's): 514
Education specialist degree enrollment: 49
Doctoral degree enrollment: 245

FINANCIAL INFORMATION
Financial aid phone number: (505) 646-4105
Tuition, 2003-2004 academic year: Full-time in-state:
$3,624; out-of-state: $11,550, Part-time in-state:
$151/credit hour; out-of-state: $481
Fees: $954, Room and board: $5,856, Books and supplies:
$760, Miscellaneous expenses: $2,916
Number of teaching assistant positions: 71
Number of research assistant positions: 12

ACADEMIC PROGRAMS
Total full-time tenured or tenure-track faculty (fall 2003): 51
Areas of specialization: curriculum and instruction, education administration and supervision, educational psychology, elementary teacher education, secondary teacher education, special education.
Professional development/partnership school(s) are used by students in all of the teaching programs.
During their internships, peer groups of students meet regularly to discuss instructional techniques in all of the teaching programs.
All of the students in their internships are mentored.
Courses that prepare teachers to pass the National Board of Professional Teaching Standards are not offered.
Teacher preparation programs: Four-year baccalaureate-degree program leading to initial licensure that includes either a major or minor in education and practice teaching. Master's program preparing college graduates for initial licensure; includes practice teaching. Alternative program for college graduates leading to provisional licensure.
The education program is currently accredited by the National Council for Accreditation of Teacher Education.

LICENSING TEST
Pass rate on state's teacher licensing test for 2002-2003: 96%
State average pass rate: 94%

University of New Mexico

■ **College of Education, Albuquerque, NM 87131**
■ **Website:** http://www.unm.edu
■ **Public**
■ **Degrees offered:** bachelor's, master's, education specialist, Ph.D., Ed.D.

ADMISSIONS
Admissions phone number: (505) 277-7401
Application website: *http://www.applyweb.com/apply/unm/*
Application fee: $40

Fall 2005 application deadline: 3/1
Test requirements: **GRE or MAT**
Test of English as Foreign Language (TOEFL) is required
for international students.
Minimum TOEFL score required for paper test: 550
Minimum TOEFL score required for computer test: 213

Fall 2003
Acceptance rate for master's degree programs: 67%
Acceptance rate for education specialist degree programs:
94%
Acceptance rate for doctoral programs: 39%
Average GRE verbal: 525, Average GRE quantitative: 517,
Average MAT: 48
Total 2003 enrollment: 1,290
Master's degree enrollment: 880
Teacher preparation program enrollment (master's): 708
Education specialist degree enrollment: 43
Doctoral degree enrollment: 367

FINANCIAL INFORMATION
Financial aid phone number: (505) 277-7395
Tuition, 2003-2004 academic year: Full-time in-state:
$3,048; out-of-state: **$11,716**, Part-time in-state:
$127/credit hour; out-of-state: **$488/credit hour**
Fees: **$25/credit hour**, Room and board: **$5,450**, Books and
supplies: **$882**, Miscellaneous expenses: **$3,866**
Number of fellowships awarded to graduate students dur-
ing the 2003-2004 academic year: 7
Number of teaching assistant positions: 114
Number of research assistant positions: 15
Number of other paid appointments: 29

ACADEMIC PROGRAMS
Total full-time tenured or tenure-track faculty (fall 2003):
96, Total part-time faculty (fall 2003): 106
Areas of specialization: curriculum and instruction, education administration and supervision, educational psychology, elementary teacher education, secondary
teacher education, special education, student counseling
and personnel services.
Professional development/partnership school(s) are used
by students in some of the teaching programs.
During their internships, peer groups of students meet
regularly to discuss instructional techniques in some of
the teaching programs.
Some of the students in their internships are mentored.
Courses that prepare teachers to pass the National Board of
Professional Teaching Standards are offered.
Teacher preparation programs: Four-year baccalaureate-
degree program leading to initial licensure that includes
either a major or minor in education and practice teach-
ing. Master's program preparing college graduates for
initial licensure; includes practice teaching.
The education program is currently accredited by the
National Council for Accreditation of Teacher Education.

LICENSING TEST
Pass rate on state's teacher licensing test for 2002-2003:
93%
State average pass rate: 94%

Western New Mexico University

- Box 680, Silver City, NM 88062
- **Website:** http://www.wnmu.edu/
- Public

LICENSING TEST
Pass rate on state's teacher licensing test for 2002-2003:
100%
State average pass rate: 94%

NEW YORK

TEACHER TESTING IN NEW YORK
Teacher licensure rules vary widely from state to state, but almost all states require tests. The exams typically cover the basics of reading, writing and math, although some states mandate in-depth, subject-specific teacher tests. For information on where to go in your state for specific academic requirements, see Chapter 6 on page 67. Note: Some schools require students to pass exams by graduation, and thus automatically report pass rates of 100 percent.

- This state **does** require a basic skills test in order to obtain a teaching license.
- This state **does** require a subject-knowledge test in order to obtain a middle school teaching license.
- This state **does** require a subject-knowledge test in order to obtain a high school teaching license.
- This state **does not** require a subject-specific pedagogy test in order to obtain a teaching license.

Adelphi University

- **1 South Avenue, Garden City, NY 11530**
- **Website:** http://www.adelphi.edu/
- **Private**

LICENSING TEST
Pass rate on state's teacher licensing test for 2002-2003: 92%
State average pass rate: **94%**

Alfred University

- **Saxon Drive, Alfred, NY 14802**
- **Website:** http://www.alfred.edu/gradschool
- **Private**
- **Degrees offered:** bachelor's, master's

ADMISSIONS
Admissions phone number: **(607) 871-2141**
Admissions email address: *gradinquiry@alfred.edu*
Application website: *http://www.alfred.edu*
Application fee: **$50**
Fall 2005 application deadline: **rolling**
Test of English as Foreign Language (TOEFL) is required for international students.
Minimum TOEFL score required for paper test: 590
Minimum TOEFL score required for computer test: 243

Fall 2003
Acceptance rate for master's degree programs: 66%
Total 2003 enrollment: 70
Master's degree enrollment: 70
  Teacher preparation program enrollment (master's): 30

FINANCIAL INFORMATION
Financial aid phone number: **(607) 871-2159**
Tuition, 2003-2004 academic year: Full-time: **$25,944**;
  Part-time: **$498/credit hour**

Fees: **$780**, Room and board: **$9,012**

ACADEMIC PROGRAMS
Areas of specialization: curriculum and instruction, student counseling and personnel services.
Professional development/partnership school(s) are used by students in all of the teaching programs.
During their internships, peer groups of students meet regularly to discuss instructional techniques in all of the teaching programs.
All of the students in their internships are mentored.
Teacher preparation programs: Four-year baccalaureate-degree program leading to initial licensure that includes either a major or minor in education and practice teaching. Master's program preparing college graduates for initial licensure; includes practice teaching.

LICENSING TEST
Pass rate on state's teacher licensing test for 2002-2003: 96%
State average pass rate: **94%**

Bank Street College of Education

- **610 West 112th Street, New York, NY 10025**
- **Website:** http://www.bankstreet.edu
- **Private**
- **Degrees offered:** master's

ADMISSIONS
Admissions phone number: **(212) 875-4404**
Admissions email address: *gradcourses@bankstreet.edu*
Application website: *http://www.bankstreet.edu/gems/gs/gradap.pdf*
Application fee: **$50**
Fall 2005 application deadline: **3/1**
Test requirements: **None**
Test of English as Foreign Language (TOEFL) is required for international students.

Minimum TOEFL score required for paper test: 550
Minimum TOEFL score required for computer test: 220

Fall 2003
Acceptance rate for master's degree programs: 78%
Total 2003 enrollment: 853
Master's degree enrollment: 853
   Teacher preparation program enrollment (master's): 660

FINANCIAL INFORMATION
Financial aid phone number: (212) 875-4408
Tuition, 2003-2004 academic year: Full-time: $795/credit hour; Part-time: $795/credit hour
Fees: $250, Room and board: $14,300, Books and supplies: $1,200
Number of fellowships awarded to graduate students during the 2003-2004 academic year: 5
Number of teaching assistant positions: 110
Number of research assistant positions: 0
Number of other paid appointments: 17

ACADEMIC PROGRAMS
Areas of specialization: curriculum and instruction, education administration and supervision, elementary teacher education, special education.
Professional development/partnership school(s) are used by students in some of the teaching programs.
During their internships, peer groups of students meet regularly to discuss instructional techniques in all of the teaching programs.
All of the students in their internships are mentored.
Courses that prepare teachers to pass the National Board of Professional Teaching Standards are not offered.
Teacher preparation programs: Master's degree in education, including internship/practice teaching and preparation for initial licensure.
The education program is currently accredited by the National Council for Accreditation of Teacher Education.

LICENSING TEST
Pass rate on state's teacher licensing test for 2002-2003: 97%
State average pass rate: 94%

Binghamton University

■ School of Education & Human Development, Binghamton, NY 13902-6000
■ **Website:** http://www.binghamton.edu
■ **Public**
■ **Degrees offered:** master's, Ed.D.

ADMISSIONS
Admissions phone number: (607) 777-2151
Admissions email address: *gradad@binghamton.edu*
Application website: *http://gradschool.binghamton.edu/graduate/Gradapp.htm*

Application fee: $45
Test requirements: **GRE**
Test of English as Foreign Language (TOEFL) is required for international students.
Minimum TOEFL score required for paper test: 550
Minimum TOEFL score required for computer test: 213

Fall 2003
Acceptance rate for master's degree programs: 48%
Acceptance rate for doctoral programs: 39%
Average GRE verbal: 492, Average GRE quantitative: 543, Average GRE analytical: 565
Total 2003 enrollment: 422
Master's degree enrollment: 337
   Teacher preparation program enrollment (master's): 337
Doctoral degree enrollment: 85

FINANCIAL INFORMATION
Financial aid phone number: (607) 777-2428
Tuition, 2003-2004 academic year: Full-time in-state: $6,900; out-of-state: $10,500, Part-time in-state: $288/credit hour; out-of-state: $438/credit hour
Fees: $870, Room and board: $8,584, Books and supplies: $1,025, Miscellaneous expenses: $4,000
Number of fellowships awarded to graduate students during the 2003-2004 academic year: 9
Number of teaching assistant positions: 6
Number of research assistant positions: 6
Number of other paid appointments: 15

ACADEMIC PROGRAMS
Total full-time tenured or tenure-track faculty (fall 2003): 15
   Total part-time faculty (fall 2003): 6
Areas of specialization: curriculum and instruction, elementary teacher education, secondary teacher education, special education.
Professional development/partnership school(s) are used by students in some of the teaching programs.
During their internships, peer groups of students meet regularly to discuss instructional techniques in all of the teaching programs.
All of the students in their internships are mentored.
Courses that prepare teachers to pass the National Board of Professional Teaching Standards are not offered.
Teacher preparation programs: Master's degree in education, including internship/practice teaching and preparation for initial licensure.

LICENSING TEST
Pass rate on state's teacher licensing test for 2002-2003: 100%
State average pass rate: 94%

Buffalo State College– SUNY

- 1300 Elmwood Avenue, Buffalo, NY 14222
- Website: http://www.buffalostate.edu/
- Public

LICENSING TEST
Pass rate on state's teacher licensing test for 2002-2003: 94%
State average pass rate: 94%

Canisius College

- 2001 Main Street, Buffalo, NY 14208
- Website: http://www.canisius.edu/
- Private

LICENSING TEST
Pass rate on state's teacher licensing test for 2002-2003: 96%
State average pass rate: 94%

Colgate University

- 13 Oak Drive, Hamilton, NY 13346
- Website: http://www.colgate.edu
- Private
- Degrees offered: bachelor's, master's

ADMISSIONS
Admissions phone number: (315) 228-7256
Admissions email address: *jpagano@mail.colgate.edu*
Application fee: $50
Fall 2005 application deadline: 3/15

FINANCIAL INFORMATION
Financial aid phone number: (315) 228-7431
Tuition, 2003-2004 academic year: $29,740
Fees: $200

LICENSING TEST
State average pass rate: 94%

College of Mount St. Vincent

- 6301 Riverdale Avenue, Riverdale, NY 10471
- Website: http://www.cmsv.edu/
- Private

LICENSING TEST
Pass rate on state's teacher licensing test for 2002-2003: 90%
State average pass rate: 94%

College of New Rochelle

- Castle Place, New Rochelle, NY 10805-2338
- Website: http://www.cnr.edu/
- Private

LICENSING TEST
Pass rate on state's teacher licensing test for 2002-2003: 92%
State average pass rate: 94%

College of St. Rose

- 432 Western Avenue, Albany, NY 12203-1490
- Website: http://www.strose.edu
- Private
- Degrees offered: bachelor's, master's, education specialist

ADMISSIONS
Admissions phone number: (518) 354-5143
Admissions email address:
  http://www.strose.edu/Future_Students/Graduate_Adm
Application website:
  https://apply.embark.com/grad/strose/domestic/53/
Application fee: $35
Fall 2005 application deadline: 3/15
Test of English as Foreign Language (TOEFL) is required for international students.
Minimum TOEFL score required for paper test: 550
Minimum TOEFL score required for computer test: 213

Fall 2003
Acceptance rate for master's degree programs: 75%
Total 2003 enrollment: 1,362
Master's degree enrollment: 1,362
  Teacher preparation program enrollment (master's): 770

FINANCIAL INFORMATION
Financial aid phone number: (518) 458-5417

Tuition, 2003-2004 academic year: Full-time: **$430/credit hour**; Part-time: **$430/credit hour**
Fees: **$396**
Number of fellowships awarded to graduate students during the 2003-2004 academic year: **0**
Number of teaching assistant positions: **0**
Number of research assistant positions: **0**
Number of other paid appointments: **53**

ACADEMIC PROGRAMS
Total full-time tenured or tenure-track faculty (fall 2003): **154**, Total part-time faculty (fall 2003): **259**
Areas of specialization: education administration and supervision, educational psychology, elementary teacher education, secondary teacher education, special education.
Professional development/partnership school(s) are used by students in some of the teaching programs.
During their internships, peer groups of students meet regularly to discuss instructional techniques in all of the teaching programs.
All of the students in their internships are mentored.
Courses that prepare teachers to pass the National Board of Professional Teaching Standards are not offered.
Teacher preparation programs: Four-year baccalaureate-degree program leading to initial licensure that includes either a major or minor in education and practice teaching. Master's program preparing college graduates for initial licensure; includes practice teaching. Alternative program for college graduates leading to provisional licensure.

LICENSING TEST
Pass rate on state's teacher licensing test for 2002-2003: **94%**
State average pass rate: **94%**

Cornell University

- **Kennedy Hall, Ithaca, NY 14853**
- **Website:** http://www.cals.cornell.edu/dept/education
- **Private**
- **Degrees offered:** bachelor's, master's, Ph.D.
- **Overall rank in the 2005 U.S. News education schools with doctoral programs: 33**

ADMISSIONS
Admissions phone number: **(607) 255-4278**
Admissions email address: *edgrfld@cornell.edu*
Application website: *http://www.gradschool.cornell.edu/*
Application fee: **$70**
Fall 2005 application deadline: **2/15**
Test requirements: **GRE**
Test of English as Foreign Language (TOEFL) is required for international students.
Minimum TOEFL score required for paper test: **550**
Minimum TOEFL score required for computer test: **213**

Fall 2003
Acceptance rate for master's degree programs: **46%**
Acceptance rate for doctoral programs: **24%**
Average GRE verbal: **541**, Average GRE quantitative: **640**, Average GRE analytical: **648**
Total 2003 enrollment: **80**
Master's degree enrollment: **45**
  Teacher preparation program enrollment (master's): **36**
Doctoral degree enrollment: **35**

FINANCIAL INFORMATION
Financial aid phone number: **(607) 255-0441**
Tuition, 2003-2004 academic year: **$16,600**
Fees: **$50**, Room and board: **$11,205**, Books and supplies: **$780**, Miscellaneous expenses: **$4,350**
Number of fellowships awarded to graduate students during the 2003-2004 academic year: **1**
Number of teaching assistant positions: **17**
Number of research assistant positions: **10**
Number of other paid appointments: **8**

ACADEMIC PROGRAMS
Total full-time tenured or tenure-track faculty (fall 2003): **11**, Total part-time faculty (fall 2003): **1**
Areas of specialization: curriculum and instruction, secondary teacher education.
Professional development/partnership school(s) are used by students in none of the teaching programs.
During their internships, peer groups of students meet regularly to discuss instructional techniques in all of the teaching programs.
All of the students in their internships are mentored.
Courses that prepare teachers to pass the National Board of Professional Teaching Standards are not offered.
Teacher preparation programs: Four-year baccalaureate-degree program leading to initial licensure that includes either a major or minor in education and practice teaching. Five-year program leading to initial licensure that results in a baccalaureate degree (with a major or minor in education) plus a master's degree and includes practice teaching. Master's program preparing college graduates for initial licensure; includes practice teaching.

LICENSING TEST
Pass rate on state's teacher licensing test for 2002-2003: **100%**
State average pass rate: **94%**

CUNY–Brooklyn College

- **2900 Bedford Avenue, Brooklyn, NY 11210**
- **Website:** http://www.brooklyn.cuny.edu/
- **Public**

LICENSING TEST
Pass rate on state's teacher licensing test for 2002-2003: **87%**
State average pass rate: **94%**

CUNY–City College

■ **Convent Avenue at 138th Street, New York, NY 10031**
■ **Website:** http://www.cuny.edu
■ **Public**
■ **Degrees offered:** bachelor's, master's

ADMISSIONS

Admissions phone number: **(212) 650-6296**
Admissions email address: *edgradadm@ccny.cuny.edu*
Application website:
  *http://www.ccny.cuny.edu/admissions/gradapp03_
  shoolofed.pdf*
Application fee: **$50**
Fall 2005 application deadline: 3/15
Test of English as Foreign Language (TOEFL) is required
  for international students.
Minimum TOEFL score required for paper test: **500**
Minimum TOEFL score required for computer test: **173**

Fall 2003
Acceptance rate for master's degree programs: **84%**
Total 2003 enrollment: **1,636**
Master's degree enrollment: **1,636**
  Teacher preparation program enrollment (master's):
  1,559

FINANCIAL INFORMATION

Financial aid phone number: **(212) 650-5812**
Tuition, 2003-2004 academic year: Full-time in-state:
  $2,720; out-of-state: **$425/credit hour**, Part-time in-state:
  $230/credit hour; out-of-state: **$425/credit hour**
Fees: **$20**
Number of fellowships awarded to graduate students dur-
  ing the 2003-2004 academic year: **0**
Number of teaching assistant positions: **0**
Number of research assistant positions: **0**
Number of other paid appointments: **3**

ACADEMIC PROGRAMS

Total full-time tenured or tenure-track faculty (fall 2003): **36**
  Total part-time faculty (fall 2003): **0**
Professional development/partnership school(s) are used
  by students in all of the teaching programs.
During their internships, peer groups of students meet
  regularly to discuss instructional techniques in all of the
  teaching programs.
All of the students in their internships are mentored.
Courses that prepare teachers to pass the National Board of
  Professional Teaching Standards are not offered.
Teacher preparation programs: Four-year baccalaureate-
  degree program leading to initial licensure that includes
  either a major or minor in education and practice teaching. Master's program preparing college graduates for
  initial licensure; includes practice teaching. Alternative
  program for college graduates leading to provisional
  licensure.

LICENSING TEST

Pass rate on state's teacher licensing test for 2002-2003:
  87%
State average pass rate: **94%**

CUNY–College of Staten Island

■ **2800 Victory Blvd., Staten Island, NY 10314**
■ **Website:** http://www.csi.cuny.edu
■ **Public**
■ **Degrees offered:** bachelor's, master's

ADMISSIONS

Admissions phone number: **(718) 982-2010**
Admissions email address:
  recruitment@postbox.csi.cuny.edu
Application website: *http://www.csi.cuny.edu/graduatestudies*
Application fee: **$50**
Fall 2005 application deadline: **rolling**
Test of English as Foreign Language (TOEFL) is required
  for international students.
Minimum TOEFL score required for paper test: **550**
Minimum TOEFL score required for computer test: **213**

Fall 2003
Acceptance rate for master's degree programs: **85%**
Total 2003 enrollment: **740**
Master's degree enrollment: **673**
  Teacher preparation program enrollment (master's): **673**
Education specialist degree enrollment: **67**

FINANCIAL INFORMATION

Financial aid phone number: **(718) 982-2030**
Tuition, 2003-2004 academic year: Full-time in-state:
  $5,440; out-of-state: **$425/credit hour**, Part-time in-state:
  $230/credit hour; out-of-state: **$425/credit hour**
Fees: **$308**, Books and supplies: **$759**

ACADEMIC PROGRAMS

Total full-time tenured or tenure-track faculty (fall 2003): **20**
  Total part-time faculty (fall 2003): **37**
Areas of specialization: education administration and
  supervision, elementary teacher education, secondary
  teacher education, special education.
Professional development/partnership school(s) are used
  by students in all of the teaching programs.
During their internships, peer groups of students meet
  regularly to discuss instructional techniques in all of the
  teaching programs.
Some of the students in their internships are mentored.
Courses that prepare teachers to pass the National Board of
  Professional Teaching Standards are not offered.
Teacher preparation programs: Four-year baccalaureate-
  degree program leading to initial licensure that includes
  either a major or minor in education and practice teaching. Master's program preparing college graduates for

initial licensure; includes practice teaching. Alternative program for college graduates leading to provisional licensure.

LICENSING TEST

Pass rate on state's teacher licensing test for 2002-2003: 98%

State average pass rate: 94%

CUNY–Graduate Center

■ 365 Fifth Avenue, New York, NY 10016
■ Website: http://www.gc.cuny.edu
■ Public
■ Degrees offered: Ph.D.

ADMISSIONS

Admissions phone number: (212) 817-7470
Admissions email address: *admissions@gc.cuny.edu*
Application fee: $50
Test requirements: GRE
Test of English as Foreign Language (TOEFL) is required for international students.
Minimum TOEFL score required for paper test: 600
Minimum TOEFL score required for computer test: 250

Fall 2003
Acceptance rate for doctoral programs: 34%
Average GRE verbal: 540, Average GRE quantitative: 608, Average GRE analytical: 550
Total 2003 enrollment: 99
Doctoral degree enrollment: 99

FINANCIAL INFORMATION

Financial aid phone number: (212) 817-7460
Tuition, 2003-2004 academic year: Full-time in-state: $4,870; out-of-state: $9,500, Part-time in-state: $275/credit hour; out-of-state: $475/credit hour
Fees: $219

ACADEMIC PROGRAMS

Total full-time tenured or tenure-track faculty (fall 2003): 21
Areas of specialization: education policy, educational psychology.

CUNY–Hunter College

■ 695 Park Avenue, New York, NY 10021
■ Website: http://www.hunter.cuny.edu
■ Public
■ Degrees offered: bachelor's, master's

ADMISSIONS

Admissions phone number: (212) 772-4482
Admissions email address: *admissions@hunter.cuny.edu*

Application website:
   http://admissions.hunter.cuny.edu/~graduate/request.html
Application fee: $50
Fall 2005 application deadline: 4/1
Test of English as Foreign Language (TOEFL) is required for international students.
Minimum TOEFL score required for paper test: 575
Minimum TOEFL score required for computer test: 233

Fall 2003
Acceptance rate for master's degree programs: 44%
Total 2003 enrollment: 1,699
Master's degree enrollment: 1,699
   Teacher preparation program enrollment (master's): 1,573

FINANCIAL INFORMATION

Financial aid phone number: (212) 772-4820
Tuition, 2003-2004 academic year: Full-time in-state: $2,720; out-of-state: $5,100, Part-time in-state: $250/credit hour; out-of-state: $425/credit hour
Fees: $45, Books and supplies: $692, Miscellaneous expenses: $771

ACADEMIC PROGRAMS

Total full-time tenured or tenure-track faculty (fall 2003): 53, Total part-time faculty (fall 2003): 91
Areas of specialization: curriculum and instruction, education administration and supervision, educational psychology, elementary teacher education, secondary teacher education, special education, student counseling and personnel services.
Professional development/partnership school(s) are used by students in some of the teaching programs.
During their internships, peer groups of students meet regularly to discuss instructional techniques in some of the teaching programs.
Some of the students in their internships are mentored.
Courses that prepare teachers to pass the National Board of Professional Teaching Standards are not offered.
Teacher preparation programs: Four-year baccalaureate-degree program leading to initial licensure that includes either a major or minor in education and practice teaching. Five-year program leading to initial licensure that results in a baccalaureate degree (with a major or minor in education) plus a master's degree and includes practice teaching. Master's program preparing college graduates for initial licensure; includes practice teaching. Alternative program for college graduates leading to provisional licensure.

LICENSING TEST

Pass rate on state's teacher licensing test for 2002-2003: 96%
State average pass rate: 94%

CUNY–Lehman College

■ 250 Bedford Park Boulevard West, Bronx, NY 10468
■ Website: http://www.lehman.cuny.edu
■ Public
■ Degrees offered: master's

ADMISSIONS
Admissions phone number: (718) 960-8706
Admissions email address: *enroll@lehman.cuny.edu*
Application website: *http://www.lehman.cuny.edu*
Application fee: $50
Fall 2005 application deadline: **rolling**
Test of English as Foreign Language (TOEFL) is required
 for international students.
Minimum TOEFL score required for paper test: 500

Fall 2003
Total 2003 enrollment: 848
Master's degree enrollment: 848
 Teacher preparation program enrollment (master's):
 809

FINANCIAL INFORMATION
Financial aid phone number: (718) 960-8545
Tuition, 2003-2004 academic year: Full-time in-state:
 $5,440; out-of-state: $425/credit hour, Part-time in-state:
 $230/credit hour; out-of-state: $425/credit hour
Fees: $190, Books and supplies: $500, Miscellaneous
 expenses: $2,850

ACADEMIC PROGRAMS
Total full-time tenured or tenure-track faculty (fall 2003):
 38
Areas of specialization: elementary teacher education, sec-
 ondary teacher education, special education, student
 counseling and personnel services.
Professional development/partnership school(s) are used
 by students in all of the teaching programs.
During their internships, peer groups of students meet
 regularly to discuss instructional techniques in some of
 the teaching programs.
All of the students in their internships are mentored.
Courses that prepare teachers to pass the National Board of
 Professional Teaching Standards are not offered.
Teacher preparation programs: Master's degree in education, including internship/practice teaching and preparation for initial licensure. Education minor for
 undergraduate students. Alternative program for college
 graduates leading to provisional licensure.
The education program is currently accredited by the
 National Council for Accreditation of Teacher Education.

LICENSING TEST
Pass rate on state's teacher licensing test for 2002-2003:
 92%
State average pass rate: 94%

CUNY–Queens College

■ 65-30 Kissena Boulevard, Flushing, NY 11367
■ Website: http://www.qc.edu/
■ Public

LICENSING TEST
Pass rate on state's teacher licensing test for 2002-2003:
 93%
State average pass rate: 94%

Daemen College

■ 4380 Main Street, Amherst, NY 14226
■ Website: http://www.daemen.edu
■ Private
■ Degrees offered: bachelor's, master's

ADMISSIONS
Admissions phone number: (716) 839-8225
Admissions email address: *www.admissions@daemen.edu*
Application website: *http://www.daemen.edu*
Application fee: $25
Fall 2005 application deadline: 4/30
Test requirements: GRE

Fall 2003
Acceptance rate for master's degree programs: 90%
Total 2003 enrollment: 44
Master's degree enrollment: 44
 Teacher preparation program enrollment (master's): 44

FINANCIAL INFORMATION
Financial aid phone number: (716) 839-8254
Tuition, 2003-2004 academic year: Full-time: $560/credit
 hour; Part-time: $560/credit hour
Fees: $11/credit hour, Room and board: $3,835, Books and
 supplies: $300, Miscellaneous expenses: $200
Number of fellowships awarded to graduate students dur-
 ing the 2003-2004 academic year: 0
Number of teaching assistant positions: 0
Number of research assistant positions: 16
Number of other paid appointments: 0

ACADEMIC PROGRAMS
Total full-time tenured or tenure-track faculty (fall 2003): 8
 Total part-time faculty (fall 2003): 22
Areas of specialization: elementary teacher education, sec-
 ondary teacher education, special education.
Professional development/partnership school(s) are used
 by students in all of the teaching programs.
During their internships, peer groups of students meet
 regularly to discuss instructional techniques in all of the
 teaching programs.
All of the students in their internships are mentored.

Courses that prepare teachers to pass the National Board of Professional Teaching Standards are not offered.

Teacher preparation programs: Four-year baccalaureate-degree program leading to initial licensure that includes either a major or minor in education and practice teaching. Five-year program leading to initial licensure that results in a baccalaureate degree (with a major or minor in education) plus graduate credit and includes practice teaching. Five-year program leading to initial licensure that results in a baccalaureate degree (with a major or minor in education) plus a master's degree and includes practice teaching. Master's program preparing college graduates for initial licensure; includes practice teaching. Alternative program for college graduates leading to provisional licensure.

LICENSING TEST

Pass rate on state's teacher licensing test for 2002-2003: **98%**
State average pass rate: **94%**

Dominican College of Blauvelt

■ **470 Western Hwy., Orangeburg, NY 10962-1210**
■ **Website:** http://www.dc.edu
■ **Private**
■ **Degrees offered:** bachelor's, master's

ADMISSIONS

Admissions phone number: **(866) 432-4636**
Admissions email address: *admissions@dc.edu*
Application website: *http://www.dc.edu/applic.html*
Application fee: **$35**
Fall 2005 application deadline: **rolling**
Test of English as Foreign Language (TOEFL) is required for international students.
Minimum TOEFL score required for paper test: **550**
Minimum TOEFL score required for computer test: **213**

Fall 2003
Acceptance rate for master's degree programs: **89%**
Total 2003 enrollment: **47**
Master's degree enrollment: **47**
    Teacher preparation program enrollment (master's): **47**

FINANCIAL INFORMATION

Financial aid phone number: **(845) 359-7800**
Tuition, 2003-2004 academic year: Full-time: **$525/credit hour**; Part-time: **$525/credit hour**
Fees: **$300**, Books and supplies: **$53**
Number of fellowships awarded to graduate students during the 2003-2004 academic year: **0**
Number of teaching assistant positions: **0**
Number of research assistant positions: **0**
Number of other paid appointments: **0**

ACADEMIC PROGRAMS

Total full-time tenured or tenure-track faculty (fall 2003): **3**
    Total part-time faculty (fall 2003): **8**
Areas of specialization: special education.
Professional development/partnership school(s) are used by students in all of the teaching programs.
During their internships, peer groups of students meet regularly to discuss instructional techniques in all of the teaching programs.
All of the students in their internships are mentored.
Teacher preparation programs: Four-year baccalaureate-degree program leading to initial licensure that includes either a major or minor in education and practice teaching.

LICENSING TEST

Pass rate on state's teacher licensing test for 2002-2003: **83%**
State average pass rate: **94%**

Dowling College

■ **Idle Hour Blvd., Oakdale Long Island, NY 11769**
■ **Website:** http://www.dowling.edu/
■ **Private**

LICENSING TEST

Pass rate on state's teacher licensing test for 2002-2003: **86%**
State average pass rate: **94%**

D'Youville College

■ **One D'Youville Square 320 Porter Avenue, Buffalo, NY 14201-1084**
■ **Website:** http://www.dyc.edu
■ **Private**
■ **Degrees offered:** master's

ADMISSIONS

Admissions phone number: **(716) 881-7676**
Admissions email address: *graduateadmissions@dyc.edu*
Application website: *http://www.dyc.edu*
Application fee: **$25**
Fall 2005 application deadline: **rolling**
Test of English as Foreign Language (TOEFL) is required for international students.
Minimum TOEFL score required for paper test: **500**
Minimum TOEFL score required for computer test: **173**

Fall 2003
Acceptance rate for master's degree programs: **52%**
Total 2003 enrollment: **1,093**
Master's degree enrollment: **1,093**
    Teacher preparation program enrollment (master's): **1,093**

FINANCIAL INFORMATION

Financial aid phone number: **(716) 881-7691**

Tuition, 2003-2004 academic year: Full-time: **$490/credit hour**; Part-time: **$490/credit hour**

Fees: **$200**

Number of fellowships awarded to graduate students during the 2003-2004 academic year: **0**

Number of teaching assistant positions: **0**

Number of research assistant positions: **1**

Number of other paid appointments: **0**

ACADEMIC PROGRAMS

Total full-time tenured or tenure-track faculty (fall 2003): **16**, Total part-time faculty (fall 2003): **37**

Areas of specialization: elementary teacher education, secondary teacher education, special education.

Professional development/partnership school(s) are used by students in some of the teaching programs.

During their internships, peer groups of students meet regularly to discuss instructional techniques in all of the teaching programs.

All of the students in their internships are mentored.

Courses that prepare teachers to pass the National Board of Professional Teaching Standards are not offered.

Teacher preparation programs: Master's degree in education, including internship/practice teaching and preparation for initial licensure.

LICENSING TEST

Pass rate on state's teacher licensing test for 2002-2003: **98%**

State average pass rate: **94%**

Elmira College

- 1 Park Place, Elmira, NY 14901
- **Website:** http://www.elmira.edu/
- **Private**

LICENSING TEST

Pass rate on state's teacher licensing test for 2002-2003: **95%**

State average pass rate: **94%**

Fordham University

- 113 W. 60th Street, New York, NY 10023
- **Website:** http://www.fordham.edu/gse
- **Private**
- **Degrees offered:** master's, education specialist, Ph.D., Ed.D.
- **Overall rank in the 2005 U.S. News education schools with doctoral programs:** 51

ADMISSIONS

Admissions phone number: **(212) 636-6400**

Admissions email address: *gse_admiss@fordham.edu*

Application fee: **$65**

Test requirements: **GRE or MAT**

Test of English as Foreign Language (TOEFL) is required for international students.

Minimum TOEFL score required for paper test: **575**

Minimum TOEFL score required for computer test: **230**

Fall 2003

Acceptance rate for master's degree programs: **87%**

Acceptance rate for education specialist degree programs: **60%**

Acceptance rate for doctoral programs: **32%**

Average GRE verbal: **532**, Average GRE quantitative: **594**, Average GRE analytical: **593**, Average MAT: **46**

Total 2003 enrollment: **1,593**

Master's degree enrollment: **1,168**

    Teacher preparation program enrollment (master's): **776**

Education specialist degree enrollment: **96**

Doctoral degree enrollment: **329**

FINANCIAL INFORMATION

Financial aid phone number: **(212) 636-6400**

Tuition, 2003-2004 academic year: Full-time: **$690/credit hour**; Part-time: **$690/credit hour**

Fees: **$296**, Room and board: **$14,220**, Books and supplies: **$850**, Miscellaneous expenses: **$2,960**

Number of research assistant positions: **52**

ACADEMIC PROGRAMS

Total full-time tenured or tenure-track faculty (fall 2003): **37**, Total part-time faculty (fall 2003): **70**

Areas of specialization: curriculum and instruction, education administration and supervision, educational psychology, elementary teacher education, secondary teacher education, special education, student counseling and personnel services.

Professional development/partnership school(s) are used by students in some of the teaching programs.

During their internships, peer groups of students meet regularly to discuss instructional techniques in all of the teaching programs.

All of the students in their internships are mentored.

Courses that prepare teachers to pass the National Board of Professional Teaching Standards are not offered.

Teacher preparation programs: Master's degree in education, including internship/practice teaching and preparation for initial licensure. Education minor for undergraduate students. Alternative program for college graduates leading to provisional licensure.

The education program is currently accredited by the National Council for Accreditation of Teacher Education.

LICENSING TEST

Pass rate on state's teacher licensing test for 2002-2003: **95%**

State average pass rate: **94%**

Graduate College of Union University

■ 807 Union Street; Lamont House, Schenectady, NY 12309
■ Website: http://www.graduatecollege.union.edu
■ Private
■ Degrees offered: master's

ADMISSIONS

Admissions phone number: (518) 388-6238
Admissions email address: *sheehanr@union.edu*
Application website: *http://www.graduatecollege.union.edu/
   gradadmin/index.htm*
Application fee: **$60**
Fall 2005 application deadline: **rolling**
Test of English as Foreign Language (TOEFL) is required
   for international students.
Minimum TOEFL score required for paper test: **550**
Minimum TOEFL score required for computer test: **213**

Fall 2003
Acceptance rate for master's degree programs: **50%**
Total 2003 enrollment: **71**
Master's degree enrollment: **71**
   Teacher preparation program enrollment (master's): **71**

FINANCIAL INFORMATION

Financial aid phone number: (518) 388-6123
Tuition, 2003-2004 academic year: Full-time: **$436/credit
   hour**; Part-time: **$436/credit hour**
Room and board: **$8,800**, Books and supplies: **$1,200**,
   Miscellaneous expenses: **$3,500**
Number of fellowships awarded to graduate students dur-
   ing the 2003-2004 academic year: **0**
Number of teaching assistant positions: **0**
Number of research assistant positions: **0**
Number of other paid appointments: **15**

ACADEMIC PROGRAMS

Total full-time tenured or tenure-track faculty (fall 2003): **3**
   Total part-time faculty (fall 2003): **15**
Areas of specialization: curriculum and instruction, sec-
   ondary teacher education.
Professional development/partnership school(s) are used
   by students in some of the teaching programs.
During their internships, peer groups of students meet
   regularly to discuss instructional techniques in all of the
   teaching programs.
All of the students in their internships are mentored.
Courses that prepare teachers to pass the National Board of
   Professional Teaching Standards are offered.
Teacher preparation programs: Master's degree in educa-
   tion, including internship/practice teaching and prepara-
   tion for initial licensure.
The education program is currently accredited by the
   Teacher Education Accreditation Council.

LICENSING TEST

Pass rate on state's teacher licensing test for 2002-2003:
   100%
State average pass rate: **94%**

Hofstra University

■ Hagerdorn Hall, Hempstead, NY 11549
■ Website: http://www.hofstra.edu/graduatestudies
■ Private
■ Degrees offered: bachelor's, master's, Ph.D., Ed.D.

ADMISSIONS

Admissions phone number: (516) 463-4723
Admissions email address: *gradstudent@hofstra.edu*
Application website: *http://www.hofstra.edu/academics/
   graduate/GS_admissions/gs_admissions_applying.cfm*
Application fee: **$60**
Fall 2005 application deadline: **rolling**
Test requirements: **GRE or MAT**
Test of English as Foreign Language (TOEFL) is required
   for international students.
Minimum TOEFL score required for paper test: **550**
Minimum TOEFL score required for computer test: **213**

Fall 2003
Acceptance rate for master's degree programs: **58%**
Acceptance rate for doctoral programs: **39%**
Total 2003 enrollment: **1,559**
Master's degree enrollment: **1,466**
   Teacher preparation program enrollment (master's):
   1,202
Doctoral degree enrollment: **93**

FINANCIAL INFORMATION

Financial aid phone number: (516) 463-6680
Tuition, 2003-2004 academic year: Full-time: **$600/credit
   hour**; Part-time: **$600/credit hour**
Fees: **$920**, Room and board: **$8,590**, Books and supplies:
   $581, Miscellaneous expenses: **$2,100**
Number of fellowships awarded to graduate students dur-
   ing the 2003-2004 academic year: **0**
Number of teaching assistant positions: **0**
Number of research assistant positions: **0**
Number of other paid appointments: **0**

ACADEMIC PROGRAMS

Total full-time tenured or tenure-track faculty (fall 2003):
   69, Total part-time faculty (fall 2003): **246**
Areas of specialization: curriculum and instruction, education administration and supervision, education policy,
   elementary teacher education, secondary teacher education, special education, student counseling and personnel services.
Professional development/partnership school(s) are used
   by students in some of the teaching programs.

During their internships, peer groups of students meet regularly to discuss instructional techniques in all of the teaching programs.

All of the students in their internships are mentored.

Courses that prepare teachers to pass the National Board of Professional Teaching Standards are not offered.

Teacher preparation programs: Four-year baccalaureate-degree program leading to initial licensure that includes either a major or minor in education and practice teaching. Master's program preparing college graduates for initial licensure; includes practice teaching.

The education program is currently accredited by the National Council for Accreditation of Teacher Education.

LICENSING TEST

Pass rate on state's teacher licensing test for 2002-2003: 97%

State average pass rate: 94%

Iona College

- **715 North Avenue, New Rochelle, NY 10801**
- **Website:** http://www.iona.edu
- **Private**
- **Degrees offered:** bachelor's, master's

ADMISSIONS

Admissions phone number: **(914) 633-2502**

Admissions email address: *admissions@iona.edu*

Application website: *http://www.iona.edu/admissions.htm*

Application fee: **$50**

Fall 2005 application deadline: **rolling**

Test of English as Foreign Language (TOEFL) is required for international students.

Minimum TOEFL score required for paper test: **550**

Minimum TOEFL score required for computer test: **213**

Fall 2003

Acceptance rate for master's degree programs: **76%**

Total 2003 enrollment: **235**

Master's degree enrollment: **235**

  Teacher preparation program enrollment (master's): **128**

FINANCIAL INFORMATION

Financial aid phone number: **(914) 633-2497**

Tuition, 2003-2004 academic year: Full-time: **$540/credit hour**; Part-time: **$540/credit hour**

Fees: **$130**, Books and supplies: **$700**

ACADEMIC PROGRAMS

Total full-time tenured or tenure-track faculty (fall 2003): **9**

  Total part-time faculty (fall 2003): **6**

Areas of specialization: education administration and supervision, educational psychology, elementary teacher education, secondary teacher education, student counseling and personnel services.

Professional development/partnership school(s) are used by students in some of the teaching programs.

During their internships, peer groups of students meet regularly to discuss instructional techniques in some of the teaching programs.

All of the students in their internships are mentored.

Courses that prepare teachers to pass the National Board of Professional Teaching Standards are not offered.

Teacher preparation programs: Four-year baccalaureate-degree program leading to initial licensure that includes either a major or minor in education and practice teaching. Master's program preparing college graduates for initial licensure; includes practice teaching. Alternative program for college graduates leading to provisional licensure.

The education program is currently accredited by the National Council for Accreditation of Teacher Education.

LICENSING TEST

Pass rate on state's teacher licensing test for 2002-2003: **94%**

State average pass rate: **94%**

Ithaca College

- **111 Towers Concourse, Ithaca, NY 14850**
- **Website:** http://www.ithaca.edu/gradstudies
- **Private**
- **Degrees offered:** bachelor's, master's

ADMISSIONS

Admissions phone number: **(607) 274-3527**

Admissions email address: *gradstudies@ithaca.edu*

Application fee: **$40**

Fall 2005 application deadline: **2/1**

Test of English as Foreign Language (TOEFL) is required for international students.

Minimum TOEFL score required for paper test: **550**

Minimum TOEFL score required for computer test: **213**

FINANCIAL INFORMATION

Financial aid phone number: **(607) 274-3131**

Tuition, 2003-2004 academic year: Full-time: **$696/credit hour**; Part-time: **$696/credit hour**

ACADEMIC PROGRAMS

Professional development/partnership school(s) are used by students in some of the teaching programs.

During their internships, peer groups of students meet regularly to discuss instructional techniques in some of the teaching programs.

Some of the students in their internships are mentored.

Courses that prepare teachers to pass the National Board of Professional Teaching Standards are not offered.

Teacher preparation programs: Four-year baccalaureate-degree program leading to initial licensure that includes either a major or minor in education and practice teaching.

LICENSING TEST

Pass rate on state's teacher licensing test for 2002-2003: **98%**

State average pass rate: **94%**

Le Moyne College

- **1419 Salt Springs Road, Syracuse, NY 13214**
- **Website:** http://www.lemoyne.edu/
- **Private**

LICENSING TEST

Pass rate on state's teacher licensing test for 2002-2003: 98%

State average pass rate: **94%**

Long Island University–Brentwood

- **100 Second Avenue, Brentwood, NY 11717**
- **Website:** http://www.liu.edu/liu_start.html
- **Private**

LICENSING TEST

Pass rate on state's teacher licensing test for 2002-2003: 97%

State average pass rate: **94%**

Long Island University–Brooklyn

- **1 University Plaza, Brooklyn, NY 11201**
- **Website:** http://www.liu.edu/liu_start.html
- **Private**

LICENSING TEST

Pass rate on state's teacher licensing test for 2002-2003: 100%

State average pass rate: **94%**

Long Island Univeristy–C.W. Post Campus

- **720 Northern Boulevard, Brookville, NY 11548**
- **Website:** http://www.liu.edu/cwpost
- **Private**
- **Degrees offered:** bachelor's, master's, education specialist

ADMISSIONS

Admissions phone number: **(516) 299-2000**
Admissions email address: *enroll@cwpost.liu.edu*
Application website: *http://www.cwpost.liu.edu/cwis/cwp/ admissions/graduate/howtoapplyg.html*

Application fee: **$30**
Fall 2005 application deadline: **rolling**
Test requirements: **GRE or MAT**
Test of English as Foreign Language (TOEFL) is required for international students.
Minimum TOEFL score required for paper test: **525**
Minimum TOEFL score required for computer test: **197**

Fall 2003
Acceptance rate for master's degree programs: **73%**
Acceptance rate for education specialist degree programs: **68%**
Total 2003 enrollment: **2,086**
Master's degree enrollment: **2,009**
Education specialist degree enrollment: **77**

FINANCIAL INFORMATION

Financial aid phone number: **(516) 299-2338**
Tuition, 2003-2004 academic year: **$15,792**
Fees: **$980**, Room and board: **$7,730**, Books and supplies: **$600**, Miscellaneous expenses: **$2,100**
Number of fellowships awarded to graduate students during the 2003-2004 academic year: **0**
Number of teaching assistant positions: **0**
Number of research assistant positions: **0**
Number of other paid appointments: **29**

ACADEMIC PROGRAMS

Total full-time tenured or tenure-track faculty (fall 2003): 62, Total part-time faculty (fall 2003): **266**
Areas of specialization: curriculum and instruction, education administration and supervision, educational psychology, elementary teacher education, secondary teacher education, special education, student counseling and personnel services.
Professional development/partnership school(s) are used by students in some of the teaching programs.
During their internships, peer groups of students meet regularly to discuss instructional techniques in all of the teaching programs.
All of the students in their internships are mentored.
Courses that prepare teachers to pass the National Board of Professional Teaching Standards are not offered.
Teacher preparation programs: Four-year baccalaureate-degree program leading to initial licensure that includes either a major or minor in education and practice teaching. Five-year program leading to initial licensure that results in a baccalaureate degree (with a major or minor in education) plus a master's degree and includes practice teaching. Master's program preparing college graduates for initial licensure; includes practice teaching.

LICENSING TEST

Pass rate on state's teacher licensing test for 2002-2003: **90%**
State average pass rate: **94%**

Long Island University–Southampton

- 239 Montauk Highway, Southampton, NY 11968
- Website: http://www.liu.edu/liu_starthtml
- Private

LICENSING TEST

Pass rate on state's teacher licensing test for 2002-2003:
93%
State average pass rate: 94%

Manhattan College

- Manhattan College Parkway, Bronx, NY 10471
- Website: http://www.manhattan.edu/
- Private

LICENSING TEST

Pass rate on state's teacher licensing test for 2002-2003:
89%
State average pass rate: 94%

Manhattanville College

- 2900 Purchase Street, Purchase, NY 10577
- Website: http://www.mville.edu/
- Private

LICENSING TEST

Pass rate on state's teacher licensing test for 2002-2003:
97%
State average pass rate: 94%

Marist College

- 3399 North Road, Poughkeepsie, NY 12590
- Website: http://www.marist.edu
- Private
- Degrees offered: bachelor's, master's

ADMISSIONS

Admissions phone number: (845) 575-3800
Admissions email address: *graduate@marist.edu*
Application website: *http://www.marist.edu/graduate*
Application fee: $30
Fall 2005 application deadline: 8/1
Test requirements: GRE
Test of English as Foreign Language (TOEFL) is required
for international students.
Minimum TOEFL score required for paper test: 550

Minimum TOEFL score required for computer test: 213

Fall 2003
Total 2003 enrollment: 140
Master's degree enrollment: 140

FINANCIAL INFORMATION

Financial aid phone number: (845) 575-3230
Tuition, 2003-2004 academic year: Full-time: $530/credit
hour; Part-time: $530/credit hour
Fees: $60, Books and supplies: $850, Miscellaneous
expenses: $700
Number of research assistant positions: 12

ACADEMIC PROGRAMS

Total full-time tenured or tenure-track faculty (fall 2003): 9
Total part-time faculty (fall 2003): 20
Areas of specialization: educational psychology.
Professional development/partnership school(s) are used
by students in all of the teaching programs.
During their internships, peer groups of students meet
regularly to discuss instructional techniques in some of
the teaching programs.
All of the students in their internships are mentored.
Courses that prepare teachers to pass the National Board of
Professional Teaching Standards are not offered.
Teacher preparation programs: Four-year baccalaureate-
degree program leading to initial licensure that includes
either a major or minor in education and practice teaching.

LICENSING TEST

Pass rate on state's teacher licensing test for 2002-2003:
98%
State average pass rate: 94%

Medaille College

- 18 Agassiz Circle, Buffalo, NY 14214
- Website: http://www.medaille.edu/
- Private

LICENSING TEST

Pass rate on state's teacher licensing test for 2002-2003:
97%
State average pass rate: 94%

Mercy College

- 555 Broadway, Dobbs Ferry, NY 10522
- Website: http://www.mercy.edu
- Private
- Degrees offered: bachelor's, master's

ADMISSIONS

Admissions phone number: (914) 674-5358
Admissions email address: *mnoblitt@mercy.edu*

Application fee: **$35**
Fall 2005 application deadline: **rolling**

Fall 2003
Total 2003 enrollment: 2,162
Master's degree enrollment: 2,162
   Teacher preparation program enrollment (master's):
   1,934

FINANCIAL INFORMATION
Financial aid phone number: **(914) 378-3421**
Tuition, 2003-2004 academic year: **$495/credit hour**

ACADEMIC PROGRAMS
Professional development/partnership school(s) are used
   by students in some of the teaching programs.
During their internships, peer groups of students meet
   regularly to discuss instructional techniques in some of
   the teaching programs.
All of the students in their internships are mentored.
Courses that prepare teachers to pass the National Board of
   Professional Teaching Standards are not offered.

LICENSING TEST
Pass rate on state's teacher licensing test for 2002-2003:
   85%
State average pass rate: **94%**

Molloy College

■ **1000 Hempstead Avenue, PO Box 5002, Rockville Center,
   NY 11571**
■ **Website:** http://www.molloy.edu
■ **Private**
■ **Degrees offered:** bachelor's, master's

ADMISSIONS
Admissions phone number: **(516) 678-5000**
Admissions email address: *mlane@molloy.edu*
Application fee: **$60**
Fall 2005 application deadline: **rolling**
Test of English as Foreign Language (TOEFL) is required
   for international students.
Minimum TOEFL score required for paper test: **500**

Fall 2003
Acceptance rate for master's degree programs: **79%**
Total 2003 enrollment: 414
Master's degree enrollment: 414
   Teacher preparation program enrollment (master's): 414

FINANCIAL INFORMATION
Financial aid phone number: **(516) 678-5000**
Tuition, 2003-2004 academic year: Full-time: **$555/credit
   hour**; Part-time: **$555/credit hour**
Fees: **$620**
Number of fellowships awarded to graduate students dur-
   ing the 2003-2004 academic year: **0**

Number of teaching assistant positions: **0**
Number of research assistant positions: **4**
Number of other paid appointments: **0**

ACADEMIC PROGRAMS
Total full-time tenured or tenure-track faculty (fall 2003): **10**
Areas of specialization: elementary teacher education, sec-
   ondary teacher education, special education.
Professional development/partnership school(s) are used
   by students in none of the teaching programs.
During their internships, peer groups of students meet
   regularly to discuss instructional techniques in some of
   the teaching programs.
None of the students in their internships are mentored.
Courses that prepare teachers to pass the National Board of
   Professional Teaching Standards are not offered.
Teacher preparation programs: Four-year baccalaureate-
   degree program leading to initial licensure that includes
   either a major or minor in education and practice teaching. Master's program preparing college graduates for
   initial licensure; includes practice teaching.

LICENSING TEST
Pass rate on state's teacher licensing test for 2002-2003:
   94%
State average pass rate: **94%**

Mount St. Mary College

■ **330 Powell Avenue, Newburgh, NY 12550**
■ **Website:** http://www.msmc.edu
■ **Private**
■ **Degrees offered:** bachelor's, master's

ADMISSIONS
Admissions phone number: **(845) 569-3149**
Admissions email address: *sadoski@msmc.edu*
Application fee: **$35**
Fall 2005 application deadline: **rolling**
Test of English as Foreign Language (TOEFL) is required
   for international students.
Minimum TOEFL score required for paper test: **550**

Fall 2003
Acceptance rate for master's degree programs: **80%**
Total 2003 enrollment: 357
Master's degree enrollment: 357
   Teacher preparation program enrollment (master's): 357

FINANCIAL INFORMATION
Financial aid phone number: **(845) 569-3194**
Tuition, 2003-2004 academic year: Full-time: **$495/credit
   hour**; Part-time: **$495/credit hour**
Fees: **$60**
Number of other paid appointments: **10**

ACADEMIC PROGRAMS

Total full-time tenured or tenure-track faculty (fall 2003): 11, Total part-time faculty (fall 2003): 17

Areas of specialization: elementary teacher education, secondary teacher education, special education.

Professional development/partnership school(s) are used by students in all of the teaching programs.

During their internships, peer groups of students meet regularly to discuss instructional techniques in all of the teaching programs.

All of the students in their internships are mentored.

Courses that prepare teachers to pass the National Board of Professional Teaching Standards are not offered.

Teacher preparation programs: Four-year baccalaureate-degree program leading to initial licensure that includes either a major or minor in education and practice teaching.

LICENSING TEST

Pass rate on state's teacher licensing test for 2002-2003: 97%

State average pass rate: 94%

Nazareth College of Rochester

- 4245 East Avenue, Rochester, NY 14618
- **Website:** http://www.naz.edu
- **Private**
- **Degrees offered:** bachelor's, master's

ADMISSIONS

Admissions phone number: (585) 389-2818
Admissions email address: *jbaker518@naz.edu*
Application website: *http://www.naz.edu/dept/grad_studies/*
Application fee: **$40**
Fall 2005 application deadline: 3/1
Test of English as Foreign Language (TOEFL) is required for international students.
Minimum TOEFL score required for paper test: 535
Minimum TOEFL score required for computer test: 213

Fall 2003
Acceptance rate for master's degree programs: 94%
Total 2003 enrollment: 745
Master's degree enrollment: 745
  Teacher preparation program enrollment (master's): 745

FINANCIAL INFORMATION

Financial aid phone number: (585) 389-2310
Tuition, 2003-2004 academic year: Full-time: **$498/credit hour**; Part-time: **$498/credit hour**
Room and board: **$8,000**, Books and supplies: **$650**, Miscellaneous expenses: **$1,500**
Number of teaching assistant positions: 0
Number of research assistant positions: 25

ACADEMIC PROGRAMS

Total full-time tenured or tenure-track faculty (fall 2003): 135

Areas of specialization: elementary teacher education, secondary teacher education, special education.

Professional development/partnership school(s) are used by students in all of the teaching programs.

During their internships, peer groups of students meet regularly to discuss instructional techniques in all of the teaching programs.

All of the students in their internships are mentored.

Courses that prepare teachers to pass the National Board of Professional Teaching Standards are not offered.

Teacher preparation programs: Four-year baccalaureate-degree program leading to initial licensure that includes either a major or minor in education and practice teaching. Master's program preparing college graduates for initial licensure; includes practice teaching. Alternative program for college graduates leading to provisional licensure.

LICENSING TEST

Pass rate on state's teacher licensing test for 2002-2003: 97%

State average pass rate: 94%

New York Institute of Technology–Manhattan

- PO Box 8000, Old Westbury, NY 11568-8000
- **Website:** http://www.nyit.edu/
- **Private**

LICENSING TEST

Pass rate on state's teacher licensing test for 2002-2003: 97%

State average pass rate: 94%

New York Institute of Technology–Old Westbury

- P.O. Box 8000, Old Westbury, NY 11568
- **Website:** http://www.nyit.edu/
- **Private**

New York University

- 82 Washington Square E, Fourth Floor, New York, NY 10003
- **Website:** http://www.education.nyu.edu/
- **Private**
- **Degrees offered:** bachelor's, master's, Ph.D., Ed.D.
- **Overall rank in the 2005 U.S. News education schools with doctoral programs:** 13
- **Overall rank in the 2005 U.S. News education school specialty rankings:** elementary education: 21, higher education administration: 18

ADMISSIONS

Admissions phone number: **(212) 998-5030**
Admissions email address: *ed.gradadmissions@nyu.edu*
Application website: *http://www.education.nyu.edu/ graduate.admissions*
Application fee: **$50**
Fall 2005 application deadline: **1/15**
Test requirements: **GRE**
Test of English as Foreign Language (TOEFL) is required for international students.
Minimum TOEFL score required for paper test: **600**
Minimum TOEFL score required for computer test: **250**

Fall 2003
Acceptance rate for master's degree programs: **50%**
Acceptance rate for doctoral programs: **17%**
Average GRE verbal: **563**, Average GRE quantitative: **609**
Total 2003 enrollment: **4,074**
Master's degree enrollment: **3,370**
    Teacher preparation program enrollment (master's): **566**
Doctoral degree enrollment: **704**

FINANCIAL INFORMATION

Financial aid phone number: **(212) 998-4444**
Tuition, 2003-2004 academic year: Full-time: **$23,202**; Part-time: **$900/credit hour**
Fees: **$1,812**, Room and board: **$15,200**, Books and supplies: **$721**, Miscellaneous expenses: **$3,723**
Number of fellowships awarded to graduate students during the 2003-2004 academic year: **42**
Number of teaching assistant positions: **65**
Number of research assistant positions: **28**
Number of other paid appointments: **680**

ACADEMIC PROGRAMS

Total full-time tenured or tenure-track faculty (fall 2003): **168**, Total part-time faculty (fall 2003): **718**
Areas of specialization: curriculum and instruction, education administration and supervision, education policy, educational psychology, elementary teacher education, higher education administration, secondary teacher education, special education, student counseling and personnel services.
Professional development/partnership school(s) are used by students in some of the teaching programs.

During their internships, peer groups of students meet regularly to discuss instructional techniques in all of the teaching programs.
All of the students in their internships are mentored.
Courses that prepare teachers to pass the National Board of Professional Teaching Standards are not offered.
Teacher preparation programs: Four-year baccalaureate-degree program leading to initial licensure that includes either a major or minor in education and practice teaching. Master's program preparing college graduates for initial licensure; includes practice teaching.

LICENSING TEST

Pass rate on state's teacher licensing test for 2002-2003: **98%**
State average pass rate: **94%**

Niagara University

- PO Box 1930, Niagara University, NY 14109
- **Website:** http://www.niagara.edu
- **Private**
- **Degrees offered:** bachelor's, master's

ADMISSIONS

Admissions phone number: **(716) 286-8336**
Admissions email address: *epierce@niagara.edu*
Application fee: **$30**
Fall 2005 application deadline: **rolling**
Test requirements: **MAT**
Test of English as Foreign Language (TOEFL) is required for international students.
Minimum TOEFL score required for paper test: **520**
Minimum TOEFL score required for computer test: **200**

Fall 2003
Average MAT: **43**
Total 2003 enrollment: **715**
Master's degree enrollment: **715**
    Teacher preparation program enrollment (master's): **538**

FINANCIAL INFORMATION

Financial aid phone number: **(716) 286-8673**
Tuition, 2003-2004 academic year: **$455/credit hour**
Fees: **$150**, Books and supplies: **$1,500**, Miscellaneous expenses: **$500**
Number of research assistant positions: **2**

ACADEMIC PROGRAMS

Total full-time tenured or tenure-track faculty (fall 2003): **27**, Total part-time faculty (fall 2003): **53**
Areas of specialization: curriculum and instruction, education administration and supervision, education policy, educational psychology, elementary teacher education, secondary teacher education, special education, student counseling and personnel services.
Professional development/partnership school(s) are used by students in all of the teaching programs.

During their internships, peer groups of students meet regularly to discuss instructional techniques in some of the teaching programs.

All of the students in their internships are mentored.

Courses that prepare teachers to pass the National Board of Professional Teaching Standards are offered.

The education program is currently accredited by the National Council for Accreditation of Teacher Education.

LICENSING TEST

Pass rate on state's teacher licensing test for 2002-2003: 98%

State average pass rate: 94%

Nyack College

- 1 South Boulevard, Nyack, NY 10960
- **Website:** http://www.nyackcollege.edu
- Private
- **Degrees offered:** bachelor's, master's

ADMISSIONS

Admissions phone number: (845) 358-1710

Admissions email address: *eduenroll@nyack.edu*

Application fee: $30

Fall 2005 application deadline: **rolling**

Test requirements: **GRE**

Test of English as Foreign Language (TOEFL) is required for international students.

Minimum TOEFL score required for paper test: 550

Minimum TOEFL score required for computer test: 213

Fall 2003

Acceptance rate for master's degree programs: 100%

Total 2003 enrollment: 8

Master's degree enrollment: 8

Teacher preparation program enrollment (master's): 8

FINANCIAL INFORMATION

Financial aid phone number: (845) 358-1710

Tuition, 2003-2004 academic year: Full-time: **$470/credit hour**; Part-time: **$470/credit hour**

Fees: $10/credit hour, Room and board: $7,000, Books and supplies: $1,000, Miscellaneous expenses: $125

Number of fellowships awarded to graduate students during the 2003-2004 academic year: 0

Number of teaching assistant positions: 0

Number of research assistant positions: 0

Number of other paid appointments: 0

ACADEMIC PROGRAMS

Total full-time tenured or tenure-track faculty (fall 2003): 1

Total part-time faculty (fall 2003): 3

Areas of specialization: curriculum and instruction, educational psychology, elementary teacher education, secondary teacher education, special education.

Professional development/partnership school(s) are used by students in all of the teaching programs.

During their internships, peer groups of students meet regularly to discuss instructional techniques in all of the teaching programs.

All of the students in their internships are mentored.

Teacher preparation programs: Four-year baccalaureate-degree program leading to initial licensure that includes either a major or minor in education and practice teaching.

LICENSING TEST

Pass rate on state's teacher licensing test for 2002-2003: 83%

State average pass rate: 94%

Pace University

- One Pace Plaza, New York, NY 10038
- **Website:** http://www.pace.edu
- Private
- **Degrees offered:** bachelor's, master's

ADMISSIONS

Admissions phone number: (914) 422-4283

Admissions email address: *gradwp@pace.edu*

Application website: *http://www.pace.edu*

Application fee: $65

Fall 2005 application deadline: **rolling**

Test of English as Foreign Language (TOEFL) is required for international students.

Minimum TOEFL score required for paper test: 550

Minimum TOEFL score required for computer test: 213

Fall 2003

Acceptance rate for master's degree programs: 81%

Total 2003 enrollment: 1,066

Master's degree enrollment: 1,066

Teacher preparation program enrollment (master's): 1,029

FINANCIAL INFORMATION

Financial aid phone number: (212) 346-1300

Tuition, 2003-2004 academic year: Full-time: **$610/credit hour**; Part-time: **$610/credit hour**

Fees: $412, Room and board: $12,570, Books and supplies: $720, Miscellaneous expenses: $2,780

Number of fellowships awarded to graduate students during the 2003-2004 academic year: 0

Number of teaching assistant positions: 0

Number of research assistant positions: 0

Number of other paid appointments: 15

ACADEMIC PROGRAMS

Total full-time tenured or tenure-track faculty (fall 2003): 17, Total part-time faculty (fall 2003): 50

Areas of specialization: curriculum and instruction, education administration and supervision, educational psychology, elementary teacher education, secondary teacher education, special education.

Professional development/partnership school(s) are used by students in some of the teaching programs.

During their internships, peer groups of students meet regularly to discuss instructional techniques in some of the teaching programs.

All of the students in their internships are mentored.

Courses that prepare teachers to pass the National Board of Professional Teaching Standards are not offered.

Teacher preparation programs: Four-year baccalaureate-degree program leading to initial licensure that includes either a major or minor in education and practice teaching. Five-year program leading to initial licensure that results in a baccalaureate degree (with a major or minor in education) plus a master's degree and includes practice teaching. Master's program preparing college graduates for initial licensure; includes practice teaching.

LICENSING TEST
Pass rate on state's teacher licensing test for 2002-2003: 98%
State average pass rate: 94%

Pratt Institute

- 200 Willoughby Avenue, Brooklyn, NY 11205
- **Website:** http://www.pratt.edu
- **Private**
- **Degrees offered:** bachelor's, master's

ADMISSIONS
Admissions phone number: **(718) 636-3669**
Admissions email address: *admissions@pratt.edu*
Application website: *http://www.pratt.edu/admiss/apply*
Application fee: **$40**
Fall 2005 application deadline: 2/1
Test of English as Foreign Language (TOEFL) is required for international students.
Minimum TOEFL score required for paper test: **550**

Fall 2003
Acceptance rate for master's degree programs: **56%**
Total 2003 enrollment: **40**
Master's degree enrollment: **40**
 Teacher preparation program enrollment (master's): **40**

FINANCIAL INFORMATION
Financial aid phone number: **(718) 636-3599**
Tuition, 2003-2004 academic year: Full-time: **$850/credit hour**; Part-time: **$850/credit hour**
Fees: **$850**, Room and board: **$10,026**, Books and supplies: **$2,500**, Miscellaneous expenses: **$2,800**
Number of fellowships awarded to graduate students during the 2003-2004 academic year: **4**

ACADEMIC PROGRAMS
Total full-time tenured or tenure-track faculty (fall 2003): **1**
 Total part-time faculty (fall 2003): **16**

Areas of specialization: curriculum and instruction, elementary teacher education, secondary teacher education, special education.

Professional development/partnership school(s) are used by students in some of the teaching programs.

During their internships, peer groups of students meet regularly to discuss instructional techniques in all of the teaching programs.

All of the students in their internships are mentored.

Courses that prepare teachers to pass the National Board of Professional Teaching Standards are not offered.

Teacher preparation programs: Four-year baccalaureate-degree program leading to initial licensure that includes either a major or minor in education and practice teaching. Five-year program leading to initial licensure that results in a baccalaureate degree (with a major or minor in education) plus a master's degree and includes practice teaching.

LICENSING TEST
Pass rate on state's teacher licensing test for 2002-2003: 77%
State average pass rate: 94%

Roberts Wesleyan College

- 2301 Westside Drive, Rochester, NY 14624
- **Website:** http://www.roberts.edu
- **Private**
- **Degrees offered:** bachelor's, master's

ADMISSIONS
Admissions phone number: **(585) 594-5651**
Admissions email address: *2301 Westside Drive, Rochester, NY 14624*
Application website: *http://www.roberts.edu*
Application fee: **$35**
Fall 2005 application deadline: 7/1
Test of English as Foreign Language (TOEFL) is required for international students.

Fall 2003
Total 2003 enrollment: **288**
Master's degree enrollment: **288**
 Teacher preparation program enrollment (master's): **288**

FINANCIAL INFORMATION
Financial aid phone number: **(585) 594-6150**
Tuition, 2003-2004 academic year: Full-time: **$470/credit hour**; Part-time: **$470/credit hour**
Fees: **$150**
Number of fellowships awarded to graduate students during the 2003-2004 academic year: **0**
Number of teaching assistant positions: **0**
Number of research assistant positions: **0**
Number of other paid appointments: **0**

ACADEMIC PROGRAMS

Total full-time tenured or tenure-track faculty (fall 2003): 13, Total part-time faculty (fall 2003): 50

Areas of specialization: educational psychology, elementary teacher education, secondary teacher education, special education, student counseling and personnel services.

Professional development/partnership school(s) are used by students in some of the teaching programs.

During their internships, peer groups of students meet regularly to discuss instructional techniques in some of the teaching programs.

Some of the students in their internships are mentored.

Courses that prepare teachers to pass the National Board of Professional Teaching Standards are not offered.

Teacher preparation programs: Four-year baccalaureate-degree program leading to initial licensure that includes either a major or minor in education and practice teaching. Master's program preparing college graduates for initial licensure; includes practice teaching. Alternative program for college graduates leading to provisional licensure.

LICENSING TEST

Pass rate on state's teacher licensing test for 2002-2003: 96%

State average pass rate: 94%

Rochester Institute of Technology

■ 1 Lomb Memorial Drive, Rochester, NY 14623
■ **Website:** http://www.rit.edu/
■ Private

LICENSING TEST

Pass rate on state's teacher licensing test for 2002-2003: 89%

State average pass rate: 94%

Sarah Lawrence College

■ One Mead Way, Bronxville, NY 10708
■ **Website:** http://www.sarahlawrence.edu
■ Private
■ **Degrees offered:** master's

ADMISSIONS

Admissions phone number: **(914) 395-2371**
Admissions email address: *grad@slc.edu*
Application website: *http://www.sarahlawrence.edu/ graduate/data/gradContact.asp*
Application fee: **$50**
Fall 2005 application deadline: **3/31**
Test of English as Foreign Language (TOEFL) is required for international students.

Minimum TOEFL score required for paper test: 550
Minimum TOEFL score required for computer test: 300

Fall 2003
Acceptance rate for master's degree programs: 88%
Total 2003 enrollment: 22
Master's degree enrollment: 22
    Teacher preparation program enrollment (master's): 22

FINANCIAL INFORMATION

Financial aid phone number: **(914) 395-2570**
Tuition, 2003-2004 academic year: Full-time: **$17,208**; Part-time: **$8,604**
Room and board: **$10,000**, Books and supplies: **$500**, Miscellaneous expenses: **$500**
Number of fellowships awarded to graduate students during the 2003-2004 academic year: 0
Number of teaching assistant positions: 0
Number of research assistant positions: 0
Number of other paid appointments: 0

ACADEMIC PROGRAMS

Total full-time tenured or tenure-track faculty (fall 2003): 2
    Total part-time faculty (fall 2003): 5
Professional development/partnership school(s) are used by students in some of the teaching programs.
During their internships, peer groups of students meet regularly to discuss instructional techniques in all of the teaching programs.
All of the students in their internships are mentored.
Courses that prepare teachers to pass the National Board of Professional Teaching Standards are not offered.

Teacher preparation programs: Master's degree in education, including internship/practice teaching and preparation for initial licensure.

St. Bonaventure University

■ Route 417, St. Bonaventure, NY 14778
■ **Website:** http://www.sbu.edu/
■ Private

LICENSING TEST

Pass rate on state's teacher licensing test for 2002-2003: 97%

State average pass rate: 94%

St. John's University

- 8000 Utopia Parkway, Jamaica, NY 11439
- **Website:** http://www.stjohns.edu
- **Private**
- **Degrees offered:** bachelor's, master's, education specialist, Ed.D.
- **Overall rank in the 2005 U.S. News education schools with doctoral programs:** 69

ADMISSIONS

Admissions phone number: **(718) 990-2304**
Admissions email address: *ronaynek@stjohns.edu*
Application website:
https://apply.embark.com/grad/stjohns/42
Application fee: **$40**
Fall 2005 application deadline: **rolling**
Test requirements: **GRE**
Test of English as Foreign Language (TOEFL) is required for international students.
Minimum TOEFL score required for paper test: **500**
Minimum TOEFL score required for computer test: **173**

Fall 2003
Acceptance rate for master's degree programs: **84%**
Acceptance rate for education specialist degree programs: **93%**
Acceptance rate for doctoral programs: **60%**
Average GRE verbal: **524**, Average GRE quantitative: **564**
Total 2003 enrollment: **1,382**
Master's degree enrollment: **1,102**
　　Teacher preparation program enrollment (master's): **893**
Education specialist degree enrollment: **129**
Doctoral degree enrollment: **151**

FINANCIAL INFORMATION

Financial aid phone number: **(718) 990-2000**
Tuition, 2003-2004 academic year: Full-time: **$15,840**;
　　Part-time: **$660/credit hour**
Fees: **$200**, Room and board: **$6,300**, Books and supplies: **$1,000**, Miscellaneous expenses: **$1,800**
Number of fellowships awarded to graduate students during the 2003-2004 academic year: **7**
Number of teaching assistant positions: **2**
Number of other paid appointments: **12**

ACADEMIC PROGRAMS

Total full-time tenured or tenure-track faculty (fall 2003): **35**, Total part-time faculty (fall 2003): **65**
Areas of specialization: curriculum and instruction, education administration and supervision, elementary teacher education, higher education administration, secondary teacher education, special education, student counseling and personnel services.
Professional development/partnership school(s) are used by students in all of the teaching programs.
During their internships, peer groups of students meet regularly to discuss instructional techniques in all of the teaching programs.

All of the students in their internships are mentored.
Courses that prepare teachers to pass the National Board of Professional Teaching Standards are not offered.
Teacher preparation programs: Four-year baccalaureate-degree program leading to initial licensure that includes either a major or minor in education and practice teaching. Master's program preparing college graduates for initial licensure; includes practice teaching.

LICENSING TEST

Pass rate on state's teacher licensing test for 2002-2003: **88%**
State average pass rate: **94%**

St. Joseph's College– Suffolk

- 155 W. Roe Blvd., Patchogue, NY 11772
- **Website:** http://www.sjcny.edu
- **Private**
- **Degrees offered:** bachelor's, master's

ADMISSIONS

Admissions phone number: **(631) 447-3216**
Application fee: **$25**
Fall 2005 application deadline: **rolling**

FINANCIAL INFORMATION

Financial aid phone number: **(631) 447-3211**
Tuition, 2003-2004 academic year: **$445/credit hour**
Fees: **$11/credit hour**

LICENSING TEST

Pass rate on state's teacher licensing test for 2002-2003: **95%**
State average pass rate: **94%**

St. Lawrence University

- Department of Education, Atwood Hall, SLU, Canton, NY 13617
- **Website:** http://web.stlawu.edu/
- **Private**
- **Degrees offered:** master's, education specialist

ADMISSIONS

Admissions phone number: **(315) 229-5861**
Admissions email address: *nteneyck@stlawu.edu*
Application fee: **$0**
Fall 2005 application deadline: **rolling**
Test of English as Foreign Language (TOEFL) is required for international students.
Minimum TOEFL score required for paper test: **650**

Fall 2003
Total 2003 enrollment: **129**

FINANCIAL INFORMATION

Financial aid phone number: **(315) 229-5265**
Tuition, 2003-2004 academic year: **$585/credit hour**
Fees: **$50**
Number of teaching assistant positions: **4**

ACADEMIC PROGRAMS

Total full-time tenured or tenure-track faculty (fall 2003): **6**
Total part-time faculty (fall 2003): **22**
Areas of specialization: education administration and supervision, secondary teacher education, student counseling and personnel services.
Professional development/partnership school(s) are used by students in all of the teaching programs.
During their internships, peer groups of students meet regularly to discuss instructional techniques in all of the teaching programs.
All of the students in their internships are mentored.
Courses that prepare teachers to pass the National Board of Professional Teaching Standards are not offered.
Teacher preparation programs: Four-year baccalaureate-degree program leading to initial licensure that includes either a major or minor in education and practice teaching. Five-year program leading to initial licensure that results in a baccalaureate degree (with a major or minor in education) plus graduate credit and includes practice teaching. Five-year program leading to initial licensure that results in a baccalaureate degree (with a major or minor in education) plus a master's degree and includes practice teaching. Master's program preparing college graduates for initial licensure; includes practice teaching.

LICENSING TEST

Pass rate on state's teacher licensing test for 2002-2003: **97%**
State average pass rate: **94%**

St. Thomas Aquinas College

- **125 Route 340, Sparkill, NY 10976**
- **Website:** http://www.stac.edu/
- **Private**

LICENSING TEST

Pass rate on state's teacher licensing test for 2002-2003: **95%**
State average pass rate: **94%**

Sunbridge College

- **285 Hungry Hollow Rd, Spring Valley, NY 10977**
- **Website:** http://www.sunbridge.edu
- **Private**
- **Degrees offered:** master's, education specialist

ADMISSIONS

Admissions phone number: **(845) 425-0055**
Admissions email address: *mburns@sunbridge.edu*
Application website:
  http://www.sunbridge.edu/sunbridge/inforequest.htm
Application fee: **$50**
Fall 2005 application deadline: **4/15**
Test of English as Foreign Language (TOEFL) is required for international students.
Minimum TOEFL score required for paper test: **550**
Minimum TOEFL score required for computer test: **250**

Fall 2003

Total 2003 enrollment: **65**
Master's degree enrollment: **65**
  Teacher preparation program enrollment (master's): **49**

FINANCIAL INFORMATION

Financial aid phone number: **(845) 425-0055**
Tuition, 2003-2004 academic year: Full-time: **$16,100**; Part-time: **$17,800**
Room and board: **$6,500**, Books and supplies: **$300**, Miscellaneous expenses: **$100**

ACADEMIC PROGRAMS

Teacher preparation programs: Master's degree in education, including internship/practice teaching and preparation for initial licensure.

SUNY–Albany

- **1400 Washington Avenue, ED 212, Albany, NY 12222**
- **Website:** http://www.albany.edu
- **Public**
- **Degrees offered:** master's, education specialist, Ph.D.
- **Overall rank in the 2005 U.S. News education schools with doctoral programs:** 36

ADMISSIONS

Admissions phone number: **(518) 442-3980**
Admissions email address: *graduate@uamail.albany.edu*
Application website:
  http://www.albany.edu/graduate/index.html
Application fee: **$60**
Fall 2005 application deadline: **rolling**
Test requirements: **GRE**
Test of English as Foreign Language (TOEFL) is required for international students.
Minimum TOEFL score required for paper test: **550**

Minimum TOEFL score required for computer test: 213

Fall 2003
Acceptance rate for master's degree programs: 57%
Acceptance rate for education specialist degree programs: 53%
Acceptance rate for doctoral programs: 24%
Average GRE verbal: 520, Average GRE quantitative: 586, Average GRE analytical: 587
Total 2003 enrollment: 1,338
Master's degree enrollment: 904
   Teacher preparation program enrollment (master's): 558
Education specialist degree enrollment: 114
Doctoral degree enrollment: 320

FINANCIAL INFORMATION
Financial aid phone number: (518) 442-5757
Tuition, 2003-2004 academic year: Full-time in-state: $6,900; out-of-state: $10,500, Part-time in-state: $288/credit hour; out-of-state: $438/credit hour
Fees: $990, Room and board: $6,923, Books and supplies: $800, Miscellaneous expenses: $1,542
Number of fellowships awarded to graduate students during the 2003-2004 academic year: 32
Number of teaching assistant positions: 4
Number of research assistant positions: 112
Number of other paid appointments: 7

ACADEMIC PROGRAMS
Total full-time tenured or tenure-track faculty (fall 2003): 57, Total part-time faculty (fall 2003): 81
Areas of specialization: curriculum and instruction, education administration and supervision, education policy, educational psychology, higher education administration, secondary teacher education, special education, student counseling and personnel services.
Professional development/partnership school(s) are used by students in some of the teaching programs.
During their internships, peer groups of students meet regularly to discuss instructional techniques in all of the teaching programs.
All of the students in their internships are mentored.
Courses that prepare teachers to pass the National Board of Professional Teaching Standards are not offered.
Teacher preparation programs: Master's degree in education, including internship/practice teaching and preparation for initial licensure. Education minor for undergraduate students.

LICENSING TEST
Pass rate on state's teacher licensing test for 2002-2003: 100%
State average pass rate: 94%

SUNY–Brockport

- 350 New Campus Drive, Brockport, NY 14420
- **Website:** http://www.brockport.edu/
- Public

LICENSING TEST
Pass rate on state's teacher licensing test for 2002-2003: 92%
State average pass rate: 94%

SUNY College–Fredonia

- 810 Maytum Hall, Fredonia, NY 14063-1136
- **Website:** http://www.fredonia.edu
- Public
- **Degrees offered:** bachelor's, master's, education specialist

ADMISSIONS
Admissions phone number: (716) 673-3808
Admissions email address: *graduate.studies@fredonia.edu*
Application fee: $50
Fall 2005 application deadline: 4/1
Test requirements: **GRE or MAT**
Test of English as Foreign Language (TOEFL) is required for international students.
Minimum TOEFL score required for paper test: 500
Minimum TOEFL score required for computer test: 173

Fall 2003
Acceptance rate for master's degree programs: 89%
Acceptance rate for education specialist degree programs: 23%
Total 2003 enrollment: 347
Master's degree enrollment: 324
   Teacher preparation program enrollment (master's): 295
Education specialist degree enrollment: 23

FINANCIAL INFORMATION
Financial aid phone number: (716) 673-3253
Tuition, 2003-2004 academic year: Full-time in-state: $6,900; out-of-state: $10,500, Part-time in-state: $3,456; out-of-state: $5,256
Fees: $1,012, Room and board: $6,510, Books and supplies: $820, Miscellaneous expenses: $578
Number of fellowships awarded to graduate students during the 2003-2004 academic year: 5
Number of teaching assistant positions: 20
Number of research assistant positions: 15
Number of other paid appointments: 11

ACADEMIC PROGRAMS
Total full-time tenured or tenure-track faculty (fall 2003): 131, Total part-time faculty (fall 2003): 108

Areas of specialization: curriculum and instruction, education administration and supervision, elementary teacher education, secondary teacher education.

Professional development/partnership school(s) are used by students in some of the teaching programs.

During their internships, peer groups of students meet regularly to discuss instructional techniques in some of the teaching programs.

All of the students in their internships are mentored.

Courses that prepare teachers to pass the National Board of Professional Teaching Standards are not offered.

Teacher preparation programs: Four-year baccalaureate-degree program leading to initial licensure that includes either a major or minor in education and practice teaching.

LICENSING TEST

Pass rate on state's teacher licensing test for 2002-2003: 98%

State average pass rate: 94%

SUNY College–Geneseo

- ■ 1 College Circle, Geneseo, NY 14454
- ■ **Website:** http://www.geneseo.edu
- ■ Public
- ■ **Degrees offered:** bachelor's, master's

ADMISSIONS

Admissions phone number: **(585) 245-5571**

Admissions email address: *admissions@geneseo.edu*

Application website: *http://admissions.geneseo.edu*

Application fee: **$40**

Fall 2005 application deadline: 1/15

Test requirements: **GRE**

Test of English as Foreign Language (TOEFL) is required for international students.

Minimum TOEFL score required for paper test: **525**

Minimum TOEFL score required for computer test: **197**

Fall 2003

Acceptance rate for master's degree programs: 79%

Average GRE verbal: 454, Average GRE quantitative: 544

Total 2003 enrollment: 161

Master's degree enrollment: 161

Teacher preparation program enrollment (master's): 161

FINANCIAL INFORMATION

Financial aid phone number: **(585) 245-5731**

Tuition, 2003-2004 academic year: Full-time in-state: **$4,350**; out-of-state: **$10,300**, Part-time in-state: **$181/credit hour**; out-of-state: **$429/credit hour**

Fees: **$1,040**, Room and board: **$6,350**, Books and supplies: **$700**, Miscellaneous expenses: **$1,300**

Number of other paid appointments: 6

ACADEMIC PROGRAMS

Total full-time tenured or tenure-track faculty (fall 2003): 23

Total part-time faculty (fall 2003): 30

Areas of specialization: elementary teacher education, secondary teacher education, special education.

Professional development/partnership school(s) are used by students in some of the teaching programs.

During their internships, peer groups of students meet regularly to discuss instructional techniques in some of the teaching programs.

All of the students in their internships are mentored.

Courses that prepare teachers to pass the National Board of Professional Teaching Standards are not offered.

Teacher preparation programs: Four-year baccalaureate-degree program leading to initial licensure that includes either a major or minor in education and practice teaching.

LICENSING TEST

Pass rate on state's teacher licensing test for 2002-2003: 99%

State average pass rate: 94%

SUNY College–Oswego

- ■ 200 Poucher Hall, Oswego, NY 13126
- ■ **Website:** http://www.oswego.edu/~gradoff
- ■ Public
- ■ **Degrees offered:** bachelor's, master's

ADMISSIONS

Admissions phone number: (315) 312-3152

Admissions email address: *gradoff@oswego.edu*

Application fee: **$50**

Fall 2005 application deadline: 2/1

Test requirements: **GRE**

Test of English as Foreign Language (TOEFL) is required for international students.

Minimum TOEFL score required for paper test: 550

Minimum TOEFL score required for computer test: 213

Fall 2003

Acceptance rate for master's degree programs: 82%

Total 2003 enrollment: 1,284

Master's degree enrollment: 1,284

Teacher preparation program enrollment (master's): 618

FINANCIAL INFORMATION

Financial aid phone number: (315) 312-2248

Tuition, 2003-2004 academic year: Full-time in-state: **$6,900**; out-of-state: **$10,500**, Part-time in-state: **$288/credit hour**; out-of-state: **$438/credit hour**

Fees: **$616**, Room and board: **$7,540**, Books and supplies: **$800**, Miscellaneous expenses: **$1,700**

Number of fellowships awarded to graduate students during the 2003-2004 academic year: 10

Number of other paid appointments: 110

ACADEMIC PROGRAMS

Total full-time tenured or tenure-track faculty (fall 2003): 263, Total part-time faculty (fall 2003): 180

Areas of specialization: curriculum and instruction, education administration and supervision, elementary teacher education, higher education administration, secondary teacher education, special education, teacher education.

Professional development/partnership school(s) are used by students in some of the teaching programs.

During their internships, peer groups of students meet regularly to discuss instructional techniques in all of the teaching programs.

All of the students in their internships are mentored.

Courses that prepare teachers to pass the National Board of Professional Teaching Standards are not offered.

Teacher preparation programs: Four-year baccalaureate-degree program leading to initial licensure that includes either a major or minor in education and practice teaching. Master's program preparing college graduates for initial licensure; includes practice teaching.

The education program is currently accredited by the National Council for Accreditation of Teacher Education.

The education program is currently accredited by the Teacher Education Accreditation Council.

LICENSING TEST

Pass rate on state's teacher licensing test for 2002-2003: 92%

State average pass rate: 94%

SUNY–Cortland

- ■ PO Box 2000 Brockway Hall 122, Cortland, NY 13045
- ■ Website: http://www.cortland.edu/gradstudies
- ■ Public
- ■ Degrees offered: bachelor's, master's

ADMISSIONS

Admissions phone number: **(607) 753-4800**

Admissions email address: *gradstudies@cortland.edu*

Application fee: **$65**

Fall 2005 application deadline: **7/1**

Test requirements: **GRE**

Test of English as Foreign Language (TOEFL) is required for international students.

Minimum TOEFL score required for paper test: **550**

Minimum TOEFL score required for computer test: **213**

Fall 2003

Total 2003 enrollment: **1,534**

Master's degree enrollment: **1,534**

    Teacher preparation program enrollment (master's): **1,160**

FINANCIAL INFORMATION

Financial aid phone number: **(607) 753-4718**

Tuition, 2003-2004 academic year: Full-time in-state: **$288/credit hour**; out-of-state: **$438/credit hour**, Part-time in-state: **$288/credit hour**; out-of-state: **$438/credit hour**

Fees: **$37/credit hour**

Number of research assistant positions: **30**

ACADEMIC PROGRAMS

Total full-time tenured or tenure-track faculty (fall 2003): **259**

Areas of specialization: education administration and supervision, elementary teacher education, secondary teacher education, special education.

Professional development/partnership school(s) are used by students in some of the teaching programs.

During their internships, peer groups of students meet regularly to discuss instructional techniques in some of the teaching programs.

Some of the students in their internships are mentored.

Courses that prepare teachers to pass the National Board of Professional Teaching Standards are not offered.

LICENSING TEST

Pass rate on state's teacher licensing test for 2002-2003: 94%

State average pass rate: 94%

SUNY–New Paltz

- ■ 75 S. Manheim Boulevard, Suite 9, New Paltz, NY 12561-2443
- ■ Website: http://www.newpaltz.edu/graduate/index.cfm
- ■ Public
- ■ Degrees offered: bachelor's, master's

ADMISSIONS

Admissions phone number: **(845) 257-3285**

Admissions email address: *gradschool@newpaltz.edu*

Application website: *http://www.newpaltz.edu/graduate/applications.cfm*

Application fee: **$50**

Fall 2005 application deadline: **rolling**

Test requirements: **GRE or MAT**

Test of English as Foreign Language (TOEFL) is required for international students.

Minimum TOEFL score required for paper test: **550**

Minimum TOEFL score required for computer test: **213**

Fall 2003

Acceptance rate for master's degree programs: **68%**

Average GRE verbal: **457**, Average GRE quantitative: **530**, Average GRE analytical: **525**

Total 2003 enrollment: **688**

Master's degree enrollment: **688**

    Teacher preparation program enrollment (master's): **681**

FINANCIAL INFORMATION

Financial aid phone number: **(845) 257-3250**

Tuition, 2003-2004 academic year: Full-time in-state: **$6,900**; out-of-state: **$10,500**, Part-time in-state: **$213/credit hour**; out-of-state: **$351/credit hour**

Fees: **$795**, Room and board: **$6,420**, Books and supplies: **$1,100**, Miscellaneous expenses: **$1,000**

Number of fellowships awarded to graduate students during the 2003-2004 academic year: **0**

Number of teaching assistant positions: 0
Number of research assistant positions: 0
Number of other paid appointments: 17

ACADEMIC PROGRAMS

Total full-time tenured or tenure-track faculty (fall 2003): 31, Total part-time faculty (fall 2003): 82

Areas of specialization: education administration and supervision, elementary teacher education, secondary teacher education, special education, teacher education.

Professional development/partnership school(s) are used by students in some of the teaching programs.

During their internships, peer groups of students meet regularly to discuss instructional techniques in some of the teaching programs.

All of the students in their internships are mentored.

Courses that prepare teachers to pass the National Board of Professional Teaching Standards are not offered.

Teacher preparation programs: Four-year baccalaureate-degree program leading to initial licensure that includes either a major or minor in education and practice teaching. Master's program preparing college graduates for initial licensure; includes practice teaching.

The education program is currently accredited by the National Council for Accreditation of Teacher Education.

LICENSING TEST

Pass rate on state's teacher licensing test for 2002-2003: 96%

State average pass rate: 94%

SUNY–Oneonta

- Ravine Parkway, Oneonta, NY 13820
- **Website:** http://www.oneonta.edu/highbwindex.asp
- Public

LICENSING TEST

Pass rate on state's teacher licensing test for 2002-2003: 96%

State average pass rate: 94%

SUNY–Plattsburgh

- 101 Broad Street, Plattsburgh, NY 12901-2697
- **Website:** http://www.plattsburgh.edu/
- Public

LICENSING TEST

Pass rate on state's teacher licensing test for 2002-2003: 94%

State average pass rate: 94%

SUNY–Potsdam

- **44 Pierrepont Avenue, Potsdam, NY 13676**
- **Website:** http://www.potsdam.edu
- **Public**
- **Degrees offered:** bachelor's, master's

ADMISSIONS

Admissions phone number: (315) 267-2165
Admissions email address: *graduate@potsdam.edu*
Application fee: $50
Fall 2005 application deadline: **rolling**
Test of English as Foreign Language (TOEFL) is required for international students.
Minimum TOEFL score required for paper test: 550
Minimum TOEFL score required for computer test: 213

Fall 2003

Acceptance rate for master's degree programs: 86%
Total 2003 enrollment: 825
Master's degree enrollment: 825
    Teacher preparation program enrollment (master's): 743

FINANCIAL INFORMATION

Financial aid phone number: (315) 267-2162
Tuition, 2003-2004 academic year: Full-time in-state: **$6,900**; out-of-state: **$10,500**, Part-time in-state: **$288/credit hour**; out-of-state: **$438/credit hour**
Fees: **$610**, Room and board: **$6,970**, Books and supplies: **$900**, Miscellaneous expenses: **$1,800**
Number of fellowships awarded to graduate students during the 2003-2004 academic year: 2
Number of teaching assistant positions: 0
Number of research assistant positions: 0
Number of other paid appointments: 10

ACADEMIC PROGRAMS

Total full-time tenured or tenure-track faculty (fall 2003): 47, Total part-time faculty (fall 2003): 31

Areas of specialization: elementary teacher education, secondary teacher education, special education.

Professional development/partnership school(s) are used by students in some of the teaching programs.

During their internships, peer groups of students meet regularly to discuss instructional techniques in all of the teaching programs.

Some of the students in their internships are mentored.

Courses that prepare teachers to pass the National Board of Professional Teaching Standards are not offered.

Teacher preparation programs: Four-year baccalaureate-degree program leading to initial licensure that includes either a major or minor in education and practice teaching. Master's program preparing college graduates for initial licensure; includes practice teaching.

The education program is currently accredited by the National Council for Accreditation of Teacher Education.

LICENSING TEST

Pass rate on state's teacher licensing test for 2002-2003: 96%

State average pass rate: 94%

SUNY–Stony Brook

- Stony Brook, NY 11794
- Website: http://ws.cc.sunysb.edu/spd/
- Public
- Degrees offered: bachelor's, master's

ADMISSIONS

Admissions phone number: (631) 632-7055
Admissions email address: spd@stonybrook.edu
Application fee: $100
Test requirements: GRE
Fall 2005 application deadline: 4/15
Test of English as Foreign Language (TOEFL) is required for international students.
Minimum TOEFL score required for paper test: 550

Fall 2003
Total 2003 enrollment: 198
Master's degree enrollment: 198
    Teacher preparation program enrollment (master's): 198

FINANCIAL INFORMATION

Financial aid phone number: (631) 632-6840
Tuition, 2003-2004 academic year: Full-time in-state: $6,900; out-of-state: $10,500, Part-time in-state: $288/credit hour; out-of-state: $438/credit hour
Fees: $485, Room and board: $7,458, Books and supplies: $900, Miscellaneous expenses: $3,080

ACADEMIC PROGRAMS

Total full-time tenured or tenure-track faculty (fall 2003): 11
Areas of specialization: secondary teacher education.
Professional development/partnership school(s) are used by students in all of the teaching programs.
During their internships, peer groups of students meet regularly to discuss instructional techniques in all of the teaching programs.
All of the students in their internships are mentored.
Courses that prepare teachers to pass the National Board of Professional Teaching Standards are not offered.
Teacher preparation programs: Four-year baccalaureate-degree program leading to initial licensure that includes either a major or minor in education and practice teaching. Master's program preparing college graduates for initial licensure; includes practice teaching.

LICENSING TEST

Pass rate on state's teacher licensing test for 2002-2003: 96%

State average pass rate: 94%

Syracuse University

- 230 Huntington Hall, Syracuse, NY 13244-2340
- Website: http://soeweb.syr.edu
- Private
- Degrees offered: bachelor's, master's, Ph.D., Ed.D.
- Overall rank in the 2005 U.S. News education schools with doctoral programs: 44
- Overall rank in the 2005 U.S. News education school specialty rankings: special education: 12

ADMISSIONS

Admissions phone number: (315) 443-2505
Admissions email address: gradrcrt@gwmail.syr.edu
Application website: https://apply.embark.com/grad/syracuse
Application fee: $65
Fall 2005 application deadline: 2/1
Test requirements: GRE
Test of English as Foreign Language (TOEFL) is required for international students.
Minimum TOEFL score required for paper test: 600
Minimum TOEFL score required for computer test: 250

Fall 2003
Acceptance rate for master's degree programs: 68%
Acceptance rate for doctoral programs: 34%
Average GRE verbal: 499, Average GRE quantitative: 584, Average GRE analytical: 578
Total 2003 enrollment: 703
Master's degree enrollment: 469
    Teacher preparation program enrollment (master's): 239
Doctoral degree enrollment: 234

FINANCIAL INFORMATION

Financial aid phone number: (315) 443-1513
Tuition, 2003-2004 academic year: $742/credit hour$742/credit hour
Fees: $494, Room and board: $10,700, Books and supplies: $1,154, Miscellaneous expenses: $4,234
Number of fellowships awarded to graduate students during the 2003-2004 academic year: 34
Number of teaching assistant positions: 51
Number of research assistant positions: 46
Number of other paid appointments: 97

ACADEMIC PROGRAMS

Total full-time tenured or tenure-track faculty (fall 2003): 51, Total part-time faculty (fall 2003): 16
Areas of specialization: curriculum and instruction, education administration and supervision, elementary teacher education, higher education administration, secondary teacher education, special education, student counseling and personnel services.
Professional development/partnership school(s) are used by students in all of the teaching programs.
During their internships, peer groups of students meet regularly to discuss instructional techniques in all of the teaching programs.

All of the students in their internships are mentored. Courses that prepare teachers to pass the National Board of Professional Teaching Standards are not offered.

Teacher preparation programs: Four-year baccalaureate-degree program leading to initial licensure that includes either a major or minor in education and practice teaching. Master's program preparing college graduates for initial licensure; includes practice teaching.

LICENSING TEST
Pass rate on state's teacher licensing test for 2002-2003: 99%
State average pass rate: 94%

Teachers College, Columbia University

- 525 W. 120th Street, New York, NY 10027
- **Website:** http://www.tc.columbia.edu/
- Private
- **Degrees offered:** master's, Ph.D., Ed.D.
- **Overall rank in the 2005 U.S. News education schools with doctoral programs:** 4
- **Overall rank in the 2005 U.S. News education school specialty rankings:** administration/supervision: 7, counseling/personnel: 15, curriculum/instruction: 3, education policy: 6, educational psychology: 10, elementary education: 3, higher education administration: 9, secondary education: 5, special education: 14

ADMISSIONS
Admissions phone number: (212) 678-3710
Admissions email address: tcinfo@tc.columbia.edu
Application website: http://www.tc.columbia.edu/admissions/
Application fee: $60
Fall 2005 application deadline: **Columbia University**
Test requirements: **GRE or MAT**
Test of English as Foreign Language (TOEFL) is required for international students.
Minimum TOEFL score required for paper test: 600
Minimum TOEFL score required for computer test: 250

Fall 2003
Acceptance rate for master's degree programs: 57%
Acceptance rate for doctoral programs: 27%
Average GRE verbal: 541, Average GRE quantitative: 619, Average GRE analytical: 634
Total 2003 enrollment: 4,676
Master's degree enrollment: 2,932
   Teacher preparation program enrollment (master's): 1,488
Doctoral degree enrollment: 1,744

FINANCIAL INFORMATION
Financial aid phone number: (212) 678-3714

Tuition, 2003-2004 academic year: Full-time: **$825/credit hour**; Part-time: **$825/credit hour**
Fees: **$380**, Room and board: **$11,700**, Books and supplies: **$2,810**, Miscellaneous expenses: **$4,700**
Number of fellowships awarded to graduate students during the 2003-2004 academic year: 1,600
Number of teaching assistant positions: 300
Number of research assistant positions: 100

ACADEMIC PROGRAMS
Total full-time tenured or tenure-track faculty (fall 2003): 154, Total part-time faculty (fall 2003): 105
Areas of specialization: curriculum and instruction, education administration and supervision, education policy, educational psychology, elementary teacher education, higher education administration, secondary teacher education, special education, student counseling and personnel services.
Professional development/partnership school(s) are used by students in some of the teaching programs.
During their internships, peer groups of students meet regularly to discuss instructional techniques in all of the teaching programs.
All of the students in their internships are mentored.
Courses that prepare teachers to pass the National Board of Professional Teaching Standards are not offered.
Teacher preparation programs: Master's degree in education, including internship/practice teaching and preparation for initial licensure. Alternative program for college graduates leading to provisional licensure.

LICENSING TEST
Pass rate on state's teacher licensing test for 2002-2003: 99%
State average pass rate: 94%

Touro College

- 27th West Street, New York, NY 10010
- **Website:** http://www.touro.edu
- Private
- **Degrees offered:** master's

ADMISSIONS
Admissions phone number: (212) 463-0400
Admissions email address: Andreba@touro.edu
Application fee: $50
Fall 2005 application deadline: **rolling**
Test requirements: **None**

Fall 2003
Acceptance rate for master's degree programs: 100%
Total 2003 enrollment: 3,044
Master's degree enrollment: 3,044
   Teacher preparation program enrollment (master's): 2,401

FINANCIAL INFORMATION

Financial aid phone number: (718) 421-8020

Tuition, 2003-2004 academic year: Full-time: **$375/credit hour**; Part-time: **$375/credit hour**

Fees: **$100**

LICENSING TEST

Pass rate on state's teacher licensing test for 2002-2003: 89%

State average pass rate: 94%

University at Buffalo– SUNY

- **367 Baldy Hall, Buffalo, NY 14260-1000**
- **Website:** http://www.gse.buffalo.edu
- **Public**
- **Degrees offered:** master's, Ph.D., Ed.D.
- **Overall rank in the 2005 U.S. News education schools with doctoral programs:** 62

ADMISSIONS

Admissions phone number: (716) 645-2110

Admissions email address: *gse-info@buffalo.edu*

Application website: *http://www.gse.buffalo.edu*

Application fee: **$50**

Fall 2005 application deadline: **rolling**

Test requirements: **GRE or MAT**

Test of English as Foreign Language (TOEFL) is required for international students.

Minimum TOEFL score required for paper test: 550

Minimum TOEFL score required for computer test: 213

Fall 2003

Acceptance rate for master's degree programs: 68%

Acceptance rate for doctoral programs: 47%

Average GRE verbal: 514, Average GRE quantitative: 597, Average GRE analytical: 598, Average MAT: 53

Total 2003 enrollment: 1,269

Master's degree enrollment: 899

Teacher preparation program enrollment (master's): 650

Doctoral degree enrollment: 370

FINANCIAL INFORMATION

Financial aid phone number: (716) 645-2450

Tuition, 2003-2004 academic year: Full-time in-state: **$6,900**; out-of-state: **$10,500**, Part-time in-state: **$288/credit hour**; out-of-state: **$438/credit hour**

Fees: **$1,092**, Room and board: **$4,590**, Books and supplies: **$966**, Miscellaneous expenses: **$2,595**

Number of fellowships awarded to graduate students during the 2003-2004 academic year: 13

Number of teaching assistant positions: 85

Number of research assistant positions: 31

Number of other paid appointments: 16

ACADEMIC PROGRAMS

Total full-time tenured or tenure-track faculty (fall 2003): 55, Total part-time faculty (fall 2003): 78

Areas of specialization: curriculum and instruction, education administration and supervision, education policy, educational psychology, elementary teacher education, higher education administration, secondary teacher education, special education, student counseling and personnel services.

Professional development/partnership school(s) are used by students in all of the teaching programs.

During their internships, peer groups of students meet regularly to discuss instructional techniques in all of the teaching programs.

All of the students in their internships are mentored.

Courses that prepare teachers to pass the National Board of Professional Teaching Standards are not offered.

Teacher preparation programs: Master's degree in education, including internship/practice teaching and preparation for initial licensure. Education minor for undergraduate students.

LICENSING TEST

Pass rate on state's teacher licensing test for 2002-2003: 100%

State average pass rate: 94%

University of Rochester (Warner)

- **2-147 Dewey Hall, Rochester, NY 14627**
- **Website:** http://www.rochester.edu/warner/
- **Private**

ADMISSIONS

Admissions phone number: (716) 275-3950

Admissions email address: *tmug@dbl.cc.rochester.edu*

FINANCIAL INFORMATION

Financial aid phone number: (716) 275-3226

LICENSING TEST

Pass rate on state's teacher licensing test for 2002-2003: 100%

State average pass rate: 94%

Utica College of Syracuse University

- **1600 Burrstone Road, Utica, NY 13502**
- **Website:** http://www.utica.edu/gce
- **Private**
- **Degrees offered:** bachelor's, master's

ADMISSIONS

Admissions phone number: (315) 792-3001
Admissions email address: *gradstudies@utica.edu*
Application website: *http://www.utica.edu/gce*
Application fee: $50
Fall 2005 application deadline: **rolling**
Test of English as Foreign Language (TOEFL) is required for international students.
Minimum TOEFL score required for paper test: 550

Fall 2003

Acceptance rate for master's degree programs: 67%
Average GRE verbal: 450, Average GRE quantitative: 450, Average GRE analytical: 450
Total 2003 enrollment: 294
Master's degree enrollment: 294
   Teacher preparation program enrollment (master's): 148

FINANCIAL INFORMATION

Financial aid phone number: (315) 792-3179
Tuition, 2003-2004 academic year: Full-time: **$17,688**; Part-time: **$475/credit hour**
Fees: $180, Room and board: $8,070, Books and supplies: $800
Number of other paid appointments: 2

ACADEMIC PROGRAMS

Areas of specialization: elementary teacher education.
Professional development/partnership school(s) are used by students in some of the teaching programs.
During their internships, peer groups of students meet regularly to discuss instructional techniques in some of the teaching programs.
Some of the students in their internships are mentored.
Courses that prepare teachers to pass the National Board of Professional Teaching Standards are offered.

LICENSING TEST

Pass rate on state's teacher licensing test for 2002-2003: 98%
State average pass rate: 94%

Wagner College

■ 1 Campus Road, Staten Island, NY 10301
■ **Website:** http://www.wagner.edu
■ **Private**
■ **Degrees offered:** bachelor's, master's

ADMISSIONS

Admissions phone number: (718) 390-3411
Admissions email address: *Ldepasca@wagner.edu*
Application fee: $50
Fall 2005 application deadline: 8/1
Test of English as Foreign Language (TOEFL) is required for international students.
Minimum TOEFL score required for paper test: 550
Minimum TOEFL score required for computer test: 217

Fall 2003

Acceptance rate for master's degree programs: 74%
Total 2003 enrollment: 99
Master's degree enrollment: 99
   Teacher preparation program enrollment (master's): 54

FINANCIAL INFORMATION

Financial aid phone number: (718) 390-3183
Tuition, 2003-2004 academic year: Full-time: **$780/credit hour**; Part-time: **$780/credit hour**
Books and supplies: $600
Number of teaching assistant positions: 14

ACADEMIC PROGRAMS

Total full-time tenured or tenure-track faculty (fall 2003): 8
   Total part-time faculty (fall 2003): 12
Areas of specialization: elementary teacher education, secondary teacher education.
Professional development/partnership school(s) are used by students in all of the teaching programs.
During their internships, peer groups of students meet regularly to discuss instructional techniques in all of the teaching programs.
All of the students in their internships are mentored.
Courses that prepare teachers to pass the National Board of Professional Teaching Standards are not offered.
Teacher preparation programs: Four-year baccalaureate-degree program leading to initial licensure that includes either a major or minor in education and practice teaching. Master's program preparing college graduates for initial licensure; includes practice teaching.

LICENSING TEST

Pass rate on state's teacher licensing test for 2002-2003: 90%
State average pass rate: 94%

Yeshiva University (Azrieli)

■ **245 Lexington Avenue, New York, NY 10016**
■ **Website:** http://www.yu.edu/azrieli/
■ **Private**

ADMISSIONS

Admissions phone number: (212) 340-7705
Test of English as Foreign Language (TOEFL) is required for international students.
Minimum TOEFL score required for paper test: 500
Minimum TOEFL score required for computer test: 173

FINANCIAL INFORMATION

Financial aid phone number: (212) 960-5269

LICENSING TEST

Pass rate on state's teacher licensing test for 2002-2003: 100%
State average pass rate: 94%

NORTH CAROLINA

Appalachian State University

- Boone, NC 28608-2068
- **Website:** http://www.graduate.appstate.edu
- **Public**
- **Degrees offered:** bachelor's, master's, education specialist, Ed.D.

ADMISSIONS
Admissions phone number: **(828) 262-2130**
Admissions email address: *chambersbk@appstate.edu*
Application website: *http://www.graduate.appstate.edu*
Application fee: **$35**
Fall 2005 application deadline: **7/1**
Test requirements: **GRE or MAT**
Test of English as Foreign Language (TOEFL) is required for international students.
Minimum TOEFL score required for paper test: **570**
Minimum TOEFL score required for computer test: **230**

Fall 2003
Acceptance rate for master's degree programs: **71%**
Acceptance rate for education specialist degree programs: **93%**
Acceptance rate for doctoral programs: **71%**
Total 2003 enrollment: **980**
Master's degree enrollment: **898**
 Teacher preparation program enrollment (master's): **185**
Education specialist degree enrollment: **28**
Doctoral degree enrollment: **54**

FINANCIAL INFORMATION
Financial aid phone number: **(828) 262-2190**
Tuition, 2003-2004 academic year: Full-time in-state: **$1,668**; out-of-state: **$11,176**, Part-time in-state: **$93/credit hour**; out-of-state: **$621/credit hour**
Fees: **$1,361**, Room and board: **$4,500**, Books and supplies: **$1,500**, Miscellaneous expenses: **$1,500**

Number of fellowships awarded to graduate students during the 2003-2004 academic year: **6**
Number of teaching assistant positions: **4**
Number of research assistant positions: **14**
Number of other paid appointments: **36**

ACADEMIC PROGRAMS
Areas of specialization: curriculum and instruction, education administration and supervision, elementary teacher education, higher education administration, secondary teacher education, special education, student counseling and personnel services.
Professional development/partnership school(s) are used by students in some of the teaching programs.
During their internships, peer groups of students meet regularly to discuss instructional techniques in all of the teaching programs.
All of the students in their internships are mentored.
Courses that prepare teachers to pass the National Board of Professional Teaching Standards are not offered.
The education program is currently accredited by the National Council for Accreditation of Teacher Education.

LICENSING TEST
Pass rate on state's teacher licensing test for 2002-2003: **93%**
State average pass rate: **92%**

Campbell University

- PO Box 546, Buies Creek, NC 27506
- **Website:** http://www.campbell.edu/
- **Private**

LICENSING TEST
Pass rate on state's teacher licensing test for 2002-2003: **96%**
State average pass rate: **92%**

Catawba College

■ 2300 W. Innes Street, Salisbury, NC 28144
■ Website:
  http://www.catawba.edu/dept/teached/index.htm
■ Private

LICENSING TEST
Pass rate on state's teacher licensing test for 2002-2003:
  100%
State average pass rate: 92%

Duke University

■ Box 90093, Durham, NC 27708
■ Website: http://www.gradschool.duke.edu
■ Private
■ Degrees offered: master's

ADMISSIONS
Admissions phone number: (919) 684-3913
Admissions email address: *grad-admissions@duke.edu*
Application website:
  https://app.applyyourself.com/?id=dukegrad
Application fee: $75
Fall 2005 application deadline: 12/31
Test requirements: GRE
Test of English as Foreign Language (TOEFL) is required
  for international students.
Minimum TOEFL score required for paper test: 600
Minimum TOEFL score required for computer test: 213

Fall 2003
Acceptance rate for master's degree programs: 52%
Average GRE verbal: 612, Average GRE quantitative: 671
Total 2003 enrollment: 16
Master's degree enrollment: 16
  Teacher preparation program enrollment (master's): 16

FINANCIAL INFORMATION
Financial aid phone number: (919) 681-1552
Tuition, 2003-2004 academic year: Full-time: $20,040;
  Part-time: $835/credit hour
Fees: $4,954, Room and board: $7,614, Books and sup-
  plies: $1,000, Miscellaneous expenses: $3,441
Number of fellowships awarded to graduate students dur-
  ing the 2003-2004 academic year: 15
Number of teaching assistant positions: 0
Number of research assistant positions: 0
Number of other paid appointments: 0

ACADEMIC PROGRAMS
Total full-time tenured or tenure-track faculty (fall 2003): 0
  Total part-time faculty (fall 2003): 5
Areas of specialization: secondary teacher education.

Professional development/partnership school(s) are used
  by students in none of the teaching programs.
During their internships, peer groups of students meet
  regularly to discuss instructional techniques in all of the
  teaching programs.
All of the students in their internships are mentored.
Courses that prepare teachers to pass the National Board of
  Professional Teaching Standards are not offered.
Teacher preparation programs: Master's program prepar-
  ing college graduates for initial licensure; includes prac-
  tice teaching. Alternative program for college graduates
  leading to provisional licensure.
The education program is currently accredited by the
  National Council for Accreditation of Teacher Education.

LICENSING TEST
Pass rate on state's teacher licensing test for 2002-2003:
  100%
State average pass rate: 92%

East Carolina University

■ E. Fifth Street, Greenville, NC 27858
■ Website: http://www.ecu.edu/gradschool/
■ Public

LICENSING TEST
Pass rate on state's teacher licensing test for 2002-2003: 90%
State average pass rate: 92%

Elizabeth City State University

■ 1704 Weeksville Road, Elizabeth City, NC 27909
■ Website: http://tep.ecsu.edu/
■ Public

LICENSING TEST
Pass rate on state's teacher licensing test for 2002-2003:
  88%
State average pass rate: 92%

Elon University

■ 2700 Campus Box, Elon, NC 27244
■ Website: http://www.elon.edu/academics/graduate/
■ Private
■ Degrees offered: bachelor's, master's

ADMISSIONS
Admissions phone number: (336) 278-7600
Admissions email address: *gradadm@elon.edu*
Application website: *https://www.applyweb.com/aw?elon/*

Application fee: $35
Fall 2005 application deadline: **rolling**
Test requirements: **GRE or MAT**
Test of English as Foreign Language (TOEFL) is required for international students.

Fall 2003
Average GRE verbal: 417, Average GRE quantitative: 500, Average GRE analytical: 645, Average MAT: 43
Total 2003 enrollment: 20
Master's degree enrollment: 20
   Teacher preparation program enrollment (master's): 20

FINANCIAL INFORMATION
Financial aid phone number: (336) 278-7640
Tuition, 2003-2004 academic year: **$288/credit hour**
Number of fellowships awarded to graduate students during the 2003-2004 academic year: 0
Number of teaching assistant positions: 0
Number of research assistant positions: 0
Number of other paid appointments: 0

ACADEMIC PROGRAMS
Total full-time tenured or tenure-track faculty (fall 2003): 11, Total part-time faculty (fall 2003): 0
Areas of specialization: elementary teacher education, special education.
Professional development/partnership school(s) are used by students in some of the teaching programs.
During their internships, peer groups of students meet regularly to discuss instructional techniques in all of the teaching programs.
All of the students in their internships are mentored.
Courses that prepare teachers to pass the National Board of Professional Teaching Standards are not offered.
Teacher preparation programs: Four-year baccalaureate-degree program leading to initial licensure that includes either a major or minor in education and practice teaching.
The education program is currently accredited by the National Council for Accreditation of Teacher Education.

LICENSING TEST
Pass rate on state's teacher licensing test for 2002-2003: 93%
State average pass rate: 92%

Fayetteville State University

- **1200 Murchison Road, Fayetteville, NC 28301**
- **Website:** http://www.uncfsu.edu/
- **Public**

LICENSING TEST
Pass rate on state's teacher licensing test for 2002-2003: 74%
State average pass rate: 92%

Gardner-Webb University

- **Main Street, Boiling Springs, NC 28017**
- **Website:** http://www.gardner-webb.edu
- **Private**
- **Degrees offered:** master's, Ed.D.

ADMISSIONS
Admissions phone number: (800) 492-4723
Admissions email address: *gradschool@gardner-webb.edu*
Application website: *http://www.gradschool.gardner-webb.edu*
Application fee: $25
Fall 2005 application deadline: **rolling**

Fall 2003
Total 2003 enrollment: 481
Master's degree enrollment: 466
   Teacher preparation program enrollment (master's): 84
Doctoral degree enrollment: 15

FINANCIAL INFORMATION
Financial aid phone number: (704) 406-3271
Tuition, 2003-2004 academic year: Full-time: **$230/credit hour**; Part-time: **$230/credit hour**
Books and supplies: $120, Miscellaneous expenses: $30

LICENSING TEST
Pass rate on state's teacher licensing test for 2002-2003: 82%
State average pass rate: 92%

Lenoir-Rhyne College

- **PO Box 7163, Hickory, NC 28603-7163**
- **Website:** http://www.lrc.edu/grad/
- **Private**
- **Degrees offered:** bachelor's, master's

ACADEMIC PROGRAMS
Areas of specialization: educational psychology, student counseling and personnel services.

LICENSING TEST
Pass rate on state's teacher licensing test for 2002-2003: 94%
State average pass rate: 92%

Meredith College

- **3800 Hillsborough Street, Raleigh, NC 27607**
- **Website:** http://www.meredith.edu/graduate
- **Private**
- **Degrees offered:** master's

ADMISSIONS

Admissions phone number: **(919) 760-8423**
Admissions email address: *graduate@meredith.edu*
Application fee: **$50**
Fall 2005 application deadline: **7/1**
Test requirements: **GRE or MAT**
Test of English as Foreign Language (TOEFL) is required for international students.

Fall 2003

Acceptance rate for master's degree programs: **71%**
Average GRE verbal: **555**, Average GRE quantitative: **510**, Average MAT: **55**
Total 2003 enrollment: **15**
Master's degree enrollment: **15**
  Teacher preparation program enrollment (master's): **15**

FINANCIAL INFORMATION

Financial aid phone number: **(919) 760-8595**
Tuition, 2003-2004 academic year: Full-time: **$345/credit hour**; Part-time: **$345/credit hour**
Fees: **$345/credit hour**, Books and supplies: **$150**
Number of fellowships awarded to graduate students during the 2003-2004 academic year: **0**
Number of teaching assistant positions: **0**
Number of research assistant positions: **0**
Number of other paid appointments: **0**

ACADEMIC PROGRAMS

Total full-time tenured or tenure-track faculty (fall 2003): **5**
  Total part-time faculty (fall 2003): **2**
Areas of specialization: curriculum and instruction, educational psychology, elementary teacher education.
Professional development/partnership school(s) are used by students in some of the teaching programs.
During their internships, peer groups of students meet regularly to discuss instructional techniques in all of the teaching programs.
All of the students in their internships are mentored.
Courses that prepare teachers to pass the National Board of Professional Teaching Standards are not offered.
The education program is currently accredited by the National Council for Accreditation of Teacher Education.

LICENSING TEST

Pass rate on state's teacher licensing test for 2002-2003: **99%**
State average pass rate: **92%**

North Carolina A&T State University

■ **1601 E. Market Street, Greensboro, NC 27411**
■ **Website:** http://www.ncat.edu/~schofed/
■ **Public**

LICENSING TEST

Pass rate on state's teacher licensing test for 2002-2003: **100%**
State average pass rate: **92%**

North Carolina Central University

■ **1801 Fayetteville Street, Durham, NC 27707**
■ **Website:** http://www.nccu.edu/soe/welcome.htm
■ **Public**

ADMISSIONS

Admissions phone number: **(919) 530-5118**
Application fee: **$30**
Fall 2005 application deadline: **3/1**

LICENSING TEST

Pass rate on state's teacher licensing test for 2002-2003: **87%**
State average pass rate: **92%**

North Carolina State University–Raleigh

■ **College of Education, Box 7801, Raleigh, NC 27695-7801**
■ **Website:** http://ced.ncsu.edu/
■ **Public**
■ **Degrees offered:** bachelor's, master's, Ph.D., Ed.D.

ADMISSIONS

Admissions phone number: **(919) 515-2872**
Admissions email address: *graduate_admissions@ncsu.edu*
Application website:
  http://www2.acs.ncsu.edu/grad/prospect.htm
Application fee: **$55**
Test requirements: **GRE or MAT**
Test of English as Foreign Language (TOEFL) is required for international students.
Minimum TOEFL score required for paper test: **550**
Minimum TOEFL score required for computer test: **213**

Fall 2003

Acceptance rate for master's degree programs: **55%**
Acceptance rate for doctoral programs: **42%**
Average GRE verbal: **484**, Average GRE quantitative: **559**, Average GRE analytical: **600**
Total 2003 enrollment: **932**
Master's degree enrollment: **556**
  Teacher preparation program enrollment (master's): **310**
Education specialist degree enrollment: **0**
Doctoral degree enrollment: **376**

FINANCIAL INFORMATION

Financial aid phone number: **(919) 515-3325**

Tuition, 2003-2004 academic year: Full-time in-state: **$3,163**; out-of-state: **$15,161**, Part-time in-state: **$1,582**; out-of-state: **$7,580**

Fees: **$1,026**, Room and board: **$6,000**, Books and supplies: **$700**, Miscellaneous expenses: **$2,000**

Number of fellowships awarded to graduate students during the 2003-2004 academic year: **7**

Number of teaching assistant positions: **24**

Number of research assistant positions: **35**

Number of other paid appointments: **21**

ACADEMIC PROGRAMS

Total full-time tenured or tenure-track faculty (fall 2003): **71**, Total part-time faculty (fall 2003): **31**

Areas of specialization: curriculum and instruction, education administration and supervision, education policy, elementary teacher education, higher education administration, secondary teacher education, special education, student counseling and personnel services.

Professional development/partnership school(s) are used by students in all of the teaching programs.

During their internships, peer groups of students meet regularly to discuss instructional techniques in all of the teaching programs.

All of the students in their internships are mentored.

Courses that prepare teachers to pass the National Board of Professional Teaching Standards are not offered.

Teacher preparation programs: Four-year baccalaureate-degree program leading to initial licensure that includes either a major or minor in education and practice teaching. Master's program preparing college graduates for initial licensure; includes practice teaching. Alternative program for college graduates leading to provisional licensure.

The education program is currently accredited by the National Council for Accreditation of Teacher Education.

LICENSING TEST

Pass rate on state's teacher licensing test for 2002-2003: **94%**

State average pass rate: **92%**

Pfeiffer University

■ **4701 Park Road, Charlotte, NC 28209**
■ **Website:** http://www.pfeiffer.edu
■ **Private**
■ **Degrees offered:** bachelor's, master's

ADMISSIONS

Admissions phone number: **(704) 521-9116**

Admissions email address: *charcamp@pfeiffer.edu*

Application website: *http://www.pfeiffer.edu*

Application fee: **$75**

Test of English as Foreign Language (TOEFL) is required for international students.

Fall 2003

Total 2003 enrollment: **110**

Master's degree enrollment: **110**

Teacher preparation program enrollment (master's): **110**

FINANCIAL INFORMATION

Financial aid phone number: **(704) 463-2070**

Tuition, 2003-2004 academic year: Full-time: **$310/credit hour**; Part-time: **$310/credit hour**

ACADEMIC PROGRAMS

Total full-time tenured or tenure-track faculty (fall 2003): **7** Total part-time faculty (fall 2003): **0**

Areas of specialization: curriculum and instruction, educational psychology, elementary teacher education, secondary teacher education, special education.

Professional development/partnership school(s) are used by students in all of the teaching programs.

During their internships, peer groups of students meet regularly to discuss instructional techniques in all of the teaching programs.

All of the students in their internships are mentored.

Courses that prepare teachers to pass the National Board of Professional Teaching Standards are offered.

Teacher preparation programs: Four-year baccalaureate-degree program leading to initial licensure that includes either a major or minor in education and practice teaching. Master's program preparing college graduates for initial licensure; includes practice teaching. Alternative program for college graduates leading to provisional licensure.

The education program is currently accredited by the National Council for Accreditation of Teacher Education.

The education program is currently accredited by the Teacher Education Accreditation Council.

LICENSING TEST

Pass rate on state's teacher licensing test for 2002-2003: **85%**

State average pass rate: **92%**

Queens University of Charlotte

■ **1900 Selwyn Ave., Charlotte, NC 28274**
■ **Website:** http://www.queens.edu
■ **Private**
■ **Degrees offered:** bachelor's, master's

ADMISSIONS

Admissions phone number: **(704) 337-2314**

Admissions email address: *hayworth@queens.edu*

Application website: *http://www.queens.edu/default_page.asp?cont_id=508*

Application fee: **$25**

Fall 2005 application deadline: **rolling**

Test requirements: **GRE**

Test of English as Foreign Language (TOEFL) is required for international students.
Minimum TOEFL score required for paper test: 550
Minimum TOEFL score required for computer test: 213

Fall 2003
Acceptance rate for master's degree programs: 54%
Total 2003 enrollment: 132
Master's degree enrollment: 132
   Teacher preparation program enrollment (master's): 96

FINANCIAL INFORMATION
Financial aid phone number: **(704) 337-2225**
Tuition, 2003-2004 academic year: Full-time: **$225/credit hour**; Part-time: **$225/credit hour**
Number of fellowships awarded to graduate students during the 2003-2004 academic year: 10
Number of teaching assistant positions: 0
Number of research assistant positions: 0
Number of other paid appointments: 0

ACADEMIC PROGRAMS
Total full-time tenured or tenure-track faculty (fall 2003): 5
   Total part-time faculty (fall 2003): 4
Areas of specialization: elementary teacher education, secondary teacher education.
Professional development/partnership school(s) are used by students in all of the teaching programs.
During their internships, peer groups of students meet regularly to discuss instructional techniques in all of the teaching programs.
All of the students in their internships are mentored.
Courses that prepare teachers to pass the National Board of Professional Teaching Standards are not offered.
Teacher preparation programs: Four-year baccalaureate-degree program leading to initial licensure that includes either a major or minor in education and practice teaching. Master's program preparing college graduates for initial licensure; includes practice teaching.
The education program is currently accredited by the National Council for Accreditation of Teacher Education.

LICENSING TEST
Pass rate on state's teacher licensing test for 2002-2003: 93%
State average pass rate: 92%

Salem College

- **P.O. Box 10548, Winston-Salem, NC 27108**
- **Website:** http://www.salem.edu/
- **Private**

LICENSING TEST
Pass rate on state's teacher licensing test for 2002-2003: 95%
State average pass rate: 92%

University of North Carolina–Chapel Hill

- **CB#3500, 101 Peabody Hall, Chapel Hill, NC 27599-3500**
- **Website:** http://www.unc.edu/depts/ed/
- **Public**
- **Degrees offered:** bachelor's, master's, Ph.D., Ed.D.
- **Overall rank in the 2005 U.S. News education schools with doctoral programs:** 30
- **Overall rank in the 2005 U.S. News education school specialty rankings:** administration/supervision: 22, curriculum/instruction: 21, education policy: 21, educational psychology: 19

ADMISSIONS
Admissions phone number: **(919) 966-7000**
Admissions email address: *ed@unc.edu*
Application website: *http://gradschool.unc.edu*
Application fee: **$60**
Fall 2005 application deadline: 3/1
Test requirements: **GRE or MAT**
Test of English as Foreign Language (TOEFL) is required for international students.
Minimum TOEFL score required for paper test: 550
Minimum TOEFL score required for computer test: 213

Fall 2003
Acceptance rate for master's degree programs: 56%
Acceptance rate for doctoral programs: 46%
Average GRE verbal: 524, Average GRE quantitative: 608, Average MAT: 40
Total 2003 enrollment: 566
Master's degree enrollment: 345
   Teacher preparation program enrollment (master's): 197
Education specialist degree enrollment: 0
Doctoral degree enrollment: 221

FINANCIAL INFORMATION
Financial aid phone number: **(919) 966-1346**
Tuition, 2003-2004 academic year: Full-time in-state: **$3,163**; out-of-state: **$15,161**, Part-time in-state: **$2,372**; out-of-state: **$11,371**
Fees: **$1,106**, Room and board: **$10,392**, Books and supplies: **$900**, Miscellaneous expenses: **$2,626**
Number of fellowships awarded to graduate students during the 2003-2004 academic year: 13
Number of teaching assistant positions: 26
Number of research assistant positions: 61
Number of other paid appointments: 5

ACADEMIC PROGRAMS
Total full-time tenured or tenure-track faculty (fall 2003): 49, Total part-time faculty (fall 2003): 32
Areas of specialization: curriculum and instruction, education administration and supervision, education policy, educational psychology, elementary teacher education,

secondary teacher education, special education, student counseling and personnel services.

Professional development/partnership school(s) are used by students in some of the teaching programs.

During their internships, peer groups of students meet regularly to discuss instructional techniques in all of the teaching programs.

All of the students in their internships are mentored.

Courses that prepare teachers to pass the National Board of Professional Teaching Standards are not offered.

Teacher preparation programs: Four-year baccalaureate-degree program leading to initial licensure that includes either a major or minor in education and practice teaching. Master's program preparing college graduates for initial licensure; includes practice teaching.

The education program is currently accredited by the National Council for Accreditation of Teacher Education.

LICENSING TEST

Pass rate on state's teacher licensing test for 2002-2003: 100%

State average pass rate: 92%

University of North Carolina–Charlotte

■ 9201 University City Blvd, Charlotte, NC 28223
■ Website: http://www.uncc.edu/
■ Public

LICENSING TEST

Pass rate on state's teacher licensing test for 2002-2003: 93%

State average pass rate: 92%

University of North Carolina–Greensboro

■ 329 Curry Building, Greensboro, NC 27402
■ Website: http://www.uncg.edu/grs
■ Public
■ Degrees offered: bachelor's, master's, education specialist, Ph.D., Ed.D.
■ Overall rank in the 2005 U.S. News education schools with doctoral programs: 40
■ Overall rank in the 2005 U.S. News education school specialty rankings: counseling/personnel: 6

ADMISSIONS

Admissions phone number: (336) 334-5596
Admissions email address: *inquiries@uncg.edu*
Application website: *http://www.uncg.edu/grs*
Application fee: $35
Fall 2005 application deadline: 7/1

Test requirements: **GRE**

Test of English as Foreign Language (TOEFL) is required for international students.

Minimum TOEFL score required for paper test: 550

Minimum TOEFL score required for computer test: 213

Fall 2003

Acceptance rate for master's degree programs: 67%

Acceptance rate for education specialist degree programs: 100%

Acceptance rate for doctoral programs: 40%

Average GRE verbal: 495, Average GRE quantitative: 558, Average GRE analytical: 531

Total 2003 enrollment: 907

Master's degree enrollment: 682

Education specialist degree enrollment: 2

Doctoral degree enrollment: 223

FINANCIAL INFORMATION

Financial aid phone number: (336) 334-5702

Tuition, 2003-2004 academic year: Full-time in-state: $1,887; out-of-state: $12,862, Part-time in-state: $944; out-of-state: $6,432

Fees: $1,321, Room and board: $4,820, Books and supplies: $1,136, Miscellaneous expenses: $2,007

Number of fellowships awarded to graduate students during the 2003-2004 academic year: 12

Number of teaching assistant positions: 28

Number of research assistant positions: 8

Number of other paid appointments: 92

ACADEMIC PROGRAMS

Total full-time tenured or tenure-track faculty (fall 2003): 53, Total part-time faculty (fall 2003): 23

Areas of specialization: curriculum and instruction, education administration and supervision, elementary teacher education, higher education administration, secondary teacher education, special education, student counseling and personnel services.

Professional development/partnership school(s) are used by students in some of the teaching programs.

During their internships, peer groups of students meet regularly to discuss instructional techniques in some of the teaching programs.

All of the students in their internships are mentored.

Courses that prepare teachers to pass the National Board of Professional Teaching Standards are offered.

Teacher preparation programs: Four-year baccalaureate-degree program leading to initial licensure that includes either a major or minor in education and practice teaching. Master's program preparing college graduates for initial licensure; includes practice teaching. Alternative program for college graduates leading to provisional licensure.

The education program is currently accredited by the National Council for Accreditation of Teacher Education.

LICENSING TEST

Pass rate on state's teacher licensing test for 2002-2003: 97%

State average pass rate: 92%

University of North Carolina—Pembroke

- **One University Drive, Pembroke, NC 228372**
- **Website:** http://www.uncp.edu
- **Public**
- **Degrees offered:** bachelor's, master's

ADMISSIONS

Admissions phone number: **(910) 521-6260**
Admissions email address: *lela.clark@uncp.edu*
Application website: *http://www.uncp.edu/grad*
Application fee: **$40**
Fall 2005 application deadline: **5/1**
Test of English as Foreign Language (TOEFL) is required for international students.
Minimum TOEFL score required for paper test: **550**
Minimum TOEFL score required for computer test: **213**

Fall 2003
Average MAT: **50**
Total 2003 enrollment: **367**
Master's degree enrollment: **367**
 Teacher preparation program enrollment (master's): **140**

FINANCIAL INFORMATION

Financial aid phone number: **(910) 521-6000**
Tuition, 2003-2004 academic year: Full-time in-state: **$2,880**; out-of-state: **$11,045**, Part-time in-state: **$79/credit hour**; out-of-state: **$547/credit hour**
Fees: **$413**, Room and board: **$4,464**, Books and supplies: **$800**
Number of fellowships awarded to graduate students during the 2003-2004 academic year: **15**
Number of teaching assistant positions: **5**

ACADEMIC PROGRAMS

Total full-time tenured or tenure-track faculty (fall 2003): **141**
Areas of specialization: curriculum and instruction, education administration and supervision, elementary teacher education, secondary teacher education, student counseling and personnel services.
Professional development/partnership school(s) are used by students in all of the teaching programs.
During their internships, peer groups of students meet regularly to discuss instructional techniques in all of the teaching programs.
All of the students in their internships are mentored.
Courses that prepare teachers to pass the National Board of Professional Teaching Standards are offered.
Teacher preparation programs: Four-year baccalaureate-degree program leading to initial licensure that includes either a major or minor in education and practice teaching. Master's program preparing college graduates for initial licensure; includes practice teaching.

The education program is currently accredited by the National Council for Accreditation of Teacher Education.

LICENSING TEST

Pass rate on state's teacher licensing test for 2002-2003: **87%**
State average pass rate: **92%**

University of North Carolina—Wilmington

- **601 S. College Road, Wilmington, NC 28403**
- **Website:** http://www.uncw.edu/grad
- **Public**
- **Degrees offered:** bachelor's, master's

ADMISSIONS

Admissions phone number: **(910) 962-3135**
Admissions email address: *roer@uncw.edu*
Application website: *http://www.uncw.edu/grad_info/index.htm*
Application fee: **$45**
Fall 2005 application deadline: **5/1**
Test requirements: **GRE or MAT**
Test of English as Foreign Language (TOEFL) is required for international students.
Minimum TOEFL score required for paper test: **550**
Minimum TOEFL score required for computer test: **213**

Fall 2003
Average GRE verbal: **480**, Average GRE quantitative: **340**, Average MAT: **51**

FINANCIAL INFORMATION

Financial aid phone number: **(910) 962-1112**
Tuition, 2003-2004 academic year: Full-time in-state: **$1,779**; out-of-state: **$11,481**, Part-time in-state: **$890**; out-of-state: **$5,741**
Fees: **$1,659**, Room and board: **$2,004**, Books and supplies: **$300**, Miscellaneous expenses: **$200**
Number of fellowships awarded to graduate students during the 2003-2004 academic year: **5**
Number of teaching assistant positions: **21**

ACADEMIC PROGRAMS

Total full-time tenured or tenure-track faculty (fall 2003): **45**
Areas of specialization: curriculum and instruction, education administration and supervision, elementary teacher education, secondary teacher education, special education.
Professional development/partnership school(s) are used by students in all of the teaching programs.
During their internships, peer groups of students meet regularly to discuss instructional techniques in all of the teaching programs.
All of the students in their internships are mentored.

Courses that prepare teachers to pass the National Board of Professional Teaching Standards are not offered.

Teacher preparation programs: Four-year baccalaureate-degree program leading to initial licensure that includes either a major or minor in education and practice teaching. Master's program preparing college graduates for initial licensure; includes practice teaching. Alternative program for college graduates leading to provisional licensure.

The education program is currently accredited by the National Council for Accreditation of Teacher Education.

LICENSING TEST

Pass rate on state's teacher licensing test for 2002-2003: 98%

State average pass rate: 92%

Wake Forest University

■ Box 7266, Reynolda Station, Winston-Salem, NC 27109
■ **Website:** http://www.bgsm.edu/graduate/
■ **Private**
■ **Degrees offered:** bachelor's, master's

ADMISSIONS

Admissions phone number: **(336) 758-5301**
Admissions email address: *gradschl@wfu.edu*
Application website: *http://www.bgsm.edu/graduate/application.html*
Application fee: **$25**
Fall 2005 application deadline: **1/15**
Test requirements: **GRE**
Test of English as Foreign Language (TOEFL) is required for international students.
Minimum TOEFL score required for paper test: **550**
Minimum TOEFL score required for computer test: **213**

Fall 2003

Acceptance rate for master's degree programs: **41%**
Average GRE verbal: **581**, Average GRE quantitative: **662**, Average GRE analytical: **642**
Total 2003 enrollment: **52**
Master's degree enrollment: **52**
 Teacher preparation program enrollment (master's): **52**

FINANCIAL INFORMATION

Financial aid phone number: **(336) 758-5154**
Tuition, 2003-2004 academic year: Full-time: **$23,310**; Part-time: **$830/credit hour**
Fees: **$60**, Books and supplies: **$500**, Miscellaneous expenses: **$100**
Number of fellowships awarded to graduate students during the 2003-2004 academic year: **26**
Number of teaching assistant positions: **2**
Number of other paid appointments: **3**

ACADEMIC PROGRAMS

Total full-time tenured or tenure-track faculty (fall 2003): **7**
 Total part-time faculty (fall 2003): **5**
Areas of specialization: secondary teacher education.
Professional development/partnership school(s) are used by students in all of the teaching programs.
During their internships, peer groups of students meet regularly to discuss instructional techniques in all of the teaching programs.
Courses that prepare teachers to pass the National Board of Professional Teaching Standards are not offered.
Teacher preparation programs: Four-year baccalaureate-degree program leading to initial licensure that includes either a major or minor in education and practice teaching. Master's program preparing college graduates for initial licensure; includes practice teaching.
The education program is currently accredited by the National Council for Accreditation of Teacher Education.

LICENSING TEST

Pass rate on state's teacher licensing test for 2002-2003: 100%

State average pass rate: 92%

Western Carolina University

■ Cullowhee, NC 28723
■ **Website:** http://www.wcu.edu/
■ **Public**

LICENSING TEST

Pass rate on state's teacher licensing test for 2002-2003: 92%

State average pass rate: 92%

Winston-Salem State University

■ 601 Martin Luther King Jr. Drive, Winston-Salem, NC 27110
■ **Website:** http://www.wssu.edu/
■ **Public**
■ **Degrees offered:** bachelor's, master's

ADMISSIONS

Admissions phone number: **(336) 750-2250**
Admissions email address: *jones@wssu.edu*
Application website: *http://www.wssu.edu*
Application fee: **$40**
Fall 2005 application deadline: **7/15**
Test requirements: **GRE or MAT**
Test of English as Foreign Language (TOEFL) is required for international students.

Minimum TOEFL score required for paper test: 550
Minimum TOEFL score required for computer test: 300

Fall 2003
Acceptance rate for master's degree programs: 52%
Total 2003 enrollment: 39
Master's degree enrollment: 39
  Teacher preparation program enrollment (master's): 39

FINANCIAL INFORMATION
Financial aid phone number: (336) 750-3280

ACADEMIC PROGRAMS
Total full-time tenured or tenure-track faculty (fall 2003): 4
  Total part-time faculty (fall 2003): 3
Areas of specialization: elementary teacher education.
Professional development/partnership school(s) are used
  by students in all of the teaching programs.

During their internships, peer groups of students meet
  regularly to discuss instructional techniques in all of the
  teaching programs.
All of the students in their internships are mentored.
Courses that prepare teachers to pass the National Board of
  Professional Teaching Standards are not offered.
Teacher preparation programs: Four-year baccalaureate-
  degree program leading to initial licensure that includes
  either a major or minor in education and practice teaching. Alternative program for college graduates leading to
  provisional licensure.
The education program is currently accredited by the
  National Council for Accreditation of Teacher Education.

LICENSING TEST
Pass rate on state's teacher licensing test for 2002-2003:
  67%
State average pass rate: 92%

NORTH DAKOTA

Minot State University

- 500 University Avenue, W, Minot, ND 58707
- **Website:** http://www.minotstateu.edu
- Public
- **Degrees offered:** bachelor's, master's, education specialist

ADMISSIONS
Admissions phone number: **(701) 858-3350**
Admissions email address: *www.misu.nodak.edu/enroll/*
Application website:
  http://www.rdb.und.nodak.edu/www_ea/plsql/ea_home
Application fee: **$35**
Fall 2005 application deadline: **9/1**
Test of English as Foreign Language (TOEFL) is required for international students.
Minimum TOEFL score required for paper test: **525**
Minimum TOEFL score required for computer test: **195**

Fall 2003
Total 2003 enrollment: **55**
Master's degree enrollment: **40**
  Teacher preparation program enrollment (master's): **40**
Education specialist degree enrollment: **15**

FINANCIAL INFORMATION
Financial aid phone number: **(701) 858-3375**
Tuition, 2003-2004 academic year: Full-time in-state: **$2,730**; out-of-state: **$7,289**
Fees: **$498**, Room and board: **$3,454**, Books and supplies: **$750**, Miscellaneous expenses: **$2,116**

ACADEMIC PROGRAMS
Courses that prepare teachers to pass the National Board of Professional Teaching Standards are not offered.
Teacher preparation programs: Four-year baccalaureate-degree program leading to initial licensure that includes either a major or minor in education and practice teaching. Alternative program for college graduates leading to provisional licensure.

The education program is currently accredited by the National Council for Accreditation of Teacher Education.

North Dakota State University

- P.O. Box 5057, Fargo, ND 58105
- **Website:** http://www.ndsu.edu/gradschool/
- Public
- **Degrees offered:** bachelor's, master's, education specialist, Ph.D., Ed.D.

ADMISSIONS
Admissions phone number: **(702) 231-7033**
Admissions email address:
  ndsu.grad.school@ndsu.nodak.edu
Application website:
  http://www.ndsu.edu/ndsu/academic/bulletin/graduate/gradbulletin
Application fee: **$35**
Fall 2005 application deadline: **rolling**
Test of English as Foreign Language (TOEFL) is required for international students.
Minimum TOEFL score required for paper test: **525**
Minimum TOEFL score required for computer test: **193**

Fall 2003
Acceptance rate for master's degree programs: **87%**
Acceptance rate for education specialist degree programs: **100%**
Acceptance rate for doctoral programs: **82%**
Total 2003 enrollment: **323**
Master's degree enrollment: **235**
  Teacher preparation program enrollment (master's): **41**
Education specialist degree enrollment: **50**
Doctoral degree enrollment: **38**

FINANCIAL INFORMATION
Financial aid phone number: **(701) 231-7533**

Tuition, 2003-2004 academic year: Full-time in-state: **$3,604**; out-of-state: **$9,648**, Part-time in-state: **$175/credit hour**; out-of-state: **$427/credit hour**

Fees: **$602**, Room and board: **$4,471**, Books and supplies: **$800**, Miscellaneous expenses: **$2,500**

Number of research assistant positions: **9**

ACADEMIC PROGRAMS

Total full-time tenured or tenure-track faculty (fall 2003): **12**, Total part-time faculty (fall 2003): **9**

Areas of specialization: curriculum and instruction, education administration and supervision, education policy, educational psychology, secondary teacher education, student counseling and personnel services, teacher education.

Professional development/partnership school(s) are used by students in some of the teaching programs.

During their internships, peer groups of students meet regularly to discuss instructional techniques in all of the teaching programs.

None of the students in their internships are mentored.

Courses that prepare teachers to pass the National Board of Professional Teaching Standards are not offered.

Teacher preparation programs: Four-year baccalaureate-degree program leading to initial licensure that includes either a major or minor in education and practice teaching.

The education program is currently accredited by the National Council for Accreditation of Teacher Education.

University of Mary

- **7500 University Drive, Bismarck, ND 58504**
- **Website:** http://www.umary.edu
- **Private**
- **Degrees offered:** master's, education specialist

ADMISSIONS

Admissions phone number: **(701) 355-8187**
Application website: *http://www.umary.edu/~edudept/*
Application fee: **$40**
Fall 2005 application deadline: **rolling**

FINANCIAL INFORMATION

Financial aid phone number: **(701) 355-8079**
Tuition, 2003-2004 academic year: Full-time: **$325/credit hour**; Part-time: **$325/credit hour**
Room and board: **$180**, Books and supplies: **$340**, Miscellaneous expenses: **$12**

University of North Dakota

- **Box 7189, Grand Forks, ND 58202-7189**
- **Website:** http://www.und.edu/dept/grad
- **Public**

- **Degrees offered:** bachelor's, master's, education specialist, Ph.D., Ed.D.

ADMISSIONS

Admissions phone number: **(701) 777-2945**
Admissions email address: *gradschool@und.edu*
Application website:
http://www.und.edu/dept/grad/gradapp.htm
Application fee: **$35**
Fall 2005 application deadline: **3/15**
Test requirements: **GRE or MAT**
Test of English as Foreign Language (TOEFL) is required for international students.
Minimum TOEFL score required for paper test: **550**
Minimum TOEFL score required for computer test: **213**

Fall 2003

Acceptance rate for master's degree programs: **93%**
Acceptance rate for education specialist degree programs: **100%**
Acceptance rate for doctoral programs: **56%**
Average GRE verbal: **437**, Average GRE quantitative: **528**, Average GRE analytical: **608**
Total 2003 enrollment: **461**
Master's degree enrollment: **263**
Education specialist degree enrollment: **10**
Doctoral degree enrollment: **188**

FINANCIAL INFORMATION

Financial aid phone number: **(701) 777-3121**
Tuition, 2003-2004 academic year: Full-time in-state: **$4,418**; out-of-state: **$10,604**, Part-time in-state: **$205/credit hour**; out-of-state: **$463/credit hour**
Fees: **$715**, Room and board: **$8,100**, Books and supplies: **$800**, Miscellaneous expenses: **$4,442**
Number of fellowships awarded to graduate students during the 2003-2004 academic year: **0**
Number of teaching assistant positions: **29**
Number of research assistant positions: **12**
Number of other paid appointments: **42**

ACADEMIC PROGRAMS

Total full-time tenured or tenure-track faculty (fall 2003): **29**, Total part-time faculty (fall 2003): **18**

Areas of specialization: education administration and supervision, elementary teacher education, higher education administration, special education.

Professional development/partnership school(s) are used by students in some of the teaching programs.

During their internships, peer groups of students meet regularly to discuss instructional techniques in some of the teaching programs.

All of the students in their internships are mentored.

Courses that prepare teachers to pass the National Board of Professional Teaching Standards are not offered.

Teacher preparation programs: Four-year baccalaureate-degree program leading to initial licensure that includes either a major or minor in education and practice teaching.

The education program is currently accredited by the National Council for Accreditation of Teacher Education.

OHIO

Antioch University (McGregor)

- 795 Livermore Street, Yellow Springs, OH 45387
- **Website:** http://www.mcgregor.edu/
- Private

LICENSING TEST

Pass rate on state's teacher licensing test for 2002-2003: 100%

State average pass rate: 91%

Ashland University

- 401 College Avenue, Ashland, OH 44805
- **Website:** http://www.ashland.edu
- Private
- **Degrees offered:** bachelor's, master's, Ed.D.

ADMISSIONS

Admissions phone number: **(419) 289-5386**
Admissions email address: *fslater@ashland.edu*
Application fee: **$25**
Fall 2005 application deadline: **rolling**
Test of English as Foreign Language (TOEFL) is required for international students.

Fall 2003
Total 2003 enrollment: 3,838
Master's degree enrollment: 3,780
Doctoral degree enrollment: 58

FINANCIAL INFORMATION

Financial aid phone number: **(419) 289-5002**
Tuition, 2003-2004 academic year: Full-time: **$347/credit hour**; Part-time: **$347/credit hour**
Number of fellowships awarded to graduate students during the 2003-2004 academic year: o

Number of teaching assistant positions: 4
Number of research assistant positions: o
Number of other paid appointments: o

ACADEMIC PROGRAMS

Total full-time tenured or tenure-track faculty (fall 2003): 51, Total part-time faculty (fall 2003): 7
Areas of specialization: curriculum and instruction, education administration and supervision, special education.
Professional development/partnership school(s) are used by students in some of the teaching programs.
During their internships, peer groups of students meet regularly to discuss instructional techniques in all of the teaching programs.
Some of the students in their internships are mentored.
Courses that prepare teachers to pass the National Board of Professional Teaching Standards are offered.
Teacher preparation programs: Four-year baccalaureate-degree program leading to initial licensure that includes either a major or minor in education and practice teaching. Five-year program leading to initial licensure that results in a baccalaureate degree (with a major or minor in education) plus graduate credit and includes practice teaching.
The education program is currently accredited by the National Council for Accreditation of Teacher Education.

LICENSING TEST

Pass rate on state's teacher licensing test for 2002-2003: 91%

State average pass rate: 91%

Baldwin-Wallace College

- Department of Graduate Education, Wheeler Hall, Berea, OH 44017
- **Website:** http://www.bw.edu/admission/
- Private
- **Degrees offered:** bachelor's, master's

ADMISSIONS

Admissions phone number: **(440) 826-2222**
Admissions email address: *admission@bw.edu*
Application fee: **$15**
Fall 2005 application deadline: **rolling**
Test requirements: **MAT**
Test of English as Foreign Language (TOEFL) is required for international students.
Minimum TOEFL score required for paper test: **500**

Fall 2003

Acceptance rate for master's degree programs: **89%**
Average MAT: **44**
Total 2003 enrollment: **453**
Master's degree enrollment: **453**
    Teacher preparation program enrollment (master's): **81**

FINANCIAL INFORMATION

Financial aid phone number: **(440) 826-2108**
Tuition, 2003-2004 academic year: Full-time: **$6,580**; Part-time: **$6,580**

ACADEMIC PROGRAMS

Total full-time tenured or tenure-track faculty (fall 2003): **17**, Total part-time faculty (fall 2003): **22**
Areas of specialization: curriculum and instruction, education administration and supervision, educational psychology, elementary teacher education, secondary teacher education, special education, student counseling and personnel services.
Professional development/partnership school(s) are used by students in all of the teaching programs.
All of the students in their internships are mentored.
Courses that prepare teachers to pass the National Board of Professional Teaching Standards are not offered.
Teacher preparation programs: Four-year baccalaureate-degree program leading to initial licensure that includes either a major or minor in education and practice teaching. Master's program preparing college graduates for initial licensure; includes practice teaching.
The education program is currently accredited by the National Council for Accreditation of Teacher Education.

LICENSING TEST

Pass rate on state's teacher licensing test for 2002-2003: **96%**
State average pass rate: **91%**

Bluffton College

- **280 W. College Avenue, Suite 1, Bluffton, OH 45817**
- **Website:** http://www.bluffton.edu/
- **Private**

LICENSING TEST

Pass rate on state's teacher licensing test for 2002-2003: **91%**
State average pass rate: **91%**

Bowling Green State University

- **444 Education Building, Bowling Green, OH 43403**
- **Website:** http://www.bgsu.edu/colleges/gradcol/
- **Public**
- **Overall rank in the 2005 U.S. News education school specialty rankings:** counseling/personnel: 15

ADMISSIONS

Admissions phone number: **(419) 372-2791**
Admissions email address: *prospct@bgnet.bgsu.edu*
Application website:
    http://www.bgsu.edu/colleges/gradcol/adms/admsindex.html
Test requirements: **GRE**
Test of English as Foreign Language (TOEFL) is required for international students.
Minimum TOEFL score required for paper test: **550**

FINANCIAL INFORMATION

Financial aid phone number: **(419) 372-2651**

ACADEMIC PROGRAMS

The education program is currently accredited by the National Council for Accreditation of Teacher Education.

LICENSING TEST

Pass rate on state's teacher licensing test for 2002-2003: **87%**
State average pass rate: **91%**

Capital University

- **2199 E. Main Street, Columbus, OH 43209**
- **Website:** http://www.capital.edu/
- **Private**

LICENSING TEST

Pass rate on state's teacher licensing test for 2002-2003: **89%**
State average pass rate: **91%**

Cedarville College

- **251 N. Main St., Cedarville, OH 45314**
- **Website:** http://www.cedarville.edu/dept/graduate/
- **Private**
- **Degrees offered:** bachelor's, master's

ADMISSIONS

Admissions phone number: **(888) 233-2784**
Admissions email address: *admissions@cedarville.edu*
Application website: *http://www.cedarville.edu/dept/graduate/admission.htm*

Application fee: **$20**

Fall 2005 application deadline: **rolling**

Test of English as Foreign Language (TOEFL) is required for international students.

Minimum TOEFL score required for paper test: **550**

Minimum TOEFL score required for computer test: **213**

FINANCIAL INFORMATION

Financial aid phone number: **(800) 444-2433**

Tuition, 2003-2004 academic year: Full-time: **$275/credit hour**; Part-time: **$275/credit hour**

LICENSING TEST

Pass rate on state's teacher licensing test for 2002-2003: **91%**

State average pass rate: **91%**

Central State University

■ **PO Box 1004, Wilberforce, OH 45384**
■ **Website:** http://www.centralstate.edu/
■ **Public**

LICENSING TEST

Pass rate on state's teacher licensing test for 2002-2003: **43%**

State average pass rate: **91%**

Cleveland State University

■ **2121 Euclid Avenue, RT 1416, Cleveland, OH 44115**
■ **Website:** http://www.csuohio.edu/coe/
■ **Public**

LICENSING TEST

Pass rate on state's teacher licensing test for 2002-2003: **91%**

State average pass rate: **91%**

College of Mount St. Joseph

■ **5701 Delhi Rd., Cincinnati, OH 45233**
■ **Website:** http://www.msj.edu
■ **Private**
■ **Degrees offered:** bachelor's, master's, education specialist

ADMISSIONS

Admissions phone number: **(513) 244-4814**

Admissions email address: *peggy_minnich@mail.msj.edu*

Application website: *http://www.msj.edu/academics/masters.html*

Application fee: **$25**

Fall 2005 application deadline: **rolling**

Test requirements: **GRE or MAT**

Fall 2003

Total 2003 enrollment: **163**

Master's degree enrollment: **163**

FINANCIAL INFORMATION

Financial aid phone number: **(513) 244-4418**

Tuition, 2003-2004 academic year: Full-time: **$400/credit hour**; Part-time: **$400/credit hour**

Fees: **$140**, Room and board: **$5,745**, Books and supplies: **$600**, Miscellaneous expenses: **$600**

ACADEMIC PROGRAMS

Total full-time tenured or tenure-track faculty (fall 2003): **14**, Total part-time faculty (fall 2003): **100**

Areas of specialization: curriculum and instruction, education administration and supervision, elementary teacher education, higher education administration, secondary teacher education, special education, student counseling and personnel services.

Courses that prepare teachers to pass the National Board of Professional Teaching Standards are offered.

Teacher preparation programs: Four-year baccalaureate-degree program leading to initial licensure that includes either a major or minor in education and practice teaching. Master's program preparing college graduates for initial licensure; includes practice teaching. Alternative program for college graduates leading to provisional licensure.

LICENSING TEST

Pass rate on state's teacher licensing test for 2002-2003: **91%**

State average pass rate: **91%**

Defiance College

■ **701 N. Clinton Street, Defiance, OH 43512**
■ **Website:** http://www.defiance.edu/
■ **Private**

LICENSING TEST

Pass rate on state's teacher licensing test for 2002-2003: **85%**

State average pass rate: **91%**

Franciscan University of Steubenville

- 1235 University Boulevard, Steubenville, OH 43952-1763
- **Website:** http://www.franciscan.edu
- **Private**
- **Degrees offered:** bachelor's, master's

ADMISSIONS
Admissions phone number: **(740) 283-6226**
Admissions email address: *admissions@franciscan.edu*
Application fee: **$20**
Fall 2005 application deadline: **rolling**
Test of English as Foreign Language (TOEFL) is required for international students.
Minimum TOEFL score required for paper test: **550**
Minimum TOEFL score required for computer test: **213**

Fall 2003
Acceptance rate for master's degree programs: **95%**
Total 2003 enrollment: **173**
Master's degree enrollment: **173**
    Teacher preparation program enrollment (master's): **123**

FINANCIAL INFORMATION
Financial aid phone number: **(740) 283-6226**
Tuition, 2003-2004 academic year: **$220/credit hour**
Fees: **$10/credit hour**, Books and supplies: **$300**
Number of fellowships awarded to graduate students during the 2003-2004 academic year: **0**
Number of teaching assistant positions: **0**
Number of research assistant positions: **0**
Number of other paid appointments: **0**

ACADEMIC PROGRAMS
Total full-time tenured or tenure-track faculty (fall 2003): **4**
    Total part-time faculty (fall 2003): **6**
Areas of specialization: curriculum and instruction, education administration and supervision, educational psychology, elementary teacher education, secondary teacher education, special education.
Professional development/partnership school(s) are used by students in all of the teaching programs.
During their internships, peer groups of students meet regularly to discuss instructional techniques in some of the teaching programs.
All of the students in their internships are mentored.
Courses that prepare teachers to pass the National Board of Professional Teaching Standards are not offered.

LICENSING TEST
Pass rate on state's teacher licensing test for 2002-2003: **92%**
State average pass rate: **91%**

Heidelberg College

- 310 E. Market St., Tiffin, OH 44883
- **Website:** http://www.heidelberg.edu
- **Private**
- **Degrees offered:** bachelor's, master's

ADMISSIONS
Admissions phone number: **(419) 448-2330**
Admissions email address: *jtroha@heidelberg.edu*
Application fee: **$25**
Fall 2005 application deadline: **8/15**
Test of English as Foreign Language (TOEFL) is required for international students.
Minimum TOEFL score required for paper test: **550**

Fall 2003
Total 2003 enrollment: **203**
Master's degree enrollment: **203**
    Teacher preparation program enrollment (master's): **88**

FINANCIAL INFORMATION
Financial aid phone number: **(419) 448-2293**
Tuition, 2003-2004 academic year: Full-time: **$315/credit hour**; Part-time: **$315/credit hour**
Books and supplies: **$150**, Miscellaneous expenses: **$200**

ACADEMIC PROGRAMS
Total full-time tenured or tenure-track faculty (fall 2003): **4**
    Total part-time faculty (fall 2003): **8**
Areas of specialization: curriculum and instruction, educational psychology, elementary teacher education, secondary teacher education, student counseling and personnel services.
Professional development/partnership school(s) are used by students in some of the teaching programs.
During their internships, peer groups of students meet regularly to discuss instructional techniques in all of the teaching programs.
All of the students in their internships are mentored.
Courses that prepare teachers to pass the National Board of Professional Teaching Standards are not offered.
The education program is currently accredited by the Teacher Education Accreditation Council.

LICENSING TEST
Pass rate on state's teacher licensing test for 2002-2003: **77%**
State average pass rate: **91%**

John Carroll University

- 20700 North Park Blvd., University Hts., OH 44118
- Website: http://www.jcu.edu
- Private
- Degrees offered: bachelor's, master's

ADMISSIONS

Admissions phone number: (216) 397-4218
Admissions email address: *epeck@jcu.edu*
Application website: *http://explore.jcu.edu*
Application fee: $25
Fall 2005 application deadline: 2/1
Test requirements: GRE or MAT

Fall 2003

Acceptance rate for master's degree programs: 50%
Total 2003 enrollment: 164
Master's degree enrollment: 164
   Teacher preparation program enrollment master's: 44
Education specialist degree enrollment: 0
Doctoral degree enrollment: 0

FINANCIAL INFORMATION

Financial aid phone number: (216) 397-4248
Tuition, 2003-2004 academic year: Full-time: $645/credit hour; Part-time: $645/credit hour
Fees: $200, Books and supplies: $1,000
Number of fellowships awarded to graduate students during the 2003-2004 academic year: 0
Number of teaching assistant positions: 0
Number of research assistant positions: 7
Number of other paid appointments: 0

ACADEMIC PROGRAMS

Total full-time tenured or tenure-track faculty (fall 2003): 29, Total part-time faculty (fall 2003): 47
Areas of specialization: curriculum and instruction, education administration and supervision, educational psychology, elementary teacher education, secondary teacher education, student counseling and personnel services.
Professional development/partnership school(s) are used by students in some of the teaching programs.
During their internships, peer groups of students meet regularly to discuss instructional techniques in all of the teaching programs.
All of the students in their internships are mentored.
Teacher preparation programs: Four-year baccalaureate-degree program leading to initial licensure that includes either a major or minor in education and practice teaching. Master's program preparing college graduates for initial licensure; includes practice teaching.
The education program is currently accredited by the National Council for Accreditation of Teacher Education.

LICENSING TEST

Pass rate on state's teacher licensing test for 2002-2003: 96%
State average pass rate: 91%

Kent State University

- PO Box 5190, Kent, OH 44242-0001
- Website: http://www.educ.kent.edu
- Public
- Degrees offered: bachelor's, master's, education specialist, Ph.D.

ADMISSIONS

Admissions phone number: (330) 672-2576
Admissions email address: *oas@educ.kent.edu*
Application website: *http://oas.educ.kent.edu*
Application fee: $30
Fall 2005 application deadline: rolling
Test requirements: GRE
Test of English as Foreign Language (TOEFL) is required for international students.
Minimum TOEFL score required for paper test: 550
Minimum TOEFL score required for computer test: 197

Fall 2003

Acceptance rate for master's degree programs: 75%
Acceptance rate for education specialist degree programs: 57%
Acceptance rate for doctoral programs: 49%
Average GRE verbal: 488, Average GRE quantitative: 524, Average GRE analytical: 568
Total 2003 enrollment: 1,339
Master's degree enrollment: 922
   Teacher preparation program enrollment (master's): 449
Education specialist degree enrollment: 71
Doctoral degree enrollment: 346

FINANCIAL INFORMATION

Financial aid phone number: (330) 672-2972
Tuition, 2003-2004 academic year: Full-time in-state: $334/credit hour; out-of-state: $627/credit hour, Part-time in-state: $334/credit hour; out-of-state: $627/credit hour
Room and board: $7,460, Books and supplies: $1,000, Miscellaneous expenses: $500
Number of fellowships awarded to graduate students during the 2003-2004 academic year: 16
Number of teaching assistant positions: 26
Number of research assistant positions: 88

ACADEMIC PROGRAMS

Total full-time tenured or tenure-track faculty (fall 2003): 93
   Total part-time faculty (fall 2003): 68
Areas of specialization: curriculum and instruction, education administration and supervision, educational psychology, elementary teacher education, higher education administration, secondary teacher education, special

education, student counseling and personnel services, teacher education.

Professional development/partnership school(s) are used by students in all of the teaching programs.

During their internships, peer groups of students meet regularly to discuss instructional techniques in all of the teaching programs.

All of the students in their internships are mentored.

Courses that prepare teachers to pass the National Board of Professional Teaching Standards are offered.

Teacher preparation programs: Four-year baccalaureate-degree program leading to initial licensure that includes either a major or minor in education and practice teaching. Five-year program leading to initial licensure that results in a baccalaureate degree (with a major or minor in education) plus a master's degree and includes practice teaching. Master's program preparing college graduates for initial licensure; includes practice teaching.

The education program is currently accredited by the National Council for Accreditation of Teacher Education.

The education program is currently accredited by the Teacher Education Accreditation Council.

LICENSING TEST

Pass rate on state's teacher licensing test for 2002-2003: 91%

State average pass rate: 91%

Lake Erie College

- 391 W. Washington Street, Painesville, OH 44077
- Website: http://www.lec.edu/
- Private

LICENSING TEST

Pass rate on state's teacher licensing test for 2002-2003: 100%

State average pass rate: 91%

Malone College

- 515 25th Street, NW, Canton, OH 44709
- Website: http://www.malone.edu
- Private
- Degrees offered: bachelor's, master's

ADMISSIONS

Admissions phone number: (330) 471-8447

Admissions email address: *gradschool@malone.edu*

Application fee: $25

Fall 2005 application deadline: 8/29

Test of English as Foreign Language (TOEFL) is required for international students.

Minimum TOEFL score required for paper test: 550

Minimum TOEFL score required for computer test: 213

Fall 2003

Acceptance rate for master's degree programs: 100%

Total 2003 enrollment: 98

Master's degree enrollment: 98

Teacher preparation program enrollment (master's): 62

FINANCIAL INFORMATION

Financial aid phone number: (330) 471-8159

Tuition, 2003-2004 academic year: Full-time: $360/credit hour; Part-time: $360/credit hour

Room and board: $2,201, Books and supplies: $450, Miscellaneous expenses: $1,296

Number of fellowships awarded to graduate students during the 2003-2004 academic year: 0

Number of teaching assistant positions: 0

Number of research assistant positions: 0

Number of other paid appointments: 5

ACADEMIC PROGRAMS

Total full-time tenured or tenure-track faculty (fall 2003): 6

Total part-time faculty (fall 2003): 17

Areas of specialization: curriculum and instruction, education administration and supervision, special education, student counseling and personnel services.

Professional development/partnership school(s) are used by students in some of the teaching programs.

During their internships, peer groups of students meet regularly to discuss instructional techniques in all of the teaching programs.

All of the students in their internships are mentored.

Courses that prepare teachers to pass the National Board of Professional Teaching Standards are not offered.

Teacher preparation programs: Four-year baccalaureate-degree program leading to initial licensure that includes either a major or minor in education and practice teaching.

LICENSING TEST

Pass rate on state's teacher licensing test for 2002-2003: 98%

State average pass rate: 91%

Marietta College

- 301 Erwin Hall, Marietta, OH 45750
- Website: http://www.marietta.edu
- Private
- Degrees offered: bachelor's, master's

ADMISSIONS

Admissions phone number: (740) 376-4768

Admissions email address: *bauerm@marietta.edu*

Application website: *http://www.marietta.edu*

Application fee: $25

Fall 2005 application deadline: **rolling**

Test of English as Foreign Language (TOEFL) is required for international students.

Fall 2003
Total 2003 enrollment: 54
Master's degree enrollment: 54
Teacher preparation program enrollment (master's): 54

FINANCIAL INFORMATION
Financial aid phone number: **(740) 376-4643**
Tuition, 2003-2004 academic year: Full-time: **$331/credit hour**; Part-time: **$331/credit hour**

ACADEMIC PROGRAMS
Teacher preparation programs: Four-year baccalaureate-degree program leading to initial licensure that includes either a major or minor in education and practice teaching. The education program is currently accredited by the National Council for Accreditation of Teacher Education.

LICENSING TEST
Pass rate on state's teacher licensing test for 2002-2003: 100%
State average pass rate: 91%

Miami University–Oxford

- 200 McGuffey Hall, Oxford, OH 45056
- **Website:** http://www.muohio.edu/graduateschool/
- **Public**
- **Degrees offered:** bachelor's, master's, education specialist, Ph.D., Ed.D.

ADMISSIONS
Admissions phone number: **(513) 529-4125**
Admissions email address: *gradschool@muohio.edu*
Application fee: **$35**
Test requirements: **GRE or MAT**
Test of English as Foreign Language (TOEFL) is required for international students.
Minimum TOEFL score required for paper test: 550
Minimum TOEFL score required for computer test: 213

Fall 2003
Acceptance rate for education specialist degree programs: 19%
Acceptance rate for doctoral programs: **74%**
Average GRE verbal: **483**, Average GRE quantitative: **600**, Average GRE analytical: **629**
Total 2003 enrollment: 462
Master's degree enrollment: 381
Teacher preparation program enrollment (master's): 125
Education specialist degree enrollment: 33
Doctoral degree enrollment: 48

FINANCIAL INFORMATION
Financial aid phone number: **(513) 529-8734**

Tuition, 2003-2004 academic year: Full-time in-state: **$8,544**; out-of-state: **$18,294**, Part-time in-state: **$356/credit hour**; out-of-state: **$762/credit hour**
Room and board: **$6,680**, Books and supplies: **$1,080**, Miscellaneous expenses: **$3,375**
Number of fellowships awarded to graduate students during the 2003-2004 academic year: 0
Number of teaching assistant positions: 13
Number of research assistant positions: 64
Number of other paid appointments: 2

ACADEMIC PROGRAMS
Total full-time tenured or tenure-track faculty (fall 2003): 85, Total part-time faculty (fall 2003): 28
Areas of specialization: curriculum and instruction, education administration and supervision, educational psychology, elementary teacher education, higher education administration, secondary teacher education, special education, student counseling and personnel services.
Professional development/partnership school(s) are used by students in some of the teaching programs.
During their internships, peer groups of students meet regularly to discuss instructional techniques in all of the teaching programs.
All of the students in their internships are mentored.
Courses that prepare teachers to pass the National Board of Professional Teaching Standards are not offered.
Teacher preparation programs: Four-year baccalaureate-degree program leading to initial licensure that includes either a major or minor in education and practice teaching. Master's program preparing college graduates for initial licensure; includes practice teaching.
The education program is currently accredited by the National Council for Accreditation of Teacher Education.

LICENSING TEST
Pass rate on state's teacher licensing test for 2002-2003: 90%
State average pass rate: 91%

Mount Vernon Nazarene University

- 800 Martinsburg Rd., Mount Vernon, OH 43050
- **Website:** http://www.mvnu.edu/excell
- **Private**
- **Degrees offered:** bachelor's, master's

ADMISSIONS
Admissions phone number: **(740) 392-6868**
Admissions email address: *cheryl.furniss@mvnu.edu*
Application fee: **$0**
Fall 2005 application deadline: 8/15
Test of English as Foreign Language (TOEFL) is required for international students.
Minimum TOEFL score required for paper test: 500

Fall 2003
Acceptance rate for master's degree programs: 85%
Total 2003 enrollment: 146
Master's degree enrollment: 146
  Teacher preparation program enrollment (master's): 146

FINANCIAL INFORMATION
Financial aid phone number: **(740) 392-6868**
Tuition, 2003-2004 academic year: Full-time: **$301/credit hour**; Part-time: **$301/credit hour**
Books and supplies: **$400**
Number of fellowships awarded to graduate students during the 2003-2004 academic year: 0
Number of teaching assistant positions: 0
Number of research assistant positions: 0
Number of other paid appointments: 0

ACADEMIC PROGRAMS
Total full-time tenured or tenure-track faculty (fall 2003): 1
  Total part-time faculty (fall 2003): 15
Areas of specialization: curriculum and instruction, elementary teacher education, secondary teacher education.
Professional development/partnership school(s) are used by students in some of the teaching programs.
During their internships, peer groups of students meet regularly to discuss instructional techniques in all of the teaching programs.
All of the students in their internships are mentored.
Courses that prepare teachers to pass the National Board of Professional Teaching Standards are offered.
Teacher preparation programs: Four-year baccalaureate-degree program leading to initial licensure that includes either a major or minor in education and practice teaching. Master's program preparing college graduates for initial licensure; includes practice teaching.

LICENSING TEST
Pass rate on state's teacher licensing test for 2002-2003: 95%
State average pass rate: 91%

Muskingum College

■ **163 Stormont Street, New Concord, OH 43762**
■ **Website:** http://fates.cns.muskingum.edu/external/
■ **Private**

LICENSING TEST
Pass rate on state's teacher licensing test for 2002-2003: 81%
State average pass rate: 91%

Notre Dame College of Ohio

■ **4545 College Road, Cleveland, OH 44121**
■ **Website:** http://www.notredamecollege.edu/
■ **Private**

LICENSING TEST
Pass rate on state's teacher licensing test for 2002-2003: 95%
State average pass rate: 91%

Ohio Northern University

■ **525 S. Main Street, Ada, OH 45810**
■ **Website:** http://www.onu.edu
■ **Private**
■ **Degrees offered:** bachelor's, master's

ADMISSIONS
Admissions phone number: **(419) 772-2260**
Admissions email address: *admissions-ug@onu.edu*
Application website: *http://www.met.onu.edu/documentation.html*
Application fee: **$30**
Fall 2005 application deadline: **4/1**
Test of English as Foreign Language (TOEFL) is required for international students.
Minimum TOEFL score required for paper test: 550
Minimum TOEFL score required for computer test: 213

Fall 2003
Acceptance rate for master's degree programs: 100%
Total 2003 enrollment: 9
Master's degree enrollment: 9
  Teacher preparation program enrollment (master's): 9

FINANCIAL INFORMATION
Financial aid phone number: **(419) 772-2272**
Tuition, 2003-2004 academic year: **$200/credit hour**
Fees: **$60**, Books and supplies: **$400**, Miscellaneous expenses: **$1,000**
Number of fellowships awarded to graduate students during the 2003-2004 academic year: 0
Number of teaching assistant positions: 0
Number of research assistant positions: 0
Number of other paid appointments: 0

ACADEMIC PROGRAMS
Total full-time tenured or tenure-track faculty (fall 2003): 7
  Total part-time faculty (fall 2003): 2
Areas of specialization: curriculum and instruction.

Professional development/partnership school(s) are used by students in all of the teaching programs.

During their internships, peer groups of students meet regularly to discuss instructional techniques in some of the teaching programs.

All of the students in their internships are mentored.

Courses that prepare teachers to pass the National Board of Professional Teaching Standards are not offered.

Teacher preparation programs: Four-year baccalaureate-degree program leading to initial licensure that includes either a major or minor in education and practice teaching.

The education program is currently accredited by the National Council for Accreditation of Teacher Education.

LICENSING TEST

Pass rate on state's teacher licensing test for 2002-2003: **96%**
State average pass rate: **91%**

Ohio State University– Columbus

■ **1945 N. High Street, Columbus, OH 43210-1172**
■ **Website:** http://www.coe.ohio-state.edu
■ **Public**
■ **Degrees offered:** bachelor's, master's, Ph.D.
■ **Overall rank in the 2005 U.S. News education schools with doctoral programs:** 17
■ **Overall rank in the 2005 U.S. News education school specialty rankings:** administration/supervision: 3, counseling/personnel: 2, curriculum/instruction: 4, education policy: 18, elementary education: 5, higher education administration: 11, secondary education: 5, special education: 13, vocational/technical: 1

ADMISSIONS

Admissions phone number: **(614) 292-9444**
Admissions email address: *domestic.grad@osu.edu*
Application website: *http://www-afa.adm.ohio-state.edu/grad/index.html*
Application fee: **$40**
Fall 2005 application deadline: **1/1**
Test requirements: **GRE**
Test of English as Foreign Language (TOEFL) is required for international students.
Minimum TOEFL score required for paper test: **550**
Minimum TOEFL score required for computer test: **213**

Fall 2003
Acceptance rate for master's degree programs: **54%**
Acceptance rate for doctoral programs: **37%**
Average GRE verbal: **468**, Average GRE quantitative: **576**, Average GRE analytical: **574**
Total 2003 enrollment: **1,231**
Master's degree enrollment: **849**
Teacher preparation program enrollment (master's): **384**
Doctoral degree enrollment: **382**

FINANCIAL INFORMATION

Financial aid phone number: **(614) 292-0300**
Tuition, 2003-2004 academic year: Full-time in-state: **$7,278**; out-of-state: **$18,489**, Part-time in-state: **$312/credit hour**; out-of-state: **$686/credit hour**
Fees: **$141**, Room and board: **$9,393**, Books and supplies: **$525**, Miscellaneous expenses: **$1,900**
Number of fellowships awarded to graduate students during the 2003-2004 academic year: **42**
Number of teaching assistant positions: **140**
Number of research assistant positions: **65**
Number of other paid appointments: **90**

ACADEMIC PROGRAMS

Total full-time tenured or tenure-track faculty (fall 2003): **134**, Total part-time faculty (fall 2003): **2**
Areas of specialization: curriculum and instruction, education administration and supervision, education policy, educational psychology, elementary teacher education, higher education administration, secondary teacher education, special education, student counseling and personnel services, teacher education.

Professional development/partnership school(s) are used by students in all of the teaching programs.

During their internships, peer groups of students meet regularly to discuss instructional techniques in all of the teaching programs.

All of the students in their internships are mentored.

Courses that prepare teachers to pass the National Board of Professional Teaching Standards are offered.

Teacher preparation programs: Four-year baccalaureate-degree program leading to initial licensure that includes either a major or minor in education and practice teaching. Master's program preparing college graduates for initial licensure; includes practice teaching.

The education program is currently accredited by the National Council for Accreditation of Teacher Education.

LICENSING TEST

Pass rate on state's teacher licensing test for 2002-2003: **95%**
State average pass rate: **91%**

Ohio University

■ **133 McCracken Hall, Athens, OH 45701**
■ **Website:** http://www.ohiou.edu/graduate
■ **Public**
■ **Degrees offered:** bachelor's, master's, Ph.D., Ed.D.

ADMISSIONS

Admissions phone number: **(740) 593-2800**
Admissions email address: *gradstu@www.ohiou.edu*
Application website: *http://www.ohio.edu/graduate/apps.htm*
Application fee: **$30**
Fall 2005 application deadline: **2/1**
Test requirements: **GRE or MAT**

Test of English as Foreign Language (TOEFL) is required for international students.
Minimum TOEFL score required for paper test: 550
Minimum TOEFL score required for computer test: 213

Fall 2003
Acceptance rate for master's degree programs: 91%
Acceptance rate for doctoral programs: 83%
Average GRE verbal: 496, Average GRE quantitative: 571, Average MAT: 47
Total 2003 enrollment: 483
Master's degree enrollment: 348
  Teacher preparation program enrollment (master's): 133
Education specialist degree enrollment: 1
Doctoral degree enrollment: 134

FINANCIAL INFORMATION
Financial aid phone number: (740) 593-4141
Tuition, 2003-2004 academic year: Full-time in-state: $2,651; out-of-state: $5,095, Part-time in-state: $328/credit hour; out-of-state: $632/credit hour
Fees: $1,944, Room and board: $7,320, Books and supplies: $1,000, Miscellaneous expenses: $500
Number of fellowships awarded to graduate students during the 2003-2004 academic year: 8
Number of teaching assistant positions: 14
Number of research assistant positions: 21
Number of other paid appointments: 36

ACADEMIC PROGRAMS
Total full-time tenured or tenure-track faculty (fall 2003): 43, Total part-time faculty (fall 2003): 11
Areas of specialization: curriculum and instruction, education administration and supervision, elementary teacher education, higher education administration, secondary teacher education, special education, student counseling and personnel services.
Professional development/partnership school(s) are used by students in all of the teaching programs.
During their internships, peer groups of students meet regularly to discuss instructional techniques in all of the teaching programs.
All of the students in their internships are mentored.
Courses that prepare teachers to pass the National Board of Professional Teaching Standards are offered.
Teacher preparation programs: Four-year baccalaureate-degree program leading to initial licensure that includes either a major or minor in education and practice teaching. Master's program preparing college graduates for initial licensure; includes practice teaching.
The education program is currently accredited by the National Council for Accreditation of Teacher Education.

LICENSING TEST
Pass rate on state's teacher licensing test for 2002-2003: 90%
State average pass rate: 91%

Otterbein College

■ One Otterbein College, Westerville, OH 43081
■ **Website:** http://www.otterbein.edu/admission/graduate
■ **Private**
■ **Degrees offered:** bachelor's, master's

ADMISSIONS
Admissions phone number: (614) 823-3210
Application fee: $0
Fall 2005 application deadline: **rolling**
Test requirements: **GRE**
Test of English as Foreign Language (TOEFL) is required for international students.
Minimum TOEFL score required for paper test: 550
Minimum TOEFL score required for computer test: 213

Fall 2003
Total 2003 enrollment: 88
Master's degree enrollment: 88
  Teacher preparation program enrollment (master's): 88

FINANCIAL INFORMATION
Financial aid phone number: (614) 823-1502
Tuition, 2003-2004 academic year: Full-time: $20,133; Part-time: $254/credit hour
Number of fellowships awarded to graduate students during the 2003-2004 academic year: 0
Number of teaching assistant positions: 0
Number of research assistant positions: 0
Number of other paid appointments: 0

ACADEMIC PROGRAMS
Total full-time tenured or tenure-track faculty (fall 2003): 13
Areas of specialization: curriculum and instruction.
Professional development/partnership school(s) are used by students in none of the teaching programs.
During their internships, peer groups of students meet regularly to discuss instructional techniques in all of the teaching programs.
Courses that prepare teachers to pass the National Board of Professional Teaching Standards are offered.
Teacher preparation programs: Four-year baccalaureate-degree program leading to initial licensure that includes either a major or minor in education and practice teaching. Master's program preparing college graduates for initial licensure; includes practice teaching.
The education program is currently accredited by the National Council for Accreditation of Teacher Education.

LICENSING TEST
Pass rate on state's teacher licensing test for 2002-2003: 95%
State average pass rate: 91%

Union Institute and University

- 440 E. McMillan Street, Cincinnati, OH 45206
- **Website:** http://www.tui.edu/
- **Private**

University of Akron

- **College of Education Graduate Studies, Akron, OH 44325-4703**
- **Website:** http://www.uakron.edu/gradsch
- **Public**
- **Degrees offered:** bachelor's, master's, education specialist, Ph.D., Ed.D.

ADMISSIONS

Admissions phone number: **(330) 972-7663**
Admissions email address: *gradschool@uakron.edu*
Application website:
   http://www.uakron.edu/gradsch/index.html
Application fee: **$40**
Test requirements: **GRE or MAT**
Test of English as Foreign Language (TOEFL) is required
   for international students.
Minimum TOEFL score required for paper test: **550**
Minimum TOEFL score required for computer test: **213**

Fall 2003
Acceptance rate for master's degree programs: **92%**
Acceptance rate for doctoral programs: **59%**
Average GRE verbal: **487**, Average GRE quantitative: **528**,
   Average GRE analytical: **462**, Average MAT: **59**
Total 2003 enrollment: **1,130**
Master's degree enrollment: **935**
   Teacher preparation program enrollment (master's): **573**
Doctoral degree enrollment: **195**

FINANCIAL INFORMATION

Financial aid phone number: **(330) 972-7032**
Tuition, 2003-2004 academic year: Full-time in-state:
   $277/credit hour; out-of-state: **$476/credit hour**, Part-
   time in-state: **$277/credit hour**; out-of-state: **$476/credit
   hour**
Fees: **$20/credit hour**, Room and board: **$6,268**, Books
   and supplies: **$800**, Miscellaneous expenses: **$2,504**
Number of teaching assistant positions: **16**
Number of research assistant positions: **68**
Number of other paid appointments: **4**

ACADEMIC PROGRAMS

Total full-time tenured or tenure-track faculty (fall 2003):
   63, Total part-time faculty (fall 2003): **112**

Areas of specialization: curriculum and instruction, education administration and supervision, educational psychology, elementary teacher education, higher education
administration, secondary teacher education, special
education, student counseling and personnel services,
teacher education.
Professional development/partnership school(s) are used
by students in some of the teaching programs.
During their internships, peer groups of students meet
regularly to discuss instructional techniques in all of the
teaching programs.
All of the students in their internships are mentored.
Courses that prepare teachers to pass the National Board of
Professional Teaching Standards are offered.
Teacher preparation programs: Four-year baccalaureate-
degree program leading to initial licensure that includes
either a major or minor in education and practice teaching. Master's program preparing college graduates for
initial licensure; includes practice teaching. Alternative
program for college graduates leading to provisional
licensure.
The education program is currently accredited by the
National Council for Accreditation of Teacher Education.

LICENSING TEST

Pass rate on state's teacher licensing test for 2002-2003: **90%**
State average pass rate: **91%**

University of Cincinnati

- **PO Box 210002, Cincinnati, OH 45221-0002**
- **Website:** http://www.education.uc.edu
- **Public**
- **Degrees offered:** bachelor's, master's, education specialist, Ph.D., Ed.D.

ADMISSIONS

Admissions phone number: **(513) 556-3857**
Admissions email address: *donald.wagner@uc.edu*
Application website:
   http://www.grad.uc.edu/content/gradapp.cfm
Application fee: **$40**
Fall 2005 application deadline: **rolling**
Test requirements: **GRE**
Test of English as Foreign Language (TOEFL) is required
   for international students.
Minimum TOEFL score required for paper test: **550**
Minimum TOEFL score required for computer test: **190**

Fall 2003
Acceptance rate for master's degree programs: **51%**
Acceptance rate for doctoral programs: **25%**
Average GRE verbal: **461**, Average GRE quantitative: **521**,
   Average GRE analytical: **557**
Total 2003 enrollment: **1,121**
Master's degree enrollment: **860**
   Teacher preparation program enrollment (master's): **256**
Doctoral degree enrollment: **261**

FINANCIAL INFORMATION

Financial aid phone number: **(513) 556-6982**

Tuition, 2003-2004 academic year: Full-time in-state: **$7,698**; out-of-state: **$5,291**, Part-time in-state: **$300/credit hour**; out-of-state: **$553/credit hour**

Fees: **$1,287**, Room and board: **$12,000**, Books and supplies: **$1,200**, Miscellaneous expenses: **$1,100**

Number of fellowships awarded to graduate students during the 2003-2004 academic year: **2**

Number of teaching assistant positions: **46**

Number of research assistant positions: **38**

Number of other paid appointments: **47**

ACADEMIC PROGRAMS

Total full-time tenured or tenure-track faculty (fall 2003): **101**, Total part-time faculty (fall 2003): **81**

Areas of specialization: curriculum and instruction, education administration and supervision, education policy, educational psychology, elementary teacher education, secondary teacher education, special education, student counseling and personnel services.

Professional development/partnership school(s) are used by students in some of the teaching programs.

During their internships, peer groups of students meet regularly to discuss instructional techniques in all of the teaching programs.

All of the students in their internships are mentored.

Courses that prepare teachers to pass the National Board of Professional Teaching Standards are not offered.

Teacher preparation programs: Five-year program leading to initial licensure that results in a baccalaureate degree (with a major or minor in education) plus graduate credit and includes practice teaching. Master's program preparing college graduates for initial licensure; includes practice teaching.

The education program is currently accredited by the National Council for Accreditation of Teacher Education.

LICENSING TEST

Pass rate on state's teacher licensing test for 2002-2003: **100%**

State average pass rate: **91%**

University of Dayton

■ **300 College Park, Dayton, OH 45469-0510**
■ **Website:** http://www.udayton.edu/~gradsch/main.htm
■ **Private**
■ **Degrees offered:** bachelor's, master's, education specialist, Ph.D.

ADMISSIONS

Admissions phone number: **(937) 229-2398**

Admissions email address:
Nancy.Wilson@notes.udayton.edu

Application website: *http://gradadmission.udayton.edu/application/default.asp*

Application fee: **$0**

Fall 2005 application deadline: **rolling**

Test requirements: **GRE or MAT**

Test of English as Foreign Language (TOEFL) is required for international students.

Minimum TOEFL score required for paper test: **550**

Minimum TOEFL score required for computer test: **213**

Fall 2003

Acceptance rate for master's degree programs: **65%**

Acceptance rate for education specialist degree programs: **83%**

Acceptance rate for doctoral programs: **36%**

Average GRE verbal: **364**, Average GRE analytical: **456**, Average MAT: **45**

Total 2003 enrollment: **1,060**

Master's degree enrollment: **1,004**
   Teacher preparation program enrollment (master's): **298**

Education specialist degree enrollment: **20**

Doctoral degree enrollment: **36**

FINANCIAL INFORMATION

Financial aid phone number: **(937) 229-4311**

Tuition, 2003-2004 academic year: Full-time: **$320/credit hour**; Part-time: **$320/credit hour**

Number of fellowships awarded to graduate students during the 2003-2004 academic year: **0**

Number of teaching assistant positions: **19**

Number of research assistant positions: **0**

Number of other paid appointments: **0**

ACADEMIC PROGRAMS

Total full-time tenured or tenure-track faculty (fall 2003): **56**, Total part-time faculty (fall 2003): **79**

Areas of specialization: curriculum and instruction, education administration and supervision, education policy, educational psychology, elementary teacher education, higher education administration, secondary teacher education, special education, student counseling and personnel services.

Professional development/partnership school(s) are used by students in all of the teaching programs.

During their internships, peer groups of students meet regularly to discuss instructional techniques in some of the teaching programs.

All of the students in their internships are mentored.

Courses that prepare teachers to pass the National Board of Professional Teaching Standards are offered.

Teacher preparation programs: Four-year baccalaureate-degree program leading to initial licensure that includes either a major or minor in education and practice teaching. Master's program preparing college graduates for initial licensure; includes practice teaching.

The education program is currently accredited by the National Council for Accreditation of Teacher Education.

LICENSING TEST

Pass rate on state's teacher licensing test for 2002-2003: **98%**

State average pass rate: **91%**

University of Findlay

- 1000 N, Main St., Findlay, OH 45840
- **Website:** http://www.findlay.edu
- **Private**
- **Degrees offered:** bachelor's, master's

ADMISSIONS
Admissions phone number: **(419) 434-5516**
Application website: *http://gcampus.findlay.edu*
Application fee: **$25**
Fall 2005 application deadline: **rolling**
Test of English as Foreign Language (TOEFL) is required for international students.
Minimum TOEFL score required for paper test: **550**

Fall 2003
Acceptance rate for master's degree programs: **100%**
Total 2003 enrollment: **272**
Master's degree enrollment: **272**
    Teacher preparation program enrollment (master's): **230**

FINANCIAL INFORMATION
Financial aid phone number: **(419) 434-4791**

ACADEMIC PROGRAMS
Total full-time tenured or tenure-track faculty (fall 2003): **10**, Total part-time faculty (fall 2003): **13**
Areas of specialization: education administration and supervision, elementary teacher education, secondary teacher education, special education.
Courses that prepare teachers to pass the National Board of Professional Teaching Standards are offered.
Teacher preparation programs: Four-year baccalaureate-degree program leading to initial licensure that includes either a major or minor in education and practice teaching. Master's program preparing college graduates for initial licensure; includes practice teaching.
The education program is currently accredited by the National Council for Accreditation of Teacher Education.

LICENSING TEST
Pass rate on state's teacher licensing test for 2002-2003: **99%**
State average pass rate: **91%**

University of Rio Grande

- P.O. Box 500 F1009, Rio Grande, OH 45674
- **Website:** http://www.rio.edu
- **Private**
- **Degrees offered:** master's

ADMISSIONS
Admissions phone number: **(740) 245-7208**
Admissions email address: *mabell@rio.edu*

Application website: *http://www.rio.edu/admissions/*
Application fee: **$25**
Test of English as Foreign Language (TOEFL) is required for international students.
Minimum TOEFL score required for paper test: **500**

Fall 2003
Total 2003 enrollment: **231**
Master's degree enrollment: **231**
    Teacher preparation program enrollment (master's): **231**

FINANCIAL INFORMATION
Financial aid phone number: **(740) 245-7218**
Tuition, 2003-2004 academic year: Full-time: **$349/credit hour**; Part-time: **$349/credit hour**
Fees: **$349/credit hour**
Number of fellowships awarded to graduate students during the 2003-2004 academic year: **0**
Number of teaching assistant positions: **0**
Number of research assistant positions: **0**
Number of other paid appointments: **0**

ACADEMIC PROGRAMS
Total full-time tenured or tenure-track faculty (fall 2003): **17**
Areas of specialization: curriculum and instruction.
Professional development/partnership school(s) are used by students in all of the teaching programs.
During their internships, peer groups of students meet regularly to discuss instructional techniques in all of the teaching programs.
All of the students in their internships are mentored.
Courses that prepare teachers to pass the National Board of Professional Teaching Standards are not offered.
Teacher preparation programs: Four-year baccalaureate-degree program leading to initial licensure that includes either a major or minor in education and practice teaching.

LICENSING TEST
Pass rate on state's teacher licensing test for 2002-2003: **83%**
State average pass rate: **91%**

University of Toledo

- 2801 W. Bancroft Street, Toledo, OH 43606
- **Website:** http://gradschool.utoledo.edu
- **Public**
- **Degrees offered:** bachelor's, master's, education specialist, Ph.D., Ed.D.

ADMISSIONS
Admissions phone number: **(419) 530-4723**
Admissions email address: *grdsch@utnet.utoledo.edu*
Application website: *http://www.utoledo.edu/grad-school/siteMap.html*
Application fee: **$40**
Fall 2005 application deadline: **rolling**
Test requirements: **GRE**

Test of English as Foreign Language (TOEFL) is required for international students.
Minimum TOEFL score required for paper test: 550
Minimum TOEFL score required for computer test: 213

Fall 2003
Acceptance rate for master's degree programs: 67%
Acceptance rate for education specialist degree programs: 80%
Acceptance rate for doctoral programs: 46%
Average GRE verbal: 461, Average GRE quantitative: 570, Average GRE analytical: 467
Total 2003 enrollment: 713
Master's degree enrollment: 613
   Teacher preparation program enrollment (master's): 482
Education specialist degree enrollment: 22
Doctoral degree enrollment: 78

FINANCIAL INFORMATION
Financial aid phone number: (419) 530-5812
Tuition, 2003-2004 academic year: Full-time in-state: $7,714; out-of-state: $16,353, Part-time in-state: $321/credit hour; out-of-state: $681/credit hour
Room and board: $4,598, Books and supplies: $729, Miscellaneous expenses: $2,191
Number of fellowships awarded to graduate students during the 2003-2004 academic year: 0
Number of teaching assistant positions: 13
Number of research assistant positions: 23
Number of other paid appointments: 13

ACADEMIC PROGRAMS
Total full-time tenured or tenure-track faculty (fall 2003): 60, Total part-time faculty (fall 2003): 44
Areas of specialization: curriculum and instruction, education administration and supervision, education policy, educational psychology, elementary teacher education, higher education administration, secondary teacher education, special education, student counseling and personnel services, teacher education.
Professional development/partnership school(s) are used by students in some of the teaching programs.
During their internships, peer groups of students meet regularly to discuss instructional techniques in some of the teaching programs.
Some of the students in their internships are mentored.
Courses that prepare teachers to pass the National Board of Professional Teaching Standards are not offered.
Teacher preparation programs: Four-year baccalaureate-degree program leading to initial licensure that includes either a major or minor in education and practice teaching. Master's program preparing college graduates for initial licensure; includes practice teaching.
The education program is currently accredited by the National Council for Accreditation of Teacher Education.

LICENSING TEST
Pass rate on state's teacher licensing test for 2002-2003: 87%
State average pass rate: 91%

Urbana University

- 579 College Way, Urbana, OH 43078
- **Website:** http://www.urbana.edu
- **Private**
- **Degrees offered:** bachelor's, master's

ADMISSIONS
Admissions phone number: (937) 484-1360
Admissions email address: *mtolle@urbana.edu*
Application fee: $25

Fall 2003
Total 2003 enrollment: 110
Master's degree enrollment: 110
   Teacher preparation program enrollment (master's): 110

FINANCIAL INFORMATION
Financial aid phone number: (937) 484-1230
Tuition, 2003-2004 academic year: $320/credit hour

ACADEMIC PROGRAMS
Total full-time tenured or tenure-track faculty (fall 2003): 25
Professional development/partnership school(s) are used by students in all of the teaching programs.
During their internships, peer groups of students meet regularly to discuss instructional techniques in all of the teaching programs.
All of the students in their internships are mentored.
Courses that prepare teachers to pass the National Board of Professional Teaching Standards are offered.
The education program is currently accredited by the National Council for Accreditation of Teacher Education.

LICENSING TEST
Pass rate on state's teacher licensing test for 2002-2003: 84%
State average pass rate: 91%

Ursuline College

- 2550 Lander Road, Pepper Pike, OH 44124
- **Website:** http://www.ursuline.edu/grad_studies
- **Private**
- **Degrees offered:** bachelor's, master's

ADMISSIONS
Admissions phone number: (440) 646-8119
Admissions email address: *gradsch@ursuline.edu*
Application fee: $25
Fall 2005 application deadline: **rolling**
Test of English as Foreign Language (TOEFL) is required for international students.
Minimum TOEFL score required for paper test: 500
Minimum TOEFL score required for computer test: 173

Fall 2003
Acceptance rate for master's degree programs: 100%
Total 2003 enrollment: 123
Master's degree enrollment: 123
    Teacher preparation program enrollment (master's): 71

FINANCIAL INFORMATION
Financial aid phone number: (440) 646-8309
Tuition, 2003-2004 academic year: $12,300
Fees: $170, Room and board: $5,458, Books and supplies: $800, Miscellaneous expenses: $1,242
Number of fellowships awarded to graduate students during the 2003-2004 academic year: 0
Number of teaching assistant positions: 0
Number of research assistant positions: 0
Number of other paid appointments: 0

ACADEMIC PROGRAMS
Total full-time tenured or tenure-track faculty (fall 2003): 5
    Total part-time faculty (fall 2003): 3
Areas of specialization: education administration and supervision, elementary teacher education, secondary teacher education.
Professional development/partnership school(s) are used by students in some of the teaching programs.
During their internships, peer groups of students meet regularly to discuss instructional techniques in all of the teaching programs.
All of the students in their internships are mentored.
Courses that prepare teachers to pass the National Board of Professional Teaching Standards are not offered.
Teacher preparation programs: Four-year baccalaureate-degree program leading to initial licensure that includes either a major or minor in education and practice teaching. Master's program preparing college graduates for initial licensure; includes practice teaching.

LICENSING TEST
Pass rate on state's teacher licensing test for 2002-2003: 94%
State average pass rate: 91%

Walsh University

■ 2020 East Maple, North Canton, OH 44720
■ **Website:** http://www.walsh.edu
■ Private
■ **Degrees offered:** bachelor's, master's

ADMISSIONS
Admissions phone number: (330) 490-7174
Admissions email address: *lsuffron@walsh.edu*
Application fee: $25
Fall 2005 application deadline: **rolling**
Test requirements: MAT
Test of English as Foreign Language (TOEFL) is required for international students.
Minimum TOEFL score required for paper test: 510
Minimum TOEFL score required for computer test: 173

Fall 2003
Total 2003 enrollment: 56
Master's degree enrollment: 56

FINANCIAL INFORMATION
Financial aid phone number: (330) 490-7146
Tuition, 2003-2004 academic year: Full-time: $450/credit hour; Part-time: $450/credit hour
Fees: $15/credit hour, Room and board: $5,300, Books and supplies: $800, Miscellaneous expenses: $2,686
Number of teaching assistant positions: 1

ACADEMIC PROGRAMS
Total full-time tenured or tenure-track faculty (fall 2003): 5
    Total part-time faculty (fall 2003): 5
Areas of specialization: curriculum and instruction, education policy, educational psychology, elementary teacher education, secondary teacher education, student counseling and personnel services.
Professional development/partnership school(s) are used by students in all of the teaching programs.
During their internships, peer groups of students meet regularly to discuss instructional techniques in all of the teaching programs.
All of the students in their internships are mentored.
Courses that prepare teachers to pass the National Board of Professional Teaching Standards are offered.
Teacher preparation programs: Four-year baccalaureate-degree program leading to initial licensure that includes either a major or minor in education and practice teaching. Alternative program for college graduates leading to provisional licensure.

LICENSING TEST
Pass rate on state's teacher licensing test for 2002-2003: 91%
State average pass rate: 91%

Wright State University

■ 3640 Colonel Glenn Highway, Dayton, OH 45435
■ **Website:** http://www.wright.edu
■ Public
■ **Degrees offered:** bachelor's, master's, education specialist

ADMISSIONS
Admissions phone number: (937) 775-2976
Admissions email address: *sogs@wright.edu*
Application website: *http://www.applyweb.com/aw/wrightg*
Application fee: $25
Fall 2005 application deadline: **rolling**
Test of English as Foreign Language (TOEFL) is required for international students.

Fall 2003
Total 2003 enrollment: 858
Master's degree enrollment: 858

FINANCIAL INFORMATION

Financial aid phone number: **(937) 775-5721**

Tuition, 2003-2004 academic year: Full-time in-state:
$1,964; out-of-state: **$3,788**, Part-time in-state:
$182/credit hour; out-of-state: **$352/credit hour**

Room and board: **$6,019**, Books and supplies: **$900**

ACADEMIC PROGRAMS

Total full-time tenured or tenure-track faculty (fall 2003): **47**
Total part-time faculty (fall 2003): **172**

Areas of specialization: curriculum and instruction, education administration and supervision, elementary teacher education, higher education administration, secondary teacher education, special education, student counseling and personnel services, teacher education.

Professional development/partnership school(s) are used by students in some of the teaching programs.

During their internships, peer groups of students meet regularly to discuss instructional techniques in some of the teaching programs.

All of the students in their internships are mentored.

Courses that prepare teachers to pass the National Board of Professional Teaching Standards are offered.

Teacher preparation programs: Four-year baccalaureate-degree program leading to initial licensure that includes either a major or minor in education and practice teaching. Five-year program leading to initial licensure that results in a baccalaureate degree (with a major or minor in education) plus graduate credit and includes practice teaching. Master's program preparing college graduates for initial licensure; includes practice teaching. Alternative program for college graduates leading to provisional licensure.

The education program is currently accredited by the National Council for Accreditation of Teacher Education.

LICENSING TEST

Pass rate on state's teacher licensing test for 2002-2003: **90%**
State average pass rate: **91%**

Xavier University

- 3800 Victory Parkway, Cincinnati, OH 45207
- **Website:** http://www.xavier.edu/graduate_admission/
- **Private**
- **Degrees offered:** bachelor's, master's

ADMISSIONS

Admissions phone number: **(800) 344-4698**
Admissions email address: *xugrad@xavier.edu*
Application website: *http://www.xavier.edu/graduate_admission/grad_apps.cfm*
Application fee: **$35**
Fall 2005 application deadline: **rolling**
Test requirements: **GRE or MAT**
Test of English as Foreign Language (TOEFL) is required for international students.
Minimum TOEFL score required for paper test: **550**

Minimum TOEFL score required for computer test: **213**

Fall 2003

Acceptance rate for master's degree programs: **56%**
Total 2003 enrollment: **924**
Master's degree enrollment: **924**
Teacher preparation program enrollment (master's): **487**

FINANCIAL INFORMATION

Financial aid phone number: **(513) 745-3142**
Tuition, 2003-2004 academic year: Full-time: **$405/credit hour**; Part-time: **$405/credit hour**

ACADEMIC PROGRAMS

Total full-time tenured or tenure-track faculty (fall 2003): **25**, Total part-time faculty (fall 2003): **114**

Areas of specialization: curriculum and instruction, education administration and supervision, educational psychology, elementary teacher education, secondary teacher education, special education, student counseling and personnel services.

Professional development/partnership school(s) are used by students in some of the teaching programs.

During their internships, peer groups of students meet regularly to discuss instructional techniques in all of the teaching programs.

All of the students in their internships are mentored.

Courses that prepare teachers to pass the National Board of Professional Teaching Standards are not offered.

Teacher preparation programs: Four-year baccalaureate-degree program leading to initial licensure that includes either a major or minor in education and practice teaching. Master's program preparing college graduates for initial licensure; includes practice teaching. Alternative program for college graduates leading to provisional licensure.

LICENSING TEST

Pass rate on state's teacher licensing test for 2002-2003: **99%**
State average pass rate: **91%**

Youngstown State University

- 1 University Plaza, Youngstown, OH 44555
- **Website:** http://www.coe.ysu.edu/
- **Public**

ADMISSIONS

Admissions phone number: **(330) 742-3091**
Admissions email address: *graduateschool@cc.ysu.edu*

FINANCIAL INFORMATION

Financial aid phone number: **(330) 941-3505**

LICENSING TEST

Pass rate on state's teacher licensing test for 2002-2003: **80%**
State average pass rate: **91%**

OKLAHOMA

Cameron University

■ 2800 W. Gore Blvd., Lawton, OK 73505
■ **Website:** http://www.cameron.edu/
■ **Public**

LICENSING TEST
Pass rate on state's teacher licensing test for 2002-2003: 97%
State average pass rate: 94%

East Central University

■ 14th Street and Francis Avenue, Ada, OK 74820
■ **Website:** http://www.ecok.edu/
■ **Public**

LICENSING TEST
Pass rate on state's teacher licensing test for 2002-2003: 89%
State average pass rate: 94%

Langston University

■ P.O. Box 907, Langston, OK 73050
■ **Website:** http://www.lunet.edu/
■ **Public**

LICENSING TEST
Pass rate on state's teacher licensing test for 2002-2003: 73%
State average pass rate: 94%

Northeastern State University

■ 600 N. Grand, Tahlequah, OK 74464
■ **Website:** http://www.nsuok.edu/
■ **Public**

LICENSING TEST
Pass rate on state's teacher licensing test for 2002-2003: 93%
State average pass rate: 94%

Northwestern Oklahoma State University

■ 709 Oklahoma Boulevard, Alva, OK 73717
■ **Website:** http://www.nwosu.edu/
■ **Public**

LICENSING TEST
Pass rate on state's teacher licensing test for 2002-2003: 89%
State average pass rate: 94%

Oklahoma City University

■ 2501 N. Blackwelder, Oklahoma City, OK 73106-1493
■ **Website:** http://www.okcu.edu/
■ **Private**

LICENSING TEST
Pass rate on state's teacher licensing test for 2002-2003: 93%
State average pass rate: 94%

Oklahoma State University

- 339 Willard, Stillwater, OK 74078-4033
- Website: http://www.pio.okstate.edu
- Public
- Degrees offered: bachelor's, master's, education specialist, Ph.D., Ed.D.
- Overall rank in the 2005 U.S. News education schools with doctoral programs: 73
- Overall rank in the 2005 U.S. News education school specialty rankings: vocational/technical: 10

ADMISSIONS
Admissions phone number: (405) 744-6368
Admissions email address: *grad-i@okstate.edu*
Application fee: $25
Fall 2005 application deadline: rolling
Test requirements: GRE or MAT
Test of English as Foreign Language (TOEFL) is required for international students.
Minimum TOEFL score required for paper test: 550
Minimum TOEFL score required for computer test: 213

Fall 2003
Acceptance rate for master's degree programs: 58%
Acceptance rate for education specialist degree programs: 44%
Acceptance rate for doctoral programs: 49%
Average GRE verbal: 446, Average GRE quantitative: 511, Average GRE analytical: 543, Average MAT: 52
Total 2003 enrollment: 849
Master's degree enrollment: 496
    Teacher preparation program enrollment (master's): 237
Education specialist degree enrollment: 15
Doctoral degree enrollment: 338

FINANCIAL INFORMATION
Financial aid phone number: (405) 744-6604
Tuition, 2003-2004 academic year: Full-time in-state: $118/credit hour; out-of-state: $275/credit hour, Part-time in-state: $118/credit hour; out-of-state: $275/credit hour
Fees: $139, Room and board: $2,575, Books and supplies: $360, Miscellaneous expenses: $1,365
Number of fellowships awarded to graduate students during the 2003-2004 academic year: 1
Number of teaching assistant positions: 68
Number of research assistant positions: 38
Number of other paid appointments: 9

ACADEMIC PROGRAMS
Total full-time tenured or tenure-track faculty (fall 2003): 87, Total part-time faculty (fall 2003): 41
Areas of specialization: curriculum and instruction, education administration and supervision, education policy, educational psychology, elementary teacher education, higher education administration, secondary teacher edu-

cation, special education, student counseling and personnel services.
Professional development/partnership school(s) are used by students in some of the teaching programs.
During their internships, peer groups of students meet regularly to discuss instructional techniques in some of the teaching programs.
All of the students in their internships are mentored.
Courses that prepare teachers to pass the National Board of Professional Teaching Standards are offered.
Teacher preparation programs: Four-year baccalaureate-degree program leading to initial licensure that includes either a major or minor in education and practice teaching.
The education program is currently accredited by the National Council for Accreditation of Teacher Education.

LICENSING TEST
Pass rate on state's teacher licensing test for 2002-2003: 97%
State average pass rate: 94%

Oral Roberts University

- 7777 S. Lewis Avenue, Tulsa, OK 74171
- Website: http://www.oru.edu/
- Private

LICENSING TEST
Pass rate on state's teacher licensing test for 2002-2003: 97%
State average pass rate: 94%

Southeastern Oklahoma State University

- 1405 N 4th PMB 4137, Durant, OK 74701
- Website: http://www.sosu.edu
- Public
- Degrees offered: bachelor's, master's

ADMISSIONS
Admissions phone number: (580) 745-2186
Admissions email address: *admissions@sosu.edu*
Application website: *http://www.sosu.edu/futurestudents/policy*
Application fee: $20
Fall 2005 application deadline: rolling
Test requirements: None
Test of English as Foreign Language (TOEFL) is required for international students.
Minimum TOEFL score required for paper test: 550
Minimum TOEFL score required for computer test: 213

Fall 2003
Acceptance rate for master's degree programs: 98%

Total 2003 enrollment: **180**
Master's degree enrollment: **180**
Teacher preparation program enrollment (master's): **87**

FINANCIAL INFORMATION
Financial aid phone number: **(580) 745-2186**
Tuition, 2003-2004 academic year: Full-time in-state:
$85/credit hour; out-of-state: **$240/credit hour**, Part-time
in-state: **$85/credit hour**; out-of-state: **$240/credit hour**
Fees: **$97/credit hour**, Room and board: **$1,200**, Books and
supplies: **$300**, Miscellaneous expenses: **$780**
Number of fellowships awarded to graduate students dur-
ing the 2003-2004 academic year: **0**
Number of teaching assistant positions: **0**
Number of research assistant positions: **0**
Number of other paid appointments: **0**

ACADEMIC PROGRAMS
Total full-time tenured or tenure-track faculty (fall 2003): **114**
Total part-time faculty (fall 2003): **70**
Areas of specialization: education administration and
supervision, elementary teacher education, higher educa-
tion administration, secondary teacher education, special
education, student counseling and personnel services,
teacher education.
Professional development/partnership school(s) are used
by students in none of the teaching programs.
During their internships, peer groups of students meet
regularly to discuss instructional techniques in all of the
teaching programs.
All of the students in their internships are mentored.
Courses that prepare teachers to pass the National Board of
Professional Teaching Standards are not offered.
The education program is currently accredited by the
National Council for Accreditation of Teacher Education.

LICENSING TEST
Pass rate on state's teacher licensing test for 2002-2003: **91%**
State average pass rate: **94%**

Southern Nazarene University

■ **6729 N.W. 39th Expressway, Bethany, OK 73008**
■ **Website:** http://www.snu.edu/home.asp
■ **Private**

LICENSING TEST
Pass rate on state's teacher licensing test for 2002-2003: **97%**
State average pass rate: **94%**

Southwestern Oklahoma State University

■ **100 Campus Drive, Weatherford, OK 73096-3098**
■ **Website:** http://www.swosu.edu/
■ **Public**

LICENSING TEST
Pass rate on state's teacher licensing test for 2002-2003:
89%
State average pass rate: **94%**

University of Central Oklahoma

■ **100 N University Drive, Edmond, OK 73034**
■ **Website:** http://www.ucok.edu/graduate/
■ **Public**
■ **Degrees offered:** bachelor's, master's

ADMISSIONS
Admissions phone number: **(405) 974-3341**
Admissions email address: *gradcoll@ucok.edu*
Application fee: **$25**
Fall 2005 application deadline: **rolling**
Test requirements: **GRE**
Test of English as Foreign Language (TOEFL) is required
for international students.
Minimum TOEFL score required for paper test: **500**
Minimum TOEFL score required for computer test: **173**

Fall 2003
Acceptance rate for master's degree programs: **71%**
Total 2003 enrollment: **3,154**
Master's degree enrollment: **3,154**
Teacher preparation program enrollment (master's):
1,571

FINANCIAL INFORMATION
Financial aid phone number: **(405) 974-3334**
Tuition, 2003-2004 academic year: Full-time in-state:
$1,950; out-of-state: **$5,850**, Part-time in-state: **$65/credit
hour**; out-of-state: **$195/credit hour**
Fees: **$699**, Room and board: **$3,670**, Books and supplies:
$1,000, Miscellaneous expenses: **$3,000**
Number of other paid appointments: **9**

ACADEMIC PROGRAMS
Total full-time tenured or tenure-track faculty (fall 2003):
69, Total part-time faculty (fall 2003): **84**
Areas of specialization: curriculum and instruction, education administration and supervision, elementary teacher
education, secondary teacher education, special educa-

tion, student counseling and personnel services, teacher education.

Professional development/partnership school(s) are used by students in all of the teaching programs.

During their internships, peer groups of students meet regularly to discuss instructional techniques in all of the teaching programs.

All of the students in their internships are mentored.

Courses that prepare teachers to pass the National Board of Professional Teaching Standards are not offered.

Teacher preparation programs: Four-year baccalaureate-degree program leading to initial licensure that includes either a major or minor in education and practice teaching. Master's program preparing college graduates for initial licensure; includes practice teaching.

The education program is currently accredited by the National Council for Accreditation of Teacher Education.

LICENSING TEST
Pass rate on state's teacher licensing test for 2002-2003: 99%
State average pass rate: 94%

University of Oklahoma

- 820 Van Vleet Oval, No. 100, Norman, OK 73019-2041
- Website: http://www.ou.edu/education
- Public
- Degrees offered: bachelor's, master's, Ph.D., Ed.D.
- Overall rank in the 2005 U.S. News education schools with doctoral programs: 58

ADMISSIONS
Admissions phone number: (405) 325-2252
Admissions email address: *admission@ou.edu*
Application website: *http://www.ou.edu/bulletins/ application/grad.htm*
Application fee: **$25**
Fall 2005 application deadline: **6/1**
Test requirements: **GRE or MAT**
Test of English as Foreign Language (TOEFL) is required for international students.
Minimum TOEFL score required for paper test: **550**
Minimum TOEFL score required for computer test: **213**

Fall 2003
Acceptance rate for master's degree programs: **23%**
Acceptance rate for doctoral programs: **13%**
Average GRE verbal: **500**, Average GRE quantitative: **550**, Average GRE analytical: **570**
Total 2003 enrollment: **660**
Master's degree enrollment: **372**
  Teacher preparation program enrollment (master's): **174**
Doctoral degree enrollment: **288**

FINANCIAL INFORMATION
Financial aid phone number: **(405) 325-4521**

Tuition, 2003-2004 academic year: Full-time in-state: **$2,774**; out-of-state: **$9,571**, Part-time in-state: **$116/credit hour**; out-of-state: **$399/credit hour**
Fees: **$953**, Room and board: **$7,605**, Books and supplies: **$936**, Miscellaneous expenses: **$4,104**
Number of fellowships awarded to graduate students during the 2003-2004 academic year: **10**
Number of teaching assistant positions: **46**
Number of research assistant positions: **71**
Number of other paid appointments: **63**

ACADEMIC PROGRAMS
Total full-time tenured or tenure-track faculty (fall 2003): **56**, Total part-time faculty (fall 2003): **18**
Areas of specialization: curriculum and instruction, education administration and supervision, education policy, educational psychology, elementary teacher education, higher education administration, secondary teacher education, special education, student counseling and personnel services.

Professional development/partnership school(s) are used by students in none of the teaching programs.

During their internships, peer groups of students meet regularly to discuss instructional techniques in some of the teaching programs.

All of the students in their internships are mentored.

Courses that prepare teachers to pass the National Board of Professional Teaching Standards are not offered.

Teacher preparation programs: Five-year program leading to initial licensure that results in a baccalaureate degree (with a major or minor in education) plus graduate credit and includes practice teaching.

The education program is currently accredited by the National Council for Accreditation of Teacher Education.

LICENSING TEST
Pass rate on state's teacher licensing test for 2002-2003: 99%
State average pass rate: 94%

University of Tulsa

- 600 S. College Avenue, Tulsa, OK 74104
- Website: http://www.utulsa.edu
- Private
- Degrees offered: bachelor's, master's

ADMISSIONS
Admissions phone number: (918) 631-2336
Admissions email address: *grad@utulsa.edu*
Application website: *http://www.utulsa.edu/graduate/*
Application fee: **$30**
Fall 2005 application deadline: **2/1**
Test requirements: **GRE**
Test of English as Foreign Language (TOEFL) is required for international students.
Minimum TOEFL score required for paper test: **550**

Fall 2003

Acceptance rate for master's degree programs: 52%

Average GRE verbal: 410, Average GRE quantitative: 460, Average GRE analytical: 570

Total 2003 enrollment: 46

Master's degree enrollment: 46

FINANCIAL INFORMATION

Financial aid phone number: (918) 631-2526

Tuition, 2003-2004 academic year: Full-time: **$588/credit hour**; Part-time: **$588/credit hour**

Fees: **$325**, Room and board: **$4,200**, Books and supplies: **$800**, Miscellaneous expenses: **$100**

Number of fellowships awarded to graduate students during the 2003-2004 academic year: 10

ACADEMIC PROGRAMS

Total full-time tenured or tenure-track faculty (fall 2003): 6 Total part-time faculty (fall 2003): 5

Areas of specialization: curriculum and instruction, education policy, educational psychology, elementary teacher education, secondary teacher education.

Professional development/partnership school(s) are used by students in none of the teaching programs.

During their internships, peer groups of students meet regularly to discuss instructional techniques in all of the teaching programs.

All of the students in their internships are mentored.

Courses that prepare teachers to pass the National Board of Professional Teaching Standards are not offered.

Teacher preparation programs: Four-year baccalaureate-degree program leading to initial licensure that includes either a major or minor in education and practice teaching. Master's program preparing college graduates for initial licensure; includes practice teaching. Alternative program for college graduates leading to provisional licensure.

The education program is currently accredited by the National Council for Accreditation of Teacher Education.

LICENSING TEST

Pass rate on state's teacher licensing test for 2002-2003: 86%

State average pass rate: 94%

OREGON

Concordia University

- **2811 NE Holman St., Portland, OR 97211**
- **Website:** http://www.cu-portland.edu/
- **Private**
- **Degrees offered:** bachelor's, master's

ADMISSIONS
Admissions phone number: **(503) 280-8501**
Admissions email address: *admissions@cu-portland.edu*
Application website: *https://acme.cu-portland.edu/AdmissApp/*
Application fee: **$35**
Fall 2005 application deadline: **rolling**
Test of English as Foreign Language (TOEFL) is required for international students.
Minimum TOEFL score required for paper test: **570**
Minimum TOEFL score required for computer test: **230**

Fall 2003
Total 2003 enrollment: **100**
Master's degree enrollment: **100**
    Teacher preparation program enrollment (master's): **90**

FINANCIAL INFORMATION
Financial aid phone number: **(503) 280-8514**
Tuition, 2003-2004 academic year: Full-time: **$450/credit hour**; Part-time: **$450/credit hour**
Fees: **$60**, Room and board: **$9,100**, Books and supplies: **$1,050**, Miscellaneous expenses: **$2,600**
Number of fellowships awarded to graduate students during the 2003-2004 academic year: **0**
Number of teaching assistant positions: **0**
Number of research assistant positions: **0**
Number of other paid appointments: **0**

ACADEMIC PROGRAMS
Total full-time tenured or tenure-track faculty (fall 2003): **45**, Total part-time faculty (fall 2003): **24**

Areas of specialization: curriculum and instruction, education administration and supervision, elementary teacher education, secondary teacher education.
Professional development/partnership school(s) are used by students in all of the teaching programs.
During their internships, peer groups of students meet regularly to discuss instructional techniques in some of the teaching programs.
All of the students in their internships are mentored.
Courses that prepare teachers to pass the National Board of Professional Teaching Standards are not offered.
Teacher preparation programs: Four-year baccalaureate-degree program leading to initial licensure that includes either a major or minor in education and practice teaching. Master's program preparing college graduates for initial licensure; includes practice teaching.

LICENSING TEST
Pass rate on state's teacher licensing test for 2002-2003: **100%**
State average pass rate: **100%**

Eastern Oregon University

- **1 University Boulevard, La Grande, OR 97850**
- **Website:** http://www.eou.edu/
- **Public**

LICENSING TEST
Pass rate on state's teacher licensing test for 2002-2003: **100%**
State average pass rate: **100%**

George Fox University

■ 414 N. Meridian Street, Newberg, OR 97132
■ **Website:** http://www.georgefox.edu/
■ Private

LICENSING TEST

Pass rate on state's teacher licensing test for 2002-2003:
100%
State average pass rate: 100%

Lewis and Clark College

■ 0615 SW Palatine Hill Rd., Portland, OR 97219-7899
■ **Website:** http://www.lclark.edu/dept/gseadmit/
■ Private
■ **Degrees offered:** master's

ADMISSIONS

Admissions phone number: (503) 768-6200
Admissions email address: *gseadmit@lclark.edu*
Application website: *http://education.lclark.edu/*
Application fee: $50
Fall 2005 application deadline: 1/3
Test requirements: **GRE or MAT**
Test of English as Foreign Language (TOEFL) is required
for international students.
Minimum TOEFL score required for paper test: 550

Fall 2003
Acceptance rate for master's degree programs: 92%
Average GRE verbal: 497, Average GRE quantitative: 523,
Average GRE analytical: 568
Total 2003 enrollment: 561
Master's degree enrollment: 561
Teacher preparation program enrollment (master's): 148

FINANCIAL INFORMATION

Financial aid phone number: (503) 768-7090
Tuition, 2003-2004 academic year: Full-time: **$550/credit
hour**; Part-time: **$550/credit hour**
Books and supplies: $800
Number of fellowships awarded to graduate students dur-
ing the 2003-2004 academic year: 0
Number of teaching assistant positions: 0
Number of research assistant positions: 0
Number of other paid appointments: 0

ACADEMIC PROGRAMS

Total full-time tenured or tenure-track faculty (fall 2003):
20, Total part-time faculty (fall 2003): 14
Areas of specialization: curriculum and instruction, education administration and supervision, education policy,
educational psychology, elementary teacher education,
higher education administration, secondary teacher edu-

cation, special education, student counseling and per-
sonnel services.
Professional development/partnership school(s) are used
by students in none of the teaching programs.
During their internships, peer groups of students meet
regularly to discuss instructional techniques in all of the
teaching programs.
All of the students in their internships are mentored.
Courses that prepare teachers to pass the National Board of
Professional Teaching Standards are not offered.
Teacher preparation programs: Master's degree in education, including internship/practice teaching and preparation for initial licensure.

LICENSING TEST

Pass rate on state's teacher licensing test for 2002-2003:
100%
State average pass rate: 100%

Northwest Christian College

■ 828 E. 11th Avenue, Eugene, OR 97401
■ **Website:** http://www.nwcc.edu
■ Private
■ **Degrees offered:** bachelor's, master's

ADMISSIONS

Admissions phone number: (541) 684-7201
Admissions email address: *admissions@nwcc.edu*
Application fee: $35
Fall 2005 application deadline: **rolling**
Test of English as Foreign Language (TOEFL) is required
for international students.
Minimum TOEFL score required for paper test: 550

Fall 2003
Total 2003 enrollment: 62
Master's degree enrollment: 62

FINANCIAL INFORMATION

Financial aid phone number: (541) 684-7323
Tuition, 2003-2004 academic year: Full-time: **$396/credit
hour**; Part-time: **$396/credit hour**
Books and supplies: $825, Miscellaneous expenses: $1,800

ACADEMIC PROGRAMS

Areas of specialization: student counseling and personnel
services.
Professional development/partnership school(s) are used
by students in all of the teaching programs.
During their internships, peer groups of students meet
regularly to discuss instructional techniques in some of
the teaching programs.
All of the students in their internships are mentored.
Courses that prepare teachers to pass the National Board of
Professional Teaching Standards are not offered.

LICENSING TEST

Pass rate on state's teacher licensing test for 2002-2003: 100%

State average pass rate: 100%

Oregon State University

- **School of Education, Corvallis, OR 97331-3502**
- **Website:** http://oregonstate.edu/admissions
- **Public**
- **Degrees offered:** bachelor's, master's, Ph.D., Ed.D.

ADMISSIONS

Admissions phone number: **(541) 737-4411**
Admissions email address: *osuadmit@oregonstate.edu*
Application fee: **$50**
Fall 2005 application deadline: **6/15**
Test of English as Foreign Language (TOEFL) is required for international students.
Minimum TOEFL score required for paper test: **550**
Minimum TOEFL score required for computer test: **213**

Fall 2003

Total 2003 enrollment: **290**
Master's degree enrollment: **198**
   Teacher preparation program enrollment (master's): **51**
Doctoral degree enrollment: **92**

FINANCIAL INFORMATION

Financial aid phone number: **(541) 737-2241**
Tuition, 2003-2004 academic year: Full-time in-state: **$8,139**; out-of-state: **$14,376**, Part-time in-state: **$301/credit hour**; out-of-state: **$532/credit hour**
Fees: **$1,227**, Room and board: **$6,336**, Books and supplies: **$1,350**, Miscellaneous expenses: **$2,082**

ACADEMIC PROGRAMS

Total full-time tenured or tenure-track faculty (fall 2003): **29**
   Total part-time faculty (fall 2003): **16**
Professional development/partnership school(s) are used by students in all of the teaching programs.
During their internships, peer groups of students meet regularly to discuss instructional techniques in all of the teaching programs.
All of the students in their internships are mentored.
Courses that prepare teachers to pass the National Board of Professional Teaching Standards are offered.
Teacher preparation programs: Four-year baccalaureate-degree program leading to initial licensure that includes either a major or minor in education and practice teaching. Master's program preparing college graduates for initial licensure; includes practice teaching.
The education program is currently accredited by the National Council for Accreditation of Teacher Education.

LICENSING TEST

Pass rate on state's teacher licensing test for 2002-2003: **100%**
State average pass rate: **100%**

Pacific University

- **2043 College Way, Forest Grove, OR 97116**
- **Website:** http://ed.pacificu.edu
- **Private**
- **Degrees offered:** bachelor's, master's

ADMISSIONS

Admissions phone number: **(503) 352-2958**
Admissions email address: *teach@pacificu.edu*
Application fee: **$35**
Fall 2005 application deadline: **rolling**
Test of English as Foreign Language (TOEFL) is required for international students.
Minimum TOEFL score required for paper test: **600**

FINANCIAL INFORMATION

Financial aid phone number: **(503) 352-2222**

LICENSING TEST

Pass rate on state's teacher licensing test for 2002-2003: **100%**
State average pass rate: **100%**

Portland State University

- **PO Box 751, Portland, OR 97207-0751**
- **Website:** http://www.pdx.edu
- **Public**
- **Degrees offered:** master's, Ed.D.

ADMISSIONS

Admissions phone number: **(503) 725-3511**
Admissions email address: *adm@pdx.edu*
Application website: *http://www.ed.pdx.edu*
Application fee: **$50**
Fall 2005 application deadline: **rolling**
Test requirements: **GRE or MAT**
Test of English as Foreign Language (TOEFL) is required for international students.
Minimum TOEFL score required for paper test: **550**

Fall 2003

Acceptance rate for master's degree programs: **93%**
Acceptance rate for doctoral programs: **54%**
Average GRE verbal: **508**, Average GRE quantitative: **527**, Average GRE analytical: **583**
Total 2003 enrollment: **899**
Master's degree enrollment: **807**
   Teacher preparation program enrollment (master's): **529**
Doctoral degree enrollment: **92**

FINANCIAL INFORMATION

Financial aid phone number: **(503) 725-3461**

Tuition, 2003-2004 academic year: Full-time in-state: $6,588; out-of-state: $12,060, Part-time in-state: $244/credit hour; out-of-state: $244/credit hour
Fees: $1,041, Room and board: $8,175, Books and supplies: $1,200, Miscellaneous expenses: $1,950
Number of teaching assistant positions: 1
Number of research assistant positions: 4
Number of other paid appointments: 28

ACADEMIC PROGRAMS

Total full-time tenured or tenure-track faculty (fall 2003): 37, Total part-time faculty (fall 2003): 47
Areas of specialization: curriculum and instruction, education administration and supervision, education policy, elementary teacher education, higher education administration, secondary teacher education, special education, student counseling and personnel services.
Professional development/partnership school(s) are used by students in some of the teaching programs.
During their internships, peer groups of students meet regularly to discuss instructional techniques in all of the teaching programs.
All of the students in their internships are mentored.
Courses that prepare teachers to pass the National Board of Professional Teaching Standards are offered.
Teacher preparation programs: Master's degree in education, including internship/practice teaching and preparation for initial licensure.
The education program is currently accredited by the National Council for Accreditation of Teacher Education.

LICENSING TEST

Pass rate on state's teacher licensing test for 2002-2003: 100%
State average pass rate: 100%

Southern Oregon University

■ **1250 Siskiyou Blvd, Ashland, OR 97520**
■ **Website:** http://www.sou.edu/education/
■ **Public**
■ **Degrees offered:** master's

ADMISSIONS

Admissions phone number: **(541) 552-6411**
Admissions email address: *admissions@sou.edu*
Application website:
http://wwwsou.edu/education/med/apply.html
Application fee: **$50**
Fall 2005 application deadline: **rolling**
Test of English as Foreign Language (TOEFL) is required for international students.

Fall 2003
Acceptance rate for master's degree programs: **87%**
Total 2003 enrollment: **169**

Master's degree enrollment: **169**
Teacher preparation program enrollment (master's): **169**

FINANCIAL INFORMATION

Financial aid phone number: **(541) 552-6161**
Tuition, 2003-2004 academic year: Full-time in-state: $6,306; out-of-state: $11,556, Part-time in-state: $230/credit hour; out-of-state: $230/credit hour
Fees: $1,015, Room and board: $6,039, Books and supplies: $1,068, Miscellaneous expenses: $2,700

ACADEMIC PROGRAMS

Total full-time tenured or tenure-track faculty (fall 2003): 11, Total part-time faculty (fall 2003): 2
Areas of specialization: curriculum and instruction, education administration and supervision, educational psychology, elementary teacher education, secondary teacher education, special education, student counseling and personnel services.
Professional development/partnership school(s) are used by students in some of the teaching programs.
During their internships, peer groups of students meet regularly to discuss instructional techniques in all of the teaching programs.
All of the students in their internships are mentored.
Courses that prepare teachers to pass the National Board of Professional Teaching Standards are not offered.
Teacher preparation programs: Master's degree in education, including internship/practice teaching and preparation for initial licensure. Education minor for undergraduate students.

LICENSING TEST

Pass rate on state's teacher licensing test for 2002-2003: **100%**
State average pass rate: **100%**

University of Oregon

■ **1215 University of Oregon, Eugene, OR 97403-1215**
■ **Website:**
http://education.uoregon.edu/path.htm?setpath=19
■ **Public**
■ **Degrees offered:** bachelor's, master's, Ph.D., Ed.D.
■ **Overall rank in the 2005 U.S. News education schools with doctoral programs:** 8
■ **Overall rank in the 2005 U.S. News education school specialty rankings:** special education: 3

ADMISSIONS

Admissions phone number: **(541) 346-3201**
Admissions email address: *uoadmit@oregon.uoregon.edu*
Application fee: **$50**
Fall 2005 application deadline: **5/13**
Test requirements: **GRE or MAT**
Test of English as Foreign Language (TOEFL) is required for international students.
Minimum TOEFL score required for paper test: **500**
Minimum TOEFL score required for computer test: **173**

Fall 2003
Acceptance rate for master's degree programs: **60%**
Acceptance rate for doctoral programs: **21%**
Average GRE verbal: **547**, Average GRE quantitative: **594**, Average GRE analytical: **578**
Total 2003 enrollment: **713**
Master's degree enrollment: **507**
    Teacher preparation program enrollment (master's): **126**
Doctoral degree enrollment: **206**

FINANCIAL INFORMATION
Financial aid phone number: **(541) 346-3221**
Tuition, 2003-2004 academic year: Full-time in-state: **$7,587**; out-of-state: **$12,363**, Part-time in-state: **$281/credit hour**; out-of-state: **$458/credit hour**
Fees: **$1,326**, Room and board: **$6,570**, Books and supplies: **$900**, Miscellaneous expenses: **$2,660**
Number of fellowships awarded to graduate students during the 2003-2004 academic year: **125**

ACADEMIC PROGRAMS
Total full-time tenured or tenure-track faculty (fall 2003): **53**, Total part-time faculty (fall 2003): **9**
Areas of specialization: education administration and supervision, education policy, elementary teacher education, higher education administration, secondary teacher education, special education, student counseling and personnel services.
Professional development/partnership school(s) are used by students in some of the teaching programs.
During their internships, peer groups of students meet regularly to discuss instructional techniques in some of the teaching programs.
All of the students in their internships are mentored.
Courses that prepare teachers to pass the National Board of Professional Teaching Standards are not offered.
Teacher preparation programs: Master's degree in education, including internship/practice teaching and preparation for initial licensure.

LICENSING TEST
Pass rate on state's teacher licensing test for 2002-2003: **100%**
State average pass rate: **100%**

University of Portland

■ **5000 N. Willamette Blvd., Portland, OR 97203**
■ **Website:** http://www.up.edu
■ **Private**
■ **Degrees offered:** bachelor's, master's, education specialist

ADMISSIONS
Admissions phone number: **(503) 943-7107**
Admissions email address: *chadwick@up.edu*
Application fee: **$45**
Fall 2005 application deadline: **rolling**

Test requirements: **GRE or MAT**
Test of English as Foreign Language (TOEFL) is required for international students.
Minimum TOEFL score required for paper test: **550**

Fall 2003
Total 2003 enrollment: **309**
Master's degree enrollment: **309**

FINANCIAL INFORMATION
Financial aid phone number: **(503) 943-7311**
Tuition, 2003-2004 academic year: Full-time: **$340/credit hour**; Part-time: **$340/credit hour**

ACADEMIC PROGRAMS
Areas of specialization: education administration and supervision, higher education administration, special education.
Teacher preparation programs: Four-year baccalaureate-degree program leading to initial licensure that includes either a major or minor in education and practice teaching. Master's program preparing college graduates for initial licensure; includes practice teaching.
The education program is currently accredited by the National Council for Accreditation of Teacher Education.

LICENSING TEST
Pass rate on state's teacher licensing test for 2002-2003: **100%**
State average pass rate: **100%**

Western Oregon University

■ **345 N Monmouth Ave, Monmouth, OR 97361**
■ **Website:** http://www.wou.edu
■ **Public**
■ **Degrees offered:** bachelor's, master's

ADMISSIONS
Admissions phone number: **(503) 838-8211**
Admissions email address: *wolfgram@wou.edu*
Application fee: **$50**
Fall 2005 application deadline: **rolling**
Test of English as Foreign Language (TOEFL) is required for international students.
Minimum TOEFL score required for paper test: **550**
Minimum TOEFL score required for computer test: **213**

Fall 2003
Acceptance rate for master's degree programs: **75%**
Total 2003 enrollment: **400**
Master's degree enrollment: **400**
    Teacher preparation program enrollment (master's): **400**

FINANCIAL INFORMATION

Financial aid phone number: (503) 838-8475
Tuition, 2003-2004 academic year: Full-time in-state:
$6,549; out-of-state: $11,793, Part-time in-state:
$243/credit hour; out-of-state: $437/credit hour
Fees: $1,065, Room and board: $5,976, Books and supplies: $1,080, Miscellaneous expenses: $2,175
Number of teaching assistant positions: 14

ACADEMIC PROGRAMS

Areas of specialization: curriculum and instruction, educational psychology, elementary teacher education, secondary teacher education, special education.
Courses that prepare teachers to pass the National Board of
Professional Teaching Standards are not offered.
Teacher preparation programs: Four-year baccalaureate-
degree program leading to initial licensure that includes
either a major or minor in education and practice teaching. Master's program preparing college graduates for
initial licensure; includes practice teaching.
The education program is currently accredited by the
National Council for Accreditation of Teacher Education.

LICENSING TEST

Pass rate on state's teacher licensing test for 2002-2003:
100%
State average pass rate: 100%

Willamette University

- 900 State Street, Salem, OR 97301
- **Website:** http://www.willamette.edu/mat
- **Private**
- **Degrees offered:** master's

ADMISSIONS

Admissions phone number: (503) 375-5453

Admissions email address: *cbowles@willamette.edu*
Application website: *http://www.willamette.edu/mat/
application.html*
Application fee: $35
Fall 2005 application deadline: 2/1

Fall 2003

Acceptance rate for master's degree programs: 77%
Total 2003 enrollment: 70
Master's degree enrollment: 70
　　Teacher preparation program enrollment (master's): 70

FINANCIAL INFORMATION

Financial aid phone number: (503) 370-6273
Tuition, 2003-2004 academic year: $18,450

ACADEMIC PROGRAMS

Total full-time tenured or tenure-track faculty (fall 2003): 7
　　Total part-time faculty (fall 2003): 15
Areas of specialization: curriculum and instruction, education
policy, educational psychology, elementary teacher educa-
tion, secondary teacher education, special education.
Professional development/partnership school(s) are used
by students in all of the teaching programs.
During their internships, peer groups of students meet
regularly to discuss instructional techniques in all of the
teaching programs.
All of the students in their internships are mentored.
Courses that prepare teachers to pass the National Board of
Professional Teaching Standards are not offered.
Teacher preparation programs: Master's degree in educa-
tion, including internship/practice teaching and preparation for initial licensure.

LICENSING TEST

Pass rate on state's teacher licensing test for 2002-2003:
100%
State average pass rate: 100%

PENNSYLVANIA

TEACHER TESTING IN PENNSYLVANIA

Teacher licensure rules vary widely from state to state, but almost all states require tests. The exams typically cover the basics of reading, writing and math, although some states mandate in-depth, subject-specific teacher tests. For information on where to go in your state for specific academic requirements, see Chapter 6 on page 67. Note: Some schools require students to pass exams by graduation, and thus automatically report pass rates of 100 percent.

- This state **does** require a basic skills test in order to obtain a teaching license.
- This state **does** require a subject-knowledge test in order to obtain a middle school teaching license.
- This state **does** require a subject-knowledge test in order to obtain a high school teaching license.
- This state **does** require a subject-specific pedagogy test in order to obtain a teaching license.

Alvernia College

- **400 St. Bernardine Street, Reading, PA 19607-1799**
- **Website:** http://www.alvernia.edu/
- **Private**

LICENSING TEST

Pass rate on state's teacher licensing test for 2002-2003: 81%

State average pass rate: 85%

Arcadia University

- **450 S. Easton Road, Glenside, PA 19038-3295**
- **Website:** http://www.arcadia.edu
- **Private**
- **Degrees offered:** bachelor's, master's, education specialist, Ed.D.

ADMISSIONS

Admissions phone number: **(215) 572-2925**
Admissions email address: *admiss@arcadia.edu*
Application website:
http://www.arcadia.edu/default.asp?t=1&pmid=1&m=74:540 &pid=1445
Application fee: **$35**
Fall 2005 application deadline: 6/15
Test requirements: **GRE**
Test of English as Foreign Language (TOEFL) is required for international students.
Minimum TOEFL score required for paper test: 550
Minimum TOEFL score required for computer test: 213

Fall 2003
Acceptance rate for master's degree programs: 32%
Total 2003 enrollment: 663
Master's degree enrollment: 642
   Teacher preparation program enrollment (master's): 608

Doctoral degree enrollment: 21

FINANCIAL INFORMATION

Financial aid phone number: **(215) 572-2980**
Tuition, 2003-2004 academic year: **$460/credit hour**
Room and board: **$14,000**, Books and supplies: **$300**
Number of other paid appointments: 35

ACADEMIC PROGRAMS

Total full-time tenured or tenure-track faculty (fall 2003): 12, Total part-time faculty (fall 2003): 67
Areas of specialization: curriculum and instruction, elementary teacher education, secondary teacher education, special education, student counseling and personnel services.
Professional development/partnership school(s) are used by students in all of the teaching programs.
During their internships, peer groups of students meet regularly to discuss instructional techniques in all of the teaching programs.
All of the students in their internships are mentored.
Courses that prepare teachers to pass the National Board of Professional Teaching Standards are not offered.
The education program is currently accredited by the Teacher Education Accreditation Council.

LICENSING TEST

Pass rate on state's teacher licensing test for 2002-2003: 90%
State average pass rate: 85%

Bloomsburg University of Pennsylvania

- **400 E. Second St., Bloomsburg, PA 17815**
- **Website:** http://www.bloomu.edu/gradschool/
- **Public**
- **Degrees offered:** bachelor's, master's

ADMISSIONS

Admissions phone number: (570) 389-4015
Admissions email address: *carnold@bloomu.edu*
Application website:
  http://www.bloomu.edu/admissions/apply_gradhtm
Application fee: $30
Fall 2005 application deadline: **rolling**
Test of English as Foreign Language (TOEFL) is required
  for international students.
Minimum TOEFL score required for paper test: 550
Minimum TOEFL score required for computer test: 213

Fall 2003
Total 2003 enrollment: 328
Master's degree enrollment: 328
  Teacher preparation program enrollment (master's): 283

FINANCIAL INFORMATION

Financial aid phone number: (570) 389-4297
Tuition, 2003-2004 academic year: Full-time in-state:
  $307/credit hour; out-of-state: **$491/credit hour**, Part-
  time in-state: **$307/credit hour**; out-of-state: **$491/credit
  hour**
Number of other paid appointments: 124

ACADEMIC PROGRAMS

Areas of specialization: education administration and
  supervision, elementary teacher education, secondary
  teacher education, special education, teacher education.
The education program is currently accredited by the
  National Council for Accreditation of Teacher Education.

LICENSING TEST

Pass rate on state's teacher licensing test for 2002-2003:
  81%
State average pass rate: 85%

Bucknell University

- **701 Moore Avenue, Lewisburg, PA 17837**
- **Website:**
  http://www.departments.bucknell.edu/education/
- **Private**

ADMISSIONS

Admissions phone number: (570) 577-3655
Admissions email address: *gradstds@bucknell.edu*
Application website:
  *http://www.bucknell.edu/Offices_Resources/Offices/
  Graduate_Studies/Admissions/Graduate_Studies_Appli*
Application fee: $25
Fall 2005 application deadline: **rolling**

LICENSING TEST

Pass rate on state's teacher licensing test for 2002-2003:
  100%
State average pass rate: 85%

Cabrini College

- **610 King of Prussia Road, Radnor, PA 19087**
- **Website:**
  http://www.cabrini.edu/Primary/Graduate/default.asp
- **Private**
- **Degrees offered:** bachelor's, master's

ADMISSIONS

Admissions phone number: (610) 902-8592
Admissions email address: *gpsadmit@cabrini.edu*
Application website: *http://www.applyweb.com/aw?cabrini/*
Application fee: $25
Fall 2005 application deadline: **rolling**
Test of English as Foreign Language (TOEFL) is required
  for international students.

Fall 2003
Acceptance rate for master's degree programs: 64%
Total 2003 enrollment: 417
Master's degree enrollment: 417
  Teacher preparation program enrollment (master's): 398

FINANCIAL INFORMATION

Financial aid phone number: (610) 902-8420
Tuition, 2003-2004 academic year: Full-time: **$447/credit
  hour**; Part-time: **$447/credit hour**
Fees: $90

ACADEMIC PROGRAMS

Total full-time tenured or tenure-track faculty (fall 2003): 1
  Total part-time faculty (fall 2003): 21
Areas of specialization: curriculum and instruction, educa-
  tion administration and supervision, education policy,
  elementary teacher education, secondary teacher educa-
  tion, special education.
Professional development/partnership school(s) are used
  by students in all of the teaching programs.
During their internships, peer groups of students meet
  regularly to discuss instructional techniques in all of the
  teaching programs.
All of the students in their internships are mentored.
Courses that prepare teachers to pass the National Board of
  Professional Teaching Standards are not offered.
Teacher preparation programs: Four-year baccalaureate-
  degree program leading to initial licensure that includes
  either a major or minor in education and practice teaching. Master's program preparing college graduates for
  initial licensure; includes practice teaching.

LICENSING TEST

Pass rate on state's teacher licensing test for 2002-2003:
  95%
State average pass rate: 85%

California University of Pennsylvania

- 250 University Avenue, California, PA 15419
- Website: http://www.cup.edu/graduate
- Public
- Degrees offered: bachelor's, master's

ADMISSIONS
Admissions phone number: (724) 938-4187
Admissions email address: *gradschool@cup.edu*
Application fee: $25
Fall 2005 application deadline: rolling
Test of English as Foreign Language (TOEFL) is required for international students.
Minimum TOEFL score required for paper test: 550
Minimum TOEFL score required for computer test: 213

FINANCIAL INFORMATION
Financial aid phone number: (724) 938-4415

LICENSING TEST
Pass rate on state's teacher licensing test for 2002-2003: 82%
State average pass rate: 85%

Carlow College

- 3333 Fifth Avenue, Pittsburgh, PA 15213
- Website: http://www.carlow.edu/
- Private

LICENSING TEST
Pass rate on state's teacher licensing test for 2002-2003: 62%
State average pass rate: 85%

Chatham College

- Woodland Road, Pittsburgh, PA 15232
- Website: http://www.chatham.edu/
- Private

LICENSING TEST
Pass rate on state's teacher licensing test for 2002-2003: 95%
State average pass rate: 85%

Chestnut Hill College

- 9601 Germantown Avenue, Philadelphia, PA 19118-2693
- Website: http://www.chc.edu/
- Private

LICENSING TEST
Pass rate on state's teacher licensing test for 2002-2003: 67%
State average pass rate: 85%

Cheyney University of Pennsylvania

- 701 Market Street, 3rd floor, Philadelphia, PA 19106
- Website: http://www.cheyney.edu
- Public
- Degrees offered: bachelor's, master's

ADMISSIONS
Admissions phone number: (610) 399-2000
Admissions email address: *gstemly@cheyney.edu*
Application website: *http://www.cheyney.edu*
Application fee: $25
Fall 2005 application deadline: 6/30
Test of English as Foreign Language (TOEFL) is required for international students.
Minimum TOEFL score required for paper test: 500

Fall 2003
Acceptance rate for master's degree programs: 60%
Total 2003 enrollment: 285
Master's degree enrollment: 285
    Teacher preparation program enrollment (master's): 164

FINANCIAL INFORMATION
Financial aid phone number: (610) 399-2302
Tuition, 2003-2004 academic year: Full-time in-state: $4,598; out-of-state: $11,496, Part-time in-state: $192/credit hour; out-of-state: $479/credit hour
Fees: $755, Room and board: $5,383, Books and supplies: $1,000, Miscellaneous expenses: $1,889
Number of other paid appointments: 2

ACADEMIC PROGRAMS
Areas of specialization: education administration and supervision, elementary teacher education, secondary teacher education, special education.
The education program is currently accredited by the National Council for Accreditation of Teacher Education.

LICENSING TEST
Pass rate on state's teacher licensing test for 2002-2003: 51%
State average pass rate: 85%

Clarion University of Pennsylvania

- ■ 101 Stevens Hall, Clarion, PA 16214
- ■ **Website:** http://www.clarion.edu
- ■ Public
- ■ **Degrees offered:** bachelor's, master's, education specialist

ADMISSIONS

Admissions phone number: **(814) 393-2337**
Admissions email address: *bdede@clarion.edu*
Application website: *http://www.clarion.edu/graduatestudies/request_form.htm*
Application fee: **$30**
Fall 2005 application deadline: **rolling**
Test requirements: **GRE or MAT**
Test of English as Foreign Language (TOEFL) is required for international students.
Minimum TOEFL score required for paper test: **600**
Minimum TOEFL score required for computer test: **250**

Fall 2003
Acceptance rate for master's degree programs: **76%**
Acceptance rate for education specialist degree programs: **89%**
Total 2003 enrollment: **391**
Master's degree enrollment: **391**
   Teacher preparation program enrollment (master's): **73**

FINANCIAL INFORMATION

Financial aid phone number: **(814) 393-2315**
Tuition, 2003-2004 academic year: Full-time in-state: **$5,518**; out-of-state: **$8,830**, Part-time in-state: **$307/credit hour**; out-of-state: **$491/credit hour**
Fees: **$113/credit hour**, Room and board: **$2,994**, Books and supplies: **$1,800**, Miscellaneous expenses: **$3,919**
Number of fellowships awarded to graduate students during the 2003-2004 academic year: **0**
Number of teaching assistant positions: **0**
Number of research assistant positions: **31**
Number of other paid appointments: **0**

ACADEMIC PROGRAMS

Total full-time tenured or tenure-track faculty (fall 2003): **42**, Total part-time faculty (fall 2003): **0**
Areas of specialization: curriculum and instruction, education administration and supervision, secondary teacher education, special education.
Professional development/partnership school(s) are used by students in some of the teaching programs.
During their internships, peer groups of students meet regularly to discuss instructional techniques in some of the teaching programs.
All of the students in their internships are mentored.
Courses that prepare teachers to pass the National Board of Professional Teaching Standards are not offered.

Teacher preparation programs: Four-year baccalaureate-degree program leading to initial licensure that includes either a major or minor in education and practice teaching. Five-year program leading to initial licensure that results in a baccalaureate degree (with a major or minor in education) plus a master's degree and includes practice teaching.
The education program is currently accredited by the National Council for Accreditation of Teacher Education.

LICENSING TEST

Pass rate on state's teacher licensing test for 2002-2003: **81%**
State average pass rate: **85%**

Delaware Valley College

- ■ 700 East Butler Avenue, Doylestown, PA 18901
- ■ **Website:** http://www.devalcol.edu/edleadership
- ■ Private
- ■ **Degrees offered:** bachelor's, master's, education specialist

ADMISSIONS

Admissions phone number: **(215) 489-4833**
Admissions email address: *Kleml@devalcol.edu*
Application fee: **$50**
Fall 2005 application deadline: **rolling**
Test requirements: **GRE or MAT**
Test of English as Foreign Language (TOEFL) is required for international students.

Fall 2003
Acceptance rate for master's degree programs: **100%**
Average GRE verbal: **320**, Average GRE quantitative: **690**
Total 2003 enrollment: **79**
Master's degree enrollment: **70**
Education specialist degree enrollment: **9**

FINANCIAL INFORMATION

Financial aid phone number: **(215) 489-2297**
Tuition, 2003-2004 academic year: **$385/credit hour**

ACADEMIC PROGRAMS

Areas of specialization: curriculum and instruction, education administration and supervision.
Professional development/partnership school(s) are used by students in some of the teaching programs.
During their internships, peer groups of students meet regularly to discuss instructional techniques in all of the teaching programs.
All of the students in their internships are mentored.
Courses that prepare teachers to pass the National Board of Professional Teaching Standards are not offered.
Teacher preparation programs: Four-year baccalaureate-degree program leading to initial licensure that includes either a major or minor in education and practice teaching.

State average pass rate: 85%

DeSales University

- **2755 Station Avenue, Center Valley, PA 18034-9568**
- **Website:**
  http://www.desales.edu/servlet/RetrievePage?site=Desal
  esu&page=home
- **Private**
- **Degrees offered:** bachelor's, master's

ADMISSIONS
Admissions phone number: **(610) 282-1100**
Admissions email address: *med@desales.edu*
Application website: *http://desales.edu/med*
Application fee: **$35**
Fall 2005 application deadline: **rolling**
Test of English as Foreign Language (TOEFL) is required
  for international students.
Minimum TOEFL score required for paper test: **610**

Fall 2003
Total 2003 enrollment: **156**
Master's degree enrollment: **156**
  Teacher preparation program enrollment (master's): **156**

FINANCIAL INFORMATION
Financial aid phone number: **(610) 282-4443**
Tuition, 2003-2004 academic year: **$320/credit hour**

ACADEMIC PROGRAMS
Total full-time tenured or tenure-track faculty (fall 2003): **7**
Areas of specialization: elementary teacher education, sec-
  ondary teacher education, special education.
Professional development/partnership school(s) are used
  by students in all of the teaching programs.
During their internships, peer groups of students meet
  regularly to discuss instructional techniques in all of the
  teaching programs.
All of the students in their internships are mentored.
Courses that prepare teachers to pass the National Board of
  Professional Teaching Standards are not offered.
Teacher preparation programs: Four-year baccalaureate-
  degree program leading to initial licensure that includes
  either a major or minor in education and practice teaching. Master's program preparing college graduates for
  initial licensure; includes practice teaching.

Drexel University

- **3141 Chestnut Street, Philadelphia, PA 19104**
- **Website:** http://www.drexel.edu/teachered
- **Private**
- **Degrees offered:** bachelor's, master's, education
  specialist, Ph.D.

ADMISSIONS
Admissions phone number: **(215) 895-2400**
Admissions email address: *admissions@drexel.edu*
Application website: *http://www.drexel.edu*
Application fee: **$50**
Fall 2005 application deadline: **rolling**
Test requirements: **GRE**
Test of English as Foreign Language (TOEFL) is required
  for international students.
Minimum TOEFL score required for paper test: **550**
Minimum TOEFL score required for computer test: **213**

Fall 2003
Acceptance rate for master's degree programs: **97%**
Acceptance rate for education specialist degree programs:
  86%
Acceptance rate for doctoral programs: **44%**
Total 2003 enrollment: **310**
Master's degree enrollment: **222**
  Teacher preparation program enrollment (master's): **214**
Education specialist degree enrollment: **45**
Doctoral degree enrollment: **43**

FINANCIAL INFORMATION
Financial aid phone number: **(215) 895-1627**
Tuition, 2003-2004 academic year: Full-time: **$700/credit
  hour**; Part-time: **$700/credit hour**
Fees: **$180**
Number of fellowships awarded to graduate students dur-
  ing the 2003-2004 academic year: **0**
Number of teaching assistant positions: **0**
Number of research assistant positions: **0**
Number of other paid appointments: **0**

ACADEMIC PROGRAMS
Total full-time tenured or tenure-track faculty (fall 2003): **5**
  Total part-time faculty (fall 2003): **30**
Areas of specialization: curriculum and instruction, educa-
  tion administration and supervision, elementary teacher
  education, secondary teacher education.
Professional development/partnership school(s) are used
  by students in all of the teaching programs.
During their internships, peer groups of students meet
  regularly to discuss instructional techniques in all of the
  teaching programs.
All of the students in their internships are mentored.
Courses that prepare teachers to pass the National Board of
  Professional Teaching Standards are not offered.
Teacher preparation programs: Four-year baccalaureate-
  degree program leading to initial licensure that includes

either a major or minor in education and practice teaching. Five-year program leading to initial licensure that results in a baccalaureate degree (with a major or minor in education) plus graduate credit and includes practice teaching. Master's program preparing college graduates for initial licensure; includes practice teaching. Alternative program for college graduates leading to provisional licensure.

LICENSING TEST
Pass rate on state's teacher licensing test for 2002-2003: 97%
State average pass rate: 85%

Duquesne University

■ 600 Forbes Avenue, Pittsburgh, PA 15282
■ Website: http://www.duq.edu/
■ Private

LICENSING TEST
Pass rate on state's teacher licensing test for 2002-2003: 94%
State average pass rate: 85%

Eastern University

■ 1300 Eagle Road, St. Davids, PA 19087-3696
■ Website: http://www.eastern.edu/
■ Private

LICENSING TEST
Pass rate on state's teacher licensing test for 2002-2003: 81%
State average pass rate: 85%

East Stroudsburg University of Pennsylvania

■ 200 Prospect Street, East Stroudsburg, PA 18301-2999
■ Website: http://www.esu.edu
■ Public

LICENSING TEST
Pass rate on state's teacher licensing test for 2002-2003: 87%
State average pass rate: 85%

Edinboro University of Pennsylvania

■ Office of Graduate Studies and Research, Reeder Hall, Edinboro University of PA, Edinboro, PA 16444
■ Website: http://www.edinboro.edu
■ Public
■ Degrees offered: bachelor's, master's, education specialist

ADMISSIONS
Admissions phone number: (814) 732-2856
Admissions email address: *gradstudies@edinboro.edu*
Application website:
   http://www.edinboro.edu/cwis/acaff/gradstudy/Pages/ graduate_admissions_form.htm
Application fee: $25
Fall 2005 application deadline: **rolling**
Test requirements: **GRE or MAT**
Test of English as Foreign Language (TOEFL) is required for international students.
Minimum TOEFL score required for paper test: 550
Minimum TOEFL score required for computer test: 213

Fall 2003
Acceptance rate for master's degree programs: 57%
Acceptance rate for education specialist degree programs: 62%
Average GRE verbal: 444, Average GRE quantitative: 491, Average GRE analytical: 537
Total 2003 enrollment: 649
Master's degree enrollment: 482
   Teacher preparation program enrollment (master's): 283
Education specialist degree enrollment: 167

FINANCIAL INFORMATION
Financial aid phone number: (814) 732-5555
Tuition, 2003-2004 academic year: Full-time in-state: $307/credit hour; out-of-state: $491/credit hour, Part-time in-state: $307/credit hour; out-of-state: $491/credit hour
Room and board: $5,086, Books and supplies: $750, Miscellaneous expenses: $1,200
Number of research assistant positions: 150

ACADEMIC PROGRAMS
Total full-time tenured or tenure-track faculty (fall 2003): 63, Total part-time faculty (fall 2003): 36
Areas of specialization: curriculum and instruction, education administration and supervision, educational psychology, elementary teacher education, higher education administration, secondary teacher education, special education, student counseling and personnel services.
Professional development/partnership school(s) are used by students in all of the teaching programs.

During their internships, peer groups of students meet regularly to discuss instructional techniques in none of the teaching programs.

All of the students in their internships are mentored.

Courses that prepare teachers to pass the National Board of Professional Teaching Standards are offered.

Teacher preparation programs: Four-year baccalaureate-degree program leading to initial licensure that includes either a major or minor in education and practice teaching. Master's program preparing college graduates for initial licensure; includes practice teaching.

The education program is currently accredited by the National Council for Accreditation of Teacher Education.

LICENSING TEST

Pass rate on state's teacher licensing test for 2002-2003: **85%**
State average pass rate: **85%**

Gannon University

- University Square, Erie, PA 16541
- Website: http://www.gannon.edu/
- Private

LICENSING TEST

Pass rate on state's teacher licensing test for 2002-2003: **74%**
State average pass rate: **85%**

Geneva College

- 3200 Geneva Avenue, Beaver Falls, PA 15010
- Website: http://www.geneva.edu/
- Private
- Degrees offered: bachelor's, master's

ACADEMIC PROGRAMS

Areas of specialization: higher education administration, special education, student counseling and personnel services.

LICENSING TEST

Pass rate on state's teacher licensing test for 2002-2003: **86%**
State average pass rate: **85%**

Gwynedd-Mercy College

- 1325 Sumneytown Pike, Gwynedd Valley, PA 19437
- Website: http://www.gmc.edu/academic/schools/education/academics/graduate.htm
- Private
- Degrees offered: bachelor's, master's

ADMISSIONS

Admissions phone number: **(215) 646-7300**
Application website:
   http://www.gmc.edu/admissions/grad_edu_app.html
Fall 2005 application deadline: **rolling**
Test requirements: **GRE or MAT**

Fall 2003

Total 2003 enrollment: **296**
Master's degree enrollment: **296**
   Teacher preparation program enrollment (master's): **86**

FINANCIAL INFORMATION

Tuition, 2003-2004 academic year: **$365/credit hour**

ACADEMIC PROGRAMS

Total full-time tenured or tenure-track faculty (fall 2003): **1**
   Total part-time faculty (fall 2003): **40**
Areas of specialization: curriculum and instruction, education administration and supervision, education policy, elementary teacher education, higher education administration, special education, student counseling and personnel services.

Professional development/partnership school(s) are used by students in all of the teaching programs.

During their internships, peer groups of students meet regularly to discuss instructional techniques in all of the teaching programs.

All of the students in their internships are mentored.

Courses that prepare teachers to pass the National Board of Professional Teaching Standards are offered.

Teacher preparation programs: Four-year baccalaureate-degree program leading to initial licensure that includes either a major or minor in education and practice teaching. Five-year program leading to initial licensure that results in a baccalaureate degree (with a major or minor in education) plus graduate credit and includes practice teaching. Five-year program leading to initial licensure that results in a baccalaureate degree (with a major or minor in education) plus a master's degree and includes practice teaching. Master's program preparing college graduates for initial licensure; includes practice teaching. Alternative program for college graduates leading to provisional licensure.

LICENSING TEST

Pass rate on state's teacher licensing test for 2002-2003: **96%**
State average pass rate: **85%**

Holy Family University

- Grant and Frankford Avenues, Philadelphia, PA 19114
- Website: http://www.hfc.edu/
- Private

LICENSING TEST

Pass rate on state's teacher licensing test for 2002-2003: **74%**
State average pass rate: **85%**

Indiana University of Pennsylvania

- 104 Stouffer Hall, Indiana, PA 15705-1083
- **Website:** http://www.iup.edu/graduate
- Public

ADMISSIONS

Admissions phone number: **(724) 357-2222**
Admissions email address: *graduate-admissions@iup.edu*
Application website: *http://www.iup.edu/graduate/admit*
Test requirements: **GRE or MAT**
Test of English as Foreign Language (TOEFL) is required for international students.
Minimum TOEFL score required for paper test: **500**

FINANCIAL INFORMATION

Financial aid phone number: **(724) 357-2218**

LICENSING TEST

Pass rate on state's teacher licensing test for 2002-2003: **81%**
State average pass rate: **85%**

King's College

- 133 North River Street, Wilkes-Barre, PA 18711
- **Website:** http://www.kings.edu
- Private
- **Degrees offered:** bachelor's, master's

ADMISSIONS

Admissions phone number: **(570) 208-5991**
Admissions email address: *eslott@kings.edu*
Application fee: **$35**
Fall 2005 application deadline: **rolling**
Test of English as Foreign Language (TOEFL) is required for international students.

Fall 2003
Total 2003 enrollment: **49**
Master's degree enrollment: **49**
    Teacher preparation program enrollment (master's): **49**

FINANCIAL INFORMATION

Financial aid phone number: **(570) 208-5868**
Tuition, 2003-2004 academic year: **$560/credit hour**

LICENSING TEST

Pass rate on state's teacher licensing test for 2002-2003: **83%**
State average pass rate: **85%**

Kutztown University of Pennsylvania

- 15200 Kutztown Road, Kutztown, PA 19530
- **Website:** http://www.kutztown.edu
- Public
- **Degrees offered:** bachelor's, master's

ADMISSIONS

Admissions phone number: **(610) 683-4201**
Admissions email address: *Graduate@kutztown.edu*
Application website:
    http://www.kutztown.edu/academics/grduate/index.shtml
Application fee: **$35**
Fall 2005 application deadline: **3/1**
Test requirements: **GRE**
Test of English as Foreign Language (TOEFL) is required for international students.
Minimum TOEFL score required for paper test: **550**

Fall 2003
Acceptance rate for master's degree programs: **67%**
Acceptance rate for education specialist degree programs: **67%**
Average GRE verbal: **442**, Average GRE quantitative: **493**, Average GRE analytical: **544**
Total 2003 enrollment: **740**
Master's degree enrollment: **673**
    Teacher preparation program enrollment (master's): **405**
Education specialist degree enrollment: **67**

FINANCIAL INFORMATION

Financial aid phone number: **(610) 683-4027**
Tuition, 2003-2004 academic year: Full-time in-state: **$5,518**; out-of-state: **$8,830**, Part-time in-state: **$307/credit hour**; out-of-state: **$491/credit hour**
Fees: **$1,129**, Room and board: **$5,110**, Books and supplies: **$500**, Miscellaneous expenses: **$1,200**
Number of research assistant positions: **60**

ACADEMIC PROGRAMS

Total full-time tenured or tenure-track faculty (fall 2003): **334**, Total part-time faculty (fall 2003): **123**
Areas of specialization: curriculum and instruction, elementary teacher education, secondary teacher education, student counseling and personnel services.
Professional development/partnership school(s) are used by students in some of the teaching programs.
During their internships, peer groups of students meet regularly to discuss instructional techniques in all of the teaching programs.
All of the students in their internships are mentored.
Courses that prepare teachers to pass the National Board of Professional Teaching Standards are offered.
Teacher preparation programs: Four-year baccalaureate-degree program leading to initial licensure that includes either a major or minor in education and practice teach-

ing. Master's program preparing college graduates for initial licensure; includes practice teaching.

The education program is currently accredited by the National Council for Accreditation of Teacher Education.

LICENSING TEST

Pass rate on state's teacher licensing test for 2002-2003: 81%
State average pass rate: 85%

La Salle University

- 1900 W. Olney Ave., Philadelphia, PA 19141
- Website: http://www.lasalle.edu/academ/grad/?referrer= Homepage%20
- Private
- Degrees offered: bachelor's, master's, education specialist

ADMISSIONS

Admissions phone number: (215) 951-1196
Admissions email address: *mosca@lasalle.edu*
Application website: *http://www.lasalle.edu/admiss/ undergrad2.htm*
Application fee: $35
Fall 2005 application deadline: rolling
Test requirements: GRE or MAT
Test of English as Foreign Language (TOEFL) is required for international students.
Minimum TOEFL score required for computer test: 213

Fall 2003

Acceptance rate for master's degree programs: 90%
Average MAT: 47
Total 2003 enrollment: 208
Master's degree enrollment: 208
    Teacher preparation program enrollment (master's): 208

FINANCIAL INFORMATION

Financial aid phone number: (215) 951-1974
Tuition, 2003-2004 academic year: $498/credit hour
Number of teaching assistant positions: 0
Number of research assistant positions: 12
Number of other paid appointments: 0

ACADEMIC PROGRAMS

Total full-time tenured or tenure-track faculty (fall 2003): 15, Total part-time faculty (fall 2003): 10
Areas of specialization: elementary teacher education, secondary teacher education, special education.
Professional development/partnership school(s) are used by students in some of the teaching programs.
During their internships, peer groups of students meet regularly to discuss instructional techniques in all of the teaching programs.
All of the students in their internships are mentored.
Courses that prepare teachers to pass the National Board of Professional Teaching Standards are not offered.

Teacher preparation programs: Four-year baccalaureate-degree program leading to initial licensure that includes either a major or minor in education and practice teaching. Master's program preparing college graduates for initial licensure; includes practice teaching.

LICENSING TEST

Pass rate on state's teacher licensing test for 2002-2003: 85%
State average pass rate: 85%

Lebanon Valley College

- P.O. Box R 101 N College Avenue, Annville, PA 17003
- Website: http://www.lvc.edu/index.aspx?bhiw=907
- Private
- Degrees offered: bachelor's, master's

ADMISSIONS

Fall 2003

Acceptance rate for master's degree programs: 100%
Total 2003 enrollment: 140
Master's degree enrollment: 140
    Teacher preparation program enrollment (master's): 140

FINANCIAL INFORMATION

Tuition, 2003-2004 academic year: $335/credit hour
Books and supplies: $500
Number of fellowships awarded to graduate students during the 2003-2004 academic year: 0
Number of teaching assistant positions: 0
Number of research assistant positions: 0
Number of other paid appointments: 0

ACADEMIC PROGRAMS

Total full-time tenured or tenure-track faculty (fall 2003): 16, Total part-time faculty (fall 2003): 5
Professional development/partnership school(s) are used by students in none of the teaching programs.
During their internships, peer groups of students meet regularly to discuss instructional techniques in some of the teaching programs.
All of the students in their internships are mentored.
Courses that prepare teachers to pass the National Board of Professional Teaching Standards are offered.

LICENSING TEST

Pass rate on state's teacher licensing test for 2002-2003: 88%
State average pass rate: 85%

Lehigh University

- 111 Research Drive, Bethlehem, PA 18015
- **Website:** http://www.lehigh.edu/collegeofeducation
- Private
- **Degrees offered:** master's, education specialist, Ph.D., Ed.D.
- **Overall rank in the 2005 U.S. News education schools with doctoral programs:** 38

ADMISSIONS

Admissions phone number: **(610) 758-3231**
Admissions email address: *ineduc@lehigh.edu*
Application fee: **$50**
Fall 2005 application deadline: **rolling**
Test requirements: **GRE or MAT**
Test of English as Foreign Language (TOEFL) is required for international students.
Minimum TOEFL score required for paper test: **600**
Minimum TOEFL score required for computer test: **250**

Fall 2003
Acceptance rate for master's degree programs: **69%**
Acceptance rate for education specialist degree programs: **22%**
Acceptance rate for doctoral programs: **17%**
Average GRE verbal: **543**, Average GRE quantitative: **632**, Average GRE analytical: **647**
Total 2003 enrollment: **550**
Master's degree enrollment: **390**
    Teacher preparation program enrollment (master's): **90**
Education specialist degree enrollment: **20**
Doctoral degree enrollment: **140**

FINANCIAL INFORMATION

Financial aid phone number: **(610) 758-3181**
Tuition, 2003-2004 academic year: Full-time: **$490/credit hour**; Part-time: **$490/credit hour**
Fees: **$200**, Room and board: **$7,820**, Books and supplies: **$1,600**, Miscellaneous expenses: **$1,250**
Number of fellowships awarded to graduate students during the 2003-2004 academic year: **2**
Number of teaching assistant positions: **0**
Number of research assistant positions: **69**
Number of other paid appointments: **114**

ACADEMIC PROGRAMS

Total full-time tenured or tenure-track faculty (fall 2003): **28**, Total part-time faculty (fall 2003): **20**
Areas of specialization: curriculum and instruction, education administration and supervision, educational psychology, elementary teacher education, secondary teacher education, special education, student counseling and personnel services.
Professional development/partnership school(s) are used by students in some of the teaching programs.

During their internships, peer groups of students meet regularly to discuss instructional techniques in all of the teaching programs.
All of the students in their internships are mentored.
Courses that prepare teachers to pass the National Board of Professional Teaching Standards are not offered.
Teacher preparation programs: Master's degree in education, including internship/practice teaching and preparation for initial licensure. Education minor for undergraduate students.

LICENSING TEST

Pass rate on state's teacher licensing test for 2002-2003: **96%**
State average pass rate: **85%**

Lincoln University

- PO Box 179, Lincoln University, PA 19352
- **Website:** http://www.lincoln.edu/
- Public

ADMISSIONS

Application fee: **$50**

Fall 2003
Total 2003 enrollment: **84**
Master's degree enrollment: **84**
    Teacher preparation program enrollment (master's): **80**

FINANCIAL INFORMATION

Tuition, 2003-2004 academic year: Full-time in-state: **$7,004**; out-of-state: **$12,514**, Part-time in-state: **$349/credit hour**; out-of-state: **$625/credit hour**
Fees: **$904**
Number of teaching assistant positions: **3**

ACADEMIC PROGRAMS

Professional development/partnership school(s) are used by students in all of the teaching programs.
During their internships, peer groups of students meet regularly to discuss instructional techniques in all of the teaching programs.
All of the students in their internships are mentored.
Courses that prepare teachers to pass the National Board of Professional Teaching Standards are not offered.

LICENSING TEST

Pass rate on state's teacher licensing test for 2002-2003: **75%**
State average pass rate: **85%**

Lock Haven University of Pennsylvania

- North Fairview Street, Lock Haven, PA 17745
- **Website:** http://www.lhup.edu
- Public
- **Degrees offered:** bachelor's, master's

ADMISSIONS

Admissions phone number: **(570) 893-2027**
Admissions email address: *admissions@lhup.edu*
Application website: *http://www.lhup.edu/academic/ acad_affairs/gradedu_admission.htm*
Application fee: **$25**
Fall 2005 application deadline: **rolling**

Fall 2003
Acceptance rate for master's degree programs: **97%**
Total 2003 enrollment: **85**
Master's degree enrollment: **85**
   Teacher preparation program enrollment (master's): **14**

FINANCIAL INFORMATION

Financial aid phone number: **(570) 893-2344**
Tuition, 2003-2004 academic year: Full-time in-state: **$5,581**; out-of-state: **$8,830**, Part-time in-state: **$307/credit hour**; out-of-state: **$491/credit hour**
Fees: **$1,164**, Room and board: **$4,936**, Books and supplies: **$900**

ACADEMIC PROGRAMS

Total full-time tenured or tenure-track faculty (fall 2003): **5**
Areas of specialization: curriculum and instruction.
Professional development/partnership school(s) are used by students in all of the teaching programs.
During their internships, peer groups of students meet regularly to discuss instructional techniques in all of the teaching programs.
All of the students in their internships are mentored.
Courses that prepare teachers to pass the National Board of Professional Teaching Standards are offered.
Teacher preparation programs: Four-year baccalaureate-degree program leading to initial licensure that includes either a major or minor in education and practice teaching. Master's program preparing college graduates for initial licensure; includes practice teaching.
The education program is currently accredited by the National Council for Accreditation of Teacher Education.

LICENSING TEST

Pass rate on state's teacher licensing test for 2002-2003: **100%**
State average pass rate: **85%**

Mansfield University of Pennsylvania

- Academy, Mansfield, PA 16933
- **Website:** http://www.mansfield.edu
- Public
- **Degrees offered:** bachelor's, master's

ADMISSIONS

Admissions phone number: **(570) 662-4243**
Admissions email address: *admissns@mansfield.edu*
Application website: *http://www.mansfield.edu*
Application fee: **$25**
Fall 2005 application deadline: **rolling**

Fall 2003
Total 2003 enrollment: **352**

FINANCIAL INFORMATION

Financial aid phone number: **(570) 662-4129**

LICENSING TEST

Pass rate on state's teacher licensing test for 2002-2003: **76%**
State average pass rate: **85%**

Marywood University

- 2300 Adams Avenue, Scranton, PA 18509
- **Website:** http://www.marywood.edu/
- Private

LICENSING TEST

Pass rate on state's teacher licensing test for 2002-2003: **87%**
State average pass rate: **85%**

Mercyhurst College

- 501 East 38th Street, Erie, PA 16546
- **Website:** http://www.mercyhurst.edu
- Private
- **Degrees offered:** bachelor's, master's

ADMISSIONS

Admissions phone number: **(814) 824-2294**
Admissions email address: *lcohen@mercyhurst.edu*
Application website:
   http://www.mercyhurst.edu/Academics/AC_42.htm
Application fee: **$35**
Fall 2005 application deadline: **rolling**
Test of English as Foreign Language (TOEFL) is required for international students.
Minimum TOEFL score required for computer test: **213**

Fall 2003

Acceptance rate for master's degree programs: **97%**
Total 2003 enrollment: **83**
Master's degree enrollment: **83**
   Teacher preparation program enrollment (master's): **83**

FINANCIAL INFORMATION

Financial aid phone number: **(814) 824-2288**
Tuition, 2003-2004 academic year: Full-time: **$350/credit hour**; Part-time: **$350/credit hour**
Room and board: **$6,414**, Books and supplies: **$885**, Miscellaneous expenses: **$5,254**
Number of other paid appointments: **25**

ACADEMIC PROGRAMS

Total full-time tenured or tenure-track faculty (fall 2003): **1**
   Total part-time faculty (fall 2003): **2**
Areas of specialization: curriculum and instruction, special education.
Professional development/partnership school(s) are used by students in all of the teaching programs.
During their internships, peer groups of students meet regularly to discuss instructional techniques in none of the teaching programs.
All of the students in their internships are mentored.
Courses that prepare teachers to pass the National Board of Professional Teaching Standards are not offered.
Teacher preparation programs: Four-year baccalaureate-degree program leading to initial licensure that includes either a major or minor in education and practice teaching. Master's program preparing college graduates for initial licensure; includes practice teaching.

LICENSING TEST

Pass rate on state's teacher licensing test for 2002-2003: **86%**
State average pass rate: **85%**

Millersville University of Pennsylvania

- PO Box 1002, Millersville, PA 17551
- **Website:** http://muweb.millersville.edu/
- Public
- **Degrees offered:** bachelor's, master's, education specialist

ADMISSIONS

Admissions phone number: **(717) 872-3030**
Application website: *http://muweb.millersville.edu/ ~graduate/gradadm.html*
Application fee: **$30**
Fall 2005 application deadline: **3/1**
Test of English as Foreign Language (TOEFL) is required for international students.
Minimum TOEFL score required for paper test: **500**
Minimum TOEFL score required for computer test: **173**

Fall 2003

Acceptance rate for master's degree programs: **79%**
Total 2003 enrollment: **325**
Master's degree enrollment: **325**
   Teacher preparation program enrollment (master's): **236**
Education specialist degree enrollment: **0**

FINANCIAL INFORMATION

Financial aid phone number: **(717) 872-3026**
Tuition, 2003-2004 academic year: Full-time in-state: **$5,518**; out-of-state: **$8,830**, Part-time in-state: **$307/credit hour**; out-of-state: **$491/credit hour**
Fees: **$1,108**, Room and board: **$5,450**, Books and supplies: **$800**

ACADEMIC PROGRAMS

Total full-time tenured or tenure-track faculty (fall 2003): **86**
Areas of specialization: curriculum and instruction, education administration and supervision, education policy, educational psychology, elementary teacher education, higher education administration, secondary teacher education, special education, student counseling and personnel services.
Professional development/partnership school(s) are used by students in some of the teaching programs.
During their internships, peer groups of students meet regularly to discuss instructional techniques in some of the teaching programs.
All of the students in their internships are mentored.
Courses that prepare teachers to pass the National Board of Professional Teaching Standards are not offered.
Teacher preparation programs: Four-year baccalaureate-degree program leading to initial licensure that includes either a major or minor in education and practice teaching. Master's program preparing college graduates for initial licensure; includes practice teaching. Alternative program for college graduates leading to provisional licensure.
The education program is currently accredited by the National Council for Accreditation of Teacher Education.

LICENSING TEST

Pass rate on state's teacher licensing test for 2002-2003: **90%**
State average pass rate: **85%**

Moravian College

- 1200 Main Street, Bethlehem, PA 18018
- **Website:** http://www.moravian.edu/
- Private

LICENSING TEST

Pass rate on state's teacher licensing test for 2002-2003: **86%**
State average pass rate: **85%**

Neumann College

■ One Neumann Drive, Aston, PA 19014
■ Website: http://www.neumann.edu
■ Private
■ Degrees offered: bachelor's, master's

ADMISSIONS
Admissions phone number: **(610) 558-5612**
Application website: *http://www.neumann.edu*
Application fee: **$50**
Fall 2005 application deadline: **rolling**
Minimum TOEFL score required for paper test: **550**
Minimum TOEFL score required for computer test: **213**

Fall 2003
Acceptance rate for master's degree programs: **96%**
Total 2003 enrollment: **199**
Master's degree enrollment: **199**
   Teacher preparation program enrollment (master's): **199**

FINANCIAL INFORMATION
Financial aid phone number: **(610) 558-5521**
Tuition, 2003-2004 academic year: Full-time: **$8,280**; Part-time: **$460/credit hour**

ACADEMIC PROGRAMS
Total full-time tenured or tenure-track faculty (fall 2003): **72**, Total part-time faculty (fall 2003): **152**
Areas of specialization: higher education administration.
Professional development/partnership school(s) are used by students in all of the teaching programs.
During their internships, peer groups of students meet regularly to discuss instructional techniques in all of the teaching programs.
All of the students in their internships are mentored.
Courses that prepare teachers to pass the National Board of Professional Teaching Standards are offered.

LICENSING TEST
Pass rate on state's teacher licensing test for 2002-2003: **55%**
State average pass rate: **85%**

Pennsylvania State University–Great Valley

■ 30 East Swedesford Road, Malvern, PA 19355-1443
■ Website: http://www.gv.psu.edu/
■ Public

Pennsylvania State University–Harrisburg

■ 777 West Harrisburg Pike, Middletown, PA 17057
■ Website: http://www.hbg.psu.edu/hbg/admiss99.html
■ Public
■ Degrees offered: bachelor's, master's, Ed.D.

ADMISSIONS
Admissions phone number: **(717) 948-6250**
Admissions email address: *hbgadmit@psu.edu*
Application website: *http://www.hbg.psu.edu/hbg/admissapps.html*
Application fee: **$45**
Fall 2005 application deadline: **7/1**
Test of English as Foreign Language (TOEFL) is required for international students.
Minimum TOEFL score required for paper test: **550**
Minimum TOEFL score required for computer test: **213**

Fall 2003
Acceptance rate for master's degree programs: **87%**
Acceptance rate for doctoral programs: **50%**
Average GRE verbal: **535**, Average GRE quantitative: **532**
Total 2003 enrollment: **767**
Master's degree enrollment: **713**
   Teacher preparation program enrollment (master's): **713**
Doctoral degree enrollment: **54**

FINANCIAL INFORMATION
Financial aid phone number: **(717) 948-6307**
Tuition, 2003-2004 academic year: Full-time in-state: **$10,010**; out-of-state: **$16,512**, Part-time in-state: **$417/credit hour**; out-of-state: **$688/credit hour**
Fees: **$194**, Room and board: **$7,290**, Books and supplies: **$936**, Miscellaneous expenses: **$3,006**
Number of fellowships awarded to graduate students during the 2003-2004 academic year: **0**
Number of teaching assistant positions: **0**
Number of research assistant positions: **3**
Number of other paid appointments: **0**

ACADEMIC PROGRAMS
Total full-time tenured or tenure-track faculty (fall 2003): **10**, Total part-time faculty (fall 2003): **40**
Areas of specialization: curriculum and instruction, elementary teacher education, secondary teacher education.
Professional development/partnership school(s) are used by students in some of the teaching programs.
During their internships, peer groups of students meet regularly to discuss instructional techniques in all of the teaching programs.
All of the students in their internships are mentored.
Courses that prepare teachers to pass the National Board of Professional Teaching Standards are not offered.

Teacher preparation programs: Four-year baccalaureate-degree program leading to initial licensure that includes either a major or minor in education and practice teaching.

LICENSING TEST

Pass rate on state's teacher licensing test for 2002-2003: 86%

State average pass rate: 85%

Penn State University–University Park

- 274 Chambers Building, University Park, PA 16802-3206
- Website: http://www.ed.psu.edu
- Public
- Degrees offered: bachelor's, master's, Ph.D., Ed.D.
- Overall rank in the 2005 U.S. News education schools with doctoral programs: 28
- Overall rank in the 2005 U.S. News education school specialty rankings: administration/supervision: 8, counseling/personnel: 11, curriculum/instruction: 14, education policy: 11, educational psychology: 21, elementary education: 17, higher education administration: 3, vocational/technical: 2

ADMISSIONS

Admissions phone number: (814) 865-1795
Admissions email address: gadm@psu.edu
Application website: http://www.gradsch.psu.edu/enroll/program.cfm
Application fee: $45
Fall 2005 application deadline: rolling
Test requirements: GRE or MAT
Test of English as Foreign Language (TOEFL) is required for international students.
Minimum TOEFL score required for paper test: 550
Minimum TOEFL score required for computer test: 213

Fall 2003

Acceptance rate for master's degree programs: 60%
Acceptance rate for doctoral programs: 43%
Average GRE verbal: 488, Average GRE quantitative: 575, Average GRE analytical: 563, Average MAT: 53
Total 2003 enrollment: 897
Master's degree enrollment: 293
   Teacher preparation program enrollment (master's): 154
Doctoral degree enrollment: 604

FINANCIAL INFORMATION

Financial aid phone number: (814) 863-1489
Tuition, 2003-2004 academic year: Full-time in-state: $10,010; out-of-state: $19,830, Part-time in-state: $417/credit hour; out-of-state: $826/credit hour
Fees: $410, Room and board: $8,250, Books and supplies: $1,100, Miscellaneous expenses: $925
Number of fellowships awarded to graduate students during the 2003-2004 academic year: 33

Number of teaching assistant positions: 140
Number of research assistant positions: 40
Number of other paid appointments: 73

ACADEMIC PROGRAMS

Total full-time tenured or tenure-track faculty (fall 2003): 112, Total part-time faculty (fall 2003): 76
Areas of specialization: curriculum and instruction, education administration and supervision, education policy, educational psychology, elementary teacher education, higher education administration, secondary teacher education, special education, student counseling and personnel services, teacher education.
Professional development/partnership school(s) are used by students in all of the teaching programs.
During their internships, peer groups of students meet regularly to discuss instructional techniques in all of the teaching programs.
All of the students in their internships are mentored.
Courses that prepare teachers to pass the National Board of Professional Teaching Standards are not offered.
Teacher preparation programs: Four-year baccalaureate-degree program leading to initial licensure that includes either a major or minor in education and practice teaching. Master's program preparing college graduates for initial licensure; includes practice teaching.
The education program is currently accredited by the National Council for Accreditation of Teacher Education.

LICENSING TEST

Pass rate on state's teacher licensing test for 2002-2003: 91%

State average pass rate: 85%

Point Park College

- 201 Wood Street, Pittsburgh, PA 15222
- Website: http://www.ppc.edu/
- Private

LICENSING TEST

Pass rate on state's teacher licensing test for 2002-2003: 62%

State average pass rate: 85%

Robert Morris University

- 6001 University Boulevard, Moon Township, PA 15108-1189
- Website: http://www.rmu.edu
- Private
- Degrees offered: bachelor's, master's

ADMISSIONS

Admissions phone number: (412) 262-8235
Admissions email address: enrollmentoffice@rmu.edu

Application website: *http://www.rmu.edu*
Application fee: **$35**
Fall 2005 application deadline: 8/1
Test of English as Foreign Language (TOEFL) is required
   for international students.
Minimum TOEFL score required for paper test: 550
Minimum TOEFL score required for computer test: 213

Fall 2003
Acceptance rate for master's degree programs: 98%
Total 2003 enrollment: 112
Master's degree enrollment: 112
   Teacher preparation program enrollment (master's): 112
Education specialist degree enrollment: 0
Doctoral degree enrollment: 0

FINANCIAL INFORMATION
Financial aid phone number: **(412) 299-2450**
Tuition, 2003-2004 academic year: **$420/credit hour**
Room and board: **$6,954**, Books and supplies: **$1,000**,
   Miscellaneous expenses: **$1,000**
Number of fellowships awarded to graduate students dur-
   ing the 2003-2004 academic year: 0
Number of teaching assistant positions: 0
Number of research assistant positions: 0
Number of other paid appointments: 0

ACADEMIC PROGRAMS
Total full-time tenured or tenure-track faculty (fall 2003): 6
   Total part-time faculty (fall 2003): 11
Areas of specialization: curriculum and instruction, sec-
   ondary teacher education.
Professional development/partnership school(s) are used
   by students in all of the teaching programs.
During their internships, peer groups of students meet
   regularly to discuss instructional techniques in all of the
   teaching programs.
All of the students in their internships are mentored.
Courses that prepare teachers to pass the National Board of
   Professional Teaching Standards are not offered.
Teacher preparation programs: Four-year baccalaureate-
   degree program leading to initial licensure that includes
   either a major or minor in education and practice teaching. Master's program preparing college graduates for
   initial licensure; includes practice teaching.

LICENSING TEST
Pass rate on state's teacher licensing test for 2002-2003:
   88%
State average pass rate: 85%

Rosemont College

■ **1400 Montgomery Avenue, Rosemont, PA 19010-1699**
■ **Website:** http://www.rosemont.edu/
■ **Private**

LICENSING TEST
Pass rate on state's teacher licensing test for 2002-2003:
   93%
State average pass rate: 85%

Seton Hill College

■ **1 Seton Hill Drive, Greensburg, PA 15601**
■ **Website:** http://www.setonhill.edu
■ **Private**
■ **Degrees offered:** bachelor's, master's

ADMISSIONS
Admissions phone number: **(724) 838-4283**
Admissions email address: *gadmit@setonhill.edu*
Application website:
   http://www.setonhill.edu/admissions2/index.cfm
Application fee: **$30**
Fall 2005 application deadline: **rolling**
Test of English as Foreign Language (TOEFL) is required
   for international students.
Minimum TOEFL score required for paper test: 550
Minimum TOEFL score required for computer test: 213

Fall 2003
Acceptance rate for master's degree programs: 92%
Total 2003 enrollment: 97
Master's degree enrollment: 97
   Teacher preparation program enrollment (master's): 97

FINANCIAL INFORMATION
Financial aid phone number: **(724) 838-4293**
Tuition, 2003-2004 academic year: Full-time: **$525/credit
   hour**; Part-time: **$525/credit hour**
Fees: **$100**, Room and board: **$6,100**, Books and supplies:
   $200, Miscellaneous expenses: **$75**
Number of fellowships awarded to graduate students dur-
   ing the 2003-2004 academic year: 0
Number of teaching assistant positions: 0
Number of research assistant positions: 0
Number of other paid appointments: 0

ACADEMIC PROGRAMS
Total full-time tenured or tenure-track faculty (fall 2003): 6
   Total part-time faculty (fall 2003): 20
Areas of specialization: elementary teacher education, spe-
   cial education.
Professional development/partnership school(s) are used
   by students in none of the teaching programs.
During their internships, peer groups of students meet
   regularly to discuss instructional techniques in all of the
   teaching programs.
All of the students in their internships are mentored.
Courses that prepare teachers to pass the National Board of
   Professional Teaching Standards are not offered.
Teacher preparation programs: Master's program preparing college graduates for initial licensure; includes practice teaching.

LICENSING TEST

Pass rate on state's teacher licensing test for 2002-2003: 79%

State average pass rate: 85%

Shippensburg University of Pennsylvania

- 1871 Old Main Drive, Shippensburg, PA 17257-2299
- Website: http://www.ship.edu
- Public
- Degrees offered: bachelor's, master's

ADMISSIONS

Admissions phone number: (717) 477-1213
Admissions email address: *gradsch@ship.edu*
Application website: *http://www.applyweb.com/apply/ship*
Application fee: $30
Fall 2005 application deadline: 6/1
Test requirements: GRE or MAT
Test of English as Foreign Language (TOEFL) is required for international students.
Minimum TOEFL score required for paper test: 560
Minimum TOEFL score required for computer test: 220

Fall 2003

Acceptance rate for master's degree programs: 50%
Average GRE verbal: 436, Average GRE quantitative: 537, Average GRE analytical: 603
Total 2003 enrollment: 467
Master's degree enrollment: 467
   Teacher preparation program enrollment (master's): 202
Education specialist degree enrollment: 0
Doctoral degree enrollment: 0

FINANCIAL INFORMATION

Financial aid phone number: (717) 477-1131
Tuition, 2003-2004 academic year: Full-time in-state: $5,518; out-of-state: $8,830, Part-time in-state: $307/credit hour; out-of-state: $491/credit hour
Fees: $908, Room and board: $6,135, Books and supplies: $900, Miscellaneous expenses: $1,717
Number of fellowships awarded to graduate students during the 2003-2004 academic year: 0
Number of teaching assistant positions: 0
Number of research assistant positions: 7
Number of other paid appointments: 0

ACADEMIC PROGRAMS

Total full-time tenured or tenure-track faculty (fall 2003): 4
   Total part-time faculty (fall 2003): 3
Areas of specialization: curriculum and instruction, education administration and supervision, elementary teacher education, secondary teacher education, special education, student counseling and personnel services.
Professional development/partnership school(s) are used by students in all of the teaching programs.

During their internships, peer groups of students meet regularly to discuss instructional techniques in some of the teaching programs.
All of the students in their internships are mentored.
Courses that prepare teachers to pass the National Board of Professional Teaching Standards are not offered.
Teacher preparation programs: Four-year baccalaureate-degree program leading to initial licensure that includes either a major or minor in education and practice teaching. The education program is currently accredited by the National Council for Accreditation of Teacher Education.

LICENSING TEST

Pass rate on state's teacher licensing test for 2002-2003: 89%
State average pass rate: 85%

Slippery Rock University of Pennsylvania

- 1 Morrow Way, Slippery Rock, PA 16057
- Website: http://www.sru.edu/pages/7724.asp
- Public
- Degrees offered: bachelor's, master's, education specialist

ADMISSIONS

Admissions phone number: (724) 738-2051
Admissions email address: *graduate.studies@sru.edu*
Application website: *http://www.sru.edu/downloads/depts/gradstudies/onlineapp.htm*
Application fee: $25
Fall 2005 application deadline: rolling
Test requirements: GRE or MAT
Test of English as Foreign Language (TOEFL) is required for international students.
Minimum TOEFL score required for paper test: 500
Minimum TOEFL score required for computer test: 173

Fall 2003

Acceptance rate for master's degree programs: 49%
Acceptance rate for education specialist degree programs: 82%
Average GRE verbal: 424, Average GRE quantitative: 507, Average GRE analytical: 552
Total 2003 enrollment: 414
Master's degree enrollment: 381
   Teacher preparation program enrollment (master's): 217
Education specialist degree enrollment: 33

FINANCIAL INFORMATION

Financial aid phone number: (724) 738-2044
Tuition, 2003-2004 academic year: Full-time in-state: $5,518; out-of-state: $8,830, Part-time in-state: $307/credit hour; out-of-state: $491/credit hour
Fees: $1,619, Room and board: $4,542, Books and supplies: $1,000, Miscellaneous expenses: $1,060
Number of research assistant positions: 77

ACADEMIC PROGRAMS

Total full-time tenured or tenure-track faculty (fall 2003): 66, Total part-time faculty (fall 2003): 13

Areas of specialization: education administration and supervision, educational psychology, elementary teacher education, secondary teacher education, special education, student counseling and personnel services.

Professional development/partnership school(s) are used by students in some of the teaching programs.

During their internships, peer groups of students meet regularly to discuss instructional techniques in some of the teaching programs.

All of the students in their internships are mentored.

Courses that prepare teachers to pass the National Board of Professional Teaching Standards are not offered.

Teacher preparation programs: Four-year baccalaureate-degree program leading to initial licensure that includes either a major or minor in education and practice teaching. Master's program preparing college graduates for initial licensure; includes practice teaching.

The education program is currently accredited by the National Council for Accreditation of Teacher Education.

LICENSING TEST

Pass rate on state's teacher licensing test for 2002-2003: 87%

State average pass rate: 85%

St. Francis University

■ P.O. Box 600, Loretto, PA 15940-0600
■ **Website:** http://www.francis.edu
■ Private
■ **Degrees offered:** bachelor's, master's

ADMISSIONS

Admissions phone number: (814) 472-3058
Admissions email address: *egensante@francis.edu*
Application fee: $25
Fall 2005 application deadline: **rolling**
Test requirements: **GRE or MAT**

Fall 2003
Acceptance rate for master's degree programs: 100%
Total 2003 enrollment: 145
Master's degree enrollment: 145
   Teacher preparation program enrollment (master's): 128

FINANCIAL INFORMATION

Financial aid phone number: (814) 472-3010
Tuition, 2003-2004 academic year: Full-time: **$400/credit hour**; Part-time: **$400/credit hour**

ACADEMIC PROGRAMS

Total full-time tenured or tenure-track faculty (fall 2003): 3
   Total part-time faculty (fall 2003): 23

Areas of specialization: curriculum and instruction, education administration and supervision, education policy,

educational psychology, elementary teacher education, secondary teacher education, special education.

Professional development/partnership school(s) are used by students in all of the teaching programs.

During their internships, peer groups of students meet regularly to discuss instructional techniques in some of the teaching programs.

All of the students in their internships are mentored.

Courses that prepare teachers to pass the National Board of Professional Teaching Standards are not offered.

Teacher preparation programs: Four-year baccalaureate-degree program leading to initial licensure that includes either a major or minor in education and practice teaching.

LICENSING TEST

Pass rate on state's teacher licensing test for 2002-2003: 91%

State average pass rate: 85%

St. Joseph's University

■ 5600 City Avenue, Philadelphia, PA 19131
■ **Website:** http://www.sju.edu
■ Private
■ **Degrees offered:** bachelor's, master's, education specialist, Ed.D.

ADMISSIONS

Admissions phone number: (610) 660-1101
Admissions email address: *graduate@sju.edu*
Application website: *http://www.sju.edu/admissions/*
Application fee: $35
Fall 2005 application deadline: **rolling**
Test requirements: **GRE or MAT**
Test of English as Foreign Language (TOEFL) is required for international students.
Minimum TOEFL score required for paper test: 550
Minimum TOEFL score required for computer test: 213

FINANCIAL INFORMATION

Financial aid phone number: (610) 660-1555
Tuition, 2003-2004 academic year: Full-time: **$645/credit hour**; Part-time: **$645/credit hour**
Books and supplies: **$800**, Miscellaneous expenses: $3,900

ACADEMIC PROGRAMS

Areas of specialization: education administration and supervision, elementary teacher education, secondary teacher education, special education.

LICENSING TEST

Pass rate on state's teacher licensing test for 2002-2003: 72%

State average pass rate: 85%

Temple University

- College of Education, OSS RA238, Philadelphia, PA 19122
- Website: http://www.temple.edu/
- Public
- Degrees offered: bachelor's, master's, Ph.D., Ed.D.
- Overall rank in the 2005 U.S. News education schools with doctoral programs: 28

ADMISSIONS

Admissions phone number: (215) 204-8011
Admissions email address: *educate@blue.vm.temple.edu*
Application fee: $40
Fall 2005 application deadline: rolling
Test requirements: GRE or MAT
Test of English as Foreign Language (TOEFL) is required for international students.
Minimum TOEFL score required for paper test: 575
Minimum TOEFL score required for computer test: 230

Fall 2003
Acceptance rate for master's degree programs: 50%
Acceptance rate for doctoral programs: 36%
Average GRE verbal: 534, Average GRE quantitative: 544, Average GRE analytical: 570, Average MAT: 50
Total 2003 enrollment: 1,497
Master's degree enrollment: 931
    Teacher preparation program enrollment (master's): 664
Doctoral degree enrollment: 566

FINANCIAL INFORMATION

Financial aid phone number: (215) 204-1492
Tuition, 2003-2004 academic year: Full-time in-state: $430/credit hour; out-of-state: $626/credit hour, Part-time in-state: $430/credit hour; out-of-state: $626/credit hour
Fees: $347, Room and board: $9,400, Books and supplies: $1,400, Miscellaneous expenses: $400
Number of fellowships awarded to graduate students during the 2003-2004 academic year: 15
Number of teaching assistant positions: 49
Number of research assistant positions: 18
Number of other paid appointments: 34

ACADEMIC PROGRAMS

Total full-time tenured or tenure-track faculty (fall 2003): 72, Total part-time faculty (fall 2003): 127
Areas of specialization: curriculum and instruction, education administration and supervision, educational psychology, elementary teacher education, higher education administration, secondary teacher education, special education, student counseling and personnel services, teacher education.
Professional development/partnership school(s) are used by students in some of the teaching programs.

During their internships, peer groups of students meet regularly to discuss instructional techniques in some of the teaching programs.
All of the students in their internships are mentored.
Courses that prepare teachers to pass the National Board of Professional Teaching Standards are offered.
Teacher preparation programs: Four-year baccalaureate-degree program leading to initial licensure that includes either a major or minor in education and practice teaching. Five-year program leading to initial licensure that results in a baccalaureate degree (with a major or minor in education) plus graduate credit and includes practice teaching. Five-year program leading to initial licensure that results in a baccalaureate degree (with a major or minor in education) plus a master's degree and includes practice teaching. Master's program preparing college graduates for initial licensure; includes practice teaching.
The education program is currently accredited by the National Council for Accreditation of Teacher Education.

LICENSING TEST

Pass rate on state's teacher licensing test for 2002-2003: 70%
State average pass rate: 85%

University of Pennsylvania

- 3700 Walnut Street, Philadelphia, PA 19104-6216
- Website: http://www.gse.upenn.edu
- Private
- Degrees offered: master's, Ph.D., Ed.D.
- Overall rank in the 2005 U.S. News education schools with doctoral programs: 9
- Overall rank in the 2005 U.S. News education school specialty rankings: education policy: 10

ADMISSIONS

Admissions phone number: (215) 898-6455
Admissions email address: *admissions@gse.upenn.edu*
Application website:
    http://www.gse.upenn.edu/admissions_financial/
Test requirements: GRE
Test of English as Foreign Language (TOEFL) is required for international students.
Minimum TOEFL score required for paper test: 550
Minimum TOEFL score required for computer test: 213

Fall 2003
Acceptance rate for master's degree programs: 64%
Acceptance rate for doctoral programs: 17%
Average GRE verbal: 548, Average GRE quantitative: 621, Average GRE analytical: 641
Total 2003 enrollment: 787
Master's degree enrollment: 428
    Teacher preparation program enrollment (master's): 219
Doctoral degree enrollment: 359

FINANCIAL INFORMATION

Financial aid phone number: (215) 898-6455

Tuition, 2003-2004 academic year: Full-time: $28,040;
Part-time: $3,550/credit hour

Fees: $1,750, Room and board: $11,930, Books and supplies: $920, Miscellaneous expenses: $4,030

Number of fellowships awarded to graduate students during the 2003-2004 academic year: 20

Number of teaching assistant positions: 68

Number of research assistant positions: 85

Number of other paid appointments: 381

ACADEMIC PROGRAMS

Total full-time tenured or tenure-track faculty (fall 2003):
38, Total part-time faculty (fall 2003): 68

Areas of specialization: curriculum and instruction, education administration and supervision, education policy,
educational psychology, elementary teacher education,
higher education administration, secondary teacher education, student counseling and personnel services.

Professional development/partnership school(s) are used
by students in some of the teaching programs.

During their internships, peer groups of students meet
regularly to discuss instructional techniques in all of the
teaching programs.

All of the students in their internships are mentored.

Courses that prepare teachers to pass the National Board of
Professional Teaching Standards are not offered.

Teacher preparation programs: Master's degree in education, including internship/practice teaching and preparation for initial licensure. Education minor for
undergraduate students.

LICENSING TEST

Pass rate on state's teacher licensing test for 2002-2003: 94%

State average pass rate: 85%

University of Pittsburgh

■ 5N01 Wesley W. Posvar Hall, Pittsburgh, PA 15260
■ Website: http://www.education.pitt.edu
■ Public
■ Degrees offered: bachelor's, master's, Ph.D., Ed.D.
■ Overall rank in the 2005 U.S. News education schools
with doctoral programs: 34

ADMISSIONS

Admissions phone number: (412) 648-2230

Admissions email address: soeinfo@pitt.edu

Application website: http://www.education.pitt.edu/
students/admissions/application.asp

Application fee: $40

Fall 2005 application deadline: rolling

Test requirements: GRE

Test of English as Foreign Language (TOEFL) is required
for international students.

Minimum TOEFL score required for paper test: 550

Minimum TOEFL score required for computer test: 213

Fall 2003

Acceptance rate for master's degree programs: 73%

Acceptance rate for doctoral programs: 51%

Average GRE verbal: 500, Average GRE quantitative: 539,
Average GRE analytical: 587

Total 2003 enrollment: 1,066

Master's degree enrollment: 692
Teacher preparation program enrollment (master's): 520

Doctoral degree enrollment: 374

FINANCIAL INFORMATION

Financial aid phone number: (412) 648-2230

Tuition, 2003-2004 academic year: Full-time in-state:
$11,744; out-of-state: $22,910, Part-time in-state:
$479/credit hour; out-of-state: $941/credit hour

Fees: $560, Books and supplies: $600, Miscellaneous
expenses: $9,200

Number of fellowships awarded to graduate students during the 2003-2004 academic year: 62

Number of teaching assistant positions: 52

Number of research assistant positions: 77

ACADEMIC PROGRAMS

Total full-time tenured or tenure-track faculty (fall 2003):
77, Total part-time faculty (fall 2003): 60

Areas of specialization: curriculum and instruction, education administration and supervision, educational psychology, elementary teacher education, higher education
administration, secondary teacher education, special
education.

Professional development/partnership school(s) are used
by students in all of the teaching programs.

During their internships, peer groups of students meet
regularly to discuss instructional techniques in all of the
teaching programs.

All of the students in their internships are mentored.

Courses that prepare teachers to pass the National Board of
Professional Teaching Standards are not offered.

Teacher preparation programs: Master's degree in education, including internship/practice teaching and preparation for initial licensure. Alternative program for college
graduates leading to provisional licensure.

LICENSING TEST

Pass rate on state's teacher licensing test for 2002-2003:
100%

State average pass rate: 85%

University of Scranton

■ 800 Linden Street, Scranton, PA 18510-4632
■ Website: http://matrix.scranton.edu/
■ Private
■ Degrees offered: bachelor's, master's, education
specialist

ADMISSIONS

Admissions phone number: (570) 941-7600

Admissions email address: *goonanj1@scranton.edu*
Application website: *http://matrix.scranton.edu/academics/ac_pr_graduate.shtml*
Application fee: **$50**
Fall 2005 application deadline: **rolling**
Test of English as Foreign Language (TOEFL) is required for international students.
Minimum TOEFL score required for paper test: **500**
Minimum TOEFL score required for computer test: **173**

Fall 2003
Acceptance rate for master's degree programs: **90%**
Total 2003 enrollment: **85**
Master's degree enrollment: **75**
 Teacher preparation program enrollment (master's): **66**
Education specialist degree enrollment: **10**

FINANCIAL INFORMATION
Financial aid phone number: **(570) 941-7700**
Tuition, 2003-2004 academic year: Full-time: **$590/credit hour**; Part-time: **$590/credit hour**
Fees: **$50**
Number of teaching assistant positions: **8**

ACADEMIC PROGRAMS
Total full-time tenured or tenure-track faculty (fall 2003): **15**, Total part-time faculty (fall 2003): **16**
Areas of specialization: curriculum and instruction, education administration and supervision, education policy, educational psychology, elementary teacher education, higher education administration, secondary teacher education, special education, student counseling and personnel services.
Professional development/partnership school(s) are used by students in all of the teaching programs.
During their internships, peer groups of students meet regularly to discuss instructional techniques in all of the teaching programs.
All of the students in their internships are mentored.
Courses that prepare teachers to pass the National Board of Professional Teaching Standards are not offered.
Teacher preparation programs: Four-year baccalaureate-degree program leading to initial licensure that includes either a major or minor in education and practice teaching.
The education program is currently accredited by the National Council for Accreditation of Teacher Education.
The education program is currently accredited by the Teacher Education Accreditation Council.

LICENSING TEST
Pass rate on state's teacher licensing test for 2002-2003: **86%**
State average pass rate: **85%**

Villanova University

■ **800 Lancaster Avenue, Villanova, PA 19085**
■ **Website:** http://www.gradartsci.villanovaedu/
■ **Private**
■ **Degrees offered:** bachelor's, master's

ADMISSIONS
Admissions phone number: **(610) 519-7090**
Admissions email address: *gradinfo@villanova.edu*
Application website: *http://admission.villanova.edu/applytovu/application/artsappl.pdf*
Application fee: **$50**
Fall 2005 application deadline: **8/1**
Test of English as Foreign Language (TOEFL) is required for international students.
Minimum TOEFL score required for paper test: **550**

FINANCIAL INFORMATION
Financial aid phone number: **(610) 519-6456**
Tuition, 2003-2004 academic year: Full-time: **$480/credit hour**; Part-time: **$480/credit hour**
Fees: **$100**

ACADEMIC PROGRAMS
Professional development/partnership school(s) are used by students in all of the teaching programs.
During their internships, peer groups of students meet regularly to discuss instructional techniques in some of the teaching programs.
All of the students in their internships are mentored.
Courses that prepare teachers to pass the National Board of Professional Teaching Standards are not offered.
Teacher preparation programs: Four-year baccalaureate-degree program leading to initial licensure that includes either a major or minor in education and practice teaching. Master's program preparing college graduates for initial licensure; includes practice teaching.

LICENSING TEST
Pass rate on state's teacher licensing test for 2002-2003: **100%**
State average pass rate: **85%**

Waynesburg College

■ **51 W. College Street, Waynesburg, PA 15370**
■ **Website:** http://www.waynesburg.edu
■ **Private**
■ **Degrees offered:** bachelor's, master's

ADMISSIONS
Admissions phone number: **(888) 481-6029**
Admissions email address: *gaps@waynesburg.edu*
Application fee: **$0**
Fall 2005 application deadline: **rolling**

Test of English as Foreign Language (TOEFL) is required for international students.
Minimum TOEFL score required for computer test: 250

Fall 2003
Total 2003 enrollment: 68
Master's degree enrollment: 68
Teacher preparation program enrollment (master's): 17

FINANCIAL INFORMATION
Financial aid phone number: (800) 225-7393
Tuition, 2003-2004 academic year: Full-time: $14,400; Part-time: $400/credit hour
Room and board: $6,520, Books and supplies: $1,200, Miscellaneous expenses: $1,000

ACADEMIC PROGRAMS
Total full-time tenured or tenure-track faculty (fall 2003): 2
Total part-time faculty (fall 2003): 9
Areas of specialization: secondary teacher education.
Professional development/partnership school(s) are used by students in some of the teaching programs.
During their internships, peer groups of students meet regularly to discuss instructional techniques in some of the teaching programs.
All of the students in their internships are mentored.
Courses that prepare teachers to pass the National Board of Professional Teaching Standards are not offered.
Teacher preparation programs: Master's degree in education, including internship/practice teaching and preparation for initial licensure.

LICENSING TEST
Pass rate on state's teacher licensing test for 2002-2003: 47%
State average pass rate: 85%

West Chester University of Pennsylvania

■ University & High Street, West Chester, PA 19383
■ Website: http://www.wcupa.edu/_ACADEMICS/sch_sed
■ Public
■ Degrees offered: bachelor's, master's

ADMISSIONS
Admissions phone number: (610) 436-2943
Admissions email address: gradstudy@wcupa.edu
Application website: http://www.wcupa.edu/_ADMISSIONS/SCH_DGR/application.html
Application fee: $35
Fall 2005 application deadline: 4/15
Test requirements: GRE or MAT
Test of English as Foreign Language (TOEFL) is required for international students.
Minimum TOEFL score required for paper test: 550
Minimum TOEFL score required for computer test: 213

Fall 2003
Average GRE verbal: 428, Average GRE quantitative: 503
Total 2003 enrollment: 1,458
Master's degree enrollment: 1,458
Teacher preparation program enrollment (master's): 268

FINANCIAL INFORMATION
Financial aid phone number: (610) 436-2627
Tuition, 2003-2004 academic year: Full-time in-state: $5,518; out-of-state: $8,830, Part-time in-state: $307/credit hour; out-of-state: $491/credit hour
Fees: $902, Room and board: $5,508

ACADEMIC PROGRAMS
Areas of specialization: educational psychology, elementary teacher education, secondary teacher education, special education.
The education program is currently accredited by the National Council for Accreditation of Teacher Education.

LICENSING TEST
Pass rate on state's teacher licensing test for 2002-2003: 82%
State average pass rate: 85%

Westminster College

■ South Market Street, New Wilmington, PA 16172
■ Website: http://www.westminster.edu/home.cfm
■ Private

LICENSING TEST
Pass rate on state's teacher licensing test for 2002-2003: 99%
State average pass rate: 85%

Widener University

■ 1 University Place, Chester, PA 19013
■ Website: http://www.widener.edu
■ Private
■ Degrees offered: bachelor's, master's, Ed.D.

ADMISSIONS
Admissions phone number: (610) 499-4251
Admissions email address: j.j.edgette@widener.edu
Application website: http://www.widener.edu/?pageId=1775
Application fee: $25
Fall 2005 application deadline: rolling
Test requirements: GRE or MAT
Test of English as Foreign Language (TOEFL) is required for international students.
Minimum TOEFL score required for paper test: 550
Minimum TOEFL score required for computer test: 175

Acceptance rate for master's degree programs: 61%
Acceptance rate for doctoral programs: 73%
Average GRE verbal: 510, Average GRE quantitative: 517,
  Average GRE analytical: 512, Average MAT: 49
Total 2003 enrollment: 528
Master's degree enrollment: 259
  Teacher preparation program enrollment (master's): 146
Doctoral degree enrollment: 269

FINANCIAL INFORMATION

Financial aid phone number: (610) 499-4174
Tuition, 2003-2004 academic year: Full-time: **$435/credit hour**; Part-time: **$435/credit hour**
Fees: **$50**, Books and supplies: **$225**, Miscellaneous expenses: **$150**
Number of fellowships awarded to graduate students during the 2003-2004 academic year: 0
Number of teaching assistant positions: 0
Number of research assistant positions: 5
Number of other paid appointments: 2

ACADEMIC PROGRAMS

Total full-time tenured or tenure-track faculty (fall 2003): 25, Total part-time faculty (fall 2003): 33
Areas of specialization: curriculum and instruction, education administration and supervision, education policy, educational psychology, elementary teacher education, higher education administration, secondary teacher education, special education, student counseling and personnel services.
Professional development/partnership school(s) are used by students in some of the teaching programs.
During their internships, peer groups of students meet regularly to discuss instructional techniques in some of the teaching programs.
All of the students in their internships are mentored.
Courses that prepare teachers to pass the National Board of Professional Teaching Standards are not offered.
Teacher preparation programs: Four-year baccalaureate-degree program leading to initial licensure that includes either a major or minor in education and practice teaching. Five-year program leading to initial licensure that results in a baccalaureate degree (with a major or minor in education) plus a master's degree and includes practice teaching. Master's program preparing college graduates for initial licensure; includes practice teaching. Alternative program for college graduates leading to provisional licensure.

LICENSING TEST

Pass rate on state's teacher licensing test for 2002-2003: 100%
State average pass rate: 85%

Wilkes University

■ **PO Box 111, Wilkes-Barre, PA 18766**
■ **Website:** http://www.wilkes.edu/
■ **Private**

LICENSING TEST

Pass rate on state's teacher licensing test for 2002-2003: 71%
State average pass rate: 85%

York College of Pennsylvania

■ **Country Club Road, York, PA 17405-7199**
■ **Website:** http://www.ycp.edu
■ **Private**
■ **Degrees offered:** bachelor's, master's, education specialist

ADMISSIONS

Admissions phone number: (717) 815-6406
Admissions email address: *mlgiblin@ycp.edu*
Application website: *http://www.ycp.edu/academics/557.htm*
Application fee: **$30**
Fall 2005 application deadline: 7/15
Test of English as Foreign Language (TOEFL) is required for international students.
Minimum TOEFL score required for paper test: 530
Minimum TOEFL score required for computer test: 200

Fall 2003
Total 2003 enrollment: 26
Master's degree enrollment: 19
  Teacher preparation program enrollment (master's): 9
Education specialist degree enrollment: 7

FINANCIAL INFORMATION

Financial aid phone number: (717) 815-1226
Tuition, 2003-2004 academic year: **$365/credit hour**
Fees: **$122**, Books and supplies: **$65**

LICENSING TEST

Pass rate on state's teacher licensing test for 2002-2003: 86%
State average pass rate: 85%

RHODE ISLAND

TEACHER TESTING IN RHODE ISLAND

Teacher licensure rules vary widely from state to state, but almost all states require tests. The exams typically cover the basics of reading, writing and math, although some states mandate in-depth, subject-specific teacher tests. For information on where to go in your state for specific academic requirements, see Chapter 6 on page 67. Note: Some schools require students to pass exams by graduation, and thus automatically report pass rates of 100 percent.

- This state **does not** require a basic skills test in order to obtain a teaching license.
- This state **does not** require a subject-knowledge test in order to obtain a middle school teaching license.
- This state **does not** require a subject-knowledge test in order to obtain a high school teaching license.
- This state **does** require a subject-specific pedagogy test in order to obtain a teaching license.

Brown University

- 1 Prospect Street, Providence, RI 02912
- Website: http://www.brown.edu/
- Private

LICENSING TEST

Pass rate on state's teacher licensing test for 2002-2003: 95%
State average pass rate: 87%

Johnson and Wales University

- 8 Abbott Park Place, Providence, RI 02903-3703
- Website: http://www.jwu.edu/
- Private

Providence College

- 549 River Avenue, Providence, RI 02918
- Website: http://www.providence.edu/
- Private

LICENSING TEST

Pass rate on state's teacher licensing test for 2002-2003: 95%
State average pass rate: 87%

Roger Williams University

- One Old Ferry Road, Bristol, RI 02809
- Website: http://www.rwu.edu/education
- Private
- **Degrees offered:** bachelor's, master's, education specialist

ADMISSIONS

Admissions phone number: (401) 254-3500
Admissions email address: *gradadmit@rwu.edu*
Application website: *http://www.applyweb.com/aw?rwu*
Application fee: **$50**
Fall 2005 application deadline: **rolling**
Test requirements: **GRE or MAT**
Test of English as Foreign Language (TOEFL) is required for international students.

Fall 2003

Acceptance rate for master's degree programs: **100%**
Acceptance rate for education specialist degree programs: **100%**
Average GRE verbal: **446**, Average GRE quantitative: **486**, Average MAT: **40**
Total 2003 enrollment: **137**
Master's degree enrollment: **137**
    Teacher preparation program enrollment (master's): **116**

FINANCIAL INFORMATION

Financial aid phone number: (401) 254-3100
Tuition, 2003-2004 academic year: Full-time: **$310/credit hour**; Part-time: **$310/credit hour**
Books and supplies: **$600**, Miscellaneous expenses: **$160**
Number of fellowships awarded to graduate students during the 2003-2004 academic year: **0**
Number of teaching assistant positions: **0**
Number of research assistant positions: **0**
Number of other paid appointments: **0**

ACADEMIC PROGRAMS

Total full-time tenured or tenure-track faculty (fall 2003): 7
  Total part-time faculty (fall 2003): 14
Areas of specialization: elementary teacher education.
Professional development/partnership school(s) are used
  by students in some of the teaching programs.
During their internships, peer groups of students meet
  regularly to discuss instructional techniques in all of the
  teaching programs.
All of the students in their internships are mentored.
Courses that prepare teachers to pass the National Board of
  Professional Teaching Standards are not offered.
Teacher preparation programs: Four-year baccalaureate-
  degree program leading to initial licensure that includes
  either a major or minor in education and practice teaching. Master's program preparing college graduates for
  initial licensure; includes practice teaching.

LICENSING TEST

Pass rate on state's teacher licensing test for 2002-2003:
  82%
State average pass rate: 87%

University of Rhode Island/Rhode Island College

- 104 Horace Mann Hall, Providence, RI 02908
- **Website:** http://www.ed.uri.edu/phd_program
- **Public**

ADMISSIONS

Admissions phone number: **(401) 874-2564**
Admissions email address: *lheifetz@uri.edu*

FINANCIAL INFORMATION

Financial aid phone number: **(401) 874-4165**

LICENSING TEST

Pass rate on state's teacher licensing test for 2002-2003:
  83%
State average pass rate: 87%

SOUTH CAROLINA

Charleston Southern University

- **PO Box 118087, 9200 University Boulevard, Charleston, SC 29423**
- **Website:** http://www.csuniv.edu/
- **Private**

LICENSING TEST

Pass rate on state's teacher licensing test for 2002-2003: **100%**

State average pass rate: **94%**

The Citadel

- **171 Moultrie Street, Charleston, SC 29409**
- **Website:** http://www.citadel.edu/
- **Public**
- **Degrees offered:** bachelor's, master's, education specialist

ADMISSIONS

Admissions phone number: **(843) 953-5089**
Admissions email address: *cgps@citadel.edu*
Application website: *http://www.citadel.edu/admissions/gadmission/gadmission.html*
Application fee: **$25**
Fall 2005 application deadline: **8/1**
Test requirements: **GRE or MAT**
Test of English as Foreign Language (TOEFL) is required for international students.
Minimum TOEFL score required for paper test: **530**
Minimum TOEFL score required for computer test: **213**

Fall 2003
Average GRE verbal: **461**, Average GRE quantitative: **552**, Average MAT: **38**
Total 2003 enrollment: **440**

Master's degree enrollment: **329**
Teacher preparation program enrollment (master's): **281**
Education specialist degree enrollment: **111**

FINANCIAL INFORMATION

Financial aid phone number: **(843) 953-5187**
Tuition, 2003-2004 academic year: Full-time in-state: **$206/credit hour**; out-of-state: **$383/credit hour**, Part-time in-state: **$206/credit hour**; out-of-state: **$383/credit hour**
Fees: **$15**

ACADEMIC PROGRAMS

Total full-time tenured or tenure-track faculty (fall 2003): **15**, Total part-time faculty (fall 2003): **15**
Areas of specialization: curriculum and instruction, education administration and supervision, education policy, educational psychology, elementary teacher education, higher education administration, secondary teacher education, student counseling and personnel services.
Professional development/partnership school(s) are used by students in all of the teaching programs.
During their internships, peer groups of students meet regularly to discuss instructional techniques in all of the teaching programs.
All of the students in their internships are mentored.
Courses that prepare teachers to pass the National Board of Professional Teaching Standards are not offered.
Teacher preparation programs: Four-year baccalaureate-degree program leading to initial licensure that includes either a major or minor in education and practice teaching. Master's program preparing college graduates for initial licensure; includes practice teaching.
The education program is currently accredited by the National Council for Accreditation of Teacher Education.

LICENSING TEST

Pass rate on state's teacher licensing test for 2002-2003: **84%**
State average pass rate: **94%**

Clemson University

- 102 Tillman Hall, Clemson, SC 29634-0702
- **Website:** http://www.grad.clemson.edu
- Public
- **Degrees offered:** bachelor's, master's, education specialist, Ph.D., Ed.D.
- **Overall rank in the 2005 U.S. News education schools with doctoral programs:** 73

ADMISSIONS

Admissions phone number: **(864) 656-3195**
Admissions email address: *grdapp@clemson.edu*
Application website:
http://www.grad.clemson.edu/f_grad.html
Application fee: **$40**
Fall 2005 application deadline: **rolling**
Test requirements: **GRE or MAT**
Test of English as Foreign Language (TOEFL) is required for international students.
Minimum TOEFL score required for paper test: **500**
Minimum TOEFL score required for computer test: **173**

Fall 2003
Acceptance rate for master's degree programs: **95%**
Acceptance rate for education specialist degree programs: **100%**
Acceptance rate for doctoral programs: **81%**
Average GRE verbal: **446**, Average GRE quantitative: **512**, Average GRE analytical: **483**
Total 2003 enrollment: **550**
Master's degree enrollment: **454**
  Teacher preparation program enrollment (master's): **128**
Education specialist degree enrollment: **20**
Doctoral degree enrollment: **76**

FINANCIAL INFORMATION

Financial aid phone number: **(864) 656-2280**
Tuition, 2003-2004 academic year: Full-time in-state: **$7,256**; out-of-state: **$14,556**, Part-time in-state: **$356/credit hour**; out-of-state: **$600/credit hour**
Room and board: **$5,038**, Books and supplies: **$780**, Miscellaneous expenses: **$3,876**
Number of fellowships awarded to graduate students during the 2003-2004 academic year: **0**
Number of teaching assistant positions: **8**
Number of research assistant positions: **35**
Number of other paid appointments: **5**

ACADEMIC PROGRAMS

Total full-time tenured or tenure-track faculty (fall 2003): **48**, Total part-time faculty (fall 2003): **18**
Areas of specialization: curriculum and instruction, education administration and supervision, elementary teacher education, higher education administration, secondary teacher education, special education, student counseling and personnel services, teacher education.

Professional development/partnership school(s) are used by students in some of the teaching programs.
During their internships, peer groups of students meet regularly to discuss instructional techniques in some of the teaching programs.
All of the students in their internships are mentored.
Courses that prepare teachers to pass the National Board of Professional Teaching Standards are offered.
Teacher preparation programs: Four-year baccalaureate-degree program leading to initial licensure that includes either a major or minor in education and practice teaching. Master's program preparing college graduates for initial licensure; includes practice teaching. Alternative program for college graduates leading to provisional licensure.
The education program is currently accredited by the National Council for Accreditation of Teacher Education.

LICENSING TEST

Pass rate on state's teacher licensing test for 2002-2003: **95%**
State average pass rate: **94%**

Coastal Carolina University

- PO Box 261954, Conway, SC 29528
- **Website:** http://www.coastal.edu/graduate/
- Public
- **Degrees offered:** bachelor's, master's

ADMISSIONS

Admissions phone number: **(800) 277-7000**
Admissions email address: *admissions@coastal.edu*
Application website:
http://www.coastal.edu/admissions/applications/gradapp.pdf
Application fee: **$45**
Fall 2005 application deadline: **rolling**
Test of English as Foreign Language (TOEFL) is required for international students.
Minimum TOEFL score required for paper test: **500**
Minimum TOEFL score required for computer test: **173**

Fall 2003
Total 2003 enrollment: **1,170**
Master's degree enrollment: **1,170**
  Teacher preparation program enrollment (master's): **89**

FINANCIAL INFORMATION

Financial aid phone number: **(843) 349-2313**
Tuition, 2003-2004 academic year: Full-time in-state: **$220/credit hour**; out-of-state: **$545/credit hour**, Part-time in-state: **$220/credit hour**; out-of-state: **$545/credit hour**

ACADEMIC PROGRAMS

Areas of specialization: elementary teacher education, secondary teacher education, special education.

The education program is currently accredited by the National Council for Accreditation of Teacher Education.

LICENSING TEST

Pass rate on state's teacher licensing test for 2002-2003: 95%

State average pass rate: 94%

College of Charleston

- 66 George Street, Charleston, SC 29424-0001
- **Website:** http://www.cofc.edu/gradschool
- **Public**
- **Degrees offered:** bachelor's, master's

ADMISSIONS

Admissions phone number: **(843) 953-5614**
Admissions email address: *gradsch@cofc.edu*
Application website:
  http://www.cofc.edu/gradschool/apply/index.html
Application fee: **$45**
Test requirements: **GRE**
Test of English as Foreign Language (TOEFL) is required for international students.
Minimum TOEFL score required for paper test: **550**
Minimum TOEFL score required for computer test: **213**

Fall 2003
Acceptance rate for master's degree programs: **70%**
Average GRE verbal: **504**, Average GRE quantitative: **538**, Average GRE analytical: **601**, Average MAT: **43**
Total 2003 enrollment: **263**
Master's degree enrollment: **263**
  Teacher preparation program enrollment (master's): **263**

FINANCIAL INFORMATION

Financial aid phone number: **(843) 953-5540**
Tuition, 2003-2004 academic year: Full-time in-state: **$5,770**; out-of-state: **$13,032**, Part-time in-state: **$238/credit hour**; out-of-state: **$541/credit hour**
Fees: **$15**, Room and board: **$9,600**, Books and supplies: **$1,100**, Miscellaneous expenses: **$627**
Number of fellowships awarded to graduate students during the 2003-2004 academic year: **3**
Number of research assistant positions: **23**

ACADEMIC PROGRAMS

Total full-time tenured or tenure-track faculty (fall 2003): **39**, Total part-time faculty (fall 2003): **49**
Areas of specialization: elementary teacher education, special education.
Professional development/partnership school(s) are used by students in some of the teaching programs.

During their internships, peer groups of students meet regularly to discuss instructional techniques in all of the teaching programs.
All of the students in their internships are mentored.
Courses that prepare teachers to pass the National Board of Professional Teaching Standards are not offered.
Teacher preparation programs: Four-year baccalaureate-degree program leading to initial licensure that includes either a major or minor in education and practice teaching. Master's program preparing college graduates for initial licensure; includes practice teaching.
The education program is currently accredited by the National Council for Accreditation of Teacher Education.

LICENSING TEST

Pass rate on state's teacher licensing test for 2002-2003: 95%

State average pass rate: 94%

Columbia College

- 1301 Columbia College Drive, Columbia, SC 29203
- **Website:** http://www.columbiacollegesc.edu/admissions/index.html
- **Private**
- **Degrees offered:** bachelor's, master's

ADMISSIONS

Admissions phone number: **(803) 786-3766**
Admissions email address: *emeneker@colacoll.edu*
Application website: *http://www.columbiacollegesc.edu/graduate/application_dl.pdf*
Application fee: **$50**
Fall 2005 application deadline: **7/16**

Fall 2003
Total 2003 enrollment: **263**
Master's degree enrollment: **263**

FINANCIAL INFORMATION

Financial aid phone number: **(803) 786-3612**
Tuition, 2003-2004 academic year: Full-time: **$249/credit hour**; Part-time: **$249/credit hour**
Books and supplies: **$900**

ACADEMIC PROGRAMS

Total full-time tenured or tenure-track faculty (fall 2003): **2**
  Total part-time faculty (fall 2003): **22**
Professional development/partnership school(s) are used by students in some of the teaching programs.
During their internships, peer groups of students meet regularly to discuss instructional techniques in some of the teaching programs.
All of the students in their internships are mentored.
Courses that prepare teachers to pass the National Board of Professional Teaching Standards are not offered.

Teacher preparation programs: Four-year baccalaureate-degree program leading to initial licensure that includes either a major or minor in education and practice teaching. The education program is currently accredited by the National Council for Accreditation of Teacher Education.

LICENSING TEST

Pass rate on state's teacher licensing test for 2002-2003: 100%
State average pass rate: 94%

Francis Marion University

- **PO Box 100547, Florence, SC 29501**
- **Website:** http://www.fmarion.edu
- **Public**
- **Degrees offered:** bachelor's, master's

ADMISSIONS

Admissions phone number: **(843) 661-1231**
Admissions email address: *drussell@fmarion.edu*
Application website:
 http://www.admissions.fmarion.edu/jump/apply.asp
Application fee: **$30**
Fall 2005 application deadline: **rolling**
Test of English as Foreign Language (TOEFL) is required for international students.
Minimum TOEFL score required for paper test: **500**
Minimum TOEFL score required for computer test: **173**

Fall 2003
Acceptance rate for master's degree programs: **83%**
Total 2003 enrollment: **403**
Master's degree enrollment: **403**
 Teacher preparation program enrollment (master's): **403**

FINANCIAL INFORMATION

Financial aid phone number: **(843) 661-1190**
Tuition, 2003-2004 academic year: Full-time in-state: **$4,947**; out-of-state: **$9,894**, Part-time in-state: **$247/credit hour**; out-of-state: **$495/credit hour**
Fees: **$125**, Room and board: **$4,282**, Books and supplies: **$600**, Miscellaneous expenses: **$5,000**

ACADEMIC PROGRAMS

Total full-time tenured or tenure-track faculty (fall 2003): **18**
Areas of specialization: education administration and supervision, secondary teacher education, special education.
Professional development/partnership school(s) are used by students in all of the teaching programs.
During their internships, peer groups of students meet regularly to discuss instructional techniques in all of the teaching programs.
All of the students in their internships are mentored.
Courses that prepare teachers to pass the National Board of Professional Teaching Standards are not offered.

Teacher preparation programs: Four-year baccalaureate-degree program leading to initial licensure that includes either a major or minor in education and practice teaching. Five-year program leading to initial licensure that results in a baccalaureate degree (with a major or minor in education) plus graduate credit and includes practice teaching. Five-year program leading to initial licensure that results in a baccalaureate degree (with a major or minor in education) plus a master's degree and includes practice teaching. Master's program preparing college graduates for initial licensure; includes practice teaching. The education program is currently accredited by the National Council for Accreditation of Teacher Education.

LICENSING TEST

Pass rate on state's teacher licensing test for 2002-2003: 100%
State average pass rate: 94%

Lander University

- **320 Stanley Avenue, Greenwood, SC 29649**
- **Website:** http://www.lander.edu/
- **Public**

LICENSING TEST

Pass rate on state's teacher licensing test for 2002-2003: 94%
State average pass rate: 94%

South Carolina State University

- **School of Education, Orangeburg, SC 29117**
- **Website:** http://www.scsu.edu
- **Public**
- **Degrees offered:** bachelor's, master's, education specialist, Ed.D.

ADMISSIONS

Admissions phone number: **(803) 536-7186**
Admissions email address: *admissions@scsu.edu*
Application website: *http://www.applyweb.com/aw?scsu*
Application fee: **$25**
Test of English as Foreign Language (TOEFL) is required for international students.
Minimum TOEFL score required for paper test: **500**

FINANCIAL INFORMATION

Financial aid phone number: **(803) 536-7067**

ACADEMIC PROGRAMS

Teacher preparation programs: Four-year baccalaureate-degree program leading to initial licensure that includes either a major or minor in education and practice teach-

ing. Master's program preparing college graduates for initial licensure; includes practice teaching.

The education program is currently accredited by the National Council for Accreditation of Teacher Education.

LICENSING TEST

Pass rate on state's teacher licensing test for 2002-2003: 99%

State average pass rate: 94%

Southern Wesleyan University

- 907 Wesleyan Drive, Central, SC 29630-1020
- **Website:** http://www.swu.edu
- **Private**
- **Degrees offered:** master's

ADMISSIONS

Admissions phone number: **(800) 264-5327**

Admissions email address: *donna.spittal@apollogrp.edu*

Application fee: **$25**

Fall 2005 application deadline: **rolling**

Test of English as Foreign Language (TOEFL) is required for international students.

Minimum TOEFL score required for paper test: **550**

Minimum TOEFL score required for computer test: **213**

Fall 2003

Acceptance rate for master's degree programs: **8%**

Total 2003 enrollment: **211**

Master's degree enrollment: **211**

  Teacher preparation program enrollment (master's): **211**

FINANCIAL INFORMATION

Financial aid phone number: **(864) 644-5516**

Tuition, 2003-2004 academic year: Full-time: **$7,080**; Part-time: **$295/credit hour**

Fees: **$125**, Books and supplies: **$1,000**

Number of fellowships awarded to graduate students during the 2003-2004 academic year: **0**

Number of teaching assistant positions: **0**

Number of research assistant positions: **0**

Number of other paid appointments: **0**

ACADEMIC PROGRAMS

Total full-time tenured or tenure-track faculty (fall 2003): **4**

  Total part-time faculty (fall 2003): **17**

Areas of specialization: curriculum and instruction.

Professional development/partnership school(s) are used by students in all of the teaching programs.

During their internships, peer groups of students meet regularly to discuss instructional techniques in all of the teaching programs.

All of the students in their internships are mentored.

Courses that prepare teachers to pass the National Board of Professional Teaching Standards are not offered.

Teacher preparation programs: Four-year baccalaureate-degree program leading to initial licensure that includes either a major or minor in education and practice teaching.

LICENSING TEST

Pass rate on state's teacher licensing test for 2002-2003: **100%**

State average pass rate: **94%**

University of South Carolina–Aiken

- 471 University Parkway, Aiken, SC 29801
- **Website:** http://www.usca.edu
- **Public**
- **Degrees offered:** bachelor's, master's

ADMISSIONS

Admissions phone number: **(803) 641-3366**

Admissions email address: *admit@usca.edu*

Application website: *http://web.csd.edu/app/ugrad_aiken*

Application fee: **$40**

Fall 2005 application deadline: **rolling**

Test requirements: **GRE or MAT**

Test of English as Foreign Language (TOEFL) is required for international students.

Minimum TOEFL score required for paper test: **550**

Minimum TOEFL score required for computer test: **213**

Fall 2003

Acceptance rate for master's degree programs: **69%**

Total 2003 enrollment: **27**

Master's degree enrollment: **27**

  Teacher preparation program enrollment (master's): **27**

FINANCIAL INFORMATION

Financial aid phone number: **(803) 641-3476**

Tuition, 2003-2004 academic year: Full-time in-state: **$308/credit hour**; out-of-state: **$655/credit hour**, Part-time in-state: **$308/credit hour**; out-of-state: **$655/credit hour**

Fees: **$5/credit hour**

Number of fellowships awarded to graduate students during the 2003-2004 academic year: **0**

Number of teaching assistant positions: **0**

Number of research assistant positions: **0**

Number of other paid appointments: **0**

ACADEMIC PROGRAMS

Total full-time tenured or tenure-track faculty (fall 2003): **13**

Areas of specialization: curriculum and instruction, educational psychology, elementary teacher education.

Professional development/partnership school(s) are used by students in some of the teaching programs.

During their internships, peer groups of students meet regularly to discuss instructional techniques in all of the teaching programs.

All of the students in their internships are mentored.

Teacher preparation programs: Four-year baccalaureate-degree program leading to initial licensure that includes either a major or minor in education and practice teaching. Alternative program for college graduates leading to provisional licensure.

The education program is currently accredited by the National Council for Accreditation of Teacher Education.

LICENSING TEST

Pass rate on state's teacher licensing test for 2002-2003: 100%

State average pass rate: 94%

University of South Carolina–Columbia

- College of Education, Columbia, SC 29208
- **Website:** http://www.ed.sc.edu
- Public
- **Degrees offered:** bachelor's, master's, education specialist, Ph.D., Ed.D.

ADMISSIONS

Admissions phone number: **(803) 777-4243**
Admissions email address: *gradapp@sc.edu*
Application website: *http://www.gradschool.sc.edu*
Application fee: **$40**
Fall 2005 application deadline: **7/1**
Test requirements: **GRE or MAT**
Test of English as Foreign Language (TOEFL) is required for international students.
Minimum TOEFL score required for paper test: **570**
Minimum TOEFL score required for computer test: **230**

Fall 2003
Acceptance rate for master's degree programs: **56%**
Acceptance rate for education specialist degree programs: **35%**
Acceptance rate for doctoral programs: **49%**
Average GRE verbal: **463**, Average GRE quantitative: **540**, Average GRE analytical: **508**, Average MAT: **47**
Total 2003 enrollment: **1,085**
Master's degree enrollment: **663**
 Teacher preparation program enrollment (master's): **396**
Education specialist degree enrollment: **146**
Doctoral degree enrollment: **276**

FINANCIAL INFORMATION

Financial aid phone number: **(803) 777-8134**
Tuition, 2003-2004 academic year: Full-time in-state: **$6,210**; out-of-state: **$13,442**, Part-time in-state: **$308/credit hour**; out-of-state: **$655/credit hour**
Fees: **$50**, Room and board: **$7,290**, Books and supplies: **$720**, Miscellaneous expenses: **$2,420**
Number of fellowships awarded to graduate students during the 2003-2004 academic year: **43**

Number of teaching assistant positions: **21**
Number of research assistant positions: **109**
Number of other paid appointments: **18**

ACADEMIC PROGRAMS

Total full-time tenured or tenure-track faculty (fall 2003): **69**, Total part-time faculty (fall 2003): **1**

Areas of specialization: curriculum and instruction, education administration and supervision, educational psychology, elementary teacher education, higher education administration, secondary teacher education, special education, student counseling and personnel services.

Professional development/partnership school(s) are used by students in some of the teaching programs.

During their internships, peer groups of students meet regularly to discuss instructional techniques in some of the teaching programs.

All of the students in their internships are mentored.

Courses that prepare teachers to pass the National Board of Professional Teaching Standards are offered.

Teacher preparation programs: Four-year baccalaureate-degree program leading to initial licensure that includes either a major or minor in education and practice teaching. Five-year program leading to initial licensure that results in a baccalaureate degree (with a major or minor in education) plus a master's degree and includes practice teaching. Master's program preparing college graduates for initial licensure; includes practice teaching.

The education program is currently accredited by the National Council for Accreditation of Teacher Education.

LICENSING TEST

Pass rate on state's teacher licensing test for 2002-2003: 98%

State average pass rate: 94%

University of South Carolina–Spartanburg

- 800 University Way, Spartanburg, SC 29303
- **Website:** http://www.uscs.edu
- Public
- **Degrees offered:** bachelor's, master's

ADMISSIONS

Admissions phone number: **(864) 503-5280**
Admissions email address: *dstewart@uscs.edu*
Application website: *http://www.uscs.edu/academics/se/grad_programs/gradapp.pdf*
Application fee: **$35**
Fall 2005 application deadline: **rolling**

Fall 2003
Total 2003 enrollment: **54**
Master's degree enrollment: **54**
 Teacher preparation program enrollment (master's): **54**

FINANCIAL INFORMATION

Financial aid phone number: **(864) 503-5340**
Tuition, 2003-2004 academic year: Full-time in-state:
$6,210; out-of-state: **$13,442**, Part-time in-state:
$308/credit hour; out-of-state: **$655/credit hour**
Fees: **$6/credit hour**, Miscellaneous expenses: **$25**

ACADEMIC PROGRAMS

The education program is currently accredited by the
National Council for Accreditation of Teacher Education.

LICENSING TEST

Pass rate on state's teacher licensing test for 2002-2003:
88%
State average pass rate: **94%**

Winthrop University

■ **701 Oakland Avenue, Rock Hill, SC 29733**
■ **Website:** http://www.winthrop.edu/
■ **Public**

LICENSING TEST

Pass rate on state's teacher licensing test for 2002-2003:
97%
State average pass rate: **94%**

SOUTH DAKOTA

Augustana College

- 2001 S. Summit Avenue, Sioux Falls, SD 57197
- **Website:** http://www.augustana.edu/
- **Private**

Black Hills State University

- 1200 University St Unit 9004, Spearfish, SD 57799
- **Website:** http://www.bhsu.edu
- **Public**
- **Degrees offered:** bachelor's, master's

ADMISSIONS

Admissions phone number: **(800) 255-2478**
Admissions email address: *admissions@bhsu.edu*
Application website: *http://www.bhsu.edu/studentlife/ enrollment/admissions/index.html*
Application fee: **$35**
Fall 2005 application deadline: **rolling**
Test of English as Foreign Language (TOEFL) is required for international students.
Minimum TOEFL score required for paper test: **530**
Minimum TOEFL score required for computer test: **197**

Fall 2003
Acceptance rate for master's degree programs: **80%**
Total 2003 enrollment: **98**
Master's degree enrollment: **98**
  Teacher preparation program enrollment (master's): **98**

FINANCIAL INFORMATION

Financial aid phone number: **(605) 642-6581**
Tuition, 2003-2004 academic year: Full-time in-state: **$109/credit hour**; out-of-state: **$322/credit hour**, Part-time in-state: **$109/credit hour**; out-of-state: **$322/credit hour**
Fees: **$70/credit hour**, Room and board: **$3,194**, Books and supplies: **$800**

ACADEMIC PROGRAMS

Total full-time tenured or tenure-track faculty (fall 2003): **3**
  Total part-time faculty (fall 2003): **61**
Areas of specialization: curriculum and instruction, educational psychology, elementary teacher education, secondary teacher education, special education.
Professional development/partnership school(s) are used by students in some of the teaching programs.
During their internships, peer groups of students meet regularly to discuss instructional techniques in none of the teaching programs.
All of the students in their internships are mentored.
Courses that prepare teachers to pass the National Board of Professional Teaching Standards are offered.
Teacher preparation programs: Four-year baccalaureate-degree program leading to initial licensure that includes either a major or minor in education and practice teaching.
The education program is currently accredited by the National Council for Accreditation of Teacher Education.

Northern State University

- 1200 S Jay Street, Alberdeen, SD 57401
- **Website:** http://www.northern.edu
- **Public**
- **Degrees offered:** master's

ADMISSIONS

Admissions phone number: **(605) 626-2558**
Admissions email address: *johnsonr@northern.edu*
Application fee: **$35**
Fall 2005 application deadline: **rolling**
Test requirements: **GRE or MAT**
Minimum TOEFL score required for paper test: **550**
Minimum TOEFL score required for computer test: **250**

Fall 2003
Acceptance rate for master's degree programs: **66%**
Total 2003 enrollment: **93**
Master's degree enrollment: **93**
  Teacher preparation program enrollment (master's): **46**

FINANCIAL INFORMATION

Financial aid phone number: **(605) 626-2640**
Tuition, 2003-2004 academic year: Full-time in-state:
$109/credit hour; out-of-state: **$322/credit hour**, Part-
time in-state: **$98/credit hour**; out-of-state: **$290/credit
hour**
Fees: **$68/credit hour**, Room and board: **$2,967**, Books
and supplies: **$600**, Miscellaneous expenses: **$35**
Number of teaching assistant positions: **31**

ACADEMIC PROGRAMS

Total full-time tenured or tenure-track faculty (fall 2003): **83**
Areas of specialization: education administration and supervision, educational psychology, elementary teacher education,
secondary teacher education, special education.
Professional development/partnership school(s) are used
by students in all of the teaching programs.
During their internships, peer groups of students meet
regularly to discuss instructional techniques in none of
the teaching programs.
The education program is currently accredited by the
National Council for Accreditation of Teacher Education.

Sinte Gleska University

■ **2nd and Lincoln, PO Box 8, Mission, SD 57555**
■ **Website:** http://www.sinte.edu/
■ **Public**
■ **Degrees offered:** bachelor's, master's

ADMISSIONS

Admissions phone number: **(605) 856-2326**
Admissions email address: *cherylm@sinte.edu*
Application fee: **$0**

FINANCIAL INFORMATION

Financial aid phone number: **(605) 856-5880**
Tuition, 2003-2004 academic year: Full-time in-state:
$95/credit hour; out-of-state: **$95/credit hour**, Part-time
in-state: **$95/credit hour**; out-of-state: **$95/credit hour**

South Dakota State University

■ **College of Education and Counseling - Box 507 Wenona
Hall, Brookings, SD 57007**
■ **Website:** http://www3.sdstate.edu/
■ **Public**
■ **Degrees offered:** bachelor's, master's

Fall 2003
Acceptance rate for master's degree programs: **92%**
Total 2003 enrollment: **371**
Master's degree enrollment: **371**
  Teacher preparation program enrollment (master's): **73**

FINANCIAL INFORMATION

Tuition, 2003-2004 academic year: Full-time in-state:
$109/credit hour; out-of-state: **$322/credit hour**

ACADEMIC PROGRAMS

Total full-time tenured or tenure-track faculty (fall 2003):
25, Total part-time faculty (fall 2003): **0**
Areas of specialization: curriculum and instruction, education administration and supervision, secondary teacher
education, student counseling and personnel services.
The education program is currently accredited by the
National Council for Accreditation of Teacher Education.

University of Sioux Falls

■ **1101 W. 22nd Street, Sioux Falls, SD 57105**
■ **Website:** http://www.thecoo.edu/
■ **Private**

University of South Dakota

■ **414 E. Clark Street, Vermillion, SD 57069**
■ **Website:** http://www.usd.edu
■ **Public**
■ **Degrees offered:** bachelor's, master's, education
specialist, Ph.D., Ed.D.

ADMISSIONS

Admissions phone number: **(605) 677-6287**
Admissions email address: *gradsch@usd.edu*
Application website:
  http://www.usd.edu/gradsch/admisApp.cfm
Application fee: **$35**
Test requirements: **GRE or MAT**
Test of English as Foreign Language (TOEFL) is required
for international students.
Minimum TOEFL score required for paper test: **550**
Minimum TOEFL score required for computer test: **213**

Fall 2003
Acceptance rate for master's degree programs: **96%**
Acceptance rate for education specialist degree programs:
  90%
Acceptance rate for doctoral programs: **96%**
Average GRE verbal: **451**, Average GRE quantitative: **525**,
  Average GRE analytical: **546**, Average MAT: **49**
Total 2003 enrollment: **515**
Master's degree enrollment: **248**
  Teacher preparation program enrollment (master's): **151**
Education specialist degree enrollment: **75**
Doctoral degree enrollment: **192**

FINANCIAL INFORMATION

Financial aid phone number: **(605) 677-5446**

Tuition, 2003-2004 academic year: Full-time in-state: **$109/credit hour**; out-of-state: **$322/credit hour**, Part-time in-state: **$109/credit hour**; out-of-state: **$322/credit hour**

Fees: **$68/credit hour**, Room and board: **$3,505**, Books and supplies: **$700**, Miscellaneous expenses: **$1,000**

ACADEMIC PROGRAMS

Areas of specialization: curriculum and instruction, education administration and supervision, educational psychology, elementary teacher education, higher education administration, secondary teacher education, special education, student counseling and personnel services.

The education program is currently accredited by the National Council for Accreditation of Teacher Education.

TENNESSEE

Austin Peay State University

■ 601 College Street, Clarksville, TN 37040
■ Website: http://www.apsu.edu/
■ Public

LICENSING TEST
Pass rate on state's teacher licensing test for 2002-2003: 99%
State average pass rate: 94%

Belmont University

■ 1900 Belmont Boulevard, Nashville, TN 37212
■ Website: http://www.belmont.edu
■ Private
■ Degrees offered: master's

ADMISSIONS
Admissions phone number: (615) 460-6879
Admissions email address: *taylorj@mail.belmont.edu*
Application website: *http://www.belmont.edu/ prospectivestudents/admissions/graduate.cfm*
Application fee: **$50**
Fall 2005 application deadline: 6/30
Test of English as Foreign Language (TOEFL) is required for international students.
Minimum TOEFL score required for paper test: 550
Minimum TOEFL score required for computer test: 213

FINANCIAL INFORMATION
Financial aid phone number: (615) 460-6403
Tuition, 2003-2004 academic year: Full-time: **$590/credit hour**; Part-time: **$590/credit hour**

LICENSING TEST
Pass rate on state's teacher licensing test for 2002-2003: 95%
State average pass rate: 94%

Bethel College

■ 325 Cherry Street, McKenzie, TN 38201
■ Website: http://www.bethel-college.edu/home/index.htm
■ Private

LICENSING TEST
Pass rate on state's teacher licensing test for 2002-2003: 100%
State average pass rate: 94%

Carson-Newman College

■ 1646 Russell Street, Jefferson City, TN 37760
■ Website: http://www.cn.edu/
■ Private
■ Degrees offered: bachelor's, master's

ADMISSIONS
Admissions phone number: (865) 471-3460
Application fee: **$25**
Fall 2005 application deadline: 6/21
Test of English as Foreign Language (TOEFL) is required for international students.
Minimum TOEFL score required for paper test: 550
Minimum TOEFL score required for computer test: 210

Fall 2003
Acceptance rate for master's degree programs: 92%
Total 2003 enrollment: 173
Master's degree enrollment: 173
        Teacher preparation program enrollment (master's): 85

FINANCIAL INFORMATION
Financial aid phone number: (865) 471-3247
Tuition, 2003-2004 academic year: $225/credit hour
Fees: $220, Room and board: $2,225, Books and supplies: $500

ACADEMIC PROGRAMS
Total full-time tenured or tenure-track faculty (fall 2003): 6
Total part-time faculty (fall 2003): 19
Areas of specialization: curriculum and instruction.
Teacher preparation programs: Four-year baccalaureate-degree program leading to initial licensure that includes either a major or minor in education and practice teaching. Master's program preparing college graduates for initial licensure; includes practice teaching.
The education program is currently accredited by the National Council for Accreditation of Teacher Education.

LICENSING TEST
Pass rate on state's teacher licensing test for 2002-2003: 99%
State average pass rate: 94%

Christian Brothers University

- 650 East Parkway, S., Memphis, TN 38104
- **Website:** http://www.cbu.edu/
- Private

LICENSING TEST
Pass rate on state's teacher licensing test for 2002-2003: 81%
State average pass rate: 94%

Cumberland University

- 1 Cumberland Square, Lebanon, TN 37087
- **Website:** http://www.cumberland.edu/
- Private
- **Degrees offered:** bachelor's, master's

ADMISSIONS
Admissions phone number: (615) 444-2562
Admissions email address: *admissions@cumberland.edu*
Application fee: $50
Fall 2005 application deadline: rolling
Test of English as Foreign Language (TOEFL) is required for international students.
Minimum TOEFL score required for paper test: 500
Minimum TOEFL score required for computer test: 173

Fall 2003
Total 2003 enrollment: 365
Master's degree enrollment: 365
Teacher preparation program enrollment (master's): 365

FINANCIAL INFORMATION
Financial aid phone number: (615) 444-2562
Tuition, 2003-2004 academic year: Full-time: $516/credit hour; Part-time: $516/credit hour
Fees: $300, Books and supplies: $450

ACADEMIC PROGRAMS
Total full-time tenured or tenure-track faculty (fall 2003): 5
Total part-time faculty (fall 2003): 15
Professional development/partnership school(s) are used by students in all of the teaching programs.
During their internships, peer groups of students meet regularly to discuss instructional techniques in all of the teaching programs.
All of the students in their internships are mentored.
Courses that prepare teachers to pass the National Board of Professional Teaching Standards are not offered.
Teacher preparation programs: Four-year baccalaureate-degree program leading to initial licensure that includes either a major or minor in education and practice teaching. Master's program preparing college graduates for initial licensure; includes practice teaching. Alternative program for college graduates leading to provisional licensure.
The education program is currently accredited by the Teacher Education Accreditation Council.

LICENSING TEST
Pass rate on state's teacher licensing test for 2002-2003: 91%
State average pass rate: 94%

David Lipscomb University

- 3901-4001 Granny White Pike, Nashville, TN 37204-3951
- **Website:** http://www.lipscomb.edu/
- Private

LICENSING TEST
Pass rate on state's teacher licensing test for 2002-2003: 91%
State average pass rate: 94%

East Tennessee State University

- PO Box 70720, Graduate Studies, Johnson City, TN 37614-0720
- **Website:** http://www.etsu.edu/
- Public
- **Degrees offered:** bachelor's, master's, education specialist, Ed.D.

ADMISSIONS

Admissions phone number: **(423) 439-4221**
Admissions email address: *gradsch@etsu.edu*
Application website: *http://www.etsu.edu/gradstud*
Application fee: **$25**
Fall 2005 application deadline: **rolling**
Test requirements: **GRE**
Test of English as Foreign Language (TOEFL) is required for international students.
Minimum TOEFL score required for paper test: **550**
Minimum TOEFL score required for computer test: **213**

Fall 2003

Acceptance rate for master's degree programs: **69%**
Acceptance rate for doctoral programs: **31%**
Average GRE verbal: **424**, Average GRE quantitative: **479**, Average GRE analytical: **570**
Total 2003 enrollment: **623**
Master's degree enrollment: **469**
 Teacher preparation program enrollment (master's): **341**
Education specialist degree enrollment: **13**
Doctoral degree enrollment: **141**

FINANCIAL INFORMATION

Financial aid phone number: **(423) 439-4300**
Tuition, 2003-2004 academic year: Full-time in-state: **$4,206**; out-of-state: **$12,138**, Part-time in-state: **$222/credit hour**; out-of-state: **$566/credit hour**
Fees: **$707**, Room and board: **$4,658**, Books and supplies: **$900**, Miscellaneous expenses: **$4,195**
Number of fellowships awarded to graduate students during the 2003-2004 academic year: **0**
Number of teaching assistant positions: **25**
Number of research assistant positions: **24**
Number of other paid appointments: **80**

ACADEMIC PROGRAMS

Total full-time tenured or tenure-track faculty (fall 2003): **55**, Total part-time faculty (fall 2003): **60**
Areas of specialization: curriculum and instruction, education administration and supervision, education policy, educational psychology, elementary teacher education, higher education administration, secondary teacher education, special education, student counseling and personnel services.
Professional development/partnership school(s) are used by students in some of the teaching programs.
During their internships, peer groups of students meet regularly to discuss instructional techniques in all of the teaching programs.
All of the students in their internships are mentored.
Courses that prepare teachers to pass the National Board of Professional Teaching Standards are offered.
Teacher preparation programs: Four-year baccalaureate-degree program leading to initial licensure that includes either a major or minor in education and practice teaching. Master's program preparing college graduates for initial licensure; includes practice teaching. Alternative program for college graduates leading to provisional licensure.

The education program is currently accredited by the National Council for Accreditation of Teacher Education.

LICENSING TEST

Pass rate on state's teacher licensing test for 2002-2003: **100%**
State average pass rate: **94%**

Freed-Hardeman University

■ **158 E. Main Street, Henderson, TN 38340**
■ **Website:** http://www.fhu.edu
■ **Private**
■ **Degrees offered:** bachelor's, master's, education specialist

ADMISSIONS

Admissions phone number: **(731) 989-6082**
Admissions email address: *jmurphy@fhu.edu*
Application fee: **$30**
Fall 2005 application deadline: **rolling**
Test requirements: **GRE or MAT**
Test of English as Foreign Language (TOEFL) is required for international students.
Minimum TOEFL score required for paper test: **500**
Minimum TOEFL score required for computer test: **173**

Fall 2003

Total 2003 enrollment: **368**
Master's degree enrollment: **368**

FINANCIAL INFORMATION

Financial aid phone number: **(731) 989-6662**
Tuition, 2003-2004 academic year: Full-time: **$265/credit hour**; Part-time: **$265/credit hour**
Fees: **$10/credit hour**, Room and board: **$2,760**

ACADEMIC PROGRAMS

Areas of specialization: curriculum and instruction, education administration and supervision, education policy, educational psychology, elementary teacher education, secondary teacher education, special education, student counseling and personnel services.
The education program is currently accredited by the National Council for Accreditation of Teacher Education.

LICENSING TEST

Pass rate on state's teacher licensing test for 2002-2003: **75%**
State average pass rate: **94%**

Lee University

- PO Box 3450, Cleveland, TN 37320
- **Website:** http://www.leeuniversity.edu
- Private
- **Degrees offered:** bachelor's, master's

ADMISSIONS

Admissions phone number: **(423) 614-8500**
Admissions email address: *admissions@leeuniversity.edu*
Application fee: **$25**
Fall 2005 application deadline: **4/1**
Test requirements: **GRE or MAT**
Test of English as Foreign Language (TOEFL) is required
for international students.
Minimum TOEFL score required for paper test: **450**
Minimum TOEFL score required for computer test: **133**

Fall 2003

Acceptance rate for master's degree programs: **91%**
Average GRE verbal: **419**, Average GRE quantitative: **575**,
Average GRE analytical: **519**, Average MAT: **40**
Total 2003 enrollment: **150**
Master's degree enrollment: **150**
Teacher preparation program enrollment (master's): **100**

FINANCIAL INFORMATION

Financial aid phone number: **(423) 614-8304**
Tuition, 2003-2004 academic year: **$8,950$355/credit hour**
Fees: **$170**, Room and board: **$4,950**, Books and supplies:
$700, Miscellaneous expenses: **$1,510**
Number of teaching assistant positions: **2**
Number of research assistant positions: **1**
Number of other paid appointments: **5**

ACADEMIC PROGRAMS

Total full-time tenured or tenure-track faculty (fall 2003):
15, Total part-time faculty (fall 2003): **29**
Areas of specialization: curriculum and instruction, education administration and supervision, elementary teacher
education, secondary teacher education, special education, student counseling and personnel services.
Professional development/partnership school(s) are used
by students in some of the teaching programs.
During their internships, peer groups of students meet
regularly to discuss instructional techniques in all of the
teaching programs.
All of the students in their internships are mentored.
Courses that prepare teachers to pass the National Board of
Professional Teaching Standards are not offered.
Teacher preparation programs: Four-year baccalaureate-
degree program leading to initial licensure that includes
either a major or minor in education and practice teaching. Master's program preparing college graduates for
initial licensure; includes practice teaching.

LICENSING TEST

Pass rate on state's teacher licensing test for 2002-2003:
97%
State average pass rate: **94%**

Lincoln Memorial University

- 6965 Cumberland Gap Parkway, Harrogateq, TN 37752
- **Website:** http://www.lmunet.edu/
- Private
- **Degrees offered:** master's, education specialist

ADMISSIONS

Admissions phone number: **(423) 869-6279**
Admissions email address: *admissions@lmunet.edu*
Application fee: **$25**
Fall 2005 application deadline: **7/15**
Test of English as Foreign Language (TOEFL) is required
for international students.
Minimum TOEFL score required for paper test: **500**

FINANCIAL INFORMATION

Financial aid phone number: **(423) 869-6388**
Tuition, 2003-2004 academic year: Full-time: **$300/credit
hour**; Part-time: **$300/credit hour**
Room and board: **$4,480**, Books and supplies: **$650**,
Miscellaneous expenses: **$1,875**

LICENSING TEST

Pass rate on state's teacher licensing test for 2002-2003:
100%
State average pass rate: **94%**

Middle Tennessee State University

- 1301 E. Main Street; CAB Room 205, Murfreesboro, TN 37132
- **Website:** http://www.mtsu.edu/
- Public

LICENSING TEST

Pass rate on state's teacher licensing test for 2002-2003:
89%
State average pass rate: **94%**

Milligan College

■ P. O. Box 309, Milligan College, TN 37682
■ **Website:** http://www.milligan.edu
■ **Private**
■ **Degrees offered:** bachelor's, master's

ADMISSIONS

Admissions phone number: **(423) 461-8306**
Admissions email address: *cdavidson@milligan.edu*
Application website: *http://www.milligan.edu*
Application fee: **$30**
Fall 2005 application deadline: **rolling**
Test requirements: **GRE or MAT**

Fall 2003

Acceptance rate for master's degree programs: **89%**
Total 2003 enrollment: **66**
Master's degree enrollment: **66**
   Teacher preparation program enrollment (master's): **66**

FINANCIAL INFORMATION

Financial aid phone number: **(423) 461-8713**
Tuition, 2003-2004 academic year: Full-time: **$260/credit hour**; Part-time: **$260/credit hour**
Fees: **$570**, Room and board: **$2,300**, Miscellaneous expenses: **$255**

ACADEMIC PROGRAMS

Total full-time tenured or tenure-track faculty (fall 2003): **7**
   Total part-time faculty (fall 2003): **13**
Areas of specialization: curriculum and instruction, education administration and supervision, educational psychology, elementary teacher education, secondary teacher education.
Professional development/partnership school(s) are used by students in all of the teaching programs.
During their internships, peer groups of students meet regularly to discuss instructional techniques in all of the teaching programs.
All of the students in their internships are mentored.
Courses that prepare teachers to pass the National Board of Professional Teaching Standards are offered.
Teacher preparation programs: Four-year baccalaureate-degree program leading to initial licensure that includes either a major or minor in education and practice teaching. Master's program preparing college graduates for initial licensure; includes practice teaching. Alternative program for college graduates leading to provisional licensure.
The education program is currently accredited by the National Council for Accreditation of Teacher Education.

LICENSING TEST

Pass rate on state's teacher licensing test for 2002-2003: **98%**
State average pass rate: **94%**

Southern Adventist University

■ PO Box 370, Collegedale, TN 37315
■ **Website:**
   http://www.southern.edu/?page=admissions/graduate/index.php
■ **Private**
■ **Degrees offered:** bachelor's, master's

ADMISSIONS

Admissions phone number: **(423) 238-2844**
Admissions email address: *admissions@southern.edu*
Application website: *http://www.southern.edu/?page=admissions/graduate/apply.php*
Application fee: **$25**
Fall 2005 application deadline: **rolling**
Test requirements: **GRE**
Test of English as Foreign Language (TOEFL) is required for international students.
Minimum TOEFL score required for paper test: **600**
Minimum TOEFL score required for computer test: **53**

Fall 2003

Acceptance rate for master's degree programs: **69%**
Average GRE verbal: **450**, Average GRE quantitative: **470**, Average GRE analytical: **500**
Total 2003 enrollment: **30**
Master's degree enrollment: **30**

FINANCIAL INFORMATION

Financial aid phone number: **(423) 238-2835**
Tuition, 2003-2004 academic year: Full-time: **$360/credit hour**; Part-time: **$360/credit hour**
Fees: **$360/credit hour**, Room and board: **$8,100**, Books and supplies: **$945**, Miscellaneous expenses: **$2,700**
Number of fellowships awarded to graduate students during the 2003-2004 academic year: **0**
Number of teaching assistant positions: **0**
Number of research assistant positions: **0**
Number of other paid appointments: **2**

ACADEMIC PROGRAMS

Total full-time tenured or tenure-track faculty (fall 2003): **12**, Total part-time faculty (fall 2003): **5**
Areas of specialization: curriculum and instruction, education administration and supervision.
Professional development/partnership school(s) are used by students in all of the teaching programs.
During their internships, peer groups of students meet regularly to discuss instructional techniques in some of the teaching programs.
All of the students in their internships are mentored.
Courses that prepare teachers to pass the National Board of Professional Teaching Standards are not offered.

Teacher preparation programs: Four-year baccalaureate-degree program leading to initial licensure that includes either a major or minor in education and practice teaching. The education program is currently accredited by the National Council for Accreditation of Teacher Education.

LICENSING TEST

Pass rate on state's teacher licensing test for 2002-2003: 100%
State average pass rate: 94%

Tennessee State University

- 3500 John A. Merritt Boulevard, Nashville, TN 37209
- **Website:** http://www.tnstate.edu
- **Public**
- **Degrees offered:** bachelor's, master's, education specialist, Ph.D., Ed.D.

ADMISSIONS

Admissions phone number: (615) 963-5901
Admissions email address: *gradschool@tnstate.edu*
Application fee: $25
Fall 2005 application deadline: 7/1
Test requirements: **GRE or MAT**
Test of English as Foreign Language (TOEFL) is required for international students.
Minimum TOEFL score required for paper test: 500
Minimum TOEFL score required for computer test: 173

Fall 2003
Acceptance rate for master's degree programs: 100%
Acceptance rate for education specialist degree programs: 100%
Acceptance rate for doctoral programs: 100%
Average GRE verbal: 400, Average GRE quantitative: 433, Average MAT: 36
Total 2003 enrollment: 1,000
Master's degree enrollment: 684
   Teacher preparation program enrollment (master's): 338
Education specialist degree enrollment: 81
Doctoral degree enrollment: 235

FINANCIAL INFORMATION

Financial aid phone number: (615) 963-5701
Tuition, 2003-2004 academic year: Full-time in-state: $3,132; out-of-state: $11,064, Part-time in-state: $783; out-of-state: $2,766
Fees: $343, Room and board: $4,270, Books and supplies: $1,000, Miscellaneous expenses: $3,484
Number of fellowships awarded to graduate students during the 2003-2004 academic year: 0
Number of teaching assistant positions: 17
Number of research assistant positions: 0
Number of other paid appointments: 0

ACADEMIC PROGRAMS

Total full-time tenured or tenure-track faculty (fall 2003): 63, Total part-time faculty (fall 2003): 125
Areas of specialization: curriculum and instruction, education administration and supervision, elementary teacher education, higher education administration, secondary teacher education, special education, student counseling and personnel services.
Professional development/partnership school(s) are used by students in some of the teaching programs.
During their internships, peer groups of students meet regularly to discuss instructional techniques in all of the teaching programs.
All of the students in their internships are mentored.
Courses that prepare teachers to pass the National Board of Professional Teaching Standards are not offered.
Teacher preparation programs: Four-year baccalaureate-degree program leading to initial licensure that includes either a major or minor in education and practice teaching. Master's program preparing college graduates for initial licensure; includes practice teaching. Alternative program for college graduates leading to provisional licensure.
The education program is currently accredited by the National Council for Accreditation of Teacher Education.

LICENSING TEST

Pass rate on state's teacher licensing test for 2002-2003: 98%
State average pass rate: 94%

Tennessee Technological University

- Box 5116, Cookeville, TN 38505
- **Website:** http://www.tntech.edu/
- **Public**
- **Degrees offered:** bachelor's, master's, education specialist, Ph.D.

ADMISSIONS

Admissions phone number: (931) 372-3233
Admissions email address: *g_admissions@tntech.edu*
Application website: *http://www.tntech.edu/graduatestudies/*
Application fee: $25
Test requirements: **GRE or MAT**
Test of English as Foreign Language (TOEFL) is required for international students.
Minimum TOEFL score required for paper test: 550
Minimum TOEFL score required for computer test: 213

Fall 2003
Total 2003 enrollment: 921
Master's degree enrollment: 608
Education specialist degree enrollment: 286
Doctoral degree enrollment: 27

FINANCIAL INFORMATION

Financial aid phone number: **(931) 372-3233**
Tuition, 2003-2004 academic year: Full-time in-state:
$2,412; out-of-state: **$6,378**, Part-time in-state:
$263/credit hour; out-of-state: **$607/credit hour**

ACADEMIC PROGRAMS

Total full-time tenured or tenure-track faculty (fall 2003): **91**
Areas of specialization: curriculum and instruction, education administration and supervision, educational psychology, elementary teacher education, secondary teacher education, special education, student counseling and personnel services.
The education program is currently accredited by the National Council for Accreditation of Teacher Education.

LICENSING TEST

Pass rate on state's teacher licensing test for 2002-2003:
92%
State average pass rate: **94%**

Tennessee Temple University

- 1815 Union Avenue, Chattanooga, TN 37404
- **Website:** http://www.tntemple.edu/
- **Private**

Trevecca Nazarene University

- 333 Murfreesboro Road, Nashville, TN 37210
- **Website:** http://www.trevecca.edu
- **Private**
- **Degrees offered:** bachelor's, master's, Ed.D.

ADMISSIONS

Admissions phone number: **(800) 284-1594**
Admissions email address: *admissions_ged.@trevecca.edu*
Application website: *http://www.trevecca.edu*
Application fee: **$50**
Fall 2005 application deadline: **rolling**
Test requirements: **GRE or MAT**
Test of English as Foreign Language (TOEFL) is required for international students.
Minimum TOEFL score required for paper test: **500**
Minimum TOEFL score required for computer test: **173**

Fall 2003

Acceptance rate for master's degree programs: **83%**
Acceptance rate for doctoral programs: **25%**
Average GRE verbal: **430**, Average GRE quantitative: **468**,
Average GRE analytical: **437**, Average MAT: **38**

Total 2003 enrollment: **250**
Master's degree enrollment: **179**
    Teacher preparation program enrollment (master's): **24**
Doctoral degree enrollment: **71**

FINANCIAL INFORMATION

Financial aid phone number: **(615) 248-1242**
Tuition, 2003-2004 academic year: Full-time: **$298/credit hour**; Part-time: **$298/credit hour**
Books and supplies: **$110**, Miscellaneous expenses: **$85**

ACADEMIC PROGRAMS

Total full-time tenured or tenure-track faculty (fall 2003):
    10, Total part-time faculty (fall 2003): **13**
Areas of specialization: curriculum and instruction, education administration and supervision.
Professional development/partnership school(s) are used by students in none of the teaching programs.
During their internships, peer groups of students meet regularly to discuss instructional techniques in all of the teaching programs.
All of the students in their internships are mentored.
Courses that prepare teachers to pass the National Board of Professional Teaching Standards are not offered.
Teacher preparation programs: Four-year baccalaureate-degree program leading to initial licensure that includes either a major or minor in education and practice teaching. Master's program preparing college graduates for initial licensure; includes practice teaching.

LICENSING TEST

Pass rate on state's teacher licensing test for 2002-2003:
90%
State average pass rate: **94%**

Tusculum College

- PO Box 5035, Greeneville, TN 37743
- **Website:** http://www.tusculum.edu
- **Private**
- **Degrees offered:** bachelor's, master's

ADMISSIONS

Admissions phone number: **(423) 581-5002**
Admissions email address: *ksimpson@tusculum.edu*
Application website: *http://www.tusculum.edu*
Application fee: **$0**
Fall 2005 application deadline: **rolling**
Test requirements: **GRE or MAT**
Test of English as Foreign Language (TOEFL) is required for international students.
Minimum TOEFL score required for paper test: **550**

Fall 2003

Total 2003 enrollment: **161**
Master's degree enrollment: **161**
    Teacher preparation program enrollment (master's): **161**

FINANCIAL INFORMATION

Financial aid phone number: **(800) 729-0256**

Tuition, 2003-2004 academic year: Full-time: **$5,565**: Part-time: **$265/credit hour**

ACADEMIC PROGRAMS

Areas of specialization: elementary teacher education, secondary teacher education.

Professional development/partnership school(s) are used by students in all of the teaching programs.

During their internships, peer groups of students meet regularly to discuss instructional techniques in some of the teaching programs.

All of the students in their internships are mentored.

Courses that prepare teachers to pass the National Board of Professional Teaching Standards are not offered.

Teacher preparation programs: Four-year baccalaureate-degree program leading to initial licensure that includes either a major or minor in education and practice teaching.

LICENSING TEST

Pass rate on state's teacher licensing test for 2002-2003: **76%**

State average pass rate: **94%**

Union University

- **1050 Union University Drive, Jackson, TN 38305**
- **Website:** http://www.uu.edu/
- **Private**
- **Degrees offered:** bachelor's, master's, education specialist, Ed.D.

ADMISSIONS

Admissions phone number: **(731) 661-5374**

Admissions email address: *hbutler@uu.edu*

Application website: *http://www.uu.edu/academics*

Application fee: **$25**

Fall 2005 application deadline: **rolling**

Test of English as Foreign Language (TOEFL) is required for international students.

Minimum TOEFL score required for paper test: **560**

Minimum TOEFL score required for computer test: **220**

Fall 2003

Total 2003 enrollment: **404**

Master's degree enrollment: **274**

　Teacher preparation program enrollment (master's): **274**

Education specialist degree enrollment: **69**

Doctoral degree enrollment: **61**

FINANCIAL INFORMATION

Financial aid phone number: **(731) 661-5015**

Tuition, 2003-2004 academic year: Full-time: **$240/credit hour**; Part-time: **$240/credit hour**

Number of research assistant positions: **3**

ACADEMIC PROGRAMS

Total full-time tenured or tenure-track faculty (fall 2003): **13**, Total part-time faculty (fall 2003): **18**

Areas of specialization: curriculum and instruction, education administration and supervision, elementary teacher education, secondary teacher education, special education.

Professional development/partnership school(s) are used by students in all of the teaching programs.

During their internships, peer groups of students meet regularly to discuss instructional techniques in all of the teaching programs.

All of the students in their internships are mentored.

Courses that prepare teachers to pass the National Board of Professional Teaching Standards are not offered.

Teacher preparation programs: Four-year baccalaureate-degree program leading to initial licensure that includes either a major or minor in education and practice teaching. Alternative program for college graduates leading to provisional licensure.

The education program is currently accredited by the National Council for Accreditation of Teacher Education.

LICENSING TEST

Pass rate on state's teacher licensing test for 2002-2003: **100%**

State average pass rate: **94%**

University of Memphis

- **215 Ball Hall, Memphis, TN 38152-6015**
- **Website:** http://www.memphis.edu/
- **Public**

ADMISSIONS

Admissions phone number: **(901) 678-2911**

Admissions email address: *gradsch@memphis.edu*

Application website: *http://www.enrollment.memphis.edu/admissions/ applications/graduate*

Test requirements: **GRE or MAT**

Test of English as Foreign Language (TOEFL) is required for international students.

Minimum TOEFL score required for paper test: **550**

Minimum TOEFL score required for computer test: **210**

FINANCIAL INFORMATION

Financial aid phone number: **(901) 678-4825**

LICENSING TEST

Pass rate on state's teacher licensing test for 2002-2003: **91%**

State average pass rate: **94%**

University of Tennessee–Chattanooga

- 615 McCallie Avenue, Chattanooga, TN 37403
- **Website:** http://www.utc.edu/gradstudies
- **Public**
- **Degrees offered:** bachelor's, master's, education specialist

ADMISSIONS

Admissions phone number: **(423) 425-4666**
Admissions email address: *jeanie-watkins@utc.edu*
Application website: *https://secure.utc.edu/GraduateSchool*
Application fee: **$25**
Fall 2005 application deadline: **rolling**
Test requirements: **MAT**
Test of English as Foreign Language (TOEFL) is required for international students.
Minimum TOEFL score required for paper test: 550
Minimum TOEFL score required for computer test: 213

Fall 2003
Acceptance rate for master's degree programs: 97%
Acceptance rate for education specialist degree programs: 100%
Average MAT: 38
Total 2003 enrollment: 412
Master's degree enrollment: 378
    Teacher preparation program enrollment (master's): 311
Education specialist degree enrollment: 34

FINANCIAL INFORMATION

Financial aid phone number: **(423) 425-4677**
Tuition, 2003-2004 academic year: Full-time in-state: **$4,456**; out-of-state: **$12,108**, Part-time in-state: **$288/credit hour**; out-of-state: **$713/credit hour**
Fees: **$29/credit hour**, Room and board: **$1,018**, Books and supplies: **$450**, Miscellaneous expenses: **$50**

ACADEMIC PROGRAMS

Total full-time tenured or tenure-track faculty (fall 2003): 10, Total part-time faculty (fall 2003): 6
Areas of specialization: education administration and supervision, educational psychology, elementary teacher education, secondary teacher education, special education, student counseling and personnel services.
Professional development/partnership school(s) are used by students in all of the teaching programs.
During their internships, peer groups of students meet regularly to discuss instructional techniques in all of the teaching programs.
All of the students in their internships are mentored.
Courses that prepare teachers to pass the National Board of Professional Teaching Standards are not offered.
Teacher preparation programs: Four-year baccalaureate-degree program leading to initial licensure that includes either a major or minor in education and practice teach-

ing. Master's program preparing college graduates for initial licensure; includes practice teaching. Alternative program for college graduates leading to provisional licensure.
The education program is currently accredited by the National Council for Accreditation of Teacher Education.

LICENSING TEST

Pass rate on state's teacher licensing test for 2002-2003: 99%
State average pass rate: 94%

University of Tennessee–Knoxville

- 335 Claxton Complex, Knoxville, TN 37996-3400
- **Website:** http://cehhs.utk.edu
- **Public**
- **Degrees offered:** bachelor's, master's, education specialist, Ph.D., Ed.D.
- **Overall rank in the 2005 U.S. News education schools with doctoral programs:** 40

ADMISSIONS

Admissions phone number: **(865) 974-4118**
Admissions email address: *nfox@utk.edu*
Application fee: **$35**
Fall 2005 application deadline: **rolling**
Test requirements: **GRE**
Test of English as Foreign Language (TOEFL) is required for international students.
Minimum TOEFL score required for paper test: 550
Minimum TOEFL score required for computer test: 213

Fall 2003
Acceptance rate for master's degree programs: 86%
Acceptance rate for education specialist degree programs: 90%
Acceptance rate for doctoral programs: 68%
Average GRE verbal: 518, Average GRE quantitative: 578, Average GRE analytical: 570
Total 2003 enrollment: 795
Master's degree enrollment: 508
    Teacher preparation program enrollment (master's): 383
Education specialist degree enrollment: 32
Doctoral degree enrollment: 255

FINANCIAL INFORMATION

Financial aid phone number: **(865) 974-3131**
Tuition, 2003-2004 academic year: Full-time in-state: **$6,555**; out-of-state: **$19,803**, Part-time in-state: **$243/credit hour**; out-of-state: **$734/credit hour**
Fees: **$827**, Room and board: **$7,098**, Books and supplies: **$1,320**, Miscellaneous expenses: **$2,742**
Number of fellowships awarded to graduate students during the 2003-2004 academic year: 38
Number of teaching assistant positions: 116

Number of research assistant positions: 4
Number of other paid appointments: 92

ACADEMIC PROGRAMS

Total full-time tenured or tenure-track faculty (fall 2003): 128, Total part-time faculty (fall 2003): 57

Areas of specialization: curriculum and instruction, education administration and supervision, education policy, educational psychology, elementary teacher education, higher education administration, secondary teacher education, special education, student counseling and personnel services.

Professional development/partnership school(s) are used by students in all of the teaching programs.

During their internships, peer groups of students meet regularly to discuss instructional techniques in all of the teaching programs.

All of the students in their internships are mentored.

Courses that prepare teachers to pass the National Board of Professional Teaching Standards are not offered.

Teacher preparation programs: Four-year baccalaureate-degree program leading to initial licensure that includes either a major or minor in education and practice teaching. Five-year program leading to initial licensure that results in a baccalaureate degree (with a major or minor in education) plus graduate credit and includes practice teaching. Five-year program leading to initial licensure that results in a baccalaureate degree (with a major or minor in education) plus a master's degree and includes practice teaching. Master's program preparing college graduates for initial licensure; includes practice teaching. Alternative program for college graduates leading to provisional licensure.

The education program is currently accredited by the National Council for Accreditation of Teacher Education.

LICENSING TEST

Pass rate on state's teacher licensing test for 2002-2003: 97%
State average pass rate: 94%

University of Tennessee–Martin

- University Street, Martin, TN 38238
- **Website:** http://www.utm.edu
- Public
- **Degrees offered:** bachelor's, master's

ADMISSIONS

Admissions phone number: (731) 587-7012
Application fee: $25
Test of English as Foreign Language (TOEFL) is required for international students.
Minimum TOEFL score required for paper test: 525
Minimum TOEFL score required for computer test: 197

Fall 2003
Total 2003 enrollment: 229
Master's degree enrollment: 229
Teacher preparation program enrollment (master's): 153

FINANCIAL INFORMATION

Financial aid phone number: (731) 587-7040
Tuition, 2003-2004 academic year: Full-time in-state: $3,214; out-of-state: $9,744, Part-time in-state: ; out-of-state: $179/credit hour
Fees: $363/credit hour

ACADEMIC PROGRAMS

Total full-time tenured or tenure-track faculty (fall 2003): 17, Total part-time faculty (fall 2003): 4

Areas of specialization: education administration and supervision, elementary teacher education, secondary teacher education, student counseling and personnel services.

Professional development/partnership school(s) are used by students in some of the teaching programs.

During their internships, peer groups of students meet regularly to discuss instructional techniques in none of the teaching programs.

All of the students in their internships are mentored.

Courses that prepare teachers to pass the National Board of Professional Teaching Standards are not offered.

Teacher preparation programs: Four-year baccalaureate-degree program leading to initial licensure that includes either a major or minor in education and practice teaching. Master's program preparing college graduates for initial licensure; includes practice teaching.

The education program is currently accredited by the National Council for Accreditation of Teacher Education.

LICENSING TEST

Pass rate on state's teacher licensing test for 2002-2003: 100%
State average pass rate: 94%

Vanderbilt University (Peabody)

- PO Box 327, Nashville, TN 37203
- **Website:** http://peabody.vanderbilt.edu
- Private
- **Degrees offered:** bachelor's, master's, Ph.D., Ed.D.
- **Overall rank in the 2005 U.S. News education schools with doctoral programs:** 4
- **Overall rank in the 2005 U.S. News education school specialty rankings:** administration/supervision: 4, curriculum/instruction: 9, education policy: 7, educational psychology: 10, elementary education: 7, higher education administration: 11, secondary education: 12, special education: 1

ADMISSIONS

Admissions phone number: **(615) 322-8410**

Admissions email address:
peabody.admissions@vanderbilt.edu

Application website: *http://peabody.vanderbilt.edu/ admissions/apply_online.htm*

Application fee: **$0**

Fall 2005 application deadline: **12/31**

Test requirements: **GRE or MAT**

Test of English as Foreign Language (TOEFL) is required for international students.

Minimum TOEFL score required for paper test: **550**

Minimum TOEFL score required for computer test: **213**

Fall 2003

Acceptance rate for master's degree programs: **68%**

Acceptance rate for doctoral programs: **15%**

Average GRE verbal: **561**, Average GRE quantitative: **645**, Average GRE analytical: **668**, Average MAT: **57**

Total 2003 enrollment: **609**

Master's degree enrollment: **308**
   Teacher preparation program enrollment (master's): **153**

Doctoral degree enrollment: **301**

FINANCIAL INFORMATION

Financial aid phone number: **(615) 322-8410**

Tuition, 2003-2004 academic year: Full-time: **$1,155/credit hour**; Part-time: **$1,155/credit hour**

Fees: **$1,510**, Room and board: **$10,300**, Books and supplies: **$1,370**, Miscellaneous expenses: **$4,290**

Number of fellowships awarded to graduate students during the 2003-2004 academic year: **74**

Number of teaching assistant positions: **89**

Number of research assistant positions: **147**

Number of other paid appointments: **61**

ACADEMIC PROGRAMS

Total full-time tenured or tenure-track faculty (fall 2003): **79**, Total part-time faculty (fall 2003): **37**

Areas of specialization: curriculum and instruction, education administration and supervision, education policy, educational psychology, elementary teacher education, higher education administration, secondary teacher education, special education, student counseling and personnel services.

Professional development/partnership school(s) are used by students in some of the teaching programs.

During their internships, peer groups of students meet regularly to discuss instructional techniques in all of the teaching programs.

All of the students in their internships are mentored.

Courses that prepare teachers to pass the National Board of Professional Teaching Standards are not offered.

Teacher preparation programs: Four-year baccalaureate-degree program leading to initial licensure that includes either a major or minor in education and practice teaching. Five-year program leading to initial licensure that results in a baccalaureate degree (with a major or minor in education) plus a master's degree and includes practice teaching. Master's program preparing college graduates for initial licensure; includes practice teaching. Alternative program for college graduates leading to provisional licensure.

The education program is currently accredited by the National Council for Accreditation of Teacher Education.

LICENSING TEST

Pass rate on state's teacher licensing test for 2002-2003: **100%**

State average pass rate: **94%**

TEXAS

TEACHER TESTING IN TEXAS
Teacher licensure rules vary widely from state to state, but almost all states require tests. The exams typically cover the basics of reading, writing and math, although some states mandate in-depth, subject-specific teacher tests. For information on where to go in your state for specific academic requirements, see Chapter 6 on page 67. Note: Some schools require students to pass exams by graduation, and thus automatically report pass rates of 100 percent.

- This state **does not** require a basic skills test in order to obtain a teaching license.
- This state **does** require a subject-knowledge test in order to obtain a middle school teaching license.
- This state **does** require a subject-knowledge test in order to obtain a high school teaching license.
- This state **does** require a subject-specific pedagogy test in order to obtain a teaching license.

Abilene Christian University

- **ACU Box 29000, Abilene, TX 79699**
- **Website:** http://www.acu.edu/
- **Private**

LICENSING TEST
Pass rate on state's teacher licensing test for 2002-2003: 89%
State average pass rate: 92%

Angelo State University

- **2601 West. Ave. N., San Angelo, TX 76909**
- **Website:** http://www.angelo.edu/gradschool
- **Public**
- **Degrees offered:** bachelor's, master's

ADMISSIONS
Admissions phone number: (325) 942-2169
Admissions email address: *graduate.school@angelo.edu*
Application website:
   http://www.angelo.edu/forms/pdf/grad_admis_app.pdf
Application fee: $25
Fall 2005 application deadline: 7/15
Test of English as Foreign Language (TOEFL) is required for international students.
Minimum TOEFL score required for paper test: 550
Minimum TOEFL score required for computer test: 213

Fall 2003
Acceptance rate for master's degree programs: 100%
Total 2003 enrollment: 113
Master's degree enrollment: 113
   Teacher preparation program enrollment (master's): 19

FINANCIAL INFORMATION
Financial aid phone number: (325) 942-2246
Tuition, 2003-2004 academic year: Full-time in-state: **$184/credit hour**; out-of-state: **$401/credit hour**, Part-time in-state: **$184/credit hour**; out-of-state: **$401/credit hour**
Room and board: **$4,001**, Books and supplies: **$1,000**, Miscellaneous expenses: **$1,500**

ACADEMIC PROGRAMS
Total full-time tenured or tenure-track faculty (fall 2003): 13, Total part-time faculty (fall 2003): 5
Professional development/partnership school(s) are used by students in all of the teaching programs.
During their internships, peer groups of students meet regularly to discuss instructional techniques in all of the teaching programs.
All of the students in their internships are mentored.
Courses that prepare teachers to pass the National Board of Professional Teaching Standards are not offered.

LICENSING TEST
Pass rate on state's teacher licensing test for 2002-2003: 95%
State average pass rate: 92%

Austin College

- **900 N Grand Ave, Sherman, TX 75090-4400**
- **Website:** http://www.austincollege.edu
- **Private**
- **Degrees offered:** master's

ADMISSIONS
Admissions phone number: (903) 813-2327
Admissions email address: *admission@austincollege.edu*
Application fee: $35

Fall 2003
Total 2003 enrollment: 38
Master's degree enrollment: 38
   Teacher preparation program enrollment (master's): 38

FINANCIAL INFORMATION

Financial aid phone number: **(903) 813-2900**
Tuition, 2003-2004 academic year: Full-time: **$20,970**;
Part-time: **$643/credit hour**
Fees: **$160**, Room and board: **$6,822**, Books and supplies:
$800, Miscellaneous expenses: **$1,200**

ACADEMIC PROGRAMS

Total full-time tenured or tenure-track faculty (fall 2003): **6**
Total part-time faculty (fall 2003): **1**
Areas of specialization: elementary teacher education, secondary teacher education.
Professional development/partnership school(s) are used by students in all of the teaching programs.
During their internships, peer groups of students meet regularly to discuss instructional techniques in all of the teaching programs.
All of the students in their internships are mentored.
Courses that prepare teachers to pass the National Board of Professional Teaching Standards are not offered.
Teacher preparation programs: Master's degree in education, including internship/practice teaching and preparation for initial licensure.
The education program is currently accredited by the Teacher Education Accreditation Council.

LICENSING TEST

Pass rate on state's teacher licensing test for 2002-2003: **100%**
State average pass rate: **92%**

Baylor University

- ■ **PO Box 97304, Waco, TX 76798-7304**
- ■ **Website:** http://www.baylor.edu/SOE/
- ■ **Private**
- ■ **Degrees offered:** bachelor's, master's, education specialist, Ph.D., Ed.D.
- ■ **Overall rank in the 2005 U.S. News education schools with doctoral programs:** 73

ADMISSIONS

Admissions phone number: **(254) 710-3584**
Admissions email address: *lisa_manis@baylor.edu*
Application website: *https://www1.baylor.edu/graduate/application/home.asp*
Application fee: **$40**
Fall 2005 application deadline: **2/15**
Test requirements: **GRE or MAT**
Test of English as Foreign Language (TOEFL) is required for international students.
Minimum TOEFL score required for paper test: **550**
Minimum TOEFL score required for computer test: **213**

Fall 2003
Acceptance rate for master's degree programs: **76%**
Acceptance rate for education specialist degree programs: **100%**

Acceptance rate for doctoral programs: **36%**
Average GRE verbal: **474**, Average GRE quantitative: **582**,
Average GRE analytical: **457**
Total 2003 enrollment: **303**
Master's degree enrollment: **167**
Teacher preparation program enrollment (master's): **37**
Education specialist degree enrollment: **9**
Doctoral degree enrollment: **127**

FINANCIAL INFORMATION

Financial aid phone number: **(254) 710-2611**
Tuition, 2003-2004 academic year: Full-time: **$698/credit hour**; Part-time: **$698/credit hour**
Fees: **$1,144**, Room and board: **$6,404**, Books and supplies: **$940**
Number of fellowships awarded to graduate students during the 2003-2004 academic year: **67**
Number of teaching assistant positions: **53**
Number of research assistant positions: **26**
Number of other paid appointments: **0**

ACADEMIC PROGRAMS

Total full-time tenured or tenure-track faculty (fall 2003): **45**
Areas of specialization: curriculum and instruction, education administration and supervision, education policy, educational psychology, elementary teacher education, higher education administration, secondary teacher education, special education, student counseling and personnel services.
Professional development/partnership school(s) are used by students in all of the teaching programs.
During their internships, peer groups of students meet regularly to discuss instructional techniques in all of the teaching programs.
All of the students in their internships are mentored.
Courses that prepare teachers to pass the National Board of Professional Teaching Standards are offered.
Teacher preparation programs: Four-year baccalaureate-degree program leading to initial licensure that includes either a major or minor in education and practice teaching. Master's program preparing college graduates for initial licensure; includes practice teaching.
The education program is currently accredited by the National Council for Accreditation of Teacher Education.

LICENSING TEST

Pass rate on state's teacher licensing test for 2002-2003: **92%**
State average pass rate: **92%**

Concordia University– Austin

- 3400 Interstate 35 North, Austin, TX 78705
- **Website:** http://www.concordia.edu/
- **Private**

LICENSING TEST
Pass rate on state's teacher licensing test for 2002-2003: 94%
State average pass rate: 92%

Dallas Baptist University

- 3000 Mountain Creek Parkway, Dallas, TX 75211-9299
- **Website:** http://www.dbu.edu/
- **Private**
- **Degrees offered:** master's, education specialist

ADMISSIONS
Admissions phone number: (214) 333-5242
Admissions email address: *graduate@dbu.edu*
Application fee: **$25**
Fall 2005 application deadline: **rolling**
Minimum TOEFL score required for paper test: 525
Minimum TOEFL score required for computer test: 197

Fall 2003
Acceptance rate for master's degree programs: 100%
Total 2003 enrollment: 217
Master's degree enrollment: 184
Education specialist degree enrollment: 33

FINANCIAL INFORMATION
Financial aid phone number: (214) 333-5363
Tuition, 2003-2004 academic year: Full-time: $6,786; Part-time: $3,393
Room and board: $4,160, Books and supplies: $731, Miscellaneous expenses: $2,021

ACADEMIC PROGRAMS
Courses that prepare teachers to pass the National Board of Professional Teaching Standards are not offered.
Teacher preparation programs: Four-year baccalaureate-degree program leading to initial licensure that includes either a major or minor in education and practice teaching. Master's program preparing college graduates for initial licensure; includes practice teaching.

LICENSING TEST
Pass rate on state's teacher licensing test for 2002-2003: 96%
State average pass rate: 92%

Hardin-Simmons University

- Box 16225, Abilene, TX 79698
- **Website:** http://www.hsutx.edu/
- **Private**
- **Degrees offered:** bachelor's, master's

ADMISSIONS
Admissions phone number: (325) 670-1298
Admissions email address: *gradoff@hsutx.edu*
Application website: http://hsutx.edu/academics/graduate/grad/generalapp.pdf
Application fee: **$50**
Fall 2005 application deadline: **rolling**
Test requirements: **GRE**
Test of English as Foreign Language (TOEFL) is required for international students.
Minimum TOEFL score required for paper test: 550

Fall 2003
Acceptance rate for master's degree programs: 86%
Average GRE verbal: 463, Average GRE quantitative: 513
Total 2003 enrollment: 151
Master's degree enrollment: 151
    Teacher preparation program enrollment (master's): 44

FINANCIAL INFORMATION
Financial aid phone number: (325) 670-1206
Tuition, 2003-2004 academic year: Full-time: $7,020; Part-time: **$390/credit hour**
Fees: $756, Room and board: $3,699, Books and supplies: $750, Miscellaneous expenses: $1,482
Number of fellowships awarded to graduate students during the 2003-2004 academic year: 23
Number of teaching assistant positions: 11
Number of research assistant positions: 0
Number of other paid appointments: 10

ACADEMIC PROGRAMS
Total full-time tenured or tenure-track faculty (fall 2003): 14
    Total part-time faculty (fall 2003): 2
Areas of specialization: curriculum and instruction, elementary teacher education, secondary teacher education, special education, student counseling and personnel services.
Professional development/partnership school(s) are used by students in all of the teaching programs.
During their internships, peer groups of students meet regularly to discuss instructional techniques in all of the teaching programs.
All of the students in their internships are mentored.
Courses that prepare teachers to pass the National Board of Professional Teaching Standards are not offered.
Teacher preparation programs: Four-year baccalaureate-degree program leading to initial licensure that includes either a major or minor in education and practice teaching.

LICENSING TEST

Pass rate on state's teacher licensing test for 2002-2003: 93%
State average pass rate: 92%

Houston Baptist University

- 7502 Fondren Road, Houston, TX 77074-3298
- Website: http://www.hbu.edu/
- Private

LICENSING TEST

Pass rate on state's teacher licensing test for 2002-2003: 100%
State average pass rate: 92%

Lamar University

- PO Box 10034, Lamar University Station, Beaumont, TX 77710
- Website: http://www.lamar.edu
- Public
- Degrees offered: bachelor's, master's

ADMISSIONS

Admissions phone number: (409) 880-8356
Admissions email address: *gradmissions@hal.lamar.edu*
Application website:
http://dept.lamar.edu/graduatestudies/Admissions.htm
Fall 2005 application deadline: rolling
Test requirements: GRE
Test of English as Foreign Language (TOEFL) is required for international students.
Minimum TOEFL score required for paper test: 525
Minimum TOEFL score required for computer test: 197

Fall 2003

Acceptance rate for master's degree programs: 70%
Average GRE verbal: 469, Average GRE quantitative: 512, Average GRE analytical: 500
Total 2003 enrollment: 347
Master's degree enrollment: 347
  Teacher preparation program enrollment (master's): 89

FINANCIAL INFORMATION

Financial aid phone number: (409) 880-8450
Tuition, 2003-2004 academic year: Full-time in-state: $2,236; out-of-state: $8,372, Part-time in-state: $86/credit hour; out-of-state: $322/credit hour
Fees: $847, Room and board: $5,012, Books and supplies: $662
Number of fellowships awarded to graduate students during the 2003-2004 academic year: 0

Number of teaching assistant positions: 10
Number of research assistant positions: 3
Number of other paid appointments: 0

ACADEMIC PROGRAMS

Total full-time tenured or tenure-track faculty (fall 2003): 38, Total part-time faculty (fall 2003): 25
Areas of specialization: education administration and supervision, elementary teacher education, secondary teacher education, special education, student counseling and personnel services.
Professional development/partnership school(s) are used by students in all of the teaching programs.
During their internships, peer groups of students meet regularly to discuss instructional techniques in all of the teaching programs.
All of the students in their internships are mentored.
Courses that prepare teachers to pass the National Board of Professional Teaching Standards are not offered.
Teacher preparation programs: Four-year baccalaureate-degree program leading to initial licensure that includes either a major or minor in education and practice teaching. Alternative program for college graduates leading to provisional licensure.

LICENSING TEST

Pass rate on state's teacher licensing test for 2002-2003: 98%
State average pass rate: 92%

Lubbock Christian University

- 5601 19th Street, Lubbock, TX 79407
- Website: http://www.lcu.edu/
- Private

LICENSING TEST

Pass rate on state's teacher licensing test for 2002-2003: 83%
State average pass rate: 92%

Midwestern State University

- 3410 Taft Boulevard, Wichita Falls, TX 76308-2099
- Website: http://www.mwsu.edu/
- Public
- Degrees offered: bachelor's, master's

ADMISSIONS

Admissions phone number: (940) 397-4334
Admissions email address: *admissions@mwsu.edu*
Application website: *http://admissions.mwsu.edu/apply.asp*

Application fee: **$0**

Fall 2005 application deadline: 8/7

Test requirements: **GRE or MAT**

Test of English as Foreign Language (TOEFL) is required for international students.

Minimum TOEFL score required for paper test: 550

Minimum TOEFL score required for computer test: 213

Fall 2003

Average GRE verbal: 407, Average GRE quantitative: 473, Average GRE analytical: 513, Average MAT: 35

Total 2003 enrollment: 284

Master's degree enrollment: 284

   Teacher preparation program enrollment (master's): 81

FINANCIAL INFORMATION

Financial aid phone number: **(940) 397-4214**

Tuition, 2003-2004 academic year: Full-time in-state: **$1,368**; out-of-state: **$5,616**, Part-time in-state: **$76/credit hour**; out-of-state: **$312/credit hour**

Fees: **$1,270**, Room and board: **$4,630**, Books and supplies: **$945**, Miscellaneous expenses: **$315**

ACADEMIC PROGRAMS

Total full-time tenured or tenure-track faculty (fall 2003): 13, Total part-time faculty (fall 2003): 8

LICENSING TEST

Pass rate on state's teacher licensing test for 2002-2003: 92%

State average pass rate: 92%

Our Lady of the Lake University

- **411 S.W. 24th Street, San Antonio, TX 78207**
- **Website:** http://www.ollusa.edu
- **Private**
- **Degrees offered:** bachelor's, master's, Ph.D., Ed.D.

ADMISSIONS

Admissions phone number: **(210) 431-3961**

Admissions email address: *gradadm@lake.ollusa.edu*

Application website: *http://www.ollusa.edu/_graduate_ admissions/index.asp*

Application fee: **$25**

Fall 2005 application deadline: **rolling**

Test of English as Foreign Language (TOEFL) is required for international students.

Minimum TOEFL score required for paper test: 525

Minimum TOEFL score required for computer test: 197

Fall 2003

Acceptance rate for master's degree programs: 80%

Acceptance rate for doctoral programs: 50%

Total 2003 enrollment: 587

Master's degree enrollment: 476

Teacher preparation program enrollment (master's): 258

Doctoral degree enrollment: 111

FINANCIAL INFORMATION

Financial aid phone number: **(210) 431-3960**

Tuition, 2003-2004 academic year: Full-time: **$514/credit hour**; Part-time: **$514/credit hour**

Room and board: **$2,551**, Books and supplies: **$500**

Number of fellowships awarded to graduate students during the 2003-2004 academic year: 0

Number of teaching assistant positions: 0

Number of research assistant positions: 3

Number of other paid appointments: 0

ACADEMIC PROGRAMS

Total full-time tenured or tenure-track faculty (fall 2003): 5
   Total part-time faculty (fall 2003): 10

Areas of specialization: curriculum and instruction, education administration and supervision, elementary teacher education, secondary teacher education, special education, student counseling and personnel services.

Professional development/partnership school(s) are used by students in some of the teaching programs.

During their internships, peer groups of students meet regularly to discuss instructional techniques in some of the teaching programs.

Some of the students in their internships are mentored.

Courses that prepare teachers to pass the National Board of Professional Teaching Standards are not offered.

Teacher preparation programs: Four-year baccalaureate-degree program leading to initial licensure that includes either a major or minor in education and practice teaching. Master's program preparing college graduates for initial licensure; includes practice teaching.

LICENSING TEST

Pass rate on state's teacher licensing test for 2002-2003: 80%

State average pass rate: 92%

Prairie View A&M University

- **PO Box 3089, Office of Admissions and Records, Prairie View, TX 77446-0188**
- **Website:** http://www.pvamu.edu/
- **Public**

LICENSING TEST

Pass rate on state's teacher licensing test for 2002-2003: 81%

State average pass rate: 92%

Rice University

- PO Box 1892, Houston, TX 77251-1892
- Website: http://www.rice.edu/
- Private

Sam Houston State University

- Box 2119, Huntsville, TX 77341
- Website: http://www.shsu.edu/~grs_www
- Public
- Degrees offered: bachelor's, master's, education specialist, Ph.D., Ed.D.

ADMISSIONS

Admissions phone number: (936) 294-1971
Admissions email address: *mmuehsam@shsu.edu*
Application website:
  http://www.shsu.edu/~grs_www/forms/gradadm.html
Application fee: $20
Fall 2005 application deadline: 8/1
Test requirements: GRE or MAT
Test of English as Foreign Language (TOEFL) is required for international students.
Minimum TOEFL score required for paper test: 550
Minimum TOEFL score required for computer test: 213

Fall 2003
Acceptance rate for master's degree programs: 88%
Acceptance rate for education specialist degree programs: 97%
Acceptance rate for doctoral programs: 33%
Total 2003 enrollment: 746
Master's degree enrollment: 714
  Teacher preparation program enrollment (master's): 258
Doctoral degree enrollment: 32

FINANCIAL INFORMATION

Financial aid phone number: (936) 294-1724
Tuition, 2003-2004 academic year: Full-time in-state: $2,304; out-of-state: $7,968, Part-time in-state: $96/credit hour; out-of-state: $332/credit hour
Fees: $490, Room and board: $1,312, Books and supplies: $400, Miscellaneous expenses: $1,024
Number of fellowships awarded to graduate students during the 2003-2004 academic year: 2
Number of teaching assistant positions: 0
Number of research assistant positions: 11
Number of other paid appointments: 3

ACADEMIC PROGRAMS

Total full-time tenured or tenure-track faculty (fall 2003): 45
  Total part-time faculty (fall 2003): 70

Areas of specialization: curriculum and instruction, education administration and supervision, educational psychology, elementary teacher education, higher education administration, secondary teacher education, special education, student counseling and personnel services, teacher education.
Professional development/partnership school(s) are used by students in all of the teaching programs.
During their internships, peer groups of students meet regularly to discuss instructional techniques in all of the teaching programs.
All of the students in their internships are mentored.
Courses that prepare teachers to pass the National Board of Professional Teaching Standards are not offered.
Teacher preparation programs: Four-year baccalaureate-degree program leading to initial licensure that includes either a major or minor in education and practice teaching. Alternative program for college graduates leading to provisional licensure.
The education program is currently accredited by the National Council for Accreditation of Teacher Education.

LICENSING TEST

Pass rate on state's teacher licensing test for 2002-2003: 100%
State average pass rate: 92%

Schreiner College

- 2100 Memorial Blvd., Kerrville, TX 78028
- Website: http://www.schreiner.edu
- Private
- Degrees offered: bachelor's, master's

ADMISSIONS

Admissions phone number: (830) 792-7223
Admissions email address: *SKSpeed@schreiner.edu*
Application fee: $25
Fall 2005 application deadline: 7/1
Test requirements: GRE

Fall 2003
Total 2003 enrollment: 48
Master's degree enrollment: 48
  Teacher preparation program enrollment (master's): 38

FINANCIAL INFORMATION

Financial aid phone number: (830) 792-7229
Tuition, 2003-2004 academic year: Full-time: $300/credit hour; Part-time: $300/credit hour
Fees: $100, Books and supplies: $150
Number of fellowships awarded to graduate students during the 2003-2004 academic year: 0
Number of teaching assistant positions: 0
Number of research assistant positions: 0
Number of other paid appointments: 0

ACADEMIC PROGRAMS

Total full-time tenured or tenure-track faculty (fall 2003): 1
  Total part-time faculty (fall 2003): 1
Areas of specialization: curriculum and instruction, education administration and supervision.
Professional development/partnership school(s) are used by students in all of the teaching programs.
During their internships, peer groups of students meet regularly to discuss instructional techniques in all of the teaching programs.
All of the students in their internships are mentored.
Courses that prepare teachers to pass the National Board of Professional Teaching Standards are not offered.
Teacher preparation programs: Four-year baccalaureate-degree program leading to initial licensure that includes either a major or minor in education and practice teaching. Master's program preparing college graduates for initial licensure; includes practice teaching.

LICENSING TEST

Pass rate on state's teacher licensing test for 2002-2003: 100%
State average pass rate: 92%

Southern Methodist University

■ PO Box 750181, Dallas, TX 75275-0181
■ Website:
  http://www.smu.edu/teacher_education/
  gradprograms.asp
■ Private
■ **Degrees offered:** master's

ADMISSIONS

Admissions phone number: **(214) 768-2346**
Admissions email address: *teacher@smu.edu*
Application website: *http://www.smu.edu/teacher_education/
  PDF/master_ed_app.pdf*
Application fee: **$50**
Fall 2005 application deadline: 6/30
Test requirements: **GRE**
Test of English as Foreign Language (TOEFL) is required for international students.
Minimum TOEFL score required for paper test: 550
Minimum TOEFL score required for computer test: 214

Fall 2003
Acceptance rate for master's degree programs: **89%**
Average GRE verbal: **460**, Average GRE quantitative: **760**, Average GRE analytical: **670**
Total 2003 enrollment: **144**
Master's degree enrollment: **144**
  Teacher preparation program enrollment (master's): 30

FINANCIAL INFORMATION

Financial aid phone number: **(214) 768-3417**

Tuition, 2003-2004 academic year: Full-time: **$299/credit hour**; Part-time: **$299/credit hour**
Books and supplies: **$100**, Miscellaneous expenses: **$50**
Number of fellowships awarded to graduate students during the 2003-2004 academic year: 0
Number of teaching assistant positions: 0
Number of research assistant positions: 7
Number of other paid appointments: 0

ACADEMIC PROGRAMS

Total full-time tenured or tenure-track faculty (fall 2003): 9
  Total part-time faculty (fall 2003): 15
Professional development/partnership school(s) are used by students in all of the teaching programs.
During their internships, peer groups of students meet regularly to discuss instructional techniques in all of the teaching programs.
All of the students in their internships are mentored.
Courses that prepare teachers to pass the National Board of Professional Teaching Standards are not offered.

LICENSING TEST

Pass rate on state's teacher licensing test for 2002-2003: 90%
State average pass rate: 92%

Southwestern Adventist University

■ PO Box 567, Keene, TX 76059
■ Website: http://www.swau.edu/
■ Private

LICENSING TEST

Pass rate on state's teacher licensing test for 2002-2003: 100%
State average pass rate: 92%

Stephen F. Austin State University

■ P.O. Box 13024, SFA Station, Nacogdoches, TX 75962
■ Website: http://www.sfasu.edu/
■ Public
■ **Degrees offered:** bachelor's, master's, Ed.D.

ADMISSIONS

Admissions phone number: **(936) 468-2807**
Admissions email address: *gschool@sfasu.edu*
Application website: http://www.sfasu.edu/graduate/
  appforms.html
Application fee: **$25**
Fall 2005 application deadline: 6/1

Test of English as Foreign Language (TOEFL) is required
for international students.
Minimum TOEFL score required for paper test: 550
Minimum TOEFL score required for computer test: 213

FINANCIAL INFORMATION

Financial aid phone number: **(936) 468-2403**
Tuition, 2003-2004 academic year: Full-time in-state:
$46/credit hour; out-of-state: **$256/credit hour**, Part-time
in-state: **$46/credit hour**; out-of-state: **$256/credit hour**
Fees: **$70/credit hour**, Room and board: **$2,598**, Books and
supplies: **$400**, Miscellaneous expenses: **$900**

ACADEMIC PROGRAMS

Teacher preparation programs: Four-year baccalaureate-
degree program leading to initial licensure that includes
either a major or minor in education and practice teaching. Master's program preparing college graduates for
initial licensure; includes practice teaching. Alternative
program for college graduates leading to provisional
licensure.
The education program is currently accredited by the
National Council for Accreditation of Teacher Education.

LICENSING TEST

Pass rate on state's teacher licensing test for 2002-2003:
98%
State average pass rate: **92%**

St. Mary's University of San Antonio

- **One Camino Santa Maria, San Antonio, TX 78228**
- **Website:** http://www.stmarytx.edu/
- **Private**
- **Degrees offered:** master's

ADMISSIONS

Admissions phone number: **(210) 436-3101**
Admissions email address: *gradsch@stmarytx.edu*
Application fee: **$30**
Fall 2005 application deadline: **6/1**
Test of English as Foreign Language (TOEFL) is required
for international students.
Minimum TOEFL score required for paper test: 550
Minimum TOEFL score required for computer test: 213

Fall 2003
Total 2003 enrollment: **807**
Master's degree enrollment: **741**
Teacher preparation program enrollment (master's): **38**
Doctoral degree enrollment: **66**

FINANCIAL INFORMATION

Financial aid phone number: **(210) 436-3141**
Tuition, 2003-2004 academic year: Full-time: **$512/credit
hour**; Part-time: **$512/credit hour**

Room and board: **$1,846**, Books and supplies: **$1,600**,
Miscellaneous expenses: **$400**

ACADEMIC PROGRAMS

Total full-time tenured or tenure-track faculty (fall 2003): **4**
Total part-time faculty (fall 2003): **2**

LICENSING TEST

Pass rate on state's teacher licensing test for 2002-2003:
95%
State average pass rate: **92%**

Sul Ross State University

- **Box C-115, Alpine, TX 79832**
- **Website:** http://www.sulross.edu
- **Public**
- **Degrees offered:** bachelor's, master's

ADMISSIONS

Admissions phone number: **(432) 837-8052**
Application website: *http://www.sulross.edu/pages/182.asp*
Application fee: **$25**
Fall 2005 application deadline: **8/20**
Test of English as Foreign Language (TOEFL) is required
for international students.
Minimum TOEFL score required for paper test: 520
Minimum TOEFL score required for computer test: 190

FINANCIAL INFORMATION

Financial aid phone number: **(453) 837-8056**

ACADEMIC PROGRAMS

Total full-time tenured or tenure-track faculty (fall 2003): **11**
Total part-time faculty (fall 2003): **3**
Areas of specialization: curriculum and instruction, education administration and supervision, educational psychology, elementary teacher education, secondary
teacher education, special education, student counseling
and personnel services.
Professional development/partnership school(s) are used
by students in all of the teaching programs.
During their internships, peer groups of students meet
regularly to discuss instructional techniques in all of the
teaching programs.
All of the students in their internships are mentored.
Courses that prepare teachers to pass the National Board of
Professional Teaching Standards are not offered.

LICENSING TEST

Pass rate on state's teacher licensing test for 2002-2003:
68%
State average pass rate: **92%**

Tarleton State University

- Box T-0350, Stephenville, TX 76402
- **Website:** http://www.tarleton.edu/~graduate
- Public
- **Degrees offered:** bachelor's, master's, education specialist, Ed.D.

ADMISSIONS

Admissions phone number: **(254) 968-9104**
Admissions email address: *ljones@tarleton.edu*
Application website: *http://www.tarleton.edu/~graduate*
Application fee: **$25**
Fall 2005 application deadline: 8/1
Test of English as Foreign Language (TOEFL) is required for international students.
Minimum TOEFL score required for paper test: 550
Minimum TOEFL score required for computer test: 210

Fall 2003
Acceptance rate for master's degree programs: 89%
Acceptance rate for doctoral programs: 65%
Total 2003 enrollment: 975
Master's degree enrollment: 877
   Teacher preparation program enrollment (master's): 260
Education specialist degree enrollment: 83
Doctoral degree enrollment: 15

FINANCIAL INFORMATION

Financial aid phone number: **(254) 968-9070**
Tuition, 2003-2004 academic year: Full-time in-state: **$90/credit hour**; out-of-state: **$298/credit hour**, Part-time in-state: **$90/credit hour**; out-of-state: **$283/credit hour**
Number of fellowships awarded to graduate students during the 2003-2004 academic year: 1
Number of teaching assistant positions: 18
Number of research assistant positions: 124

ACADEMIC PROGRAMS

Total full-time tenured or tenure-track faculty (fall 2003): 61, Total part-time faculty (fall 2003): 43
Areas of specialization: curriculum and instruction, education administration and supervision, educational psychology, elementary teacher education, higher education administration, special education, student counseling and personnel services.
Professional development/partnership school(s) are used by students in all of the teaching programs.
During their internships, peer groups of students meet regularly to discuss instructional techniques in all of the teaching programs.
All of the students in their internships are mentored.
Courses that prepare teachers to pass the National Board of Professional Teaching Standards are offered.

LICENSING TEST

Pass rate on state's teacher licensing test for 2002-2003: 96%
State average pass rate: 92%

Texas A&M International University

- 5201 University Blvd., Laredo, TX 78041
- **Website:** http://www.tamiu.edu/
- Public

LICENSING TEST

Pass rate on state's teacher licensing test for 2002-2003: 86%
State average pass rate: 92%

Texas A&M University– College Station

- College of Education, 4222 TAMUS, College Station, TX 77843-4222
- **Website:** http://www.coe.tamu.edu/
- Public
- **Degrees offered:** bachelor's, master's, Ph.D., Ed.D.
- **Overall rank in the 2005 U.S. News education schools with doctoral programs:** 42
- **Overall rank in the 2005 U.S. News education school specialty rankings:** administration/supervision: 25, educational psychology: 18, higher education administration: 22, vocational/technical: 10

ADMISSIONS

Admissions phone number: **(979) 845-5311**
Admissions email address: *admissions@tamu.edu*
Application website: *http://www.tamu.edu/admissions/grad*
Application fee: **$50**
Fall 2005 application deadline: 8/1
Test requirements: **GRE**
Test of English as Foreign Language (TOEFL) is required for international students.
Minimum TOEFL score required for paper test: 550

Fall 2003
Acceptance rate for master's degree programs: 59%
Acceptance rate for doctoral programs: 54%
Average GRE verbal: 465, Average GRE quantitative: 567, Average GRE analytical: 550
Total 2003 enrollment: 1,110
Master's degree enrollment: 435
   Teacher preparation program enrollment (master's): 83
Doctoral degree enrollment: 675

FINANCIAL INFORMATION

Financial aid phone number: **(979) 845-3236**
Tuition, 2003-2004 academic year: Full-time in-state: **$138/credit hour**; out-of-state: **$374/credit hour**, Part-time in-state: **$138/credit hour**; out-of-state: **$374/credit hour**

Fees: **$1,861**, Room and board: **$6,880**, Books and supplies: **$950**, Miscellaneous expenses: **$1,640**

Number of fellowships awarded to graduate students during the 2003-2004 academic year: **56**

Number of teaching assistant positions: **37**

Number of research assistant positions: **7**

Number of other paid appointments: **89**

ACADEMIC PROGRAMS

Total full-time tenured or tenure-track faculty (fall 2003): **106**, Total part-time faculty (fall 2003): **65**

Areas of specialization: curriculum and instruction, education administration and supervision, educational psychology, elementary teacher education, higher education administration, secondary teacher education, special education, student counseling and personnel services.

Professional development/partnership school(s) are used by students in all of the teaching programs.

During their internships, peer groups of students meet regularly to discuss instructional techniques in all of the teaching programs.

Some of the students in their internships are mentored.

Courses that prepare teachers to pass the National Board of Professional Teaching Standards are not offered.

Teacher preparation programs: Four-year baccalaureate-degree program leading to initial licensure that includes either a major or minor in education and practice teaching. Alternative program for college graduates leading to provisional licensure.

The education program is currently accredited by the National Council for Accreditation of Teacher Education.

LICENSING TEST

Pass rate on state's teacher licensing test for 2002-2003: **98%**

State average pass rate: **92%**

Texas A&M University– Commerce

- **PO Box 3011, Commerce, TX 75429-3011**
- **Website:** http://www.tamu-commerce.edu
- **Public**
- **Degrees offered:** bachelor's, master's, education specialist, Ph.D., Ed.D.

ADMISSIONS

Admissions phone number: **(903) 886-5167**

Admissions email address: *graduate_school@tamu-commerce.edu*

Application website: http://www7.tamu-commerce.edu/admissions/application.asp

Application fee: **$35**

Test requirements: **GRE**

Test of English as Foreign Language (TOEFL) is required for international students.

Minimum TOEFL score required for paper test: **500**

Minimum TOEFL score required for computer test: **173**

FINANCIAL INFORMATION

Financial aid phone number: **(903) 886-5096**

Tuition, 2003-2004 academic year: Full-time in-state: **$2,788**; out-of-state: **$7,036**, Part-time in-state: **$1,960**; out-of-state: **$4,792**

Fees: **$754**, Room and board: **$5,004**, Books and supplies: **$900**, Miscellaneous expenses: **$2,730**

ACADEMIC PROGRAMS

Areas of specialization: education administration and supervision, educational psychology, elementary teacher education, higher education administration, secondary teacher education, special education, student counseling and personnel services.

LICENSING TEST

Pass rate on state's teacher licensing test for 2002-2003: **92%**

State average pass rate: **92%**

Texas A&M University– Corpus Christi

- **6300 Ocean Drive, Corpus Christi, TX 78412**
- **Website:** http://www.tamucc.edu/~gradweb
- **Public**
- **Degrees offered:** bachelor's, master's, Ed.D.

ADMISSIONS

Admissions phone number: **(361) 825-2177**

Admissions email address: *Harvey.Knull@mail.tamucc.edu*

Application fee: **$30**

Fall 2005 application deadline: **7/15**

Test of English as Foreign Language (TOEFL) is required for international students.

Fall 2003

Total 2003 enrollment: **1,590**

Master's degree enrollment: **1,500**

Teacher preparation program enrollment (master's): **750**

Doctoral degree enrollment: **90**

FINANCIAL INFORMATION

Financial aid phone number: **(361) 825-5549**

Number of fellowships awarded to graduate students during the 2003-2004 academic year: **0**

ACADEMIC PROGRAMS

Total full-time tenured or tenure-track faculty (fall 2003): **48**

Areas of specialization: curriculum and instruction, education administration and supervision, elementary teacher education, higher education administration, secondary teacher education, special education, student counseling and personnel services, teacher education.

Professional development/partnership school(s) are used by students in all of the teaching programs.

All of the students in their internships are mentored.

Courses that prepare teachers to pass the National Board of Professional Teaching Standards are not offered.

Teacher preparation programs: Four-year baccalaureate-degree program leading to initial licensure that includes either a major or minor in education and practice teaching. Master's program preparing college graduates for initial licensure; includes practice teaching.

LICENSING TEST

Pass rate on state's teacher licensing test for 2002-2003: 98%
State average pass rate: 92%

Texas A&M University–Kingsville

- 700 University Boulevard, Kingsville, TX 78363
- **Website:** http://www.tamuk.edu
- **Public**
- **Degrees offered:** bachelor's, master's, education specialist, Ed.D.

ADMISSIONS

Admissions phone number: **(361) 593-2811**
Application fee: **$15**
Fall 2005 application deadline: **rolling**
Test of English as Foreign Language (TOEFL) is required for international students.
Minimum TOEFL score required for paper test: **500**

Fall 2003

Acceptance rate for master's degree programs: **74%**
Acceptance rate for doctoral programs: **78%**
Total 2003 enrollment: **580**
Master's degree enrollment: **452**
   Teacher preparation program enrollment (master's): **60**
Doctoral degree enrollment: **128**

FINANCIAL INFORMATION

Financial aid phone number: **(361) 593-3911**
Tuition, 2003-2004 academic year: Full-time in-state: **$818**; out-of-state: **$4,554**, Part-time in-state: **$276**; out-of-state: **$1,518**
Room and board: **$3,464**, Books and supplies: **$614**, Miscellaneous expenses: **$2,107**

ACADEMIC PROGRAMS

Total full-time tenured or tenure-track faculty (fall 2003): **237**
   Total part-time faculty (fall 2003): **119**
Professional development/partnership school(s) are used by students in all of the teaching programs.
During their internships, peer groups of students meet regularly to discuss instructional techniques in all of the teaching programs.
All of the students in their internships are mentored.
Courses that prepare teachers to pass the National Board of Professional Teaching Standards are not offered.

Teacher preparation programs: Four-year baccalaureate-degree program leading to initial licensure that includes either a major or minor in education and practice teaching. Master's program preparing college graduates for initial licensure; includes practice teaching. Alternative program for college graduates leading to provisional licensure.

LICENSING TEST

Pass rate on state's teacher licensing test for 2002-2003: 72%
State average pass rate: 92%

Texas A&M University–Texarkana

- 2600 North Robison Road, Texarkana, TX 75501
- **Website:** http://www.tamut.edu/
- **Public**

LICENSING TEST

Pass rate on state's teacher licensing test for 2002-2003: 93%
State average pass rate: 92%

Texas Christian University

- 3000 Bellaire Ave, Ft Worth, TX 76129
- **Website:** http://www.sofe.tcu.edu
- **Private**
- **Degrees offered:** bachelor's, master's

ADMISSIONS

Admissions phone number: **(817) 257-7661**
Admissions email address: *ed_grad@TCU.edu*
Application website: *http://www.sofe.tcu.edu*
Application fee: **$50**
Fall 2005 application deadline: **7/16**
Test requirements: **None**
Test of English as Foreign Language (TOEFL) is required for international students.
Minimum TOEFL score required for paper test: **550**
Minimum TOEFL score required for computer test: **213**

Fall 2003

Total 2003 enrollment: **292**
Master's degree enrollment: **292**
   Teacher preparation program enrollment (master's): **103**

FINANCIAL INFORMATION

Financial aid phone number: **(817) 257-7872**
Tuition, 2003-2004 academic year: Full-time: **$490/credit hour** Part-time: **$490/credit hour**

Fees: **$1,890**, Room and board: **$7,400**, Books and supplies: **$750**, Miscellaneous expenses: **$4,185**
Number of fellowships awarded to graduate students during the 2003-2004 academic year: **0**
Number of teaching assistant positions: **9**
Number of research assistant positions: **17**
Number of other paid appointments: **0**

ACADEMIC PROGRAMS

Total full-time tenured or tenure-track faculty (fall 2003): **18**
  Total part-time faculty (fall 2003): **25**
Areas of specialization: education administration and supervision, elementary teacher education, secondary teacher education, special education, student counseling and personnel services.
Professional development/partnership school(s) are used by students in all of the teaching programs.
During their internships, peer groups of students meet regularly to discuss instructional techniques in all of the teaching programs.
All of the students in their internships are mentored.
Courses that prepare teachers to pass the National Board of Professional Teaching Standards are not offered.
Teacher preparation programs: Four-year baccalaureate-degree program leading to initial licensure that includes either a major or minor in education and practice teaching. Master's program preparing college graduates for initial licensure; includes practice teaching.

LICENSING TEST

Pass rate on state's teacher licensing test for 2002-2003: **94%**
State average pass rate: **92%**

Texas State University– San Marcos

■ **601 University Drive, San Marcos, TX 78666**
■ **Website:** http://www.txstate.edu
■ **Public**
■ **Degrees offered:** bachelor's, master's, Ph.D.

ADMISSIONS

Admissions phone number: **(512) 245-2581**
Admissions email address: *gradcollege@txstate.edu.*
Application website: *http://www.gradcollege.txstate.edu/applicationproc.html*
Application fee: **$40**
Fall 2005 application deadline: **6/15**
Test requirements: **GRE**
Test of English as Foreign Language (TOEFL) is required for international students.
Minimum TOEFL score required for paper test: **550**
Minimum TOEFL score required for computer test: **213**

Fall 2003
Acceptance rate for master's degree programs: **84%**

Acceptance rate for doctoral programs: **56%**
Average GRE verbal: **463**, Average GRE quantitative: **516**, Average GRE analytical: **528**
Total 2003 enrollment: **1,179**
Master's degree enrollment: **1,125**
  Teacher preparation program enrollment (master's): **653**
Doctoral degree enrollment: **54**

FINANCIAL INFORMATION

Financial aid phone number: **(512) 245-2315**
Tuition, 2003-2004 academic year: Full-time in-state: **$2,484**; out-of-state: **$6,732**, Part-time in-state: **$138/credit hour**; out-of-state: **$374**
Fees: **$948**, Room and board: **$5,310**, Books and supplies: **$770**, Miscellaneous expenses: **$3,250**
Number of teaching assistant positions: **11**
Number of research assistant positions: **39**
Number of other paid appointments: **8**

ACADEMIC PROGRAMS

Total full-time tenured or tenure-track faculty (fall 2003): **69**, Total part-time faculty (fall 2003): **128**
Areas of specialization: curriculum and instruction, education administration and supervision, educational psychology, elementary teacher education, higher education administration, secondary teacher education, special education, student counseling and personnel services, teacher education.
Professional development/partnership school(s) are used by students in all of the teaching programs.
During their internships, peer groups of students meet regularly to discuss instructional techniques in none of the teaching programs.
All of the students in their internships are mentored.
Courses that prepare teachers to pass the National Board of Professional Teaching Standards are not offered.
Teacher preparation programs: Four-year baccalaureate-degree program leading to initial licensure that includes either a major or minor in education and practice teaching. Five-year program leading to initial licensure that results in a baccalaureate degree (with a major or minor in education) plus graduate credit and includes practice teaching.

LICENSING TEST

Pass rate on state's teacher licensing test for 2002-2003: **92%**
State average pass rate: **92%**

Texas Southern University

■ **College of Education, Houston, TX 77004**
■ **Website:** http://www.tsu.edu/education
■ **Public**

ADMISSIONS

Admissions phone number: **(713) 313-7435**
Admissions email address: *admissions@tsu.edu*

FINANCIAL INFORMATION

Financial aid phone number: **(713) 313-7530**

LICENSING TEST

Pass rate on state's teacher licensing test for 2002-2003: 100%

State average pass rate: **92%**

Texas Tech University

- Box 41071, Lubbock, TX 79409-1071
- **Website:** http://www.educ.ttu.edu/
- Public
- **Degrees offered:** bachelor's, master's, Ph.D., Ed.D.

ADMISSIONS

Admissions phone number: **(806) 742-2787**
Admissions email address: *gradschool@ttu.edu*
Application website: *http://www.ttu.edu/gradschool/*
Application fee: **$50**
Fall 2005 application deadline: 2/1
Test requirements: **GRE**
Test of English as Foreign Language (TOEFL) is required for international students.
Minimum TOEFL score required for paper test: **550**
Minimum TOEFL score required for computer test: **213**

Fall 2003
Acceptance rate for master's degree programs: **49%**
Acceptance rate for doctoral programs: **63%**
Average GRE verbal: **467**, Average GRE quantitative: **481**, Average GRE analytical: **482**
Total 2003 enrollment: **558**
Master's degree enrollment: **331**
  Teacher preparation program enrollment (master's): **142**
Education specialist degree enrollment: **0**
Doctoral degree enrollment: **227**

FINANCIAL INFORMATION

Financial aid phone number: **(806) 742-3681**
Tuition, 2003-2004 academic year: Full-time in-state: **$138/credit hour**; out-of-state: **$374/credit hour**, Part-time in-state: **$138/credit hour**; out-of-state: **$374/credit hour**
Fees: **$1,745**, Room and board: **$6,023**, Books and supplies: **$1,100**
Number of fellowships awarded to graduate students during the 2003-2004 academic year: **0**
Number of teaching assistant positions: **5**
Number of research assistant positions: **38**
Number of other paid appointments: **9**

ACADEMIC PROGRAMS

Total full-time tenured or tenure-track faculty (fall 2003): **56**, Total part-time faculty (fall 2003): **42**
Areas of specialization: curriculum and instruction, education administration and supervision, education policy, educational psychology, elementary teacher education,

higher education administration, secondary teacher education, special education, student counseling and personnel services.

Professional development/partnership school(s) are used by students in some of the teaching programs.

During their internships, peer groups of students meet regularly to discuss instructional techniques in all of the teaching programs.

All of the students in their internships are mentored.

Courses that prepare teachers to pass the National Board of Professional Teaching Standards are not offered.

Teacher preparation programs: Four-year baccalaureate-degree program leading to initial licensure that includes either a major or minor in education and practice teaching.

The education program is currently accredited by the National Council for Accreditation of Teacher Education.

LICENSING TEST

Pass rate on state's teacher licensing test for 2002-2003: 91%

State average pass rate: **92%**

Texas Wesleyan University

- 1201 Wesleyan, Fort Worth, TX 76105
- **Website:** http://www.txwes.edu/
- Private
- **Degrees offered:** master's

ADMISSIONS

Application fee: **$50**
Fall 2005 application deadline: **rolling**

Fall 2003
Acceptance rate for master's degree programs: **100%**
Total 2003 enrollment: **49**
Master's degree enrollment: **49**
  Teacher preparation program enrollment (master's): **49**

FINANCIAL INFORMATION

Financial aid phone number: **(817) 531-4420**
Tuition, 2003-2004 academic year: Full-time: **$260/credit** ; Part-time: **hour$260/credit hour**
Fees: **$40/credit hour**, Room and board: **$4,322**, Books and supplies: **$700**, Miscellaneous expenses: **$2,500**

LICENSING TEST

Pass rate on state's teacher licensing test for 2002-2003: 100%

State average pass rate: **92%**

Texas Woman's University

■ **P.O. Box 425589, Denton, TX 76204**
■ **Website:** http://www.twu.edu/admissions/
■ **Public**
■ **Degrees offered:** bachelor's, master's, Ph.D., Ed.D.

ADMISSIONS

Admissions phone number: **(940) 898-3188**
Admissions email address: *admissions@twu.edu*
Application website:
    http://www.twu.edu/admissions/apply.htm
Application fee: **$30**
Fall 2005 application deadline: 6/30
Test requirements: **GRE**
Test of English as Foreign Language (TOEFL) is required
    for international students.
Minimum TOEFL score required for paper test: 550
Minimum TOEFL score required for computer test: 213

Fall 2003
Acceptance rate for master's degree programs: **74%**
Acceptance rate for doctoral programs: **67%**
Average GRE verbal: **417**, Average GRE quantitative: **476**,
    Average GRE analytical: **468**
Total 2003 enrollment: **924**
Master's degree enrollment: **876**
    Teacher preparation program enrollment (master's): **75**
Doctoral degree enrollment: **48**

FINANCIAL INFORMATION

Financial aid phone number: **(940) 898-3050**
Tuition, 2003-2004 academic year: Full-time in-state:
    $2,016; out-of-state: **$6,264**, Part-time in-state: **$1,344**;
    out-of-state: **$2,088**
Fees: **$756**, Room and board: **$4,780**, Books and supplies:
    $720, Miscellaneous expenses: **$3,987**
Number of fellowships awarded to graduate students dur-
    ing the 2003-2004 academic year: **0**
Number of teaching assistant positions: **0**
Number of research assistant positions: **0**
Number of other paid appointments: **9**

ACADEMIC PROGRAMS

Total full-time tenured or tenure-track faculty (fall 2003):
    14, Total part-time faculty (fall 2003): **20**
Areas of specialization: education administration and
    supervision, elementary teacher education, secondary
    teacher education, special education, student counseling
    and personnel services.
Professional development/partnership school(s) are used
    by students in all of the teaching programs.
During their internships, peer groups of students meet
    regularly to discuss instructional techniques in some of
    the teaching programs.
All of the students in their internships are mentored.

Courses that prepare teachers to pass the National Board of
    Professional Teaching Standards are not offered.
Teacher preparation programs: Four-year baccalaureate-
    degree program leading to initial licensure that includes
    either a major or minor in education and practice teach-
    ing. Master's program preparing college graduates for
    initial licensure; includes practice teaching. Alternative
    program for college graduates leading to provisional
    licensure.

LICENSING TEST

Pass rate on state's teacher licensing test for 2002-2003:
    96%
State average pass rate: 92%

Trinity University

■ **1 Trinity Place, San Antonio, TX 78212-7200**
■ **Website:** http://www.trinity.edu/
■ **Private**

LICENSING TEST

Pass rate on state's teacher licensing test for 2002-2003:
    100%
State average pass rate: 92%

University of Houston–Clear Lake

■ **2700 Bay Area Blvd., Houston, TX 77058**
■ **Website:** http://www.cl.uh.edu/
■ **Public**

LICENSING TEST

Pass rate on state's teacher licensing test for 2002-2003:
    90%
State average pass rate: 92%

University of Houston–Main Campus

■ **4800 Calhoun, Farish Hall, Houston, TX 77204-5023**
■ **Website:** http://www.uh.edu/grad_catalog/edu/
■ **Public**
■ **Degrees offered:** bachelor's, master's, Ph.D., Ed.D.
■ **Overall rank in the 2005 U.S. News education schools
    with doctoral programs:** 69

ADMISSIONS

Admissions phone number: **(713) 743-1010**
Admissions email address: *admissions@uh.edu*
Application fee: **$45**

Fall 2005 application deadline: 7/2
Test requirements: **GRE or MAT**
Test of English as Foreign Language (TOEFL) is required for international students.
Minimum TOEFL score required for paper test: 550
Minimum TOEFL score required for computer test: 213

Fall 2003
Acceptance rate for master's degree programs: 61%
Acceptance rate for doctoral programs: 42%
Average GRE verbal: 487, Average GRE quantitative: 583, Average GRE analytical: 593, Average MAT: 47
Total 2003 enrollment: 1,040
Master's degree enrollment: 678
   Teacher preparation program enrollment (master's): 352
Doctoral degree enrollment: 362

FINANCIAL INFORMATION
Financial aid phone number: **(713) 743-9090**
Tuition, 2003-2004 academic year: Full-time in-state: **$92/credit hour**; out-of-state: **$328/credit hour**, Part-time in-state: **$92/credit hour**; out-of-state: **$328/credit hour**
Fees: **$1,704**, Room and board: **$6,266**, Books and supplies: **$1,000**, Miscellaneous expenses: **$5,194**
Number of fellowships awarded to graduate students during the 2003-2004 academic year: 0
Number of teaching assistant positions: 44
Number of research assistant positions: 21
Number of other paid appointments: 25

ACADEMIC PROGRAMS
Total full-time tenured or tenure-track faculty (fall 2003): 71, Total part-time faculty (fall 2003): 68
Areas of specialization: curriculum and instruction, education administration and supervision, educational psychology, elementary teacher education, higher education administration, secondary teacher education, special education.
Professional development/partnership school(s) are used by students in some of the teaching programs.
During their internships, peer groups of students meet regularly to discuss instructional techniques in some of the teaching programs.
All of the students in their internships are mentored.
Courses that prepare teachers to pass the National Board of Professional Teaching Standards are not offered.
Teacher preparation programs: Four-year baccalaureate-degree program leading to initial licensure that includes either a major or minor in education and practice teaching. Alternative program for college graduates leading to provisional licensure.
The education program is currently accredited by the National Council for Accreditation of Teacher Education.

LICENSING TEST
Pass rate on state's teacher licensing test for 2002-2003: 94%
State average pass rate: 92%

University of Houston–Victoria

- 3007 N. Ben Wilson, Victoria, TX 77901
- **Website:** http://www.uhv.edu/oar/index.htm
- Public
- **Degrees offered:** bachelor's, master's

ADMISSIONS
Admissions phone number: **(361) 570-4110**
Admissions email address: *admissions@uhv.edu*
Application website:
   http://www.uhv.edu/oar/pdf/UHV%20 ADMISSIONS%20APPLICATION%200203.pdf
Application fee: **$0**
Fall 2005 application deadline: **rolling**
Test requirements: **GRE or MAT**
Test of English as Foreign Language (TOEFL) is required for international students.
Minimum TOEFL score required for paper test: 550
Minimum TOEFL score required for computer test: 213

Fall 2003
Acceptance rate for master's degree programs: 100%
Average GRE verbal: 428, Average GRE quantitative: 473, Average GRE analytical: 441, Average MAT: 39
Total 2003 enrollment: 605
Master's degree enrollment: 605
   Teacher preparation program enrollment (master's): 89

FINANCIAL INFORMATION
Financial aid phone number: **(361) 570-4131**
Tuition, 2003-2004 academic year: Full-time in-state: **$138/credit hour**; out-of-state: **$328/credit hour**, Part-time in-state: **$138/credit hour**; out-of-state: **$328/credit hour**
Fees: **$35/credit hour**, Miscellaneous expenses: **$10**
Number of fellowships awarded to graduate students during the 2003-2004 academic year: 0
Number of teaching assistant positions: 0
Number of research assistant positions: 0
Number of other paid appointments: 0

ACADEMIC PROGRAMS
Total full-time tenured or tenure-track faculty (fall 2003): 21, Total part-time faculty (fall 2003): 0
Areas of specialization: curriculum and instruction, education administration and supervision, education policy, educational psychology, higher education administration, special education, student counseling and personnel services.
Professional development/partnership school(s) are used by students in some of the teaching programs.
During their internships, peer groups of students meet regularly to discuss instructional techniques in some of the teaching programs.
All of the students in their internships are mentored.

Courses that prepare teachers to pass the National Board of Professional Teaching Standards are not offered.

LICENSING TEST

Pass rate on state's teacher licensing test for 2002-2003: 92%
State average pass rate: 92%

University of Mary Hardin-Baylor

- ■ UMHB Box 8017 900 College Street, Belton, TX 76513
- ■ **Website:** http://www.umhb.edu
- ■ **Private**
- ■ **Degrees offered:** bachelor's, master's

ADMISSIONS

Admissions phone number: (254) 295-4520
Admissions email address: *stheordore@umhb.edu*
Application website: *http://www.umhb.edu*
Application fee: **$35**
Fall 2005 application deadline: **rolling**

Fall 2003
Total 2003 enrollment: 76
Master's degree enrollment: 76
Teacher preparation program enrollment (master's): 26

FINANCIAL INFORMATION

Financial aid phone number: (254) 295-4516
Tuition, 2003-2004 academic year: Full-time: **$385/credit hour**; Part-time: **$385/credit hour**
Fees: **$28/credit hour**, Books and supplies: **$450**, Miscellaneous expenses: **$50**

LICENSING TEST

Pass rate on state's teacher licensing test for 2002-2003: 88%
State average pass rate: 92%

University of North Texas

- ■ PO Box 311337, Denton, TX 76203
- ■ **Website:** http://www.unt.edu
- ■ **Public**
- ■ **Degrees offered:** bachelor's, master's, Ph.D., Ed.D.
- ■ **Overall rank in the 2005 U.S. News education school specialty rankings:** counseling/personnel: 18

ADMISSIONS

Admissions phone number: (940) 565-2383
Admissions email address: *gradsch@unt.edu*
Application website: *http://www.applytexas.org*
Application fee: **$50**
Fall 2005 application deadline: **7/15**

Test requirements: **GRE or MAT**
Test of English as Foreign Language (TOEFL) is required for international students.
Minimum TOEFL score required for paper test: 550
Minimum TOEFL score required for computer test: 213

Fall 2003
Acceptance rate for master's degree programs: 97%
Acceptance rate for doctoral programs: 96%
Total 2003 enrollment: 1,709
Master's degree enrollment: 1,258
Teacher preparation program enrollment (master's): 189
Doctoral degree enrollment: 451

FINANCIAL INFORMATION

Financial aid phone number: (940) 565-2302
Tuition, 2003-2004 academic year: Full-time in-state: **$2,484**; out-of-state: **$6,732**, Part-time in-state: **$138/credit hour**; out-of-state: **$374/credit hour**
Fees: **$1,268**, Room and board: **$5,530**, Books and supplies: **$1,010**, Miscellaneous expenses: **$3,150**
Number of fellowships awarded to graduate students during the 2003-2004 academic year: 15
Number of teaching assistant positions: 15
Number of research assistant positions: 2
Number of other paid appointments: 25

ACADEMIC PROGRAMS

Total full-time tenured or tenure-track faculty (fall 2003): 106
Total part-time faculty (fall 2003): 30
Areas of specialization: curriculum and instruction, education administration and supervision, educational psychology, elementary teacher education, higher education administration, secondary teacher education, special education, student counseling and personnel services.
Professional development/partnership school(s) are used by students in some of the teaching programs.
During their internships, peer groups of students meet regularly to discuss instructional techniques in all of the teaching programs.
All of the students in their internships are mentored.
Courses that prepare teachers to pass the National Board of Professional Teaching Standards are not offered.
Teacher preparation programs: Four-year baccalaureate-degree program leading to initial licensure that includes either a major or minor in education and practice teaching. Five-year program leading to initial licensure that results in a baccalaureate degree (with a major or minor in education) plus graduate credit and includes practice teaching. Five-year program leading to initial licensure that results in a baccalaureate degree (with a major or minor in education) plus a master's degree and includes practice teaching. Master's program preparing college graduates for initial licensure; includes practice teaching. Alternative program for college graduates leading to provisional licensure.
The education program is currently accredited by the National Council for Accreditation of Teacher Education.

Pass rate on state's teacher licensing test for 2002-2003: **95%**
State average pass rate: **92%**

University of St. Thomas

- 3800 Montrose Blvd, Houston, TX 77006-4696
- Website:
  http://www.stthom.edu/education/graduate.html
- Private
- Degrees offered: bachelor's, master's

ADMISSIONS

Admissions phone number: **(713) 525-3541**
Admissions email address: *hollisp@stthom.edu*
Application fee: **$35**
Fall 2005 application deadline: **rolling**
Test requirements: **GRE**

Fall 2003
Acceptance rate for master's degree programs: **100%**
Total 2003 enrollment: **166**
Master's degree enrollment: **166**
  Teacher preparation program enrollment (master's): **101**

FINANCIAL INFORMATION

Financial aid phone number: **(713) 942-3465**
Tuition, 2003-2004 academic year: Full-time: **$9,000**; Part-time: **$500/credit hour**
Fees: **$33**, Room and board: **$6,840**, Books and supplies: **$800**, Miscellaneous expenses: **$3,324**

ACADEMIC PROGRAMS

Total full-time tenured or tenure-track faculty (fall 2003): **10**, Total part-time faculty (fall 2003): **50**
Areas of specialization: curriculum and instruction, education administration and supervision, educational psychology, elementary teacher education, secondary teacher education, special education, student counseling and personnel services.
Professional development/partnership school(s) are used by students in some of the teaching programs.
During their internships, peer groups of students meet regularly to discuss instructional techniques in some of the teaching programs.
All of the students in their internships are mentored.
Courses that prepare teachers to pass the National Board of Professional Teaching Standards are not offered.
Teacher preparation programs: Four-year baccalaureate-degree program leading to initial licensure that includes either a major or minor in education and practice teaching. Master's program preparing college graduates for initial licensure; includes practice teaching. Alternative program for college graduates leading to provisional licensure.

Pass rate on state's teacher licensing test for 2002-2003: **96%**
State average pass rate: **92%**

University of Texas–Arlington

- 701 S. Nedderman Drive, Arlington, TX 76019
- Website: http://www.uta.edu/coed/
- Public

LICENSING TEST

Pass rate on state's teacher licensing test for 2002-2003: **100%**
State average pass rate: **92%**

University of Texas–Austin

- 1 University Station, D5000, Sanchez Building Room 210, Austin, TX 78712
- Website: http://www.utexas.edu/student/admissions
- Public
- Degrees offered: bachelor's, master's, Ph.D., Ed.D.
- Overall rank in the 2005 U.S. News education schools with doctoral programs: 15
- Overall rank in the 2005 U.S. News education school specialty rankings: administration/supervision: 4, curriculum/instruction: 11, education policy: 18, educational psychology: 13, elementary education: 13, higher education administration: 13, secondary education: 13, special education: 8

ADMISSIONS

Admissions phone number: **(512) 475-7398**
Admissions email address: *adgrd@utxdp.dp.utexas.edu*
Application website: https://www.applytexas.org/adappc/commonapp.wb
Application fee: **$50**
Fall 2005 application deadline: **2/1**
Test requirements: **GRE**
Test of English as Foreign Language (TOEFL) is required for international students.
Minimum TOEFL score required for paper test: **550**
Minimum TOEFL score required for computer test: **213**

Fall 2003
Acceptance rate for master's degree programs: **61%**
Acceptance rate for doctoral programs: **44%**
Average GRE verbal: **535**, Average GRE quantitative: **601**
  Average GRE analytical: **561**
Total 2003 enrollment: **1,351**
Master's degree enrollment: **484**

Teacher preparation program enrollment (master's): 139
Doctoral degree enrollment: 867

FINANCIAL INFORMATION
Financial aid phone number: (512) 471-7213
Tuition, 2003-2004 academic year: Full-time in-state:
$3,312; out-of-state: $8,976, Part-time in-state: $2,070;
out-of-state: $5,610
Fees: $1,998, Room and board: $6,082, Books and supplies: $748, Miscellaneous expenses: $2,798
Number of fellowships awarded to graduate students during the 2003-2004 academic year: 144
Number of teaching assistant positions: 266
Number of research assistant positions: 182
Number of other paid appointments: 422

ACADEMIC PROGRAMS
Total full-time tenured or tenure-track faculty (fall 2003): 125
  Total part-time faculty (fall 2003): 79
Areas of specialization: curriculum and instruction, education administration and supervision, education policy, educational psychology, higher education administration, special education, student counseling and personnel services.
Professional development/partnership school(s) are used by students in all of the teaching programs.
During their internships, peer groups of students meet regularly to discuss instructional techniques in some of the teaching programs.
All of the students in their internships are mentored.
Courses that prepare teachers to pass the National Board of Professional Teaching Standards are not offered.
Teacher preparation programs: Four-year baccalaureate-degree program leading to initial licensure that includes either a major or minor in education and practice teaching.

LICENSING TEST
Pass rate on state's teacher licensing test for 2002-2003: 100%
State average pass rate: 92%

University of Texas–Brownsville

■ 80 Fort Brown, Brownsville, TX 78520
■ **Website:** http://www.utb.edu/
■ **Public**

LICENSING TEST
Pass rate on state's teacher licensing test for 2002-2003:
  79%
State average pass rate: 92%

University of Texas–El Paso

■ **500 W. University, 414 College of Education, El Paso, TX 79968**
■ **Website:** http://www.education.utep.edu
■ **Public**

ADMISSIONS
Admissions phone number: (915) 747-5572
Admissions email address: *gradschool@utep.edu*
Application website:
  http://www.utep.edu/graduate/forms/index.html

FINANCIAL INFORMATION
Financial aid phone number: (915) 747-5204

LICENSING TEST
Pass rate on state's teacher licensing test for 2002-2003:
  80%
State average pass rate: 92%

University of Texas–Pan American

■ **1201 W. University Drive, Edinburg, TX 78541-2999**
■ **Website:** http://www.panam.edu
■ **Public**
■ **Degrees offered:** bachelor's, master's, Ed.D.

ADMISSIONS
Admissions phone number: (956) 381-2201
Admissions email address: *admissions@panam.edu*
Application website: *http://www.panam.edu/admissions*
Application fee: $0
Fall 2005 application deadline: 8/10
Test of English as Foreign Language (TOEFL) is required for international students.
Minimum TOEFL score required for paper test: 500
Minimum TOEFL score required for computer test: 173

Fall 2003
Average GRE verbal: 391, Average GRE quantitative: 403
Total 2003 enrollment: 1,022
Master's degree enrollment: 982
  Teacher preparation program enrollment (master's): 214
Doctoral degree enrollment: 40

FINANCIAL INFORMATION
Financial aid phone number: (956) 381-2501
Tuition, 2003-2004 academic year: Full-time in-state:
  $2,074; out-of-state: $5,998, Part-time in-state:
  $165/credit hour; out-of-state: **$381/credit hour**

Fees: **$454**, Room and board: **$4,333**, Books and supplies: **$600**, Miscellaneous expenses: **$3,000**
Number of fellowships awarded to graduate students during the 2003-2004 academic year: **6**
Number of research assistant positions: **8**
Number of other paid appointments: **2**

ACADEMIC PROGRAMS

Total full-time tenured or tenure-track faculty (fall 2003): **53**, Total part-time faculty (fall 2003): **70**
Areas of specialization: curriculum and instruction, education administration and supervision, education policy, educational psychology, elementary teacher education, secondary teacher education, special education, student counseling and personnel services.
Professional development/partnership school(s) are used by students in all of the teaching programs.
During their internships, peer groups of students meet regularly to discuss instructional techniques in all of the teaching programs.
All of the students in their internships are mentored.
Courses that prepare teachers to pass the National Board of Professional Teaching Standards are not offered.
Teacher preparation programs: Four-year baccalaureate-degree program leading to initial licensure that includes either a major or minor in education and practice teaching. Five-year program leading to initial licensure that results in a baccalaureate degree (with a major or minor in education) plus graduate credit and includes practice teaching. Master's program preparing college graduates for initial licensure; includes practice teaching. Alternative program for college graduates leading to provisional licensure.
The education program is currently accredited by the Teacher Education Accreditation Council.

LICENSING TEST

Pass rate on state's teacher licensing test for 2002-2003: **70%**
State average pass rate: **92%**

University of Texas– Permian Basin

■ **4901 E. University Boulevard, Odessa, TX 79762-0001**
■ **Website:** http://www.utpb.edu
■ **Public**
■ **Degrees offered:** master's

ADMISSIONS

Admissions phone number: **(432) 552-2605**
Admissions email address: *admissions@utpb.edu*
Application website: http://www.utpb.edu/utpb_student/students/s2_prospective_student.htm
Application fee: **$0**
Fall 2005 application deadline: **7/15**
Test requirements: **GRE**

Test of English as Foreign Language (TOEFL) is required for international students.
Minimum TOEFL score required for paper test: **550**
Minimum TOEFL score required for computer test: **213**

Fall 2003
Total 2003 enrollment: **171**
Master's degree enrollment: **171**
  Teacher preparation program enrollment (master's): **94**

FINANCIAL INFORMATION

Financial aid phone number: **(432) 552-2620**
Tuition, 2003-2004 academic year: Full-time in-state: **$1,944**; out-of-state: **$5,940**, Part-time in-state: **$140/credit hour**; out-of-state: **$362/credit hour**
Fees: **$571**, Room and board: **$4,034**, Books and supplies: **$800**, Miscellaneous expenses: **$2,410**
Number of fellowships awarded to graduate students during the 2003-2004 academic year: **0**
Number of teaching assistant positions: **0**
Number of research assistant positions: **0**
Number of other paid appointments: **0**

ACADEMIC PROGRAMS

Total full-time tenured or tenure-track faculty (fall 2003): **11**, Total part-time faculty (fall 2003): **20**
Areas of specialization: curriculum and instruction, education administration and supervision, education policy, educational psychology, elementary teacher education, secondary teacher education, special education, student counseling and personnel services.
Professional development/partnership school(s) are used by students in all of the teaching programs.
During their internships, peer groups of students meet regularly to discuss instructional techniques in all of the teaching programs.
All of the students in their internships are mentored.
Courses that prepare teachers to pass the National Board of Professional Teaching Standards are not offered.

LICENSING TEST

Pass rate on state's teacher licensing test for 2002-2003: **89%**
State average pass rate: **92%**

University of Texas– San Antonio

■ **6900 N. Loop 1604, W., San Antonio, TX 78209**
■ **Website:** http://www.utsa.edu/
■ **Public**

LICENSING TEST

Pass rate on state's teacher licensing test for 2002-2003: **97%**
State average pass rate: **92%**

University of Texas–Tyler

- 3900 University Avenue, Tyler, TX 75799
- **Website:** http://www.uttyler.edu/
- **Public**

ADMISSIONS
Admissions phone number: **(903) 566-7339**
Test of English as Foreign Language (TOEFL) is required for international students.
Minimum TOEFL score required for paper test: **550**
Minimum TOEFL score required for computer test: **213**

Fall 2003
Total 2003 enrollment: **286**

FINANCIAL INFORMATION
Tuition, 2003-2004 academic year: Full-time in-state: **$2,700**; out-of-state: **$9,180**, Part-time in-state: **$540**; out-of-state: **$1,836**
Fees: **$742**, Room and board: **$5,280**, Books and supplies: **$700**, Miscellaneous expenses: **$1,882**

ACADEMIC PROGRAMS
Courses that prepare teachers to pass the National Board of Professional Teaching Standards are not offered.

LICENSING TEST
Pass rate on state's teacher licensing test for 2002-2003: **99%**
State average pass rate: **92%**

University of the Incarnate Word

- 4301 Broadway, San Antonio, TX 78209
- **Website:** http://www.uiw.edu
- **Private**
- **Degrees offered:** bachelor's, master's, Ph.D.

ADMISSIONS
Admissions phone number: **(210) 829-6005**
Admissions email address: *admis@universe.uiwtx.edu*
Application website: *http://www.uiw.edu*
Application fee: **$20**
Fall 2005 application deadline: **rolling**

Fall 2003
Total 2003 enrollment: **250**
Master's degree enrollment: **90**
  Teacher preparation program enrollment (master's): **33**
Doctoral degree enrollment: **160**

FINANCIAL INFORMATION
Financial aid phone number: **(210) 829-6008**

Tuition, 2003-2004 academic year: **$495/credit hour**
Room and board: **$5,586**, Books and supplies: **$800**, Miscellaneous expenses: **$1,450**

ACADEMIC PROGRAMS
Areas of specialization: elementary teacher education.

LICENSING TEST
Pass rate on state's teacher licensing test for 2002-2003: **100%**
State average pass rate: **92%**

Wayland Baptist University

- 1900 W. Seventh Street, Plainview, TX 79072
- **Website:** http://www.wbu.edu/
- **Private**

LICENSING TEST
Pass rate on state's teacher licensing test for 2002-2003: **98%**
State average pass rate: **92%**

West Texas A&M University

- WTAMU BOX 60296, Canyon, TX 79016
- **Website:** http://www.wtamu.edu
- **Public**
- **Degrees offered:** bachelor's, master's

ADMISSIONS
Admissions phone number: **(806) 651-2020**
Admissions email address: *admissons@mail.wtamu.edu*
Application fee: **$25**
Fall 2005 application deadline: **rolling**
Test requirements: **GRE**
Test of English as Foreign Language (TOEFL) is required for international students.
Minimum TOEFL score required for paper test: **550**
Minimum TOEFL score required for computer test: **213**

Fall 2003
Acceptance rate for master's degree programs: **76%**
Total 2003 enrollment: **248**
Master's degree enrollment: **248**

FINANCIAL INFORMATION
Financial aid phone number: **(806) 651-2055**
Tuition, 2003-2004 academic year: Full-time in-state: **$56/credit hour**; out-of-state: **$292/credit hour**, Part-time in-state: **$56/credit hour**; out-of-state: **$292/credit hour**

Fees: **$1,248**, Room and board: **$5,238**, Books and supplies: **$400**, Miscellaneous expenses: **$100**

ACADEMIC PROGRAMS

Total full-time tenured or tenure-track faculty (fall 2003): **20**

Areas of specialization: curriculum and instruction, education administration and supervision, special education, student counseling and personnel services.

Professional development/partnership school(s) are used by students in all of the teaching programs.

During their internships, peer groups of students meet regularly to discuss instructional techniques in some of the teaching programs.

All of the students in their internships are mentored.

Courses that prepare teachers to pass the National Board of Professional Teaching Standards are not offered.

LICENSING TEST

Pass rate on state's teacher licensing test for 2002-2003: **86%**

State average pass rate: **92%**

UTAH

TEACHER TESTING IN UTAH
The state is currently developing teacher licensure exams. For information on where to go in your state for specific academic requirements, see Chapter 6 on page 67.

Brigham Young University—Provo

- 237 MCKB, Provo, UT 84602
- **Website:** http://www.byu.edu/gradstudies
- Private

ADMISSIONS
Admissions phone number: **(801) 422-4091**
Admissions email address: *james_crane@byu.edu*
Application website: *https://app.applyyourself.com/?id=byugrad*
Test requirements: **GRE or MAT**
Test of English as Foreign Language (TOEFL) is required for international students.
Minimum TOEFL score required for paper test: **550**
Minimum TOEFL score required for computer test: **213**

FINANCIAL INFORMATION
Financial aid phone number: **(801) 422-4104**

Southern Utah University

- 351 W. Center Street, Cedar City, UT 84720
- **Website:** http://www.suu.edu/
- Public

University of Utah

- 1705 Campus Center Drive, Room 225, Salt Lake City, UT 84112-9251
- **Website:** http://www.sa.utah.edu/admiss/index.htm
- Public
- **Degrees offered:** bachelor's, master's, Ph.D., Ed.D.
- **Overall rank in the 2005 U.S. News education school specialty rankings:** administration/supervision: 19, special education: 19

ADMISSIONS
Admissions phone number: **(801) 581-7281**
Admissions email address: *uadmiss@sa.utah.edu*

Application website: http://www.sa.utah.edu/admiss/appdownload/index.htm
Application fee: **$35**
Fall 2005 application deadline: **4/1**
Test requirements: **GRE**
Test of English as Foreign Language (TOEFL) is required for international students.
Minimum TOEFL score required for paper test: **500**
Minimum TOEFL score required for computer test: **173**

Fall 2003
Acceptance rate for master's degree programs: **53%**
Acceptance rate for doctoral programs: **43%**
Average GRE verbal: **485**, Average GRE quantitative: **539**, Average GRE analytical: **570**, Average MAT: **45**
Total 2003 enrollment: **551**
Master's degree enrollment: **336**
   Teacher preparation program enrollment (master's): **87**
Doctoral degree enrollment: **215**

FINANCIAL INFORMATION
Financial aid phone number: **(801) 581-6211**
Tuition, 2003-2004 academic year: Full-time in-state: **$3,058**; out-of-state: **$10,704**, Part-time in-state: **$1,511**; out-of-state: **$5,387**
Fees: **$589**, Room and board: **$5,036**, Books and supplies: **$1,086**, Miscellaneous expenses: **$3,528**
Number of fellowships awarded to graduate students during the 2003-2004 academic year: **46**
Number of teaching assistant positions: **21**
Number of research assistant positions: **24**
Number of other paid appointments: **19**

ACADEMIC PROGRAMS
Total full-time tenured or tenure-track faculty (fall 2003): **56**
   Total part-time faculty (fall 2003): **1**
Areas of specialization: curriculum and instruction, education administration and supervision, education policy, educational psychology, elementary teacher education, higher education administration, secondary teacher education, special education, student counseling and personnel services.
Professional development/partnership school(s) are used by students in some of the teaching programs.
During their internships, peer groups of students meet regularly to discuss instructional techniques in all of the teaching programs.
All of the students in their internships are mentored.

Courses that prepare teachers to pass the National Board of Professional Teaching Standards are not offered.

Utah State University

■ **College of Education and Human Services, 2800 Old Main Hill, Logan, UT 84322-2800**
■ **Website:** http://www.usu.edu/gradsch/home.html
■ **Public**
■ **Degrees offered:** bachelor's, master's, education specialist, Ph.D., Ed.D.
■ **Overall rank in the 2005 U.S. News education schools with doctoral programs:** 38
■ **Overall rank in the 2005 U.S. News education school specialty rankings:** special education: 15

ADMISSIONS
Admissions phone number: **(435) 797-1189**
Admissions email address: *gradsch@cc.usu.edu*
Application website:
  http://www.usu.edu/gradsch/approcdr.html
Application fee: **$50**
Test requirements: **GRE or MAT**
Test of English as Foreign Language (TOEFL) is required for international students.
Minimum TOEFL score required for paper test: **550**
Minimum TOEFL score required for computer test: **213**

Fall 2003
Acceptance rate for master's degree programs: **65%**
Acceptance rate for doctoral programs: **35%**
Average GRE verbal: **519**, Average GRE quantitative: **620**, Average MAT: **52**
Total 2003 enrollment: **924**
Master's degree enrollment: **679**
  Teacher preparation program enrollment (master's): **524**
Doctoral degree enrollment: **245**

FINANCIAL INFORMATION
Financial aid phone number: **(435) 797-0173**
Tuition, 2003-2004 academic year: Full-time in-state: **$2,237**; out-of-state: **$7,830**, Part-time in-state: **$1,389**; out-of-state: **$4,862**
Fees: **$517**, Room and board: **$7,538**, Books and supplies: **$900**, Miscellaneous expenses: **$1,944**
Number of fellowships awarded to graduate students during the 2003-2004 academic year: **8**
Number of teaching assistant positions: **22**
Number of research assistant positions: **63**
Number of other paid appointments: **51**

ACADEMIC PROGRAMS
Total full-time tenured or tenure-track faculty (fall 2003): **101**, Total part-time faculty (fall 2003): **10**
Areas of specialization: curriculum and instruction, elementary teacher education, secondary teacher education, special education, student counseling and personnel services.

Professional development/partnership school(s) are used by students in none of the teaching programs.
During their internships, peer groups of students meet regularly to discuss instructional techniques in all of the teaching programs.
All of the students in their internships are mentored.
Courses that prepare teachers to pass the National Board of Professional Teaching Standards are not offered.
Teacher preparation programs: Four-year baccalaureate-degree program leading to initial licensure that includes either a major or minor in education and practice teaching. Five-year program leading to initial licensure that results in a baccalaureate degree (with a major or minor in education) plus a master's degree and includes practice teaching. Master's program preparing college graduates for initial licensure; includes practice teaching. Alternative program for college graduates leading to provisional licensure.
The education program is currently accredited by the National Council for Accreditation of Teacher Education.

Weber State University

■ **1302 University Circle, Ogden, UT 84408-1302**
■ **Website:** http://departments.weber.edu/meduc/
■ **Public**
■ **Degrees offered:** bachelor's, master's

ADMISSIONS
Admissions phone number: **(801) 626-6626**
Admissions email address: *jmitchell@weber.edu*
Application website:
  http://departments.weber.edu/meduc/forms.htm
Application fee: **$25**
Fall 2005 application deadline: **7/1**
Test requirements: **GRE or MAT**
Test of English as Foreign Language (TOEFL) is required for international students.
Minimum TOEFL score required for paper test: **550**

Fall 2003
Acceptance rate for master's degree programs: **96%**
Average MAT: **53**
Total 2003 enrollment: **146**
Master's degree enrollment: **146**
  Teacher preparation program enrollment (master's): **146**

FINANCIAL INFORMATION
Financial aid phone number: **(801) 626-6586**
Tuition, 2003-2004 academic year: Full-time in-state: **$2,038**; out-of-state: **$7,130**
Fees: **$476**, Room and board: **$5,313**, Books and supplies: **$900**, Miscellaneous expenses: **$3,722**
Number of other paid appointments: **1**

ACADEMIC PROGRAMS
Total full-time tenured or tenure-track faculty (fall 2003): **22**, Total part-time faculty (fall 2003): **6**

Areas of specialization: curriculum and instruction.

Professional development/partnership school(s) are used by students in none of the teaching programs.

During their internships, peer groups of students meet regularly to discuss instructional techniques in all of the teaching programs.

All of the students in their internships are mentored.

Courses that prepare teachers to pass the National Board of Professional Teaching Standards are not offered.

The education program is currently accredited by the National Council for Accreditation of Teacher Education.

Westminster College

■ 1840 S. 1300, E, Salt Lake City, UT 84105-3697
■ **Website:** http://www.westminstercollege.edu/
■ **Private**

VERMONT

Castleton State College

- Seminary Street, Castleton, VT 05735
- **Website:** http://www.castleton.edu
- Public
- **Degrees offered:** master's

ADMISSIONS

Admissions phone number: **(802) 468-1213**
Admissions email address: *info@castleton.edu*
Application website: *http://www.castleton.edu/admissions*
Application fee: **$30**
Fall 2005 application deadline: **rolling**

Fall 2003
Total 2003 enrollment: **57**
Master's degree enrollment: **57**

FINANCIAL INFORMATION

Financial aid phone number: **(802) 468-1286**
Tuition, 2003-2004 academic year: Full-time in-state:
   $7,058; out-of-state: **$15,250**, Part-time in-state:
   $297/credit hour; out-of-state: **$638/credit hour**

LICENSING TEST

Pass rate on state's teacher licensing test for 2002-2003:
   93%
State average pass rate: **97%**

College of St. Joseph

- 71 Clement Road, Rutland, VT 05701
- **Website:** http://www.sjc.edu/
- Private

LICENSING TEST

Pass rate on state's teacher licensing test for 2002-2003:
   97%
State average pass rate: **97%**

Goddard College

- 123 Pitkin Road, Plainfield, VT 05667
- **Website:** http://www.goddard.edu/
- Private

LICENSING TEST

Pass rate on state's teacher licensing test for 2002-2003:
   100%
State average pass rate: **97%**

Johnson State College

- 337 College Hill, Johnson, VT 05656-9405
- **Website:** http://www.jsc.vsc.edu
- Public
- **Degrees offered:** bachelor's, master's

ADMISSIONS

Admissions phone number: **(802) 635-1219**
Admissions email address: *jscapply@jsc.vsc.edu*
Application fee: **$30**
Fall 2005 application deadline: **4/1**
Test of English as Foreign Language (TOEFL) is required
   for international students.
Minimum TOEFL score required for paper test: **500**

Fall 2003
Total 2003 enrollment: **212**
Master's degree enrollment: **212**
   Teacher preparation program enrollment (master's): **183**

FINANCIAL INFORMATION

Financial aid phone number: **(802) 635-1380**
Tuition, 2003-2004 academic year: Full-time in-state:
   $297/credit hour; out-of-state: **$638/credit hour**, Part-
   time in-state: **$297/credit hour**; out-of-state: **$638/credit
   hour**
Fees: **$18/credit hour**

ACADEMIC PROGRAMS

Professional development/partnership school(s) are used by students in all of the teaching programs.

During their internships, peer groups of students meet regularly to discuss instructional techniques in some of the teaching programs.

All of the students in their internships are mentored.

Courses that prepare teachers to pass the National Board of Professional Teaching Standards are not offered.

Teacher preparation programs: Four-year baccalaureate-degree program leading to initial licensure that includes either a major or minor in education and practice teaching. Five-year program leading to initial licensure that results in a baccalaureate degree (with a major or minor in education) plus graduate credit and includes practice teaching. Master's program preparing college graduates for initial licensure; includes practice teaching.

LICENSING TEST

Pass rate on state's teacher licensing test for 2002-2003: 92%

State average pass rate: 97%

Lyndon State College

- PO Box 919, Lyndonville, VT 05851
- **Website:** http://www.lyndonstate.edu/
- Public
- **Degrees offered:** bachelor's, master's

ADMISSIONS

Admissions phone number: **(800) 225-1998**
Admissions email address: *admissions@lyndonstate.edu*
Application website: *http://www.applyweb.com/aw?lyndon*
Application fee: **$32**
Fall 2005 application deadline: **rolling**

FINANCIAL INFORMATION

Financial aid phone number: **(802) 626-6216**
Tuition, 2003-2004 academic year: Full-time in-state: **$297/credit hour**; out-of-state: **$638/credit hour**, Part-time in-state: **$297/credit hour**; out-of-state: **$638/credit hour**
Fees: **$58**

ACADEMIC PROGRAMS

Total full-time tenured or tenure-track faculty (fall 2003): **11**, Total part-time faculty (fall 2003): **4**

Areas of specialization: curriculum and instruction, education administration and supervision, education policy, educational psychology, elementary teacher education, higher education administration, secondary teacher education, special education, student counseling and personnel services.

Professional development/partnership school(s) are used by students in all of the teaching programs.

During their internships, peer groups of students meet regularly to discuss instructional techniques in all of the teaching programs.

All of the students in their internships are mentored.

Courses that prepare teachers to pass the National Board of Professional Teaching Standards are not offered.

Teacher preparation programs: Four-year baccalaureate-degree program leading to initial licensure that includes either a major or minor in education and practice teaching. Master's program preparing college graduates for initial licensure; includes practice teaching. Alternative program for college graduates leading to provisional licensure.

LICENSING TEST

Pass rate on state's teacher licensing test for 2002-2003: 100%

State average pass rate: 97%

School for International Training

- Kipling Road-P.O. Box 676, Brattleboro, VT 05302-0676
- **Website:** http://www.sit.edu
- Private
- **Degrees offered:** master's, education specialist

ADMISSIONS

Admissions phone number: **(800) 336-1616**
Admissions email address: *admissions@sit.edu*
Application website: http://www.sit.edu/graduate/admissions/index.html
Application fee: **$45**
Fall 2005 application deadline: **rolling**
Test of English as Foreign Language (TOEFL) is required for international students.
Minimum TOEFL score required for paper test: **550**
Minimum TOEFL score required for computer test: **213**

Fall 2003

Acceptance rate for master's degree programs: **73%**
Total 2003 enrollment: **126**
Master's degree enrollment: **126**
    Teacher preparation program enrollment (master's): **126**

FINANCIAL INFORMATION

Financial aid phone number: **(802) 258-3281**
Tuition, 2003-2004 academic year: **$21,320**
Fees: **$1,952**, Room and board: **$5,756**, Books and supplies: **$1,000**, Miscellaneous expenses: **$5,690**

ACADEMIC PROGRAMS

Total full-time tenured or tenure-track faculty (fall 2003): **10**, Total part-time faculty (fall 2003): **7**

Professional development/partnership school(s) are used by students in some of the teaching programs.

During their internships, peer groups of students meet regularly to discuss instructional techniques in all of the teaching programs.

All of the students in their internships are mentored.

Courses that prepare teachers to pass the National Board of Professional Teaching Standards are not offered.

Teacher preparation programs: Master's degree in education, including internship/practice teaching and preparation for initial licensure.

LICENSING TEST

Pass rate on state's teacher licensing test for 2002-2003: 100%

State average pass rate: 97%

St. Michael's College

- 1 Winooski Park, Colchester, VT 05439
- **Website:** http://www.smcvt.edu
- **Private**
- **Degrees offered:** bachelor's, master's, education specialist

ADMISSIONS

Admissions phone number: **(802) 654-2251**

Admissions email address: *dgoodrich@smcvt.edu*

Application website:
http://www2.smcvt.edu/pdf/GradProgram_Application/2003_Grad_Application.pdf

Application fee: **$35**

Fall 2005 application deadline: **rolling**

Test of English as Foreign Language (TOEFL) is required for international students.

Minimum TOEFL score required for paper test: 550

Minimum TOEFL score required for computer test: 213

FINANCIAL INFORMATION

Financial aid phone number: **(802) 654-3243**

Tuition, 2003-2004 academic year: Full-time: **$410/credit hour**; Part-time: **$410/credit hour**

ACADEMIC PROGRAMS

Professional development/partnership school(s) are used by students in some of the teaching programs.

During their internships, peer groups of students meet regularly to discuss instructional techniques in all of the teaching programs.

All of the students in their internships are mentored.

Courses that prepare teachers to pass the National Board of Professional Teaching Standards are offered.

Teacher preparation programs: Four-year baccalaureate-degree program leading to initial licensure that includes either a major or minor in education and practice teaching. Master's program preparing college graduates for initial licensure; includes practice teaching.

LICENSING TEST

Pass rate on state's teacher licensing test for 2002-2003: 100%

State average pass rate: 97%

University of Vermont

- 309 Waterman Building, Burlington, VT 05405-0160
- **Website:** http://www.uvm.edu/~gradcoll
- **Public**
- **Degrees offered:** bachelor's, master's, education specialist, Ed.D.

ADMISSIONS

Admissions phone number: **(802) 656-2699**

Admissions email address: *graduate.admissions@uvm.edu*

Application website:
http://www.applyweb.com/apply/uvmg/menu.html

Application fee: **$25**

Test requirements: **GRE**

Test of English as Foreign Language (TOEFL) is required for international students.

Minimum TOEFL score required for paper test: 550

Minimum TOEFL score required for computer test: 213

Fall 2003

Acceptance rate for master's degree programs: **61%**

Acceptance rate for doctoral programs: **51%**

Average GRE verbal: **526**, Average GRE quantitative: **493**, Average GRE analytical: **587**

Total 2003 enrollment: **441**

Master's degree enrollment: **373**
    Teacher preparation program enrollment (master's): **136**

Doctoral degree enrollment: **68**

FINANCIAL INFORMATION

Financial aid phone number: **(802) 656-3156**

Tuition, 2003-2004 academic year: Full-time in-state: **$8,696**; out-of-state: **$21,748**, Part-time in-state: **$362/credit hour**; out-of-state: **$906/credit hour**

Fees: **$812**, Room and board: **$6,704**, Books and supplies: **$800**

Number of fellowships awarded to graduate students during the 2003-2004 academic year: **13**

Number of teaching assistant positions: **23**

Number of research assistant positions: **9**

Number of other paid appointments: **26**

ACADEMIC PROGRAMS

Total full-time tenured or tenure-track faculty (fall 2003): **42**
    Total part-time faculty (fall 2003): **28**

Areas of specialization: curriculum and instruction, education administration and supervision, education policy, elementary teacher education, higher education administration, secondary teacher education, special education, student counseling and personnel services.

Professional development/partnership school(s) are used by students in all of the teaching programs.

During their internships, peer groups of students meet regularly to discuss instructional techniques in all of the teaching programs.

All of the students in their internships are mentored.

Courses that prepare teachers to pass the National Board of Professional Teaching Standards are offered.

Teacher preparation programs: Four-year baccalaureate-degree program leading to initial licensure that includes either a major or minor in education and practice teaching. Master's program preparing college graduates for initial licensure; includes practice teaching.

The education program is currently accredited by the National Council for Accreditation of Teacher Education.

LICENSING TEST

Pass rate on state's teacher licensing test for 2002-2003: **96%**

State average pass rate: **97%**

VIRGINIA

Averett University

■ **420 West Main Street, Danville, VA 24541**
■ **Website:** http://www.averett.edu/html/edgrad.html
■ **Private**
■ **Degrees offered:** bachelor's, master's

ADMISSIONS
Admissions phone number: **(434) 791-5657**
Admissions email address: *randy.cromwell@averett.edu*
Application fee: **$20**
Fall 2005 application deadline: **8/1**
Test requirements: **GRE or MAT**

Fall 2003
Acceptance rate for master's degree programs: **93%**
Total 2003 enrollment: **77**
Master's degree enrollment: **77**
    Teacher preparation program enrollment (master's): **77**

FINANCIAL INFORMATION
Financial aid phone number: **(434) 791-5646**
Tuition, 2003-2004 academic year: Full-time: **$165/credit hour**; Part-time: **$165/credit hour**
Books and supplies: **$100**, Miscellaneous expenses: **$50**
Number of fellowships awarded to graduate students during the 2003-2004 academic year: **0**
Number of teaching assistant positions: **0**
Number of research assistant positions: **0**
Number of other paid appointments: **0**

ACADEMIC PROGRAMS
Total full-time tenured or tenure-track faculty (fall 2003): **68**
    Total part-time faculty (fall 2003): **186**
Areas of specialization: curriculum and instruction, elementary teacher education, secondary teacher education, special education.
Professional development/partnership school(s) are used by students in all of the teaching programs.

During their internships, peer groups of students meet regularly to discuss instructional techniques in some of the teaching programs.
All of the students in their internships are mentored.
Courses that prepare teachers to pass the National Board of Professional Teaching Standards are not offered.
Teacher preparation programs: Four-year baccalaureate-degree program leading to initial licensure that includes either a major or minor in education and practice teaching. Five-year program leading to initial licensure that results in a baccalaureate degree (with a major or minor in education) plus a master's degree and includes practice teaching. Master's program preparing college graduates for initial licensure; includes practice teaching. Alternative program for college graduates leading to provisional licensure.

LICENSING TEST
Pass rate on state's teacher licensing test for 2002-2003: **100%**
State average pass rate: **94%**

Christopher Newport University

■ **1 University Place, Newport News, VA 23606-2998**
■ **Website:** http://www.cnu.edu/mat
■ **Public**
■ **Degrees offered:** master's

ADMISSIONS
Admissions phone number: **(757) 594-7544**
Admissions email address: *gradstdy@cnu.edu*
Application website: *http://www.cnu.edu/gradstudies*
Application fee: **$40**
Fall 2005 application deadline: **4/15**
Test of English as Foreign Language (TOEFL) is required for international students.
Minimum TOEFL score required for paper test: **580**
Minimum TOEFL score required for computer test: **237**

FINANCIAL INFORMATION

Financial aid phone number: **(757) 594-7170**

Tuition, 2003-2004 academic year: Full-time in-state: **$213/credit hour**; out-of-state: **$524/credit hour**, Part-time in-state: **$213/credit hour**; out-of-state: **$524/credit hour**

Fees: **$150**, Room and board: **$6,350**, Books and supplies: **$400**

ACADEMIC PROGRAMS

Courses that prepare teachers to pass the National Board of Professional Teaching Standards are not offered.

Teacher preparation programs: Master's degree in education, including internship/practice teaching and preparation for initial licensure.

LICENSING TEST

Pass rate on state's teacher licensing test for 2002-2003: **100%**

State average pass rate: **94%**

College of William and Mary

- ■ PO Box 8795, Williamsburg, VA 23187-8795
- ■ **Website:** http://www.wm.edu/education/index.html
- ■ **Public**
- ■ **Degrees offered:** master's, education specialist, Ph.D., Ed.D.
- ■ **Overall rank in the 2005 U.S. News education schools with doctoral programs:** 47

ADMISSIONS

Admissions phone number: **(757) 221-2317**

Admissions email address: *GradEd@wm.edu*

Application fee: **$30**

Fall 2005 application deadline: **2/1**

Test requirements: **GRE or MAT**

Test of English as Foreign Language (TOEFL) is required for international students.

Fall 2003

Acceptance rate for master's degree programs: **49%**

Acceptance rate for education specialist degree programs: **83%**

Acceptance rate for doctoral programs: **52%**

Average GRE verbal: **538**, Average GRE quantitative: **586**, Average GRE analytical: **634**, Average MAT: **53**

Total 2003 enrollment: **378**

Master's degree enrollment: **244**

Teacher preparation program enrollment (master's): **109**

Education specialist degree enrollment: **19**

Doctoral degree enrollment: **115**

FINANCIAL INFORMATION

Financial aid phone number: **(757) 221-2317**

Tuition, 2003-2004 academic year: Full-time in-state: **$7,532**; out-of-state: **$19,196**, Part-time in-state: **$222/credit hour**; out-of-state: **$618/credit hour**

Fees: **$2,620**, Room and board: **$6,652**, Books and supplies: **$2,000**, Miscellaneous expenses: **$2,000**

Number of fellowships awarded to graduate students during the 2003-2004 academic year: **0**

Number of teaching assistant positions: **96**

Number of research assistant positions: **0**

Number of other paid appointments: **1**

ACADEMIC PROGRAMS

Total full-time tenured or tenure-track faculty (fall 2003): **35**, Total part-time faculty (fall 2003): **25**

Areas of specialization: curriculum and instruction, education administration and supervision, education policy, elementary teacher education, higher education administration, secondary teacher education, special education, student counseling and personnel services.

Professional development/partnership school(s) are used by students in some of the teaching programs.

During their internships, peer groups of students meet regularly to discuss instructional techniques in all of the teaching programs.

All of the students in their internships are mentored.

Courses that prepare teachers to pass the National Board of Professional Teaching Standards are not offered.

Teacher preparation programs: Four-year baccalaureate-degree program leading to initial licensure that includes either a major or minor in education and practice teaching. Master's program preparing college graduates for initial licensure; includes practice teaching.

The education program is currently accredited by the National Council for Accreditation of Teacher Education.

LICENSING TEST

Pass rate on state's teacher licensing test for 2002-2003: **89%**

State average pass rate: **94%**

Eastern Mennonite University

- ■ **1200 Park Road, Harrisonburg, VA 22802**
- ■ **Website:** http://www.emu.edu/maed
- ■ **Private**
- ■ **Degrees offered:** bachelor's, master's

ADMISSIONS

Admissions phone number: **(540) 432-4257**

Admissions email address: *yoderda@emu.edu*

Application fee: **$25**

Fall 2005 application deadline: **2/15**

Test of English as Foreign Language (TOEFL) is required for international students.

Minimum TOEFL score required for paper test: **550**

Minimum TOEFL score required for computer test: **213**

Fall 2003

Total 2003 enrollment: **75**

Master's degree enrollment: **75**

FINANCIAL INFORMATION

Financial aid phone number: **(540) 432-4081**
Tuition, 2003-2004 academic year: Full-time: **$285/credit hour**; Part-time: **$285/credit hour**
Fees: **$46**

LICENSING TEST

Pass rate on state's teacher licensing test for 2002-2003: **100%**
State average pass rate: **94%**

George Mason University

- **4400 University Drive, MSN 2F1, Fairfax, VA 22030-4444**
- **Website:** http://gse.gmu.edu
- **Public**
- **Degrees offered:** master's, Ph.D.
- **Overall rank in the 2005 U.S. News education schools with doctoral programs:** 62

ADMISSIONS

Admissions phone number: **(703) 993-2010**
Admissions email address: *gseadmit@gmu.edu*
Application website: *http://www.admissions.gmu.edu*
Application fee: **$60**
Fall 2005 application deadline: **3/1**
Test requirements: **GRE**
Test of English as Foreign Language (TOEFL) is required for international students.
Minimum TOEFL score required for paper test: **575**
Minimum TOEFL score required for computer test: **230**

Fall 2003
Acceptance rate for master's degree programs: **69%**
Acceptance rate for doctoral programs: **51%**
Average GRE verbal: **515**, Average GRE quantitative: **538**
Total 2003 enrollment: **2,211**
Master's degree enrollment: **2,045**
 Teacher preparation program enrollment (master's): **1,593**
Doctoral degree enrollment: **166**

FINANCIAL INFORMATION

Financial aid phone number: **(703) 993-2353**
Tuition, 2003-2004 academic year: Full-time in-state: **$245/credit hour**; out-of-state: **$623/credit hour**, Part-time in-state: **$245/credit hour**; out-of-state: **$623/credit hour**
Room and board: **$6,832**, Books and supplies: **$1,000**, Miscellaneous expenses: **$5,870**
Number of fellowships awarded to graduate students during the 2003-2004 academic year: **81**
Number of teaching assistant positions: **0**
Number of research assistant positions: **85**
Number of other paid appointments: **0**

ACADEMIC PROGRAMS

Total full-time tenured or tenure-track faculty (fall 2003): **81**, Total part-time faculty (fall 2003): **13**
Areas of specialization: curriculum and instruction, education administration and supervision, education policy, educational psychology, elementary teacher education, higher education administration, secondary teacher education, special education, student counseling and personnel services.
Professional development/partnership school(s) are used by students in some of the teaching programs.
During their internships, peer groups of students meet regularly to discuss instructional techniques in some of the teaching programs.
All of the students in their internships are mentored.
Courses that prepare teachers to pass the National Board of Professional Teaching Standards are offered.
Teacher preparation programs: Master's degree in education, including internship/practice teaching and preparation for initial licensure. Education minor for undergraduate students. Alternative program for college graduates leading to provisional licensure.
The education program is currently accredited by the National Council for Accreditation of Teacher Education.

LICENSING TEST

Pass rate on state's teacher licensing test for 2002-2003: **84%**
State average pass rate: **94%**

Hampton University

- **Graduate College, Hampton, VA 23668**
- **Website:**
  http://www.hamptonu.edu/GraduateCollege/home.html
- **Private**
- **Degrees offered:** master's

ADMISSIONS

Admissions phone number: **(757) 727-5454**
Admissions email address: *hugrad@hamptonu.edu*
Application website:
 http://www.hamptonu.edu/admissions/application.htm
Application fee: **$25**
Fall 2005 application deadline: **6/1**
Test requirements: **GRE**
Test of English as Foreign Language (TOEFL) is required for international students.
Minimum TOEFL score required for paper test: **525**
Minimum TOEFL score required for computer test: **200**

Fall 2003
Acceptance rate for master's degree programs: **93%**
Average GRE verbal: **374**, Average GRE quantitative: **401**, Average GRE analytical: **407**
Total 2003 enrollment: **73**
Master's degree enrollment: **73**
 Teacher preparation program enrollment (master's): **39**

FINANCIAL INFORMATION

Financial aid phone number: **(757) 727-5332**
Tuition, 2003-2004 academic year: **$5,220$290/credit hour**
Fees: **$70**, Room and board: **$6,850**, Books and supplies: **$770**, Miscellaneous expenses: **$5,120**
Number of fellowships awarded to graduate students during the 2003-2004 academic year: **0**
Number of teaching assistant positions: **0**
Number of other paid appointments: **0**

ACADEMIC PROGRAMS

Total full-time tenured or tenure-track faculty (fall 2003): **8**
Total part-time faculty (fall 2003): **4**
Areas of specialization: curriculum and instruction, education administration and supervision, education policy, educational psychology, elementary teacher education, secondary teacher education, special education, student counseling and personnel services.
Professional development/partnership school(s) are used by students in all of the teaching programs.
During their internships, peer groups of students meet regularly to discuss instructional techniques in all of the teaching programs.
All of the students in their internships are mentored.
Courses that prepare teachers to pass the National Board of Professional Teaching Standards are not offered.
Teacher preparation programs: Master's degree in education, including internship/practice teaching and preparation for initial licensure. Alternative program for college graduates leading to provisional licensure.
The education program is currently accredited by the National Council for Accreditation of Teacher Education.

LICENSING TEST

Pass rate on state's teacher licensing test for 2002-2003: **100%**
State average pass rate: **94%**

James Madison University

■ **17 West Grace Street, MSC 6702, Harrisonburg, VA 22807**
■ **Website:** http://www.jmu.edu/cgapp
■ **Public**
■ **Degrees offered:** bachelor's, master's, education specialist

ADMISSIONS

Admissions phone number: **(540) 568-6395**
Admissions email address: *grad_programs@jmu.edu*
Application website: *http://www.applyweb.com/aw?jmug*
Application fee: **$55**
Fall 2005 application deadline: **7/1**
Test requirements: **GRE or MAT**
Test of English as Foreign Language (TOEFL) is required for international students.
Minimum TOEFL score required for paper test: **570**
Minimum TOEFL score required for computer test: **230**

Fall 2003
Total 2003 enrollment: **250**
Master's degree enrollment: **207**
Teacher preparation program enrollment (master's): **135**
Education specialist degree enrollment: **43**

FINANCIAL INFORMATION

Financial aid phone number: **(540) 568-7820**
Tuition, 2003-2004 academic year: Full-time in-state: **$201/credit hour**; out-of-state: **$605**, Part-time in-state: **$201/credit hour**; out-of-state: **$605/credit hour**
Number of teaching assistant positions: **16**

ACADEMIC PROGRAMS

Total full-time tenured or tenure-track faculty (fall 2003): **26**
Areas of specialization: curriculum and instruction, education administration and supervision, educational psychology, elementary teacher education, higher education administration, secondary teacher education, special education, student counseling and personnel services.
Professional development/partnership school(s) are used by students in some of the teaching programs.
During their internships, peer groups of students meet regularly to discuss instructional techniques in some of the teaching programs.
All of the students in their internships are mentored.
Courses that prepare teachers to pass the National Board of Professional Teaching Standards are offered.
Teacher preparation programs: Four-year baccalaureate-degree program leading to initial licensure that includes either a major or minor in education and practice teaching. Five-year program leading to initial licensure that results in a baccalaureate degree (with a major or minor in education) plus graduate credit and includes practice teaching. Five-year program leading to initial licensure that results in a baccalaureate degree (with a major or minor in education) plus a master's degree and includes practice teaching. Master's program preparing college graduates for initial licensure; includes practice teaching.
The education program is currently accredited by the National Council for Accreditation of Teacher Education.

LICENSING TEST

Pass rate on state's teacher licensing test for 2002-2003: **100%**
State average pass rate: **94%**

Liberty University

■ **1971 University Blvd, Lynchburg, VA 24550**
■ **Website:** http://www.liberty.edu/academics/graduate
■ **Private**
■ **Degrees offered:** master's, education specialist, Ed.D.

ADMISSIONS

Admissions phone number: **(800) 424-9596**
Admissions email address: *gradadmissions@liberty.edu*

Application website: *http://www.liberty.edu/gradforms*
Application fee: $35
Fall 2005 application deadline: 8/1
Test requirements: **GRE**
Test of English as Foreign Language (TOEFL) is required for international students.
Minimum TOEFL score required for paper test: **600**
Minimum TOEFL score required for computer test: **250**

Fall 2003
Acceptance rate for master's degree programs: **37%**
Acceptance rate for education specialist degree programs: **47%**
Acceptance rate for doctoral programs: **33%**
Average GRE verbal: **538**, Average GRE quantitative: **492**, Average GRE analytical: **533**
Total 2003 enrollment: **784**
Master's degree enrollment: **591**
  Teacher preparation program enrollment (master's): **488**
Education specialist degree enrollment: **16**
Doctoral degree enrollment: **177**

FINANCIAL INFORMATION
Financial aid phone number: **(434) 582-2270**
Tuition, 2003-2004 academic year: Full-time: **$260/credit hour**; Part-time: **$260/credit hour**
Fees: **$200**, Books and supplies: **$242**
Number of fellowships awarded to graduate students during the 2003-2004 academic year: **0**
Number of teaching assistant positions: **0**
Number of research assistant positions: **0**
Number of other paid appointments: **2**

ACADEMIC PROGRAMS
Total full-time tenured or tenure-track faculty (fall 2003): **8**
  Total part-time faculty (fall 2003): **2**
Areas of specialization: curriculum and instruction, education administration and supervision, education policy, educational psychology, elementary teacher education, secondary teacher education, special education, student counseling and personnel services.
Professional development/partnership school(s) are used by students in some of the teaching programs.
During their internships, peer groups of students meet regularly to discuss instructional techniques in all of the teaching programs.
Some of the students in their internships are mentored.
Courses that prepare teachers to pass the National Board of Professional Teaching Standards are not offered.
Teacher preparation programs: Four-year baccalaureate-degree program leading to initial licensure that includes either a major or minor in education and practice teaching. Master's program preparing college graduates for initial licensure; includes practice teaching.
The education program is currently accredited by the National Council for Accreditation of Teacher Education.

LICENSING TEST
Pass rate on state's teacher licensing test for 2002-2003: **100%**
State average pass rate: **94%**

Longwood University

■ **201 High Street, Farmville, VA 23909**
■ **Website:** http://www.longwood.edu/
■ **Public**

LICENSING TEST
Pass rate on state's teacher licensing test for 2002-2003: **89%**
State average pass rate: **94%**

Lynchburg College

■ **1501 Lakeside Drive, Lynchburg, VA 24501**
■ **Website:** http://www.lynchburg.edu/enroll/
■ **Private**
■ **Degrees offered:** bachelor's, master's

ADMISSIONS
Admissions phone number: **(434) 544-8300**
Admissions email address: *admissions@lynchburg.edu*
Application fee: **$30**
Fall 2005 application deadline: **7/31**
Test of English as Foreign Language (TOEFL) is required for international students.
Minimum TOEFL score required for paper test: **525**
Minimum TOEFL score required for computer test: **197**

FINANCIAL INFORMATION
Financial aid phone number: **(434) 544-8228**
Tuition, 2003-2004 academic year: Full-time: **$310/credit hour**; Part-time: **$310/credit hour**
Fees: **$50**
Number of other paid appointments: **35**

ACADEMIC PROGRAMS
Total full-time tenured or tenure-track faculty (fall 2003): **16**
  Total part-time faculty (fall 2003): **4**
Areas of specialization: education administration and supervision, special education, student counseling and personnel services.
Professional development/partnership school(s) are used by students in some of the teaching programs.
During their internships, peer groups of students meet regularly to discuss instructional techniques in some of the teaching programs.
All of the students in their internships are mentored.
Courses that prepare teachers to pass the National Board of Professional Teaching Standards are not offered.
Teacher preparation programs: Four-year baccalaureate-degree program leading to initial licensure that includes either a major or minor in education and practice teaching. Master's program preparing college graduates for initial licensure; includes practice teaching. Alternative program for college graduates leading to provisional licensure.

LICENSING TEST

Pass rate on state's teacher licensing test for 2002-2003: **91%**
State average pass rate: **94%**

Mary Baldwin College

- Mary Baldiwn College, Staunton, VA 24401
- **Website:** http://www.mbc.edu/
- Private
- **Degrees offered:** master's

ADMISSIONS

Admissions phone number: **(540) 887-7333**
Admissions email address: *cgrove@mbc.edu*
Application fee: **$35**
Fall 2005 application deadline: **rolling**

Fall 2003
Acceptance rate for master's degree programs: **93%**
Total 2003 enrollment: **125**
Master's degree enrollment: **125**
    Teacher preparation program enrollment (master's): **125**

FINANCIAL INFORMATION

Financial aid phone number: **(540) 887-7228**
Tuition, 2003-2004 academic year: Full-time: **$355/credit hour**; Part-time: **$355/credit hour**
Fees: **$80**, Books and supplies: **$700**

ACADEMIC PROGRAMS

Total full-time tenured or tenure-track faculty (fall 2003): **2**
    Total part-time faculty (fall 2003): **35**
Areas of specialization: curriculum and instruction.
Professional development/partnership school(s) are used by students in all of the teaching programs.
During their internships, peer groups of students meet regularly to discuss instructional techniques in all of the teaching programs.
All of the students in their internships are mentored.
Courses that prepare teachers to pass the National Board of Professional Teaching Standards are offered.

LICENSING TEST

Pass rate on state's teacher licensing test for 2002-2003: **100%**
State average pass rate: **94%**

Marymount University

- 2807 N. Glebe Road, Arlington, VA 22207
- **Website:** http://www.marymount.edu/
- Private

LICENSING TEST

Pass rate on state's teacher licensing test for 2002-2003: **100%**
State average pass rate: **94%**

Norfolk State University

- 700 Park Avenue, Norfolk, VA 23504
- **Website:** http://www.nsu.edu/
- Public

LICENSING TEST

Pass rate on state's teacher licensing test for 2002-2003: **91%**
State average pass rate: **94%**

Old Dominion University

- Hampton Boulevard, Norfolk, VA 23529
- **Website:**
  http://www.odu.edu/educ/education/index.html
- Public
- **Degrees offered:** bachelor's, master's, education specialist, Ph.D.

ADMISSIONS

Admissions phone number: **(757) 683-3685**
Admissions email address: *admit@odu.edu*
Application website:
    http://www.odu.edu/ao/admissions/docs/applications.html
Application fee: **$40**
Fall 2005 application deadline: **3/15**
Test requirements: **GRE or MAT**
Test of English as Foreign Language (TOEFL) is required for international students.
Minimum TOEFL score required for paper test: **550**
Minimum TOEFL score required for computer test: **213**

Fall 2003
Acceptance rate for master's degree programs: **49%**
Acceptance rate for education specialist degree programs: **58%**
Acceptance rate for doctoral programs: **38%**
Average GRE verbal: **460**, Average GRE quantitative: **500**, Average MAT: **46**
Total 2003 enrollment: **1,364**
Master's degree enrollment: **1,246**
    Teacher preparation program enrollment (master's): **1,028**
Education specialist degree enrollment: **55**
Doctoral degree enrollment: **63**

FINANCIAL INFORMATION

Financial aid phone number: **(757) 683-3683**
Tuition, 2003-2004 academic year: Full-time in-state: **$235/credit hour**; out-of-state: **$603/credit hour**, Part-time in-state: **$235/credit hour**; out-of-state: **$603/credit hour**
Fees: **$62**, Room and board: **$5,513**, Books and supplies: **$800**, Miscellaneous expenses: **$2,875**
Number of teaching assistant positions: **9**
Number of research assistant positions: **81**
Number of other paid appointments: **46**

ACADEMIC PROGRAMS

Total full-time tenured or tenure-track faculty (fall 2003): 64, Total part-time faculty (fall 2003): 120

Areas of specialization: curriculum and instruction, education administration and supervision, elementary teacher education, higher education administration, secondary teacher education, special education, student counseling and personnel services, teacher education.

Professional development/partnership school(s) are used by students in some of the teaching programs.

During their internships, peer groups of students meet regularly to discuss instructional techniques in some of the teaching programs.

All of the students in their internships are mentored.

Courses that prepare teachers to pass the National Board of Professional Teaching Standards are not offered.

Teacher preparation programs: Five-year program leading to initial licensure that results in a baccalaureate degree (with a major or minor in education) plus a master's degree and includes practice teaching. Master's program preparing college graduates for initial licensure; includes practice teaching.

The education program is currently accredited by the National Council for Accreditation of Teacher Education.

LICENSING TEST

Pass rate on state's teacher licensing test for 2002-2003: 96%
State average pass rate: 94%

Radford University

■ P.O. Box 6890, RU Station, Radford, VA 24142
■ **Website:** http://www.radford.edu
■ **Public**
■ **Degrees offered:** bachelor's, master's, education specialist

ADMISSIONS

Admissions phone number: **(540) 831-5431**
Admissions email address: *gradcoll@radford.edu*
Application website: *http://www.radford.edu/~gradcoll*
Application fee: **$40**
Fall 2005 application deadline: **3/1**
Test of English as Foreign Language (TOEFL) is required for international students.
Minimum TOEFL score required for paper test: **550**
Minimum TOEFL score required for computer test: **213**

Fall 2003
Total 2003 enrollment: **375**
Master's degree enrollment: **350**
Education specialist degree enrollment: **25**

FINANCIAL INFORMATION

Financial aid phone number: **(540) 831-5408**
Tuition, 2003-2004 academic year: Full-time in-state: **$215/credit hour**; out-of-state: **$397/credit hour**, Part-time in-state: **$215/credit hour**; out-of-state: **$397/credit hour**

Room and board: **$5,660**, Books and supplies: **$700**, Miscellaneous expenses: **$3,112**

ACADEMIC PROGRAMS

Courses that prepare teachers to pass the National Board of Professional Teaching Standards are not offered.

Teacher preparation programs: Four-year baccalaureate-degree program leading to initial licensure that includes either a major or minor in education and practice teaching. Five-year program leading to initial licensure that results in a baccalaureate degree (with a major or minor in education) plus graduate credit and includes practice teaching. Five-year program leading to initial licensure that results in a baccalaureate degree (with a major or minor in education) plus a master's degree and includes practice teaching.

The education program is currently accredited by the National Council for Accreditation of Teacher Education.

LICENSING TEST

Pass rate on state's teacher licensing test for 2002-2003: 100%
State average pass rate: 94%

Regent University

■ **1000 Regent University Drive, Virginia Beach, VA 23693**
■ **Website:** http://www.regent.edu
■ **Private**
■ **Degrees offered:** master's, Ed.D.

ADMISSIONS

Admissions phone number: **(800) 373-5504**
Admissions email address: *admissions@regent.edu*
Application website: *http://www.regent.edu/admissions/*
Application fee: **$50**
Fall 2005 application deadline: **8/1**
Test requirements: **GRE or MAT**
Test of English as Foreign Language (TOEFL) is required for international students.
Minimum TOEFL score required for paper test: **577**
Minimum TOEFL score required for computer test: **233**

Fall 2003
Acceptance rate for master's degree programs: **86%**
Acceptance rate for doctoral programs: **32%**
Average GRE verbal: **477**, Average GRE quantitative: **476**
Total 2003 enrollment: **681**
Master's degree enrollment: **575**
Teacher preparation program enrollment (master's): **46**
Education specialist degree enrollment: **0**
Doctoral degree enrollment: **106**

FINANCIAL INFORMATION

Financial aid phone number: **(757) 226-4140**
Tuition, 2003-2004 academic year: Full-time: **$420/credit hour**; Part-time: **$420/credit hour**
Fees: **$369**, Books and supplies: **$3,000**

ACADEMIC PROGRAMS

Total full-time tenured or tenure-track faculty (fall 2003): 18

Areas of specialization: curriculum and instruction, education administration and supervision, education policy, educational psychology, elementary teacher education, higher education administration, special education.

Professional development/partnership school(s) are used by students in some of the teaching programs.

During their internships, peer groups of students meet regularly to discuss instructional techniques in all of the teaching programs.

All of the students in their internships are mentored.

Courses that prepare teachers to pass the National Board of Professional Teaching Standards are not offered.

Teacher preparation programs: Master's degree in education, including internship/practice teaching and preparation for initial licensure. Alternative program for college graduates leading to provisional licensure.

Shenandoah University

■ 1460 University Drive, Winchester, VA 22601
■ **Website:** http://www.su.edu
■ **Private**
■ **Degrees offered:** master's, Ed.D.

ADMISSIONS

Admissions phone number: **(540) 665-4581**
Admissions email address: *admit@su.edu*
Application website: *http://www.su.edu*
Application fee: **$30**
Fall 2005 application deadline: **rolling**
Test of English as Foreign Language (TOEFL) is required for international students.
Minimum TOEFL score required for paper test: **550**
Minimum TOEFL score required for computer test: **213**

Fall 2003
Acceptance rate for master's degree programs: **91%**
Acceptance rate for doctoral programs: **100%**
Total 2003 enrollment: **279**
Master's degree enrollment: **244**
  Teacher preparation program enrollment (master's): **46**
Doctoral degree enrollment: **35**

FINANCIAL INFORMATION

Financial aid phone number: **(540) 665-4538**
Tuition, 2003-2004 academic year: Full-time: **$10,080**; Part-time: **$560/credit hour**
Fees: **$80**, Room and board: **$6,800**, Books and supplies: **$2,000**, Miscellaneous expenses: **$2,100**
Number of fellowships awarded to graduate students during the 2003-2004 academic year: **279**

ACADEMIC PROGRAMS

Total full-time tenured or tenure-track faculty (fall 2003): **11**, Total part-time faculty (fall 2003): **15**

Areas of specialization: curriculum and instruction, education administration and supervision, education policy, educational psychology, elementary teacher education, secondary teacher education.

Professional development/partnership school(s) are used by students in all of the teaching programs.

During their internships, peer groups of students meet regularly to discuss instructional techniques in none of the teaching programs.

All of the students in their internships are mentored.

Courses that prepare teachers to pass the National Board of Professional Teaching Standards are not offered.

Teacher preparation programs: Master's degree in education, including internship/practice teaching and preparation for initial licensure.

LICENSING TEST

Pass rate on state's teacher licensing test for 2002-2003: **81%**
State average pass rate: **94%**

University of Virginia (Curry)

■ 405 Emmet Street S, Charlottesville, VA 22903-2495
■ **Website:** http://curry.edschool.virginia.edu/
■ **Public**
■ **Degrees offered:** bachelor's, master's, education specialist, Ph.D., Ed.D.
■ **Overall rank in the 2005 U.S. News education schools with doctoral programs: 20**
■ **Overall rank in the 2005 U.S. News education school specialty rankings:** administration/supervision: 22, counseling/personnel: 18, curriculum/instruction: 14, elementary education: 11, higher education administration: 22, secondary education: 10, special education: 4

ADMISSIONS

Admissions phone number: **(434) 924-3334**
Admissions email address: *curry@virginia.edu*
Application website: *https://www.applyweb.com/aw?uvaed*
Application fee: **$40**
Fall 2005 application deadline: **rolling**
Test requirements: **GRE**
Test of English as Foreign Language (TOEFL) is required for international students.
Minimum TOEFL score required for paper test: **600**
Minimum TOEFL score required for computer test: **250**

Fall 2003
Acceptance rate for master's degree programs: **61%**
Acceptance rate for education specialist degree programs: **91%**
Acceptance rate for doctoral programs: **60%**
Average GRE verbal: **528**, Average GRE quantitative: **583**, Average GRE analytical: **588**

Total 2003 enrollment: 899
Master's degree enrollment: 456
    Teacher preparation program enrollment (master's): 368
Education specialist degree enrollment: 12
Doctoral degree enrollment: 431

FINANCIAL INFORMATION
Financial aid phone number: **(434) 982-6000**
Tuition, 2003-2004 academic year: Full-time in-state:
    $6,476; out-of-state: **$18,534**, Part-time in-state: **$2,830**;
    out-of-state: **$6,874**
Fees: **$1,390**, Room and board: **$9,077**, Books and sup-
    plies: **$1,875**, Miscellaneous expenses: **$2,938**
Number of fellowships awarded to graduate students dur-
    ing the 2003-2004 academic year: **349**
Number of teaching assistant positions: **57**
Number of research assistant positions: **47**
Number of other paid appointments: **21**

ACADEMIC PROGRAMS
Total full-time tenured or tenure-track faculty (fall 2003): **85**
    Total part-time faculty (fall 2003): **25**
Areas of specialization: curriculum and instruction, educa-
    tion administration and supervision, education policy,
    educational psychology, elementary teacher education,
    higher education administration, secondary teacher edu-
    cation, special education, student counseling and per-
    sonnel services.
Professional development/partnership school(s) are used
    by students in none of the teaching programs.
During their internships, peer groups of students meet
    regularly to discuss instructional techniques in all of the
    teaching programs.
All of the students in their internships are mentored.
Courses that prepare teachers to pass the National Board of
    Professional Teaching Standards are not offered.
Teacher preparation programs: Master's program prepar-
    ing college graduates for initial licensure; includes prac-
    tice teaching.
The education program is currently accredited by the
    National Council for Accreditation of Teacher Education.
The education program is currently accredited by the
    Teacher Education Accreditation Council.

LICENSING TEST
Pass rate on state's teacher licensing test for 2002-2003:
    99%
State average pass rate: **94%**

Virginia Commonwealth University

■ **1015 W. Main Street, PO Box 842020, Richmond, VA
23284-2020**
■ **Website:** http://www.soe.vcu.edu
■ **Public**
■ **Degrees offered:** bachelor's, master's, Ph.D.

■ **Overall rank in the 2005 U.S. News education schools
with doctoral programs:** 47

ADMISSIONS
Admissions phone number: **(804) 828-3382**
Admissions email address: *mddavis@vcu.edu*
Application website: http://www.vcu.edu/graduate/pdfs/
    application.pdf
Application fee: **$50**
Fall 2005 application deadline: **5/15**
Test requirements: **GRE or MAT**
Test of English as Foreign Language (TOEFL) is required
    for international students.
Minimum TOEFL score required for paper test: **600**
Minimum TOEFL score required for computer test: **250**

Fall 2003
Acceptance rate for master's degree programs: **78%**
Acceptance rate for doctoral programs: **56%**
Average GRE verbal: **453**, Average GRE quantitative: **511**,
    Average MAT: **38**
Total 2003 enrollment: **747**
Master's degree enrollment: **658**
    Teacher preparation program enrollment (master's): **487**
Doctoral degree enrollment: **89**

FINANCIAL INFORMATION
Financial aid phone number: **(804) 828-6181**
Tuition, 2003-2004 academic year: Full-time in-state:
    $5,498; out-of-state: **$15,905**, Part-time in-state:
    $611/credit hour; out-of-state: **$1,678/credit hour**
Fees: **$1,220**, Room and board: **$7,440**, Books and sup-
    plies: **$850**, Miscellaneous expenses: **$2,390**
Number of fellowships awarded to graduate students dur-
    ing the 2003-2004 academic year: **4**
Number of teaching assistant positions: **0**
Number of research assistant positions: **10**
Number of other paid appointments: **6**

ACADEMIC PROGRAMS
Total full-time tenured or tenure-track faculty (fall 2003): **43**
    Total part-time faculty (fall 2003): **55**
Areas of specialization: curriculum and instruction, educa-
    tion administration and supervision, education policy,
    educational psychology, elementary teacher education,
    higher education administration, secondary teacher edu-
    cation, special education, student counseling and per-
    sonnel services.
Professional development/partnership school(s) are used
    by students in some of the teaching programs.
During their internships, peer groups of students meet
    regularly to discuss instructional techniques in some of
    the teaching programs.
All of the students in their internships are mentored.
Courses that prepare teachers to pass the National Board of
    Professional Teaching Standards are offered.
Teacher preparation programs: Four-year baccalaureate-
    degree program leading to initial licensure that includes
    either a major or minor in education and practice teaching.
    Five-year program leading to initial licensure that results in

a baccalaureate degree (with a major or minor in education) plus a master's degree and includes practice teaching. Master's program preparing college graduates for initial licensure; includes practice teaching. Alternative program for college graduates leading to provisional licensure. The education program is currently accredited by the National Council for Accreditation of Teacher Education.

LICENSING TEST
Pass rate on state's teacher licensing test for 2002-2003: **84%**
State average pass rate: **94%**

Virginia State University

■ 1 Hayden Street, Petersburg, VA 23806
■ **Website:** http://www.vsu.edu/
■ **Public**

LICENSING TEST
Pass rate on state's teacher licensing test for 2002-2003: **80%**
State average pass rate: **94%**

Virginia Tech

■ 260 Wallace Hall, Blacksburg, VA 24061-0426
■ **Website:** http://www.grads.vt.edu/
■ **Public**
■ **Degrees offered:** bachelor's, master's, education specialist, Ph.D., Ed.D.
■ **Overall rank in the 2005 U.S. News education school specialty rankings:** vocational/technical: 5

ADMISSIONS
Admissions phone number: **(540) 231-6691**
Admissions email address: *awwebb@vt.edu*
Application website: *http://www.grads.vt.edu/homeapply.html*
Application fee: **$45**
Fall 2005 application deadline: **rolling**
Test requirements: **GRE**
Test of English as Foreign Language (TOEFL) is required for international students.
Minimum TOEFL score required for paper test: **550**
Minimum TOEFL score required for computer test: **213**

Fall 2003
Acceptance rate for master's degree programs: **68%**
Acceptance rate for education specialist degree programs: **100%**
Acceptance rate for doctoral programs: **62%**

Total 2003 enrollment: **1,115**
Master's degree enrollment: **639**
    Teacher preparation program enrollment (master's): **469**
Education specialist degree enrollment: **48**
Doctoral degree enrollment: **428**

FINANCIAL INFORMATION
Financial aid phone number: **(540) 231-4558**
Tuition, 2003-2004 academic year: Full-time in-state: **$6,039**; out-of-state: **$9,708**, Part-time in-state: **$336/credit hour**; out-of-state: **$539/credit hour**
Fees: **$905**, Room and board: **$5,200**, Books and supplies: **$1,000**, Miscellaneous expenses: **$1,000**
Number of fellowships awarded to graduate students during the 2003-2004 academic year: **0**
Number of teaching assistant positions: **19**
Number of research assistant positions: **4**
Number of other paid appointments: **37**

ACADEMIC PROGRAMS
Total full-time tenured or tenure-track faculty (fall 2003): **56**
    Total part-time faculty (fall 2003): **27**
Areas of specialization: curriculum and instruction, education administration and supervision, education policy, educational psychology, elementary teacher education, higher education administration, secondary teacher education, special education, student counseling and personnel services.
Professional development/partnership school(s) are used by students in some of the teaching programs.
During their internships, peer groups of students meet regularly to discuss instructional techniques in all of the teaching programs.
All of the students in their internships are mentored.
Courses that prepare teachers to pass the National Board of Professional Teaching Standards are offered.
Teacher preparation programs: Four-year baccalaureate-degree program leading to initial licensure that includes either a major or minor in education and practice teaching. Five-year program leading to initial licensure that results in a baccalaureate degree (with a major or minor in education) plus graduate credit and includes practice teaching. Five-year program leading to initial licensure that results in a baccalaureate degree (with a major or minor in education) plus a master's degree and includes practice teaching. Master's program preparing college graduates for initial licensure; includes practice teaching.
The education program is currently accredited by the National Council for Accreditation of Teacher Education.

LICENSING TEST
Pass rate on state's teacher licensing test for 2002-2003: **94%**
State average pass rate: **94%**

WASHINGTON

TEACHER TESTING IN WASHINGTON

Teacher licensure rules vary widely from state to state, but almost all states require tests. Washington has recently instituted a licensure exam. The exams typically cover the basics of reading, writing and math, although some states mandate in-depth, subject-specific teacher tests. For information on where to go in your state for specific academic requirements, see Chapter 6 on page 67. Note: Some schools require students to pass exams by graduation, and thus automatically report pass rates of 100 percent.

- This state **does** require a basic skills test in order to obtain a teaching license.
- This state **does not** require a subject-knowledge test in order to obtain a middle school teaching license.
- This state **does not** require a subject-knowledge test in order to obtain a high school teaching license.
- This state **does not** require a subject-specific pedagogy test in order to obtain a teaching license.

Antioch University–Seattle

- **2326 Sixth Ave, Seattle, WA 98121**
- **Website:** http://www.aus.edu
- **Private**
- **Degrees offered:** bachelor's, master's

ADMISSIONS

Admissions phone number: **(888) 268-4477**
Admissions email address: *admissions@antiochsea.edu*
Application website: http://www.antiochsea.edu/admit/index.html
Application fee: **$50**
Fall 2005 application deadline: **rolling**
Test of English as Foreign Language (TOEFL) is required for international students.
Minimum TOEFL score required for paper test: **600**
Minimum TOEFL score required for computer test: **250**

Fall 2003
Total 2003 enrollment: **400**
Master's degree enrollment: **400**

FINANCIAL INFORMATION

Financial aid phone number: **(206) 268-4010**
Tuition, 2003-2004 academic year: **$340/credit hour**
Number of teaching assistant positions: **2**

ACADEMIC PROGRAMS

Areas of specialization: curriculum and instruction, education policy, elementary teacher education, secondary teacher education, special education.
Professional development/partnership school(s) are used by students in some of the teaching programs.
During their internships, peer groups of students meet regularly to discuss instructional techniques in all of the teaching programs.
All of the students in their internships are mentored.

Courses that prepare teachers to pass the National Board of Professional Teaching Standards are offered.
Teacher preparation programs: Four-year baccalaureate-degree program leading to initial licensure that includes either a major or minor in education and practice teaching. Master's program preparing college graduates for initial licensure; includes practice teaching.

Central Washington University

- **400 East University Way, Ellensburg, WA 98926-7415**
- **Website:** http://www.cwu.edu
- **Public**
- **Degrees offered:** bachelor's, master's

ADMISSIONS

Admissions phone number: **(509) 963-3103**
Admissions email address: *masters@cwu.edu*
Application website: http://www.applyweb.com/apply/cwu/index.html
Application fee: **$35**
Fall 2005 application deadline: **4/1**
Test requirements: **GRE**
Test of English as Foreign Language (TOEFL) is required for international students.
Minimum TOEFL score required for paper test: **550**
Minimum TOEFL score required for computer test: **213**

Fall 2003
Acceptance rate for master's degree programs: **80%**
Average GRE verbal: **497**, Average GRE quantitative: **555**, Average GRE analytical: **576**
Total 2003 enrollment: **168**
Master's degree enrollment: **168**
Teacher preparation program enrollment (master's): **115**

FINANCIAL INFORMATION

Financial aid phone number: **(509) 963-1611**

Tuition, 2003-2004 academic year: Full-time in-state:
    $5,493; out-of-state: $11,430, Part-time in-state:
    $183/credit hour; out-of-state: $381/credit hour
Fees: $369, Room and board: $5,745, Books and supplies:
    $738, Miscellaneous expenses: $2,058
Number of teaching assistant positions: 69
Number of research assistant positions: 16
Number of other paid appointments: 34

ACADEMIC PROGRAMS

Total full-time tenured or tenure-track faculty (fall 2003): 106
    Total part-time faculty (fall 2003): 26
Areas of specialization: curriculum and instruction, educa-
    tion administration and supervision, educational psy-
    chology, elementary teacher education, secondary
    teacher education, special education, student counseling
    and personnel services.
Professional development/partnership school(s) are used
    by students in some of the teaching programs.
During their internships, peer groups of students meet
    regularly to discuss instructional techniques in some of
    the teaching programs.
All of the students in their internships are mentored.
Courses that prepare teachers to pass the National Board of
    Professional Teaching Standards are not offered.
The education program is currently accredited by the
    National Council for Accreditation of Teacher Education.

City University

■ 11900 N.E. First Street, Bellevue, WA 98005
■ **Website:** http://www.cityu.edu/fla.asp
■ **Private**

Eastern Washington University

■ 526 Fifth Street, Cheney, WA 99004
■ **Website:**
    http://cehd.edu/education/graduate/GraduateProgram
    .html
■ **Public**
■ **Degrees offered:** bachelor's, master's, education specialist

ADMISSIONS

Admissions phone number: **(509) 359-6094**
Admissions email address: *nancy.todd@mailserver.ewu.edu*
Application website: *http://www.ewu.edu*
Application fee: **$35**
Fall 2005 application deadline: **3/1**
Test of English as Foreign Language (TOEFL) is required
    for international students.
Minimum TOEFL score required for paper test: **580**
Minimum TOEFL score required for computer test: **237**

FINANCIAL INFORMATION

Financial aid phone number: **(509) 359-2314**
Tuition, 2003-2004 academic year: Full-time in-state:
    $5,772; out-of-state: $17,085, Part-time in-state:
    $192/credit hour; out-of-state: $570/credit hour
Fees: $230, Room and board: $5,200, Books and supplies:
    $798, Miscellaneous expenses: $3,348

ACADEMIC PROGRAMS

Areas of specialization: curriculum and instruction, educa-
    tion administration and supervision, education policy,
    educational psychology, elementary teacher education,
    secondary teacher education, special education, student
    counseling and personnel services.
The education program is currently accredited by the
    National Council for Accreditation of Teacher Education.

Evergreen State College

■ **2700 Evergreen Parkway, NW, Olympia, WA 98505**
■ **Website:** http://www.evergreen.edu/
■ **Public**
■ **Degrees offered:** master's

ADMISSIONS

Admissions phone number: **(360) 867-6176**
Admissions email address: *admissions@evergreen.edu*
Application fee: **$37**
Fall 2005 application deadline: **4/15**

Fall 2003
Acceptance rate for master's degree programs: 51%
Total 2003 enrollment: 83
Master's degree enrollment: 83
    Teacher preparation program enrollment (master's): 83

FINANCIAL INFORMATION

Financial aid phone number: **(360) 867-6205**
Tuition, 2003-2004 academic year: Full-time in-state:
    $5,979; out-of-state: $18,306
Fees: $153, Room and board: $5,722, Books and supplies:
    $891, Miscellaneous expenses: $2,058

ACADEMIC PROGRAMS

Total full-time tenured or tenure-track faculty (fall 2003): 6
Areas of specialization: elementary teacher education, sec-
    ondary teacher education.
Professional development/partnership school(s) are used
    by students in all of the teaching programs.
During their internships, peer groups of students meet
    regularly to discuss instructional techniques in all of the
    teaching programs.
All of the students in their internships are mentored.
Courses that prepare teachers to pass the National Board of
    Professional Teaching Standards are not offered.
Teacher preparation programs: Master's degree in educa-
    tion, including internship/practice teaching and prepara-
    tion for initial licensure.

The education program is currently accredited by the National Council for Accreditation of Teacher Education.

Gonzaga University

- 502 E. Boone Avenue, Spokane, WA 99258-0025
- Website:
  http://www.gonzaga.edu/Academics/Graduate/default.htm
- Private

ADMISSIONS

Admissions phone number: (509) 323-6572
Admissions email address: *soriet@soe.gonzaga.edu*
Test requirements: **GRE or MAT**
Test of English as Foreign Language (TOEFL) is required for international students.
Minimum TOEFL score required for paper test: 550
Minimum TOEFL score required for computer test: 213

FINANCIAL INFORMATION

Financial aid phone number: (509) 323-6582

Heritage College

- 3240 Fort Road, Toppenish, WA 98948
- Website: http://www.heritage.edu
- Private
- **Degrees offered:** bachelor's, master's, education specialist

ADMISSIONS

Admissions phone number: (509) 865-8508
Admissions email address: *3w_Admissions@heritage.edu*
Application website:
  http://www.heritage.edu/admisfinan/topadmisfinan.htm
Application fee: **$45**
Fall 2005 application deadline: **9/1**
Test of English as Foreign Language (TOEFL) is required for international students.
Minimum TOEFL score required for paper test: 550
Minimum TOEFL score required for computer test: 213

Fall 2003

Acceptance rate for master's degree programs: 92%
Total 2003 enrollment: 732
Master's degree enrollment: 732
  Teacher preparation program enrollment (master's): 286
Education specialist degree enrollment: 0

FINANCIAL INFORMATION

Financial aid phone number: (509) 865-8647
Tuition, 2003-2004 academic year: Full-time: **$365/credit hour**; Part-time: **$365/credit hour**
Room and board: **$6,365**, Books and supplies: **$396**, Miscellaneous expenses: **$2,294**

ACADEMIC PROGRAMS

Total full-time tenured or tenure-track faculty (fall 2003): 10
Areas of specialization: curriculum and instruction, education administration and supervision, education policy, educational psychology, elementary teacher education, secondary teacher education, special education, student counseling and personnel services.

Pacific Lutheran University

- Tacoma, WA 98447
- Website: http://www.plu.edu/external/
- Private

Seattle Pacific University

- 3307 Third Avenue W, Seattle, WA 98119-1997
- Website: http://www.spu.edu
- Private

ADMISSIONS

Admissions phone number: (206) 281-2378
Admissions email address: *blomqa@spu.edu*
Test requirements: **GRE or MAT**
Test of English as Foreign Language (TOEFL) is required for international students.
Minimum TOEFL score required for paper test: 550

FINANCIAL INFORMATION

Financial aid phone number: (206) 281-2469

Seattle University

- 900 Broadway, Seattle, WA 98122
- Website: http://www.seattleu.edu/soe/
- Private

St. Martin's College

- 5300 Pacific Ave SE, Lacey, WA 98503
- Website: http://www.stmartin.edu
- Private
- **Degrees offered:** bachelor's, master's

ADMISSIONS

Admissions phone number: (360) 438-4333
Admissions email address: *cjacobs@stmartin.edu*
Application fee: **$25**

Fall 2005 application deadline: **rolling**
Test requirements: **GRE or MAT**
Test of English as Foreign Language (TOEFL) is required for international students.
Minimum TOEFL score required for paper test: 525
Minimum TOEFL score required for computer test: 195

Fall 2003
Acceptance rate for master's degree programs: 100%
Average GRE verbal: 506, Average GRE quantitative: 536, Average GRE analytical: 480, Average MAT: 54
Total 2003 enrollment: 56
Master's degree enrollment: 56
    Teacher preparation program enrollment (master's): 42

FINANCIAL INFORMATION
Financial aid phone number: (360) 438-4397
Tuition, 2003-2004 academic year: Full-time: **$17,600**; Part-time: **$587/credit hour**
Fees: **$370**, Room and board: **$5,355**, Books and supplies: **$1,000**, Miscellaneous expenses: **$100**
Number of fellowships awarded to graduate students during the 2003-2004 academic year: 0
Number of teaching assistant positions: 0
Number of research assistant positions: 0
Number of other paid appointments: 0

ACADEMIC PROGRAMS
Total full-time tenured or tenure-track faculty (fall 2003): 11
Areas of specialization: curriculum and instruction, elementary teacher education, secondary teacher education, special education, student counseling and personnel services.
Professional development/partnership school(s) are used by students in some of the teaching programs.
During their internships, peer groups of students meet regularly to discuss instructional techniques in some of the teaching programs.
All of the students in their internships are mentored.
Courses that prepare teachers to pass the National Board of Professional Teaching Standards are not offered.
Teacher preparation programs: Four-year baccalaureate-degree program leading to initial licensure that includes either a major or minor in education and practice teaching. Master's program preparing college graduates for initial licensure; includes practice teaching. Alternative program for college graduates leading to provisional licensure.

University of Puget Sound

- **7011 226th Place, SW, Mountlake Terrace, WA 98043**
- **Website:** http://www.ups.edu/external_homes/
- **Private**

University of Washington

- **206 Miller Box 353600, Seattle, WA 98195-3600**
- **Website:** http://www.educ.washington.edu/COEWebSite/
- **Public**
- **Degrees offered:** master's, Ph.D., Ed.D.
- **Overall rank in the 2005 U.S. News education schools with doctoral programs:** 31
- **Overall rank in the 2005 U.S. News education school specialty rankings:** administration/supervision: 12, curriculum/instruction: 16, education policy: 13, elementary education: 10, secondary education: 9, special education: 10

ADMISSIONS
Admissions phone number: (206) 543-7834
Admissions email address: *edinfo@u.washington.edu*
Application website: http://www.educ.washington.edu/COEWebSite/students/prospective/admissions.html
Application fee: **$45**
Test requirements: **GRE**
Test of English as Foreign Language (TOEFL) is required for international students.
Minimum TOEFL score required for paper test: 580
Minimum TOEFL score required for computer test: 237

Fall 2003
Acceptance rate for master's degree programs: 43%
Acceptance rate for doctoral programs: 37%
Average GRE verbal: 530, Average GRE quantitative: 580, Average GRE analytical: 615
Total 2003 enrollment: 768
Master's degree enrollment: 528
    Teacher preparation program enrollment (master's): 205
Doctoral degree enrollment: 240

FINANCIAL INFORMATION
Financial aid phone number: (206) 543-7834
Tuition, 2003-2004 academic year: Full-time in-state: **$6,822**; out-of-state: **$16,545**, Part-time in-state: **$325/credit hour**; out-of-state: **$788/credit hour**
Fees: **$105**, Room and board: **$12,812**, Books and supplies: **$1,400**, Miscellaneous expenses: **$3,004**
Number of fellowships awarded to graduate students during the 2003-2004 academic year: 2
Number of teaching assistant positions: 51
Number of research assistant positions: 51
Number of other paid appointments: 45

ACADEMIC PROGRAMS
Total full-time tenured or tenure-track faculty (fall 2003): 53
Areas of specialization: curriculum and instruction, education administration and supervision, education policy, educational psychology, elementary teacher education, higher education administration, secondary teacher education, special education.

Professional development/partnership school(s) are used by students in all of the teaching programs.

During their internships, peer groups of students meet regularly to discuss instructional techniques in all of the teaching programs.

All of the students in their internships are mentored.

Courses that prepare teachers to pass the National Board of Professional Teaching Standards are offered.

Teacher preparation programs: Master's degree in education, including internship/practice teaching and preparation for initial licensure.

The education program is currently accredited by the National Council for Accreditation of Teacher Education.

Walla Walla College

- 204 S. College Avenue, College Place, WA 99324-1198
- **Website:** http://www.wwc.edu/
- Private

Washington State University

- **College of Education PO Box 642114, Pullman, WA 99164-2114**
- **Website:** http://www.wsu.edu/~gradsch/
- **Public**

ADMISSIONS

Admissions phone number: **(509) 335-1446**
Admissions email address: *gradsch@wsu.edu*
Test requirements: **GRE**
Test of English as Foreign Language (TOEFL) is required for international students.
Minimum TOEFL score required for paper test: **550**
Minimum TOEFL score required for computer test: **213**

FINANCIAL INFORMATION

Financial aid phone number: **(509) 335-9711**

Western Washington University

- 516 High Street, Bellingham, WA 98225
- **Website:** http://www.wwu.edu/home.shtml
- **Public**
- **Degrees offered:** master's

ADMISSIONS

Admissions phone number: **(360) 650-3170**
Admissions email address: *gradschl@wwu.edu*

Application fee: **$35**
Fall 2005 application deadline: **6/1**
Test requirements: **GRE or MAT**
Test of English as Foreign Language (TOEFL) is required for international students.
Minimum TOEFL score required for paper test: **567**
Minimum TOEFL score required for computer test: **227**

Fall 2003
Acceptance rate for master's degree programs: **64%**
Total 2003 enrollment: **375**
Master's degree enrollment: **375**
    Teacher preparation program enrollment (master's): **167**

FINANCIAL INFORMATION

Financial aid phone number: **(360) 650-3470**
Tuition, 2003-2004 academic year: Full-time in-state: **$5,151**; out-of-state: **$15,678**, Part-time in-state: **$172/credit hour**; out-of-state: **$523/credit hour**
Fees: **$543**, Room and board: **$1,956**, Books and supplies: **$240**, Miscellaneous expenses: **$888**
Number of fellowships awarded to graduate students during the 2003-2004 academic year: **0**
Number of teaching assistant positions: **11**
Number of research assistant positions: **0**
Number of other paid appointments: **0**

ACADEMIC PROGRAMS

Total full-time tenured or tenure-track faculty (fall 2003): **21**
    Total part-time faculty (fall 2003): **24**
Areas of specialization: education administration and supervision, elementary teacher education, secondary teacher education, special education, student counseling and personnel services.
Professional development/partnership school(s) are used by students in some of the teaching programs.
During their internships, peer groups of students meet regularly to discuss instructional techniques in some of the teaching programs.
All of the students in their internships are mentored.
Courses that prepare teachers to pass the National Board of Professional Teaching Standards are offered.
Teacher preparation programs: Four-year baccalaureate-degree program leading to initial licensure that includes either a major or minor in education and practice teaching. Master's program preparing college graduates for initial licensure; includes practice teaching.
The education program is currently accredited by the National Council for Accreditation of Teacher Education.

Whitworth College

- 300 W. Hawthorne Road, Spokane, WA 99251
- **Website:** http://www.whitworth.edu
- Private
- **Degrees offered:** bachelor's, master's

ADMISSIONS

Admissions phone number: **(509) 777-3228**
Admissions email address: *gse@whitworth.edu*
Application fee: **$35**
Fall 2005 application deadline: **rolling**
Test of English as Foreign Language (TOEFL) is required
for international students.
Minimum TOEFL score required for paper test: **550**

Fall 2003

Total 2003 enrollment: **169**
Master's degree enrollment: **169**
  Teacher preparation program enrollment (master's): **52**

FINANCIAL INFORMATION

Financial aid phone number: **(800) 533-4668**
Tuition, 2003-2004 academic year: Full-time: **$350/credit
  hour**; Part-time: **$350/credit hour**
Fees: **$150**, Books and supplies: **$500**, Miscellaneous
  expenses: **$500**
Number of other paid appointments: **4**

ACADEMIC PROGRAMS

Total full-time tenured or tenure-track faculty (fall 2003):
  14
Areas of specialization: curriculum and instruction, education administration and supervision, education policy, educational psychology, elementary teacher education, secondary teacher education, special education, student counseling and personnel services.
Professional development/partnership school(s) are used by students in all of the teaching programs.
During their internships, peer groups of students meet regularly to discuss instructional techniques in all of the teaching programs.
All of the students in their internships are mentored.
Courses that prepare teachers to pass the National Board of Professional Teaching Standards are not offered.
Teacher preparation programs: Four-year baccalaureate-degree program leading to initial licensure that includes either a major or minor in education and practice teaching. Master's program preparing college graduates for initial licensure; includes practice teaching.
The education program is currently accredited by the National Council for Accreditation of Teacher Education.

WEST VIRGINIA

Marshall University

■ 1 John Marshall Drive, Huntington, WV 25755
■ **Website:** http://www.marshall.edu/muge
■ Public
■ **Degrees offered:** master's, education specialist, Ed.D.

ADMISSIONS

Admissions phone number: **(304) 746-1900**
Admissions email address: *services@marshall.edu*
Application website: *http://www.marshall.edu/muge*
Application fee: **$30**
Fall 2005 application deadline: **rolling**
Test requirements: **GRE or MAT**
Test of English as Foreign Language (TOEFL) is required for international students.
Minimum TOEFL score required for paper test: 550
Minimum TOEFL score required for computer test: 197

Fall 2003

Acceptance rate for master's degree programs: 94%
Acceptance rate for education specialist degree programs: 86%
Acceptance rate for doctoral programs: 53%
Average GRE verbal: 401, Average GRE quantitative: 457, Average GRE analytical: 421, Average MAT: 41
Total 2003 enrollment: 1,999
Master's degree enrollment: 1,839
   Teacher preparation program enrollment (master's): 1,385
Education specialist degree enrollment: 119
Doctoral degree enrollment: 41

FINANCIAL INFORMATION

Financial aid phone number: (304) 696-3162
Tuition, 2003-2004 academic year: Full-time in-state: **$164/credit hour**; out-of-state: **$528/credit hour**, Part-time in-state: **$164/credit hour**; out-of-state: **$528/credit hour**
Fees: **$29**, Room and board: **$5,856**, Books and supplies: **$800**, Miscellaneous expenses: **$2,378**

Number of fellowships awarded to graduate students during the 2003-2004 academic year: 0
Number of teaching assistant positions: 0
Number of research assistant positions: 0
Number of other paid appointments: 0

ACADEMIC PROGRAMS

Total full-time tenured or tenure-track faculty (fall 2003): 86
   Total part-time faculty (fall 2003): 110
Areas of specialization: curriculum and instruction, education administration and supervision, education policy, educational psychology, elementary teacher education, higher education administration, secondary teacher education, special education, student counseling and personnel services, teacher education.
Professional development/partnership school(s) are used by students in some of the teaching programs.
During their internships, peer groups of students meet regularly to discuss instructional techniques in some of the teaching programs.
All of the students in their internships are mentored.
Courses that prepare teachers to pass the National Board of Professional Teaching Standards are offered.
The education program is currently accredited by the National Council for Accreditation of Teacher Education.

LICENSING TEST

Pass rate on state's teacher licensing test for 2002-2003: 100%
State average pass rate: 100%

Salem International University

■ 223 W. Main Street, Salem, WV 26426
■ **Website:** http://www.salemiu.edu/
■ Private

West Virginia University

- 802 Allen Hall PO Box 6122, Morgantown, WV 26506-6122
- **Website:** http://www.wvu.edu
- **Public**
- **Degrees offered:** bachelor's, master's, Ph.D., Ed.D.

ADMISSIONS

Admissions phone number: **(304) 293-2124**
Application website: *http://www.applyweb.com/apply/wvu/*
Application fee: **$50**
Fall 2005 application deadline: **rolling**
Test requirements: **GRE or MAT**
Test of English as Foreign Language (TOEFL) is required for international students.
Minimum TOEFL score required for paper test: **550**
Minimum TOEFL score required for computer test: **213**

Fall 2003

Acceptance rate for master's degree programs: **82%**
Acceptance rate for doctoral programs: **52%**
Average GRE verbal: **512**, Average GRE quantitative: **556**, Average GRE analytical: **558**, Average MAT: **54**
Total 2003 enrollment: **1,486**
Master's degree enrollment: **1,194**
Teacher preparation program enrollment (master's): **733**
Doctoral degree enrollment: **292**

FINANCIAL INFORMATION

Financial aid phone number: **(304) 293-5242**
Tuition, 2003-2004 academic year: Full-time in-state: **$3,902**; out-of-state: **$11,108**, Part-time in-state: **$220/credit hour**; out-of-state: **$620/credit hour**

Room and board: **$7,535**, Books and supplies: **$740**, Miscellaneous expenses: **$2,470**
Number of fellowships awarded to graduate students during the 2003-2004 academic year: **3**
Number of teaching assistant positions: **28**
Number of research assistant positions: **36**
Number of other paid appointments: **23**

Total full-time tenured or tenure-track faculty (fall 2003): **54**
Total part-time faculty (fall 2003): **4**
Areas of specialization: curriculum and instruction, education administration and supervision, educational psychology, elementary teacher education, secondary teacher education, special education, student counseling and personnel services, teacher education.
Professional development/partnership school(s) are used by students in some of the teaching programs.
During their internships, peer groups of students meet regularly to discuss instructional techniques in some of the teaching programs.
Some of the students in their internships are mentored.
Courses that prepare teachers to pass the National Board of Professional Teaching Standards are offered.
Teacher preparation programs: Master's degree in education, including internship/practice teaching and preparation for initial licensure.
The education program is currently accredited by the National Council for Accreditation of Teacher Education.

LICENSING TEST

Pass rate on state's teacher licensing test for 2002-2003: **100%**
State average pass rate: **100%**

WISCONSIN

Alverno College

■ 3400 South 43 Street, PO Box 343922, Milwaukee, WI 53234-3922
■ Website: http://www.alverno.edu
■ Private
■ Degrees offered: bachelor's, master's

ADMISSIONS

Admissions phone number: **(414) 382-6100**
Admissions email address: *admissions@alverno.edu*
Application fee: **$20**
Fall 2005 application deadline: **rolling**
Test of English as Foreign Language (TOEFL) is required for international students.
Minimum TOEFL score required for paper test: **500**
Minimum TOEFL score required for computer test: **173**

Fall 2003
Acceptance rate for master's degree programs: **100%**
Total 2003 enrollment: **209**
Master's degree enrollment: **209**

FINANCIAL INFORMATION

Financial aid phone number: **(414) 382-6046**
Tuition, 2003-2004 academic year: Full-time: **$6,976**; Part-time: **$436/credit hour**
Fees: **$200**, Room and board: **$5,500**, Books and supplies: **$1,000**, Miscellaneous expenses: **$2,500**
Number of fellowships awarded to graduate students during the 2003-2004 academic year: **0**
Number of teaching assistant positions: **0**
Number of research assistant positions: **0**
Number of other paid appointments: **0**

ACADEMIC PROGRAMS

Total full-time tenured or tenure-track faculty (fall 2003): **104**
Total part-time faculty (fall 2003): **101**
Areas of specialization: curriculum and instruction, education administration and supervision, elementary teacher education, secondary teacher education.

Professional development/partnership school(s) are used by students in none of the teaching programs.
During their internships, peer groups of students meet regularly to discuss instructional techniques in some of the teaching programs.
All of the students in their internships are mentored.
Courses that prepare teachers to pass the National Board of Professional Teaching Standards are offered.
Teacher preparation programs: Four-year baccalaureate-degree program leading to initial licensure that includes either a major or minor in education and practice teaching. Alternative program for college graduates leading to provisional licensure.
The education program is currently accredited by the National Council for Accreditation of Teacher Education.

Cardinal Stritch University

■ 6801 N. Yates Road, Milwaukee, WI 53217
■ Website: http://www.stritch.edu/
■ Private

Carroll College

■ 100 N. East Avenue, Waukesha, WI 53186
■ Website: http://www.cc.edu/
■ Private

Carthage College

- 2001 Alford Park Dr., Kenosha, WI 53140
- **Website:** http://www.carthage.edu
- **Private**
- **Degrees offered:** bachelor's, master's

ADMISSIONS
Admissions phone number: **(262) 551-6001**
Test requirements: **MAT**

Fall 2003
Acceptance rate for master's degree programs: **100%**
Total 2003 enrollment: **120**
Master's degree enrollment: **120**
    Teacher preparation program enrollment (master's): **120**

FINANCIAL INFORMATION
Financial aid phone number: **(262) 551-6001**
Number of teaching assistant positions: **9**

ACADEMIC PROGRAMS
Professional development/partnership school(s) are used by students in some of the teaching programs.
During their internships, peer groups of students meet regularly to discuss instructional techniques in all of the teaching programs.
All of the students in their internships are mentored.
Courses that prepare teachers to pass the National Board of Professional Teaching Standards are not offered.

Concordia University Wisconsin

- 12800 N. Lake Shore Drive, Mequon, WI 53097
- **Website:** http://www.cuw.edu
- **Private**
- **Degrees offered:** bachelor's, master's

ADMISSIONS
Admissions phone number: **(262) 243-4551**
Application fee: **$35**
Fall 2005 application deadline: **rolling**
Test of English as Foreign Language (TOEFL) is required for international students.
Minimum TOEFL score required for paper test: **550**

Fall 2003
Total 2003 enrollment: **515**
Master's degree enrollment: **515**
    Teacher preparation program enrollment (master's): **205**

FINANCIAL INFORMATION
Financial aid phone number: **(262) 243-4392**

Tuition, 2003-2004 academic year: Full-time: **$400/credit hour**; Part-time: **$400/credit hour**

ACADEMIC PROGRAMS
Total full-time tenured or tenure-track faculty (fall 2003): **33**
    Total part-time faculty (fall 2003): **116**
Areas of specialization: curriculum and instruction, education administration and supervision, elementary teacher education, higher education administration, secondary teacher education, student counseling and personnel services.
Professional development/partnership school(s) are used by students in some of the teaching programs.
During their internships, peer groups of students meet regularly to discuss instructional techniques in some of the teaching programs.
All of the students in their internships are mentored.
Courses that prepare teachers to pass the National Board of Professional Teaching Standards are not offered.

Edgewood College

- 1000 Edgewood College Drive, Madison, WI 53711
- **Website:** http://www.edgewood.edu
- **Private**
- **Degrees offered:** bachelor's, master's, Ed.D.

ADMISSIONS
Admissions phone number: **(608) 663-2294**
Admissions email address: *admissions@edgewood.edu*
Application website:
    http://www.edgewood.edu/students/applying.htm
Application fee: **$25**
Fall 2005 application deadline: **8/20**
Test of English as Foreign Language (TOEFL) is required for international students.
Minimum TOEFL score required for paper test: **550**
Minimum TOEFL score required for computer test: **213**

Fall 2003
Total 2003 enrollment: **162**
Master's degree enrollment: **126**
    Teacher preparation program enrollment (master's): **43**
Doctoral degree enrollment: **36**

FINANCIAL INFORMATION
Financial aid phone number: **(608) 663-2206**
Tuition, 2003-2004 academic year: Full-time: **$485/credit hour**; Part-time: **$485/credit hour**
Room and board: **$5,420**, Books and supplies: **$750**, Miscellaneous expenses: **$2,253**

ACADEMIC PROGRAMS
Total full-time tenured or tenure-track faculty (fall 2003): **8**
    Total part-time faculty (fall 2003): **11**
Areas of specialization: curriculum and instruction, education administration and supervision, education policy,

elementary teacher education, higher education administration, secondary teacher education, special education.
Professional development/partnership school(s) are used by students in some of the teaching programs.
During their internships, peer groups of students meet regularly to discuss instructional techniques in all of the teaching programs.
All of the students in their internships are mentored.
Courses that prepare teachers to pass the National Board of Professional Teaching Standards are not offered.
Teacher preparation programs: Four-year baccalaureate-degree program leading to initial licensure that includes either a major or minor in education and practice teaching. Five-year program leading to initial licensure that results in a baccalaureate degree (with a major or minor in education) plus graduate credit and includes practice teaching. Five-year program leading to initial licensure that results in a baccalaureate degree (with a major or minor in education) plus a master's degree and includes practice teaching. Master's program preparing college graduates for initial licensure; includes practice teaching.
The education program is currently accredited by the National Council for Accreditation of Teacher Education.

Lakeland College

■ PO Box 359, Sheboygan, WI 53082
■ **Website:** http://www.lakeland.edu/
■ Private

Marian College of Fond Du Lac

■ 45 S. National Avenue, Fond du Lac, WI 54935
■ **Website:** http://www.mariancoll.edu/
■ Private

Marquette University

■ Schroeder Complex Box 1881, Milwaukee, WI 53201
■ **Website:** http://www.grad.marquette.edu
■ Private
■ **Degrees offered:** master's, Ph.D.
■ **Overall rank in the 2005 U.S. News education schools with doctoral programs:** 68

ADMISSIONS
Admissions phone number: **(414) 288-7137**
Admissions email address: *mugs@marquette.edu*
Application website: *http://www.grad.marquette.edu*
Application fee: **$40**

Fall 2005 application deadline: **rolling**
Test requirements: **GRE or MAT**
Test of English as Foreign Language (TOEFL) is required for international students.
Minimum TOEFL score required for paper test: **550**
Minimum TOEFL score required for computer test: **213**

Fall 2003
Acceptance rate for master's degree programs: **75%**
Acceptance rate for doctoral programs: **34%**
Average GRE verbal: **500**, Average GRE quantitative: **550**, Average GRE analytical: **590**
Total 2003 enrollment: **233**
Master's degree enrollment: **145**
  Teacher preparation program enrollment (master's): **78**
Doctoral degree enrollment: **88**

FINANCIAL INFORMATION
Financial aid phone number: **(414) 288-5325**
Tuition, 2003-2004 academic year: Full-time: **$470/credit hour**; Part-time: **$470/credit hour**
Room and board: **$7,500**, Books and supplies: **$660**, Miscellaneous expenses: **$3,000**
Number of fellowships awarded to graduate students during the 2003-2004 academic year: **32**
Number of teaching assistant positions: **33**
Number of research assistant positions: **7**
Number of other paid appointments: **39**

ACADEMIC PROGRAMS
Total full-time tenured or tenure-track faculty (fall 2003): **17**, Total part-time faculty (fall 2003): **21**
Areas of specialization: curriculum and instruction, education administration and supervision, education policy, educational psychology, elementary teacher education, higher education administration, secondary teacher education, student counseling and personnel services.
Professional development/partnership school(s) are used by students in some of the teaching programs.
During their internships, peer groups of students meet regularly to discuss instructional techniques in some of the teaching programs.
All of the students in their internships are mentored.
Courses that prepare teachers to pass the National Board of Professional Teaching Standards are not offered.
Teacher preparation programs: Four-year baccalaureate-degree program leading to initial licensure that includes either a major or minor in education and practice teaching. Master's program preparing college graduates for initial licensure; includes practice teaching.
The education program is currently accredited by the National Council for Accreditation of Teacher Education.

Mount Mary College

- 2900 N. Menomonee River Parkway, Milwaukee, WI 53222
- Website: http://www.mtmary.edu/
- Private

Silver Lake College

- 2406 S. Alverno Road, Manitowoc, WI 54220
- Website: http://www.sl.edu/graded
- Private
- Degrees offered: master's

ADMISSIONS

Application fee: $35
Fall 2005 application deadline: **rolling**
Test of English as Foreign Language (TOEFL) is required for international students.

FINANCIAL INFORMATION

Financial aid phone number: (920) 686-6127
Tuition, 2003-2004 academic year: Full-time: **$185/credit hour**; Part-time: **$185/credit hour**
Books and supplies: $250, Miscellaneous expenses: $250
Number of fellowships awarded to graduate students during the 2003-2004 academic year: 0
Number of teaching assistant positions: 0
Number of research assistant positions: 0
Number of other paid appointments: 0

ACADEMIC PROGRAMS

Areas of specialization: curriculum and instruction, education administration and supervision, elementary teacher education, secondary teacher education, teacher education.

St. Norbert College

- 100 Grant Street, De Pere, WI 54115-2099
- Website: http://www.snc.edu/
- Private

University of Wisconsin–Eau Claire

- 105 Garfield Avenue, Eau Claire, WI 54701
- Website: http://www.uwec.edu
- Public
- Degrees offered: bachelor's, master's, education specialist

ADMISSIONS

Admissions phone number: **(715) 836-5415**
Admissions email address: *admissions@uwec.edu*
Application website: *http://apply.wisconsin.edu/graduate/eau*
Application fee: $45
Fall 2005 application deadline: **rolling**
Test of English as Foreign Language (TOEFL) is required for international students.
Minimum TOEFL score required for paper test: 550
Minimum TOEFL score required for computer test: 213

Fall 2003
Acceptance rate for master's degree programs: 86%
Acceptance rate for education specialist degree programs: 65%
Total 2003 enrollment: 152
Master's degree enrollment: 131
  Teacher preparation program enrollment (master's): 127
Education specialist degree enrollment: 21

FINANCIAL INFORMATION

Financial aid phone number: (715) 836-3373
Tuition, 2003-2004 academic year: Full-time in-state: **$5,383**; out-of-state: **$15,993**, Part-time in-state: **$299/credit hour**; out-of-state: **$888/credit hour**
Room and board: **$4,150**, Books and supplies: **$494**
Number of other paid appointments: 16

ACADEMIC PROGRAMS

Total full-time tenured or tenure-track faculty (fall 2003): 344, Total part-time faculty (fall 2003): 5
Areas of specialization: curriculum and instruction, educational psychology, elementary teacher education, secondary teacher education, special education.
Professional development/partnership school(s) are used by students in some of the teaching programs.
During their internships, peer groups of students meet regularly to discuss instructional techniques in some of the teaching programs.
All of the students in their internships are mentored.
Courses that prepare teachers to pass the National Board of Professional Teaching Standards are not offered.

University of Wisconsin–Green Bay

- 2420 Nicolet Drive, Green Bay, WI 54311
- **Website:** http://www.uwgb.edu
- **Public**
- **Degrees offered:** bachelor's, master's

ADMISSIONS

Admissions phone number: **(920) 465-2964**
Admissions email address: *kaufmant@uwgb.edu*
Application website:
   http://www.uwgb.edu/gradstu/online_application_form.htm
Application fee: **$45**
Fall 2005 application deadline: **8/1**

FINANCIAL INFORMATION

Financial aid phone number: **(920) 465-2075**
Tuition, 2003-2004 academic year: Full-time in-state:
   $333/credit hour; out-of-state: **$922/credit hour**, Part-
   time in-state: **$333/credit hour**; out-of-state: **$922/credit
   hour**
Books and supplies: **$400**, Miscellaneous expenses: **$100**

ACADEMIC PROGRAMS

Total full-time tenured or tenure-track faculty (fall 2003): **12**
   Total part-time faculty (fall 2003): **8**
Areas of specialization: curriculum and instruction, ele-
   mentary teacher education, secondary teacher education.
Professional development/partnership school(s) are used
   by students in all of the teaching programs.
During their internships, peer groups of students meet
   regularly to discuss instructional techniques in some of
   the teaching programs.
Some of the students in their internships are mentored.
Courses that prepare teachers to pass the National Board of
   Professional Teaching Standards are not offered.
The education program is currently accredited by the
   National Council for Accreditation of Teacher Education.

University of Wisconsin–La Crosse

- 1725 State Street, La Crosse, WI 54601
- **Website:** http://www.uwlax.edu
- **Public**
- **Degrees offered:** bachelor's, master's, education
   specialist

ADMISSIONS

Admissions phone number: **(608) 785-8939**
Admissions email address: *admissions@uwlax.edu*
Application fee: **$40**
Fall 2005 application deadline: **3/1**

Test requirements: **GRE**
Test of English as Foreign Language (TOEFL) is required
   for international students.
Minimum TOEFL score required for paper test: **550**
Minimum TOEFL score required for computer test: **213**

Fall 2003
Acceptance rate for master's degree programs: **80%**
Acceptance rate for education specialist degree programs:
   32%
Total 2003 enrollment: **174**
Master's degree enrollment: **150**
   Teacher preparation program enrollment (master's): **150**
Education specialist degree enrollment: **24**

FINANCIAL INFORMATION

Financial aid phone number: **(608) 785-8120**
Tuition, 2003-2004 academic year: Full-time in-state:
   $307/credit hour; out-of-state: **$897/credit hour**, Part-
   time in-state: **$307/credit hour**; out-of-state: **$897/credit
   hour**
Number of teaching assistant positions: **20**

ACADEMIC PROGRAMS

Total full-time tenured or tenure-track faculty (fall 2003):
   14, Total part-time faculty (fall 2003): **23**
Areas of specialization: curriculum and instruction, education administration and supervision, education policy,
   educational psychology, elementary teacher education,
   secondary teacher education, special education, student
   counseling and personnel services, teacher education.
During their internships, peer groups of students meet
   regularly to discuss instructional techniques in all of the
   teaching programs.
Some of the students in their internships are mentored.
Courses that prepare teachers to pass the National Board of
   Professional Teaching Standards are not offered.
Teacher preparation programs: Four-year baccalaureate-
   degree program leading to initial licensure that includes
   either a major or minor in education and practice teach-
   ing. Master's program preparing college graduates for
   initial licensure; includes practice teaching.
The education program is currently accredited by the
   National Council for Accreditation of Teacher Education.

University of Wisconsin–Madison

- 123 Education Building, Madison, WI 53706-1398
- **Website:** http://www.wisc.edu/grad
- **Public**
- **Degrees offered:** bachelor's, master's, Ph.D.
- **Overall rank in the 2005 U.S. News education schools
   with doctoral programs:** 6
- **Overall rank in the 2005 U.S. News education school
   specialty rankings:** administration/supervision: 2,
   counseling/personnel: 6, curriculum/instruction: 1,

education policy: 3, educational psychology: 1, elementary education: 2, higher education administration: 13, secondary education: 2, special education: 11, vocational/technical: 7

ADMISSIONS

Admissions phone number: **(608) 262-2433**
Admissions email address: *gradadmiss@bascom.wisc.edu*
Application website:
  http://www.wisc.edu/grad/eapp/indexhtml
Application fee: **$45**
Fall 2005 application deadline: **rolling**
Test requirements: **GRE**
Test of English as Foreign Language (TOEFL) is required for international students.
Minimum TOEFL score required for paper test: **550**
Minimum TOEFL score required for computer test: **213**

Fall 2003

Acceptance rate for master's degree programs: **42%**
Acceptance rate for doctoral programs: **34%**
Average GRE verbal: **542**, Average GRE quantitative: **651**, Average GRE analytical: **588**
Total 2003 enrollment: **1,024**
Master's degree enrollment: **492**
Doctoral degree enrollment: **532**

FINANCIAL INFORMATION

Financial aid phone number: (608) 262-3060
Tuition, 2003-2004 academic year: Full-time in-state: **$7,590**; out-of-state: **$22,860**, Part-time in-state: **$475/credit hour**; out-of-state: **$1,430/credit hour**
Room and board: **$5,700**, Books and supplies: **$680**, Miscellaneous expenses: **$500**
Number of fellowships awarded to graduate students during the 2003-2004 academic year: **81**
Number of teaching assistant positions: **144**
Number of research assistant positions: **7**
Number of other paid appointments: **222**

ACADEMIC PROGRAMS

Total full-time tenured or tenure-track faculty (fall 2003): **159**
  Total part-time faculty (fall 2003): **0**
Areas of specialization: curriculum and instruction, education administration and supervision, education policy, educational psychology, elementary teacher education, higher education administration, secondary teacher education, special education, student counseling and personnel services, teacher education.
Professional development/partnership school(s) are used by students in some of the teaching programs.
During their internships, peer groups of students meet regularly to discuss instructional techniques in some of the teaching programs.
All of the students in their internships are mentored.
Courses that prepare teachers to pass the National Board of Professional Teaching Standards are not offered.
Teacher preparation programs: Four-year baccalaureate-degree program leading to initial licensure that includes either a major or minor in education and practice teach-

ing. Master's program preparing college graduates for initial licensure; includes practice teaching.

University of Wisconsin– Milwaukee

- ■ PO Box 413, Milwaukee, WI 53201
- ■ **Website:** http://www.uwm.edu
- ■ **Public**
- ■ **Degrees offered:** bachelor's, master's, education specialist, Ph.D.
- ■ **Overall rank in the 2005 U.S. News education school specialty rankings:** elementary education: 16

ADMISSIONS

Admissions phone number: **(414) 229-4729**
Admissions email address: *marshah@uwm.edu*
Application website:
  http://www.uwm.edu/Dept/Grad_Sch/Prospective/
  onlineapp.html
Application fee: **$45**
Fall 2005 application deadline: **rolling**
Test requirements: **GRE**
Test of English as Foreign Language (TOEFL) is required for international students.
Minimum TOEFL score required for paper test: **550**
Minimum TOEFL score required for computer test: **213**

Fall 2003

Acceptance rate for master's degree programs: **66%**
Acceptance rate for doctoral programs: **59%**
Average GRE verbal: **458**, Average GRE quantitative: **506**, Average GRE analytical: **556**
Total 2003 enrollment: **725**
Master's degree enrollment: **557**
  Teacher preparation program enrollment (master's): **214**
Doctoral degree enrollment: **168**

FINANCIAL INFORMATION

Financial aid phone number: **(414) 229-5840**
Tuition, 2003-2004 academic year: Full-time in-state: **$7,403**; out-of-state: **$21,768**, Part-time in-state: **$634/credit hour**; out-of-state: **$1,531/credit hour**
Fees: **$618**, Room and board: **$5,106**, Books and supplies: **$800**, Miscellaneous expenses: **$1,444**
Number of fellowships awarded to graduate students during the 2003-2004 academic year: **12**
Number of teaching assistant positions: **4**
Number of other paid appointments: **39**

ACADEMIC PROGRAMS

Total full-time tenured or tenure-track faculty (fall 2003): **75**
  Total part-time faculty (fall 2003): **134**
Areas of specialization: curriculum and instruction, education administration and supervision, educational psychology, special education, student counseling and personnel services.

Professional development/partnership school(s) are used by students in all of the teaching programs.

During their internships, peer groups of students meet regularly to discuss instructional techniques in some of the teaching programs.

All of the students in their internships are mentored.

Courses that prepare teachers to pass the National Board of Professional Teaching Standards are not offered.

Teacher preparation programs: Four-year baccalaureate-degree program leading to initial licensure that includes either a major or minor in education and practice teaching.

University of Wisconsin–Oshkosh

- 800 Algoma Boulevard, Oshkosh, WI 54901
- Website: http://www.uwosh.edu/grad_school/
- Public
- Degrees offered: bachelor's, master's

ADMISSIONS

Admissions phone number: **(920) 424-1223**
Admissions email address: *gradschool@uwosh.edu*
Application website:
   http://www.uwosh.edu/grad_school/admissionmain.htm
Application fee: **$45**
Fall 2005 application deadline: **rolling**
Test of English as Foreign Language (TOEFL) is required for international students.
Minimum TOEFL score required for paper test: **550**
Minimum TOEFL score required for computer test: **213**

FINANCIAL INFORMATION

Financial aid phone number: **(920) 424-3377**
Tuition, 2003-2004 academic year: Full-time in-state:
   $5,334; out-of-state: **$15,945**, Part-time in-state:
   $298/credit hour; out-of-state: **$887/credit hour**
Room and board: **$4,800**, Books and supplies: **$4,300**,
   Miscellaneous expenses: **$2,500**

ACADEMIC PROGRAMS

Courses that prepare teachers to pass the National Board of Professional Teaching Standards are offered.

Teacher preparation programs: Five-year program leading to initial licensure that results in a baccalaureate degree (with a major or minor in education) plus graduate credit and includes practice teaching. Master's program preparing college graduates for initial licensure; includes practice teaching.

The education program is currently accredited by the National Council for Accreditation of Teacher Education.

University of Wisconsin–Platteville

- 1 University Plaza, Platteville, WI 53818
- Website: http://www.uwplatt.edu/
- Public
- Degrees offered: bachelor's, master's

Fall 2003
Total 2003 enrollment: 562
Master's degree enrollment: 562
   Teacher preparation program enrollment (master's): 154

FINANCIAL INFORMATION

Tuition, 2003-2004 academic year: Full-time in-state:
   $4,842; out-of-state: **$15,452**, Part-time in-state:
   $269/credit hour; out-of-state: **$858/credit hour**
Fees: **$31/credit hour**, Room and board: **$2,120**
Number of fellowships awarded to graduate students during the 2003-2004 academic year: **0**
Number of research assistant positions: **26**

ACADEMIC PROGRAMS

Areas of specialization: curriculum and instruction, education administration and supervision, education policy, educational psychology, elementary teacher education, higher education administration, secondary teacher education, special education, student counseling and personnel services, teacher education.

Teacher preparation programs: Four-year baccalaureate-degree program leading to initial licensure that includes either a major or minor in education and practice teaching. Master's program preparing college graduates for initial licensure; includes practice teaching. Alternative program for college graduates leading to provisional licensure.

The education program is currently accredited by the National Council for Accreditation of Teacher Education.

The education program is currently accredited by the Teacher Education Accreditation Council.

University of Wisconsin–River Falls

- 410 S. Third Street, River Falls, WI 54022
- Website: http://www.uwrf.edu/ogs/
- Public
- Degrees offered: bachelor's, master's, education specialist

ADMISSIONS

Admissions phone number: **(715) 425-3843**
Application website: http://www.uwrf.edu/ogs/
   grad_registration_form.pdf

Application fee: **$45**
Fall 2005 application deadline: 2/1
Test requirements: **MAT**
Test of English as Foreign Language (TOEFL) is required
for international students.
Minimum TOEFL score required for paper test: 500

Fall 2003
Total 2003 enrollment: 322
Master's degree enrollment: 316
    Teacher preparation program enrollment (master's): 176
Education specialist degree enrollment: 6

FINANCIAL INFORMATION
Financial aid phone number: **(715) 425-3141**
Tuition, 2003-2004 academic year: Full-time in-state:
    $5,452; out-of-state: **$16,062**, Part-time in-state:
    $342/credit hour; out-of-state: **$931/credit hour**
Room and board: **$3,908**, Books and supplies: **$200**,
    Miscellaneous expenses: **$2,112**

ACADEMIC PROGRAMS
Areas of specialization: education administration and
    supervision, elementary teacher education, secondary
    teacher education, student counseling and personnel
    services.
Professional development/partnership school(s) are used
    by students in some of the teaching programs.
During their internships, peer groups of students meet
    regularly to discuss instructional techniques in all of the
    teaching programs.
All of the students in their internships are mentored.
Courses that prepare teachers to pass the National Board of
    Professional Teaching Standards are not offered.
Teacher preparation programs: Four-year baccalaureate-
    degree program leading to initial licensure that includes
    either a major or minor in education and practice teach-
    ing. Master's program preparing college graduates for
    initial licensure; includes practice teaching.
The education program is currently accredited by the
    National Council for Accreditation of Teacher Education.

University of Wisconsin– Stevens Point

■ **2100 Main St., Stevens Point, WI 54481**
■ **Website:** http://www.uwsp.edu/
■ **Public**
■ **Degrees offered:** bachelor's, master's

ADMISSIONS
Admissions phone number: **(715) 346-2441**
Admissions email address: *admiss@uwsp.edu*
Application website: *http://apply.wisconsin.edu*
Application fee: **$45**
Fall 2005 application deadline: 8/1

Test of English as Foreign Language (TOEFL) is required
    for international students.
Minimum TOEFL score required for paper test: **523**
Minimum TOEFL score required for computer test: **193**

Fall 2003
Acceptance rate for master's degree programs: **67%**
Total 2003 enrollment: **106**
Master's degree enrollment: **106**
    Teacher preparation program enrollment (master's): **106**

FINANCIAL INFORMATION
Financial aid phone number: **(715) 346-4771**
Tuition, 2003-2004 academic year: Full-time in-state:
    $4,842; out-of-state: **$15,452**, Part-time in-state:
    $322/credit hour; out-of-state: **$911/credit hour**
Fees: **$521**, Room and board: **$4,195**, Books and supplies:
    $450, Miscellaneous expenses: **$1,800**
Number of fellowships awarded to graduate students dur-
    ing the 2003-2004 academic year: **0**
Number of teaching assistant positions: **0**
Number of research assistant positions: **4**
Number of other paid appointments: **0**

ACADEMIC PROGRAMS
Total full-time tenured or tenure-track faculty (fall 2003): **14**
    Total part-time faculty (fall 2003): **2**
Areas of specialization: curriculum and instruction, ele-
    mentary teacher education, secondary teacher education,
    special education.
Professional development/partnership school(s) are used
    by students in some of the teaching programs.
During their internships, peer groups of students meet
    regularly to discuss instructional techniques in all of the
    teaching programs.
All of the students in their internships are mentored.
Courses that prepare teachers to pass the National Board of
    Professional Teaching Standards are not offered.

University of Wisconsin– Stout

■ **1 Clock Tower Plaza, Menomonie, WI 54751**
■ **Website:** http://www.uwstout.edu
■ **Public**
■ **Degrees offered:** bachelor's, master's, education
    specialist

ADMISSIONS
Admissions phone number: **(715) 232-2211**
Admissions email address: *gradschool@uwstout.edu*
Application website: *http://www.uwstout.edu/grad/apply.htm*
Application fee: **$45**
Fall 2005 application deadline: **rolling**
Test requirements: **None**
Test of English as Foreign Language (TOEFL) is required
    for international students.

Minimum TOEFL score required for paper test: **500**
Minimum TOEFL score required for computer test: **173**

Fall 2003
Acceptance rate for master's degree programs: **56%**
Acceptance rate for education specialist degree programs: **50%**
Total 2003 enrollment: **184**
Master's degree enrollment: **161**
Education specialist degree enrollment: **23**

FINANCIAL INFORMATION
Financial aid phone number: **(715) 232-1363**
Tuition, 2003-2004 academic year: Full-time in-state: **$5,084**; out-of-state: **$15,694**, Part-time in-state: **$282/credit hour**; out-of-state: **$872**
Fees: **$600**, Room and board: **$4,038**, Books and supplies: **$300**, Miscellaneous expenses: **$2,000**
Number of teaching assistant positions: **3**
Number of research assistant positions: **11**

ACADEMIC PROGRAMS
Total full-time tenured or tenure-track faculty (fall 2003): **25**, Total part-time faculty (fall 2003): **0**
Areas of specialization: curriculum and instruction, education administration and supervision, education policy, higher education administration, secondary teacher education, special education, student counseling and personnel services, teacher education.
Professional development/partnership school(s) are used by students in some of the teaching programs.
During their internships, peer groups of students meet regularly to discuss instructional techniques in some of the teaching programs.
All of the students in their internships are mentored.
Courses that prepare teachers to pass the National Board of Professional Teaching Standards are offered.
Teacher preparation programs: Four-year baccalaureate-degree program leading to initial licensure that includes either a major or minor in education and practice teaching. Master's program preparing college graduates for initial licensure; includes practice teaching.

University of Wisconsin–Superior

■ Belknap and Catlin, P.O. Box 2000, Superior, WI 54880
■ **Website:** http://www.uwsuper.edu
■ **Public**
■ **Degrees offered:** bachelor's, master's, education specialist

ADMISSIONS
Admissions phone number: **(715) 394-8295**
Admissions email address: *gradstudy@uwsuper.edu*
Application website:
 http://www.uwsuper.edu/admissions/apply/index.html
Application fee: **$45**

Fall 2005 application deadline: **rolling**
Test of English as Foreign Language (TOEFL) is required for international students.
Minimum TOEFL score required for paper test: **550**
Minimum TOEFL score required for computer test: **213**

Fall 2003
Acceptance rate for master's degree programs: **81%**
Acceptance rate for education specialist degree programs: **64%**
Average GRE verbal: **400**, Average GRE quantitative: **552**, Average GRE analytical: **306**, Average MAT: **38**
Total 2003 enrollment: **223**
Master's degree enrollment: **195**
 Teacher preparation program enrollment (master's): **73**
Education specialist degree enrollment: **28**

FINANCIAL INFORMATION
Financial aid phone number: **(715) 394-8200**
Tuition, 2003-2004 academic year: Full-time in-state: **$5,467**; out-of-state: **$16,077**, Part-time in-state: **$389/credit hour**; out-of-state: **$978/credit hour**
Room and board: **$5,314**, Books and supplies: **$750**, Miscellaneous expenses: **$2,000**
Number of fellowships awarded to graduate students during the 2003-2004 academic year: **2**
Number of other paid appointments: **2**

ACADEMIC PROGRAMS
Total full-time tenured or tenure-track faculty (fall 2003): **10**, Total part-time faculty (fall 2003): **6**
Areas of specialization: curriculum and instruction, education administration and supervision, elementary teacher education, higher education administration, secondary teacher education, special education, student counseling and personnel services.
Professional development/partnership school(s) are used by students in all of the teaching programs.
During their internships, peer groups of students meet regularly to discuss instructional techniques in some of the teaching programs.
All of the students in their internships are mentored.
Courses that prepare teachers to pass the National Board of Professional Teaching Standards are offered.
Teacher preparation programs: Four-year baccalaureate-degree program leading to initial licensure that includes either a major or minor in education and practice teaching. Master's program preparing college graduates for initial licensure; includes practice teaching.

University of Wisconsin–Whitewater

- 800 W Main Street, Whitewater, WI 53190
- **Website:** http://www.uww.edu/gradstudies/
- **Public**
- **Degrees offered:** bachelor's, master's, education specialist

ADMISSIONS

Admissions phone number: **(262) 472-1006**
Admissions email address: *gradschl@uww.edu*
Application website:
 http://www.uww.edu/gradstudies/addapps.html
Application fee: **$45**
Fall 2005 application deadline: **7/15**
Test requirements: **None**
Test of English as Foreign Language (TOEFL) is required for international students.
Minimum TOEFL score required for paper test: **550**
Minimum TOEFL score required for computer test: **213**

Fall 2003
Acceptance rate for master's degree programs: **85%**
Acceptance rate for education specialist degree programs: **100%**
Total 2003 enrollment: **631**
Master's degree enrollment: **607**
 Teacher preparation program enrollment (master's): **385**
Education specialist degree enrollment: **24**

FINANCIAL INFORMATION

Financial aid phone number: **(262) 472-1130**
Tuition, 2003-2004 academic year: Full-time in-state: **$299/credit hour**; out-of-state: **$889/credit hour**, Part-time in-state: **$299/credit hour**; out-of-state: **$889/credit hour**
Room and board: **$8,000**, Books and supplies: **$1,000**, Miscellaneous expenses: **$1,000**
Number of fellowships awarded to graduate students during the 2003-2004 academic year: **0**
Number of teaching assistant positions: **0**
Number of research assistant positions: **10**
Number of other paid appointments: **0**

ACADEMIC PROGRAMS

Total full-time tenured or tenure-track faculty (fall 2003): **74**
Areas of specialization: curriculum and instruction, educational psychology, elementary teacher education, higher education administration, secondary teacher education, special education, student counseling and personnel services, teacher education.
Professional development/partnership school(s) are used by students in some of the teaching programs.
During their internships, peer groups of students meet regularly to discuss instructional techniques in some of the teaching programs.
All of the students in their internships are mentored.
Courses that prepare teachers to pass the National Board of Professional Teaching Standards are offered.
Teacher preparation programs: Four-year baccalaureate-degree program leading to initial licensure that includes either a major or minor in education and practice teaching. Five-year program leading to initial licensure that results in a baccalaureate degree (with a major or minor in education) plus a master's degree and includes practice teaching.
The education program is currently accredited by the National Council for Accreditation of Teacher Education.

Viterbo College

- 900 Viterbo Drive, La Crosse, WI 54601
- **Website:** http://www.viterbo.edu
- **Private**

ADMISSIONS

Admissions phone number: **(608) 796-3384**
Admissions email address: *smfrick@viterbo.edu*
Application website:
 http://www.viterbo.edu/academic/gr/educ/index.htm
Application fee: **$50**
Fall 2005 application deadline: **rolling**

FINANCIAL INFORMATION

Financial aid phone number: **(608) 796-3900**
Tuition, 2003-2004 academic year: Full-time: **$210/credit hour**; Part-time: **$210/credit hour**

WYOMING

TEACHER TESTING IN WYOMING
Wyoming does not require a teacher licensing test. For information on where to go in your state for academic requirements, see Chapter 6 on page 67.

University of Wyoming

- **Dept 3374, 1000 E. University Ave., Laramie, WY 82071**
- **Website:** http://uwadmnweb.uwyo.edu/uwgrad/
- **Public**
- **Degrees offered:** bachelor's, master's, Ph.D., Ed.D.

ADMISSIONS

Admissions phone number: **(307) 766-2287**
Admissions email address: *uwgrad@uwyo.edu*
Application website:
   http://uwadmnweb.uwyo.edu/uwgrad/app_index.htm
Application fee: **$40**
Fall 2005 application deadline: **12/30**
Test requirements: **GRE**
Test of English as Foreign Language (TOEFL) is required
   for international students.
Minimum TOEFL score required for paper test: **525**
Minimum TOEFL score required for computer test: **197**

Fall 2003
Acceptance rate for master's degree programs: **92%**
Acceptance rate for doctoral programs: **90%**
Average GRE verbal: **486**, Average GRE quantitative: **562**,
   Average GRE analytical: **577**
Total 2003 enrollment: **375**
Master's degree enrollment: **239**
   Teacher preparation program enrollment (master's): **145**
Doctoral degree enrollment: **136**

FINANCIAL INFORMATION

Financial aid phone number: **(307) 766-2118**
Tuition, 2003-2004 academic year: Full-time in-state:
   $142/credit hour; out-of-state: **$408/credit hour**, Part-
   time in-state: **$142/credit hour**; out-of-state: **$408/credit
   hour**
Fees: **$570**, Room and board: **$5,546**, Books and supplies:
   $1,000, Miscellaneous expenses: **$2,676**

ACADEMIC PROGRAMS

Total full-time tenured or tenure-track faculty (fall 2003): **50**
   Total part-time faculty (fall 2003): **0**
Areas of specialization: curriculum and instruction, education administration and supervision, education policy,
   educational psychology, elementary teacher education,
   higher education administration, secondary teacher education, special education, student counseling and personnel services.
Professional development/partnership school(s) are used
   by students in all of the teaching programs.
During their internships, peer groups of students meet
   regularly to discuss instructional techniques in some of
   the teaching programs.
All of the students in their internships are mentored.
Courses that prepare teachers to pass the National Board of
   Professional Teaching Standards are offered.
Teacher preparation programs: Four-year baccalaureate-
   degree program leading to initial licensure that includes
   either a major or minor in education and practice teach-
   ing. Alternative program for college graduates leading to
   provisional licensure.
The education program is currently accredited by the
   National Council for Accreditation of Teacher Education.

Index of Schools

Abilene Christian University, 448

Adams State College, 169

Adelphi University, 335

Agnes Scott College, 197

Alabama A&M University, 126

Alabama State University, 126

Alaska Pacific University, 135

Albany State University, 197

Alcorn State University, 297

Alfred University, 335

Alliant International University–San Diego, 145

Alvernia College, 403

Alverno College, 494

American International College, 269

American University, 182

Anderson University, 226

Andrews University, 281

Angelo State University, 448

Anna Maria College, 269

Antioch New England Graduate School, 321

Antioch University (McGregor), 376

Antioch University–Seattle, 486

Appalachian State University, 364

Aquinas College, 282

Arcadia University, 403

Arizona State University–Main Campus, 137

Arizona State University–West, 138

Arkansas State University, 141

Arkansas Tech University, 141

Armstrong Atlantic State University, 197

Asbury College, 245

Ashland University, 376

Assumption College, 269

Auburn University–Main Campus, 126

Auburn University–Montgomery, 127

Augsburg College, 290

Augusta State University, 198

Augustana College, 434

Aurora University, 211

Austin College, 448

Austin Peay State University, 437

Averett University, 476

Avila College, 301

Azusa Pacific University, 146

Baker University College of Arts and Sciences, 241

Baldwin-Wallace College, 376

Ball State University, 226

Bank Street College of Education, 335

Barry University, 186

Baylor University, 449

Belhaven College, 297

Bellarmine University, 245

Belmont University, 437

Bemidji State University, 290

Benedictine College, 241

Benedictine University, 211

Berry College, 198

Bethany College of the Assemblies of God, 145

Bethel College, MN, 290

Bethel College, TN, 437

Binghamton University, 336

Biola University, 146

Black Hills State University, 434

Bloomsburg University of Pennsylvania, 403

Bluffton College, 377

Boise State University, 209

Boston College (Lynch), 270

Boston University, 270

Bowie State University, 262

Bowling Green State University, 377

Bradley University, 212

Brenau University, 199

Brescia University, 246

Bridgewater State College, 271

Brigham Young University–Provo, 469

Brown University, 425

Bucknell University, 404

Buena Vista University, 236

Buffalo State College–SUNY, 337

Butler University, 226

Cabrini College, 404

Cal Poly–San Luis Obispo, 151

Caldwell College, 323

California Baptist University, 147

California State Polytechnic
   University–Pomona, 147

California State University–Bakersfield, 147

California State University–Chico, 147

California State University–Dominguez Hills,
   148

California State University–Fresno, 148

California State University–Fullerton, 148

California State University–Hayward, 149

California State University–Long Beach, 149

California State University–Los Angeles, 150

California State University–Nothridge, 150

California State University–Sacramento, 150

California State University–San Bernardino,
   150

California State University–San Marcos, 151

California State University–Stanislaus, 151

California University of Pennsylvania, 405

Cambridge College, 272

Cameron University, 392

Campbell University, 364

Campbellsville University, 246

Canisius College, 337

Capital University, 377

Cardinal Stritch University, 494

Carlow College, 405

Carroll College, 494

Carson-Newman College, 437

Carthage College, 495

Castleton State College, 472

Catawba College, 365

Catholic University of America, 182

Cedarville College, 377

Centenary College, 323

Centenary College of Louisiana, 252

Central Connecticut State University, 174

Central Methodist College, 301

Central Michigan University, 282

Central Missouri State University, 301

Central State University, 378

Central Washington University, 486

Chadron State College, 315

Chaminade University of Honolulu, 207

Chapman University, 152

Charleston Southern University, 427

Chatham College, 405

Chestnut Hill College, 405

Cheyney University of Pennsylvania, 405

Chicago State University, 212

Christian Brothers University, 438

Christopher Newport University, 476

City University, 487

Claremont Graduate University, 152

Clarion University of Pennsylvania , 406

Clark Atlanta University, 199

Clark University, 272

Clarke College, 236

Clemson University, 428

Cleveland State University, 378
Coastal Carolina University, 428
Colgate University, 337
College of Charleston, 429
College of Mount St. Joseph, 378
College of Mount St. Vincent, 337
College of New Jersey, 324
College of New Rochelle, 337
College of Notre Dame, 153
College of Notre Dame of Maryland, 262
College of Our Lady of the Elms, 272
College of Santa Fe, 331
College of St. Catherine, 291
College of St. Elizabeth, 324
College of St. Joseph, 472
College of St. Rose, 337
College of St. Scholastica, 291
College of the Southwest, 331
College of William and Mary, 477
Colorado Christian College, 169
Colorado College, 169
Colorado State University, 170
Columbia College, 429
Columbia College, 302
Columbia College Chicago, 213
Columbus State University, 199
Concordia University, 153
Concordia University, 213
Concordia University, 315
Concordia University, 397
Concordia University, 495
Concordia University–Austin, 450
Coppin State College, 263
Cornell University, 338
Cornerstone University, 282
Covenant College, 199
Creighton University, 316
Cumberland College, 246

Cumberland University, 438
CUNY–Brooklyn College, 338
CUNY–City College, 339
CUNY–College of Staten Island, 339
CUNY–Graduate Center, 340
CUNY–Hunter College, 340
CUNY–Lehman College, 341
CUNY–Queens College, 341
Curry College, 272

D'Youville College, 342
Daemen College, 341
Dallas Baptist University, 450
David Lipscomb University, 438
Defiance College, 378
Delaware State University, 180
Delaware Valley College, 406
Delta State University, 297
DePaul University, 213
DeSales University, 407
Doane College, 316
Dominican College of Blauvelt, 342
Dominican College of San Rafael, 154
Dominican University, 214
Dordt College, 236
Dowling College, 342
Drake University, 237
Drexel University, 407
Drury College, 302
Duke University, 365
Duquesne University, 408

Earlham College, 227
East Carolina uNiversity, 365
East Central University, 392
East Stroudsburg University of Pennsylvania, 408
East Tennessee State University, 438

Eastern Connecticut State University, 174

Eastern Illinois University, 214

Eastern Kentucky University, 246

Eastern Mennonite University, 477

Eastern Michigan University, 282

Eastern Nazarene College, 273

Eastern New Mexico University, 332

Eastern Oregon University, 397

Eastern University, 408

Eastern Washington University, 487

Edgewood College, 495

Edinboro University of Pennsylvania, 408

Elizabeth City State University, 365

Elmhurst College, 214

Elmira College, 343

Elon University, 365

Emmanuel College, 273

Emory Universy, 199

Emporia State University, 241

Endicott College, 273

Evangel University, 302

Evergreen State College, 487

Fairfield University, 175

Fairleigh Dickinson University, 325

Fayetteville State University, 366

Ferris State University, 283

Fielding Graduate Institute, 154

Fitchburg State College, 273

Florida A&M University, 186

Florida Atlantic University, 186

Florida Institue of Technology–Melbourne, 187

Florida International University, 187

Florida State University, 188

Fontbonne University, 303

Fordham University, 343

Fort Hays State University, 241

Fort Valley State University, 200

Framingham State College, 273

Francis Marion University, 430

Franciscan University of Steubenville, 379

Freed-Hardeman University, 439

Fresno Pacific University, 154

Friends University, 242

Frostburg State University, 263

Gallaudet University, 183

Gannon University, 409

Gardner-Webb University, 366

Geneva College, 409

George Fox University, 398

George Mason University, 478

George Washington University, 183

Georgetown College, 247

Georgia College and State University, 200

Georgia Southern University, 201

Georgia Southwestern State University, 201

Georgia State University, 201

Georgian Court College, 325

Goddard College, 472

Gonzaga University, 488

Gordon College, 274

Goucher College, 263

Governors State University, 214

Graceland College, 237

Graduate College of Union University, 344

Grambling State University, 252

Grand Canyon University, 138

Grand Valley State University, 283

Greenville College, 215

Gwynedd-Mercy College, 409

Hamline University, 292

Hampton University, 478

Hardin-Simmons University, 450

Harding University, 141

Harvard University, 274

Hastings College, 316
Heidelberg College, 379
Henderson State University, 142
Heritage College, 488
Hofstra University, 344
Holy Family University, 409
Holy Names College, 155
Hood College, 264
Hope International University, 155
Houston Baptist University, 450
Howard University, 184
Humboldt State University, 156

Idaho State University, 209
Illinois State University, 215
Indiana State University, 227
Indiana University of Pennsylvania, 410
Indiana University–Purdue University–Fort
　Wayne, 230
Indiana University–Purdue
　University–Indianapolis, 230
Indiana University–Bloomingtom, 229
Indiana University–Kokomo, 229
Indiana University–Northwest, 229
Indiana University–South Bend, 230
Indiana University–Southeast, 231
Indiana Wesleyan University, 232
Iona College, 345
Iowa State University, 237
Ithaca College, 345

Jackson State University, 298
Jacksonville State University, 127
Jacksonville University, 189
James Madison University, 479
John Carroll University, 380
John F. Kennedy University, 156
Johns Hopkins University, 264

Johnson and Wales University, 425
Johnson State College, 472

Kansas State University, 242
Kean University, 326
Keene State College, 321
Kennesaw State University, 202
Kent State University, 380
Kentucky State University, 247
King's College, 410
Kutztown University of Pennsylvania, 410

La Salle University, 411
La Sierra University, 156
LaGrange College, 202
Lake Erie College, 381
Lakeland College, 496
Lamar University, 451
Lander University, 430
Langston University, 392
Le Moyne College, 346
Lebanon Valley College, 411
Lee University, 440
Lehigh University, 412
Lenoir-Rhyne College, 366
Lesley University, 275
Lewis and Clark College, 398
Lewis University, 216
Liberty University, 479
Lincoln Memorial University, 440
Lincoln University, 303
Lincoln University, 412
Lindenwood University, 303
Lindsey Wilson College, 247
Lock Haven University of Pennsylvania, 413
Long Island University–Brentwood, 346
Long Island University–Brooklyn, 346
Long Island University–C.W. Post Campus, 346

Long Island University–Southampton, 347

Longwood University, 480

Loras College, 238

Louisiana State University–Baton Rouge, 252

Louisiana State University–Shreveport, 253

Louisiana Tech University, 253

Loyola College in Maryland, 264

Loyola Marymount University, 156

Loyola University Chicago, 216

Loyola University New Orleans, 254

Lubbock Christian University, 451

Lynchburg College, 480

Lyndon State College, 473

Lynn University, 189

Madonna University, 284

Maharishi University of Management, 238

Malone College, 381

Manhattan College, 347

Manhattanville College, 347

Mansfield University of Pennsylvania, 413

Marian College of Fond Du Lac, 496

Marietta College, 381

Marist College, 347

Marquette University, 496

Marshall University, 492

Mary Baldwin College, 481

Marygrove College, 284

Marymount University, 481

Maryville University of St. Louis, 304

Marywood University, 413

McNeese State University, 254

Medaille College, 347

Mercer University, 203

Mercy College, 347

Mercyhurst College, 413

Meredith College, 366

Miami University–Oxford, 382

Michigan State University, 285

MidAmerica Nazarene University, 242

Middle Tennessee State University, 440

Midwestern State University, 451

Millersville University of Pennsylvania, 414

Milligan College, 441

Mills College, 157

Minnesota State University–Mankato, 292

Minnesota State University–Moorhead, 292

Minot State University, 374

Mississippi College, 298

Mississippi State University, 298

Mississippi University for Women, 299

Mississippi Valley State University, 299

Missouri Baptist College, 304

Molloy College, 348

Monmouth University, 326

Montana State University, 313

Montana State University–Billings, 313

Montana State University–Northern, 314

Montclair State University, 326

Moravian College, 414

Morehead State University, 247

Morgan State University, 265

Morningside College, 239

Mount Holyoke College, 275

Mount Mary College, 497

Mount St. Mary College, 348

Mount St. Mary's College, 157

Mount St. Mary's College, 265

Mount Vernon Nazarene University, 382

Murray State University, 247

Muskingum College, 383

National University, 158

National-Lewis University, 217

Nazareth College of Rochester, 349

Neumann College, 415

New Jersey City University, 327

New Mexico Highlands University, 332

New Mexico State University, 333

New York Institute of Technology–Manhattan, 349

New York Institute of Technology–Old Westbury, 349

New York University, 350

Newman University, 242

Niagra University, 350

Nicholls State University, 254

Norfolk State University, 481

North Carolina A&T State University, 367

North Carolina Central University, 367

North Carolina State University–Raleigh, 367

North Central College, 217

North Dakota State University, 374

North Georgia College and State University, 203

North Park University, 219

Northeastern Illinois University, 218

Northeastern State University, 392

Northeastern University, 276

Northern Arizona University, 138

Northern Illinois University, 218

Northern Kentucky University, 248

Northern Michigan University, 285

Northern State University, 434

Northwest Christian College, 398

Northwest Missouri State University, 304

Northwest Nazarene University, 210

Northwestern Oklahoma State University, 392

Northwestern State University of Louisiana, 255

Northwestern University, 219

Notre Dame College of Ohio, 383

Nova Southeastern University, 190

Nyack College, 351

Oakland City University, 232

Oakland University, 285

Occidental College, 158

Oglethorpe University, 203

Ohio Nothern University, 383

Ohio State University–Columbus, 384

Ohio University, 384

Oklahoma City University, 392

Oklahoma State University, 393

Old Dominion University, 481

Olivet Nazarene University, 220

Oral Roberts University, 393

Oregon State University, 399

Otterbein College, 385

Our Lady of Holy Cross College, 255

Our Lady of the Lake University, 452

Pace University, 351

Pacific Lutheran University, 488

Pacific University, 399

Palm Beach Atlantic College, 190

Park University, 305

Patten College, 158

Penn State University–University Park, 416

Pennsylvania State University–Great Valley, 415

Pennsylvania State University–Harrisburg, 415

Pepperdine University, 158

Peru State College, 316

Pfeiffer University, 368

Piedmont College, 204

Pittsburg State University, 243

Plymouth State University, 321

Point Loma Nazarene University, 158

Point Park College, 416

Portland State University, 399

Prairie View A&M University, 452

Pratt Institute, 352

Prescott College, 139

Providence College, 425
Purdue University–Calumet, 232
Purdue University–West Lafayette, 233

Queens University of Charlotte, 368
Quincy University, 220
Quinnipiac University, 175

Radford University, 482
Regent University, 482
Regis College, 276
Regis University, 170
Rice University, 452
Rider University, 327
Rivier College, 322
Robert Morris University, 416
Roberts Wesleyan College, 352
Rochester Institute of Technology, 353
Rockford College, 220
Rockhurst University, 305
Roger Williams University, 425
Rollins College, 191
Roosevelt University, 220
Rosemont College, 417
Rowan University, 327
Rutgers State University–New Brunswick, 328

Sacred Heart University, 176
Saginaw Valley State University, 286
Salem College, 369
Salem International University, 492
Salem State College, 276
Salisbury University, 265
Sam Houston State University, 453
Samford University, 128
San Diego State University, 158
San Francisco State University, 159
San Jose State University, 159

Santa Clara University, 159
Sarah Lawrence College, 353
School for International Training, 473
Schreiner College, 453
Seattle Pacific University, 488
Seattle University, 488
Seton Hall University, 328
Seton Hill College, 417
Shenandoah University, 483
Shippensburg University of Pennsylvania, 418
Siena Heights College, 286
Silver Lake College, 497
Simmons College, 277
Simpson College, 160
Sinte Gleska University, 435
Slippery Rock University of Pennsylvania, 418
Smith College, 277
Sonoma State University, 160
South Carolina State University, 430
South Dakota State University, 435
Southeast Missouri State University, 306
Southeastern Louisiana University, 256
Southeastern Oklahoma State University, 393
Southern Adventist University, 441
Southern Arkansas University, 142
Southern Connecticut State University, 176
Southern Illinois University–Carbondale, 221
Southern Illinois University–Edwardsville, 222
Southern Methodist University, 454
Southern Nazarene University, 394
Southern Oregon University, 400
Southern University and A&M College, 256
Southern Utah University, 469
Southern Wesleyan University, 431
Southwest Baptist University, 307
Southwest Minnesota State University, 292
Southwest Missouri State University, 307
Southwestern Adventist University, 454

Southwestern College, 243

Southwestern Oklahoma State University, 394

Spalding University, 249

Spring Arbor College, 286

Spring Hill College, 128

Springfield College, 277

St. Ambrose University, 239

St. Bonaventure, 353

St. Cloud State University, 293

St. Francis University, 419

St. John's University, 354

St. Joseph College, 177

St. Joseph's College, 259

St. Joseph's College–Suffolk, 354

St. Joseph's University, 419

St. Lawrence University, 354

St. Leo University, 192

St. Louis University, 307

St. Martin's College, 488

St. Mary's College of California, 160

St. Mary's University of Minnesota, 293

St. Mary's University of San Antonio, 455

St. Michael's College, 474

St. Norbert College, 497

St. Peter's College, 329

St. Thomas University, 192

St. Xavier University, 222

St. Thomas Aquinas, 355

Stanford University, 161

State University of West Georgia, 204

Stephen F. Austin State University, 454

Stephens College, 307

Stetson University, 191

Suffolk University, 277

Sul Ross State University, 455

Sunbridge College, 355

SUNY College–Fredonia, 356

SUNY College–Geneseo, 357

SUNY College–Oswego, 357

SUNY–Albany, 355

SUNY–Brockport, 356

SUNY–Cortland, 358

SUNY–New Paltz, 358

SUNY–Oneonta, 359

SUNY–Plattsburgh, 359

SUNY–Potsdam, 359

SUNY–Stony Brook, 360

Syracuse University, 360

Tarleton State University, 456

Teachers College, Columbia University, 361

Temple University, 420

Tennessee State University, 442

Tennessee Technological University, 442

Tennessee Temple University, 443

Texas A&M International University, 456

Texas A&M University—College Station, 456

Texas A&M University–Commerce, 457

Texas A&M University–Corpus Christi, 457

Texas A&M University–Kingsville, 458

Texas A&M University–Texarkana, 458

Texas Christian University, 459

Texas Southern University, 459

Texas State University–San Marcos, 459

Texas Tech University, 460

Texas Wesleyan University, 460

Texas Woman's University, 460

The Citadel, 427

Touro College, 361

Towson University, 266

Trevecca Nazarene University, 443

Trinity Baptist College, 192

Trinity College, 184

Trinity International University, 193

Trinity University, 461

Troy State University–Dothan, 129

Troy State University–Main Campus, 129
Troy State University–Montgomery, 130
Truman State University, 307
Tufts University, 277
Tusculum College, 443

Union College, 249
Union Institute and University, 386
Union University, 444
University at Buffalo–SUNY, 362
University of Akron, 386
University of Alabama–Birmingham, 130
University of Alabama–Tuscaloosa, 131
University of Alaska–Anchorage, 135
University of Alaska–Fairbanks, 135
University of Alaska–Southeast, 136
University of Arizona, 139
University of Arkansas–Fayetteville, 142
University of Arkansas–Little Rock, 143
University of Arkansas–Monticello, 143
University of Bridgeport, 177
University of California–Berkeley, 161
University of California–Davis, 162
University of California–Irvine, 162
University of California–Los Angeles, 163
University of California–Riverside, 164
University of California–San Diego, 164
University of California–Santa Barbara
  (Gevirtz), 164
University of California–Santa Cruz, 165
University of Central Arkansas, 143
University of Central Florida, 193
University of Central Oklahoma, 394
University of Cincinnati, 386
University of Colorado–Boulder, 170
University of Colorado–Colorado Springs, 171
University of Colorado–Denver, 171
University of Connecticut (Neag), 178

University of Dayton, 387
University of Delaware, 180
University of Denver, 172
University of Detroit Mercy, 287
University of Findlay, 388
University of Florida, 193
University of Georgia, 205
University of Great Falls, 314
University of Hartford, 178
University of Hawaii–Hilo, 207
University of Hawaii–Manoa, 207
University of Houston–Clear Lake, 461
University of Houston–Main Campus, 461
University of Houston–Victoria, 462
University of Idaho, 210
University of Illinois–Chicago, 222
University of Illinois–Springfield, 223
University of Illinois–Urbana-Champaign, 223
University of Indianapolis, 233
University of Iowa, 239
University of Judaism, 165
University of Kansas, 243
University of Kentucky, 249
University of La Verne, 165
University of Louisiana–Lafayette, 257
University of Louisiana–Monroe, 257
University of Louisville, 250
University of Maine–Orono, 259
University of Mary, 375
University of Mary Hardin–Baylor, 463
University of Maryland–Baltimore County, 266
University of Maryland–College Park, 267
University of Maryland–Eastern Shore, 268
University of Massachusetts–Amherst, 277
University of Massachusetts–Boston, 278
University of Massachusetts–Dartmouth, 278
University of Massachusetts–Lowell, 278
University of Memphis, 444

University of Miami, 194

University of Michigan–Ann Arbor, 287

University of Michigan–Dearborn, 287

University of Michigan–Flint, 288

University of Minnesota–Duluth, 293

University of Minnesota–Twin Cities, 294

University of Mississippi, 299

University of Missouri–Columbia, 308

University of Missouri–Kansas City, 309

University of Missouri–St. Louis, 310

University of Mobile, 132

University of Montana, 314

University of Montevallo, 132

University of Nebraska–Kearney, 316

University of Nebraska–Lincoln, 317

University of Nebraska–Omaha, 317

University of Nevada–Las Vegas, 319

University of Nevada–Reno, 319

University of New England, 260

University of New Hampshire, 322

University of New Haven, 179

University of New Mexico, 333

University of New Orleans, 258

University of North Alabama, 132

University of North Carolina–Chapel Hill, 369

University of North Carolina–Charlotte, 370

University of North Carolina–Greensboro, 370

University of North Carolina–Pembroke, 371

University of North Carolina–Wilmington, 371

University of North Dakota, 375

University of North Florida, 195

University of North Texas, 463

University of Northern Colorado, 172

University of Northern Iowa, 240

University of Oklahoma, 395

University of Oregon, 400

University of Pennsylvania, 420

University of Pittsburgh, 421

University of Portland, 401

University of Puget Sound, 489

University of Redlands, 167

University of Rhode Island/Rhode Island College, 426

University of Rio Grande, 388

University of San Diego, 167

University of San Francisco, 167

University of Scranton, 421

University of Sioux Falls, 435

University of South Alabama, 133

University of South Carolina–Aiken, 431

University of South Carolina–Columbia, 432

University of South Carolina–Spartanburg, 432

University of South Dakota, 435

University of South Florida, 195

University of Southern California (Rossier), 168

University of Southern Indiana, 234

University of Southern Maine, 260

University of Southern Mississippi, 300

University of St. Francis, 224

University of St. Francis, 234

University of St. Thomas, 294

University of St. Thomas, 464

University of Tennessee–Chattanooga, 445

University of Tennessee–Knoxville, 445

University of Tennessee–Martin, 446

University of Texas–Arlington, 464

University of Texas–Austin, 464

University of Texas–Brownsville, 465

University of Texas–El Paso, 465

University of Texas–Pan American, 465

University of Texas–Permain Basin, 466

University of Texas–San Antonio, 466

University of Texas–Tyler, 467

University of the District of Columbia, 185

University of the Incarnate Word, 467

University of the Pacific, 166
University of Toledo, 388
University of Tulsa, 395
University of Utah, 469
University of Vermont, 474
University of Virginia (Curry), 483
University of Washington, 489
University of West Alabama, 133
University of West Florida, 196
University of Wisconsin–Eau Claire, 497
University of Wisconsin–Green Bay, 498
University of Wisconsin–La Crosse, 498
University of Wisconsin–Madison, 498
University of Wisconsin–Milwaukee, 499
University of Wisconsin–Oshkosh, 500
University of Wisconsin–River Falls, 500
University of Wisconsin–Stevens Point, 501
University of Wisconsin–Stout, 501
University of Wisconsin–Superior, 502
University of Wisconsin–Whitewater, 502
University of Wyoming, 504
University of Rochester (Warner), 362
Urbana University, 389
Ursuline College, 389
Utah State University, 470
Utica College of Syracuse University, 362

Valdosta State University, 205
Valparaiso University, 235
Vanderbilt University (Peabody), 446
Villanova University, 422
Virginia Commonwealth University, 484
Virginia State University, 485
Virginia Tech, 485
Viterbo College, 503

Wagner College, 363
Wake Forest University, 372

Walden University, 295
Walla Walla College, 490
Walsh University, 390
Washburn University, 243
Washington State University, 490
Washington University in St. Louis, 310
Wayland Baptist University, 467
Wayne State College, 318
Wayne State University, 288
Waynesburg College, 422
Weber State University, 470
Webster University, 311
Wesley College, 181
Wesleyan College, 206
West Chester University of Pennsylvania, 423
West Texas A&M University, 467
West Virginia University, 493
Western Carolina University, 372
Western Connecticut State University, 179
Western Illinois University, 225
Western Kentucky University, 251
Western Michigan University, 289
Western New Mexico University, 334
Western Oregon University, 401
Western Washington University, 490
Westfield State College, 279
Westminster College, 423
Westminster College, 471
Wheaton College, 225
Wheelock College, 279
Whittier College, 168
Whitworth College, 490
Wichita State University, 244
Widener University, 423
Wilkes University, 424
Willamette University, 402
William Carey College, 300
William Paterson University, 329

William Woods University, 311
Wilmington College, 181
Winona State University, 295
Winston-Salem State University, 372
Winthrop University, 433
Worcester State College, 280
Wright State University, 390

Xavier University, 391
Xavier University of Louisiana, 258

Yeshiva University (Azrieli), 363
York College of Pennsylvania, 424
Youngstown State University, 391

About the Authors & Editors

Founded in 1933, Washington, D.C.–based *U.S.News & World Report* delivers a unique brand of weekly magazine journalism to its 12.2 million readers. In 1983, *U.S. News* began its exclusive annual rankings of American colleges and universities. The *U.S. News* education franchise is second to none; its annual college and graduate school rankings are among the most eagerly anticipated magazine issues in the country.

Ben Wildavsky, the book's lead author, is a longtime education journalist and a deputy editor at *U.S.News & World Report*, where he helps plan and edit coverage of education and culture for the magazine's weekly Science & Society section. He is also a deputy editor of "America's Best Colleges" and "America's Best Graduate Schools." Previously, he covered economic policy for *National Journal*, wrote on higher education for *The San Francisco Chronicle*, and was executive editor of *The Public Interest*. He has also written for *The New Republic*, *The Wall Street Journal*, and *The Christian Science Monitor*, and was a writer and editor for "Teaching at Risk: A Call to Action," a 2004 report by the nonprofit Teaching Commission.

Anne McGrath, editor, is a senior writer at *U.S.News & World Report* covering higher education as well as primary and secondary education. Previously, she was managing editor of "America's Best Colleges" and "America's Best Graduate Schools."

Robert Morse is the director of data research at *U.S.News & World Report*. He is in charge of the research, data collection, methodologies, and survey design for the annual "America's Best Colleges" rankings and the "America's Best Graduate Schools" rankings.

Ulrich Boser is an associate editor at *U.S.News & World Report*, where he writes about higher education as well as primary and secondary education for the magazine's Science & Society section.

Sara Sklaroff is the education editor of *U.S.News & World Report*, where she manages the magazine's education journalism, both in the weekly magazine and in "America's Best Colleges" and other guides. She is also an editor of the magazine's weekly Science & Society section. Sklaroff has written for *Education Week* and *The Chronicle of Higher Education*, among other publications.

Brian Kelly is the executive editor of *U.S.News & World Report*. As the magazine's No. 2 editor, he oversees the weekly magazine, the website, and a series of newsstand books. He is a former editor at *The Washington Post* and the author of three books.

Other writers who contributed chapters or passages to the book are **Carolyn Kleiner Butler, Kristin Davis, Justin Ewers, Dan Gilgoff, Caroline Hsu, Rachel Hartigan Shea**, and **Betsy Streisand**. The work involved in producing the directory and *U.S. News* Insider's Index was handled by senior research analyst **Sam Flanigan**, with associate research analyst **Meadow Yerkie**. Thanks to **David Griffin**, creative director at the magazine, for his work in designing the book, and to members of the *U.S. News* **factchecking team** for making sure we got it right.

Find out where the story is going…not simply where it's been

Subscribe to *U.S. News* for only 40¢ an issue

News and events can affect you in a very personal way, whether something happens on the other side of the world or in your own community. And that's where *U.S.News & World Report* can help you. You get valuable information you can use to make better choices for yourself and your family.

And now you can get *U.S. News* at the special rate of just 40¢ an issue. That's over a year (60 issues) for only $24—you **SAVE 90%** off the cover price. Plus, by subscribing you also receive our Special Guides on *Best Colleges, Best Hospitals, Careers, Retirement*, and more.

So call today and get ahead of the news for only 40¢ a copy.

To subscribe, call:

1-800-436-6520 *(MENTION CODE: 04SPE4)*

*Savings off the cover price. *U.S. News* publishes weekly except for six special double issues per year.

Looking to simplify your graduate school search?

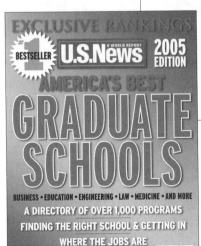